A HISTORY OF THE MODERN BRITISH ISLES, 1529–1603

The Two Kingdoms

Mark Nicholls

D1387486

BLACKWELL Publishers

First published 1999

2 4 6 8 10 9 7 5 3 1

Blackwell Publishers Ltd
108 Cowley Road
Oxford OX4 1JF
UK

Blackwell Publishers Inc.
350 Main Street
Malden, Massachusetts 02148
USA

British Library Cataloguing in Publication Data

A CIP catalogue record for this book is available from the British Library.

Library of Congress Cataloging-in-Publication Data

Nicholls, Mark, 1959–
    A history of the modern British Isles, 1529–1603: the two kingdoms / Mark Nicholls.
        p.   cm. – (A history of the modern British Isles)
    Includes bibliographical references and index.
    ISBN 0–631–19333–2 (HB: alk. paper). – ISBN 0–631–19334–0 (PB: alk. paper)
    1. Great Britain – History – Tudors, 1485–1603.   2. Scotland – History –
    16th century.   I. Title.   II. Series.
DA315.N53   1999
942.05–dc21   98–21301
                                                                                           CIP

Commissioning Editor: Tessa Harvey
Desk Editor: Brigitte Lee
Production Controller: Brian Johnson
Picture Researcher: Leanda Shrimpton

Typeset in 10 on 12 pt Plantin by Graphicraft Limited, Hong Kong

Printed in Great Britain by T. J. International, Padstow, Cornwall

This book is printed on acid-free paper

For Guy

Contents

CONTENTS

Plates

List of Maps

Acknowledgements

My grateful thanks go to Dr Paul Ayris, Professor David Loades, Professor Wallace MacCaffrey, Dr Hiram Morgan, Mr John Wells and Dr Jenny Wormald, all of whom read and commented on extensive sections of various drafts. It is, of course, necessary to note at this point that the views expressed are my own, and that I implicate none of these scholars in my errors, misjudgements and omissions. The founding editor of this series, Sir Geoffrey Elton, was always typically generous with his advice and encouragement. His successor, Dr John Stevenson, has also offered help and necessary reassurance, while John Davey and Tessa Harvey at Blackwell have in expert fashion coaxed and cajoled whenever necessary. My colleagues in Cambridge University Library have asked many pertinent questions, and supplied a great deal of welcome encouragement. The Library Tea Room, with its excellent cakes and buns, has once again played a significant part in nudging a book towards completion. Most important of all, I must acknowledge the contribution of my wife Linda, whose patience has been sorely tested on far too many occasions over the past four years.

Note on Conventions

Where specific, all dates have been given in the old style, ten days behind the Gregorian calendar adopted in many parts of Catholic Europe during the 1580s. The year, however, has been considered to begin on 1 January and not 25 March. Spelling in all quotes has been modernized, while a few alterations in punctuation have been made for the sake of clarity. In the chapters on England, the unit of currency is the English pound; in those on Scotland it is the pound Scots. In chapters 10 and 14, the unit is the pound sterling *unless otherwise stated*. In the interests of Anglo-Scottish amity I have retained certain variant spellings where the preferences north and south of the border so dictate, and where clarity remains unimpaired. Stewart and Stuart is a case in point: both will be encountered in what follows.

Introduction

Before making the attempt, one must excuse the attempt. To embark upon a history of the British Isles at a time when the concept of British history is itself under particularly close scrutiny may be judged either rash or opportune. A word or two of self-justification are possibly in order.

The historian writing at the end of the twentieth century finds it hard to ignore the mood of the times. Fashion, as ever, prompts us to write of this subject, or that, just as fashion helps to set the parameters within which these topics are studied. And in one sense at least current fashion favours extremes. Local studies, of county, town or parish, flourish as never before. At the same time – and here there is surely something of a reaction against the past century and all that it has brought, for the effect is particularly noticeable in countries which have suffered most – the historian is beginning to reject the study of nation states in favour of the supra-national region and the cultural imperium. The trend is not absolute, and it may be reversed, but like other manifestations of multinationalism it is gaining ground. Our brief, therefore, in this present work, is a history not of England, or of Scotland, or of Ireland, but of the British Isles.[1]

And so, many would say, it *should* be. We are frequently reminded that an appropriate – or, some might suggest, *the* appropriate – way to study the fortunes of England or Scotland, Wales or Ireland, is to consider these and the other, smaller component parts of the British Isles as a whole. Again and again, constant political and cultural comparison and evaluation, and the deployment of broad perspectives, are urged upon us. Even its warmest supporters concede, however, that such all-embracing British history is more easily discussed in the abstract than applied to any particular period. Pioneers of this modern genre tell us *what* we should do, but *how* we should do it is still, despite a number of worthy proposals, an open issue.[2]

I certainly would not challenge the essential and frankly unchallengeable premise: that British history is a valid and vital field of study, and that the component parts of the British Isles did indeed influence one another's development, at all times, if to varying degrees. Awareness of a wider context is always desirable in the historian working at any level. A scholar labouring on the court rolls of Essex should recognize that the universe extends beyond Colchester, and that a painstakingly acquired picture of the manorial system of justice in the county may not be mirrored elsewhere. Similarly, the historian of England, Scotland, Ireland or Wales, should look for ways in which the politics, economy and culture of a nation are shaped by external influences wheresoever these may emerge. Lessons may profitably be drawn from comparisons between different experiences, but parallels and divergences should never be forced. A pan-British approach runs the risk of presupposing parallels where there is in fact nothing but coincidence, distinction or divergence. As Hiram Morgan rightly emphasizes in the context of the pre-1600 British polity, the historian's decision to view matters from a British perspective should not automatically suggest that anything approaching a 'British policy' was adopted in any part of these Isles, the persistent and unsurprising English wish to exclude overseas powers apart.[3]

When one descends, as we all must do on occasion, from the general to the particular, any holistic approach faces an especial difficulty in pinpointing some appropriate focus for the study of these particularities. Some have argued that pan-British studies should concentrate on contrasting and counterbalancing lowland against upland, or centre against periphery, the settled cores of each kingdom against the militarized borderlands and the remote, inaccessible limits of these islands. But there are problems with these approaches: the precise limits and divides separating core and periphery are seldom very satisfactorily defined, while measures of militarization are sometimes awkward and often unconvincing. On occasion, it is true, the traditional borderlands and peripheries, such as the shires which ran along both sides of the Scottish border, the Welsh 'marches', Cornwall, Ireland, and the Scottish Highlands and Islands, influenced and shaped the politics of the English and Scottish kingdoms. But during other, lengthy periods of history their perennial disquiets and factions were either ignored or comfortably downplayed by statesmen in London or Edinburgh, and the cultural, religious or social contribution of these areas to the emerging national consciousness both north and south of the Tweed is marginal indeed.

Should we not also demand to know what particular purpose might be served by focusing on the influence of peripheries? The scholar, sufficiently familiar with the politics and personalities of these islands in the early modern period, will not miss the real significance of what went on in the Cheviots, in County Wicklow or on the Isle of Skye, and he or she will no doubt find interest in the manifold strategies by which the independently minded inhabitants of these regions played off their remote, superior lords and squabbled interminably with their nearest neighbours. But the student new to the world of John Knox's Scotland or Shakespeare's England has other priorities. Given the abiding ignorance of continental history in Britain, might it not be appropriate to turn the spotlight elsewhere, and to ask whether, as beginners, we would learn most about the development of, say, France through the study of ways in which the absorption of Brittany or Burgundy affected the realm, or through a study of the growing authority wielded by successive kings and statesmen in the central court at Paris, down the centuries? No sensible person would wish to disparage any credible means of shedding light upon the doubtful panoramas of the past, but perhaps the concept of core and periphery is only useful in the Tudor or Stewart context if we limit the cores drastically, at the same time extending the peripheries – complex, inconsistent and individual as they are – to the gates of Whitehall and the banks of the Forth.

The deceptively simple concept of a British history, a British problem, also, to my mind, fails to recognize a formidable and fundamental stumbling block. The historian of the sixteenth century contemplates an age for which the records are, by modern standards, fearfully incomplete and ambiguous; elaborate theories can seldom be based upon wholly persuasive evidence. A broad historical canvas requires that the paint available is spread very thinly: generalizations are readily arrived at, but the evidence upon which those generalizations are based does not always withstand detailed scrutiny. Attempts to construct an all-encompassing British history built on an inadequate grasp of the component histories of Britain are either likely to prove fruitless, or to fuel inadvertently the romantic nationalism which many meticulous national histories and carefully researched monographs have done so much to downplay.

I have suggested that we are dealing here with fashion as much as with history, and no fashion on earth is entirely new. British history has its own ancient roots. We need not delve back into the pseudo-histories of Geoffrey of Monmouth, or the works of the martyrologist John Foxe in Queen Elizabeth's reign, or the Unionist writings of the seventeenth century; modern contempt for nineteenth-century historians obscures the fact that many of these gentleman-amateurs portrayed, in their accounts of the growth of distinct British institutions to a point at which they were carried along with the nation's culture and political traditions throughout the British Empire, a far more realistic and 'balanced' version of British history than we necessarily appreciate today. These writers should not be criticized for their failure to appreciate the transience of Empire. Their modern counterparts escape condemnation when, just as closely in keeping with current mores, they play down the astonishing expansion of British influence and control over a quarter of the globe. Nor should their habitual absorption with English history – the history of the most populous, and politically most significant British nation – automatically imply that they were blind to wider horizons, or that they failed to recognize the deeper truth that the fortunes of England and Scotland, Ireland and Wales, have ever been linked. Fashions change, but to criticize a multi-volume *History of England* for being anglocentric is surely to verge upon fashionable correctness of another kind.[4] Sometimes, it seems possible that the preoccupation of historians with the ways in which others have written history impedes their own, necessarily painstaking attempts to understand an elusive past.

There is, I believe, every reason to argue that the sixteenth century, perhaps in contrast to much that goes before and comes after, should be studied in terms of individual, developing states. National consciousness gradually becomes more pronounced with the spread of the printed word and with wars of survival, while the erosion of English royal possessions across the Channel diminishes a familiar, medieval, continental dimension. Neither have we as yet embarked upon the period in which a single monarch ruled the three constituent kingdoms of these islands: the work of four decades has now established that we are, in 1603, a far journey away from the terrible wars of the 1640s and 1650s, wars truly fought out upon a British stage.

We are, it must be conceded, still further away from any sense of nation-hood as we might understand it today. John Morrill wonders whether the emergence of Welshness, Irishness, even Scottishness, was significantly en-couraged through the process by which 'Britishness' was thrust upon the peoples living in Wales, Ireland and Scotland: the forging of a British nation is the product of seventeenth- and, particularly, eighteenth- and nineteenth-century wars, taken together with a good deal of political effort from the landed elites in all component countries within the British Isles. Maybe, however, this is less an inherently *sixteenth-century* process. England's long war against Spain in the 1580s and 1590s began to hint at such a change, though the degree and direction of that change varies in England, Scotland and in Ireland. But to keep matters in perspective, a common sense of war weariness, a lengthening series of night-terrors – invasion, destruction, con-fusion of 'true religion' – is as apparent as any developing sense of national or supra-national destiny. A man or woman born and raised in Tudor England, for example, would acknowledge that he or she was an Englishman or Eng-lishwoman, but the acknowledgement would not, perhaps, be accompanied by any quickening of the pulse. Insist to that individual that England might one day form a part of a composite nation in which Englishmen, Scots and Irish could mix freely, hailing one another as Britons, and the response might possibly be both abrupt and pithy.

Morrill also argues strongly for a paradox, that if the English are con-sidered the driving force behind an assimilation of Britishness that force was never particularly strong: 'the English are the least interested parties in thinking through, articulating, and above all redefining the relationship of the com-ponent parts' of the seventeenth-century multiple kingdom.[5] A few examples of antiquarian propaganda apart, that was indisputably the case throughout most of the sixteenth century. Henry VIII bullied, and William Cecil day-dreamed, but there was hardly any prevailing sense, either at the English court or in the English countryside, that England ought to lead the way, politically, militarily, culturally or religiously, towards a Greater British state. It is, however, also important to recognize that before 1600 the concept had only limited appeal for other parts of the Islands. The Scots began to consider some form of union only in the wake of military disaster, only when their own military weaknesses had been repeatedly and humiliatingly exposed. The Welsh gentry supported incorporation into the English state out of self-serving pragmat-ism, leaving many of their poorer countrymen either bewildered or resentful, while both the Gaelic Irish and the Anglo-Irish saw existing relationships, existing forms of limited union, under threat, and reacted accordingly.

My plan, therefore, is straightforward. It is to adapt and, let it be con-fessed, to simplify grossly for our specific purposes, the multi-national approach so capably advanced over a far longer period by Hugh Kearney,[6] and to focus in turn on both kingdoms within the British Isles, to interweave in parallel narrative the stories of England and Scotland, while introducing Ireland, itself a kingdom from 1541, though never more than a shadow crown worn by the English monarch, when discussing the British dimension in broader terms. So traditional an approach is, I would contend, appropriate for any study which breaks off with the century. We cannot ignore the facts that underpin more general theories. What works when applied to the medieval, feudal states, or in analyses of that curious multiple kingdom which brought together England, Scotland and Ireland under James VI and I and his Stuart successors, may perhaps not be so suitable in any detailed examination of the two independent and very different kingdoms encountered in the century covered in this volume.

General histories seem nowadays honour-bound to advance some grand design, to elaborate on a unifying thesis which characterizes the period under discussion. Readers will very soon become aware that imposed themes of this kind are in large part absent from this work. Concepts that succeed in illuminating an alien landscape – and for the modern reader there is a great deal that appears frighteningly remote about the sixteenth century – are doubtless valuable, but, at the risk of repeating an argument, they are only useful if they are valid, and cogent, and when they make no untoward demands on the integrity of the facts. The England of Henry VIII and Elizabeth, and the Scotland of Mary and James VI, are diverse, complex bodies politic in which the shifting balances of royal authority, regional independence and interdependence, appropriate confidence and unfounded bragging, personal survival and national insecurity insist that any generality runs the risk of oversimplifying the issues involved. Those broad generalizations advanced below, and touched upon in later chapters, are hardly original. They are put forward simply as starting points, as a loose framework in which to understand an age long past. Lack of evidence is not the only difficulty. To answer the ever more sophisticated questions now being asked by students and historians alike, we lack, in far too many instances, extensive, systematic investigation of all the evidence to hand. The historical profession in these countries is a late starter, or late developer, prone to second and third thoughts, and the processing of archives, where such archives survive in quantity, requires both patience and time.

Any superior unity this period possesses surely derives from the day-to-day uncertainties over the future of both ruling dynasties, problems which, quite unprecedentedly, lingered on throughout the seventy-four years under review, and which merged at the end into one single problem, and one single solution. Developing ideological tensions borne from the reformations which, howsoever slowly, had transformed both England and Scotland into protestant nations by 1600 both fed upon and fuelled those fears. When a king or queen is the source of political authority within a state, and indeed the embodiment of that state's pretensions to independent nationhood, the life of an individual monarch takes on a meaning that now seems all too elusive. We live in a bureaucratic era in which the passing of any one man or woman, however exalted, cannot shake the stability of the nation. Four centuries ago, it was otherwise. In the developed world of the late 1990s individual mortality has been marginalized and, if not defeated, then contained within the bounds imposed by modern medicine and culture. Again, it was otherwise in the sixteenth century. Death, an unpredictable tyrant, stalked the corridors of Whitehall or Holyrood, just as it stalked the streets of provincial Norwich, Bristol, Perth or Aberdeen; just as it trod the rushes on the floor of the meanest cottage in the remotest hamlet or crofting settlement. Faced with the untimely death of a ruler, such as that of the sixteen-year-old Edward VI in 1553, or the thirty-year-old James V in 1542, statesmen made shift to handle a dynastic crisis. But far more characteristic of this age, and far more unusual, were the occasions on which the monarch, despite inevitable health scares, lived on, without producing and without nominating an heir. The greatest alarms arise from regular contemplation of inescapable uncertainty. Just how far down the social scale these fears persisted is debatable, and it may be that the nightmares of great statesmen were seldom shared by the mass of their fellow-countrymen, more concerned with the survival and welfare of their families through another harvest. On the other hand, the injuries and depredations that might follow in the wake of a contested succession to the throne stirred anxieties far beyond the palaces and courts of London and Edinburgh.

The sixteenth century was a rough, violent age. While violence in crime and in the punishment of crime alarms the modern observer, we could argue today that although crime is a disease in society, it is a containable disease, which does not ultimately threaten the life of the body politic. Four hundred years ago citizens, and certainly statesmen, were never so sanguine. Society was, they argued, a fragile entity: it might be overturned by any number of forces, running from foreign invasion to internal unrest. Such fears were intensified by the fact that an early modern state lacked the means to impress its authority on many of its inhabitants. The law of the land can, generally speaking, be enforced today. It underpins social stability, but so too does the overwhelming bureaucracy of the late twentieth century, with its legions of officials and its numerous and ever-multiplying tiers of intrusive government. By contrast, the law of the land in Tudor England and Stewart Scotland could seldom be enforced entirely effectively, and that all-embracing bureaucracy was largely absent. Laws were disregarded, justice was delayed. The sole pressure for many to conform was peer pressure, a healthy regard for the censure and opprobrium of one's neighbours and friends. Uncertainty and incapacity breed fear and vengeance. Small wonder, then, that the early modern state sought to inflict harsh punishments on those who all too frequently flouted its authority with impunity.

Our final theme is still more specifically characteristic of its times. The sixteenth century sees religious ideology dividing both British kingdoms, shattering established customs, systems of justice and administration, and hierarchies, and setting up new and untried systems in their place. This degree of radical change in the heart of society would be extraordinary at any time, but given the fears of social upheaval, and the deference to established nobility and custom, the readiness of statesmen both north and south of the border to countenance reformation in the state religion, and to oversee repeated efforts to enforce the new faith, marks an astonishing new departure in the history of the two kingdoms, the like of which had never been seen before and has – arguably – never been seen again. Ideology developed into a major, menacing new factor on the international stage, transforming traditional alliances involving both England and Scotland, and threatening the security and integrity of both countries. The recreational exercise of royal power that underpinned French campaigning in the days of Henry VIII was replaced, throughout the grim Elizabethan conflicts of the 1590s, by costly and bitterly unpopular wars of attrition which more than once left many parts of the British Isles facing fleets and armies intent on invasion and occupation. Whereas English monarchs of the early sixteenth century might choose their battlefields, that luxury was denied their successors. In 1588, as everyone remembers, the Armada was seen off by Drake and Lord Howard of Effingham; but in 1601 more than three thousand Spanish troops landed in Ireland, and they and their Irish allies were only defeated by English forces enjoying an unreliable mixture of luck, daring and tactical good sense among the high command. As the military issue was resolved in Ireland, so the ideological question there took on ever greater significance, a matter of moment for future centuries.

Finally, a word of explanation to those who might be a little surprised that this volume – and this series – opens half way through the reigns of Henry VIII and James V. No one has yet come up with a particularly satisfactory single date at which we may start to write of modern British history. The abrupt switch from ancient to modern heralded by the departing legions in AD 410 might delight the Oxbridge classicist, but has clear disadvantages in the present context. Another candidate, 22 August 1485, has lost favour in recent years, largely, I suspect, because it was *in* favour for so long, though the concept of modern times being plucked with Richard III's crown from a thorn bush has a good deal to recommend it, just as the death of James III at Sauchieburn three years later closes and opens distinct chapters in the history of Scotland. Others believe we should move the divide into the 1460s, or even back to the Black Death of 1349, while still others would bring us forward to the era of George Washington and Napoleon Bonaparte, branding all that went before 'early modern' for want of anything more suitable. So much for labels, epochs and boundaries. Suspicions that the original series editor, whose views on the significance of the Reformation Parliament and of its chief architect need little rehearsal, might have chosen to link the dawning of the modern age with the summoning of peers, knights and burgesses to Westminster in 1529 cannot be entirely discounted, but there is a rather more pragmatic explanation to hand. As some readers will be aware, the final volume in an earlier multi-volume Blackwell series, *A History of Medieval Britain*, draws to a close in that year. Although the two series differ slightly in their approach, there seemed every point in launching the present enterprise at a moment when the king of England was edging towards decisions which permanently changed his nation's religion, and when one of Scotland's most energetic monarchs was embarking on a decade and a half of unpredictable personal rule.

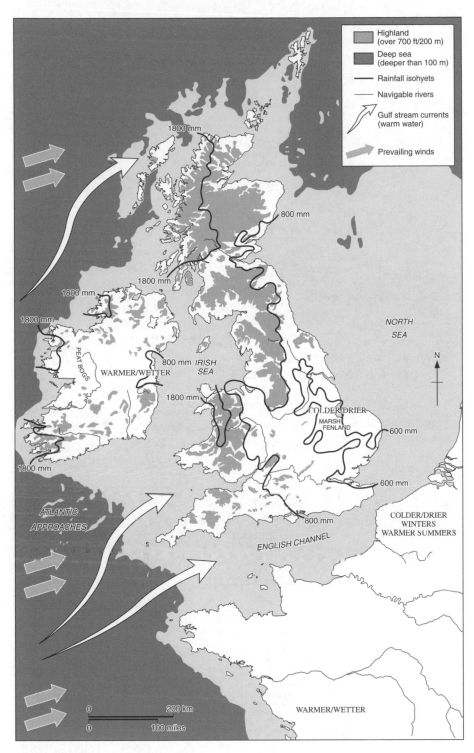

Map 1 Physical geography

Key

+ Bishoprics
⊕ Archbishoprics
--- Effective boundary of
   the English 'Pale' in 1534

1 Achonry	9 Elphin	17 Leighlin
2 Ardagh	10 Emly	18 Limerick
3 Ardfert	(to 1569)	19 Ossory
4 Clogher	11 Kildare	20 Raphoe
5 Clonfert	12 Kilfenora	21 Ross
6 Clonmacnois	13 Killala	22 Waterford
(to 1569)	14 Killaloe	and Lismore
7 Down	15 Kilmacduagh	23 Annadown
8 Dromore	16 Kilmore	(to 1555)

Map 2 Political divisions

xxii

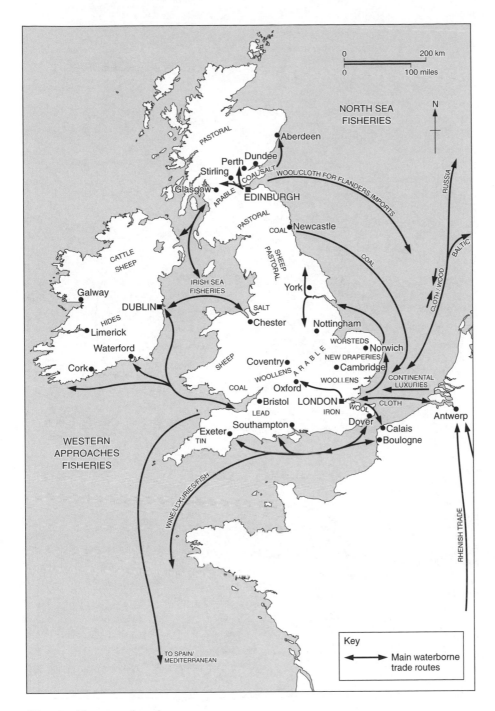

Map 3 Towns and trades

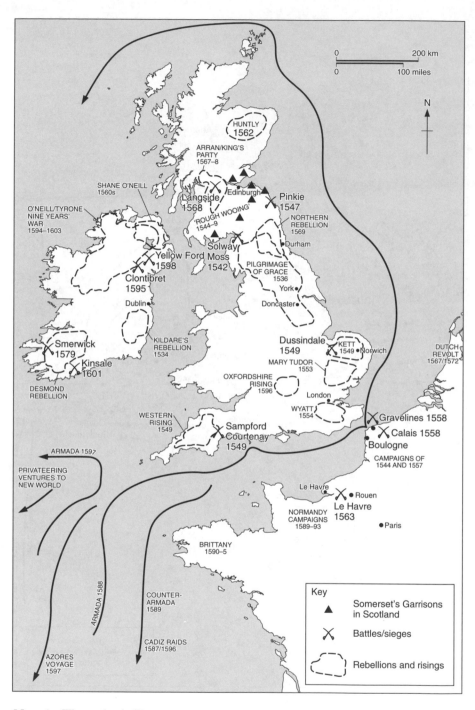

Map 4 War and rebellion

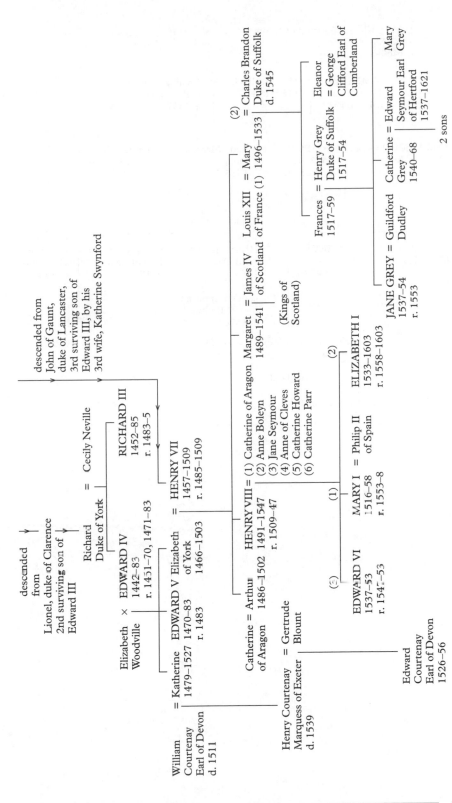

Table 1 The Tudors

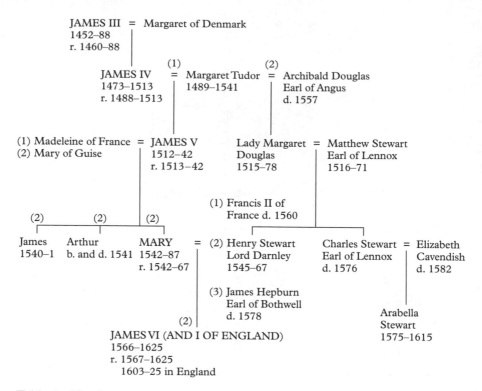

JAMES III = Margaret of Denmark
1452–88
r. 1460–88

          (1)   (2)
JAMES IV = Margaret Tudor = Archibald Douglas
1473–1513   1489–1541   Earl of Angus
r. 1488–1513   d. 1557

(1) Madeleine of France = JAMES V   Lady Margaret = Matthew Stewart
(2) Mary of Guise   1512–42   Douglas   Earl of Lennox
                     r. 1513–42   1515–78   1516–71

                              (1) Francis II of
                              France d. 1560
  (2)   (2)   (2)

James   Arthur   MARY   = (2) Henry Stewart   Charles Stewart = Elizabeth
1540–1 b. and d. 1541 1542–87   Lord Darnley   Earl of Lennox   Cavendish
                     r. 1542–67   1545–67   d. 1576   d. 1582

                              (3) James Hepburn
                              Earl of Bothwell   Arabella
                    (2)   d. 1578   Stewart
           JAMES VI (AND I OF ENGLAND)   1575–1615
            1566–1625
            r. 1567–1625
              1603–25 in England

Table 2 The Stewart dynasty

1 Sixteenth-century England

When we come to explore the England of four centuries past, we do not set out across some uncharted, alien landscape. Though stripped of pylons, wire and concrete, the skyline might not appear unfamiliar to a twentieth-century eye. Towns were smaller, roads were rougher, and there was essentially no industrial landscape, of the kind familiar to our immediate ancestors. Yet, with relatively few exceptions, both roads and towns existed where they exist today, while industries on a small scale were to be found scattered across the land.

By the middle of the century, a largely fertile country was, for the first time in two hundred years, maintaining a substantial rural population. For reasons still uncertain, but in part due to an amelioration in the worst effects of epidemic disease, the population of England had begun to grow. Although that growth attracted contemporary comment, and contributed to social difficulties, viewed over centuries it still appears as a taking up of slack rather than as a development placing intolerable burdens on resources. Population levels were still, perhaps, only half the pre-Black Death figures of two hundred years earlier, and much marginal land farmed for the first time under medieval population pressure had long been abandoned.

These lingering effects of epidemic mortality serve to underscore one fundamental fact of life four centuries ago. At every level of society, the lack of adequate preventatives or cures for disease made human existence acutely unpredictable, and the imminence of death very real. Bubonic plague, a bacterial disease caused by the micro-organism *pasteurella pestis* and transmitted most commonly by rat fleas, never quite assumed endemic proportions in the sixteenth century, yet it periodically ravaged rural and, particularly, urban populations, usually during summer months when its carriers were active. Nor was plague the only threat. That mysterious viral disease known as the 'sweat' killed more swiftly but spared rather more of its victims. The sweat recurred regularly through the first half of the century, then subsided, only to be replaced by a form of influenza which devastated England in the 1550s. While plague and sweat were particularly severe on the young adult, smallpox and other infectious diseases killed as many as one in five children before their first birthday. Survive all these perils, and a person might, with fortune, achieve a respectable age, if with rheumatism and without teeth. The words of the 90th Psalm in a mid-century translation:

> The days of our age are iij score years and ten, and though men be so strong that they come to iiij score years yet is their strength then but labour and sorrow, so soon passeth it away, and we are gone

offer a deliberately downbeat yet sufficiently accurate contemporary view on the destiny of mortal man.

This population, if we may generalize profoundly, lived in small, two-generation family units, predominantly on the land but with a low proportion in small towns. The most populated, and prosperous, parts of England were the lowlands of the south and east, but the ancient division between these regions and the wilder, upland north and west is an oversimplification. The vale of York supported agricultural patterns more closely related to those found in the Thames valley than to those prevailing on the hill farms of northern Derbyshire or Northumberland, while Breckland Suffolk, with its thin sandy soils, had more in common with the unpopulated Pennines than with the great agricultural heartland of nearby Cambridgeshire. English farming output was already highly diverse. Sheep, horses, oxen, pigs, even rabbits and bees, testified to the variety in animal husbandry, while the cultivation of wheat, oats, pulses, hay and rye underlined the beneficence of climate and soil.

Generalizations are comforting given the perils of more precise statistical calculation. Problems of evidence abound. At the start of our period, population estimates are based on tax and probate records, which by their nature detail only a proportion of more prosperous men and women.[1] From 1538, the historian of England is able to extract demographic information from parish registers, maintained by incumbents up and down the land. Though an invaluable source, the registers vary greatly in detail and accuracy, while population mobility often frustrates attempts to trace lineages from generation to generation. Many registers, moreover, have disappeared with time. With these caveats in mind, let us nevertheless attempt greater precision. England's population stood at about 2.4 million in 1529. As aptly as any other, the figure sets England in its European context: four times as many people lived in France, about twice as many in peninsular Spain. The population of the Low Countries was similar to that of England, perhaps four times greater than the nearest available, albeit even less reliable, estimate for Scotland.

The mobility of this population is often underestimated. In a society of nuclear families – which saw children put out as resident servants, which followed, despite pockets of alternative local inheritance systems, the custom of primogeniture under which younger sons were almost everywhere expected to leave home in search of their fortune, and which favoured individual choice of marriage partners – such fluidity comes as no surprise. Surviving evidence suggests an established movement of population from the north-west to the south and east, and from countryside into large villages and towns. In both cases, we are witnessing the attraction of opportunity, in particular the availability of more and better-paid work.

Physical and emotional mobility, however, are two very different concepts. The essential loyalty of a sixteenth-century Englishman lay with his 'country', the parish, town or county where he was born and raised, or where he had chosen to settle. While the word 'country' was used with deliberate ambiguity, England remained a regionalized society. Many, including, if John Aubrey is to be believed, the great Elizabethan favourite Sir Walter Ralegh, spoke in a broad local dialect, even, in Sir Walter's case, after years at the royal court. Some linguistic divisions were still more distinct. Cornish, though shrinking into the west throughout the century, remained a living language in 1603. A more successful Celtic tongue, Welsh, was sufficiently well established to secure *de facto* toleration from English governments. Further afield, the native forms of Gaelic were never seriously challenged as the principal spoken languages across broad swathes of Scotland and Ireland.

Population mobility owed nothing to an inefficient communications infrastructure. Roads were unpaved and often poorly defined. A 'road-table', the nearest thing to a road atlas that the sixteenth century possessed, printed in 1541 lists just nine arterial routes connecting London to provincial towns, and while later, more sophisticated tables describe twice that number, the actual quality and condition of highways may not have improved markedly. For those wishing to travel across country, the ways were rougher still. Only towards the end of the century do we encounter regular references, in tables and elsewhere, to major cross-country routes.

In theory, responsibility for maintaining the highways rested with the local parishes through which they ran. After an act of 1555 compelled all adult males in such parishes to work four unpaid eight-hour days each year at highway upkeep – increased to six days in 1563 – the related fines for negligence permitted some official control of this fragmented process. In practice, the degree of care exercised varied enormously. Transport by land of goods and animals was thus an expensive process, though never quite prohibitively expensive. The escalating number of complaints denouncing poorly maintained highways, in literature and litigation down into the eighteenth century, reflects increasing use of the road as well as deteriorating standards. Horse-drawn passenger coaches and long four-wheel goods wagons, novelties in 1530, were relatively common on the main radial routes out of London by 1600, and their very existence presupposes roads that were at least passable.

There is, nevertheless, a sharp contrast to be drawn between landward transport and the extensive trade and traffic made possible by England's lengthy coastline. The sea offered routes between coastal ports, while the network of estuaries and rivers open to barges and small boats left no village in the kingdom more than twenty miles or so from navigable water. Coastal traffic, unlike the export trade overseas, was shared out among the many small ships based in regional ports. Barge traffic gave Oxford, Cambridge, Nottingham, Shrewsbury and York access to the open sea, and the first attempts at systematic improvement of river navigation are seen on the Exe in the 1560s, and the Lea in the 1570s. Huge volumes of coal, grain and other commodities were shipped into London. Yet water-borne transport had its own disadvantages. Pirates at sea were more common than footpads on land, and while winter storms made both road and coastal travel hazardous, at sea, in the small wooden vessels of the age, those perils were particularly acute.

The urban population of 1520s England amounted only to around 10 per cent of the whole, rising to perhaps 15 per cent by 1600. By the end of our period, the London–Westminster conurbation – the nation's principal port, and home to royal court, parliament, law courts and the mint – was stretching away as the biggest urban concentration in the entire British Isles. Its population of some 200,000 had more than tripled in the century. Next in rank came the provincial centres, Norwich, York and Bristol, possibly Newcastle and Exeter as well. In comparison to the capital, and in real terms, these regional cities were very small. While our estimates of the populations of provincial towns can only take the form of educated guesses, not one was a fifth the size of London. No other European state displayed such an imbalance. By 1600 at least seven French and seven Dutch or Flemish cities boasted populations in excess of 40,000.

Next in the hierarchy we find about eighty 'county towns' exercising important shire functions, built round a castle, perhaps, or housing the sheriff's headquarters, or maybe with a cathedral. These towns were frequently the venues of major fairs and markets, and supported between 1500 and 7000 inhabitants. As John Leland recognized during his ambitious tour of the kingdom at the end of Henry VIII's reign, many had suffered in the past century or so, either through the general demographic decline, or from a movement outward to the unrestricted labour market of the surrounding countryside by England's pre-eminent group of industries, manufacture of woollens. Of large English towns, only Norwich and Worcester had successfully reversed this trend. Smaller still were the five hundred or so 'country towns', service points for their hinterlands. Some of these were differentiated from larger villages only by their weekly markets.

Great or small, towns shared features in common. Several enjoyed tax concessions from successive administrations eager to reverse the generally recognized urban decay of the fifteenth and early sixteenth centuries. The perceptive writer Thomas Starkey argued that a realm with shabby, unruly urban centres deserved scant respect, but the role of towns as local economic hothouses was just as important a consideration. All towns offered in some degree facilities scarce or unknown in the countryside: shops with varied merchandise, schools, taverns, entertainment, businesses such as tanning, brewing and smithies operating from backyards or domestic dwellings. Here the countryman might also find professional services, doctors for example, and lawyers. Many towns even looked the same, typically clustered together on limited, medieval sites, with close, narrow main streets, squalid backstreets and timber buildings, increasingly roofed with lead or tile rather than thatch so as to reduce the ever-present risk of fire.[2] Some retained antiquated, often ruinous walls. Only where royal money was spent on the fortifications of garrison towns – Hull, Berwick, Carlisle and Portsmouth – were such traditional defences modernized or repaired.

The round figures cited conceal the remarkable mobility of urban populations. Rich men moved out to found estates and dynasties in the countryside, while others placed their sons in more 'gentlemanly' professions than trade: in the law perhaps, or in the service of a courtier. Tradesmen sought out other towns with better prospects, while poor countrymen driven by ambition or by the dictates of daily subsistence moved in the other direction. In the cramped conditions, plague and other diseases took a disproportionate toll, producing an excess of deaths over births which in itself stimulated mobility.

Towns and cities were gradually acquiring a renewed self-respect, a positive new identity. The spate of mid-Tudor royal charters of incorporation, twenty-six in Queen Mary's reign alone, extended and renewed privileges, and established new parliamentary franchises. They also put on an official footing the prevailing form of urban government, almost invariably dominated, throughout the century, by self-perpetuating councils drawn from the ranks of richer merchants.

Whether located within or outside the town, industry was, by continental standards, both backward and limited. With few exceptions it was tied to farming production and based in an individual domestic residence. Processing of wool and hides offered a profitable sideline for smallholders and pastoral farmers. Similarly, cottage industries such as nail-making, or the manufacture of pottery in Staffordshire, offered extra income for poor families. In some localities, those sidelines might dominate, as with the cloth-making round Halifax, recognized by parliament in 1555 as vital to the subsistence of those dwelling on the poor moorland soils close to the town.

More speculative industrial ventures, which could swallow large amounts of capital for a sometimes fleeting, if potentially high return, were the preserve of wealthy risk-takers among the nobility and gentry, and, in occasional instances, the religious houses. Obvious examples are the exploitation of coal reserves at Wollaton in Nottinghamshire, on the estates of the Myddeltons and Mostyns in North Wales, and on lands of the bishopric of Durham, through the century. Coal was in increasing demand, not simply as a domestic fuel but also as a source of heat and power for industries like salt-making, the working of iron and the preparation of saltpetre for gunpowder. When mining was more than a surface operation, and pits had to be dug and supported, investment made such activity possible. Constraints were imposed by still-limited drainage and ventilation technology, and it was always a high-risk, volatile industry. As with the other established extractive industries – tin in Devon and Cornwall, lead in Somerset and Derbyshire, iron in the Weald – labour was drawn from an agrarian population making time for work in the mines from their regular pastoral callings. Much paid labour was, indeed, seasonal: apart from employment at the harvest, masonry, fishing and peddling of wares tended to be summer occupations.

As the growing demand for coal would suggest, industrialization, if very small-scale by later standards, is evident before the end of the century. A stocking-knitting industry grew from small beginnings in the 1570s to employ several thousand people part-time across a wide stretch of southern England. Pin-making, labour-intensive to a degree, reduced the need to import. Iron foundries emerged and prospered, with ready supplies of timber fuel in the Sussex weald. However, in 1600 as a century earlier, cloth remained the dominant product, and the dominant export. Cloth production, whether in the form of traditional woollens, worsteds or the more fancy 'new draperies', provided work for householders across England. Under-employment in pastoral areas with small farms, and the natural advantages of water power, combined to make the west country and the Cotswolds, East Anglia, Wiltshire and the West Riding of Yorkshire particularly important as textile-producing regions, but they were by no means alone.

Possession of the land was widely distributed. While the nobility, numerically a far smaller group, held perhaps 15 per cent, more than half the territory of England in 1529 was owned by commoners. That simple statement conceals wonderful complexities. The commoner landowners themselves came from, and saw themselves as representing, a bewildering array of social grades. These ranged from the 350 or so knights, the wealthiest men of longest lineage in each county, through the esquires, men of good birth considered capable of holding senior county offices, to the amorphous 'gentlemen' and 'yeomen', in neither case a legally provable degree, but one conferred upon the holder through a blend of his own ambition and the recognition of neighbours. Further still down the social scale we find the smallest freeholders and copyholders, men with a few acres, often no better off in real terms than their landless, wage-earning contemporaries.

In a pre-industrial society possession of land was fundamental to both status and wealth. Yet the laws upon which English titles to land rested remained complex and, in legal theory at least, disturbingly uncertain. Land was generally held of a superior landlord, under a variety of terms and conditions, from personal military service to straight cash rents, some written down, others recognized by local custom alone. An Englishman who inherited land, or who made his own way in the world, would almost certainly be obliged at some stage in his life to go to law, to defend possessions, to safeguard formal transfers of title, or to enter actions designed either to compel or avoid payment of debts. More and more men and women sought redress through the courts during the sixteenth century, and lawyers thrived commensurately, but both courts and profession were grounded on ancient foundations. The structure of redress had been in place for centuries: England had courts for every occasion. Parliament had, indeed, moved away from its original function as a court which processed petitions for justice – although erring noblemen were throughout the century and beyond tried by their peers – but the king's council still considered a wide range of legal questions, and its long-established central branches each maintained a particular sphere of expertise while competing one against the other for new business. Yorkist or early-Tudor offshoots of the council, the courts of Star Chamber and Requests, offered specific and relatively swift settlement of cases alleging violence and cases involving poor men's suits respectively.

This hierarchy of courts reached out from London to the peripheries, symbolizing both the unity of the kingdom and, in its eccentricities and anomalies, the continuing limitations set upon such unity. Of the ancient common law courts, King's Bench exercised its broad jurisdiction over criminal matters and any case that touched the monarch's interests, while

Common Pleas limited its work to property and debt litigation. Central common law was linked to the counties through the twice-yearly assizes; itinerant royal judges had for more than three centuries been authorized to dispense central justice by commission and writ. A third great court, the Exchequer, the chief crown revenue court still dealing nominally with matters affecting the crown's financial rights, kept its work centralized, developing a large bureaucracy in Westminster.

Tudor assize judges travelled circuits that had been in place since the reign of Edward III, and another form of local common law jurisdiction – the commission of the peace – had roots almost as antique. The justices of the peace (JPs), assembled at the three-monthly 'quarter sessions', were authorized to decide almost every kind of misdemeanour or civil suit, treason alone excepted. In practice, the JPs during the course of the century lost several of their judicial functions, including determination of more serious civil and criminal matters, to the assize courts, gaining by way of compensation an increased workload out of sessions. They were fast becoming the principal agents of government in the shire. To them fell such tasks as administering oath takings, overseeing Tudor social legislation, regulating alehouses, supervising highway maintenance, assisting in collecting taxes, promulgating proclamations, and general 'crisis management' in times of dearth and disease. In short, they became workhorses of an administration lacking a nationwide bureaucracy. Workhorses had to be watched, and here the assize judges served a further purpose, keeping an eye on the performance of the county justices in their respective circuits. Gentlemen on the quarter sessions bench were in any case stiffened and guided by a quorum of experienced lawyers.

Like other prominent county officials, JPs were drawn from the leading landowning families in the shire. They were chosen by the lord chancellor on the advice of the privy council, judges and, in the case of Wales, the council in the marches. The selection process, of course, was far from passive. Gentlemen sought out these positions as frequently as they complained about the burdens of office and the costs involved, once successful. This was largely a matter of prestige, but most recognized that public esteem carried with it some measure of social responsibility.

The increasing use of county divisions – groups of anciently defined 'hundreds' – in the exercise of the JPs' multiplying administrative duties, formalized by the early years of the next century a further permanent level of local justice, the petty sessions. Such county divisions emphasize the limitations of, and the cooperative effort that underpinned Tudor government. While privy council might propose their establishment – be it for reasons of tax collection, militia training or legal administration – the actual combination of hundreds was left almost entirely to local men.[3]

Other courts had evolved outside the traditional common law of England. Based originally on papal and continental forms, and initially offering speedier justice, these included the so-called equity jurisdictions of Chancery, Requests, Star Chamber, and the councils of the north and the marches. Chancery apart, these courts were relatively new, conciliar responses to perceived drawbacks in the medieval systems of English law. Within limited spheres of competence, all proved popular, although in a litigious age the common law courts also displayed flexibility, and in the relentless competition for new clients more than held their own.

There was also a separate array of ecclesiastical jurisdictions. Higher clergy down to the rank of archdeacon generally maintained their own courts, as did various 'peculiar' jurisdictions outside the established church hierarchy. Justice dispensed in all these courts was based on the canon laws of the church, and, after the reformation, on related civil law. While it might be supposed that the religious courts lost business after the great upheavals of the 1530s, that was not in fact the case. The Ecclesiastical High Commissions of England's two religious provinces, Canterbury and York, vigorously enforced the Elizabethan settlement after 1559, and attempted to resolve damaging family disputes that erupted in the wake of matrimonial, defamation and testamentary cases. These domestic concerns, and the parson's unending quest for his tithe, his due share of parishioners' annual produce, supplied the majority of ecclesiastical cases as the century wore on. Limited justice it might have been, with few penalties available beyond penance, yet the conciliation on offer was often popular, for it saved many litigants a great deal of money.

These were not, however, the jurisdictions that had greatest impact on the lives of most Englishmen. Manorial, hundredal or borough courts dispensed local justice, resolved local disputes, and endeavoured to maintain due order in rural and urban communities. There were some 50,000 manors in England. They could be large or small, compact or fragmented, but each had its own feudal overlord and, significantly, its own court. The great jurist Sir Edward Coke spoke for his fellow lawyers when he wrote early in the seventeenth century that a manorial court was 'incident to and inseparable from a Manor'; without a court the manor 'falleth to the ground'. This court served to protect the rights and enforce the obligations of both lord and tenants, rights and obligations fashioned over the years into an often quite rigid manorial custom. Custom meant security. In most parts of the country a lord would number among his tenants former bondmen or villeins, now referred to as 'copyholders', whose holdings were accorded effective protection by a record of their descent entered on the manorial court roll. Even his tenants 'at will', theoretically vulnerable to eviction at any time, were commonly protected, through the manorial court, by various forms of customary 'tenant right'. A ruthless landlord might attempt to batter or bully his way into property, but evidence suggests that few ever did so.

The wonderful formality of all these courts suggests a ready access to justice for all who sought it. This illusion, however, evaporates upon consideration of practicalities. In a society lacking any police force, in which the initiative for local harmony lay with leading local gentry and their estate officers, it is unreasonable to look for the even-handed or swift execution of justice. High and petty constables in hundred and parish were not always so conscientious or thoroughly supervised as their JP superiors. Felons fled, debtors delayed, plaintiffs met with procrastination, juries, consisting of an uneasy mix of the influential and the indebted or bribable, juggled with doubtful evidence, and justices, on occasion, judged less than impartially. Worse still, perhaps, men and women often indulged in prosecution of civil actions for the basest and most provocative motives. The very sophistication of legal process, fuelled by a rising profession competing for clients, itself contributed to such vexations.

English courts considered a bewildering variety of crimes. Offences ranged from petty instances of defamation and trespass to the capital charges of murder, rape or arson. Tudor administrations and, indeed, their successors deemed one crime especially foul. Treason, an attack upon the person or dignity of the monarch, was considered an offence against the very fabric of society, although few Englishmen felt comfortable defining what was treason and what was not. In practice, some treasons were clear-cut, others were far less obvious. But even as construed by anxious governments, treason was rare. Although the surviving evidence is again uneven, and open to statistical misrepresentation, it appears that crimes against property far outnumbered offences against the person, even in criminal cases. In lesser courts – quarter sessions and below – crimes 'without a victim' were especially numerous.

The worst crimes commanded dire penalties. Convicted traitors died a savage and grimly symbolic death: males were hanged, disembowelled and quartered, women commonly hanged and burnt. By contrast, murderers and thieves escaped lightly with a hanging. Felonies – misdemeanours involving forfeiture of lands and goods, and by common extension life itself – increased in number through the century, but again theory departed from practice. As the extreme example of the eighteenth century shows, the more petty the crime punishable by death or forfeiture, the greater the inclination to interpret offences in a less heinous light, and the greater the likelihood that a jury would acquit. Nevertheless, as many as 800 people every year were being executed on the gallows when it becomes possible to estimate figures, towards the end of the century.

Once again we are at the mercy of intermittent records. Archives of the central courts arc copious, though here too there are lacunae. The decree books of Star Chamber have been lost for over three and a half centuries. Across the localities, assize records are almost non-existent for the early sixteenth century, while many series of quarter sessions records arc notoriously incomplete. In the light of surviving evidence, Tudor England appears as a savage, pugnacious place, its population forever coming to blows over trifles. An impression of disorder cannot be set aside; per head of population almost every felony was far more common than such crimes are today. Nevertheless, accusations of violence were in many cases technicalities in court processes rather than statements of fact. The tentative statistics provide some curiosities too, for instance, the fact that domestic homicide as a proportion of all these cases stood at a half the late twentieth-century level. Perhaps we have touched here upon crimes unreported and unrecorded, though the fact that misbehaviour leaves a record, while correct carriage is mute, may stand as a counterweight to the many colourful vignettes of disorder.

Having focused at such length on crime and courts, the emergence of law as a popular, prestigious profession should come as no surprise. The number of practising barristers rose by around 200 per cent between the 1570s and 1630s. While there had been perhaps one attorney for every 20,000 head of population in 1560, there was one for every 4000 by 1606. The availability of statistics tells its own tale. Professions, lawyers, doctors, merchants of all kinds, were becoming more self-conscious, and bureaucratic. These men never fitted easily into traditional models of society based on landownership, although the professionals themselves made every effort to conform, established town tradesmen persisting in describing themselves as yeomen, and office-holding citizens expecting to be addressed as gentlemen. If one social trend is apparent in the later sixteenth century, it is that towards a greater diversity of elites – of land, of church, of trade, of industry and of law.

Sixteenth-century England was a relatively literate society. No entirely satisfactory measurement of prevailing literacy is now possible, but at least half the population could sign a name, and rather more could read simple passages from the popular cheap tracts and ballads or from the elementary religious catechisms, turned out in great numbers and endless editions later in the century. The fact that the Oxford bookseller John Dorne was selling over 170 halfpenny or penny ballads a day as early as 1520 speaks for itself. Reading was a skill more readily acquired than writing, and there were probably regional variations, with London more literate than the far north or Wales. Women were, and were expected to be, less literate than men, although towards the end of the century there is an increase in the number of publications aimed specifically at a female readership. The divisions were social also. A late sixteenth-century gentleman, especially if he aspired to the increasingly fashionable ideal of multi-talented renaissance versatility, was expected to read and write, and so too was his wife, although from the evidence of many exotically composed letters it appears that women were allowed greater latitude in spelling and grammar. Here fashion was underpinned by practicalities. In litigious times, a gentleman had to be literate if he was to contest lawsuits efficiently, while his younger sons might look to the law and other 'literate' professions as profitable and honourable ways of making a living.

We hold to traditional views of an ignorant proletariat at our peril; those seeking an education have in all ages generally been able to find one. The problem lies once again in quantification. While it is possible to count endowed grammar schools – where boys, often of some means, were schooled in Latin, the language of government and diplomacy – there were numerous other unendowed schools, every kind of private institution, and a developing tradition of parish education offering the 'three Rs'. Around formal lessons in established schools, moreover, lay a penumbra of informal education, where senior pupils taught younger or poorer children, while 'dames' – who as John Guy remarks can resemble 'child-minders by another name' – catered for the basics with varying degrees of success in their elementary schools.[4]

In the 1530s literacy, combined with the accessibility of printed works, and the chance assembly of prominent figures proficient in their native tongue, contributed to what Geoffrey Elton once called 'an epoch in the development of the English language'. Such a coming together of talent foreshadows still more remarkable developments in the 1590s. The elegance and range of vocabulary behind Archbishop Thomas Cranmer's compositions are echoed in the statesman Thomas Cromwell's surviving writings, in William Tyndale's Biblical translations, in the work of the chronicler Edward Hall, and in the verses of the poet Sir Thomas Wyatt. Spurred by debates at every intellectual level over the break with Rome, printing presses flourished. The majority – virtually all in the 1530s – were in London. While reform programmes and theological broadsides have held centre stage in the considerations of many historians, there was already a vast body of varied printed literature on other topics, from academic works in a still-vigorous Latin through translations of classical texts and endless reprints of popular native folk tales, to more original ventures, among them various works by the enterprising Sir Thomas Elyot. Elyot's writings included a medical vade-mecum, *The Castell of Health*, a Latin–English dictionary, and an organized course of education for the sons of gentlemen, *The Boke named the Governour*. London book dealers clustered around St Paul's Cathedral carried on a busy, nationwide trade. Booksellers in the provincial towns, rare birds in 1529, had multiplied by the end of the century: schools formed the bed-rock of their custom, but their large stocks, from expensive chronicles to the cheapest almanacs and broadsheets, catered for every taste.[5]

Despite the proliferation of printed texts, many works still circulated in the traditional manuscript copy. Numerous draft programmes of social reform, for example, were passed round among critical commentators. There were risks in going to press, particularly if the opinions expressed were controversial, and to this deterrent must be added a social stigma which clung persistently to the whole idea of print. In Thomas Starkey's lifetime, only his defence of the moderate united national church and state, his *Exhortation to the people*, was printed, and that only at the insistence of his powerful friend Cromwell. On the other hand, Starkey's masterpiece, the *Dialogue between Pole and Lupset*, and a number of other important works, did not appear in print for centuries.

For the Elizabethan statesman Sir Thomas Smith, choosing his words in a way which no contemporary would have questioned, the monarch was 'the life, the head, and the authority of all things that be done in the realm of England'. Personal monarchy, of course, had its weaknesses. Medieval English precedent, in the persons of Edward II, Richard II and Henry VI, reminded observers that whenever a king was incompetent, insecure or insane, the stability of the realm itself was prejudiced. Worse still, in an age of epidemic disease and sudden death, were the dangers inherent in a minority. At such times the nominal rule of a child monarch was of necessity overseen by powerful relatives and magnates. The Tudors were fortunate in avoiding many such misfortunes, yet the troubled reign of the boy king Edward VI illustrated some of the potential problems, while the subsequent succession of two women raised other doubts and anxieties in this male-dominated society.

Howsoever buttressed by the exhortations of churchmen and political theorists, obedience to the crown was still at its root a personal loyalty. Homilies on obedience, regular fare in sermons from the court to the parish church, dwelt on the evils of dissent. Sir John Cheke's *Hurt of sedition*, a work both temperate and intelligent, may be taken to represent the fears of many in authority. Men might be tempted to rebel, but to fall before such temptation was to succumb to the agents of darkness. The reformation introduced a debate on the lawfulness of resistance to a crowned monarch, though even then it took an effort of will to subscribe to theories advanced by men like the protestants Christopher Goodman, John Ponet or John Knox against the Marian regime of the 1550s, or by the Catholics William Allen and William Reynolds under Queen Elizabeth, that a ruler forcibly imposing error in religion might in conscience be opposed, even to the extremity of tyrannicide. The position adopted by Archbishop Cranmer under Queen Mary – he preferred submission and death to rebellion against a legitimate ruler – was one extreme example of the more common reaction: passive conformity to sovereign will.

The message was reinforced by royal policy, and by the careful cultivation of an awe-inspiring royal image. Royal portraiture as an art form develops rapidly during the century, particularly under Henry VIII and Elizabeth. Henry stares with splendid truculence from Holbein's masterpiece, while in a sequence of carefully composed images Elizabeth becomes ever less a woman, ever more a symbol – 'Gloriana' – embodying the spirit and superficial splendour of her country and her age.

Queen Elizabeth fought to control the iconography involved, and the resulting images are a complex composite of personal and national majesty. From the time of the first official portrait by Nicholas Hilliard in 1572, Elizabeth manipulates sunshine and storm, she towers over the defeated Armada, she surveys the map of England at her feet (as can be seen in plate 16). The contrast with more lifelike portraits of her sister Mary is instructive. Paintings were copied widely, the images they provided being duplicated in monuments, in the transient art of public pageantry, and in the spectacle of a court progress which carried the splendour of a royal entourage across southern (never northern) England. Tournaments, the theatre of participation for a young Henry VIII, became under Elizabeth a further opportunity to convey a symbolic message in which the queen in her many guises – Deborah, Gloriana, Cynthia, Astraea, the Belphoebe of Edmund Spenser's *The Faerie Queene* – vanquishes Protestant England's foes and bestows an age of plenty upon her adoring people. Sixteenth-century portraiture is crowded with the symbolism of a culture in which men and women were accustomed to interpret and recognize, if not necessarily to respect, the complicated messages thus conveyed.

Elizabeth was, though, in a very real sense 'alone of all her sex': women played a very minor part in public life. That indirect power might sometimes be exercised through informal channels, or through marriage, only emphasizes this fact. In law, male domination went one step further. When a woman married, her land and moveable possessions passed to her husband; if she subsequently took a knife to him the charge would be not murder but petty treason, a crime committed against her lord and master. A woman enjoyed an independent status only when a spinster or a widow, although for the better off a carefully drawn marriage settlement could, with increasing support from English courts, protect personal property.[6] England's sixteenth-century queens regnant were aberrations which prove the rule. We have only to note the ways in which their accessions were rationalized by contemporaries sympathetic to Mary and Elizabeth. God, argued Nicholas Ridley, argued Cranmer, argued Nicholas Bacon, had His own purposes in setting a woman to bear sway over kingdoms, and there was an overriding obligation to bend to His will, always with the consolation that male counsellors would be on hand to give sound advice. As with queens, so too with their countrywomen. No woman is found in the ranks of judges, great officials of state, or in anything but the lowest reaches of the church's hierarchy. Technically, women could become sheriffs of counties, or justices of the peace, though there remains no certain evidence that any ever did. Some appear to have attained the humble, parochial office of churchwarden, but opportunity ran no higher.[7]

The vicissitudes of personal monarchies are reflected in the fortunes of their greatest subjects. Like an unfit king, the improvident, debt-ridden, ailing or unlucky nobleman could disgrace or impoverish a house built up through generations of care and prudence. The careers of the third earl of Kent and the sixth earl of Northumberland illustrate the destructive qualities of feckless debt, premature death and childlessness.[8] On occasion the parallels were reinforced by royal design. A score of peers executed or imprisoned during these seventy years bore witness to the uncertainty of magnate power in its all-important relations with monarchy. Nevertheless, no king set out to destroy the nobility on which his authority and prestige rested. Peers were a foundation, not an embellishment of the state. The poet Fulke Greville elegantly considered them 'brave half paces between a throne and a people'.

The wealth, social status and personal capacities of this small group varied markedly. At the top, the high nobility commanded landed incomes in excess of £5000 a year, influence among the gentry of entire counties, and control of elections in particular shires and boroughs. The earl of Derby in Lancashire is a case in point. At the other end of the scale some barons, promoted beyond their means, enjoyed relatively little influence, and were indistinguishable from the ranks of the gentry whence they had risen.[9]

Such a blurring of the boundaries between nobility and gentility has rendered problematic persisting attempts to see in the late sixteenth century a rising gentry class, or, alternatively, a 'crisis' among the aristocracy. The first is clearer than the second. It never proved easy to specify the factors that made a gentleman or gentlewoman: an ability to live entirely on landed income, and the capacity to entertain on an appropriate scale, in an appropriate house, were but two, inconclusive elements. The most important 'qualifications' to gentility were ancient lineage, gentle descent and the right to bear a coat of arms. Heralds, clearly responding to demand (but not universal demand, for many old families either scorned or would not pay for the exercise) went busily about their county 'visitations', examining and approving the claims of local men to bear arms. Seven hundred and forty grants of arms are on record for the 1570s alone. In the end, though, most observers conceded that a man might emerge from the commonalty and make himself a

Plate 1 *William Brooke, tenth Lord Cobham, and his family*, British school, oil on panel, 1567. Cobham was an able career nobleman. His son and eventual heir Henry, the little boy on the left, a close friend of Sir Walter Ralegh and favourite of Elizabeth I in her last years, was convicted of treason in 1603. Mealtimes could be used by parents to teach their children good manners. They were often regarded as symbolizing due order and respect for degree.
Source: Reproduced by permission of the Marquess of Bath, Longleat House, Warminster, Wiltshire

gentleman. Sir Thomas Smith in *De Republica Anglorum* decided that a gentleman was, simply, one not constrained to manual work, who 'will bear the port, charge, and countenance of a gentleman', while the best modern study of the gentry concludes again that they were 'that body of men and women whose gentility was acknowledged by others'.[10] However defined, numbers were certainly rising. By 1600, there were perhaps as many as 15,000 families – 1 or 2 per cent of the total population – claiming the status of gentry. This figure had increased fivefold in seventy years.[11]

The element of social emulation at work here led some to overreach themselves, while others fell prey to those enduring calamities of improvidence, unwise property transactions, failure of the male line and ill-judged matrimonial alliances. The story is one of a myriad individuals, and individual fortunes. With quantification based on collective assessments of that personal experience, the extent of any crisis among the nobility becomes elusive. Economic evidence is incomplete, a small sample is prone to produce abnormal, rather meaningless statistical data, and by any measure the nobility remains the dominant social group, in 1600 and beyond. Generalizations are surely dangerous here, but if we must attempt them it seems most helpful to dwell, not on a crisis among the nobility, but rather upon the sixteenth-century prosperity of the English gentry, among which the peerage formed a small if elite subset.

Upon the shoulders of the entire landed class fell the burden of projecting royal authority at court and in the counties, the duty, and cost, of providing military leadership, the onus of giving counsel when it was required by the king. It was one of the essential arts of kingship to assess when and in what form such advice should be sought, and the extent to which, when given, it should be heeded. Man management was the key to this game. Just like his medieval predecessors, the Tudor monarch had to impress, and at the same time to appraise, his greatest subjects. Society at that high level was close, even intimate, and while it was in no one's interest to disrupt these ties, the king was clearly obliged to cultivate the skills of a diplomat and to curb the instincts of an autocrat.

Noblemen and the more prominent gentlemen had also to cement the range of formal and informal relations between themselves, their clients and retainers. One manifestation of this complicated process has in the past received a great deal of attention. Retaining – the maintenance by peers and other great men of private retinues – had been legislated against in several early Tudor parliaments, but the target on those occasions had been the independent employment of military personnel. For the nobleman of proven trust, licensed military retaining continued to be not only permitted, but often enjoined, on the understanding that these retinues were maintained for royal service. The crown thereby saved money, and valued such resources against any sudden crisis. Otherwise, provided the purpose was peaceable, it was permissible for the wealthy nobleman to gather round him a broad group of administrators, legal officers and domestic servants. These agents, often eminent county figures in their own right, were expected to render faithful service, and in return a nobleman strove to reward them financially, to assist their dynastic and legal ambitions, and to return 'good thank' for loyal endeavour.

Kings of England governed with the advice of their councils. Even here, at the heart of policy-making, a lack of evidence frustrates the investigator. No official record of debates in council was kept in Tudor England, and council records of any kind for the 1530s are also virtually non-existent. In 1540, after the fall of Thomas Cromwell, our attention is drawn to an existing 'privy' council. Henceforward, it is this intimate advisory group which not only advises the monarch but also exercises executive powers over a wide range of administrative concerns through the signed council letter. Privy counsellors were, if only through their necessarily intimate attendance on the monarch, also principal members of the royal court. However we define the terms, no man might be a counsellor who was not a courtier. The earls of Shrewsbury, resident on their northern estates, maintained agents at court and kept close watch on what happened there. Access to the monarch was all-important. The authority born of intimacy was shared by some servants of the crown outside the council. Every gentleman of the privy chamber, for example, might be employed as a trusted extension of the royal persona, carrying personal commands into his locality, conducting diplomacy and levying men for military operations.[12]

The shape and characteristics of the Tudor court changed with the years. In essence, though, it retained to 1603 a subdivision, both in organization and personnel, inherited from the distant past. The household, nominally presided over by the lord steward, provided the service and logistical requirements: kitchens, stables, and so forth. The chamber, under the lord chamberlain, attended to ceremonial aspects and, originally, to the king's own quarters. The court, though, was more than the sum of these parts. It was a place for royal display, for the cut and thrust of national politics, and also for the enjoyment of, in Daniel Javitch's splendid phrase, 'sophisticated leisure'.[13] The court was both a physical space and also a concept embodying the entire realm. It defined that realm's executive power. Never closed off from the outside world, it was rather a highly 'porous' entity, a true point of contact with the political nation. Principal courtiers lived out, maintaining houses near or in London. Henry VIII appointed some 500 chamber officials in the years to 1540, the vast majority of them honorary posts granted to leading gentlemen of the shires. In this way he developed a personal affinity along the lines of one created by Edward IV, seventy years earlier. The king gained thereby a secure local clientage, and the gentlemen involved gained prestige: a further cementing of local authority.

Increasing demands for royal privacy, and the young Henry VIII's inclination for companions of his own age, combined to separate from the chamber an increasingly significant privy chamber. Privy chamber officials controlled access to the king's private apartments, and to the king himself. Its head – whose title, groom of the [close] stool, betrayed his office's menial yet personal origins – administered the privy purse, originally a petty-cash extension of the treasurer of the chamber, but soon one of the key financial offices. From 1529 the purse by-passed chamber accounts, drawing coin from the king's own treasure chests, or privy coffers. Nevertheless, such trends were subsequently reversed under female monarchs surrounded by apolitical female attendants. Viewed over a century, the interlocking structure of household, chamber and privy chamber remained curiously constant.

Describing the structure of the Tudor court is one thing, understanding its day-to-day operation quite another. The deficiencies of evidence for the workings of the council are as nothing when compared to the ambiguous and inconsistent surviving records for court affairs. So much of this story was never written down: the passing feuds between courtiers, the irritation suffered by a king with gout, the whispered secret confided on a stair. Tradition further obscures the tale, for court politics are essentially national politics, they contribute to the story of England told for centuries in schoolbooks, and old myths die hard. These histories are replete with tales of intrigues, factional strife, grand speeches and gallant gestures. Thomas Cromwell is dragged unceremoniously from the council chamber, the duke of Northumberland manipulates a dying young king, Queen Elizabeth appears in armour at Tilbury, astride a white horse and Sir Walter Ralegh surrenders his cloak to Gloriana. Sadly, the evidence for such events is all too often circumstantial, or suspect. With reflection that should come as no surprise, for the real history of a court is secret history. It shows a public face, and may array itself in finery for coronation, diplomacy and revelry, but its true nature nevertheless lies hidden behind the obscurities of private conversation, and still more private conceit.

As a result, we depend heavily on the reports of foreign ambassadors, men whose mission it was to penetrate the inner mind of the Tudor court. Unfortunately, ambassadors were seldom well informed, and frequently inexpert in the interpretation of news coming their way. Resident envoys, unlike the noblemen sent on specific missions to foreign courts, did not often come from the very highest ranks of society. They had their own careers to consider, and their despatches can reflect an unwarranted sense of self-importance. There are more fundamental problems, too. Ambassadors' reports habitually factionalize politics, giving the king's ear first to one group of courtiers, then to another. They maintain in their helter-skelter gathering of news an unconscious if natural discrimination between those who talked to the envoy, and those who did not.

Just the same, the importance of ambassadorial evidence must not be underestimated. Envoys were present as great affairs were transacted, and interviewed the men and women who transacted them. A balance has to be struck between careful interpretation of the evidence we do have and sensible guesswork in its absence. Official records of government will influence us one way, the ambassador's report another, the uncorroborated testimony of a contemporary biographer still another. These are lessons common to the study of every period; all that must be remembered is that the story before us is subject to endless revision. There is no such thing as a definitive light.[14]

Our period opens with the summoning of what future generations were to term the Reformation Parliament, yet the quantity of government-inspired legislation passed by that assembly hardly typified the workload of a Tudor parliament. In a far more common scenario, some modest government programme – a request for a financial subsidy, or an attempt to address some specific political problem – was washed about by a sea of private legislation. The authority of statute law, laws passed with the approval of king in parliament, had come during the previous two centuries to be recognized as supreme. Queen Elizabeth's pre-eminent counsellor, William Cecil, once confessed that he doubted whether there were any laws which an English parliament could *not* pass. Parliament, moreover, remained a court. As we have seen, it was the highest court in the land. For the crown, parliament therefore offered several useful roles: it could create law, and it could pass judgement on points of law, or on prominent offenders. Less tangibly it could, like the royal court, serve as an effective sounding board, a means by which the king might demonstrate national unity of purpose. Debate was permitted, indeed, encouraged, within due bounds. Measures passed after a 'full and frank' exchange of views were considered all the stronger for having been examined by the community of England in parliament assembled. In this manner it provided a means of spreading political risk across the whole nation, a way of sanctioning legislation desired by the king.

The Tudor parliament also provided funds for a king's more costly and unforeseen projects, particularly his wars. To the modern Englishman, nothing is counted so certain as death and taxation. For his early Tudor forebear, while death lurked as an everyday companion, taxation remained an intermittent evil. He expected to pay taxes only when some unanticipated political development threatened national security and obliged the crown to find large sums for military expenditure, coming to accept this episodic burden on the understanding that the crown asked for the money in parliament, and explained the nature of a particular emergency. In response, parliament granted, and continued to grant well into the 1600s, two forms of tax. The fifteenth and tenth – a fixed sum demanded of individual towns and parishes, on scales little changed in two hundred years – promised a known return, but was unresponsive to both inflation and geographic changes in wealth. One fifteenth and tenth brought in around £30,000. This traditional levy had from 1513 been supplemented by the lay subsidy, a direct tax based on a local assessment of the incomes from lands, fees and annuities – or, if greater, on moveable possessions – of laypeople sufficiently wealthy to fall above a varying exemption limit.

The theoretical justification for taxation was to change slowly in the course of the century. What did not change was the state's inability to coerce the reluctant taxpayer, or – in an age when calculation was left to the representatives of local taxpayers themselves – to overcome deliberate underassessment. Undervaluation became ubiquitous. The crown in 1600 anticipated a return on each subsidy amounting to no more than one third the 1530 figure.[15]

There were, however, very clear limits on parliament's role as a constitutional assembly. Monarchs summoned parliament and they dissolved parliament; years passed by without a session. Through appointments to peerages and bishoprics, and through control of writs of summons, the sovereign maintained control over the House of Lords, throughout this century the most powerful chamber of parliament. The Commons, although much larger and for that reason potentially less tractable, consisted of men who owed their seats to court and local magnate connections. The election of an MP in the sixteenth century served many purposes. It expressed the local influence of landowners, and allowed the exchange of favours between crown, counsellors, and their local friends and agents. Usually, a member was returned unopposed. Elections turned into contests only when something went wrong – when consensus failed, when feuding families lacked the strength to browbeat their neighbours, or when a nominee proved particularly repugnant.

Who, then, sat in a Tudor parliament? The House of Lords was small, consisting in 1529 of some fifty lay peers and about the same number of bishops and abbots. By the end of Elizabeth's reign its strength was down to under sixty, with the lay peers in a majority after the dissolution of the monasteries had removed abbots from the roll. Numbers were not everything.

A meeting of the Lords brought together a select group of those whom the king had nominated as members of parliament, or whose presence represented the king's acquiescence in similar nominations made by his predecessors. To look at matters in this way is indeed a little anachronistic: although the oldest peerages were defined by the antiquity of their summons to parliament, the monarch seldom if ever created new peers with an eye to their performance in the Lords. Nevertheless, the nobility in parliament, old and new, represented the highest level of Tudor society. They represented loyalty too, since most noblemen owed their prominence to the Tudor dynasty. By the end of his reign, Henry VIII had created half his peerage. It was generally the case by 1529 that a peer would take his seat on succeeding to his title. Since he might thereafter give a lifetime of service the Upper House was full of experience in parliamentary process. Another circumstance emphasized that experience. Several new peers created by Henry VIII had sat previously in the Commons. Four – Lords Hussey, Tailboys, Windsor and Wentworth – were promoted from the Lower House shortly after the 1529 session began.[16]

Our impression of an experienced Upper House is further strengthened by contemporary expansion in the Commons – new seats often meant new, untried, men. That growth is very much a sixteenth-century phenomenon. The nominal strength of the Lower House in 1500 was 296: 74 knights of the shire, selected by the great men of each county, and 222 burgesses, elected under various franchises in more than a hundred towns. By 1603, 462 members were returned. Each shire in England and Wales still returned a quota of knights – normally two, although most of the Welsh counties when first enfranchised in the 1530s were allotted just one representative each. Otherwise, this growth came about as a result of crown enfranchisement of new parliamentary boroughs. Henry VIII added about forty such constituencies in the course of his reign, Edward VI and Mary together created just under thirty, while the total under Elizabeth was approximately another thirty, all of them before 1586. Again, the norm for boroughs was two members each, although an ancient precedent was revived in the 1530s with the establishment of single-member constituencies, often in poorer, smaller towns. Late Tudor growth was made possible when in 1547 the Commons moved out of its ancient quarters in the refectory or chapter house of Westminster Abbey. The acquisition of part of the old St Stephen's Chapel in the Palace of Westminster brought more space, as well as an antechamber which facilitated divisions of the House and the accurate recording of votes on disputed points. The House itself welcomed growth, only becoming worried about the representative rights of particular boroughs when discovering, to its dismay, that there were insufficient seats in the building to go round.[17]

The desire for enfranchisement was by no means universal. Some towns – Nuneaton and Birmingham, for example – actively avoided parliamentary representation. Intermittent parliaments, and consequent inexperience, meant that limited opportunities to advance a town's particular interests had to be set against the cost of maintaining ineffectual men at Westminster. On the whole, though, the matter was viewed in terms of duty and prestige. Towns frequently placed parliamentary seats at the disposal of wealthy, powerful, friendly outsiders, prepared to pay their own way.[18] In Elizabeth's ten parliaments, just one quarter of burgesses were resident in the boroughs they represented.

Inasmuch as there has been a common thread to this brief excursion through an early modern society, it lies in stressing the dangers of generalization given the imperfections of available evidence. Nowhere have ambiguities offered more scope for academic disagreement than in the many attempts to gauge the vitality of the English church on the eve of reformation. One long-dominant school of thought portrays a church spiritually and financially moribund, impoverished and illiterate in its lower reaches, proud, worldly and corrupt at the top, and deeply unpopular among an anticlerical laity. Those who challenge this interpretation suggest rather that there are many signs of spiritual and intellectual vitality in the church, and that dissatisfaction with the religious status quo, and creeping irreligion, become evident only after the Henrician reformation has stripped the church of its wealth, authority and antique mystery.

While investigations have produced many valuable regional case studies to support both arguments, the findings for no one area can be considered typical of the country as a whole. Nor is this surprising, given that there were perhaps 20,000 to 25,000 clergy, and some 9000 parishes in England in 1530, and given too that lay attitudes towards the religious are difficult to pin down. For every worldly, negligent bishop there was another both conscientious and hardworking. For every suggestion that the lesser clergy – the ordained priests who did not hold a benefice and who found work as curate or chantry priest – existed in a state of poverty, we can counter with suggestions that the level of stipends alone is unlikely to be in every case an accurate guide to a man's entire wealth.[19] One has, after all, to account for the apparent popularity of ordination in the early years of the century when set against the fact that the unbeneficed outnumbered the beneficed clergy in every English diocese. Career prospects among the lower clergy were poor, for relatively few ordained priests who lacked a benefice at the start of their careers acquired one later. Maybe 'lesser' clergy looked upon the occasional curacy or obituary-work as a useful extra income to augment a livelihood earned elsewhere. There were, in any case, realities which frustrated reform in both pre- and post-reformation England. One third of all parish churches were appropriated to religious houses, colleges or other individuals or institutions. The practice was widely criticized within the church, but served a purpose, and the drain on parochial incomes as the appropriator took a varying percentage was considered by most a necessary evil.

Nor have efforts to chart the reception of unorthodox religious ideas in England resolved disagreements over the popularity of demands for church reform. Despite the professional gloom of some clerics, medieval heresies survived on only a small scale. The native Lollard heresy was still to be found in the Chilterns, down the Thames valley and in London; individuals and families consciously shared heretical views and through intermarriage tried to preserve those beliefs, but this entrenched minority nonconformity does not amount to a national protestant movement. The emerging realization that

Lollards were disproportionately wealthy, 'respectable' men and women helps us to understand the successive persecutions led by bishops of London and Lincoln in the early sixteenth century. At the same time, the efficiency of persecution suggests that the church had the measure of its opponents.

Lollardy embraced a variety of views, and often exhibited a practical co-operation with regular parish activities that foreshadows the conformist puritan and 'church papist' of later years. Insofar as they held a coherent set of beliefs, Lollards shared doubts, scepticism and resentment. Building on the views of their fourteenth-century inspiration John Wyclif, they questioned the nature of the mass, rejected the doctrine of transubstantiation, doubted the necessity of confessing sins to a clergyman, and scorned such 'corrupt' practices as pilgrimages, fasting, purchased indulgences and prayers to saints. Some Lollards, though, allowed these observances in a purer form: barefoot pilgrimages to visit the sick and poor, for example. The more positive aspects of Lollard beliefs focused on their conviction that religion ought to be expressed verbally rather than through symbol and intercession; that individuals, lay or religious, deserved direct access to scripture, where appropriate in an English translation. While the Catholic church held fast to services in Latin, and a Latin Bible, a vernacular 'Lollard' Bible had, indeed, been in circulation in England throughout the fifteenth century.

Certainly, parallels may be noted between Lollardy and the views of the great continental reformer Martin Luther. These parallels, however, stand only limited scrutiny. Lutheranism in 1520s Germany was still essentially a clerical protest within the established church. Lollardy had started out as such, but had developed into an underground movement sustained largely by laypeople, and containing a strain of anticlericalism. Luther's central doctrines, that salvation comes solely through Christ's grace, and that men – following the later teachings of St Augustine of Hippo – are justified by faith alone, that is, they are regarded as just by God through a work of divine grace, without the necessity for good works, were not themselves Lollard beliefs. Nevertheless their anticlerical implications coincided with Lollard sentiments. Many Lollards welcomed the new interpretations, as a long-beleaguered community invariably welcomes the arrival of allies. That, however, was the point: Lollards were beleaguered, and they were a minority. Lollardy and Lutheranism both thrived on the same doubts and antagonisms harboured by a section of the population towards religious authority, but by 1529 neither had made much headway towards the conversion of the English court, or the English people.[20]

2 Divorce, Schism and Statute: England 1529–36

Chronology

October 1529	Thomas More succeeds Thomas Wolsey as lord chancellor
November 1529	Opening of the Reformation Parliament
November 1530	Wolsey dies
March 1532	Act in Restraint of Annates
May 1532	Submission of the English clergy to royal authority
January 1533	Marriage of Henry VIII to Anne Boleyn
March 1533	Thomas Cranmer consecrated archbishop of Canterbury
April 1533	Act in Restraint of Appeals
May 1533	Annulment of Henry's marriage to Catherine of Aragon
June 1533	Coronation of Anne Boleyn
September 1533	Birth of the future Elizabeth I
April 1534	Execution of Elizabeth Barton
May 1534	Rowland Lee, bishop of Coventry and Lichfield, appointed president of the council in the marches
1535	Thomas Cromwell appointed vice-gerent; compilation of the *Valor Ecclesiasticus*
May 1535	John Fisher, bishop of Rochester, created a cardinal by the pope

| June/July 1535 | Executions of John Fisher and Thomas More |
| 1535 | Publication of Stephen Gardiner's *De vera obedientia* |

In 1549, when it was safe to express an objective opinion, that elderly and perceptive observer of his times Lord Russell described the late King Henry VIII as 'a prince of much wisdom and knowledge, but very suspicious and much given to suspection'. To wisdom, learning and suspicion might be added unpredictability (which was at times premeditated), cunning, avarice and experience in the lonely exercise of personal monarchy. Towards the close of the 1520s, increasing weight and declining health had taken Henry away from the hunting field and the tiltyard, presenting him with more time for attending to affairs of state. More time, but no more inclination. That, perhaps, is one reason why the king grumbled a good deal, 'ever mixing in some complaints' into his conversations, as one French envoy observed.

In October 1529, Thomas Wolsey, Cardinal Archbishop of York since 1515, the man who had dominated court and politics for the past fifteen years, was forced to relinquish his position as lord chancellor and to retire from court. Explanations for his fall are at once complex – a whispering campaign against the cardinal had played its part – and very simple. For all his suspicion and reserve, the king placed great trust in his closest advisers, and whenever that trust was broken the rupture was painful for all concerned. By 1529 Henry had lost confidence in Wolsey's ability to deliver a solution to the twin problems of state which at that time far outweighed all others: those linked issues of the king's marriage and the succession to his throne.

What Henry wanted was a male heir. His father having come to the throne only forty-four years earlier through divisions bred by a minority in the House of York, the second Tudor king harboured fundamental suspicions, not entirely unfounded, of his subjects' loyalty. What Henry had, by the late 1520s, was one legitimate daughter, approaching her 'teens, a wife past child-bearing age, and an illegitimate son upon whom only desperate hopes might be placed. The marital harmony that had cloaked his early years with Catherine of Aragon had been forgotten. In its place was an increasing determination to set aside his queen and to wed a young woman under whose spell, from early 1526, he had fallen. That woman's name was Anne Boleyn.

Fascination and public duty combined with stubbornness – an obsessive, urgent stubbornness touched with panic. Henry would have his marriage annulled: popes had granted princes similar favours before, and would do so again. To the king, lack of a male heir amounted to a personal rejection, a chastisement at the hands of God. It was common enough at the time, at all levels of society, to equate a childless marriage with some moral deficiency in the parents. Henry had hinted at doubts over the propriety of his marriage very early on, doubts partly assuaged by the birth and survival of Princess Mary in 1516. But sons had died in infancy and now those doubts returned,

Plate 2 *Miniature of Henry VIII, aged 35,* by Lucas Horenbout, *c.*1527. Note the angels holding golden cords entwining the initials H and K for Henry and Katherine of Aragon.
Source: Fitzwilliam Museum, Cambridge

and prevailed. Catherine, daughter of Ferdinand of Aragon and Isabella of Castille, had been married before, for less than five months, to Henry's elder brother Arthur. Arthur had died aged fifteen in 1502. That previous marriage, whether or not it had ever been consummated, provided a focus for Henry's reservations, and all the excuse he needed for his actions.

Others, however, felt that his scruples were unfounded. To canon lawyers across Europe Henry's case was weak, the Bible ambiguous. Verses in Leviticus forbid marriage to a brother's widow, threatening the second husband with childlessness or – in the Hebrew rather than Latin version – the failure to beget a son and heir. A contrary verse in Deuteronomy, though, specifically encourages such marriages as a means of raising up children in memory of the dead brother. This was just the sort of debatable ground in which a papal adjudication might be sought; a dispensation had indeed been granted Henry and Catherine by Pope Julius II, years before. Catherine, however, was determined to fight against any resolution that branded her marriage unlawful and her child illegitimate. Wolsey persisted in misreading the situation to a quite astonishing degree, delighting in Catherine's discomfiture, assuming until far too late that Henry would outgrow a passing infatuation with Anne. Thereafter, he was denied any room for manoeuvre. By the beginning of 1529, as delay followed delay, the king began to sense that so adroit a servant was playing his own sly game.

While Henry was from the start prepared to reject the pope's authority to decide the issue, he would naturally have welcomed a papal ruling in accord with his own views. Perceived 'errors' in the original dispensation granted by Julius II might, in other circumstances, have proved a mutually acceptable excuse, despite Catherine's protests. Unfortunately for Henry, the pope was unable to oblige. Clement VII had been, since the sack of Rome by Spanish troops in 1527, a puppet in the control of Catherine's nephew, the Emperor Charles V. The most powerful prince in Europe – he ruled over Spain, Burgundy, the Low Countries and much of Italy – Charles saw in the situation both an obligation to assist his aunt and the delicious possibilities of frustrating an English king who had recently aligned himself with France against the Empire. As trapped as his cardinal, Clement tried to placate Henry with legatine commissions efficient only in procrastination. Time passed, and Henry's frustration grew.

The frustrations were quite as great for the women involved: Catherine, understandably bitter at the way she was now being treated, her child Mary, and the king's new love, Anne Boleyn. Anne has, through diligent and imaginative recent research, emerged as a significant political figure in her own right, a woman imbued with French culture following service at the royal courts of Flanders and France, a patron of artistic endeavour and, while it may be fair to observe that a good deal of her patronage turned on kinship rather than purely spiritual considerations, of religious reform.[1] Though a commoner by birth, Anne was well connected. Her maternal uncle, the duke of Norfolk, was a long-standing ally. Henry clearly appreciated the family's charms: he had indulged in an affair with Anne's sister Mary around 1525, and unsubstantiated, probably untrue, rumour linked him with the girls' mother, Elizabeth Howard. It was Anne, however, who in rejecting his advances fuelled his desire.

The character of Anne Boleyn remains as elusive as a reliable description of her appearance. Balancing the hostility and flattery of commentators, almost all writing after she had achieved both publicity and notoriety, we discover a woman not especially beautiful by the standards of the time, yet marked out by her vivacity, courtly accomplishments and pretty, dark eyes. Her date of birth now uncertain, she was at least ten, perhaps as much as sixteen years younger than Henry, but foreigners saw such age discrepancies in married couples as an English characteristic, and in any case Henry's need for a younger wife was obvious. The attraction between Henry and Anne was genuine and mutual, illustrated as it is by the king's very frank love letters and Anne's wistful remarks written in a shared Book of Hours.

With peace concluded between France and the Empire at Cambrai in August 1529, and with the pope's legatine court convened in London that May recalled to Rome, Henry's patience snapped. His first target was Wolsey. Few courtiers had dared to plot against the cardinal in the heyday of his power, indeed they had maintained the civil, even cordial relations Henry expected from his greatest servants. But a hint of the king's irritation and the sight of Henry in search of other counsel spurred several of them into open hostility, and into some kind of predatory alliance.

Plate 3 *Anne Boleyn*, by an anonymous artist, oil on panel.
Source: National Portrait Gallery, London

Prompting and, in turn, prompted by this groundswell of influential opinion, conscious of Wolsey's recent failings, Henry took a decisive step, albeit with a show of reluctance. The cardinal was found guilty of praemunire, technically a correct verdict at law, for Wolsey had indeed secured his powers as legate directly from Rome, against the terms of a fourteenth-century statute. Initially the king protected him: he was allowed to retain the see of York and his liberty, despite conviction for an offence punishable by life imprisonment. Nevertheless, Wolsey's power was in eclipse, and everyone knew it. Eventually, his own optimism that the king would again require his services, his negotiations with agents of France, Spain, Queen Catherine and the papacy, and the unremitting vengefulness of his enemies at court, completed Wolsey's destruction. He was arrested in November 1530, cheating a trial for treason only through his death, apparently of dysentery, later the same month.[2]

Following Wolsey's disgrace, Henry at first exercised a greater personal control of both policy and routine administrative tasks. When initial enthusiasms faded, he relied increasingly upon Wolsey's successor as chancellor, Sir Thomas More, and on three noblemen, the dukes of Norfolk and Suffolk and the earl of Wiltshire. By far the most able of the four, More was fundamentally opposed to any policy which set England against Rome. Witty and intelligent, a talented and imaginative writer, a friend of that influential 'humanist' and man of letters, Desiderius Erasmus of Rotterdam, More had enjoyed a happy career in public service and was eminently qualified for his post. An adept courtier, he possessed the necessary skills of survival. There remain, however, darker sides to his complex character, notably an at times vindictive hatred of heresy. For the next three years More busied himself in the ordering of law courts chaotically swamped with business under Wolsey, and in the relentless persecution of heretics, determinedly ignoring the most pressing problem of the day.

More's campaign against heresy, vigorously backed by most bishops, failed to stem the tide of heretical works imported from continental printing presses. Notable among these was William Tyndale's strikingly modern 1525 English translation of the New Testament. More failed in part through lack of time, in part because effective censorship was not possible given the resources available to government, but also because reform had, to a greater or lesser degree, many friends among the higher reaches of Henry's court, particularly in the circle round Anne Boleyn.

An assault on heresy was nevertheless in tune with Henry's theological opinions. Refuting Lutheranism in print, the king had been rewarded by the pope with the title *Fidei Defensor* – Defender of the Faith – in 1521. Nor did it run against the political advice of More's fellow humanists, at home and abroad. Humanism defies precise definition. Unlike *humanist*, which emerged in late fifteenth-century Italy, the word is anachronistic, a creation of the early 1800s, and adopted then for quite different purposes and causes. Suffice it to say that early sixteenth-century humanism was founded upon what Alistair Fox calls 'an enthusiasm for good letters': grammar, rhetoric, ethics, history and poetry were to be studied, for their own sake first of all, and secondly for the improvement of the student's life, and, by example and persuasion, the lives of those about him. Classical authors were admired and imitated, in both method and literary style.

Humanism, though, was less a movement than a cast of mind. The variations are numerous. Erasmus's pious and unworldly ideals appealed to many in England, but Erasmian humanism took little account of the practical problems faced by those holding offices of state. Advice to educate the prince through enlightened counsel, through the gadfly gathering of classical precepts, was all very well, but the prince might be unreceptive, or he might hold views of his own. That its most lasting influence lay in the realm of education is not to deny humanism a role in shaping Henry's policies during the 1530s, but as personified by the orthodox More, or the evangelical Thomas Starkey, it took a more pragmatic, practical form, adapting to times and circumstances and, certainly in Starkey's case, less contemptuous of the wicked world.[3]

Norfolk, Suffolk and Wiltshire were not in More's league. Wiltshire, lord privy seal, owed his position to the fact that he was Anne Boleyn's father. Lord Treasurer Norfolk, a cunning man and proficient soldier, proud and intemperate, remained loyal to the king despite a reluctance to discard traditional religion. The duke of Suffolk, who had married Henry's sister Mary, widow of Louis XII of France, displayed a dexterity in the handling of his friend the king markedly absent from any contribution he made to affairs of state.

Their pre-eminence was built upon convenience, and was not unchallenged. David Starkey sees court faction as one inevitable by-product of 'participational' monarchy. Unlike his father, or his daughter, but like James I seventy years later, so this argument goes, Henry opted for more personal involvement in court life, and that involvement bred alliances which vied for his attention. Faction resists precise definition, but a factional interpretation of events, however simplified, can help clarify the confusing court politics of the 1530s. Henry was ultimately responsible for his own actions, but he listened to advice and could be influenced; as John Foxe wrote years after, 'King Henry, according as his counsel was about him, so was he led'. Charles V's ambassador Eustace Chapuys, much closer in time, recalls an occasion on which he saw king and minister quarrelling: Cromwell stalked off in a huff, and Henry wandered about mournfully, quite at a loss what to do next.

In late 1529 a coalition of interests had determined Wolsey's downfall. Once that mutual goal had been achieved, the alliance splintered. A circle round Anne Boleyn, sharing, to put it no higher, sympathies for religious reform, can be distinguished from the 'old counsellors' among the nobility – men like Norfolk and Suffolk, though Norfolk's family ties with Anne complicated the picture – and from those who made clear their support for Queen Catherine and her daughter, the so-called 'Aragonese'. These distinctions were fluid. All served King Henry, and themselves, before any 'party ideal'. Diplomacy and discretion placed a veneer of comradeship and shared purpose over dissent, for all sides ostentatiously aligned with the king, endeavouring to cast doubt on the fidelity of others.

The summoning of a new parliament followed closely upon Wolsey's fall. Writs went out in August, but the parliament, preceded by a now shadowy assembly of 'great men' in October, did not meet until November, and when it finally did foregather there was little sign of haste or direction in its deliberations. The year 1529 has acquired in retrospect great significance. Prorogued – adjourned – many times, the assembly which historians have dubbed the Reformation Parliament was not finally dissolved until 1536, and the legislation it passed included some of the most significant measures ever debated in an English assembly. Yet early sessions hardly distinguish this parliament from its predecessors. Legislation is thin, the impetus to political life elsewhere. The first session, for example, concentrated on the enduring problems of royal finance. There was little else by way of a crown programme; even More, after making an opening speech full of dire warnings against the threat of religious diversity, produced no legislation that lent force to fine words. The Commons muttered about perceived clerical shortcomings, while the Lords – with many bishops and abbots among them – denounced intemperate legislation in this area. Canterbury convocation, the clerical assembly which met at the same time as parliament, may possibly have considered, and rejected, a proposal to dissolve the smaller religious houses, although the evidence is far from conclusive. Surviving records of early sixteenth-century convocations are thin indeed. There was, in short, not the slightest indication that parliament had been seen as the constitutional means of freeing Henry from his unhappy marriage. After December 1529, it did not meet again until January 1531.

At the turn of the decade, Henry appears to have pinned his hopes of an annulment on a fortuitous shift in the balance of power in Europe, and on the success of sustained diplomacy. Pressure upon Catherine to accept the king's will was unremitting; had she settled for a pension and the title of princess dowager, her nephew and the pope would probably have breathed a simultaneous, if secret, sigh of relief. Charles was distracted by the Ottoman Turks in Austria and the Mediterranean, and by the religious and political unrest in Germany, while Clement VII would have been spared an impossible dilemma. But Catherine did not give way. The opinions of leading European universities, sought by the king's agents following a suggestion by an up and coming Cambridge academic, Thomas Cranmer, in August 1529, and published selectively in Latin and English editions by the king's printer during 1531, were either evasive or hesitantly positive. Equally discomfiting to Henry, precious little support was forthcoming from the continental religious reformers, most of whom, Martin Luther included, opposed any annulment.

The first indications of a new approach become apparent only in the later months of that year. It is hinted at in the appeal from eighty-three leading men of the kingdom to Rome during June, a petition which suggests that, if Clement does not look more favourably on Henry's plight, the matter might be taken 'elsewhere'. By the end of the year, Henry's own declarations are promoting his 'imperial' authority, his ability to decide such matters without recourse to the pope. Was not England an empire – a sovereignty of jurisdiction? Were not the English people exempt from appeals to courts outside their kingdom? Was not their king, the legal successor of Constantine and other Roman emperors, supreme over both church and state within his own boundaries? Was not the common law at all times superior to the canon law of Rome, exercised in England?[4]

There was nothing particularly new in these rhetorical assertions, only in the ends to which they were being applied. An instinctive response to claims for papal authority, they had been advanced by common lawyers in England over many years. Like his father, and a long line of English kings before them, Henry himself had emphasized the 'imperial' dimension to his kingship at every opportunity: through the wearing of an imperial closed crown – in life as in portraiture – through pageant, stained glass, sculpture, funeral iconography, and in such incidentals as the naming of ships. This semi-mythical heritage of English kings – successors to the Roman Emperor Constantine, the legendary Arthur and the conqueror of France, Henry V – was utilized in the field of foreign diplomacy long before the reformation.

Developments elsewhere suggested that such views were gaining ground. The French model, all too familiar to Henry, offered effective royal control over the national church. Under the terms of an agreement with the papacy, France allowed no appeals from her courts to Rome. When Henry contemplated a bid for the crown of the Holy Roman Empire in 1516–17 he asked Cuthbert Tunstall if election would affect the prestige of his existing dignity. The reply from the future bishop of London and Durham was unequivocal. 'The crown of England is an Empire in itself', Tunstall wrote, 'for which cause your grace weareth a close crown.' The crown, as both Henry and Tunstall knew, was itself a powerful symbol of an accepted authority.[5]

Ideas in the king's mind were shared with and shaped by learned men about him, many of them recruited to royal service by Wolsey. Edward Fox, future bishop of Hereford, was one; others included John Stokesley, Nicholas de Burgo, Edward Lee, Stephen Gardiner and Cranmer, at that time a conventionally traditional cleric who nevertheless harboured sympathy for some ideas of the continental reformers. Another was Thomas Cromwell, brought into the council late in 1530 and already Henry's key 'business manager' one year later. The advice and deliberations of these men contributed to the process by which notions conceived as threats with which to browbeat Rome were transformed into a full reordering of the church in England.

That process was by no means inevitable. We have embarked on a period of many months where Henry's actions, and the policies pursued by his ministers, remain ambiguous. While Henry may already have been contemplating some unilateral action to settle his marital problems he was well aware that any precipitate step was fraught with danger. Edward IV's unpopular and legally dubious marriage to Elizabeth Woodville in 1464 had resulted, twenty years on, in the murder of his sons on his brother's order and the toppling of his dynasty, and Henry understood that however many children he might have by Anne Boleyn, the Tudors' grasp on the throne after his death depended ultimately on widespread recognition of that marriage's validity, and on the loyalty of peers and gentry. If we believe Chapuys, our one source, Henry took note of the negative answer returned by assembled lawyers and clergy in the autumn of 1530, when asked in the king's presence whether the privileges of the realm would allow the marriage question to be determined by the archbishop of Canterbury, regardless of the pope's stance. Blustering all the while as to what he might be forced to do, Henry persisted in his efforts to placate Rome, endeavouring to have his case referred back to England, or, at least, to 'neutral' territory. The parliamentary session of 1531 is again devoid of direct government initiative on the all-important marriage question.

Henry did, however, make a determined effort to secure recognition from convocation of his supreme status within the English church. His motives appear to have been a mixture of the financial, the legal and the political.[6] The king threatened an undefined majority of the English church with praemunire in that they had acquiesced in Wolsey's 'illegal' exercise of legatine powers, later amending this to an accusation that they had so offended simply by exercising their own spiritual jurisdiction when holding church courts. The clergy, it was made clear, would have to buy their 'pardon', both financially and through a pointed submission, recognizing Henry as 'sole protector and supreme head' of the English church and clergy.

The clerical unity that had prompted such a radical demand also, for the time, frustrated it. Not yet prepared to push matters to a head, the king and his counsellors accepted a compromise which, by adding the qualifier 'so far as the law of Christ allows' to the required declaration of Henry's supremacy, stripped from the statement some of its force. The king eventually also abandoned any claim to exercise a priestly cure of souls. The money, though, was duly granted. Canterbury agreed to give the king £100,000, and the much poorer and politically less significant archdiocese of York granted just under £19,000. Elements within both convocations, however, subsequently declared openly that nothing they had done obscured the supremacy of the pope in all spiritual matters. Some of these intransigents were subsequently exempted from the 1531 Act for the Pardon of the Clergy, and were prosecuted on charges of praemunire.

A new urgency and purpose to the lengthy third session of parliament – January to May 1532 – and the survival of planning notes and memoranda in Cromwell's hand, suggests a programme directed by Henry and his ministers. An act regulating drainage and river management was the product of government initiative, as was the first phase in a great assault by the crown on the legal device known as a use. This process – common for well over a century – enabled a landowner to pass the legal title in his lands to a body of trustees. These trustees held it solely for the use of a beneficiary whose rights in the property, irrelevant under common law, were guaranteed by the equity court of Chancery. By these means, tenants of the crown had been evading the financial feudal burdens due on the transfer of such property from father to son. Cromwell, it appears, now proposed a compromise whereby only one half of an estate would be vulnerable to feudal aids. Since the king had already come to a similar agreement with the peers in 1529, his target on this occasion seems to have been those prominent landowners represented in the Commons. But something went badly wrong. Although the precise course of debate remains uncertain owing to the brevity of the record, we know that the bill was eventually dropped. Even the attempt seems to have generated great ill-feeling, for the crown also encountered stiff resistance when it sought a much-needed subsidy. We may conveniently run ahead a little here. The loss of the bill against uses rankled with king and minister, and when the judges in Exchequer rejected the validity of uses in a test case concerning the will of Lord Dacre of the South in 1534 they returned to the attack. In a statute of 1536 uses were shorn of their attractive aspects: ownership henceforth rested with the beneficiaries of a trust, who were held responsible for feudal dues. This bull-headed solution, which also denied that land might be bequeathed by will, provoked great resentment and soon proved politically impractical.

Attending to other concerns, the Commons were much more obliging. The first significant blow against papal authority was struck in this 1532 session. Upon preferment to a diocese, bishops and archbishops owed substantial payments to the pope, known collectively as annates. A bill was now introduced which prohibited these contributions, denouncing them as a squandering of English wealth and threatening that, were the pope to retaliate by refusing confirmation for the king's nominees to high positions in the church, English bishops might act in his stead. This legislation was a warning shot rather than a broadside, the bill containing a clause which suspended implementation until the measure was confirmed by royal letters patent. Indeed, it represented a considerable refinement of the draft petition against annates, which had threatened a complete break with Rome. Even in amended form the bill encountered strong opposition in the House of Lords, where, in a small chamber, the bishops, abbots and some sympathetic lay peers wielded significant power. Henry's formidable presence during debates ensured only a narrow passage upon that rarity of the age, a vote.

If the 1532 session displayed elements of a new approach, that approach was still cautious, still oblique. Cromwell, beset as he was by difficulties over the progress of legislation on uses and taxation, attempted to introduce a petition in the Commons rehearsing all the standard lay grievances against the high clergy, and requesting the king to provide redress in the form of parliamentary legislation. This 'Supplication against the Ordinaries', obscure in its origins, and not, apparently, widely discussed among counsellors before introduction, was calculated to appeal to as many manifestations of popular anticlericalism as possible. Delays encountered in church courts, the independence of convocation and the harshness of recent proceedings against heretics were all criticized. Henry was graciously pleased to approve the initiative, and acts followed to control the legal authority of bishops outside their dioceses and to limit benefit of clergy: the right of clergymen – very broadly defined – to avoid trial in a secular court when charged with a felony.

Pressure upon the high clergy was also applied in Canterbury convocation. Increasingly alienated from his king, Archbishop William Warham was threatened with praemunire, and he and other clerics were indicted on contrived charges in the court of King's Bench. Intimidation had its effect; initial bravado in the face of Henry's demand for a response to the Supplication

soon dissolved. Fearing that the alternative would be implacable royal displeasure expressed through a hostile parliament, convocation surrendered to
Henry its independent legislative powers, a concession appropriately referred
to as the 'Submission of the Clergy'. Henceforth, new and existing clerical
legislation alike came under the scrutiny of king and, by his allowance, parliament. Convocation could now be assembled only by royal command. Though
this was no more than an open acknowledgement of long-standing reality,
and though the issue of Henry's divorce still hung fire, here was an explicit
challenge to the authority of Clement VII.

For some at court, such presumption was already intolerable. On 16 May
1532, the day on which the 'Submission' was officially approved by convocation, Henry accepted More's resignation from the chancellorship. There was
no outward animosity, the king perhaps lulled by More's disingenuous insistence that he wished to spend his remaining years in contemplation of the life
to come. Instead, More busied himself in rebutting the writings of an elderly
lawyer Christopher St German, refuting St German's attacks on the competence and methods of church courts. St German had advised the king himself during 1531, urging a divorce through act of parliament alone; his works
of the early 1530s were published by the king's printer and clearly enjoyed
royal support. Though the fact that his opponent wrote anonymously gave
More technical protection against charges that he was attacking the king's
own policy, no one was left in any doubt as to his intentions. Henry felt
increasingly betrayed.[7]

After the prorogation of parliament in the summer of 1532, a marriage was
proposed between Henry, son of Francis I of France, and Catherine de
Medici, a kinswoman of the pope. Henry hoped that this union, promoted
alongside England's alliance with France, might afford him more bargaining
power in Rome. He and Anne travelled to Calais, England's last remaining
continental possession, where they entertained a friendly and non-committally
supportive Francis. Anne finally agreed to share Henry's bed, and she was
pregnant by the end of the year. Now the king had to act; the legitimacy of
his unborn child was at stake. Whatever the risks of future instability a bold
hand had to be played: legislation in parliament, overseen by Cromwell,
would ensure the consent of the nation for his actions. Death obligingly
removed the intransigent Warham in August 1532. At Henry's insistence and
with papal approval, Cranmer, then archdeacon of Taunton, was installed as
archbishop of Canterbury. Cranmer's loyalty to the king proved a trump
card. Though the new archbishop did not officiate, Henry married Anne in a
private ceremony, probably on 25 January 1533, secure in the knowledge
that England's senior prelate would endorse the union.

During the remaining four years of the Reformation Parliament the crown
was, through a succession of acts, given legal, financial and jurisdictional
control over the English church, while the pope's authority was progressively
extinguished. If the high gamble – of his crown and of national security – was
Henry's, the logistical process behind the break with Rome was the achievement of his principal minister. Thomas Cromwell, the son of a Putney
clothworker and tavern-keeper, was about forty-seven years old in 1532.

Plate 4 *Thomas Cranmer, archbishop of Canterbury*, by Gerlach Flicke, *c.*1546.
Cranmer is portrayed as the scholarly theologian, rather than as a prince of the church.
Source: National Portrait Gallery, London

Behind him lay a varied, at times extremely obscure career as soldier in the
Italian wars, merchant, lawyer and, latterly, a trusted member of Wolsey's
household. Cromwell possessed contacts in all these communities, a person-
able disposition, a talent for debate and oratory, an aptitude for languages

and a focused ambition. Well acquainted with the Bible, he was a friend to religious reformers; indeed, he grew more and more sympathetic as the 1530s progressed. At no time, however, are his personal views easy to discern, for they are subsumed always in current political necessities. Cromwell told German protestant envoys in 1538 that although inclined to their way of thinking he would, 'as the world stood, believe even as his master the king believed'.[8] Such a statement married cynicism to common sense: once Henry suspected that his minister did not share his own opinions, all Cromwell's power and authority rapidly melted away.

Cromwell's rise had been swift, a successful conclusion to the difficult 1532 session setting the seal on that ascent. Now, with Anne married and pregnant, he was allowed scope to proceed with legislation in parliament which would – barring, even then, a change of heart in Rome – establish a quite separate English church. The timing may have been dictated by dynastic necessity, but it also proved auspicious. Parliamentary opposition in 1533 was decidedly muted. The bishops were cowed by events the previous year and preferred subjection to the king over subjection to parliament, while Catherine's lay supporters, encouraged by the indefatigable Chapuys, saw their best prospects in a cautious waiting upon events.

In April 1533, after some hesitation over the economic consequences, parliament passed an Act in Restraint of Appeals, which by preventing the appeal of any case in a church court to Rome denied Catherine the chance to take her challenge outside England. Henceforth, appeals were to be heard in English ecclesiastical courts. Any matter touching the king, moreover, might only be appealed to the Upper House of convocation. An obscure and complex drafting process raises questions concerning the bill's deeper purpose. Its tone is set by Cromwell's pithy and wide-ranging preface, which declares Henry to be the ruler of an 'empire'. Justification for this grandiose if unoriginal claim comes in the form of a vague reference to 'divers sundry old authentic histories and chronicles', and in a reminder that the church had been endowed with lands by the kings and noblemen of the nation, an implicit threat that what the king had given, he might one day take back. The substance of the bill, however, was less overtly contentious. It may represent something of a compromise between concepts of a supreme head in the all-powerful image of a Roman emperor, and ideas which placed absolute power in the hands of a king-in-parliament – a compromise, that is, between positions apparently taken up by Henry himself on the one hand, and by Cromwell, Fox and St German on the other. But, as John Guy has observed, the matter is more complex still, for there remains a sense in which both king and drafters tread carefully, reluctant to reduce too far the authority of the clergy and their courts, and more immediately, fearing any alienation of the temporal and spiritual peers. It paid rather to place hints in the minds of bishops and abbots that royal supremacy might be their best source of security in troubled times, both at the personal and the institutional level. Nevertheless, the emergent act marks a highly significant stage in England's breach with Rome. The historian of that institution, Stanford Lehmberg, is in no doubt that it was 'the most important single piece of legislation to be enacted by the Reformation Parliament'.[9]

The Act of Appeals rendered definitive Cranmer's judgement, passed in May, on the validity of Henry's two marriages. The archbishop confirmed the majority opinion expressed in convocation that April: that Catherine had, in consummating her marriage with Prince Arthur, rendered invalid her subsequent union with Arthur's brother. A marriage of more than twenty years was thereby set aside, while a by now noticeably pregnant Anne was confirmed as lawful queen of England. She was crowned amid high ceremonial on 1 June. After all this the birth of another royal princess, Elizabeth, on 7 September, came as something of an anti-climax.

Clement VII could not but respond to so flagrant a challenge. The pope excommunicated Henry in September 1533, though, still hoping for reconciliation, he suspended implementation of the sentence. The king, clearly in no mood to back down, retorted by issuing letters patent confirming the restraint of annates, his council ordering sermons to denounce the 'pretensions' of papal power. Rumbles of discontent at the setting aside of wife to marry mistress were met with a show of calculated extremity. One opponent of the annulment, Elizabeth Barton, the so-called Nun of Kent – a visionary with a considerable following – was arrested, attainted of treason and executed with five of her followers in April 1534. On the day of these executions, the day after Cranmer had consecrated three bishops, pro-Boleyn men all, in a demonstration of the new royal supremacy, the leading citizens of London swore an oath recognizing the right of succession to lie in the children of Henry and Anne. The display of bloodletting and social cohesion sent – was meant to send – a blunt message. A dangerous course had been plotted, to an uncertain destination, and everyone was expected to sit demure, silent and still within the boat.[10]

Against the background of a vigorous official preaching campaign deploring the pretensions of the papacy, the first of two busy parliamentary sessions in 1534 produced legislation attending to loose ends arising from the declaration of legal and jurisdictional independence from Rome. A succession act reflected the anxieties of king and council. It published Cranmer's judgement, warned that any writing or action against the king's title, or against his marriage, would be considered treason, and required, as we have seen, an oath upholding the act's provisions. A few high-profile opponents of the second marriage, including More and John Fisher, bishop of Rochester, refused to take the oath and were promptly thrown into prison.[11]

Parliament also enshrined the 1532 surrender of convocation in statute by embodying it in an Act for the Submission of the Clergy. Several legal and constitutional implications had to be addressed. One clause of this act envisaged a commission to oversee the systematic revision of canon law, but this initiative, like similar efforts later in the century, led nowhere. Another took the 1533 legislation on appeals one step further, placing ultimate authority over ecclesiastical cases in the hands of commissioners from the court of Chancery. Legislation also regulated the prosecution of heretics, abolished remaining payments to Rome, gave the crown complete control over the selection of new bishops, and assigned to Cranmer, supervised in more significant cases by Chancery, powers to grant licences and dispensations. Somewhat belatedly, it was made legal to question papal supremacy.

A poorly documented session that autumn helped clarify the administration's new designs. One statute remedied a defect in the Act of Succession by specifying the precise words of the required oath. More and Fisher, who refused to swear on the grounds that the wording set before them exceeded the scope of the statute, were condemned to life imprisonment. An Act for First Fruits and Tenths took one tenth of annual revenue from spiritual offices for the crown, as well as a further levy from all new holders of such preferments. Commissioners set about a valuation of all spiritual preferments, the result of their endeavours later becoming known as the *Valor Ecclesiasticus*.

The central issues were also addressed. An Act of Supremacy passed in this session declared that, from henceforth, Henry and his successors were to be accepted in turn as 'the only supreme head in Earth of the Church of England'. The king, and his agents, were acknowledged to have the authority to investigate and correct faults 'which by any manner spiritual authority or jurisdiction ought or may lawfully be reformed'. Clarification was timely. Cranmer, in his traditional role as a prince of the church, attempted to enforce his own discipline in a visitation – that is, an inspection – of the various bishoprics within his province during 1534 and 1535. But while it gathered a vast number of signatures subscribing to the oath of supremacy, no mean logistical feat, the visitation failed to impose Cranmer's own authority at the very highest level. Several bishops doubted Cranmer's right to meddle in their affairs now that the church was free from papal control, and suspected that they might win more independence from archiepiscopal interference under the new royal supremacy. So the king flexed his muscles. Perhaps in December 1534, Henry delegated his own authority over the church to Cromwell, appointing him 'vice-gerent in spirituals', initially for the specific purpose of examining the church and correcting its defects.[12]

On a different tack, Cromwell and More's replacement as chancellor, the avaricious, unlikeable but highly capable Sir Thomas Audley, introduced a new bill which defined as treason any deeds, writings or words intending harm to the king, queen or heir apparent. The fine divide between treason and lesser crimes had for centuries been the subject of concern to kings and their leading subjects. A statute of 1352 had defined certain offences as treason, but this and subsequent, unrepealed fifteenth-century legislation had only spelt out subsets of what might be considered treason at the common law. The 1534 Treason Act now supplied a fresh definition, a fresh subset, but in confirming that words alone could be construed as treason it seemed to widen the scope of the offence, even though successful prosecutions alleging words alone had been brought home in the past. Such apparent rigour prompted some misgivings in the Commons, and it was stressed that only 'malicious' words and actions should be interpreted as treason.

A subsidy act, the first since 1523, has been regarded as a radical departure in the theory of direct taxation. The preamble, or discursive introductory paragraph, does not justify the tax as such. Rather, it appeals to English men and women to express their gratitude for the years of 'wealth, unity, rest and quietness' Henry has provided by opening their purses. They are being asked, in other words, to subsidize the costs of peacetime, administrative charges, traditionally viewed as matters handled by the crown through its own revenues. Those so-called 'ordinary' receipts consisted, principally, of income from land, feudal dues from principal landowners, profits from court cases, and a life grant of customs, tunnage and poundage, voted by tradition in the first parliament of each reign, to which should now be added first fruits and tenths.

The novelty of this initiative has not passed unchallenged.[13] A more traditional justification for 'extraordinary' taxation – unavoidable military expenditure – also features in the preamble. If England stood notionally at peace everyone recognized that the times were troublesome and dangerous. Under these circumstances, defence could be interpreted broadly as an essential of ordinary royal government. The practical distinction between 'ordinary' and 'extraordinary' revenue had, indeed, never been clear. Taxation, as successive preambles pointed out, seldom covered extraordinary costs entirely, particularly in time of war, while taxation raised on the plea of military necessity was not infrequently spent on other, more peaceful, projects. From as early as 1517 the expenses of the king's council had regularly been met by the Exchequer out of tax revenue. A case can also be made for placing the 1534 preamble in an early Tudor tradition of educating subjects on the specific necessities prompting any request for a subsidy. Nevertheless, even if the act did not establish that taxation might be extended to meet the costs of normal administration, it helped make the point that changes to the structures of crown finance might not be postponed indefinitely. Inflation, and a growing bureaucracy, together insisted that a new basis for ordinary revenue was required if taxation was not to prop up administrative costs on a regular basis.

Again and again, however, Tudor administrations ducked the challenge, refusing to attempt significant reform. New taxes, indeed, refinements to old taxes, are seldom popular. Fears of consequent social upheaval always counselled caution and focused attention on more basic problems. Internal security was always a paramount concern. A year of rain, plague, bad harvests and threats of unrest, 1535 saw repeated attempts to identify and proceed against remaining supporters of the pope. Reminding local officials that mere concealment carried its own penalties, Cromwell solicited information, personally scrutinizing the evidence gathered. His judgement was generally measured, although in the trials and executions of Fisher, More and John Houghton, prior of the London Charterhouse, all in 1535, there is reason to think that the causes of propaganda and humanity were alike ill-served. Perhaps royal insecurity took over here. The dispassionate observer may see some, albeit rough, justice in the fate of Fisher, author of numerous works in support of Catherine, for he had intrigued with Chapuys and papal agents over the previous eight years. A decision by the new pope, Paul III, to make Fisher a cardinal was as foolish as it was provocative, prompting a savage rejoinder from Henry that he would send the pontiff Fisher's head, cardinal's hat and all. Yet the king's relentless determination for blood leaves a sour taste, as does Henry's presence – 'in order to laugh at his ease, and encourage the people' – at a pageant staged on 23 June 1535, the day after Fisher died. Spectators were treated to a display based on an episode in the Book of Revelation; they were able to laugh with their king at the mock executions of a number of senior clerics.[14] The limited ability of isolated prisoners such as Fisher and More to influence their countrymen when alive must be set against the revulsion, both at home and abroad, aroused by their deaths.

King Henry's cause was better served elsewhere: 1535 saw publication of the most able early defence of royal supremacy. Three years before, Stephen Gardiner, bishop of Winchester, an experienced diplomat and one of the scholars who had worked on the divorce issue from the early days, had misinterpreted the king's determination to enforce submission from the clergy; his opposition to the king in this matter had been infelicitously prolonged. That one, disastrous misjudgement had cost him the archbishopric of Canterbury, and had ever since blighted his career. Attempting to regain lost ground, Gardiner composed his *De vera obedientia*, a defence of theories placing church and state under one supreme, secular head. His book succeeded both commercially and, where it mattered, in winning Henry's approval. *De vera obedientia* was the most enduring element in a great propaganda exercise to reinforce monarchy and supremacy that summer: the king and queen embarked on a spectacular progress through the west of England, dealing out largesse to those favouring religious change. They were accompanied much of the way by Cromwell, who busied himself with personal visitations of several regional monasteries.

Not that Gardiner, forgiven yet swiftly consigned to an embassy to France which took him out of England for three years, entirely grasped the furious pace of change. His book allowed the pope, as bishop of Rome, a continuing role as exemplar. A worthy pope, in other words, might earn respect, and having earned respect he might exercise an ill-defined yet important moral authority. In the event, residual respect for the pope was decisively jettisoned by parliament in 1536. By an act which came into force that July, any defence or exercise of papal authority was declared to be praemunire.

What remained, and what continued to perplex theologians and statesmen for centuries, were ambiguities over the extent of the new royal supremacy. Could the powers exercised by a layman, albeit a sovereign layman, ever equate to those exercised by an ordained prince of the church? The king does not appear to have been troubled by such uncertainties. To Henry, what mattered above all was the breaking of subservience to papal jurisdiction. He was attracted by the reputation of a reformer, but his heart was never in widespread doctrinal or administrative change. Indeed, his tolerance for evangelical forms of religion – if we use the word as Englishmen of the 1530s were coming to do, as implying a rejection of the pope's supremacy, coupled with a wish to see doctrinal and procedural reform – waned as the 1530s wore on. He never openly laid claim to the priestly powers of administering the sacrament, preaching or excommunication. These were papal powers, of course, and the French concord which conceded to the pope a spiritual primacy shorn of political or legal power was from time to time held up to Henry as the grounds for compromise with Rome. That he made no significant attempt at reconciliation, even when changed circumstances seemed to favour it, suggests a personal resolve to preserve the new forms established by statute in the Reformation Parliament.

Though unwilling to consider radical theological reform, Henry, one senses, starts to feel comfortable in his supremacy by the mid-1530s: *his* church, still 'Catholic' in ceremonial, begins nevertheless to display a Henrician stamp. Most vulnerable in these changing circumstances were institutions, customs and studies which owed their vitality and influence to the supremacy of the pope within western Christendom. Canon law was no longer studied in the universities after 1535, and that year also witnessed the launch of Cromwell's visitation. In the light of what followed, to suggest that the latter was merely a new manifestation of the age-old system of moral scrutiny within the church, may be stretching ingenuity, or naivety, too far. Those traditional visitors – bishops, and their subordinates – were divested of their jurisdiction for the duration, and found themselves also under investigation. When they eventually recovered their powers these came explicitly from the crown, and at the cost of fees traditionally enjoyed by the higher clergy.

Most of the work involved in the monastic visitation was carried through by just four men, all capable canon lawyers, conscientious if never entirely even-handed in executing their commission. The usual efforts were made to obtain evidence on moral and institutional shortcomings, and houses were enjoined to observe their original rules of foundation, amended to reflect the new supremacy legislation, but the principal difference between this and earlier visitations lay in the uses to which all the information gathered was put. At the busy last session of the Reformation Parliament, early in 1536, Lords and Commons were presented with a bill compassing the dissolution of all religious houses valued at under £200 a year: generally speaking, that is, those with fewer than twelve members. Though none too cleverly drafted, it was passed by an assembly showing little patience for monastic ideals.

Rather curious logic justified this move. The larger houses were felt to be well run, only their smaller counterparts harboured corruptions so notorious that dissolution remained the only remedy. If the logic is curious, the intent behind this act remains elusive. What we might be seeing is an extension of Wolsey's own financially driven closure of some thirty small houses in the mid-1520s, a compromise between the opinions of those at court who rejected any need for dissolution, and others who favoured dissolution or more general clerical disendowment. That last, extreme, course may have been proposed again in parliament during the winter session of 1534, the aim being the restoration of royal finances, an ever-present incentive.

Piecemeal dissolution to finance reform had long been under discussion within the church itself: both the purposes served by religious houses and their economic viability had come into question. Many smaller houses were struggling, for their way of life was slowly going out of fashion. This implicit threat to monasticism, rumbling over many years, had itself hampered recruitment and deterred fresh benefactions and bequests, the monasteries' life-blood. Still famous for their hospitality, many houses were hard pressed to offer any further justification for their continued existence. Whatever the visitation's findings most were orderly, respectable places, but they were also undistinguished in either learning or in exemplary devotion; they were becoming marginalized, and vulnerable.

Some three hundred religious communities were now threatened with immediate closure. Their properties fell to the crown, their members were left with the choice of moving on to a surviving house, or seeking permission to serve as 'secular' priests. Heads of houses – who were provided with pensions – and nuns enjoyed no choice. To avoid accusations that the administration was being too arbitrary in its ostensible search for monastic purity, the act permitted houses to buy exemption – in effect, to purchase survival – and some forty eventually did so, hoping that the whole process might after all be a money-making exercise. Roughly the same number of small houses survived, but paid nothing, their continuing existence justified by the need to provide homes for the monks and nuns transferred from dissolved communities.

Cromwell appears to have had no patience for monasticism, but it is possible that he would have preferred a piecemeal approach to dissolution rather than the comprehensive if rather artificial legislation set forward in 1536. Henry, for his part, appears to have been torn between a desire to preserve the familiar outward forms of his church, and the counter-attractions of new wealth. But if the 1536 legislation was hesitant, and selective, it still spelt the beginning of the end for England's religious houses. An act establishing a court of augmentations of the king's revenue, set up with the purpose of administering and disposing of monastic property, provided a machinery well capable of handling further closures.

The court of augmentations was one of four new revenue courts established between 1536 and 1542, the others being the courts of wards (wards and liveries from 1542), first fruits and tenths, and general surveyors of the king's lands and revenues. Each had a legal function, and wards would handle a great deal of judicial business in Elizabeth I's reign. Each, however, in addition collected and distributed specific revenues. Considerable significance has been read into the emergence of these new 'bureaucratic' bodies, particularly when their processes are judged against those of ancient courts like the Exchequer. They offered a more flexible and rapid means of handling revenues that accrued to the crown from the breach with Rome. At the same time, however, the Exchequer was never the fossilized dinosaur of later legend: absorbing several of the new courts in 1554 it adopted the best features of each. Careful preservation of age-old systems in the Exchequer did not prevent the increasing use, at all but the final stage of accounting, of arabic numerals and paper calculations. Conversely, the new courts, which owed nothing to internal tradition, moved as new institutions tend to move from the informality of youth towards more closely defined processes, even in the course of their brief existence.

In an age when the practice of revenue administration was highly personalized, when an officer like Sir John Daunce, working from his own house, might fulfil functions as diverse as a teller, customs collector, receiver-general of wards and treasurer at war, the new courts were pragmatic means to an end. A development of medieval government through courts, they were favoured by Cromwell, who in addition to his new creations took the existing Tudor courts of Requests and Star Chamber and gave them new impetus. They also mark one stage in a series of slow, deliberate changes, responses to the financial necessities of the age, which transformed the administrative focus of government finance. Chamber domination of revenue agencies, under the direct control of Henry VII, gave way to this multiplicity of convenient revenue courts, and most of these courts in time merged with the Exchequer, under the supervision of the privy council.[15]

The 1536 parliamentary session had important consequences for Wales as well as England. Much of present-day Wales had been conquered by the Normans, and the remaining independent areas in the north and west were subjugated by the armies of Edward I late in the thirteenth century. These Edwardian conquests thereafter formed a principality, subordinate to the English crown and under the nominal authority of the prince of Wales, eldest son of the sovereign. The principality was shired to the extent that its five counties possessed sheriffs, and some framework of local administration, but at the same time those counties lacked commissions of the peace and returned no member of parliament throughout the Middle Ages. In the old Norman conquests, the frontier lands of south and east Wales, government took a rather different form. There the council in the marches, a fifteenth-century creation reinvigorated by far-reaching reforms overseen by Wolsey in 1525, supervised something like 130 marcher lordships. The principality was characterized by a hybrid legal system whereby English criminal law operated alongside a tangled mix of Welsh and English civil law. In the marches, custom dictated that the king's writ did not run. Each marcher lordship technically exercised its own broad, quasi-royal, legal powers. Nevertheless, practice and theory here differed a good deal. Strong monarchs had always enforced their prerogative authority as feudal overlords, and in the 1530s the king was by some distance the pre-eminent landowner in this borderland, since many of the lordships had fallen to the crown through attainder, forfeiture or failure in the male line. With the loyalty of the Somerset, Herbert and Devereux families, dynasties built up by the Tudors, and unshakeably subservient to the crown, this loose system of control imposed as much government on the marches as the crown was prepared to finance, or its inhabitants disposed to accept.

However, the threats of international action against England set in train by Henry's break with Rome sparked fears that foreign powers might opt to invade England through Wales. Here was a thinly populated, disorderly, religiously conservative region, with an unprotected coastline: a security risk. It was difficult to forget that when Henry VII in 1485 had marched to Bosworth to wrest the crown from Richard III, his army had landed in and advanced through the heart of Wales. How, then, could the dangers be minimized? Suggestions that Wales should be incorporated into the English state had been mooted for some time. In response to a 1531 proposal from James Denton, chancellor to the council in the marches, that the marches should be divided into counties, Henry made encouraging noises, stating that 'it were a gracious deed to reform Wales'. Only in 1534, however, were steps taken in parliament to curb the autonomous powers of the marcher lords. The council's powers were increased, and JPs from English border counties were given a broad remit to extradite criminals from the marches.

It was one thing to legislate, another to enforce new laws, even when that enforcement was directed by a new, energetic president of the council in the marches, Cromwell's friend and trusted ally the choleric Rowland Lee, bishop of Coventry and Lichfield. Lee believed that only summary justice could cow an unruly country: one untrustworthy source suggests that he hanged 5000 criminals – gentlemen, crown servants, merchants and all – in the space of six years, and though that figure may be an exaggeration such tales reflect the bishop's rough enthusiasm. 'All the thieves in Wales', he noted, after hanging several in 1536, 'quake with fear.' But there was more to Cromwell's plans for Wales than a simple purge of the criminal classes. While the threat of disorder certainly influenced his legislative initiatives, lawlessness was hard to quantify, its wider implications difficult to assess. More deep-seated was the problem of a complicated, uncertain and divided judicial structure within the country as a whole. Good lordship was not being provided, despite well-intentioned legislation, and this negligence, quite as much as petty thievery, had security implications. Further measures were introduced. Despite Lee's misgivings, Henry and Cromwell had decided on more radical reform, dependent on support from the willing workmen essential to its success, the Welsh gentry.[16]

The basis of this Tudor settlement may be viewed as an extension of principality administration, modernized and further Anglicized, to the rest of Wales. Distinctions between principality and marches were now abolished. A bill was passed extending English common law across Wales, replacing systems of justice based on native custom. The act also insisted on the use of the English language in court and government. All Wales was divided into counties, on the English pattern, each with its own sheriff, justices of the peace and its own representation in parliament. Parliamentary representation was at the same time extended to some of the more important boroughs. Welsh MPs sat from 1542, and the total number of Welsh seats was twenty-seven in 1543.[17] Theoretically all Welshmen, from all parts of the country, now enjoyed the same rights and owed the same obligations as Englishmen.

Ambitious and slowly implemented – we do not have evidence of appointments of JPs before October 1541, for example – the new Welsh statutes were at least in part a recognition of existing reality. That, no doubt, is why they proved effective. In the greater part of Wales, the changes were popular among the ruling elite, serving to place these men on equal terms with English gentlemen, establishing them in shire government, and giving them access both to London courts and to the royal court itself. Such families were already integrated with their English gentry cousins. Many were, and long remained, religious conservatives, but as with gentry across England the likes of Sir John Price at Brecon, Geoffrey Glyn at Bangor, the Owens of Plas Du and the Somerset earls of Worcester at Raglan, whatever their particular religious convictions, promptly took up leases on former religious land, or had existing leases confirmed. All the benefits of monastic dissolution, and due regard for royal authority in these matters, ensured that the majority bent with prevailing religious winds.

Legislation in 1536 in many ways consolidated a long-drawn-out process of creeping Anglicization. Parliament then decreed that the Welsh custom of dividing lands between sons should be replaced with the dominant English practice: primogeniture, or inheritance by eldest son. A gradual process extending over the past century had already seen the majority of tenancies in Wales transformed into leasehold, with an increasing adoption of primogeniture. Although the Welsh acceptance of primogeniture was never universal, these trends accelerated after 1536. The gentry's enthusiasm to harmonize law and custom had also been reflected in the growing influence of English legal systems in Wales over the past hundred years. It was illustrated too in the subsequent survival of the council in the marches, a prerogative court given statutory recognition in 1543. Throughout Elizabeth's reign the council retained, even extended, a wide and prestigious range of judicial and administrative powers. It settled at Ludlow under the long presidency of Sir Henry Sidney, operating as the most prominent arm of privy council authority across Wales and, for good measure, in many English border counties.

When the process of unification was confirmed by further, very detailed, legislation in 1543, the new act benefited considerably from Welsh contributions and recommendations. The king retained theoretical powers to make laws for Wales outside parliament, but no Tudor monarch tried to enforce them. It was the Welsh gentry, like their English counterparts, who made or broke ambitious legislation, whatever the wishes of king, council or parliament, and these gentlemen now saw it as in their best interests to undergo what George Owen at the time called a 'joyful metamorphosis'. They flocked to the English universities, resorted to the Inns of Court and studied the arcana of English law. And so, in many respects, they became Englishmen. The authority which they and their kind actually wielded in their countries, and the reactions of lesser figures in the principality, nevertheless remain far more difficult to pin down.

The so-called Act of Union complements near-simultaneous measures extending shire jurisdiction in England, and others regulating the government of Calais, which also received parliamentary representation. It seems part of a wider picture. Legislation abolished the legal independence of counties palatine such as Durham, and ancient liberties such as Hexham and Redesdale in the far north, other areas in which the king's writ had never run. Here, and in Ireland too, we see sustained attempts to tighten English border security in these uncertain times. Acts of union also served to tie the peripheries into a national system of taxation, even if early returns were modest. Just 6 per cent of the £74,000 received under the first subsidy act to embrace Wales, that of 1543, was raised there, and regular Welsh contributions to Tudor subsidies did not begin until 1576.

But is there indeed a wider picture lying beyond this coincidence of religious, financial, legal and administrative reform, and if there is, who is the artist? During the last forty years, historians have grappled with an inter-pretation placed upon English administrative history in the 1530s constructed by the late Sir Geoffrey Elton. Elton saw a 'revolution' in the forms of Tudor government, the foundation, under Cromwell's enlightened guidance, of a modern, bureaucratic state, developing at the expense of the court. Elton's ideas have beguiled and infuriated, been accepted in part, revised extensively, rejected, and reinstated. The debate turns on the accuracy of broad general-ization across long timescales, and over differing perceptions of motivation, ground which frustrates precise quantification. Where Elton saw Cromwell, armed with a programme of reform, setting about reshaping the nation state to make it less subject to the whims of an individual monarch, others see such reforms either as a reinstatement and codification of fifteenth-century and still earlier precedent, or as an inspired response to short-term circum-stances, owing everything to the wishes, or the terrors, of an unpredictable royal master.[18]

That Cromwell viewed legislation as a means to various ends is natural and self-evident. It was by the purposeful management of business that he rose to power. This pragmatism was, moreover, a shared effort. Cromwell listened to advice; he harvested the ideas of others.[19] He was, as Elton has so ably demonstrated, particularly receptive to ideas in the field of social and eco-nomic reforms. Consensus, after all, lightened the extreme burdens of govern-ment. Cromwell did his best to enlist as partners and allies conservative peers exercised by a nobleman's age-old concern: that his role as the king's 'natural counsellor' was being debased through the advancement of low-born men enjoying the ear of the king. Given Cromwell's own background, con-ciliation of this sort was unlikely to make much headway, but there is no question that he tried.[20]

One may, indeed one should, attempt to provide a pragmatic explanation for Cromwell's every move, but still there remains a sense of greater purpose, difficult to dispel. Much had changed, even by 1536. The break with Rome had been carried through, the succession to the throne radically altered, and the two houses of parliament had been accorded a role tantamount to part-nership with the crown, albeit on the crown's own terms and for the crown's own purposes, in expressing national approval to controversial claims for sovereignty. Parliament had mutated under the spotlight: its structure and procedural methods are, so far as one may tell, unchanged – rituals of assembly, procedure and dispersal remain constant throughout the century[21] – but the Commons has gained enhanced prominence, and the institution as a whole has emerged with a new, real sense of political as well as jurisdictional purpose.

Other changes are scarcely less enduring. The year 1529 marks a point of departure in fabric and in stone as well as in administrative design, in the physical nature of the court itself. Wolsey's downfall brought Henry the cardinal's magnificent palace at Whitehall. After costly rebuilding work – Henry never stinted in ostentatious building projects, tripling the number of houses owned by the crown – Whitehall served as the principal royal residence for the next century, the palace eventually sprawling over twenty-six acres. The pattern of its chambers was copied, as approximately as might be, whenever the court visited another palace or private house. While the king's old palace of Westminster, not a quarter of a mile distant, had been taken over by law courts and parliament, Whitehall provided a focus for court society, and, by extension, for Tudor government also. Significantly, the privy council, the leading administrative body of the age, met in Whitehall and continued to do so for as long as the Tudor dynasty endured.

3 Pilgrimage, Dissolution and Reform: England 1536–40

The month of January 1536 proved disastrous for Anne Boleyn.[1] Her miscarriage of a boy on the twenty-ninth had been preceded by a still more telling blow, the death, possibly from a heart attack, of Catherine of Aragon. While his first wife lived, Henry had been obliged to outface both murmurs of bigamy and the real, if distracted, hostility of Charles V. Catherine's death, however, adjusted the equation: were he to set Anne aside and take another wife, those who had all along regarded his second queen as no queen at all could only cheer the king's decision. With Henry now increasingly neglectful of Anne, and openly attracted to the daughter of a Somerset gentleman, Jane Seymour, the queen suddenly appeared very vulnerable.

On the continent, meanwhile, the French renewed their challenge to the emperor's control of northern Italy, marching into Savoy during February and March. Chapuys duly opened negotiations in April for a renewal of the Anglo-Imperial alliance. From anxiously guessing Charles V's next move, England once again enjoyed the luxury of choosing her friends, and all the consequent freedoms of action that choice entailed. Henry opted, in effect, for neutrality, calling down plagues on both French and Imperial houses. Negotiations with the Lutheran princes of Germany, which the king had pursued optimistically, were rapidly shelved; a draft treaty with the protestant Schmalkaldic League drawn up in December 1535 was already foundering amid intractable theological controversies.

All these considerations help us understand the precarious position in which Queen Anne found herself early in 1536, but they do not in themselves explain what happened next. Anne was not merely set aside in favour of her rival. She was accused of adultery with five courtiers, one of them her own brother George, Lord Rochford. In the space of twelve days, late in April and early in May, a commission was appointed to examine her conduct, a new parliament was summoned, and the suspects were all interrogated by the council and imprisoned in the Tower. Tried and convicted on 15 May, Anne was beheaded in the French fashion, by a swordsman specially brought over from Calais, four days later. Her co-defendants were put to death by the axe in more orthodox, English style. Two days before Anne died, Cranmer's ecclesiastical court ruled that the old charges advanced by Catherine's party – that Henry had enjoyed sexual relations with Mary Boleyn – constituted an impediment to union, and annulled the marriage.

Precise reasons for this hasty savagery are hard to pin down; as so often, events close to the heart of the court rest shrouded in mystery, and our interpretations of what happened are dangerously dependent on Chapuys, his fellow ambassadors, and later reminiscence. John Foxe, only a quarter of a century on, in effect threw up his hands in despair when trying to explain the queen's fall, and the passage of centuries has not made the task any easier. There are, nevertheless, one or two clues to hand. Signs that Anne's authority was weakening had for some months attracted the vultures at court, and perhaps, as Eric Ives suggests, we see another example of 'grand faction': of disparate groups and individuals united only by the scent of blood. Transferring their loyalties from mother to daughter, Catherine's supporters worked for the removal of Anne as a necessary step towards reconciliation between Henry and his eldest child. Other courtiers, including the sixth earl of Northumberland and the marquess of Exeter, had no particular regard for Mary but still detested Boleyn pretensions. They were prepared, to the best of very limited personal abilities, to lend their support. These predators had in Sir Nicholas Carew an ally within the privy chamber, a ready route to Henry's receptive ear.

Anne and her family, though, retained their strong position at court and were probably a match for such relatively feeble alliances: by 1536 the

Aragonese appear a spent force, while Northumberland and Exeter were discredited or marginalized. Henry, reviewing these painful events, regarded himself as a prince greatly wronged, driven to extremities first by his wife's indiscretions and then by the blood-lust of his advisers. Not for the first or last time he was being disingenuous. The intimacy of the English court, and the queen's outspoken manner, proved an unlucky combination, but it seems unlikely that the charges laid against Anne were true. Rather, the king desired another woman and was genuinely dismayed by the continued absence of a male heir. What we seem to observe in the tangled events that April is a wholesale desertion of Anne by every important political player, each taking his cue from the king. Amid enduring speculation, one question remains: why did Henry act when he did? Had he been biding his time since January, awaiting the convenience of a law term, or did he move on the spur of the moment, goaded by the accusations of adultery? The truth of this matter may well remain elusive.[2]

The wise servant takes his cue from the master. One moment Norfolk was Anne's champion at court, the next he was sitting in judgement upon her. Cromwell's hand in Anne's downfall is evident, both in its efficient management and in his own self-justifications to Chapuys. According to the ambassador, Cromwell finally took the decision to work against Anne as late as 18 April, prompted by a realization that harmonious relations with Chapuys's master could come about only with the removal of the emperor's bitterest critics in the English court. Chapuys believed this statement, and has been taxed by some historians with excess credulity, but we may set aside the explanation without dismissing the fact. Apparently, Cromwell felt obliged to reject a patron and principal ally at court; the ill-fortune of that ally, coupled with an instinct for self-preservation, dictated his subsequent moves. There is at least some suggestion that domestic as well as foreign policy played a hand, although intriguing theories that Anne opposed the intended diversion of monastic endowments to secular rather than religious ends, adding to her alienation from Cromwell, still need to be worked through.[3] Geoffrey Elton saw in the events of 1536 Cromwell playing a skilful game, first siding with the conservatives to remove Anne, then blocking the expectations of his former allies to ensure a future for himself and his reforms. Perhaps the day-to-day struggle for survival – in which luck played its part – may merit still greater emphasis.

Eleven days after Anne's death King Henry married Jane Seymour. With Princess Elizabeth now bastardized, the Aragonese faction expressed its hope that the king might again recognize Mary as heir presumptive and be reconciled to the pope. Mary's own stubborn attachment to Rome, however, ruined their expectations, and by rousing in Henry an ominous fury, eventually brought the princess to an abject personal submission which helped neither her friends nor her cause. Henry, by now, had digested his own anti-Roman propaganda, and was relishing his new, high role. A recognition of this helps explain how Cromwell not only survived but profited from Anne's fall: the supreme head needed his advice. Mary's submission on 15 June was followed by Cromwell's promotion to the peerage as Lord Cromwell on 9 July. Anne's

father, permitted to retire from court after the destruction of his family, relinquished the keepership of the privy seal into Cromwell's hands. Exeter suddenly found himself out of favour, and there was no augmentation of Aragonese elements in either council or privy chamber. When parliament was dissolved on 18 July, Cromwell's vice-gerency, hitherto limited to the duration of a visitation now effectively accomplished, was transformed by Henry into a general authority over religious matters, modelled on Wolsey's legatine powers but representative of, and subordinate solely to, Henry's supremacy. Cromwell, Charles Wriothesley the chronicler tells us, was that day 'made high vicar over the spirituality under the king, and sat diverse times in the Convocation house among the bishops as head over them'.[4]

Cranmer – not unwillingly – and every other bishop were for the next four years subordinate figures: the royal supremacy was directed, under the king, by Cromwell alone. The next year saw him presiding over his own synods as vice-gerent, and eventually, in May 1539, a precedence act ranked him above the archbishop of Canterbury in the House of Lords. Those 'evangelicals' who before had looked to Anne as a patron of reform, Cranmer and Hugh Latimer among them, took the safe course, formally denounced the dead queen's 'crimes', and sought favour from Cromwell. Cranmer, though, hinted at his doubts and remembered Anne's services to reform in a characteristically brave letter to the king.

The parliament that met in June 1536 was one of those rather aimless, single-issue assemblies which, summoned to confront a particular Tudor crisis, exhibit a marked absence of government foresight and planning. The contrast with later stages of the Reformation Parliament was accentuated by the short interval – just two months – between the two. When the new succession bill was finally introduced, three weeks into the session, it contained few substantial surprises. Repealing the 1534 Act, it settled the succession upon any children born to Henry and Jane, and cautiously gave the king, in default of a legitimate heir, powers to declare the succession either by letters patent or in his will. Rumour had it that Henry intended, if necessary, to entrust the crown to his illegitimate son by Elizabeth Blount, Henry, duke of Richmond. By the time the bill became law, however, young Richmond had died of tuberculosis, and the practical choice once again narrowed.

Caution was the hallmark on a definition of religion, presented to convocation for subscription on 11 July. Of these Ten Articles, or statements on matters of faith, five dealt with 'principal' questions, while the others considered 'laudable ceremonies'. Definition took a cautiously narrow form; only specific points were discussed, and these only in rather conservative terms. The article on the eucharist was short and opposed any significant concession to Lutheran views; a similar approach is found towards two other sacraments, baptism and confession. While broadly Lutheran in form, and reflecting recent negotiations in Germany between English envoys and prominent Lutherans, the article on Justification emphasized that while good works were not necessary to salvation, they were an unavoidable obligation placed upon the justified Christian. On other contentious topics, notably the four traditional sacraments rejected by Luther, silence was preferred to denunciation.

Although they gained more ground in the articles dealing with the lesser, 'laudable ceremonies', disappointment in reformist circles was patent. While Cardinal Reginald Pole, a great-nephew of Edward IV who from the relative safety of the continent had recently denounced the royal supremacy, questioned only the king's right to attempt such definitions, Alexander Alesius, Cromwell's Lutheran client, found it impossible to agree to them as they stood. Though the Ten Articles were accepted by numerous reformers as a stepping stone, and by conservatives as a bulwark against further diversity in preaching, their publication and enforcement by vice-gerential injunction did not silence the debates and discussions over forms of religion in England.

These Ten Articles were accompanied by a series of Royal Injunctions, issued by Cromwell. The Injunctions required children to receive religious instruction in English, attacked shrines and religious images as irrelevant, and demanded that rectors should provide Bibles in both Latin and English in their churches for the edification of parishioners. It bears repeating that these were hardly dangerous novelties. Despite long-held views to the contrary, little evidence links the promulgation of either Ten Articles or Injunctions to the great rebellion against Tudor rule which broke out during the autumn of 1536.

The so-called Pilgrimage of Grace began as a town riot at Louth, Lincolnshire, on 1 October. Briefly, the county blazed, with Lincoln falling to the insurgents six days later, but in the face of a small force led by Suffolk, a peer newly married to a local heiress and ambitious to stamp his authority on the county, the rebels lost their nerve, accepted a proffered pardon and returned home. The Lincolnshire slow match nevertheless spluttered sufficiently to ignite a northern powder keg. Under the leadership of an East Riding lawyer, Robert Aske, Yorkshire was soon convulsed by rebellion. York fell, and the elderly Lord Darcy, a knight of the garter with a splendid record of military service, but also an erstwhile supporter of Catherine of Aragon, surrendered Pontefract Castle without a fight. Twenty thousand Yorkshire rebels converged on Doncaster, while large assemblies in Durham, Northumberland, Lancashire and Cumberland also flouted royal authority. In response, Norfolk marched north at the head of a small, hastily assembled force. Much to Henry's disgust, the duke negotiated a truce whereby both sides agreed to disarm and withdraw, undertaking in the king's name to redress grievances.

The speed of the rising, and the ready compliance of many leading northern figures, suggest some degree of pre-planning among disaffected northern gentry.[5] Most obvious, though perhaps not especially significant, was the involvement of the Percy family, earls of Northumberland. The sixth earl, ailing, childless and burdened by debt, had recently announced his intention to leave all his lands to the king, and his disinherited brothers figure prominently in the rebellion. But the Percys seem to have seized an opportunity; there is little evidence to suggest that they created it. Darcy and his fellow Aragonese Lord Hussey and Sir Robert Constable had been considering some form of military action for the past three years, and all three now took leading roles in the rising: Darcy in the West Riding, Constable in the East, and Hussey in Lincolnshire. Several other gentlemen joined in, subsequently protesting that their tenants had encouraged them to treason at the point of a sword. In most cases this appeared to the investigating authority, as it appears to us, a lame excuse; the wonder is that so many of these rebels were spared royal vengeance.

If we admit an element of pre-planning, we can only assume that the timing of the rebellion was premature. Darcy's experienced military coterie may have hoped to delay action until the spring, when better campaigning weather would coincide with improved prospects of assistance from Catholic Europe. As it was, with Spain and France then at war, there was not the slightest chance of substantial aid from either continental power. Hopes of support from other great families proved equally vain. The great northern magnates, Northumberland, Westmorland, Shrewsbury and Derby, did not come out for the rebels. Elsewhere, apart from an embryonic rising in the vicinity of the great Norfolk pilgrimage centre of Walsingham, and some unrest in the farther reaches of Cornwall, serious disturbances were absent south of a line from the Wash to the Mersey.[6]

In particular, the great Plantagenet Catholic families of the south-west, Pole and Courtenay, made no move. Both were discontented, and in covert contact with their kinsman Reginald Pole, delegated by the pope to consider the merits and requirements of the pilgrims in January 1537. Caution, though, proved entirely futile, for Henry, attributing their apparent loyalty either to cunning or to cowardice, soon chose to believe Cromwell's discoveries of treasonous conspiracy. Fears of a Yorkist restoration lingered in his mind, and in the interests of his own dynasty he destroyed both families. The marquess of Exeter was among those executed during the winter of 1538–9.

It is, however, easier to speculate over the motives of a few discontented gentlemen than it is to account for the actions of thousands of anonymous Englishmen and women across the north during that tumultuous autumn. Loyalty to landlords and patrons cannot fully explain their readiness to risk everything in an open revolt, in blatant treason. After much debate in Pontefract the rebels, responding to Norfolk's invitation, produced a list of twenty-four grievances and demands. They called for the legitimation and acknowledgement of Mary as heir to the throne, the recall of Pole, the removal of Cromwell in favour of noble counsellors, a 'free' parliament, a restoration of monasteries and friaries, and a return to Rome. How widely the Catholic sentiment here expressed reflects the wishes of all those engaged in rebellion must, though, remain at issue. Programmes produced by Tudor rebels were inevitably compromises in which the aims of any leadership received disproportionate prominence. Aske and the other ringleaders eventually admitted that they had included articles, notably those calling for partial restoration of the papacy and for the punishment of heretics, on their own initiative. Which leaves us as puzzled as ever. No one can doubt that those who marched under a banner depicting the Five Wounds of Christ, who swore oaths to protect the monasteries, and who proceeded beyond mere words to restore at least sixteen of the dissolved religious houses, shared a hostility to religious reform. The activities of local priests, and of recently ejected monks and friars, as recruiters and inciters of the commons, doubtless help explain why the disturbances spread so rapidly. In January 1537 Sir William Fairfax, who leased the dissolved and now restored priory of Ferriby, wrote of monks, clustered in villages round their former homes, endeavouring daily to 'wag the people to put them in again'. But religion is surely just one element in a complex brew. As important to many, particularly among the better off, was the demand that the widely detested statute of uses be repealed; the hostility towards this attack on the rights of landed men to bequeath their property has too often been underestimated.[7]

Then there is evidence of agrarian discontent arising from the flouting of 'good and laudable customs'.[8] Much also points to a multitude of local grievances. The revolt in Cumberland and Westmorland, for example, was, so far as the meagre documentation allows us to judge, a popular, conservative movement which focused its anger against a leading local landowner, the first earl of Cumberland. Despite his title, Cumberland had no established power base in the region, and he was obliged to adopt a passively defiant role in the face of his tenants' fury.[9] The Lincolnshire upheaval certainly fed upon widespread unease in the face of busy investigations by no fewer than three sets of commissioners that September: subsidy commissioners, commissioners for dissolution of the smaller monasteries, and the bishop of Lincoln's agents attempting to enforce the Ten Articles and Injunctions. Concern over the innovation of a peacetime subsidy, fears of further taxation, even the coincidence of poor harvests in 1535 and 1536: none of these turns law-abiding men into rebels. At the same time, not one of these factors does much to enhance the popularity of a regime already held in low esteem.[10]

Finally, though, any simple explanation for revolt will founder on the complexities of individual motivation. Whoever might have been responsible for their circulation, many lurid examples of that particularly potent early Tudor phenomenon, the political prophecy, spread fast and wide, particularly through the lower ranks of society, providing in their obscurity justifications for some, excuses for others, some comfort for the distressed, and warnings for the cautious.[11] The Pilgrimage reflected no simple north–south divide; we may suspect hidden links with the heart of court, and observe the fears that it instilled in the many who remained either uncommitted, or loyal to the king and his administration.

Henry's government rode its good fortune. Norfolk's conciliatory tactics at Doncaster brought the necessary breathing space. In the cold of winter the rebellious north returned home. Aske was received graciously by Henry in London, but it was a very different king who considered in private the pilgrims' demands. Henry had no intention of yielding to the cries of a mob, and he waited on time to provide him with an opportunity for revenge. Time duly obliged. Further disturbances in the far north-west, and a futile commotion in Yorkshire led by an impetuous local knight, Sir Francis Bigod, allowed Norfolk to strike at the now dispersed insurgents. Now, significantly, gentlemen prominent in events of the previous autumn sensed disaster and held aloof, although caution did not save the former ringleaders. Aske, Constable, Darcy and Hussey were arrested and brought to trial in London, while elsewhere Norfolk ensured that prominent pilgrims were tried for treason in their own counties. By the standards of the day, retribution was moderate enough: perhaps 179 executions across the entire north, including Lincolnshire. Many more died after the risings of 1549 and 1569, the latter at least providing a threat of altogether lesser magnitude.

The Pilgrimage served as a catalyst for some important constitutional and legal reforms. With the court on a war footing as events in the north unfolded, leading aristocrats, as levyers and commanders of fighting men, found themselves in positions of particular authority. While Henry did not lose faith in his minister it appeared prudent, given the rebels' calls for Cromwell's head, for the king to assign him a lower profile and to highlight, as he did in replying to the rebels' demands, the noblemen and bishops in his 'pryvey counsell'. Fearing disturbances in the capital, Henry withdrew to Windsor, accompanied by a select body of advisers. During the winter of 1536–7 we see signs of this slimmed-down council, consisting of prominent peers, clergy and officers of state, operating as a day-to-day executive under the king, writing and signing letters together as a body. In its composition it bears some resemblance to the short-lived council that had followed Wolsey's fall; indeed, it may be nothing more than that very council, operating in time of crisis. Interestingly, however, its membership is close to that of the first known privy council furnished with clerk and register on recognizably late Tudor lines – the conservative, magnate-dominated body, also nineteen strong, which springs into view at Cromwell's death. Twelve men serve in both the emergency council of 1536–7 and the privy council of August 1540.

What should we make of this? Many circumstances contributed to the evolution of the late Tudor council, the supreme executive body in Elizabeth's reign. Wolsey's quest for legal business had helped, for it had furthered the mutation of Star Chamber into a regular court of law, and had overseen the birth of the court of Requests, both operating with dedicated council staff. The divorce of executive power from the chancellor in Star Chamber after 1529 had also helped regulate the distinct, legal role of the king's council. Simultaneously, the old Council Attendant of 'close', 'secret' or indeed 'privy' counsellors, for a recognizable name preceded a recognizable body, is gradually transformed into a small, exclusive group of privy counsellors armed with the power to require appearance. That body itself applied the final touch of organizational legitimacy by advising the king to appoint a council clerk in August 1540.

The source of the council's authority was, however, never in question. The privy council, like the privy chamber with which it invariably shared membership and affinity, drew strength from its privileged position of great intimacy with the monarch. The council chamber was located in the privy lodgings, physically close to the king himself. Privy counsellors swore a personal oath to their sovereign, there was no collective council responsibility, and counsellorships all lapsed on the sovereign's death.[12]

Another development augmented the powers of assize courts, the annual sessions of justice conducted in the localities in the presence of itinerant royal judges. In addition to the existing commissions of the peace, and of gaol delivery, justices of assize were, for the first time, from 1537 routinely armed with general circuit commissions of oyer and terminer, empowering them to hear and pass sentence in – here was the rationale behind the move – cases of treason. Put to the test in the aftermath of serious rebellion, the capacity of the existing system to deal with suspects under the recent treason acts was thought inadequate. The beauty of the new model lay in its simplicity. Not only might instances of treason be swiftly dealt with in the relevant shire, but the gentlemen of that shire, as JPs in the commission, would be obliged to make a public display of loyalty, under the careful scrutiny of the assize judges. With the scope of treason widening, this was an innovation never rescinded.[13]

The two years after the suppression of the Pilgrimage mark the zenith of Cromwell's authority. Eradication of the Boleyn faction, followed by that of the Aragonese rebels and the marquess of Exeter, left him with what amounted to a free hand in the royal household. Replacing Exeter as the 'chief noble' of the privy chamber, Cromwell introduced his own followers as gentlemen, among them his nephew Richard in 1539, and tightened his control of access to King Henry, the privy coffers and the selection of documents to be preferred for royal signature. Shortly before his disgrace he secured the post of lord chamberlain; he may have intended to use this as a means of exercising administrative control of the 'upstairs' household as well.

As vice-gerent Cromwell also rode the king's favour. Thanks not a little to the mediation of Heinrich Bullinger at Zurich, contacts with the Lutherans and, uneasily, with the emerging 'reformed' churches of the Rhine and northern Switzerland, who tended to oppose Luther's insistence on a real presence at communion, flourished at the highest level. Archbishop Cranmer, at that point in his career, still held Lutheran views on the eucharist, but exchanges with the Swiss reformers were very cordial, and significant for the future. The *Institution of a Christian Man* or *Bishop's Book* – somewhat reluctantly licensed for a three-year trial period by Henry and published in September 1537 – displays continental influences not seen in the earlier, less wide-ranging Ten Articles. The *Bishop's Book* is a different kind of pronouncement: a departure much copied on both sides of the religious divide in later years. It takes the form of a series of sermons or homilies designed to lead national beliefs in a new direction. At first sight there is still much that is equivocal: all seven 'Roman' sacraments are maintained to some degree, though a distinction is drawn between the three discussed in the Ten Articles – which are taken to enjoy clear scriptural support – and the rest. Nevertheless, the balances between faith and good works in the article on justification, and that between tradition and Biblical authority in the evaluation of doctrine, tilt significantly towards the evangelical position. In listing the Ten Commandments, preference was given to the 'reformed' conflation of traditional prohibitions against coveting a neighbour's family and possessions, to balance the crucial separation of injunctions to worship one God and to reject graven images. Here may be seen early steps towards the official campaign of iconoclasm which, following further Royal Injunctions in the later part of 1538 and 1539, stripped and destroyed the great Catholic shrines, Thomas Becket's at Canterbury being merely the most prominent.

The *Bishop's Book* was the work of committees, controlled by the evangelical bishops but bent upon compromise in accord with royal wishes. It tested the religious waters. Even so, it received only the most grudging support from conservatives: Gardiner, still on embassy in France, would have nothing to do with it. Henry, who had sanctioned the work rather half-heartedly, and in haste, repented of his action at leisure, disliking the book more with each reading and coming up with dozens of revisions. Cranmer may have been moving towards a belief in predestination but Henry was not travelling, and he never would travel, along the same road. That such a document could pass into circulation as a statement of the English faith testifies particularly to the vice-gerent's authority in church matters during 1537.

Again working closely with Cranmer, Cromwell's hand can also be detected behind the promulgation of an English Bible. The publication of scripture in the vernacular had long been under consideration: Thomas More and Reginald Pole had both acknowledged the desirability of a vernacular Bible, but remembering the malign influence of Wyclif's translation, and appalled that literate Englishmen might take God's word at face value, they had wished to restrict the circulation of any translation. Cromwell and Cranmer, on the other hand, were persuaded that such limitations concealed rather than promoted true religion. In 1536 the vice-gerent had instructed parish priests to obtain a vernacular Bible by 1 August 1537. Zeal here outran common sense, for there was no appropriate translation to hand. Miles Coverdale's version, published in 1535, was non-contentious but lacking in erudition: the bishops would not approve its use. Instead, Cranmer and Fox advanced the claim of William Tyndale's fine translation. This had been revised and published under the name of Thomas Mathew, apparently to avoid exciting Henry, whose hatred of the radical Tyndale was notorious.[14]

Cromwell duly secured the king's assent, putting his own money into the project and ordering distribution, but when the supply threatened to prove insufficient he instead threw more money and influence behind another Bible, the so-called 'Great Bible', which amounted to Coverdale's version amended with improved Tyndale translations. He obtained Henry's permission to publish the book in England, steered it through the superior-quality Parisian presses, and worked hard to ensure that the Bible found a place in every parish church.

The Pilgrimage of Grace both delayed and made inevitable the final stages of monastic dissolution. Several heads of monasteries suffered for their support of the rebels: the prior of Bridlington, and the abbots of Jervaulx and Fountains, all perished on the gallows. Tainted by treason, their houses, and others, suffered too. Henry himself may have remained ambivalent over the last steps in this process: when in December 1537 Chertsey Abbey surrendered the king refounded it with generous endowments. Nevertheless, everyone was aware that the remaining houses represented a source of new revenue for any government resolved on their closure, and confidence seeped away. Pessimism, rather than decay or laxity, is surely the characteristic face of monasticism in the 1530s. Cromwell's visitors found moral shortcomings, to be sure, yet so had visitations in every age, and by their own admission these jaundiced enquirers also discovered a good deal to commend in the houses they examined. On the other hand, lay bequests were dwindling, recruitment drying up, and any able careerists in the great houses looked elsewhere, even overseas, to secure a future in the church.[15]

Since the recent legislation dissolving smaller houses had recognized the relative efficiency of larger institutions, further process by statute was considered inappropriate. Parliament was not sitting, and there seemed no broader justification for its recall. From April 1537, when Furness Abbey was induced to surrender, piecemeal dissolution sealed the fate of surviving monasteries, nunneries and friaries. Few religious houses put up much of a struggle. Three heads of great houses preferred a traitor's death to surrender, but in examining the cases of the abbots of Colchester, Reading and Glastonbury, one is struck by the tardiness of events (all died at the end of 1539 or 1540), and the idiosyncratic nature of their opposition. Technically, the last surrenders were those of Rochester and Canterbury Cathedrals, both monastic foundations, during April 1540, but most houses had by then long since disappeared. A new parliament, assembling in 1539, was presented with a *fait accompli*, and duly passed a second Act of Dissolution confirming the king's right to all surrendered property. The whole process had accounted for some 800 houses, occupied by perhaps 10,000 people, a figure that includes around 2500 friars and 2000 women. No longer were the religious offered places in other houses, for now there was nowhere else for them to go. Pensions, particularly for senior clergy, were often not ungenerous, and the more compliant and fortunate walked straight into new posts, but there were many hundreds of monks who received no more than £5 a year, assuming, indeed, that they could obtain their due. Former friars, whose orders had never acquired large landed estates, went without compensatory pensions. For the likes of these, dissolution meant an uncertain, often a very difficult future.

Established to administer the former religious property, the court of augmentations worked efficiently, handling the £90,000 annual income added in this way to the royal revenues, much of it in the form of rents from existing leases. Lay landowners set about outbidding one another for the privilege of acquiring a share of these immense spoils. During the invasion scare of 1538–9 the crown had need of large sums in order to improve coastal fortifications, and by the beginning of 1540 some 240 grants of land had been made, mostly at realistic valuations and reserving rents to the crown. Thereafter, the rate of disposal increased markedly. Between 1539 and 1543, annual sales of crown land averaged £66,000.

Formerly quite restricted, the English land market became more dynamic, as wealthy men without acres, professionals and younger sons of peers competed with established noblemen and courtiers for monastic estates. Most land ended up in the hands of local families. In Devon, to take an apparently typical example, less than 10 per cent of former monastic land was held by 'outsiders' in 1558. These transactions brought profit to the lawyers, both through increased demand for conveyancing – in which they shared the benefits with the scriveners, or professional writers – and also in the mass of lawsuits spawned by a buoyant market. Increased knowledge of estates was now also valued, making work for practitioners in the new science of surveying. John Dee's pioneering advocacy of triangulation was taken up by the great mapmakers of the age, John Norden and Christopher Saxton, both of whom cut their teeth on manorial work. Norden, to the end of his life, notably in his *Surveyor's Dialogue* of 1607, publicized the advantages enjoyed by landlords possessed of accurate maps and plans.

Alienations of crown land resulted from a blend of convenience and design: the king required ready cash, and with the assistance of some judicious if still rather mysterious borrowing many leading courtiers and gentlemen were prepared to pay the competitive sums demanded. More advantageous terms were, on occasion, offered to favoured gentlemen of the privy chamber, or to senior counsellors. Interestingly, a quite ruthless attitude was taken towards the importunate nobility. Helen Miller notes in her study of the Henrician peerage that, since lords were obliged to serve the king on demand, they 'did not have to be recompensed with special favours'.[16] Having paid out a good deal, the new proprietor was prepared to defend his property. As has long been recognized, investment in monastic estates helped secure support for Henry's policies and, perhaps, eased the immediate blow imposed by the statute of uses.

The 1539 act authorized the foundation of new dioceses by letters patent, but this measure was, in part at least, an exercise in justificatory propaganda. Six new bishoprics did eventually emerge – Bristol, Chester, Gloucester, Oxford, Peterborough and, briefly, Westminster – but with war looming enlightened endowment of this nature was necessarily limited. Traditionally, monastic foundations had nurtured or patronized learning, within their walls or at the universities. While Cromwell tried in his 1536 injunctions to ensure that wealthier incumbents filled the void in this respect, little suggests that his exhortations, lacking as they did any coercive element, were taken to heart. He set a good personal example, but the shortfall remained.

By the end of 1537, Henry was once again in search of a wife. The birth of a male heir, christened Edward, in October 1537 was followed twelve days later by Jane Seymour's death from a childbirth infection. Henry grieved, genuinely and briefly. Recognizing that yet another marriage to a member of his own aristocracy might harm his international prestige, he scoured the courts of Europe for a bride. No obvious candidate, however, seemed willing to be considered: Spanish and French princesses all rejected the idea. Though Cromwell preferred the prospect of a foreign match to the elevation of another domestic family, more and more of his own time, and that of other crown officials, was absorbed in the hunt.

At this same moment, England's precarious neutrality was called into question when France and Spain moved gradually from war to peace. During 1537 and the early months of 1538 English diplomacy, substantially entrusted to the uncertain hands of the poet-diplomat Sir Thomas Wyatt and a gentleman of the privy chamber, old companion of the king and deeply religious rake Sir Francis Bryan, concentrated on exacerbating those issues that still divided the great powers, notably control of the strategic duchy of Milan. Marriage negotiations – extremely convoluted – were but one facet of their game. The kidnapping or assassination of Pole was also on their, unwritten, agenda, but the envoys, possibly not without some deliberation in Bryan's case, botched this particular enterprise.[17]

In the short term, such spoiling tactics proved unsuccessful. The monarchs of France and Spain, reconciled by the Treaties of Nice and Toledo in June 1538 and January 1539, jointly rejected the possibility of a marriage alliance with England and withdrew their envoys from London in 1539. Henry's search for a wife thus narrowed, first to the sisters and daughters of independent German princes, and finally to Anne, sister of Duke William of Cleves, ruler of a strategically important Rhineland state. As yet uncommitted to the German Lutheran alliance, William had, like Henry, rejected obedience to the papacy.

The threat of invasion, however, proved a pressing distraction and, with the prospect of a General Church Council in the air, encouraged further talks with the Lutherans. No useful consensus emerged. In December 1538, Paul III at last removed his predecessor's suspension of Henry's excommunication, provoking royal anger, military musters and a review of coastal defences all along the Channel. In the wake of this flurry of activity a number of up-to-date fortifications were constructed, costing over £300,000. A council of the west was also erected, under the newly ennobled Sir John Russell. Its brief was both to oversee the military works in Devon and Cornwall and, such at least were Cromwell's hopes, to offer a new means of exercising crown authority in that unpredictable region.

As Henry anticipated, however, the threat from France and Spain was short-lived. Neither monarch, neither court, trusted the other, and fears of practical military cooperation proved fanciful. Having listened briefly to papal calls for a joint crusade against England, Francis and Charles soon fell out once again, and a French ambassador returned to London within weeks. The council of the west, its military rationale no longer compelling, was ignored both by its president and by its leading gentry counsellors, who all preferred to follow established and mutually satisfactory practice and communicate directly with Cromwell. The council limped on into 1540, when Cromwell's fall administered a *coup de grâce*.[18]

Whereas Cromwell's answer to the threat of diplomatic isolation was to seek an understanding with the Lutheran princes of Germany, Henry preferred to adopt the pose of a religiously orthodox monarch, misunderstood by his European cousins. Frustrated by German intransigence, the king understandably preferred to move in the circles of sovereigns and emperors, men of his own degree, sound in the fundamentals of faith. He now began to feel that some definitive statement of Catholic orthodoxy was long overdue. Domestic concerns reinforced these convictions, for 'anabaptist' cells in England were attracting increasing notoriety. Anabaptists had acquired an evil reputation throughout Europe, and on both sides of the religious divide, the term as then used embracing a range of groups which shared doubts over the practice of infant baptism and which were critical of Rome, Luther and the Swiss reformers alike. After an attempt to establish a radical anabaptist state in Münster had been suppressed amid horrific savagery in 1535, no

I Russell L. Privy Seale.

with one Eye

Plate 5 *John Russell, later first earl of Bedford*, by Hans Holbein the Younger, 1530s. Russell lost his right eye at the battle of Morlaix, 1526.
Source: The Royal Collection © Her Majesty Queen Elizabeth II

government was able to ignore the threat, however remote, that such groups posed to internal stability.

In England that threat was negligible: numbers were small and confined to immigrant communities, or to those in regular contact with anabaptist cells on the continent. Most radicals had no wish to disturb the political status quo. Several anabaptists were, however, discovered among the townspeople of Calais, and his enemies were highly delighted to find upon investigation that Cromwell had personally taken steps to shield some of the more extreme protestants in the town. When, belatedly, Cromwell's actions and the 'infected' state of Calais were made known to Henry, the king's latent conservatism was stirred. Dissent of this kind could not be tolerated. During November 1538 a proclamation was issued which is known to have been drafted by Henry himself. It denounced anabaptism, and for good measure the so-called sacramentaries who followed Ulrich Zwingli in rejecting the real presence in communion. Indeed it went further, opposing clerical marriage, requiring privy council licensing of all scriptural publications, and restraining attacks on church ceremonial. For all who supported more wide-reaching reform, Henry's uncompromising pronouncements appeared ominous. They took solace in all that had been achieved so far, and kept their heads down, preserving in this way their own lives and the security of their court patrons.[19] The most prominent fell reluctantly into line, participating in the attack on anabaptism. 'I will not be a patron unto heretics,' Henry told John Lambert, when presiding over the latter's condemnation for denying the real presence in November 1538. He meant what he said: Lambert was burnt, along with numerous others, as the king of England paraded his hatred of religious unorthodoxy to the world.

In this changed climate, Cromwell appeared vulnerable. Opposition to his ascendancy had hitherto lacked an effective focus. The return of Stephen Gardiner from his ambassadorial post in France during September 1538, however, placed a conservative cleric of particular ambition at the centre of English court life. Gardiner was implacably hostile to Cromwell. He was, moreover, a man of great presence, a man to whom Henry listened. The parliament of 1539 illustrated the extent to which Henry's mind had hardened. After labouring to ensure that 'reliable' men were returned in the shires and boroughs, Cromwell boasted in March 1539 that 'your majesty had never more tractable parliament', but his brag proved hollow when that same tractability was turned against the minister himself. The intention had all along been that this parliament should establish – in the words of Cromwell's March memorandum – 'unity in religion'. London in particular was exhibiting troubling dissensions between men of various persuasions. So far as the evidence allows us to tell, Lutherans and more radical reformers were attracting men and women from all social levels, but they were also thoroughly alienating a similarly diverse group of citizens. Potential trouble in the capital could not be ignored. But even after recent clues the form such unity took surprised many. One week after the session opened, Lord Chancellor Audley announced in the Lords Henry's wish that parliament should produce legislation to curb religious dissent. Frustrating the minister's own hopes of introducing further social legislation, this demand threw the spotlight on Cromwell's own weaknesses, working against policies which he had personally espoused, but which did not command broad support in either House.

Incapacitated by sickness, Cromwell had few resources on which to draw. When he tried to play for time by referring the initial proposals to committee the duke of Norfolk, probably at Henry's bidding, and certainly with his consent, set before the Lords six doctrinal questions framed to require unequivocally Catholic responses. These questions were based on topics discussed recently with representatives of the German princes: discussions that had foundered, despite Henry's best endeavours, reminding the king of his reservations about continental manifestations of religious reform. They appear to have been drafted by Cuthbert Tunstall, bishop of Durham, a conservative cleric close to both the king and Norfolk. Reasoning that Henry could be diverted by the prospect of revenue, Cromwell tried to press ahead with the bill for a subsidy, then passing through the Commons. By this point, however, the threat of invasion had again receded, and the subsidy bill, though desirable, could be delayed for a week or two. After token consultation with divines, and due deliberation in committee, a bill was introduced on 7 June which provided the required Catholic interpretations. Communion was to be in one kind, and the eucharist was defined in conservative terms, even though the word transubstantiation was not used. Private masses and clerical celibacy were both deemed necessary. In the only significant concession to evangelical opinion, auricular confession was held to be merely 'expedient', though 'necessary to be retained and continued'. Before June was out, the bill had passed both Houses with minimal opposition.

While Henry basked in the good press these resounding statements of orthodoxy afforded him in foreign courts,[20] English reformers floundered in disarray. Of the more radical bishops, Hugh Latimer was obliged to resign the see of Worcester, Nicholas Shaxton that of Salisbury. Others subscribed to the Act of Six Articles. Cranmer, frightened, snubbed, and entirely loyal to Henry, sent his wife to the continent and remained in office, still retaining, somehow, the king's affection and support. But he now presided over a bench of bishops distinctly hostile to his own reformist inclinations.

Cromwell also bent with the wind, and Henry, obviously still mindful of the minister's utility, was content to see him retain his authority for the time being. Nevertheless, the portents were ominous. The vice-gerent had lost the initiative in matters of religion. His appointments to bishoprics in 1539–40 have about them the appearance of a man looking over his shoulder for approval. The Paul's Cross Sermon, channel of official religious expression, and unpredictably protestant under Cromwell's guidance, now attracted only the most cautious and conservative preachers, Bishop John Stokesley of London having regained control of the programme. Most telling of all, when Cromwell's Lutheran protégé Robert Barnes, translator, preacher and diplomat, presumed to criticize Gardiner at Paul's Cross, he set in motion a chain of events which carried him to the stake for heresy. Barnes's patron was quite unable to save him. Cromwell lost more freedom of action when the 1539 parliament passed an act requiring that royal proclamations might only be issued by 'the advice of the more part' of the council: council members were carefully listed, all qualified by some office, while an act of precedence ranked all office holders carefully and strictly.

Still, however, there was scope for Cromwell to outwit his enemies. His control of the court was, by late 1539, tighter than ever before. Mindful of 'balance', Henry in October approved the choice of Edmund Bonner, then a supporter of Cromwell, as bishop of London in succession to the conservative Stokesley, and backed continuing evangelical attempts to promulgate scripture in the vernacular. He set Cromwell in charge of licensing all Bible translations over the following five years, and warmly endorsed Cranmer's high-minded preface to the Great Bible, which appeared in the second impression of April 1540. Furthermore, when Francis I and Charles V indulged in yet another series of peace overtures, Henry was even moved to accept the idea of a Cleves marriage, long advocated by his minister. A treaty was signed in October 1539; in December, Anne arrived in England. Henry took an immediate dislike to her, apparently on the grounds that she lacked graceful accomplishments, although the precise reasons remain obscure. Their marriage was celebrated on 6 January 1540, but further acquaintance brought no improvement in relations. There was, all sides later agreed, no consummation, and Henry's thoughts soon lay elsewhere, specifically with Catherine Howard, about nineteen years old, and like Anne Boleyn one of Norfolk's nieces.

As Wolsey had taken alarm at the prospect of a Queen Anne, so now Cromwell could generate no enthusiasm for a Queen Catherine. Compared with the intractable difficulties over the 'divorce' of Catherine of Aragon, however, there was now no obvious legal impediment to an annulment. The diplomatic fall-out would be manageable, for Duke William was no Charles V. Indeed, his lands were under threat from the emperor and any call for aid made to his brother-in-law would prove only embarrassing. While Wolsey's excuses for delay long appeared plausible, Cromwell's foot-dragging was plain for all to see. Certainly, Henry saw it.

To all outward appearances, though, relations between king and minister were unimpaired. The king elevated Cromwell to the earldom of Essex, and to the office of chamberlain, shortly after another parliament met in April 1540. This promotion may, however, have been simply a formal recognition of Cromwell's continuing central role in what was becoming a more regulated and noble-dominated council. Successfully steering a subsidy bill through both Houses, Cromwell again tried to presume on the king's support by adding to his clientage in the privy chamber, by an attempted reconciliation with Gardiner (which led nowhere) and, once the time seemed right, by striking at his opponents through their more vulnerable associates. The latter included Arthur Plantagenet, Lord Lisle, deputy in Calais – one of whose chaplains had defected to Rome – and Richard Sampson, the conservative bishop of Chichester.

By May, London rumour was insisting that Cromwell held the measure of his enemies. Such rumours proved false. In the council, conservative influence was strong, and one senses that many of his fellow counsellors were awaiting an opportunity to bring Cromwell down. Even at court his authority was under threat, for power at court, still more than at the council table, rested on trust and intimacy with the king, and that trust Cromwell's recent actions had jeopardized. The minister's links with protestant European courts were an embarrassment for an ostensibly 'Catholic' monarch, and the disastrous Cleves union still rankled. All of a sudden – and the timing remains mysterious – Henry sanctioned action by Cromwell's opponents. On 10 June, in a scene gleefully related by Charles de Marillac the French ambassador

– who was, of course, not present – Cromwell was arrested, amid much indignity and mutual recrimination, at the council table. The initial charge, as might be expected, was one of treason. With their prey in the Tower, however, his opponents pushed a bill of attainder through parliament, charging Cromwell with a broader misuse of his authority. He had, they alleged, personally threatened noblemen who derided his origins and status, and had given constant support, ignoring Henry's express wishes, to heretics, fostering 'damnable Errors and Heresies'. The vice-gerent, they went on, had even licensed known heretics as preachers, and had been responsible for furthering the free transmission of heretical publications.

The charges were not without foundation. Cromwell had indeed helped men like Robert Barnes and the Calais protestant Adam Damplip. However, they justify without explaining. Henry, once again indulging in self-pity, would later blame malicious advisers, who through their tricks had deprived him of his 'most faithful servant'. Such statements recall his remarks after the fall of Anne Boleyn and should not be accepted at face value. There is every reason to suppose that Henry took the initiative in Cromwell's downfall. Trust had ebbed away.[21]

From his cell the condemned minister performed one final service for his master, providing testimony to the commission which, on 12 July, pronounced Henry's fourth marriage void on the grounds of non-consummation and Anne's precontract to the duke of Lorraine.[22] Sixteen days later, Henry married Catherine Howard and Cromwell went to the block. On 30 July three conservative priests were hanged, drawn and quartered for treason, while three radical protestants, Robert Barnes, Thomas Garret and William Jerome, were burnt at the stake, the culmination of a wider and none too effective campaign against heresy and sedition which served also to publicize the charges laid against the late minister. Like Cromwell, the three reformers suffered through the provisions of an act of attainder. They received no trial.

4 The Last Years of Henry VIII: England 1540–7

After Wolsey's fall, the developing divorce crisis had facilitated the rise of another pre-eminent minister. Eleven years later, with no such crisis in the offing, king and counsellors alike sought to provide against a repetition of history. The disposition of Cromwell's greatest offices points the way ahead. While William Fitzwilliam, earl of Southampton, was given the privy seal, and Thomas Wriothesley became principal secretary of state, no one secured the vice-gerency in spirituals. That high dignity has, indeed, never been filled since.

In anything but the very short term, neither Gardiner nor Norfolk won much ground by the death of their rival. Gardiner, his reputation as a diplomat again proving a doubtful asset, was in November 1540 saddled with the important but unwelcome post of ambassador to Charles V. Growing ever more determined to oppose French ambitions in Italy, the emperor was then trying, unsuccessfully, to patch together a religious peace in Germany: he was not averse to an understanding with England. Separated from court, as in the 1530s, Gardiner saw his personal influence with the king ebb away, even as he was establishing himself as England's leading advocate of a full understanding with the empire.

Norfolk, in an unnerving echo of 1536, was personally shaken and politically damaged when Catherine Howard was accused of multiple adultery in November 1541. Those charges are, unlike the Boleyn case, all too credible: the queen's hysterical confessions are remarkable principally for the excess that they reveal. Catherine, attainted and condemned without trial, lost her head in February 1542. Assorted lovers died too, while various members of the Howard family forfeited both lands and liberty. The king himself was appalled and greatly distressed by this turn of events. In failing health – an ulcer was eating away his leg, and he seems to have suffered from dropsy or some similar complaint[1] – his temper grew ever less predictable. His gradual decline could not, of course, be concealed from his court. Henry's last years are characterized by the sight of his loyal, deferential and fearful ministers looking with clearing vision to the day when a new king would reign in England.

The minister removed, and a principal source of Cromwell's hegemony denied to others, Henry's privy council springs suddenly into focus with the appointment of William Paget as its clerk, and with the opening of a minute book. Of Paget, an able man and experienced foreign diplomat employed at various times by both Gardiner and Cromwell, we shall hear more. The council book, as it develops through the century, becomes one of the most important – arguably *the* most important – source for the administrative history of late Tudor England.

Cromwell's fall claimed few other victims: Cranmer and Audley kept their high offices. Even one of his closest and most expendable friends, Ralph Sadler, suffered only a relatively brief imprisonment. The majority of Cromwell's appointments to the privy chamber retained their posts. Men like Anthony Denny and Philip Hoby served for the next six years as counterweights to the conservative inclinations of the privy council. The practical alliance and overlap between these men and the reformist minority in the council then became of crucial importance in the succession politics of 1546–7.

If, indeed, Cromwell had been dispatched in a conservative coup, it was Henry's very personal brand of religious conservatism that had triumphed. The king argued all along that his was a 'middle of the road' stance: Cromwell it was who had left 'the mean indifferent true and virtuous way' trodden by his eirenic master. Henry was conservative in that he distrusted the temptations innovation of any kind placed in the way of his subjects. He read, and wrote theology, and his religious beliefs did change, a little, over time. Diarmaid MacCulloch goes so far as to suggest that Henry 'jettisoned the past in his last decade', losing a belief in the notion of purgatory still evident in the mid-1530s, and becoming far less convinced of the sacramental nature of confession. The king did not reject change out of hand. First, any alteration had to pass the test of his conscience. Second, its benefits both to church and state had to be assessed: did it encourage subservience to Rome, or provoke unrest? Last of all came the barrier of innate caution. Some measures advanced by reformers surmounted all these obstacles, even after the vice-gerent's fall. Cromwell's order that a copy of the vernacular Great Bible should be placed in every church was reiterated by royal proclamation in May 1541, and backed up this time by financial penalties for non-compliance. The destruction of remaining shrines was ordered that October.

Together, these considerations gave shape to a reformation which, if nothing protestant by 1547, had moved both king and national church a far distance in fifteen years. After the turbulence of the 1530s, and after the hand of Cromwell is removed, the 1540s show the English reformation for what, in its early phase, it clearly was: the moulding of both church and state to the theocratic vision of a powerful king. At times the vision was ambiguous; but on occasion, too, that ambiguity was itself deliberate.[2]

Such personal fashioning had obvious consequences for Henry's church. Just as in the late 1530s, diplomatic advantage continued to shape domestic religious policy. Given the alignment of European powers in 1543, Henry wished to pose as the orthodox Catholic ally of the emperor. That May, a drastically revised version of the *Bishop's Book* was approved in convocation and duly published. The revision was largely undertaken by six theologians, most of them moderately conservative in their opinions. However, it also owed much to the personal attention of King Henry. Published with the clear royal authority its predecessor had always lacked, the new version justifiably became known as the *King's Book*.[3] The entire composition is highly conservative. Transubstantiation is implicitly justified, good works are advocated, and protestant doctrines of free will and justification by faith alone unambiguously denounced. While purgatory is condemned as a papist accretion, prayers for the dead are promoted using traditional Catholic arguments, and images, provided they are put to no superstitious or idolatrous use, are deemed acceptable. Introduction of the *King's Book* was reinforced by the passage through parliament of an Act for the Advancement of True Religion, which in endorsing all religious doctrine published under royal authority since 1540 also attempted to restrict Bible reading to men of property and – a late concession – to noble and gentry women.

Regularly portrayed as a Catholic (if not a *Roman* Catholic) monarch, the description in fact sits uneasily on Henry's shoulders. In an uncertain, threatening world, maintenance of outward, orthodox trappings had mattered a great deal to the king. By the mid-1540s, though, threats of overseas intervention had receded and what then mattered more to him was the need to avoid religious factionalism at home. If this meant the frustration of attempts to enforce religious acts he himself had pressed through his parliaments, that was a price readily paid. Personal loyalty became a touchstone of Henrician orthodoxy. Whenever a servant retained the king's trust, no attempt to question his religious credentials was likely to succeed. In 1543 the so-called Prebendaries' Plot – shorthand for a broad-based conspiracy undertaken by conservatives ranging from Gardiner, through representatives of the Kentish gentry, to a faction within the archbishop's own cathedral which maintained links with like-minded members of Oxford University – tried to destroy Cranmer by denouncing the archbishop and his followers as heretics. Henry, though, rejected accusations which, if manufactured, were no more contrived than those used to bring down Cromwell in 1540.[4] The plotting was perhaps too byzantine for its own purpose, but the most significant difference between 1540 and 1543 was that Henry trusted Cranmer whereas he had no longer trusted Cromwell – this unshakeable confidence is one of the imponderables of his reign. A year later, however, Henry also stemmed attempts to topple Gardiner, engineered in 1544 by the king's brother-in-law Edward Seymour, earl of Hertford, by Sir Anthony Denny, and by the Lord Admiral John Dudley, Lord Lisle. All these manoeuvres suggest a king moving decisively to reject aggressive extremes in the formulation of religious policy, and indeed there is no real need to seek for suggestive evidence, given the king's emotional and patently sincere appeal for charity, for adherence to his cherished 'middle way', during his address to parliament in 1545.

The king's religious orthodoxy in fact displayed quite a number of distinctive features. The long battle with forces he interpreted as anti-Christian had, it seems, moved Henry to cast himself as an Israelite king. The greatest Old Testament monarchs had not only purged their realm of idolatry, they had also offered unity to fractious tribes. Conscious that they spoke for their God, they had chastised the wicked, giving succour to those who submitted to their will. Opening the Second Book of Kings, Henry seized in particular upon the example of Josiah, the king whose initial ignorance and sin had given way to religious zeal. Just as Josiah, the scales fallen from his eyes, had promulgated the law, so Henry saw himself distributing vernacular Bibles, striking down false images, and insisting on the education of his people in the creed and Ten Commandments. Here, in its outline, was King Henry's faith.

The apparent religious reaction of 1543 suggests, on closer examination, further winding of the spring by which Henry drove his church according to his own priorities. 'Conservative' legislation contained some surprises. More latitude was permitted the recanting sinner than had been extended under the Act of Six Articles: it was now possible to recant twice before suffering the flames. The next parliament, that of early 1544, limited the scope to prosecute under the 1543 legislation, and in May 1544 an English litany was published, the first church service in English to carry unequivocal royal authority. This, indeed, was an exceptional wartime measure, designed to coordinate the national prayer effort with the military campaign against France that year, but in 1545 the penitential litany was extended to become a standard element in English church worship. During May 1545, a primer in English was given exclusive royal backing and further, abortive, efforts were made to reform canon law. These measures taken in 1544 and 1545 cannot, by any stretch of the imagination, be construed as a conservative triumph.

Changing iconography of kingship again conveys Henry's message. The English monarch is, time after time, portrayed armed with both the sword of justice and the Bible: on Hans Holbein's title page for Coverdale's Bible, for example, and on the title page of the Great Bible of 1539, where Henry is depicted handing down the Word of God, through the ranks of society, to his people. Edward VI and Elizabeth I in their turn were urged to take up the imperial duty bestowed by their father and to advance the 'fire of God's word'. Elizabeth is portrayed in John Foxe's *Acts and Monuments* as a second Emperor Constantine, putting an end to persecution of faithful Christians. She and her brother are also established as monarchs of sword and book, although the emphasis with a female monarch lies more in the hope arising from dissemination of scriptural truth than in the corrective severity of justice.[5]

Henry's closest companions adapted prudently to his often quite subtle shifts of emphasis in religion. Among the gentlemen of the privy chamber, the increasingly authoritative Sir Anthony Denny, and those rising stars Hertford and Lisle, despite their more or less obvious reformist inclinations, conformed to a faith which rested on traditional dogma while rejecting anything that smacked of Roman 'innovation'. With so much tradition emanating from past papal decrees the conflation was never easy, but it reflected the king's wishes and most worldly-wise courtiers made no difficulty over accommodation. Denny in particular seems to have successfully matched active private support of reformers with open conformity to the king's will.

In July 1543, having for eighteen months set his face against yet another marriage, Henry wed Catherine Parr, Lady Latimer. A widow in her early thirties, Catherine was the sister of an experienced if singularly untalented courtier, William Parr, earl of Essex.[6] The new queen was a woman known to favour moderate reform. She was undoubtedly pious, her chaplain Francis Goldsmith maintained with only modest exaggeration that she treated every day as a Sunday. Yet her faith was by nature direct, obvious, at times verging on the simplistic. 'I have certainly no curious learning to defend this matter withal,' she wrote, 'but a simple zeal and earnest love to the truth, inspired of God.' The considerations which prompted Henry to take a sixth wife have never been adequately investigated. The king was not given to making political statements through his marriages, and perhaps lust and loneliness played their part, but we have at least some scope to see in the union a further royal insistence on that cherished religious 'middle way'.

It has been many times argued that Catherine introduced learned men of reformist inclinations – notably John Cheke, the Regius professor of Greek at Cambridge, Richard Cox and Anthony Cooke – into influential positions overseeing the education of both Edward and Elizabeth. If the notion that Henry's two younger children shared a common education has been questioned, if doubt has been cast on the queen's direction of that education, and if there is no evidence to suggest that anything taught by these men clashed with Henrician 'dogma' while the king lived, the appointments *were* made, most probably by Henry himself. Maria Dowling perceives here a series of patronage links in play, in which the queen had no part, involving scholars of Cambridge University.[7] Perhaps these appointments were engineered through Cranmer's influence, or that of Denny, in whose household Elizabeth resided for much of this period; but such hypotheses lack proof. It is certainly true that, whoever was responsible for their placement, the arguments and examples set by these teachers had a marked influence on both royal children.

However we may assess the extent of her influence, either over her husband or over the 'evangelical' reformers, Catherine herself appears to have been targeted by religious conservatives in the summer of 1546. The evidence is thin and late, but if we accept John Foxe's version she survived through formal submission to her husband's direction in spiritual matters. The story echoes in several respects the pursuit of Cranmer by the Prebendaries' plotters, and its significance may well have been exaggerated. Nevertheless, the times were still perilous for reformers. Henry entertained a papal envoy in August 1546, and for a while considered sending delegates to a General Council, although the absence of any external threat to England dissuaded him from such passing conceits. In September, evangelical books were being burnt on London bonfires and the evangelicals themselves – the usual extremists who, in their denial of the real presence, alienated most shades of opinion at court – were everywhere harried. The king, his health rapidly declining, was in no mood for clemency and everyone at court was, as usual, observing him and drawing appropriate conclusions.

Henry's religious reforms are here considered in terms of legislation and leading characters, essentially because it is so difficult to assess the wider popularity of change. Most Englishmen and women acquiesced in what amounted to a decision of state. To resist – and for many in a generally deferential society the very thought of resistance against the dictates of a lawful sovereign was difficult to countenance – threatened livelihood, even life itself. Yet acquiescence does not amount to popularity. Some well-organized reformed communities were flourishing, in London and the southeastern counties, but even here most remained conservative, albeit insipidly, while the great majority of the kingdom appears to have rejected innovation in the fabric of their daily religion. Given the prevailing political uncertainties, and the king's age and condition, this conclusion is perhaps unsurprising. That there was, indeed, a reformation, which in the long term came to claim the loyalties of most Englishmen and women, yet remains an inescapable fact, perhaps only explicable through appreciation that fashions in popular religion do alter, through acceptance that people were disposed to take direction from the monarch in such matters, and, perhaps, through recognition that for many, the choice was neither fundamental nor particularly important. Still more pragmatically, the 'new' church had exploited the financial resources of the clergy without calling upon correspondingly increased contributions from lay members of society. In time of foreign war, heavy tax demands and inflationary debasement, laymen, particularly that influential minority of laymen who had profited from monastic dissolution, were content with this arrangement.

Henry's church does at times appear to adapt traditional, Catholic religion to new tastes in religious practice; how far these new tastes emerge in response to or independently from Henrician reforms it is hard to tell. In the field of printing, where religious books were produced both to conform with current religious policy and to meet demand, old favourites like Bonaventure's *Life of Christ*, collections of lives of saints such as the *Golden Legend*, even Thomas à Kempis's long-popular *Imitation of Christ*, lose their appeal as Henry's reign progresses, to be replaced by workaday manuals of Christianity: primers, collections of sermons and commentaries on Biblical texts. No fewer than fifteen English editions of the Psalms appeared between 1535 and 1548. One cannot really doubt the popularity of the English Bible; once the expensive translations began to appear they were purchased and read.

As the momentous events of the 1530s recede, we may ask whether the English parliament had undergone any lasting changes. It is a difficult question to answer. Structurally, parliaments of the 1540s were still not so very different from fifteenth-century predecessors. The composition of the two Houses, and the ways in which they transacted their affairs, had altered little. Elton saw in these later parliaments a lack of direction when contrasted with sessions managed by Cromwell. Perhaps. Or maybe it is the focus of such direction that has shifted. In the 1530s the king stood in need of a divorce, and the procurement of that divorce demanded constitutional change. Ten years on, the king stood in need of money – a lot of money – and if the procurement of revenue represented a return to more familiar parliamentary territory, that procurement was no less immediately important to both monarch and kingdom. In the middle of an expensive, aggressive war against France and Scotland, pressing demands for armies, weapons and supply occupied every thought. Against this background, legislation like the act establishing the court of general surveyors, that which completed the integration of Wales into Henry's kingdom in 1543, and the close-fought bill of December 1545 which empowered the king to dissolve chantries, so providing desperately needed funds, reflect the dictates of the present rather than the past. Parliament continued to matter to its wealthy, landed constituents, while a rash of improvement acts during the 1540s testifies to the social contribution of statute in meeting the aspirations and necessities of individual towns, up and down the land.[8] The simplest of statistics is perhaps the most telling. There were five parliamentary sessions in the last five years of the reign, hardly a sign of decreasing institutional significance.

With relations between Francis I and Charles V again deteriorating – no lasting solution had been found to some intractable territorial disputes – Henry once again enjoyed scope to exploit their differences. After much debate, complex diplomacy, politic hesitation and perhaps genuine uncertainty, the king chose the course advocated by Gardiner and opted for alliance with the emperor, and for war. Perhaps he was disenchanted at the marginalization that had come with neutrality, or perhaps high dreams of conquest carried the day. In July 1543, a secret treaty of mutual aid with the Empire drawn up in the previous February was published, and eighteen years of more or less enthusiastic alignment with France came to an end.

The 1540s, like the 1510s, was a decade of warfare and overseas military commitment. Once again England was pitted in uneasy alliance with the Empire against the French and the Scots, and once again the French, distracted elsewhere, surrendered a northern town – for Tournai in 1513 read Boulogne, captured in September 1544. Once again the Scots were routed in the field. As a battle, Solway Moss (November 1542) was no Flodden, but the events this near-bloodless skirmish set in train on both sides of the northern border had lasting repercussions for at least three European nations. Henry, who again crossed the Channel in person to supervise operations, may be criticized for his lack of judgement in foisting an inconsequential war on a country ill able to afford it, although at a purely military level he showed good sense in limiting campaigning to manageable goals in Picardy, and eschewing, in the face of great imperial pressure, any repeat of the duke of Suffolk's costly march on Paris in 1523.

The king had in fact acquired strategic subtlety with age. He chose war, he chose his ground, and on his own terms he was undoubtedly successful. Only his stubborn insistence on retaining Boulogne edged towards the impractical: Henry had long coveted the town, and he was not prepared to trade it away once Charles V again beat him in the race to break their always fragile alliance, negotiating a peace with France at Crépy in the same month that Boulogne fell. Eventually, England and France put an end to hostilities by the Treaty of Camp in June 1546, Boulogne remaining in English hands. The cost of garrisoning and fortifying a town with few natural defences and obsolete walls, even allowing for the restoration of French 'pension' payments in abeyance since 1533, proved a financial burden far outweighing any bargaining benefits its possession might have conferred.[9]

Cost seldom was a consideration dear to Henry's heart, but it was one that had to be faced eventually. Waging any prolonged war in sixteenth-century Europe was a ruinous business, especially when the war involved Europe's great powers. The French crown, with an established income from taxation, and – the mark of a tyranny in English eyes – a standing army, reinforced with Swiss volunteers, boasted reserves far exceeding those of England, but even France's resources appeared limited when set against those of the Habsburg giant. A smaller population, one, moreover, which had shown itself resistant to frequent taxation during the 1520s, left the English crown at a disadvantage; the need to finance campaigns which between 1542 and 1547 cost in excess of £2 million demanded unparalleled royal self-sacrifice. Three quarters of a million pounds' worth of land was sold, representing perhaps 20 per cent of all crown property. Over £100,000 was borrowed at high rates of interest from the financial houses of Antwerp. Taxation granted by parliament and forced loans from the nobility together raised a little under £1 million. Still there was a deficit, however, and Henry was obliged to pursue the precedents of Wolsey's 1526 experiment, and Cromwell's tinkering with the Irish pound in 1540, authorizing debasement of the English currency. In an age when coins contained precious metal, gold or silver, such content was reduced without altering the face value. Well over £4 million in debased coin was issued in the period 1544–51.

Debasement brought short-term gains. It resulted in a profit of some £1.3 million to the crown over the same seven-year period and helped boost exports while sterling depreciated against foreign currencies, establishing the mint as a new and highly important national revenue agency. It also, however, contributed to a loss of confidence in English coin abroad, made foreign loans harder to secure, and fuelled the worst decade of price inflation yet experienced in England. In the space of little more than ten years, average prices of foodstuffs all but doubled; wages paid to labourers rose by some 50 per cent. The hardships borne by many whenever prices either rose rapidly or fluctuated uncertainly, and whenever incomes failed to match these increases thanks to the prevalence of fixed rents and a well-supplied labour market, were recognized by several contemporary commentators.

Wartime expedients had long-term repercussions. The effects of debasement continued to plague the English economy for decades, while a crown shorn of lands accrued through dissolution required alternative sources of patronage and revenue. From 1542, few years passed free from the collection of instalments to the various parliamentary subsidies. Near-permanent military expenditure helped accustom English people to regular taxation. In a gradual yet inexorable process, subjects were conditioned to consider as old-fashioned and unpatriotic expectations that the king should 'live off his own'. The newer theories, when they found expression, were more stark. Sir Thomas Smith, a privy counsellor in the next reign, did not mince his words: 'So long as the subjects have it', said Smith, meaning money, 'so it is meet the King should have as long as they have it.'

The most significant immediate consequence of England's return to the battlefields, however, was the way in which a new generation of soldier statesmen enhanced their reputations. For his French adventure in 1544, Henry chose as his senior commanders those experienced campaigners, the dukes of Norfolk and Suffolk. Norfolk, though, failed miserably when laying siege to Henry's secondary objective, Montreuil. Suffolk succeeded in capturing Boulogne, then died in 1545. The laurels passed elsewhere. The earl of Hertford led successive expeditions against Scotland in 1544–6, while his friend and political ally, Lord Lisle, presided over a permanent Navy Board from 1546, defended the south coast against a French fleet, and kept Boulogne supplied in the face of counter-attacks. In time of war, military command brought with it political strength. Backed by the queen's brother, Essex, and by a dominant group within the privy chamber that included Sir William Herbert, Paget and Denny, Hertford's political position was, by the end of 1546, growing very strong.

There is always a temptation to divide the king's closest advisers of the 1540s into two politico-religious camps, the conservatives, under Norfolk and Gardiner, ranged against Cranmer, Hertford, Lisle and their associates. Evidence survives to illustrate personal animosities, and also the existence of groups competing for Henry's ear. But it is striking how few counsellors can now be consigned without qualification to either one side or the other. Only if a definition of faction embraces the full subtleties of lives devoted to pleasing the king, to securing a due share of the patronage and rewards on offer, and to treading carefully in conversations with colleagues, can it hope to approach reality. Faction at this almost intangible, instinctive level is the stuff of court life, and in Tudor England court life and high politics merge inseparably. Expressions of open dissent and anger are rare, and, being rare, they are seized and remarked upon. Thus, from manifestations of Gardiner's grating arrogance, or from the actions of Lisle who – so de Selve the French ambassador says – was banished from court in September 1546 for striking Gardiner in privy council, we take our clues to a hidden game. Through all these shifts and explosions, the king it was who disposed, favoured and rejected. Talk of deep-laid factional plotting succeeds in overlooking the capacity of individuals to humour, or to cross, an unpredictable master.

Such considerations are of particular relevance when assessing events at the very end of Henry's reign. In December 1546, Gardiner again misjudged Henry's mood and tried to reject an exchange of lands desired by the king. Norfolk, meanwhile, was brought down through the folly of his eldest son, Henry Howard, earl of Surrey, a notable poet but no diplomat, who had compounded a poor showing in the French war with unwise allusions to his own royal blood and to a future Howard regency. Under examination, the old duke sealed his own fate by conceding that he had revealed state secrets to the French. Both Gardiner and the Howards were clearly concerned by Hertford's growing influence; Surrey's wild talk and the duke's cack-handed duplicity smack of desperation. But if the factional divide is usually presented in terms of religious differences, there is little hint of religion in these disputes. No one, least of all, perhaps, the dying Henry, could have foreseen the adoption of a radical religious policy after his death, under a kinsman he had come to trust.

War, indeed, had brought its own tensions, and on occasion drove into conflict men otherwise closely allied. Norfolk, the military captain, charged Gardiner, the controller of supplies, with incompetence and mismanagement, carrying his criticism to the king himself. Whereas Norfolk's sympathies lay all along with France rather than the Empire, Sir Anthony Browne, master of the horse and an important figure close to the king in the privy chamber, shared Gardiner's religious conservatism and his warm approval of imperial policy. Yet even Browne was brought to criticize – openly to the whole council – the bishop's mismanagement of provisions.

Attacking a skilful administrator on such grounds promised to be a fruitless exercise and, indeed, when Hertford and Lisle deprecated Gardiner's arrangements in the north the bishop was cleared following a council investigation. Common cause could equally unite the strangest of bedfellows, as when Gardiner, Essex and Lisle together urged the zealous protestant Anne Askew to retract her denial of the real presence at communion and spare herself a martyr's death. Askew, whose embarrassing court connections may help explain this unexpected show of unity, proved resolute and was burnt in July 1546. Paget and Hertford both insisted later that they had sought to preserve Gardiner's place among the counsellors nominated for a forthcoming minority, and their assurances are by no means improbable. Gardiner's administrative skills would have been an asset to any future regime. At least in their own version of events it was Henry, late in December 1546, who insisted that the bishop was 'a wilful man, not meet to be about his son'. Positions were taken up and abandoned, brief alliances of convenience concluded, and then broken. A reign of nearly four decades was coming to an end, and no one was entirely certain who would prosper in King Edward's new world. At such times the courtier's mask seldom slips. If they could confound the contemporaries who knew them best, the opinions of many prominent figures are quite capable of resisting scrutiny from distant generations.

5 Pre-Reformation Scotland, 1528–57

Chronology

July 1528	James V begins personal rule
1532	Establishment of College of Justice
January 1537	James V marries Princess Madeleine of France
July 1537	Death of Queen Madeleine
May 1538	Marriage of James V to Mary of Guise
November 1542	Battle of Solway Moss
December 1542	Birth of the future Queen Mary; death of James V
January 1543	Earl of Arran appointed regent
July 1543	Treaty of Greenwich
December 1543	Scots parliament rejects Treaty of Greenwich
May 1544	Start of 'rough wooing'; earl of Hertford burns city of Edinburgh
May 1546	Murder of Cardinal Beaton
September 1547	Battle of Pinkie
June 1548	French troops land in Scotland
July/August 1548	Treaty of Haddington; Mary leaves for France
1549	First of three reforming church councils (others 1552, 1559)
April 1554	Arran replaced as regent by Mary of Guise

How did Scotland, as a peripheral, small and impoverished nation, prey to the condescension of almost every other European country, make its mark upon the wider sixteenth-century world? The occasional Englishman might exaggerate the virtues of its climate and geography when seeking to promote its conquest, and as England's long-standing foe it attracted the flattery of would-be allies, but there was little by way of a good press otherwise.[1] At the same time, there was a widespread, grudging admiration for the spirit, the temper and the make-do of the Scot himself, particularly when the writer was not English and when the Scot had wandered from his native shores. Whenever contemporaries indulged in that timeless pursuit of the national stereotype the Englishman was frequently portrayed as an inconstant, rebellious fellow, addicted to novelty.[2] The Scot, on the other hand, was generally acknowledged as a good fighter, in demand from the 1400s by successive kings of France and, as horizons widened and European armies grew in size, by the sixteenth- and seventeenth-century monarchs of Sweden and the Baltic coast.[3] The sterling warrior displayed a substantial self-confidence. Don Pedro d'Ayala, a Spanish envoy who reported in 1498, described the Scots as handsome people, friendly towards a foreign visitor, vain, ostentatious, 'well dressed as is possible to be in such a country as that in which they live . . . courageous, strong, quick and agile . . . envious to excess'.

Foreigners who saw the Scots as a success story when judged against unpromising circumstance also recognized that Scotland had enjoyed, in the centuries since the decline of the Viking threat, the good fortune to confront only one, often distracted, enemy power. English inability to conquer her northern neighbour nurtured in that neighbour a corresponding pride in survival, while forcing the Scots to seek more distant allies, a search that brought enduring cultural associations. Her merchants and gentlemen travelled, bringing home new architectural ideas. Her scholars took first degrees at the three fifteenth-century Scottish universities of St Andrews, Glasgow and Aberdeen, and then pursued their studies in the schools of continental Europe. From John Major [or Mair] and Hector Boece to Robert Wauchope and Alexander Alesius a century on, Scotsmen participated in the principal theological and intellectual disputes of the day. Condescension and dismissal bred a fierce determination in Boece, his sixteenth-century translator John Bellenden, Major and the legal historian Sir Thomas Craig, to establish the antiquity and respectability of Scottish civilization, even if their efforts were largely concentrated on lowland rather than highland Scotland and drew strength from comparisons between the two that became ever more dismissive of highlanders.

The independent Scottish kingdom was essentially a kingdom of the lowland Scots; Scotland, like England, possessed a culturally dominant southeastern corner. There, many Anglo-Norman customs had long been adopted. Back in the fourteenth century Robert Bruce had wrested Scotland's independence from Edward II of England, but the contending nations had fought by the same rules: Bruce had secured recognition as an independent, medieval, feudal monarch. Successful kingship depended, as in England, on the personal capacity of the ruler, but the Scottish polity was different in that the institutions of central and regional government in Scotland were less developed and less bureaucratic in their methods.

One consequence of the decentralized forms of government encountered in Scotland is the poverty in available data. Almost every attempt to quantify society in the 1500s is based on backward extrapolations from the first statistical by-products of a burgeoning bureaucracy, invisible before the 1590s, and hardly sustaining analysis for another half century or more. A best guess is that Scotland's population edged up from 500,000 to around 750,000 in the course of the sixteenth century, about one-fifth of the figure for England. Only some 3–5 per cent lived in towns of any size, and similarly cautious estimates put the population of the capital, Edinburgh, at just 15,000 by 1600. Nevertheless, towns grew and became more self-conscious and oligarchic during the course of the century. Edinburgh experienced growth resembling that of London, doubling her population between 1550 and 1625, and dominating Scotland's overseas trade. Even more than London, she grew at the expense of long-established neighbours, particularly Stirling, the old capital. Within the context of a less-urbanized society, provincial towns – Aberdeen, Dundee, Perth and the emerging Glasgow, its Atlantic economy yet to blossom – were at least as important as their English equivalents, their role as regional centres reflecting the greater decentralization imposed by geography and by history.

There were all sorts of demographic parallels with the southern neighbour. Scotland's population grew when England's grew, although that growth was, so far as we can now tell, never so buoyant. Plague proved the same intermittent, summer scourge of urban populations. Like England, too, the population in 1600, though rising, still failed to match pre-Black Death totals. Scottish society does reserve its distinctive features: high levels of emigration and, more controversially, a lower proportion of the 'middling sort' in the countryside. There appear to have been few equivalents of the English yeoman, owning land and prospering through the production of a surplus. There was, furthermore, a more pronounced emphasis on leasehold, and proportionately fewer landless people; the land market was less active. Nevertheless, the small, nuclear family predominated, north and south of the border, and prevailing inheritance customs, patterns of age at marriage and geographical mobility, commonly over quite short distances in Scotland, are similar, again, insofar as the thin evidence allows us to judge.

Scottish towns offered, in comparison with other parts of western Europe, a limited range of services and trades. They concentrated mainly on the processing of products emerging from a rural hinterland – principally hides and wool – for the ultimate purpose of export. Most Scots lived in rural communities, concentrated along the eastern littoral and in the central lowlands, while the small population and difficulties of land transport placed an emphasis on the export trade, and precluded the growth of an internal market similar to that found in England. Much later growth of industrial towns and cities has only accentuated a population distribution long established by the dictates of geography. 'The land itself,' writes Margaret Sanderson, was all-important, the food and shelter which it provided were the priorities of life. Some people had more food and more substantial and comfortable houses than others but the grain, fish and flesh, the stone, timber, turf and thatch that all needed came locally from land and river.[4]

'Lairds' and other landlords stood close to processes by which the land was made profitable, frequently exercising a personal supervision, and suffering along with farmers and tenants when bad harvests brought financial hardship and, sometimes, the threat of famine.

Scotland had its own currency, but as in England the Scottish penny multiplied into shillings and pounds. Again like her southern neighbour, Scotland's main export was wool, raw and partly finished, destined for the Low Countries market and for the Baltic ports. During the sixteenth century, wool and its products accounted for at least 60 per cent of all customs revenue, the trade dominated by Edinburgh merchants. Other commodities offered opportunities to merchants in lesser burghs: Aberdeen, for example, led the way in salmon exports, Pittenweem and its neighbours, in cod. Herring, though, was the principal fish export. Increasing levels of imports and a stalling in the demand for wool stimulated exports in salt from coastal towns, while the introduction of new continental technology for ventilating pits towards the end of the century facilitated ambitious exploitation of Scotland's more accessible coal reserves. By the early 1600s, Sir George Bruce's great coalmine at Culross, on the Fife coast, was one of the technological wonders of the age. Nevertheless, mining remained a perilous undertaking, for miner and mineowner alike.

Scotland had, and retains, its own distinct system of law. Early in the sixteenth century, however, that distinctiveness was still evolving. Scottish law – outside some of the western and northern isles, where Gaelic customs prevailed and Norse influences still lingered – came to be dominated by written codes and Roman ideas, according less weight to custom than English common law. Civil law, at least in theory, was standardized in the 1530s on the conciliar justice later formalized as the Edinburgh court of session. Nevertheless, this importance attached to Roman and Canon law, which so worried English common lawyers after 1603, reflected a sixteenth-century refinement of what had before been another essentially customary system, albeit one with its own ancient roots. The first known Scottish legal treatise, the *Regiam Majestatem*, of the early fourteenth century, had been based on the twelfth-century English treatise known as *Glanvill*.[5]

Practice was, as usual, never so straightforward as theory. In the countryside legally independent 'regalities' still flourished, while alongside both royal law court and regality the personal, private bloodfeud with its elaborate customary mechanisms for composition and redress remained an important feature of Scottish highland and lowland society, three centuries after it had vanished in southern England.[6]

In the crucial consideration of title to land there were, at all levels of society, many parallels with England. Scottish magnates held land of the king, like their English counterparts, and they owed similar feudal dues.

Custom in manor and barony gave legal security of tenure to a variety of copyholders, north and south of the border, while both societies harboured significant underclasses of the true tenant-at-will, and the landless. On closer inspection, of course, there were any number of subtle differences. Leases for three lives, encountered in many parts of England, are seldom found in Scotland, while the position of a 'kindly tenant' in Scotland – one whose tenancy was justified through kinship with former holders – appears stronger than that enjoyed by an English tenant-at-will: tenants on occasion bequeathed their 'kindness' in a property, treating it as a heritable asset.

The geographical divide noticed in England between a predominantly pastoral, highland north-west and a more populous, lowland, arable south-east is accentuated in Scotland. Between lowland and highland Scots, roughly equal in numbers, lay a wide linguistic and cultural gulf. The lowlander, speaking English,[7] and for centuries culturally assimilated into the north European mainstream, was becoming increasingly suspicious and contemptuous of his traditionally unruly Gaelic-speaking cousin. His opinions were reciprocated, and mutual suspicion aggravated by religious differences endured far beyond 1600. The historian encounters another manifestation of this divide: relative paucity of written records for lowland Scotland contrasts with an almost complete absence of such sources across the so-called Highland Line.

There were, of course, as many differences as similarities between the two nations of Britain. Scotland was an independent country, she had her own distinctive parliament, of a single chamber and three estates,[8] and her own anciently descended line of kings. Detailed sources for her institutional history frequently remain elusive. With regard to her parliament, for example, we have few significant records of sixteenth-century electoral politics, debates, speeches or procedure. No obscurity, however, attaches to the importance of the monarchy. Kingship was the cement which bound the nation together. As G. W. S. Barrow points out, 'it was through acceptance of a common kingship that the varied peoples of Scotland had gradually come to political unity'.[9] That monarchy could appear at once weak and strong. It might seem underfinanced – James V around 1530 enjoyed an annual income of just £15,000 English – and in time of minority highly vulnerable to the power-plays of the nobility. On the other hand, no sixteenth-century European monarchy flourished under a juvenile king. The reigns of the earlier Stewarts afford substantial excuses for suspecting both that the royal authority was capable of broad interpretation and that, to quote Jenny Wormald, 'when kings and magnates did conflict, kings did not always have right on their side'.[10] Scottish kings had ever been reliant on their nobility, but it is equally true that the nobility was often all too aware of its own responsibilities, and tried to live up to them. Individual responses colour general assertions, while the myth of the overmighty subject dies hard. Human nature being what it is, there were inevitably some irresponsible men in the ranks of the nobility, yet it is remarkable how few of them ever prospered in the early modern Scottish state.

The Scottish monarchy's practical weakness was, curiously, its greatest strength. For all but his greatest nobles the king was seldom a threatening presence, indeed, most subjects, including many powerful men, would live out their lives never seeing the king, never entering a royal court, and seldom if ever contributing to royal taxation. The barony, for which the nearest approximation in England is the manor, was the focus of most people's lives, and the barony court still exercised a wide jurisdiction. While the first Tudor kings were eradicating remaining English 'liberties', their Stewart counterparts hardly challenged, indeed, increased, the number of 'regalities', territories belonging to favoured peers where the royal writ did not run. Principles of give and take held sway. The king sought personal, intimate contact with the great men of his land, and he cultivated such contacts through royal progresses and a flourishing court. He toured his kingdom, surveying the justice of his lords, representing a wider, international Scottishness, but he remained a symbol rather than an ever-present burden. In contrast to England, the sixteenth century saw no popular rebellion. Grievances there were, and as in England they were directed against statesmen and noblemen rather than the person of the monarch. But in England those men clustered about the king, whereas in Scotland many were still fundamentally regional magnates.

Despite personal failings the first five Jameses, who ruled Scotland successively from 1406 to 1542, shared the energy and self-confidence that foreigners perceived in their subjects. If their ambitions toppled over on occasion into absurdity and impracticality – James III's call for chivalric adventure in France, during the 1470s, and the Flodden campaign of 1513 stand out as cases in point – their pursuit of a role in the European polity appeared to many of their more eminent subjects a necessary statement of Scottish independence. The ambitious building projects of successive kings, which stretched their financial resources but encouraged the transmission of Italian, German and French architectural ideas into Scotland, underlined that statement. James IV's stunning great hall at Stirling was equalled only by the various projects embarked upon by his successor. Ambition also lies behind the passion for up-to-date military technology which so possessed the Stewarts – James II suffered in the name of innovation when killed by a misfiring cannon at Roxburgh in 1460.

The foundations of independence, however, had suffered some telling blows, as the glories of Bannockburn – a victory made the more splendid by its rarity – dwindled ever further into the past. The all-important monarchy was particularly accident prone. Queen Victoria, in a rare attempt at humour, is said to have rejected the study of 'too many Jameses, all of them murdered', and while the murder rate among Scottish monarchs during the fifteenth century does not compare with the mayhem wreaked among England's Plantagenets, the Stewart dynasty certainly endured more than its share of untimely deaths and lengthy minorities. The appalling military disaster of Flodden in 1513, when an English army hastily assembled from northern retinues and soldiers spared from Henry VIII's campaign in France outmanoeuvred, outfought and slaughtered James IV and the cream of his nobility, produced shocks that reverberated throughout the century, sending successive Scots administrations in search of secure alliances overseas.

To whom could they turn? Scotland's world in 1530 was still in some ways that of Scandinavian Europe; the Baltic timber trade and political manoeuvrings with Norway during the fifteenth century had fostered close relations between James IV and King Hans of Denmark and Norway. Scotland provided mercenaries for Denmark's incessant wars, and a degree of technological expertise, notably in shipbuilding. Denmark, in its turn, provided the enterprising Scottish merchant with a point of access to European markets and commodities. In these ties lay the foundations of a lasting relationship. Although Denmark's preoccupation with German and Baltic politics led to the weakening of those close ties during the sixteenth century, many Danish towns retained a significant Scottish community, while James VI's marriage to the Danish Princess Anne in 1589 breathed new life into the alliance, helping counter increasingly pervasive Dutch infiltration of the Danish economy.[11]

Scotland's horizons, though, were at no time limited to the north; her long-standing alliance with France and well-established commercial links with Flanders saw to that. Evidence distilled from the custumars' accounts afford ample proof that the Scottish export trade was focused on continental outlets rather than the closer but limited markets of England and Ireland.[12] Political constraints apart, in an age of limited land communications a sea voyage to London was as difficult, and less rewarding, than one to Antwerp or Hamburg.

King James V, son of James IV and Henry VII's daughter Margaret Tudor, had succeeded to the throne when just seventeen months old. His personal rule has traditionally been dated from July 1528, when, at the age of sixteen, he entered Edinburgh in a formal demonstration of his majority. Dynastic circumstances were auspicious. James had no legitimate brother or sister, faced no effective challenge to his own authority, and also enjoyed, through his mother, a strong claim to the English throne should the Tudor line fail. This energetic and determined king still awaits his thorough, modern biography, a curious oversight, since the elusive, unpredictable James is as fit a subject for the biographer as any of his more popular forebears or successors. James was at once remorseless and subtle: it was unwise to cross him. Archibald Douglas, sixth earl of Angus, James's stepfather and powerful during the recent minority, was permitted to retire to England after an inconclusive trial of strength with the king in 1528–9, but his family, and any who attempted to mediate or communicate with them, were thereafter harried and victimized. Angus's sister, Lady Glamis, and his nephew by marriage, the Master of Forbes, were both executed in 1537 on unconvincing charges of conspiracy. In the words of his biographer, Angus's young nephew James Douglas, later earl of Morton and regent in the 1570s, 'lived obscurely' while James V lived, and 'lurked for fear of the king'.[13]

A reputation for ruthlessness did few kings harm. James was quite capable of harrying the fractious men who lived along Scotland's southern border, summarily executing a prominent reiver, John Armstrong of Liddesdale. Some rather dubious circumstances surrounding this episode impressed numerous contemporaries, which was no doubt the object: trouble from the south was minimal during the remainder of the reign. However, while strength of character was commendable, and profitable for some – Campbells in the west and

Gordons in the north-east gained ground on their rivals through coopera-tion with the adult James V – fundamental unpredictability was less easy to accommodate, and James was unpredictable to a degree.

The king's vengeful streak, in particular, verged on the irrational. It may in part be ascribed to cupidity, or the natural ambitions of a personal monarchy determined to recover from a period of minority. There is little doubt, though, that personal vindictiveness creeps into many of James's dealings with his greater subjects. The earl of Morton was pursued for over a decade before agreeing to resign his lands in favour of Douglas of Lochleven – who made the same properties over to James. Others were harassed with specious allega-tions, and then offered the chance to purchase pardons. Sir James Colville of East Wemyss is recorded as having paid £1000 to this end. Since James's four immediate predecessors had all succeeded to the throne as minors, a necessary tradition had sprung up by which Stewart kings, upon attaining their majority, saw through parliament an act of revocation, the terms of which annulled all grants made in their names during their minorities. These acts had been welcomed by the beneficiaries of such grants, for their acquisi-tions were customarily confirmed once more, but the process placed poten-tially wide powers in the hands of an adult king. James's act of revocation, passed in the 1540 parliament, was accompanied, innovatively, by selective and insistent demands for large payments to ensure his goodwill.

For some, no composition was offered. Sir James Hamilton of Finnart, long the wealthy and favoured master of building works, was executed in August 1540, ostensibly on the grounds that he had plotted with those *bêtes noires* the Douglases. But so far as many contemporaries were concerned he died because he had amassed a large fortune. The king it was who received his lands, his moveable property and his gold.

Everything, though, is relative. Many who lived through the dismal periods of minority after James's death looked back on the 1530s as a golden age, and modern historians weaned of the Mary Stewart cult also incline to magnify the father at his daughter's expense. While parallels can be found in the previous century, there is much to admire in the king's sponsorship of social legislation in parliament, his determination, through the fresh appoint-ment of a poor man's advocate, to make justice available to all levels of society. Unsurprisingly, there was a gulf between legislation and practice. Nevertheless, one cannot entirely ignore John Leslie's opinion, given later in the century, that James had earned the favour of his subjects through enabling them to live 'quietly and in rest, out of all oppression and molestation of the nobility and rich persons'. King James's building projects at Stirling, Falkland, Linlithgow and elsewhere, which cost in excess of £26,000 in the years of his personal rule, have also long been admired. Much of what went on in those buildings, however, remains mysterious. Like the king who pre-sided over it, the Scottish court of the 1530s has been neglected in recent years, and its structure, operational methods and wider political significance all await clear delineation.

Regular income of the crown increased nearly threefold between 1536 and 1542, albeit from a very low baseline: James, no doubt, would have considered that his greatest achievement. This improvement was substantially derived from coinage profiteering and from James's exploitation of sheep farming on crown estates. Two marriages into the royal house of France – to Madeleine, who died in July 1537, and to Mary in June 1538 – brought two dowries, as well as ships, armaments, a foreign pension regularly paid and international prestige. No attempt was made to impose significant lay taxation. The absence of regular warfare left James able to maintain what everyone admitted was a lavish court without recourse to such burdens. The £20,000 granted by parliament towards his expenses as a suitor in France in 1535 – he actually received about £6000 – remained exceptional.

Like other contemporary European monarchs, James considered the national church a vulnerable, valuable source of wealth. Again, circumstances worked in his favour. Grateful that Scotland had remained loyal during Henry VIII's reformation, the papacy made concessions in the face of repeated royal demands. It agreed to a clerical tax in 1531, to subsequent impositions, and to a 'request' that the Scottish crown might nominate to vacant bishoprics. In 1536 it further agreed that the Scottish church should contribute 10,000 ducats (c.£10,000 Scots) annually to the establishment of a central civil court. Sum and principle aroused opposition among leading churchmen, but since James sought monetary gain rather than legal innovation a compromise was reached by which £72,000 was to be paid as a once-for-all composition, both crown and church contributing to the maintenance of judges' salaries. Implementation was, at best, dilatory: the court of session remained one facet of the council's activity. Not until 1540 does it maintain its own register, separate from that kept for the privy council.

The Scottish church was the largest and wealthiest landowner in the kingdom. In 1560, its notional annual income was about £400,000, around ten times the crown's revenue. Generalizations on such abstract concepts as vitality and decline are once again hazardous. There are numerous instances of individual energy and piety to counter the many expressions of gloom, and there is scope to argue against the existence of any widespread, popular, reformed religion in Scotland. There was a native Lollard tradition in one or two areas – some Ayrshire families appear to have adhered to 'unorthodoxy' over several decades – but, as in England, that tradition was ultimately ineffectual. In the surviving records, much early religious dissent reflects the views of dissatisfied clerics; the degree of popular backing enjoyed by these priests is unknown, but was probably negligible. The execution in 1528 of Patrick Hamilton, burnt for his intemperate expression of Lutheran views, was sufficient to drive a few like-minded men and women overseas and to force other sympathizers into reluctant conformity.

Harsh measures against heresy appear at first sight to have swept the problem aside for a generation, but the picture is not quite so clear cut. Printing and a ready market ensured that Lutheran views – and, equally important in the fluid world of the 1530s, the views of reformers within the Catholic church – were available to significant numbers of literate Scots. The printing in question was largely foreign, for the scale of these operations in Scotland remained very small. John Gau's translation of a Danish work by

Christiern Pedersen, *The Richt Way to the kingdome of Heuine*, printed in Malmö in 1533, gave this market a weighty exposition of Lutheranism in Scots, to be followed by many less demanding works, including the *Gude and Godlie Ballattis*, published in the 1540s, John Wedderburn's popular and enterprising collection of religious songs and psalms which, as James Kirk colourfully puts it, 'encouraged Scots almost subconsciously to sing themselves into Lutheranism'. 'Contagion' from England and the continent remained a concern of all Scottish bishops, down to the reformation.[14]

Early sixteenth-century Scotland counted about forty active monastic communities. Though the general standard was unexceptional, few were culpably lax or immoderate in their regimes. Indeed, the Carthusians at Perth, like that other vigorous religious movement the Observant Franciscan friars, supported a wide range of educational and devotional institutions. Scottish monasticism displays one particular feature not found in England. As in France, and other parts of the continent, a good proportion of religious houses had from the late fifteenth century been placed, generally at the recommendation of the crown, in the hands of commendators: men who enjoyed the incomes of the monasteries for ever longer periods. Many commendators were bishops. Others were under-age members of noble families, or, as in the case of the sons of James V, royal bastards. Important standards were, it appears, maintained. Down to the reformation all commendators remained unmarried and in major clerical orders, even if they were not themselves members of religious communities.[15] Only from 1560 does the picture change. As recruitment to religious houses dried up and communities withered, so the commendators married and their commendatorships became hereditary possessions which passed readily enough to laymen.

In themselves, such appointments were not necessarily unhealthy. The proprietary nature of the office instilled in the holder a sense that here was an asset worth nurturing, while the monasteries gained prestige from the patronage of powerful men. A more pragmatic form of security was on offer, too. Given prevailing political uncertainties, the growing demands from the crown, and an increasing incidence of iconoclasm or vandalism, it made sense to shelter behind a strong secular arm. Whether this arm belonged to a commendator or a powerful lay bailie – the holder of courts of barony and regality on behalf of the institution – or whether the necessary backing was secured through bonds, pensions, grants and leases concluded between clergy and nobleman, the principle remained the same. Throughout Europe, the church was coming to depend more and more on the strength of the local nobility: in unstable or decentralized regimes that trend was all the more pronounced.[16]

However, despite all qualification, the pre-reformation church displays many serious shortcomings. We can certainly find examples of dutiful and learned parish priests, ministering to their flocks, but such men are thin on the ground. Not only was the parish seen as very much the bottom rung in the long ladder of clerical preferment, a rung which any enterprising man might hope either to step over or quit without delay, but the funding for earlier religious initiatives in a poor country – particularly the endowment of monasteries, collegiate churches in town and countryside, and the fifteenth-century universities – had all been drawn from the resources of the country church. Some 85–90 per cent of all Scotland's parishes contributed the larger part of their revenues to these institutions. No one, from the impoverished priests to their bishops, from the local congregations to the lords in parliament, considered this situation desirable, but when interests opposing significant reform included powerful institutions and their noble patrons little was likely to change. Many benefices, great and small, had acquired by the reformation a hereditary incumbent: whatever the spiritual rights and wrongs, this was a convenience, indeed, a necessity in cases of inadequate endowment. Unlike England, there was no secular land-rush at each step of the developing reformation since the lands of the church were to a great extent already in lay hands. Many Scottish families had enriched themselves upon religious property; that enrichment had begun before our period, and was well on the way to completion before the break with Rome in 1560.

James's determination to maximize income from ecclesiastical sources aggravated weaknesses in the very structure of the church in Scotland. With so many revenues appropriated, and with new bishops facing the additional burden of annual payments to the crown, clerics at all levels had to meet demands for taxation out of capital or family reserves. Obligations of this nature encouraged the ancient practice of feuing, whereby land, often for some high-minded if notional purpose such as the repair of monastic buildings following English invasion, was permanently alienated in return for a down payment, or 'grassum', and fixed annual payments and duties. Initially, and especially considering all the incidental fees involved, the feu was no cheap option, but embodied in a great variety of terms and conditions across lowland Scotland it proved very popular in the sixteenth century. During periods of stable prices these arrangements guaranteed an income to the feuors, but with the onset of rapid inflation incomes diminished in real terms, while the lands were seldom if ever recovered.

The consequences for Scottish society were considerable. Feuing allowed the crown and great families to consolidate estates and to buy political support. In time, it also turned hundreds of lesser tenants into men and women possessed of heritable property, often lands which they had hitherto leased. Sometimes, feuing was the culmination of a process which had already seen life tenancies replace tacks – leases – for terms of years. Church lands, frequently in the hands of cadet branches of noble families, were especially vulnerable to this process, as family groups gathered estates either side of the reformation. A further social complication was that tenants on ecclesiastical estates suddenly found themselves in the hands of new landlords, eager to see quick returns on their investment. The temptation to 'rack' up rents was considerable. Faced by far more pressing concerns the papacy was compliant, permitting Scottish archbishops, as legates, to confirm feu charters. Occasionally, confirmation was given on the authority of the crown alone.

James's policy towards the more remote western parts of his realm continued the traditional strategy in which Scottish kings played one competing family off against another, venturing from time to time upon a personal visit.

He kept the west under relatively close scrutiny, and with the exception of a minor rising in 1539 encountered little trouble there, maintaining an amity of convenience with the powerful Campbell earls of Argyll. In 1540 James embarked upon a 'cruise' from the Orkneys down the west coast, seizing compliant chiefs as (well-looked-after) hostages for their kinsmen's good behaviour.

Royal control over the Orkneys and Shetlands was, if anything, still more tenuous. While ignoring repeated offers from the Danish crown to redeem fifteenth-century mortgages of both island groups to Scotland, the Edinburgh government remained wary of imposing Scottish laws and customs on essentially Norse communities, inhabiting remote, unattractive land. Only in 1611 did the privy council state clearly that 'foreign' laws prevailing in the islands were henceforth to be considered 'discharged'.[17]

Scottish monarchy in the early sixteenth century thus appears a strange mixture of strengths – there were few if any theoretical bounds upon the king's power – and weaknesses – lack of bureaucracy, standing army and financial resources. In this essentially very old picture, more than in any more bureaucratic or 'constitutional' monarchy, success and failure rested on the capacity, real and perceived, of an individual king. The balance was delicate: perhaps, if James V had lived, royal power would have grown as it did in other contemporary states. And then again, perhaps not. Setbacks preyed on the king's mind, prompting not always rational responses. The assumption that he would not have sooner or later misplayed his hand is one that is dangerous to make.

There are, in several aspects of James V's reign, echoes of events under his grandfather James III. Although the younger man was clearly the more able, both kings were noted for their energy and disliked for their unpredictability, and both in the end lost the committed support of their nobility. James III was slain by rebellious nobles in 1488, not least because in the course of a twenty-year personal reign he had succeeded in alienating a large section of the political nation. For every man ranged against him on the battlefield of Sauchieburn, another ten never lifted a finger to support him in the crisis. When James V invaded England in November 1542, determined to avenge a raid led by the duke of Norfolk, the abject collapse of his powerful army at Solway Moss, near Carlisle, smacks of a similar reluctance to risk all for the policies of an unloved king. Leading Scottish noblemen appear to have surrendered without seriously contemplating a fight. James died twenty days after the battle, and six days after his French queen had given birth to their only surviving child, a daughter, baptized Mary. The streak of mental instability hinted at more than once may well help explain the curious circumstances surrounding James's death. Chroniclers blamed nervous prostration or, more poetically, a broken heart. James Melville, at the end of the century, perhaps came closer to the truth, suggesting that James died 'for displeasure'.

Whatever its causes, Scotland's defeat at Solway Moss appeared to confirm what many had long suspected: that militarily, the Scots were now no match for England, or, for that matter, France. The 'psychic numbing', to borrow John Morrill's phrase, induced by Flodden and Solway Moss encouraged

Plate 6 *James V and Mary of Guise*, King James and his second French bride, who ruled as regent for their daughter after his death.
Source: National Trust for Scotland/Falkland Palace

a belief that Scotland would in future have to accept some kind of union with another power, if only to safeguard her own identity. This paradoxical conclusion was not necessarily in accord with the sentiments of successive administrations in either Paris or London, but it did at times over the next century and a half come close to emerging as a Scottish obsession.[18]

In 1542, as in 1513, the Scottish throne passed to an infant, and this time that infant was a girl, only the second queen regnant in the nation's history. After much heated dispute and amid accusations involving forged wills, James Hamilton, earl of Arran, great-grandson of James II, prevailed over his rival Cardinal David Beaton, archbishop of St Andrews, to secure the regency in January 1543. Arran's claim was strong. Not only was he heir presumptive to the throne, he was likely to remain so for perhaps twenty years, even if the young queen survived the perils of a sixteenth-century childhood.

The new regent confronted formidable problems. By his vendetta against the Douglases, and through his backing of the Catholic church, King James had ensured that England harboured during the 1530s a Scottish exile community with influence out of all proportion to its size. From the brothers Sir George Douglas and Archibald, earl of Angus, to the reformist scholars John Knox, Alexander Alesius and George Wishart, all in some degree displayed an anglophilia last seen in Scotland before Flodden, and without any real political significance there since the death of the notoriously pro-English James III. The exiles now began to return home, and Arran, sensing that rapprochement with England might strengthen his own position, initially sought out their support. Flatly opposed to such overtures, Beaton, bishop of Mirepoix since 1537, and the queen's mother Mary of Guise, a French princess, regarded France as the least predatory guarantor of Scottish independence and, indeed, of the Stewart dynasty. Mary of Guise, in particular, begrudged the overwhelming authority arrogated by the regent, for Arran had chosen to exclude her from the ward and education of her daughter, privileges granted to queens dowager in earlier minorities.

English inability to press home the advantage gained in 1542 is commonly attributed to the blunders of Henry VIII. That, though, is to take too direct, too anglocentric, a view. Henry, in fact, played his initial cards cannily, extracting promises of support from and dispatching back to Scotland prominent prisoners taken at Solway Moss, alongside many representatives of the exile community. Contemplating fresh adventures on the continent, the English king sought recognition of his claim to feudal overlordship in Scotland – a claim pressed by his ancestors for four hundred years or more – rather than a military conquest. He presumed, optimistically yet not unreasonably, on the continuing friendship of those to whom he had granted liberty, or protection.

Early in 1543, the cohesiveness and power of this anglophile alliance climbed to its zenith. Beaton, disagreeable, canny, busy and bumptious, hated by generations of protestants for his persecution of their predecessors, and no less heartily by contemporary Catholics because of the failure of such repressive policies, was under arrest. Mary of Guise retained her liberty, but lacked experience in affairs of state. The parliament which met in March approved negotiations with England for a marriage between Mary and Prince Edward, and, in a startling about face on the policies of James V, authorized the reading of scripture in the vernacular. Whether the latter reflected protestant influence or a general desire for religious reform within the Catholic church remains unclear, but in practice a vernacular Bible meant, in Scotland, William Tyndale's English translation of the New Testament, a very protestant model. This concession was accompanied by the first serious outbreaks of iconoclasm, notably in Perth and Dundee, and assaults on religious houses in which the friars appear to have suffered disproportionately. So intemperate an expression of dissatisfaction with established church practices was to become extremely familiar over the ensuing two decades.

Negotiations with England initially made progress. Under the Treaty of Greenwich, concluded in July 1543, Scotland was guaranteed her independence as a separate kingdom, the betrothal of the two royal children specifying a proxy marriage in 1552, at which time Mary would be handed over into the care of her father-in-law. Already, however, the strengths of the anglophile grouping were proving transient. Beaton had been released, Arran's personal ineptitude was growing daily more obvious, and Mary of Guise, left at Linlithgow with the custody of the infant around whom all high negotiations revolved, retired with her daughter to Stirling in July.

Uncertain times increased the popularity of the bond of maintenance and manrent, a promise of mutual protection and support between personal landowners, great and small, which extended the ancient kin group as a basis for security. Bonds were commonly concluded for a long period – for life, or in perpetuity – but since the fifteenth century they had been complemented by short-term agreements, tying men together to achieve a common political and, later, a shared religious purpose. In the years 1542–8 five large-scale bonds of this kind are on record, as many as had been seen in the past half century, while Arran, Mary of Guise and Beaton all used the personal bond to secure political allies. Two such bonds concluded in 1543 suggest that, already, the regent was losing support. The English bogey united in opposition great earls – Huntly, Argyll, Lennox (heir presumptive should Arran's line fail), Bothwell and Sutherland – the majority of high churchmen, and a strong array of over thirty lords and lairds.

Arran all his life subjected constancy to advancement and survival. Alarmed by both the strength of opposition to an English marriage and by the increasingly tactless behaviour of Henry VIII, who was now demanding that Mary be handed over for an English upbringing, he openly repented of his 'godly fit', ceding hostages into the care of his former opponents, performing penance for sins against the church and capitulating unreservedly to Beaton, who returned as chancellor. The earl of Lennox's defection to the pro-English camp helped balance the situation, but, to all intents and purposes, the agreements concluded at Greenwich were already dead letters. Henry had, mysteriously, failed to ratify them, giving the Scots parliament a ready excuse, that December, to reject what they had recently demanded and to renew close links with France.

Ever more impatient as he grew older, the English king chafed at the impotence of his allies and saw danger in the existence of so determined a pro-French grouping, given his military and territorial ambitions in France. Efforts were made, in conjunction with Angus and Lennox, to subsidize a rebellion against the Scottish crown in the Western Isles led by the Clanranald claimant to the lordship of the Isles, Donald Dubh. The rising proved entirely futile. Lennox was forced into English exile in 1544, Donald died late in 1545, and the spectre of western insurrection receded for a generation. More directly, in May 1544, an army under the earl of Hertford was unleashed on southern Scotland, the first in a series of major raids. The so-called 'rough wooing' was essentially an admission of defeat. Henry was trying to cow an enemy rather than ease teething troubles in an enduring friendship. As Protector Somerset, Hertford continued the policy after Henry's death, and while his efforts were more single-minded, the logic that lay behind them was similar.

Neither king nor protector enjoyed lasting success. The raids of 1544 and 1545 caused a great deal of distress and devastation: Edinburgh was sacked, most prosperous east coast ports suffered from the depredations of English armies, while trade, measured by the crude statistics available for export duties, declined to levels in 1540–2 unmatched in the next three decades. Nevertheless, the Scots won both the occasional skirmish – notably at Ancrum

Plate 7 Edinburgh, 1544. Perhaps the earliest surviving depiction of the entire city, drawn by an Englishman during the 'rough wooing'.

Source: British Library MS. Cotton Augustus I, ii 56

Moor in February 1545 – and strengthening support from France. That backing initially came in the form of cash subsidies and a small military expedition, though French involvement took on a new dimension after the death of Francis I in January 1547. Like Henry VIII and Somerset, Francis's ambitious and able son Henry II understood the attractions of dynastic integration with Scotland.[19]

The rejection of an English marriage for Mary, though, did not instantly promote an alternative alliance with France. Both Arran and Lennox had eligible sons and hankered after a union with the royal house. The impediment in both cases was the existence of a rival. Resulting deadlock played into the hands of those who distrusted both earls. Beaton departed the stage, murdered in 1546 by his own countrymen, Fifeshire lords nursing individual grievances. The queen mother, however, was gaining influence and respect with experience, and she was able to exploit such divisions in her own quest for a French marriage. Still, though, there was resistance from those who distrusted Gallic ambitions.

Ironically, Somerset's military success at the Battle of Pinkie in September 1547 cost England the initiative.[20] His victory, which had exposed the Scottish army's lack of artillery and modern hand-guns, and its wholly inadequate training, came late in the campaigning season: Somerset did not have the time or the resources to follow it up effectively. Arran, showing unprecedented determination, refused to submit and set about rallying his shattered forces. That winter, the regency engaged in a dispassionate comparison of two evils. If resistance to Somerset was to be prolonged, all parties in the faction-ridden Edinburgh government conceded that French assistance would be necessary, that this assistance might only be won with the offer of Mary's hand, and that the terms would have to be generous. France, for her part, and for the first time in her history, was obliged to contemplate what might, in time, amount to an annexation of Scotland. While not every nobleman in Paris shared his views, such thoughts were decidedly congenial to Henry II. The French had shown what they could do in July 1547 by the recapture of St Andrews Castle, held for a year by the murderers of Beaton, nominal supporters and pensioners of the English crown. The operation against St Andrews had been an exemplary amphibious operation, executed with great skill and knowledge of the North Sea coast: superior French seamanship would embarrass the Somerset regime more than once over the next two years.[21]

The terms were duly agreed, and, for all that Arran and the French king never really trusted one another, proved enduring. Arran received the French duchy of Châtelherault, and French troops landed at Leith in June 1548. A treaty concluded at Haddington that July effectively guaranteed a French military presence in Scotland for the foreseeable future and consigned Mary to France, betrothed to the Dauphin Francis. Given a free choice, the Scots had declined to send Mary into England during 1543. In August 1548, lacking that choice, they handed her over to the French.

Yet the logic of restoring the 'auld alliance' in so binding a form was lost on many Scots. While court and high nobility appeared united, the English retained considerable support among lesser lords, and that support in time provided a focus for discontent. The successive disasters of Solway Moss and Pinkie, and the ravages of the rough wooing, had persuaded some that it would be wiser to befriend rather than defy a powerful neighbour, while the presence of what amounted to a French army of occupation, and the prospect of eventual subordination to the French crown, just as Brittany had been absorbed in disturbingly similar circumstances a few decades earlier, aroused those who had failed to profit from the entente with France. As England swung towards reform, amity with France also antagonized many whose religious beliefs differed from those espoused by the Scottish and French crowns.

It is easy to exaggerate the speed at which protestantism spread through Scotland. Sermons preached by Wishart, who was burnt after a show trial in 1546, and by Knox castigated the papacy as irredeemably corrupt and without doubt sparked some response. By 1550, continental heresies, encouraged by the regime in England and increasingly manifesting 'sacramentarian' or 'reformed' rather than Lutheran forms, had established a foothold in Scotland. This religious dissent may be seen as both a token of political opposition, useful to alienated nobles and gentlemen, and as a statement of dissatisfaction with the church of Rome and its local agents. The foothold, though, was still tenuous. Knox's claims, made in later years, that pockets of protestant zeal had emerged by 1559 in such regions as Angus, Fife and Ayrshire may be to credit local populations with the views of their local gentry leadership, while his insistence that eight towns, including Edinburgh, had been secured for the 'true faith' by that year can be scaled down, and then uncertainly, to Dundee and Perth. Important progress to be sure, but in Perth at least the spread of protestantism was assisted by local political factions, and was far from a manifestation of the urban religious radicalism that was helping to advance nonconformity on the continent.

Initially, therefore, the domestic church enjoyed considerable scope to set its house in order. As Jenny Wormald has put it, Scotland witnessed 'a counter-reformation taking place before the reformation itself', even though this counter-reformation hardly progressed beyond demands for greater energy and commitment in pastoral work.[22] Little attempt was made to forward these laudable ambitions through improvements in stipends paid to parish clergy. Similar campaigns of moral self-improvement were launched in France and other parts of western Europe during and after the 1530s, with equally patchy results. Beaton's successor at St Andrews, the energetic Archbishop John Hamilton, convened three councils – in 1549, 1552 and 1559 – specifically to consider the question of reform, and in 1552 he published a *Catechism*, written at Hamilton's request by the English exile Richard Marshall, which catalogued in the vernacular the fundamentals of the Catholic faith. Seven years later, in a deliberate attempt to secure a wider market, short abstracts were issued to the parish clergy in the form of a 'Godly Exhortation' upon the eucharist, popularly known as the 'Twopenny Faith'. The content of this *Catechism* is indicative of the degree to which Hamilton gathered inspiration from Catholic reformers then searching vainly for compromise with Lutheranism in Germany. It made no mention of the pope, and veered towards recognition of Lutheran views on justification and communion. As with Pole's contemporary work in England, we are still some distance away from the settled, doctrinal Catholicism that emerged in the 1560s following the Council of Trent.

Politically, too, the wind during the early 1550s seemed set fair for the status quo. In 1553, the death of Edward VI led, after some delays, to the restoration of Catholicism in England, denying Scottish protestants their most obvious source of succour and of refuge. The next year, what amounted to a French coup saw Mary of Guise replace Châtelherault[23] as regent. Technically, Mary acted on the advice of the French *parlement*, which had declared that the Scottish queen, now in her twelfth year, was of an age to select her own regent. While the Scots parliament of April 1554 huffed slightly, Châtelherault's own compliance – he had been promised an indemnity for past actions and did not suffer financially – ensured that the alteration went through without serious disagreement.

A pro-French policy had been adopted in 1548 in the face of extreme English pressure, so it is ironic that the most determined advocate of such a policy finally secured power at a moment when that pressure had been relaxed to negligible proportions. Without the life-or-death drama of English intervention, increasing numbers of Scottish noblemen began to look askance at French troops in Dunbar and Inchkeith, and at the French administrators installed at every level of court and government. By 1555 the comptrollership of the household and the vice-chancellorship were in French hands. Under the treaties of alliance, the French garrisons and much of the costs incurred by their absentee queen had to be financed from Scottish sources, and Mary of Guise in her unwontedly strong position did not hesitate to raise taxes to these ends. There was talk of regular taxation and of revising assessments for taxation so as to do away with the archaic, unrealistic, exemption-riddled 'old extent' for barons and freeholders, and 'Bagimond's Roll' for the beneficed clergy. Twenty thousand pounds Scots was called for in 1555 to pay for border fortifications at Kelso, £60,000 was raised as an aid for the queen's marriage, and £48,000 was collected for the payment of 1000 soldiers. In all, and quite without precedent, five taxes were demanded over a sixteen-month period in 1556–7.

For the moment the discontented nobles were effectively powerless, having no external friends to whom they might turn. When, however, at the outbreak of war between England and France in 1557 an army dutifully made its way to the border, the Scottish peerage refused to 'hazard battle forth of their country'. A similar refusal had occurred in 1523, under similar circumstances, but for the first time in nine years the Scots had set a definite check on French ambitions. This gave Mary of Guise food for thought, and may have encouraged Henry II to push ahead with the marriage of his son to the queen of Scots. In December 1557 the Scots parliament agreed to send commissioners to France in order to finalize the match. Of the nine men who successfully concluded terms three were known protestants. In this, and in parliament's acknowledgement of Châtelherault's continuing rights as heir presumptive, there was more than a hint of determined conciliation.

6 The Reformation and the Reign of Queen Mary: Scotland 1557–67

June 1566	Birth of James VI
December 1566	Baptism of Prince James with full Catholic ritual
February 1567	Murder of Darnley at Kirk o' Field
May 1567	Marriage between Queen Mary and the earl of Bothwell
June 1567	'Battle' of Carberry Hill
July 1567	Abdication of Queen Mary; succession of James VI

Scotland's reformation, like England's, was first made possible and afterwards facilitated by political acts of state. Its details were fashioned at parliament, in the teeth of opposition from a great European power. For both nations the breach with Rome was a tactical decision, which endured because subsequent circumstances persuaded a predominant section of the nation's governing class that their interests, and the interests of their country, were best served by its survival. Events in London during the 1530s bore the imprimatur of a powerful king and were stage-managed, in part, by a politician of dexterity and vision. In Scotland, events proceeded as they did because there was no king, because regents of whatever religious persuasion lacked the authority of a king, and because an external circumstance – the accession of Elizabeth I in England – lent the support of a neighbouring protestant power to those dissatisfied with the Francophile regime.

At the same time, it is quite impossible to describe the reformation on either side of the border in solely political terms. Men may cloak their motives in any sort of pious justification, and there is no doubt that many of those who subsequently subscribed to a succinct demand for the adoption of the new faith, the 'First Band' set forward by the self-styled 'lords of the congregation' in December 1557, did so for secular motives. But it is equally true that religious scruple and commitment to reform went hand in hand with political change. For a considerable number of Scottish gentlemen in the 1550s, the establishment of a reformed church and the elimination of Roman error formed a goal in itself not merely desirable, but essential. From their ranks emerged the Band's five signatories. That this tiny group was faithful to its beliefs needs no emphasis: it is sufficient to glance at the unpromising political scene, both at home and abroad. If these signatures standing in isolation testify to a misjudgement of the moment, they speak too for the triumph of principle over expediency.

For a while, commitment to protestant reform did not necessarily imply political opposition to the Guise regency. France, itself containing an ambitious Calvinist minority, was bent on conciliation in Scotland from the mid-1550s, and Regent Mary's own attitude to the reformed faith remained distinctly equivocal. Political advantage might be derived from offering asylum to refugees fleeing the freshly imposed Catholicism in England, and she determinedly chose to ignore every outburst of the prominent reformer John Knox, rejecting suggestions that he be tried for heresy in 1556 and preferring instead to laugh at him. For this she earned Knox's particular hatred. Mary, it seemed, could well afford to laugh. Political resistance based on religious dissent was difficult to contemplate. The regency was well established, and no assistance was to be expected from England, where the political nation had long since resigned itself to following the ruler's doctrinal inclination. Even when their complacency was shattered in April 1558 with the burning of an elderly protestant, Walter Miln, at St Andrews, most reformist noblemen continued to credit Mary's assurances of toleration within a Catholic Scotland. Much, though not all, of the opprobrium for this act of savagery fell upon the archbishop, John Hamilton.

By offering a little, the regent appeared to be securing everything she sought. In April 1558 her daughter married the Dauphin Francis, and her promises to consider the question of future religious toleration secured agreement from a Scottish parliament the following November that Francis should wear the crown matrimonial: that he should rule as well as reign. This diplomatic triumph would not have been possible without the readiness of the Scots – or at least the Scots parliament and a majority of the country's nobility – to accept the prospect of a future united inextricably to the French crown. It remains difficult to say whether such readiness represents a general loss of national self-confidence, an appreciation of the possibilities offered by an absentee monarchy, or the want of any practical alternative.

And then, at one stroke, much of the regent's careful work lay undone: Mary Tudor's death had a lasting effect upon the development of Scotland's reformation. Before 17 November 1558, a weak protestant faction in Scotland could turn only to a cagily magnanimous regent. Afterwards, the prospect of another alliance gradually opened, and that prospect disturbed the regent profoundly. Five months later, the conclusion of European peace at Câteau-Cambrésis pointed out the future even more starkly. Henry II of France, freed from continental distractions, demanded from the pope a lead against heresy in Scotland, while the policies of religious repression introduced in both Madrid and Paris so alarmed the reformed nobility of Europe that the Scottish protestants found themselves presented with a cause wider than any provincial or national struggle. The lords of the congregation now enjoyed scope to realize their dreams of an alliance with England's new protestant regime.

Against these tensions, attitudes polarized in a fashion still not altogether clear. By 1559, the Swiss doctrinal reforms proposed by Zwingli and John Calvin had prevailed among the still fragmented and often idiosyncratic protestant communities in Scotland, perhaps through the attractions of novelty, or perhaps because most exiles, whose writings became so influential in Scottish and English churches over the next three decades, had lived in those parts of the continent dominated by the 'reformed' church. Important towns such as Perth and Dundee, the target of some vigorous preaching by John

Willock and Paul Methven during the previous year, declared their support for religious reform in the spring of 1559. This reform was implemented through the introduction of preachers and a tentative adoption of the Edwardian prayer book; it was also accompanied by a spate of iconoclasm. Early that May John Knox returned, barred from his preferred home, England, by a queen incensed at his recent, appallingly ill-timed diatribe against female rule, *The First Blast of the Trumpet against the monstrous regiment of women*.[1] Knox's preaching could stir a multitude – to acts of violence as well as to spiritual zeal. He made first for Dundee, then Perth, and the brew of local factionalism in that town duly obliged him with an anti-Catholic riot and the destruction of church furnishings and local religious houses inside a fortnight of his arrival. Here, as on later occasions, Knox openly deprecated the violence aroused by his preaching, but his regret never really rings true given his enthusiasm for the eradication of image-worship, broadly defined, as a means of purifying religion. In his *History of the Reformation* in Scotland he repeatedly likened Scots to the ancient Israelites, both pursuing God's design in their respective struggles against idolatry. The message was becoming rather familiar. Enjoying support from the earl of Argyll, the queen's illegitimate half-brother Lord James Stewart, and the university and city authorities, similar results were obtained in an even more important religious centre, St Andrews, that June.

Elsewhere, however, there were few signs that Knox's 'rascal multitude' was prepared to be rascally. Coming out into open rebellion in May 1559, the leading protestant lords encountered little appetite among the population at large for a crusade against popery. They resorted increasingly to patriotism, pitching their appeal to the conservative local lairds and denouncing the French and the threat of centralized government directed and exploited by France. In particular they rejected the authority of the regent, complaining of her 'unjust tyranny'. The new regime in England cautiously offered support, but there was an inconsistency in any policy that combined alliance with one predatory foreign power, albeit one exuding promises of disinterested goodwill, to frustrate the ambition of another. In attacking a Francophile government the protestants appealed to fellow countrymen, requiring them to restore the ancient order and independence of Scotland. Their means to that end, however, were themselves a threat to ancient order, to 'heritages and houses'. It is scarcely surprising that even the most committed experienced moments of doubt, even of despair. The provost of Perth, Lord Ruthven, a zealous protestant much admired by Knox, temporarily deserted the reformers' cause in May 1559, his defection causing, Knox admitted, 'great discouragement to the hearts of many'.

So volatile a situation offered scope for individual acts of lawlessness, particularly against the monasteries and friaries which suffered looting and destruction, up and down the land. In a near bloodless revolution, the antipathy experienced by religious orders is quite startling. Nor was this violence confined to large towns and the more markedly protestant corners of the land. Banffshire was considered conservative, yet in August the Carmelite friars of Banff leased their property to a local laird, desperately seeking his protection in the face of iconoclast gangs. The friars all along endured the reformers' special hatred, in part because of their high profile in religiously divided towns, in part because their mendicant principles were viewed as beggarly in the derogatory sense of the word. Such hostility may also have fed on the calculated prejudice of successive regimes, which had themselves suggested to the papacy that monasteries, being rich and contributing little to the state, should be placed in the hands of the crown: Mary of Guise had argued for royal control of their property transactions as recently as 1556.

During the autumn and winter of 1559 Scotland descended into civil war, but it soon became obvious that neither side enjoyed the resources to defeat the other without further foreign intervention. French reinforcements were accordingly introduced. Elizabeth at first held aloof, even though support from Châtelherault afforded the rebels greater respectability in the eyes of a queen reluctant to sponsor insurrection against a crowned head. In October Mary of Guise was suspended from the regency by the protestant lords, under Châtelherault's nominal authority, but for a time, political and military realities saw to it that this fundamental decision had only marginal impact. Unpaid troops deserted, and the balance of power in all-important Edinburgh began at the onset of winter to teeter back towards the queen dowager. Stirling was occupied by French troops in December, emerging from their impregnable bases at Leith and on the island of Inchkeith. Symbolic of the uncertain times, Edinburgh Castle remained in the ambivalent hands of Lord Erskine, who refused outright support to either side.

What decided the issue was the eventual English decision to send troops north, and the French inability to break a blockade of Leith and the Forth mounted by Elizabeth's fleet from January 1560. The Treaty of Berwick, concluded that February, was multi-faceted. In a move which owes much to the English statesman William Cecil's developing vision of the British Isles as a political unit, and to their wish to curb the cost of Irish government, the English demanded in return assistance from the Campbell earl of Argyll in their attempts to bring Ulster, currently in revolt under Shane O'Neill, to submission through his influence over the Scots settlement in Antrim.[2] This, though, was a side issue. Under the principal terms of the treaty, England agreed to intervene in Scotland's civil war so as to preserve for the Scots 'their old freedom and liberties'. Religion was nowhere mentioned, and the Scots specifically undertook to obey their proper sovereigns on the understanding that those sovereigns would respect the 'liberties' of subjects. English troops laid siege to Leith in the spring, blockade and foul weather frustrated early French efforts to supply the garrison, while an explosion of political unrest in France during the summer – a foretaste of the disastrous wars of religion which blight French history for the next three decades – made further attempts unlikely. Between them, the lords of the congregation and the English army exercised a stranglehold which throttled any meaningful resistance. Stripped of their foreign military support, the Catholics sustained another grievous blow when Mary of Guise died in June 1560. Knox gloated, but other protestant leaders showed more grace, some keeping vigil at her deathbed. By the Treaty of Edinburgh, concluded in July, all English and – crucially – all French troops left Scotland. On 1 August, the so-called Reformation Parliament met in Edinburgh.

As the tide of war turned in their favour, so the rebel lords became ever more conscious of the need to appear, not as disobedient subjects, but as loyal supporters of a monarchy, pushed into unwelcome rebellion by a challenge to their religious beliefs and a conviction that their realm was being sold to the French. Militarily, the Scottish reformation was a relatively gentle affair – towns were deserted and occupied, soldiers marched and counter-marched, opening and abandoning sieges without showing any inclination to come to blows. In such an atmosphere, calls upon patriotism and other propaganda tactics were all the more telling. During May 1560, a Second Band – this time signed by nearly fifty peers and lairds – spelt out their limited aims, and ultimate obedience to the crown. As they had hoped, publication of this Band won the lords support from towns and peers fearful of further social unrest, but political calculation apart, the lords' protestations were no doubt genuine enough. Emphasis laid in the Band upon the necessity of obedience to lawful sovereigns echoes the desires of its signatories as much as those of the men to whom it was addressed.

The Reformation Parliament was attended by some hundred or so gentlemen, men below the traditional rank of the lord of parliament. High representation of lairds in a Scottish parliament was not, indeed, new – those who were tenants in chief of the crown enjoyed a strong, historical case for personal representation, and the assemblies which met in 1479, 1487 and 1488 had seen them attend in considerable numbers. What *was* unusual in 1560 was the number of lesser lairds who turned up, wrongly invoking an act of 1428 that had never been operative, but which had in fact denied them the very right of attendance they now claimed. Nevertheless, they came, and no one turned them away. Their protestant voices, and their confident participation in politics and religion, harnessed by the nobles and greater lairds who encouraged their presence, provided administrative momentum to Scottish religious reform for decades ahead. Such confidence testifies to a cautious passivity among the greater nobility, and to the fact that many early evangelicals had already fled abroad, never to return. The result of this migration was a reformed church singularly lacking in preachers and theologians during the 1560s and 1570s. English prayer books supplied the essential liturgical foundations of Scotland's reformation: first the successive Books of Common Prayer, and from its first Scottish printing in 1562 the more Calvinist Book of Common Order, used by exiles living in Switzerland during Mary Tudor's reign.

Constitutionally, this momentous session remains full of mysteries, for there is virtually no record of its debates or procedure. The 1560 parliament produced just three acts, for the most part negative in content. The mass was abolished in one measure, papal jurisdiction in another. The third act cut away that legal security enjoyed by the old church through its annulment of all acts from the past century and a half which failed to agree with 'God's holy word'. As its sole positive action, the assembly adopted a Confession of Faith, a spirited if hastily compiled and undogmatic statement of reformed beliefs, which was, thanks to the disarray and intimidation of Scottish Catholics, adopted with minimal dissent. Today we might discern a strong Calvinist input in the Confession, but English, Zwinglian, French and Lutheran influences were also in play, and the Calvinism there expressed is idiosyncratic. In 1560 Calvin was, after all, still evolving his beliefs, seeking a consensus among the protestant churches. Though never explicitly defined, justification by faith alone is assumed throughout the Confession. Predestination, in any case a notion derived from the teaching of St Paul, common to all protestant churches and with a strong Catholic tradition, is also accepted, if somewhat incidentally. There is a probable hint, but nothing more, at 'double predestination', later a benchmark of Calvinism in which the community of the elect was mirrored by a muster of the reprobate, predestined to suffer the torments of hell. A clear-cut statement of the duty of obedience to the secular power, or crown, in one article, is tacitly qualified by suggestions elsewhere that resistance to tyranny is a duty enjoined upon the faithful.[3]

The Confession, like many similar expressions of belief across the continent, emerged from a committee. Six strong, this comprised the indispensable Knox, a canon lawyer John Row, and four other experienced ministers. The committee had in fact already produced another work of lasting significance, albeit one which never enjoyed the same ready acceptance. Developing the importance placed upon it by Calvin, much emphasis in the Confession was given to religious discipline: according to two key articles discipline was, with the preaching of the Word of God and the administration of the sacraments, one of the three marks of a 'true' church. However, the so-called *First Book of Discipline*, a code of correct living commissioned by the great council in the spring of 1560, was initially ignored, then accepted with reservations by a small number of the peers and introduced grudgingly in January 1561. This unpopularity resulted from the Book's sweeping demands for lay restoration of former religious property, the better to fund ministries and educational reforms.

In contrast to England, no concerted attempt was made to abolish religious houses. Over the following decades monasteries and friaries withered slowly, closing through lack of patronage, absence of further bequests, and the frustration of career prospects in unsupported institutions. The ecclesiastical hierarchy, along with crown appointments to bishoprics, were retained, despite continuing attempts to dispense with an office considered by Calvinists to be symptomatic of latent popery. With the crown valuing such patronage, and reformers themselves divided on the issue, a compromise in 1572 left the office of bishop intact, if shorn of real power.

For all the momentous opportunism of the Reformation Parliament, the authority enjoyed by the lords of the congregation remained precarious, grounded upon the impotence of a hostile, absentee queen, and upon the inconstant support of her heir presumptive, Châtelherault. Legislation passed in 1560 was, to no one's surprise, refused ratification by Francis and Mary in France. While nominally protestant, Châtelherault remained on good terms with his half-brother, the Catholic archbishop John Hamilton, and the Hamilton family as a whole, notably cohesive and mutually supportive over the past two centuries, stood fast against religious change.[4] In the circumstances, no immediate attempt could be made to enforce conformity on parish incumbents. While some among the pre-reformation clergy may have experienced genuine conversion, others temporized, or rejected the new settlement outright. For at least a decade before the 1573 Act of Conformity – and in practice for some years after, since clergy might subscribe to the Confession of Faith and oath of supremacy for form's sake, while preserving older ways with the connivance of a compliant congregation – Scotland witnessed across her 1080 parishes the curious spectacle of a national church or 'kirk' spiritually at odds with the majority of local priests. Some conformist ministers would work with the new Calvinist religious supervisor, the 'superintendent', or with the reformist bishop; many others would not. Others still would labour fruitlessly in areas where their parishioners rejected new ways. Aberdeenshire, for example, was well supplied with reformist clergy, yet stayed staunchly Catholic down to the wars of the 1640s. The Gaelic west remained, almost entirely, conservative and unresponsive.

As in England, calls for a graduate clergy met with a slow response. No significant effort was made in the sixteenth century to deny patrons their rights of presentation, and although from 1567 they were obliged by law to seek approval from the superintendent for an appointee, they did not always do so. Despite the challenges of superintendents, bishops retained rights of collation. Thus the prevalence of readers – men authorized to read prayers but not to preach or administer the sacraments – in the post-reformation lowland church of the 1570s and 1580s, and much, much later in the west. Most readers were, indeed, former Catholic clergy deemed insufficiently worthy of a benefice, yet willing to conform, and ready to instruct and examine their flocks, Calvin's *Catechism* in hand.

To lay the political foundations of a reformation was one thing; to achieve any alteration in the ecclesiastical structure of a decentralized nation quite another. Support from the nobility was essential. Knox made free to address all levels of Scottish society, by turns reprimanding, harrying and flattering, but his foremost ambition was to spark among peers some flame of reformist zeal. He urged them to found and endow ministries, and through personal example to provide for their servants and tenants the moral guidelines of sobriety and constancy.

There were some who responded to his call. Many took no notice whatsoever. Backsliders, even more or less open Catholics, were nevertheless treated with great tolerance, as the shifts of the sixth earl of Huntly illustrate later in the century. Up to a point the kirk here acted wisely, for the local nobility, presiding over their baronies or regalities, enjoyed a great say in the advancement of religious change in Scotland. On the other hand, with much patronage in the hands of the crown, and with local authority rather more of a two-way process than the zealots might allow, there is a sense of inevitability in the spectacle of a nobility falling short of expectations. When the eminent theologian Andrew Melville denounced in the 1580s the current generation of peers, comparing them unfavourably with their stout-hearted forebears of the 1560s, he held up as shining examples men whom Knox would hardly have recognized. The church of Melville's day, more self-assured, perhaps more presbyterian, certainly more popular in Scotland's towns and villages, had changed from that established after the 1560 parliament. Through such comparisons, Melville nevertheless helped fashion an enduring vision of a noble-inspired religious revolution, still encountered today.

Aspiring to good lordship the great noble, whether Catholic or protestant, frequently reflected in his own stance the views of his clientage. The survival of Catholicism in the north-east was as much a creation of the Hays, Menzies and cadet Gordons as of the paramount Gordon earls of Huntly: the fifth earl, though conservative, was not himself a Catholic. In the long term, Wormald argues, the nobility were bound to lose authority in the face of reform, for although they were given a new, 'inspiring' image of themselves by the kirk as the natural storm-troops of religious change, they were at the same time left in no doubt that this role was exercised at the discretion of the church they served. Many peers chose to stand aloof from church politics and church government, leaving lairds to shoulder these burdens. That, however, is a line of argument which must be followed elsewhere; from our vantage point in the 1560s we are here discussing centuries yet unborn.[5]

Lacking positive direction or encouragement from the crown, the progress of the reformation in Scotland was an uneven affair, owing much to individual or civic enterprise. The reformation in the northern islands was largely accomplished under the direction of one man, Adam Bothwell, bishop of Orkney. Towns were more readily dominated by influential protestant minorities, and perhaps enjoyed readier access to the all-important printed Bibles, catechisms and psalters which nourished a bibliocentric faith. St Andrews, ironically a pilgrimage centre and the seat of the primate of Scotland, rushed to adopt reformed religion, and, with its bare church, rigorous discipline, preaching ministry, weekly exercises for Biblical discussion, pre-communion examination and catechizing, became something of a model for Scottish reform by the mid-1560s.[6]

But exemplary models alone failed to convert a majority of the Scottish people. The kingdom was not Greater Geneva, and individual cities found that the virtuous leads they offered were substantially ignored, even in their immediate hinterlands. Religious commitment within towns was in any case far from uniform. The tussle for spiritual control of Edinburgh, and for the hearts and minds of its citizens, was complicated and hard-fought. Aberdeen clung as determinedly to, and derived a sense of local unity from, the Catholic church, though the want of new, young Catholic priests later in the century gradually sapped resistance. Across the countryside the story is still more diverse. Coastal parishes of Fife displayed an adherence to reform not to be found further inland. Dunkeld diocese, under its Catholic bishop Robert Crichton, appeared conservative, yet drawing upon recently ordained recruits from nearby St Andrews, converted parish clergy and Augustinian canons, a protestant ministry was installed in most of the more accessible parishes by the time Crichton was removed from his see in 1571. In many more remote parts neither Catholic nor protestant doctrine made a great deal of impact.[7] It is tempting to fall back on statistics, which assure us that 90 per cent of parishes outside the highlands were filled by reformed clergy in 1574: but two-thirds of these clerics were readers rather than ministers, and the presence of an incumbent was no guarantee that parishioners would either attend church or adopt the new ways.

Many of the tensions between clergy and lay landowners centred, unsurprisingly, on money. The kirk deplored all the depredations thirty years of royal hostility and weak minorities had wrought upon church property, while those who had prospered from these processes, whatever their religious persuasion, feared a resurgent church. Nor was it solely the successful acquisitors who entertained such fears. Rights to a good deal of property in Scotland rested upon foundations inherited from the old church: although leading landowners held property as commendators, for example, this was an ecclesiastical title and could not in theory be bequeathed.

Disputes, however, were those of tactics rather than strategy. All sides recognized the obligation to provide a new church with 'appropriate' funding, only the level and source of that funding was at issue. When higher ideals ran up against entrenched vested interest the result was an uneasy yet enduring compromise. Under the terms of an agreement reached in February 1562, benefice holders retained two-thirds of their revenues, passing the remaining third to the crown, ostensibly for the upkeep of the kirk but also covering crown 'expenses'. Two-thirds of church income lost to the devil, Knox fulminated, and the remaining third 'must be divided betwix God and the devil'. A general survey of benefices was initiated, but from the start there were administrative difficulties. Thirds were 'remitted' for purposes which ranged from the funding of hospitals to the enrichment of relatives and political associates, while in years to come tensions developed over the share accorded to the kirk. The system seethed with jealousy, chicanery and suspicion. Nevertheless, legislation in 1567 gave priority to the payment of stipends, and the absolute destitution of many pre-reformation benefices had, thirty years after the reformation, become a thing of the past.

The emergent reformed, 'presbyterian' church of the 1560s was no monolith. It remained, for decades after, a hybrid association, which displayed a dominant strain of Calvinist theology, but which also embraced men whose views were more conservative, more Lutheran, more ecumenical. Of those who together produced the *First Book of Discipline*, no stretching of terminology can allow us to call John Winram, John Douglas or Erskine of Dun Calvinist. Unlike its successor of 1578, the *First Book* was primarily concerned with the Christian life of an individual, set within the immediate community of the godly. In 1560–1, basic unity remained to be forged among Scotland's disparate congregations. A broader, national church polity awaited more certain, settled times.[8]

In 1560, the Scottish parliament had rejected papal authority in the name of a queen who wanted no part in such presumption. A year later, that queen stood once again on Scottish soil. Again, change had arisen from the death of a French king. Francis II had succumbed to pneumonia in December 1560, and it had soon become clear that his eighteen-year-old widow did not figure in the plans laid by France's new regent, Catherine de Medici. Mary was, after all, a daughter of the house of Guise, a member of the most powerful noble family in France; as such, she was a potential threat to royal security during a minority. Her destiny, so the French had insisted, and many Scots had concurred, lay in her native country. That prospect had hardly appealed to Mary, but with no potential husband stepping forward to detain her in France, her viable options had been few.

A woman of energy and physical presence – she is said to have been, like her mother, nearly six feet tall, possessed of a good figure, elegant hands and, in youth, gold-red hair – Mary inherited both the charm and the unpredictable cunning of her father. Her marital history, and her dismal fate, have attracted novelists, composers, artists of the Romantic school and Hollywood moguls alike. No figure in Scottish history raises greater controversy, for while some see her as a victim of tragedy in its true, inevitable sense, others hold both her actions and her intentions in deep contempt.[9]

The personal reign is, however, one of the least perfectly documented periods of Mary's life, and the evidence that does survive permits more than one interpretation of several key events. For the queen's inherent caution, surprising to those raised on stories of the rash conspirator of later years, there is a good deal of evidence. Like her predecessors she eschewed taxation, inevitably a popular decision. Her income from French lands, in a currency that only strengthened against the debased Scottish pound as years passed by, went some way towards paying the regular cost of the royal household, while the embryonic system of thirds – bringing in over £32,000 in 1565 – helped still further.[10] For all the luxury and frivolity of the court so criticized by Knox, there was none of that ostentation in building that had characterized the two previous reigns. Spectacle and entertainment were in any case the stuff of a personal monarchy. Particularly after the queen's marriage, the glamour of a royal court was consciously cultivated: five new earldoms were just the pinnacle of a long 'honours list', while Sir Thomas Craig's *Epithalamium* and the charming verses preserved in manuscript by the young George Bannatyne symbolize a fashion for celebration and a new impetus in courtly literature closely modelled, as one might expect, on France.[11] Mary was herself an accomplished musician, she collected books, and the presence of skilled artists, among them the poet Alexander Scott and the Hudson family of violists and singers, added further lustre to life at court. Knox found it all too much: 'Jezebel' ruled over a court bewitched.

Not only bewitched but mobile, for Mary's energy was both remarkable and in tune with the expressed demands of her subjects. She covered over a thousand miles in the year from August 1562, venturing as far north as Inverness, and bringing majesty in person to her subjects. Over half a century earlier, parliament had recommended that James IV 'ride in proper person, once in the year, through all parts of the realm'; similar advice had been given to James III back in 1473. While both kings had paid lip-service to such counsel, Mary took it to heart.

Another familiar picture of Mary, the Catholic martyr, is strangely blurred during the years of personal rule. Like almost every contemporary monarch, the nature of her faith – in public, and so far as we can tell in private too

– was opportunistic, responsive to the dictates of political circumstances. Mary was willing to accept the gift of a vernacular Bible and prayer book, even the burning of a priestly effigy, on the occasion of her ceremonial entry into Edinburgh: that deeply symbolic occasion at which, amid much pomp and festivity, new monarchs and the populace of their capital city reaffirmed mutual obligations, assurances and responsibilities.[12] She was prepared to attend a protestant service, to fund the reformed church, to drive successive popes into wary distrust of her ambitions and her morals, and to make any fair promises she deemed expedient.

From the start Mary appeared to aim at a consensus, ostensibly refusing to consider changes to the religion she had found established on her return. For counsel she relied on protestants – the capable secretary William Maitland of Lethington, and Lord James Stewart – rejecting overtures by the earl of Huntly and John Leslie, later bishop of Ross, to front a counter-reformation from the security of the Huntly estates about Aberdeen. Indeed, the queen played a remarkably small part in the administration of her kingdom, leaving these matters to her strongly protestant council, and she was content to see that council control legislation set before the one 'normal' parliament of her reign, which met in 1563. However, to the fury of Knox and like-minded clerics, the council was also obliged by its mistress to tolerate Catholic masses within the royal chapel. Mary's domestic arrangements also gave the reformers cause for concern. She surrounded herself with a congenial household in which French and Catholic elements were prominent, and this became a source of particular tension. One may defend such distinctions between the public and private face of royalty as politic tolerance, or damn them as an irresponsible dereliction of the sixteenth-century ruler's duty to convey a particular doctrine to subjects. As with so much else in her story, the queen's actions offer an attractive ambiguity to the contentious.

Ambiguity was, perhaps, the only viable course open to her, but inescapable choices are not always unwelcome. Much criticism of Mary's stance rests upon assumptions that she was at all times committed to the eventual recovery of her realm for the Catholic church. Now, popes may have hoped, and Knox may have feared that this was the case, but assumptions of consistency are, given the available evidence, far from convincing. Her French upbringing had accustomed Mary to think of herself and her late husband as rightful rulers of the entire British Isles. In the changed circumstances of 1561, the survival of that dream demanded fortune – any children born to Elizabeth would destroy those prospects – and the promotion of opportunism and caution over conviction.

This caution manifested itself first of all in a studied amity with England. During the first four years of her reign there was little that Mary was not prepared to consider in the cause of smoothing her path to the English crown. A mission to Scotland undertaken in 1562 by the Jesuit Nicholas Floris – Nicholas de Gouda – was received warily by the queen, while not wholly unfounded rumour had her contemplating a conversion to Elizabethan protestantism, the better to establish her claim. In 1565 fresh rumours went one better, announcing her actual conversion.

The balancing of religious interests in fact angered zealots on both sides: Knox, though favouring cooperation with England, distrusted unprincipled compromise, while several lords opposed to reconciliation with the English – or on belligerent terms with supporters of that policy – proved equally intransigent. The obdurate extremes were, nevertheless, soon isolated. Among the protestant lords Châtelherault's son, James Hamilton, earl of Arran, was stricken with a mental sickness which, in due course, cost him both liberty and title.[13] Knox, for all his pithy Genevan fulminations against the idolatry and superstitious abominations implicit in Mary's open personal profession of Catholicism, remained a marginal figure so long as the queen maintained the respect of a majority among her nobles.

Until the very end of her reign, this Mary did. Her progresses witness genuine efforts to unite the political nation, efforts that proved unquestionably popular. Scotland gained international respect with the return of a court presided over by an adult ruler, and although a female upon the throne was not to everyone's taste, the extraordinary authority possessed by a Scottish monarch who was also dowager queen of France and heir presumptive to England was seldom lost on those about her.

Many of her most prominent lay opponents were, indeed, fellow Catholics. Their opposition emerged from a brew of feuding and personal disaffection, and lacked sufficient support to threaten the regime. When Huntly, infuriated by Mary's promise of the earldom of Moray to Lord James Stewart, rebelled in 1562, no peer supported him and his forces were routed by a royal army at Corrichie in October. Huntly himself perished of an apoplexy immediately after the battle. Mary seized the opportunity to establish Lord James as earl of Moray, a title formerly enjoyed by the Gordon earls of Huntly; she was, it seems, determined to demonstrate that shared religion could serve as no defence for a rebel, and Huntly's repeated attempts to invoke their mutual Catholicism may only have sealed his fate. This was arbitrary dealing, and arbitrariness in a Stewart monarch had in the past proved risky, but it worked in 1562.[14] Even when Moray, as we should now call him, turned against Mary and secured the support of Châtelherault and the fifth earl of Argyll in his opposition to the Darnley marriage, his attempt at rebellion, the appropriately named Chaseabout Raid, failed dismally in 1565. Having dodged the queen around a large part of Scotland many of the rebel lords fled across the English border, and although the militarily powerful Argyll remained defiant in the west, he was, for the time being, isolated and ignored.[15] A potentially more dangerous combination, comprising Darnley, Moray, Argyll, Morton and Ruthven, disintegrated at the first taste of determined royal opposition in 1566. Although rebellion was never easy to engineer, Mary's personal energy in moments of crisis should be allowed much of the credit for the crown's successes.

While the argument has been advanced that in her humiliations of Huntly and the Hamiltons, Mary, like James III before her, sowed the seeds of her own downfall – the nobility are supposed to have regarded these proceedings with dismay – the queen's position had, after five years of personal rule, never been stronger. Marriage in 1565 to her teenage cousin Henry Stewart,

Lord Darnley, made apparent political sense, quite apart from the physical attraction which Mary did not attempt to conceal. Darnley was the eldest son of Matthew, earl of Lennox, long an exile in England, and of his wife Margaret Douglas, daughter by a second marriage of James IV's widow and Henry VIII's sister Margaret Tudor. Though marking an end, for the time being, to the close friendship with England central to the policies of Moray and Maitland, the match united the two strongest claims to succeed Elizabeth on the English throne. It also provided Mary with an ally among her nearest kin and advanced, potentially to the crown matrimonial, a youth recently arrived from London and thus personally untainted by recent political faction.

It also reflected reality. Mary had been casting about unavailingly for a suitable husband in the courts of Europe. Guided by his mother, Charles IX of France would not have her, while Philip II of Spain, apparently disturbed by Mary's ambivalence in religion, was spared a difficult decision when his heir Don Carlos succumbed to insanity. Both the great European nations, interested more in the queen of Scots' dynastic ambitions than in the politics of Scotland, preferred the prospect of a married queen resident in her own country and free of any commitment to the other power.

Precisely why Elizabeth permitted Darnley's return to Scotland remains obscure. He was her own cousin, and a potential king of England in his own right. Just the sort of man who might need watching. If, knowing something of Darnley's character, she foresaw the course of events, her perception was not sufficiently assured to prevent second thoughts after he had left for the north. Nor did it save Darnley's mother from imprisonment when Elizabeth heard of the marriage. The Darnley match put a stop to infinitely more dangerous talk of foreign alliances with France or Spain, and also to the prospect of marriage between Mary and Robert Dudley, earl of Leicester, ostensibly the preferred course in London but hardly a desirable union from Elizabeth's own point of view. Elizabeth wanted Leicester for herself, if not as consort, then as counsellor and confidant. It was also true, of course, that support for Lennox's interests in Scotland diverted a family of the blood royal from intrigues closer to home. One persuasive theory suggests that, in the spirit of mutual intransigence which prevailed after a conference at Berwick in November 1564, Mary refused to accept Leicester for her husband without parliamentary guarantees of the succession should Elizabeth die child-less, and Elizabeth insisted that general personal assurances and a commit-ment to frustrate rivals were as far as she would go. Deadlock having been reached, Elizabeth may for once have miscalculated. Compromise restoration of the Lennox family offered Mary quite fortuitous scope to adopt a more independent policy. With the Anglo-Scottish amity based on an understand-ing between individual ministers, pressures on such friendship grew when new power brokers in the form of Lennox and his son took centre stage in Edinburgh.[16] But much of this is still supposition, and lacking essential cor-respondence between the parties involved we cannot really know for sure. Having calmed down, Elizabeth was inclined to view the whole affair as an impudent gesture, an annoyance that had its own peculiar compensations.

Marriage made little immediate difference to the queen's opaque religious policy: Mary married Darnley by Catholic rites in July 1565, but Darnley's[17] own Janus-like professions – he refused to attend the subsequent mass and preferred protestant services at St Giles – together with conciliatory gestures by the queen, allayed the fears of many reformers. Husband and wife together repeated Mary's assurances given in 1561 that the reformed church as then established in Scotland would be retained. These assurances may not have been entirely sincere, for there are reasons to believe that Mary was edging towards the restoration of Catholicism in 1565. The cooling of Anglo-Scottish relations recommended closer ties with the Catholic continental powers. If a return to Rome was indeed her aim, Mary pursued it in the only viable manner, through pleas for support from her nobles, many of whom retained strong affections for Catholicism. Given the fluidity of the 1560s, and the religious ambivalence of many notional protestants at every social level, re-conversion was not, at that moment, an impossible design.[18]

In a strategy dependent on mutual trust, however, Mary's apparent lack of principle in religious matters now worked against her. The queen's earnest appeals to Spain for assistance during the Chaseabout Raid had sowed serious doubts in the minds of loyalist reformers. These doubts were nourished by her increasing reliance on the advice of a small, exclusive group of peers – Huntly, Lennox, John Stewart, earl of Atholl, and the thirty-year-old James Hepburn, earl of Bothwell – supplemented by counsel from a circle of foreign courtiers, the Italian David Rizzio, talented musician and a secretary on the queen's French establishment, prominent among them. They were further sharpened by Mary's encouragement of Catholic devotional literature and her repeated promises made to the pope that she intended to return her realm to Catholicism. Coming at a time when a meeting between Catherine de Medici and the Spanish general, the duke of Alba, at Bayonne sparked wild rumours of a Catholic conspiracy against the protestant states of Europe, such undertakings, however tactical and financially motivated they might be, blew suspicions to new heights.

Despite all the apparent advantages, marriage to Darnley proved a catastrophic mistake. Immediate difficulties arose, not from the faiths professed by either party but from the elevation of one domestic suitor over others. While Darnley himself had no experience of Scottish politics his ambitious father, back in Scotland and dispensing royal patronage with his daughter-in-law's approval, was rapidly recovering twenty years of lost ground. Moray and the Hamiltons looked on with open dismay. Even then, as we have seen, the ensuing rebellion ended with Moray replacing Lennox in English exile, but by this time the poisonous taint of an unhappy marriage was itself corrupting the queen's authority. Gordon Donaldson's succinct dismissal of Darnley as 'morally and intellectually worthless' summarizes the verdict of contemporaries and historians from that day to this.[19] After a few months as his wife Mary herself had come to the same conclusion; she made no secret of her revulsion from the drunken, insolent, perhaps syphilitic young man. Sharing the coldness of royal neglect, Darnley and a group of lords, among them men who had originally revolted against the royal marriage and who now stood under summons to trial for rebellion, began to plot revenge.

The subsequent murder of Rizzio, under the eyes of a six-months-pregnant queen, is the stuff of melodrama. Mary, however, far from succumbing to hysteria as the murderers seem to have hoped, showed characteristic resilience, winning the feeble Darnley back to her side. Setting up a headquarters at Dunbar, the queen held out pardons to those Chaseabout Raiders not involved in the Rizzio killing, at the same time rallying all available loyalist support. Subsequently, the opposition confused and divided, she returned to Edinburgh in triumph. Many fled, but Moray and Argyll secured pardons and, amid gestures of mutual reconciliation, served on the royal council for the rest of the year. Mary's child was born on 19 June. Her son, when baptized amid innovative festivity at Stirling in December 1566, was given the names Charles James – those of the French king and of the queen's own father.[20] The ghost of a French alliance still walked, even though France was unable to reanimate the corpse.

Conscious of her recent peril, Mary adopted afresh the course of compromise and reconciliation. Further pardons were offered, no new attempt was made to persuade the nobility to participate in the mass, and minor benefices – worth under £200 per annum – were awarded to the reformed church. The importance of the monarchy was emphasized by the threat of Mary's death when she fell dangerously sick that October. Her so-called deathbed speech – an impassioned call for noble-led harmony – was widely circulated.

In the winter of 1566, therefore, Mary's position appeared very strong. The baptism of the future James VI provided an occasion on which to display the unity of her council and the subjugation of her few intransigent foes. Negotiations between kirk and crown were now following the queen's agenda; indeed, she was standing patron to both churches, restoring the imprisoned John Hamilton as archbishop of St Andrews and primate of Scotland, perhaps with an eye to future divorce proceedings. Approaches were also made to renew the friendship with England, albeit without its former openly protestant overtones.

Such harmony only makes the disasters of 1567 more astonishing. Religion alone cannot explain what happened: the zealots, whether protestant or Catholic, lacked resources sufficient to bring down a queen who seemed to offer the only hope of unity within a disparate political nation. To understand subsequent events one must turn again to the continuing, festering sore of a broken marriage, a marriage, moreover, which had now produced a son, a potential rival for the throne. Darnley skulked in the west, while Mary showed an increasingly reckless predilection for Bothwell. Though we may discount some of the wilder stories put about later by presbyterian and Jacobean propaganda, it is clear that the queen had, by the end of 1566, grown strongly attached to the earl. Humiliated and angry, Darnley ostensibly pondered the merits of foreign travel, all the while looking for a means of revenge. As Mary and her council recognized, he posed a very real threat. Some thought was given to divorce, and to judicial execution, but the queen and a majority of her counsellors were uneasy with any course that threw doubt upon James's legitimacy. Thence, by tortured and obscure ways, grew a conviction that the superfluous husband must die.

There is no certain means of determining Mary's involvement in, or knowledge of, these plans. Her release of captive Rizzio murderers in December 1566 – men with scores to settle against the turncoat Darnley – must be weighed against her efforts at a pragmatic reconciliation with her husband, early the following year. If it is extremely difficult to believe that the queen remained altogether ignorant of this bloody enterprise, Darnley's murder one night in February 1567 reduced rather than increased her scope for action. An explosion of concealed gunpowder destroyed the house on the outskirts of Edinburgh, Kirk o' Field, where Darnley was convalescing from smallpox. He staggered from the wreckage, only to be strangled in the gardens. While Mary is from time to time put forward as the principal intended victim of this Scottish gunpowder plot, it remains more likely that Darnley was targeted, either by a band drawn from the former Rizzio conspirators under Morton's leadership, by counsellors determined to dispatch an unpopular troublemaker, or by a group of assassins led by Bothwell, himself intent on marrying the queen. Or, perhaps, by all three. Suggestions that a large proportion of the Scots peerage lurked that evening in the gardens of Kirk o' Field seem not far wide of the mark. Indeed, they reinforce an impression that the crisis of 1567, like the strife of the 1480s which led to the death of James III, was a crisis of confidence in the monarchy among those key players in the game of high politics, the Scottish nobility.

Mystery still hangs over events at Kirk o' Field, but when seeking to apportion guilt many contemporaries looked no further than Bothwell. Although the earl was acquitted of regicide in a trial that April, proceedings there were blatantly rigged. The queen's unswerving determination to marry him thus appears, in its lack of elementary statecraft, quite baffling. There are several possible explanations. Mary may have been pregnant with Bothwell's child, although the primitive gynaecological evidence defies certain interpretation. She may have decided that it was necessary to secure Bothwell, mature, an experienced soldier, and obligingly flexible in his protestant beliefs, to her cause. Alternatively, she may simply have miscalculated. In past perils, the queen had seized the initiative with swift, decisive actions, and, outcome apart, the crisis of 1567 was to be no different. Mary made every effort to secure support for her marriage to the earl that May, this time conducted by reformed rites. For too many, however, the choice of Bothwell proved impossible to swallow. When confronting the inanities of a fatuous young husband she had enjoyed broad support, but in her resolve to marry an unscrupulous nobleman, lacking any particular blood claim to such an elevation and himself freshly divorced, she forfeited a great deal of that loyalty. The queen's own pretence that Bothwell had carried her off by force and raped her – making marriage inevitable – unwittingly offered a focus and a cover to those who opposed the match. Although many lords subscribed to a bond pledging to dissolve the marriage, and to protect both queen and prince, several signatories were aware from the start that deposition might prove the only viable outcome.

The speed at which resistance developed took Mary and her new husband by surprise. Among leading peers, only the conservatives Huntly and Crawford remained loyal – the newly restored Huntly very reluctantly – and when the armies raised by each side met at Carberry Hill in June 1567, the demoralization in the royalist ranks provoked mass desertion, leaving the field to the so-called 'confederate lords' without the necessity of battle. Bothwell escaped, but Mary was taken prisoner and subjected to a humiliating procession through the streets of Edinburgh. After miscarrying twins, she was forced to abdicate in favour of her son on 24 July. Young James – the 'French' first name was dropped – was crowned at Stirling five days later. Adam Bothwell, the reformist bishop of Orkney who had officiated at the marriage of Mary and Bothwell, performed the ceremony, and Knox obliged with a sermon taken from the Book of Kings. Simultaneously, Mary's chapel at Holyrood was despoiled, an act symbolizing, if only in hindsight, the end of realistic hopes for a restoration of Catholicism in Scotland.

Five days after James's coronation a General Assembly of the kirk met in Edinburgh, wholeheartedly endorsing the overthrow of an 'unfit' queen, and resolved upon further reforms. In what has been described as a second, more Calvinist reformation, the 1567 assembly sought to provide new resources for the parishes and to weed out Catholic elements in the universities. A majority of reformers still preferred the receding hope of personal conversion to the upheavals of deposition, and kirk involvement in the noble conflicts which brought Mary down had been limited. Nevertheless, in the *De Jure Regni apud Scotos* of George Buchanan, principal of St Leonard's College from 1566 and moderator of the General Assembly in 1567, it eventually provided telling theoretical justification for the deed. Written during the crisis of 1567–8, the *De Jure* was not published until 1579. An accomplished scholar and subsequent overseer of James VI's education, Buchanan argued from ancient, seldom-historical precedent that the Scots had ever dealt summarily with 'ungodly' rulers. The same opinions were aired repeatedly in Buchanan's life-work, the history of Scotland, *Rerum Scoticarum Historia*, published in 1582. What he lacked in accuracy the author supplied in a pithy and bitterly intense critique which won admirers, as surely as it antagonized his royal pupil. Buchanan's role in the emergent Scottish church was profound. Already, by the end of the 1560s, he had begun to transform St Leonard's College into a pre-eminent college of the reformed kirk, turning out a succession of men who would lead the Scottish church in the next generation.

7 Protector Somerset: England 1547–9

Building upon the views of Edward VI's first biographer John Hayward and those of A. F. Pollard, writing early this century, historians long regarded the protectorate of Edward Seymour, earl of Hertford and, from February 1547, duke of Somerset, as a brief age of enlightenment amid the sorry gloom of mid-Tudor politics. Blessed with the goodwill of moderate religious reformers, marching at the head of an army of stout commonwealth men, the 'Good Duke' was thought to have embarked upon a programme of religious and social reform which culminated on the one hand in the prayer book of 1549, and, on the other, in the parliamentary attack upon enclosures. Appreciation of the duke's 'goodness' also helped explain the otherwise baffling spectacle of his fall, a mere thirty-two months after the coup of January 1547 which brought him to power. Like all other good things, his regime was not destined to endure, running foul of entrenched vested interests, and at length falling victim to rebellion and the machinations of that prototype Iago, John Dudley, earl of Warwick. To this destructive brew, the unhappily married Hayward added the evil counsel of Somerset's wife, Anne Stanhope, truly a 'devilish woman', 'monstrous' in her pride.

Since so glib a résumé captures the essence of these arguments, their rejection in more recent, more cynical times can come as no surprise. Somerset's administration now limps from the fray, branded with the twin stigmas of incompetence and irresponsibility. The duke's personal failings, his pride, and his reluctance to contemplate advice from council and courtiers, run together with successive policy disasters. After five years of ruinously expensive war, so the indictment goes, Somerset not only passed over the chance to establish a period of financial retrenchment through peace, he must take the blame for provoking an unprecedented national crisis. Through his decision to prolong the Scottish war, the duke is held responsible for the intervention of 6000 well-equipped French troops in June 1548, for the removal of the young Queen Mary to France that August, and for the encouragement of Henry II's designs on the northern kingdom: three unwelcome developments that shaped a decade of political uncertainty in northern Europe. In his pursuit of unrealizable goals, the duke stands accused of inadvertently encouraging insurrection and then of culpable misjudgement when rebellion duly erupted, early in the summer of 1549. Far from innovatory, the protectorate is now dismissed as a sterile interlude, characterized by all the worst features of Henry VIII's last years: debasement, religious ambiguity and dangerous social unrest.

This, however, may be to carry revision too far; some of the problems Somerset encountered were inherent in the nature of his authority. The emergence of a protectorate where none had been envisaged under the terms of Henry VIII's will illustrates both the strengths and weaknesses of his position. Under the Succession Act of 1544, the crown was to pass to Edward and his heirs, or in default of such to Mary, then Elizabeth. Recognition of both sisters, branded as bastards by act of parliament a few years before, testifies to a pragmatism born of necessity. Henry had been granted powers to lay down conditions for the succession in his will and to nominate his heirs beyond his immediate children. He was also empowered to name a council which might act as a collective guardianship in the event of a minority.

Dated 30 December 1546, less than a month before his death, the king's will is a curious document. Subsequent events suggest two possible interpretations of its contents, based alike on circumstantial evidence. In one, the failing mind of a dying king is already being manipulated by those who controlled access to his person. An investigation during the 1560s first brought to general attention the fact that Henry had not signed the document with his own hand. His dry stamp had been used, by William Clerk, a clerk of the privy seal, under the directions of its keeper Sir Anthony Denny, groom of the stool. Denny was, at that time, a political ally of Hertford. Technically,

ANNO DNI · · · 5 4 4 ·

LADI MARI DOVGHTER TO
THE MOST VERTVOVS PRINCE
KING HENRI THE EIGHT

THE AGE OF XXVIII YERES

Plate 8 *Mary I as a princess*, unknown artist, attributed to 'Master John', 1544. Mary was restored to the order of succession by act of parliament that year.
Source: National Portrait Gallery, London

this was of no consequence: the dry stamp was, by 1547, an established instrument of government. All the same, its use on so important a document casts doubt on the accuracy with which Henry's wishes were being represented.

Most probably such doubts are misplaced. In the alternative interpretation, the king, though dangerously ill, is well able to lay plans for the future, throwing his weight behind those who appear most committed to his son's cause. At the same time, he trusts nobody; the will makes every effort to guard against the arrogation of power into a few, ambitious hands. Sixteen executors are to be assisted by twelve further prominent figures, and this group of twenty-eight is, as Eric Ives puts it, hermetically sealed – no provision is made for additions or replacements. What is sometimes seen as hasty drafting thus takes on a particularly thoughtful slant, coloured also by Henry's characteristic arrogance in presuming to shackle the living after his death.[1]

We must, therefore, be careful to distinguish between suggestions that Henry was marginalized before he died, and the notion that, in death, his wishes were interpreted very freely. The terms of his will in the event proved incompatible with the practicalities of national politics. Government with supreme temporal power vested in a committee was a concept alien to sixteenth-century Englishmen. In the past 130 years, a brother of the dead monarch had twice been at hand to take on the role of regent or protector at the accession of a child, and while the precedents set by Humphrey and Richard, dukes of Gloucester in the minorities of Henry VI and Edward V, were to say the least unpropitious, most members of the regency council inclined to a similar appointment in 1547.

Henry VIII, however, left no brother, and the claims of his wife and daughter failed to appeal. A female regent acting as caretaker for an absentee adult king might be tolerated, one bestowed with the authority inherent in the guardianship of a royal minor was quite another matter. Hertford, as the new king's uncle and as the most successful English military commander of his generation, emerged as a clear choice, yet he was in many ways the best from a poor field: the Seymours did not rank among the oldest aristocratic families, while his administrative skills had hardly been tested. Documentary evidence for events at the beginning of the Edwardian protectorate is frustratingly vague, dominated by the usual undigested gossip relayed by ambassadors. So far as we can now tell, however, bargaining over the form of the new government was by no means straightforward and absorbed the council's immediate labours. Henry's death was kept secret for seventy-two hours, and while a corresponding delay had occurred in 1509, this secrecy in itself is suggestive. Had there been any manipulation of Henry's will by Hertford and his colleagues, such haggling would surely have been unnecessary. At length, the collective regency promoted Hertford's appointment as protector.

Acquiescence had been won in many cases by generous promises. Henry's will included a clause empowering his council to confirm 'such grants and gifts as we have made given or promised to any, which be not yet perfected under our sign or any our seals as they ought to be'. The old king had certainly been contemplating promotions in his nobility after the fall of the Howards, and had compiled and revised a list of new creations with help from his secretary, William Paget. Confirmation of Hertford's position as protector and governor of the king's person in February was accompanied both by a lengthy catalogue of promotions and by a distribution of crown lands among counsellors. Hertford himself became duke of Somerset, while his allies William Parr, earl of Essex, and John Dudley, viscount Lisle, became, respectively, marquess of Northampton and earl of Warwick. Thomas Wriothesley, Audley's successor as lord chancellor, was advanced to the earldom of Southampton.[2] Somerset, as his son admitted years later, was 'his own carver' in the simultaneous shareout of land, but every courtier of consequence took a portion.

In accepting the protectorship, Somerset had agreed to act at all times with the advice and counsel of his fellow executors, and it is clear from the very start that he found this condition irksome. Early on, counsellor-executors appear to have shared his view, for when in March the duke was formally appointed protector by the new king, the distinction between counsellor and assistant under the terms of the will was quietly forgotten, while Somerset was permitted to draw on an unrestricted field in selecting a privy council. Amid these self-conscious efforts to strengthen the authority of an untried regime, however, the protector still appeared to onlookers a man placed on probation by his peers.

The bloodless coup of January 1547 claimed only one victim, and even this solitary case is cloaked in ambiguity. The new earl of Southampton lost the chancellorship and was removed from the council in March, a month after promotion to his earldom. While Somerset seemed bent on reform and Southampton advocated a continuation of King Henry's church settlement, it is likely, given the speed of events, that their disagreements turned more on the personal and the political: maybe they disagreed over the powers appropriate to a protector. Whatever the truth may be, Southampton's censure was half-hearted and impermanent: he retained his peerage, his share of the land 'promised' by Henry VIII was conveyed to him without demur, and he was restored to his council seat within two years. Perhaps this curious shuffle again suggests the protector's impotence, his need to seek a consensus early in the new reign.[3]

Owing his elevation to his relationship with King Edward, Somerset was particularly vulnerable to challenges from within his family. The two fifteenth-century precedents noted above differed in one significant respect, for while Richard III had, like Somerset, assumed both the protectorship of the realm and the governorship of his nephew, in 1422 the greatest offices had been divided between the brothers of Henry V and other high-ranking noblemen. Somerset's younger brother, Thomas Seymour, characterized by the future Queen Elizabeth as 'a man with much wit, and very little judgment', advanced his own claim to the governorship and spent the first eighteen months of the reign plotting to secure a division of the family spoils.

At first, Seymour was successful. He received a peerage, succeeding Warwick as lord admiral in February and securing admission to the council shortly afterwards. His hasty and disorganized attempts to buy the support of leading noblemen at court with money embezzled from the Bristol mint, however, eventually grew too much for his colleagues. Counsellors were affronted, too, by his marriage to Catherine Parr and, even before Catherine's untimely death in 1548, his none too subtle wooing of Princess Elizabeth. To some, his brags and boasts suggested that Seymour had hatched a plot to kidnap the king. Seymour was arrested, attainted in parliament for treason, and executed in March 1549. Bishop Latimer, choosing his words carefully, described Seymour after his death as 'a man the farthest from the fear of God that ever I knew or heard of in England'. Latimer spoke for the administration, but his words ring true. The protector faced an impossible situation: were he to urge a pardon he would invite charges that he was prepared to subjugate considerations of royal security and, indeed, the law of England itself, to save his brother, while a stoic acceptance of Seymour's fate, however much that fate was merited, left him open to accusations of fratricide and to suggestions that a family thus tainted stood unfit to rule.[4]

Charges that Somerset was increasingly reluctant to involve fellow counsellors in his decisions and that he obsessively pursued long-discredited policies rely heavily upon the formal accusations laid against him after his fall. They should, perhaps, be entertained with a little scepticism. Surviving records of the privy council seldom permit us to establish the opinions of counsellors on any particular subject, although they begin to suggest, in the increasing banality of the business transacted, that the important decisions were being taken, by Somerset, elsewhere. On the other hand, available evidence is ambiguous. Warwick's growing use of the duke's secretary, William Cecil, as an intermediary with Somerset, for example, may show the protector attempting to distance himself from a lifelong colleague, but it can just as easily reflect either Warwick's own absence from court owing to the ill-health that dogged him in later life or, maybe, his friendship for the promising young Cecil.

It might be supposed that the accession of a minor would have had an immediate effect upon the composition and influence of the privy chamber. The needs of an adult king were, after all, different to those of a nine-year-old boy. In practice, alteration was delayed. Somerset, it appears, as yet lacked the confidence to risk change. Once embarked on his Scottish campaign, however, the duke promoted his trusted brother-in-law, Sir Michael Stanhope, to the crucial office of first gentleman of the privy chamber. Under Stanhope's control, the chamber rapidly became what one modern historian has called 'a sub-department of the protector's household'. By 1548, Sir Michael was governor in all but name, Thomas Seymour, in one revealing confession, defining his own ambition in terms of obtaining 'the governance of [Edward VI] as Mr Stanhope had'. Successful in excluding unwelcome influences from the court, Somerset's delegation of authority to Stanhope bred its own tensions and may have fuelled the discontent which toppled him in 1549.[5]

Military operations against Scotland shaped every aspect of protectorate policy. While Somerset's war in the north was a continuation of that waged by Henry VIII since 1544, the underlying strategy changed markedly in 1547. For Henry, the struggle with France had always taken priority over operations in Scotland, but the Anglo-French peace in 1546 had now pushed Scotland to centre stage. Nevertheless, Henry and Somerset shared a belief that the logic and Divine Fitness of union, upheld vociferously by pro-Unionist evangelical Scots like John Elder and James Henrisoun, would themselves win over the Scottish nobility and gentry and render full-scale military conquest unnecessary.[6] Such a belief lies behind Somerset's key tactic: the establishment of garrisons across lowland Scotland.

Only the unavailability of necessary funds had hindered more extensive garrisoning in the past. The idea of stationing troops in a hostile countryside in order to support local loyalists and to shield the existing frontier had been hinted at in the course of earlier northern campaigns, and had also been tested on the borders of the Irish Pale in the 1530s and 1540s. After Somerset's emphatic victory at Pinkie, garrisons were established in five locations along the borders, at Inchcolm in the Firth of Forth and at Broughty Crag in the Tay. At first they prospered; in the winter of 1547–8 thousands of Scots came in person to 'assure' local garrisons of their loyalty. The idea was developed during 1548, and eventually some two dozen garrisons were set up, either by the private initiative of local officials – as at Dumfries and Jedburgh – or through the considered policy of the protectorate.

Given prevailing circumstances in 1547, the plan was sound enough. Scotland lacked resources for the standing army which alone could confound such tactics; garrisons were well suited to prolonged, small-scale, attritional warfare. There is little evidence to support suggestions that the protector saw them as instruments of government, supplying secure bases for the spread of English reformed religion in Scotland. For Somerset, the soldier, garrisons were rather a means of exerting a stranglehold on enemy territory. The map of Scotland reveals his strategy: lines of garrisons hinged upon Berwick and Haddington, advancing the frontier and cloaking the populated eastern seaboard.

But the stranglehold could not be sustained; a series of unforeseen blows wrecked the protector's plans. The arrival of French troops enabled the Scots to fight an expensive major war, while domestic troubles frustrated summer campaigning in 1549. A more resolute enemy demanded greater commitments of men and money; original estimates for the costs of maintaining garrisons soon proved wildly optimistic. The standing navy, too, continued to swallow large sums: Henry VIII had left a fleet of sixty ships, and the vessels which supplied remote garrisons had themselves to be docked, victualled, repaired and manned by capable crews. By October 1549, Somerset had spent just short of £600,000 pursuing his Scottish ambitions. With the increasing unwillingness of men to serve in Scotland, and the Scots themselves considered unreliable as garrison troops, 60 per cent of this sum had gone on the hiring of mercenaries. Over 7000 foreign soldiers served in the north during Somerset's Scottish war.

Even reinforcements on this scale proved inadequate. Demoralized by arrears in pay, and by the resilience of the foe, garrisons failed in their principal purpose. Most housed no more than one or two hundred soldiers, insufficient to offer effective protection for friendly Scots. Confidence in English arms ebbed away. In 1548, an army of some 2500 men was installed at Haddington, on the North Tyne between Dunbar and Leith. Intended to guarantee control of the Forth and its shore, dominating the key approaches to Edinburgh, Haddington proved an unwise choice, subjected to siege from the outset, awkward to defend and difficult to supply. Other large camps to deter French operations were planned but, with the shortage of available men, money and time, never materialized. Haddington was abandoned in September 1549 and some ten further garrisons were either ceded without a struggle, or fell to the enemy. About the same number survived, to be surrendered upon the conclusion of peace in 1550.

War against Scotland was supported by every member of Edward's first council, and there is little reason to accuse Somerset of inflexibility in a strategy towards Scotland not three years old. In this crucial area of policy he listened to advice, acting on Paget's recommendation to abandon Haddington, for example. Michael Bush suggests that Somerset, in choosing not to take personal charge of the campaign against the French in 1548, made a grave tactical error,[7] but it is not clear that the protector's presence would have made a significant difference: the three well-equipped armies that were dispatched north under trusted subordinates between August 1548 and July 1549 achieved nothing.

Like so many other new administrations, Somerset's government set about clearing away the less palatable legacies of its predecessor. In the first session of Edward VI's first parliament, an Act of Repeal abolished the Act of Six Articles and the Act for the Advancement of True Religion, reduced the number of crimes considered felonies, and restricted the scope of treason by statute so that words might be held treasonous only on the third offence. The bill had a complicated passage through both Houses, but such difficulties arose over proposed additions to the extensive remit of the measure, not from opposition to the principles of repeal and change. It is clear Somerset spoke for many when he told Charles V's envoy that some laws inherited from Henry VIII were 'extremely rigorous and indeed almost iniquitous in their severity'. There was, however, more to this act than the simple purchasing of goodwill; for a government headed by men of a reformist persuasion, both the termination of heresy legislation and the repeal of the Six Articles were clear declarations of intent.

Attempts to play down Somerset's personal commitment to religious reform are not entirely convincing. Statements of belief are hard to come by – Somerset as protector never commits himself to a declaration defining his personal convictions – and with no definition of orthodoxy yet provided by Rome, with the views of Luther and Zwingli at odds in key areas, and with those of Calvin still evolving, a clear picture is elusive. Any portrayal of the duke as a politique moderate, as a man persuaded through political calculation to impose a veneer of protestantism on the church, yet unwilling to press ahead with extensive reforms, sits oddly with his actions. Somerset's inclination to reformed religion appears unfeigned: numerous reformers, including Peter Martyr, accepted the sincerity of his professions, and following the duke's execution in 1552, Calvin himself expressed genuine regret.

Between 1547 and 1549, the English church underwent far-reaching alterations, both in ceremonial and in its underlying beliefs. Others besides Somerset were party to this remoulding. Archbishop Cranmer enjoyed greater influence in the shaping of religious policy, as he worked with the protector and other sympathetic council colleagues to bring about further reform. During Edward's reign, Cranmer comes out decisively against any notion of a real presence at the eucharist, and so too does the English church. If the point at which the archbishop was finally persuaded of such views rests uncertain, and if these doctrinal changes took five years or more to effect, there is yet some suggestion that both conviction and ambition were in place by January 1547.

At Edward's coronation, Cranmer belittled any deeper significance in the ancient coronation ritual: it could not, he maintained, augment the king's authority, bestowed by God alone. At the same time Cranmer urged Edward, according to the fashion of the time, to model his actions on those of his 'predecessor', Josiah, the idol-smashing boy king of Israel. All this was by way of preliminary. A royal visitation started work in August. The July 1547 religious injunctions, modelled on those issued by Cromwell nine years earlier, appeared to express moderate opinions, but again denounced religious processions and the veneration of images. A parallel book of homilies mixed, in twelve sermons, broadly Lutheran teachings on justification – the work of Cranmer's pen – with more orthodox doctrine. Parliamentary legislation introduced communion in both kinds, enforced as an interim measure by royal proclamation from April 1548, and embedded the service in a new liturgical structure, which used English for the first time. Justified by a preamble which rejected the twin superstitions of purgatory and prayers for the dead, an act of 1547 abolished chantries, confraternities and guilds, bringing in useful revenue to the crown. The sanctioning of clerical marriage the next year might have been a personal concession to Cranmer and other like-minded supporters of Somerset's regime.

Cranmer may have enjoyed a freer hand in spiritual matters, and he could once again openly acknowledge his wife. But this is not to suggest that he could, or would, have tried to impose his beliefs on either protector or monarch. As in King Henry's time, the archbishop sheltered behind a higher, secular authority. Here was systematic, measured reform, decisively enforced. In common with every other Tudor administrator, Somerset regarded uniformity of worship within the state as essential to good order. He enforced such unity at Oxford and Cambridge Universities during 1548, and in the same year banned first unlicensed, then licensed preaching. He allowed conservative bishops to express their reservations – eight entered protests in the Lords against both prayer book and clerical marriage, six opposed the abolition of chantries – but when Stephen Gardiner, and the bishop of London, Edmund Bonner, took their opposition further, preaching and writing against the changes, both were thrown into prison. These Henrician conservatives defended a weak position, because what parliament had imposed in the form of the Act of Six Articles, parliament could, and did, reject.

Like the measures that had preceded it, the settlement imposed by the 1549 Act of Uniformity suggests compromise, but a compromise now weighted against Henrician conservatism and in favour of reform. It introduced a book of common prayer which, while retaining altars, prayers for the dead, Catholic vestments and private confession, and acknowledging 'mass' as a popular synonym for lord's supper and holy communion, recast every church service in English.[8] While there was little immediate attempt at statutory enforcement, for the work of a mere two and a half years this catalogue of change suggests a high degree of commitment from all in authority, as they took the first steps on a long journey. The German theologian Martin Bucer in April 1549 was told what he wanted to hear, but also what Cranmer clearly wanted to tell him: that there was more to come.

Somerset's religious alterations took a great majority of the influential along a road they were not unwilling to travel. Numerous spiritual and temporal peers never noted for their radical convictions supported the official line. If Somerset's goal was to introduce reform despite an unfavourable international situation, this too was accomplished. The protectorate's skilful handling of relations with Charles V, whose ambassador seems all along to have believed that the religious innovations were but matters of, as Paget had it, 'forms and fashions', led in the summer of 1549 to that triumph of the regime, the ratification of the Anglo-Imperial treaty of 1543.

Revisionism is most persuasive when qualifying the supposed innovations in social policy. Old ideas that Somerset fought the corner of the small landholder against the enclosers and engrossers must be set aside. The duke courted popularity to the extent that every Tudor statesman wished to be remembered as a just and virtuous ruler; his surviving letters accompanying bills of complaint passed on to the masters of the court of Requests reflect his genuine concern that justice should reach down to all who sought it. The manifestations of such goodwill, however – his attacks on enclosures and his attempts to introduce a parliamentary programme of social and economic reform – were born of a desire to maintain the English war effort. By the 1540s, 'enclosure' had grown into a broad term, embracing all practices which might lead to depopulation, notably the conversion of former arable land to sheep pasture or to parkland. Against the background of a growing population, but without particularly strong statistical justification, it had long been regarded as a major social evil.

Enclosure, it was said, led to the loss of men from the land, or more particularly, the loss of the self-sufficient smallholder, able to muster for the wars; it was held responsible for depleting the pool of manpower available for military operations. That, the administration reasoned, helped explain how English kings in former times had been able to pursue large-scale war to better effect. Commitments in Scotland also lie behind official reluctance to restore the coinage to its pre-1544 value, even though the evils of inflation were addressed in other less problematic but less effective ways. Debasement, after all, paid half the costs of the Scottish war, a contribution beside which the rewards of chantry dissolution (around £150,000 to October 1549) and parliamentary subsidy (£189,000 towards defence for the whole of Edward's reign) were relatively insignificant.

The regime's concern for social reform was sustained by its awareness that the recent run of good harvests, which had shielded England's population from the effects of steeply rising prices, could not continue forever. It also took note of polemicists – later dignified as a 'commonwealth party' – who demanded government initiatives to halt the decay of tillage and to tackle the evils of inflation. The lamentations of men like Hugh Latimer and the returned Henrician refugees William Turner and Thomas Becon were, however, seldom matched by any practical proposals. Individual works of charity, and exhortations to a sober life, exhausted their imaginations. To the few who had thought through some form of remedial programme, notably Thomas Smith and John Hales, the administration listened with respect and attention. They were most receptive to Hales's ideas, perhaps because he was a persuasive fellow, or perhaps because his views accorded with petitions from several counties and reflected the prevailing opinions in council.

Neither Smith nor Hales looked for radical reform. Hales in particular exemplified the faith of the 'commonwealth man' in a benevolent aristocracy. Inclined to the reformed religion, he emphasized the importance of a charitable approach to the problems of the poorer classes, thus placating both God and the less stable elements among the poor themselves. For Hales, war against Scotland was both unavoidable and just; he believed that inflation was caused not by debasement but by a whole range of depopulating policies: sheep-farming, cattle grazing and marketing malpractice. There was no dissimulation here, for Hales spoke and wrote as he found too often for his own good, but there is equally no question that Somerset and the council accepted more readily advice which sought to cure the realm's social ills while recognizing the current necessity of war. Smith, who advocated immediate reform of the coinage, and, by implication, peace, was a voice in the economic wilderness before 1550.

Central to Hales's 'reforming' policies were the so-called enclosure commissions set up in 1548 and 1549. The 1548 commissions lacked powers of coercion; their remit was to survey the extent of the problem as a basis of future reform. For one reason or another, only the midland commission, with Hales its guiding spirit, began work, accomplishing little in the face of – so said Hales – widespread non-cooperation from the enclosing landlords. Somerset, however, was persuaded that commissions, armed with powers to enforce legislation, offered a way forward. In a proclamation of April 1549 subsequently attributed by his enemies to Somerset alone, he announced tough new measures against those who flouted existing agrarian legislation. During the following summer, attention once again focused on the midlands commissioners, though amid the distractions of social unrest commissions for the western counties, Cambridgeshire and – possibly – Kent were taken beyond the planning stage. It would appear that the arbitrary nature of the times transmitted itself to the instructions provided, for, without descending to particulars, the administration ordered commissions simply to reform abuses, a vague direction, posing theoretical and practical problems at law for the commissioners. Perhaps Somerset, sensing the threat to his position in 1549, had grown more enthusiastic for immediate rather than gradual action.

Given the highly tentative beginnings of 1548, and the radical change of remit in 1549, it is difficult to accept Bush's picture of a protector stubbornly adhering to policies which stood no chance of success. Certainly, there was a good deal of council opposition to the adopted measures, notably from the earl of Warwick and others who, always wary of raising unrealistic expectations, looked askance at the scribblings of commonwealth theorists. Such opposition, however, stemmed rather from fears that the methods of implementation might bring unrest in their wake than from any belief that the remedies were, in themselves, undesirable. Bush may well be correct in arguing that personal factors, such as Somerset's toleration of Hales, could have aggravated relations with his fellow counsellors. At his subsequent trial, the protectorate's social measures were used to illustrate Somerset's irresponsibility. Nevertheless, his obligation to devise workable social reforms was implicitly recognized by the duke's successors in power.

Economic measures advanced, either at the initiative or with the support of the council, during the second Edwardian session of parliament of 1548–9, met with varying success. Bills to combat inflation by preserving the quality of leather, malt and steel passed into law, as did legislation to exempt north Atlantic fishermen from duties, to restrict the export of bell metal and white ashes, and to control price fixing in certain trades. A progressive indirect tax on sheep and cloth, diversely interpreted as a fiscal response to the decline in royal revenue from the wool staple due to the increasing manufacture of domestic cloth, or as an attempt to restrict numbers of sheep in the country, so encouraging tillage, was also pushed through. Further measures, particularly those concerned with agriculture, failed in the face of alarmed vested interest: Hales's bills to promote the breeding of dairy cattle and to restrict engrossing both enjoyed the support of Somerset, as, perhaps, did legislation to limit ownership of rabbit warrens and to promote disparking. All four bills, however, were rejected by parliament. Nothing indicates that the administration, for all its rhetoric, was particularly alarmed by such wholesale rejection; in a session dominated first by debates over the Act of Uniformity, and later by efforts to secure a much-needed subsidy, social renewal came low on the list of priorities.

The rebellions that broke out in the south-west and in East Anglia during 1549 cannot be said to have resulted from any particular act of Somerset's protectorate. As with events in 1536–7, it is tempting to see broad economic and social causes prompting revolt, but interpretations of this nature fail to allow for the random, individual causation common to so many popular uprisings. The twin blights of dearth and inflation – on one index of consumables, prices were 11 per cent higher year on year in 1549 – certainly bore down on the 70 per cent of England's population that spent over 80 per cent of its income on food and drink. The introduction of services using the English prayer book in June 1549 did indeed provide useful tinder for the fire of rebellion in the south-west, while urban unrest added an increasingly volatile element to the brew. Yet few years passed in sixteenth-century England without rumours of unrest in the countryside, and while the rumours were louder and more substantial than usual in 1549, trouble was averted in the midlands and home counties, either through a blend of conciliation and threats offered by local gentry or, where necessary, through an early and efficient show of force.

Much depended on leadership. In the south-west, the organizing role of Humphry Arundell, an experienced soldier and member of one of Cornwall's leading families, was crucial, but his motives in casting aside loyalty to the Tudor crown remain obscure. Cornwall, divided by local feuds and rivalries, and heavily armed by the standards of the day, remained the powerbase of rebellion, although the shortcomings of the Devon gentry and the lord privy seal Lord Russell, the general appointed to crush the rising, combined with the protector's unwillingness to commit sufficient troops to ensure that trouble spread rapidly throughout both counties.

In Norfolk, the spark of rebellion was provided by a petty local quarrel between the brothers Robert and William Kett and an upwardly mobile lawyer, John Flowerdew of Wymondham. The flame thus kindled was fed by tensions within town hierarchies, the absence of many important gentlemen from the region in the summer of 1549 and the speed of the insurgents' initial moves. Religion hardly features: the rebels, who included some quite important evangelicals, scorned cautious overtures from Catholics like Sir Roger Woodhouse. The conservative gentry almost to a man supported the crown. More important was the widespread ill-feeling against local gentlemen who had prospered, against 'new' men who had risen in an intensely competitive county environment. Enclosures were thrown down, but it was the encloser, not the economics of his actions, who seems to have been the target. Similar disturbances flared in Suffolk, a vacuum of authority in East Anglia following the recent eclipse of the Howards further aggravating the situation. Princess Mary now wielded a good deal of local influence, but the Catholic princess was disinclined to cooperate with her brother's council and, although she did not back the rebellion, her local following was less than wholehearted in its support for the regime.

The rebels in both Norfolk and the south-west carefully listed their demands, in effect supplying their *raison d'être* for revolt. These lists are remarkably different. Each displays its own peculiar emphasis, even allowing for the inextricable contributions of later editors. The points forwarded by the western rebels are pervaded with religious conservatism, favouring a return to Henrician Catholicism: 'We will have the laws of our sovereign lord King Henry VIII concerning the six articles to be used again as in his time they were.' There is an overwhelming concern to reintroduce familiar ritual, to restore chantries and to be rid of the English Bible and prayer book, 'for we be informed that otherwise the clergy shall not of long time confound the heretics'. The list is surprisingly apolitical. We find no call for the restoration of a Roman primacy, Reginald Pole's pardon and recall being urged only on the grounds that he is 'of the king's blood'.

Such lists, however, reflect first of all the anxieties of their compilers: the western leadership included a large number of conservative local clergymen, and the reason pervading their catalogue scarcely reflects the finally inexplicable rage which infused the commons of Cornwall and Devon against their gentry superiors. In East Anglia, the articles were composed by minor gentlemen, yeoman farmers and their lawyer friends. Here the rebels, to quote Diarmaid MacCulloch, 'sought to exclude the gentry and the clergy from their world'.[9] The rapacious manorial lord is portrayed as the villain of the piece: removal of abuses in reassessing rents and prosaic attempts to adjust the existing balance of society dominate the agenda. In an attempt to curb the local custom of foldcoursing – rights to pasture sheep on lands often belonging to another party – gentlemen worth under £40 per annum are to be limited in their holdings of livestock, while none beneath the degree of esquire is to keep doves or 'unbounded coneys'. Some lawyers and their acquisitive ways come in for particular criticism. All very much like the social engineering attempted regularly through statute, and all rather conservative. The subject of enclosure appears only in the form of demands for a prohibition on further fencing for saffron cultivation, while down the list, hidden amid a welter of minor points, comes a clause much quoted: 'We pray that all bond men may be made free, for God made all free with his precious blood.' Although the duke of Norfolk had been particularly old-fashioned in this respect, serfdom affected a small minority of the population in 1549. Neither enclosure nor serfdom weighed very heavily in the scale of grievances.

Complacency and tactical naivety certainly facilitated the spread of both insurrections. Attempts to suppress the Norfolk uprising were particularly ill-managed; the marquess of Northampton, commanding the first royal army on the scene, displayed quite staggering incompetence. Norwich, near impossible to defend, had admitted Robert Kett's men. Reoccupying the city, Northampton committed his force – largely composed of cavalry – to an unequal struggle fought out in narrow city streets. He was driven into ignominious retreat. Fortunately for Somerset's administration, the Norfolk and Suffolk risings were neutralized by the rebels' indifference to concerns outside their native counties. An inclination to 'camp' rather than march reflected the leaders' conviction that their quarrel lay with the corrupt and inefficient local agents of government rather than with the government itself. The far more dangerous western rebellion was confined to the two southwestern counties only through the stubborn defence offered by the city of Exeter, which endured a month's siege.[10]

Suppression of both risings was eventually made possible by Somerset's belated recognition that Scotland would have to take second place to more urgent dangers. Italian and German mercenaries were diverted from their march north and committed to the troubled areas. Nevertheless, while Warwick quickly overran the rebels at Dussindale outside Norwich, butchering hundreds, Russell, forcing the passage to Exeter by way of Clyst St Mary, triumphed in the fiercest fighting seen in southern England during the sixteenth century. Even then, Arundell had the resources to make a final stand at Sampford Courtenay, where he suffered further heavy casualties. The aftermath of the western rising, left in the hands of Sir Anthony Kingston as provost marshal, a man with a taste for the humour of the gallows, lacked all trace of mercy. In this wretched epilogue, at least, we see efficiency from the regime.

After the outbreak of serious unrest, the protectorship lived on borrowed time. Somerset's eventual downfall is best explained in terms of the weaknesses which had dogged him since 1547. He lacked the personal authority enjoyed by kings and, thanks not a little to his arrogant mismanagement of colleagues, he was denied the committed support in council and court essential for survival in the stormy political waters whipped up by continued economic crisis, festering local unrest, the outbreak of war with France in August 1549 and the plot against him which emerged that autumn. The details of this conspiracy are obscure, but attention has traditionally focused on the part played by the earl of Warwick. Warwick was the son of Henry VII's financial minister, Edmund Dudley, whose execution had served to underline Henry VIII's rejection of his father's policies. Through faithful service and an aptitude for military command, he had shadowed Somerset's rise in favour with the late king, while as an executor of Henry's will he had enthusiastically endorsed the protectorate. Now, though, he harboured personal grievances. Even one of Somerset's supporters concedes as much, noting that the protector had unwisely ignored Warwick's requests for two offices in reversion. But Warwick was capable of higher motives: it is clear that his experiences in Norfolk that summer helped turn him against a protector who had allowed such disturbances to escalate.

Contemporaries never underestimated Warwick's talent for intrigue. Many shared Sir Richard Morison's opinion that Dudley 'seldom went about anything but he conceived first three or four purposes beforehand'. He was, of course, not the only conspirator; had he been, the coup could never have succeeded. In order to put an end to the protectorate, Warwick made common cause with more conservative counsellors – notably the earls of Southampton and Arundel, and Lord St John – who, at heart, feared him as much as they loathed Somerset. These noblemen pinned their hopes on a restoration of conciliar powers submerged under the protectorate. Implausible talk of bestowing the regency on Princess Mary helped counter Somerset's last sure weapon, his kinship with the young king. The implication was obvious enough: for all she was a woman and a Catholic, Mary would, suitably guided and advised, provide England with better leadership during the remaining years of Edward's minority.

Matters came to a head in September: the Imperial ambassador François van der Delft began relaying rumours of disputes in council. While an ambassador's report was only as good as the information on which it was based, and the sagacity with which such information was interpreted, it appears that some of the most important men in the kingdom were at this moment beating a path to van der Delft's door.[11] By 23 September Warwick was angling for Imperial support in a forthcoming coup, suggesting to the ambassador that now was the time for his master 'to come forward as the king's father'. On 5 October Somerset, learning that troops were assembling in London and perceiving at last his perilous position, publicly denounced all his council colleagues, calling upon Englishmen to defend their king. He was already too late. The counsellors responded in kind, setting themselves forward as the sole dispensers of good administration and at the same time writing to King Edward alleging that Somerset, 'too much given to his own will', was incapable of rational government. Somerset reacted to news of increasing defections with initial determination and eventual despair, his

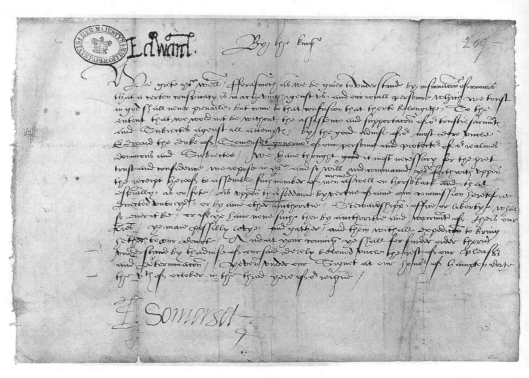

Plate 9 Warrant of Edward VI to Sir Harry Seymour, calling upon him for assistance in the crisis which preceded the protector's downfall. Somerset signs the warrant; note the use of a stamp for the king's signature.
Source: Public Record Office

position undermined by a failed bid to secure the Tower of London and by the lord mayor and Common Council's unambiguous if unenthusiastic endorsement of the counsellors' cause.

The nature of this coup is itself extremely curious. Subsequent accounts resemble an epistolary novel, as letters between the opposing camps at London and Windsor passed to and fro. The situation veered towards violence, then away again as Lord Russell, smarting over his treatment in the west that summer, refused Somerset the backing of his soldiers. Eventually, the protector capitulated, his final supporters, Paget and Cranmer, taking advantage of an opportunity to secure their own positions by negotiating his surrender. The protectorate was tacitly abandoned, and on 14 October Somerset was escorted to the Tower.[12]

Like the government of Richard III seventy years earlier, Somerset's protectorate confronts the historian with the unrewarding task of assessing – often, that is, guessing – the wisdom of policies either cut short or refashioned by later regimes. Criticism of the protector's 'stubborn' aggression in Scotland makes insufficient allowance for the importance of military success to one whose hold on a difficult office was far from secure, to a man who had established his credibility in that same office through triumph in battle. There is, moreover, a distinction to be drawn between a substantially capable administration which fell through the failure of its key policy and through the inherent, inescapable weaknesses of a minority, and the regime of an incapable, foolish man who reached out for absolute powers, only to see the authority that he craved slip from his eager hands.

8 The Dudley Supremacy and the Reign of Jane Grey: England 1549–53

Somerset's fall left power, to all appearances, firmly within the grasp of Southampton and his supporters. 'Every man', declared John Ponet, 'repaireth to Wriothesley, honoureth Wriothesley, sueth unto Wriothesley . . . and all things be done by his advice.' As late as 7 November van der Delft shared this view, informing his master that Southampton held sway at court and – the great test of power – that other peers and counsellors were constantly seeking him out, through courtesy or in search of favour.

By the end of that month, however, those same counsellors were gathering to transact business at the ailing earl of Warwick's London residence, leaving Southampton ignored upon his own sick bed. The alliance that had brought Somerset down was foundering on mutual distrust and conflicting objectives. While both sides and many onlookers saw religion as a factor dividing those contending for power, Warwick and Southampton were more concerned with the final distribution of political influence than with precise definitions of the real presence or the niceties of clerical dress. Warwick's espousal of further religious reform was most probably a political decision, taken in the face of Southampton's equally pragmatic support for the conservative interest.

Perturbed by the increasing antagonism of his allies, Warwick redoubled his efforts to win the trust of the king. Though Edward was a minor, he kept his own journal, had his own opinions and expressed his own wishes. His ministers might compete to exercise authority in the king's name, but in that perilous game Edward's willing support was already a precious asset. To this end, Warwick readily accommodated the religious preferences of the young Edward and courted those whose opinions the king valued. Working in concert with Cranmer – trusted by the king and with the most to lose in any religious reaction – he was able to persuade Edward that he held his monarch's best interests at heart. The key alliance between archbishop and minister was a partnership of convenience. Cranmer had little time for Warwick, knowing a trimmer when he saw one and fearing further despoliation of the church in the grave economic climate. Just the same, the crisis of 1549–50 bred a pact that held good for several critical months.[1]

Excluding rivals from royal trust was as important as winning it oneself. Governorship of the king was placed in the hands of a privy council commission consisting of six peers, while Sir Michael Stanhope was replaced on 15 October as groom of the stool by four 'Principal Gentlemen'. Together, these ten counsellors and gentlemen controlled the privy purse, the royal 'dry stamp' signature and, above all, access to the monarch, vital assets in any power struggle. Ostensibly selected to avoid the undue concentration of authority, these two groups included, so far as one may discern personal convictions, a majority of reformers over conservatives. More significantly, they contained several influential figures personally loyal to the earl of Warwick.

Southampton and his associates, deprived of significant access to the king, reassessed the chances of establishing Princess Mary as regent. When sounded out on the subject, Mary refused to commit herself before success was guaranteed, but so far as Warwick was concerned even the approach was ominous. Some crucial developments in November prove particularly difficult to

Plate 10 *Edward VI*, by Guillim Scrots, *c.*1550. Scrots was King's Painter to Henry VIII and his son.
Source: Réunion des Musées nationaux/Louvre

interpret.[2] Both sides strove to increase their strength in council, and in this Warwick, using his influence with the king, enjoyed greater success. Thomas Goodrich, bishop of Ely, was sworn in as a counsellor at the beginning of the month and Warwick's close ally, Henry Grey, marquess of Dorset, joined him on 29 November. Paget, initially drawn to Southampton on account of his support for an alliance with Charles V, was bought over with the promise of a peerage, and set to work convincing others that Warwick was the man to back.

The twist to the tale, while credible, depends on particularly thin evidence. During late November and early December several counsellors, Southampton prominent among them, interrogated Somerset in the Tower, and it was commonly believed that, despite assurances given him in October, the protector would be attainted and executed. Somerset, however, while denying none of the charges brought against him, reminded his examiners that the council, and Warwick in particular, had endorsed all his actions. Scenting an opportunity, Southampton and the conservative earl of Arundel stepped up their efforts to bring Somerset to public trial and execution, scheming thereby to discredit Warwick by exploiting his long, close and widely acknowledged association with the protector.

The gambit failed. One of the conspirators, Lord St John, warned Warwick of what was afoot. Warwick then refused to consider Somerset's impeachment and Southampton, his bluff called, lacked sufficient support to back his threats. St John was rewarded with the earldom of Wiltshire, while Lord Russell also swung over to the Warwick camp and was created earl of Bedford. On Christmas Day the council completely rebuffed the religious conservatives, confirming its support for the Act of Uniformity, and by 14 January 1550 it was clear to everyone that Southampton had lost the game. On that day parliament passed a bill to fine Somerset rather than to proceed against him for his life. Arundel and Southampton were ordered to leave court. Early in February, Warwick was promised the lord presidency of the council by the king, and promptly dismissed his rivals. Southampton died, it is said of grief, in July 1550. Arundel awaited happier days, Lord Paget, tainted by close ties to Somerset, eventually sharing his eclipse. In time, Warwick was reconciled to both Arundel and Paget, but he was never again able to trust either man.

Just as Somerset's stock has fallen in the face of determined revisionism, so Warwick's has risen markedly over the past three decades. Even the more telling points traditionally laid to his charge – his frenetic acquisition of personal wealth and his obvious unpopularity – have been brushed aside as misunderstandings of political life in Tudor England and as the natural consequence of harsh yet necessary measures. However, not every piece in the new jigsaw fits neatly. When his regime was put to the test in July 1553 – the popular test of support from gentlemen and nobles – it collapsed as rapidly and abjectly as had Somerset's in 1549. No amount of personal rehabilitation can obscure the essentially provisional authority of Edward VI's second administration, a fundamental weakness against which Warwick fought manfully but which, in the end, he could not overcome.

Apart, perhaps, from the very last days of his ascendancy, Warwick never aspired to the role of protector vacated by Somerset: such a course was precluded by the very process of discrediting Somerset's rule. Royal blood did not flow in his veins, and any attempt to secure so high an office would have antagonized too many influential colleagues. The offices Warwick did hold, however, were significant: as lord great master of the household he regulated access to the king, and as lord president of the council he sat as Edward's deputy in the council chamber, controlling appointments and enjoying the right to decide agendas. There the earl was a first among equals. A capable, pragmatic diplomat, he governed through the general assent given to such necessary policies as peace with France. Somerset may have neglected the council, but his successor would not and could not afford to do likewise.[3]

A catalogue of high offices and formal authority, though, is only a part of the story. Warwick's primacy was essentially intangible, based as it was on deferential yet secure control of the king and the men about the king, and on respect for the sensitivities of council colleagues. Like Somerset, his personal authority rested upon proven good service and on military reputation. Unlike the protector, he also exuded an engaging blend of resolution and, when he chose, winning candour. That authority may also have rested on the ready acceptance of a punishing workload; a sense of duty is observable throughout his career. In one of his frank and consistently melancholy letters to William Cecil, secretary of state from September 1550, Warwick lamented that 'when others went to their suppers and pastimes after their travail I went to bed, with a careful heart and a wearied body'. Perhaps it is no coincidence that Cecil, who would make his own mark on the world through painstaking labour, was schooled in the ways of government during Warwick's ascendancy.[4]

Trouble, when it came, emerged from a discredited quarter. Somerset, though recalled to the council, found it hard to come to terms with his demotion. Warwick attempted conciliation: in June 1550 his eldest son married Somerset's daughter, and the two men cooperated to introduce county lieutenancies, which administered order in the shires. They are again seen working together in negotiations with France which produced a conditional marriage alliance between Edward and Elisabeth, daughter of Henry II. Nevertheless, tensions remained. Court politics across these years are shrouded in the usual obscurity. It is possible that, during late 1550 and early 1551, Somerset was involved in a conspiracy to restore his former authority, plotting Warwick's removal and offering hints of support for conservatives at court. He might, though the evidence is ambiguous, have angled for the release of Stephen Gardiner, imprisoned in the Tower and deprived of the see of Winchester after lengthy attempts to persuade him into conformity, and he may also have made overtures to Princess Mary, whose hostility to Warwick was growing clearer every day. Such efforts, however, are difficult to evaluate. Gardiner's own motives and ambitions in this perilous time remain opaque: some see him fighting a desperate battle against religious innovation, blending defiance with compromise, while others interpret his actions as those of a conciliator, intent only on accommodation, whose overtures were spurned by a hostile council.[5]

Edward VI's journal and the Imperial ambassador's reports suggest disputes in council during April 1551, concealed by ostentatious displays of unity, and although neither source identifies any cause Warwick's appointment as earl marshal – a position once enjoyed by Somerset – may well have contributed to the tension. On 16 October, matters came to a head. Somerset was once again placed under arrest, and he was arraigned that December. Initial accusations that he had plotted to murder Warwick and raise rebellion were specious, but served their purpose. The former protector was convicted, not of treason, but of a felony, in having assembled a force for the assassination of his rival. He was beheaded in January 1552.

Some have suggested, rather unconvincingly, that Warwick desired Somerset's release but that his intentions were frustrated by the concerted bloodlust of fellow counsellors. From reports on the trial, and rumour relayed by ambassadors, it would indeed appear that distrust of Somerset, at times verging upon hatred, was rife among his former council colleagues and that Edward himself was not disposed to save his stricken uncle. On the other hand, there were counsellors, notably Cranmer, who spoke out for mercy and who appear to have lost Warwick's friendship when they did so. There can be little doubt that Warwick, fearing the threat Somerset posed to his own authority, had resolved to strike the first blow.

While Somerset lived, there was always a sense in which his relationship to the king set him apart from fellow counsellors, above all the shifts and squabbles of conciliar strife. A remarkable series of letters, written to the English ambassador at the Imperial court, Sir Philip Hoby, by his financial agent Richard Scudamore, helps us grasp the duke's enduring authority and the uncertainty that this bred after 1549.[6] Not until five days before Somerset's arrest was Warwick at last advanced to the dukedom of Northumberland, his loyal associate Dorset being raised at the same time to the dukedom of Suffolk, while more conservative colleagues in council, the earl of Wiltshire and Sir William Herbert, became marquess of Winchester and earl of Pembroke respectively. It is no coincidence that Warwick acquired his dukedom only as a part of those veiled manoeuvres which finally destroyed the duke of Somerset: developing self-confidence, ambition and an appreciation of the power emanating from prestige all dictated his elevation.

Many policies pursued by Somerset, howsoever driven by the demands of war, still carry about them the suggestion of idealistic impulse. The courses pursued by Warwick – or Northumberland, as we shall now call him – are singularly devoid of such trappings. Poorly educated, he was accustomed to accepting the formulations of policy worked through by Henry VIII, Somerset or more experienced council colleagues. In his pragmatic search for internal security, external peace and financial solvency, the essentials of such 'policies' as can be discerned are based firmly upon the studied avoidance of his predecessor's errors. Fear of disorder, in particular, lies behind many initiatives. The county lieutenancies in 1551 are a direct response to the risings two years earlier; while the introduction of household security measures and the establishment of the 'gendarmes' – standing forces raised under licence by approved courtiers but paid for by the government – counter the possibility of further conspiracies. Significant unrest did not, in fact, materialize. No group at court was sufficiently strong, or sufficiently keen, to mount a challenge, while in the countryside, despite innumerable worrying rumours, memories of Sampford Courtenay and Dussindale, the bad harvests of 1549–51, and a severe outbreak of sweating sickness, together dampened the tinder of revolt.

Peace with France and Scotland was financially imperative, whatever the enemy might demand. 'Of many evils', wrote Paget, 'let us choose the least.' Renewed conflict between Charles V and Henry II, however, gave the English a breathing space entirely absent under the protectorate, and because France, too, sought peace, the terms were not ungenerous. French control in Scotland was diplomatically fudged, though all English troops left the country, and the English were generously compensated for the inevitable return of Boulogne.[7] Warwick worked hard to develop amity with the French: amid the efforts to arrange a Valois marriage for King Edward, Henry II was created a knight of the garter and unresolved issues between England and Scotland were settled in June 1551. When France and the Empire fell once again to war in September 1551, England preserved her neutrality.

A restoration of the currency was also necessary by 1551, although the council drew back from an expensive redemption of all base coin and, desperate for cash, resorted to the discredited panacea one last time. Nevertheless, a subsequent issue of coinage restored silver content to early 1540s levels. The administration's wider commitment to reducing expenditure can be illustrated by the mothballing of some coastal fortifications, the discharging of numerous mercenary contingents and by the swift abandonment of the gendarmes experiment, a decision that may have cost Northumberland his life in 1553. 'To have his majesty out of debt' was the duke's explicit goal. Implementation of so laudable if unoriginal a policy was left to the marquess of Winchester, lord treasurer from February 1550, and to William Cecil, whose surviving papers illustrate the combination of uncompromising debt collection and stricter financial accounting eventually adopted. Drawing upon the precedent of Henry VIII's privy coffer war-chest, which had been used to finance conflict with France, building projects and royal gifts, the Northumberland regime began to develop a second household treasury, supplementing the by now purely domestic privy purse. Avoiding the slow procedures of accounting in more established courts of receipt, this cash reserve could be exploited rapidly to pursue the king's 'special affairs' and to repay short-term loans. All the same, ordinary revenues still had to be augmented with land sales, a trend encouraged by the insecurities of a minority regime quite prepared to purchase support.[8]

The formulation of religious policy was again an exercise in pragmatism: conservative elements in council and court included Northumberland's personal rivals, while the king was closing fast upon his majority and, under Cranmer's influence, showing every sign of backing further radical reform. Northumberland had long accepted the maxim that royal will should establish the precise form of a national creed. His contributions to parliamentary debates in December 1548 on the bill for uniformity in religion illustrate in their shallowness his subordination of doctrinal considerations and personal conviction to the demands of state security and, at the same time, his inclination to support the reformers, other factors apart. Many fellow counsellors, not noted for their radical sympathies, went along with change for similar reasons. The path of principled resistance was left to a group of conservative bishops. Gardiner lost his see and ended up in prison, while George Day in Chichester, Nicholas Heath in Worcester and Cuthbert Tunstall in Durham, like Bishop Bonner of London back in 1549, all took their stand over some point or other of the new reforms and endured deprivation as a result.

Fresh episcopal appointments now move decisively towards the evangelical: Nicholas Ridley becomes bishop of London, John Ponet, Miles Coverdale and John Hooper bishops of Winchester, Exeter and Gloucester respectively. The new bishops shared a commitment to further reform, beyond the limits envisaged in the first Edwardian Act of Uniformity, and, in Hooper's case, beyond anything Cranmer could tolerate. As a result of his refusal to wear traditional clerical garb at his consecration, the argumentative Hooper spent a short time in the Fleet prison, eventually backing down when he appreciated his isolation on the subject. No new Edwardian bishop aspired to a central role in national politics, but all were competent preachers and diocesan administrators who found themselves singularly well placed to influence the course of the English reformation.[9]

Religious reforms introduced between 1549 and 1553 were the most radical seen in England at any time before the Civil War. As early as January 1550, the appointment of a committee to devise an English ordination service shows the way in which events are moving. The new ordinal appeared in March, accompanied by steps to abolish minor religious orders. Local initiatives by reformist bishops, possibly following Ridley's lead, led to the replacement of altars with tables in many parts of England, and the grumbling discontent this roused encouraged the council, as it had done over the images controversy two years earlier, to step in and give official sanction to such changes in November 1550, for the sake of preserving public order. In the vast majority of parishes that decision was accepted without fuss, although Ludlow was not the only place to set its altar stones carefully on one side, against the possibility of further change. Such provision was itself a concession of the right of the king's ministers – and, increasingly, the young king himself – to settle external forms of religion.

The April 1552 Act of Uniformity, and the prayer book annexed thereto which was introduced the following November, provided just such a lead. In reformed quarters, 1549 had all along been seen as a compromise: only the pace of further change was at issue. Cranmer, though considering the retention of certain ceremonies a mere sop for a people 'not having yet learned Christ', advised caution, mindful of the distinction between religious change dictated by a powerful, adult king and innovation that might be construed as the imposition of a protestant faction during a minority. The existing prayer book, though, had outlived its day. Most of the conservative bishops involved in its compilation had lost influence, and while continental protestants mocked its half-hearted innovations, Gardiner, much to Cranmer's annoyance, initially 'approved of' the 1549 book and subsequently cited it in his defence of the real presence in communion, a notion now discredited by every leading figure within the English church.

Drafted with input from Cranmer, Ridley, Martin Bucer and Peter Martyr, the new prayer book swept away remaining Catholic ceremonies, developed and enhanced the services of matins and evensong in a tacit recognition that not everyone felt comfortable with a weekly communion, and introduced significant alterations to the sacraments of baptism, confirmation and burial. Prayers for the dead went unmentioned, and a reshaped funeral service destroyed, in Diarmaid MacCulloch's words, 'the sense of continuing communion between living and dead which had been such a striking feature of late medieval religion'.[10] The most radical changes of all, however, were reserved for the communion service, which no longer bore much resemblance to the Catholic mass: prayers were omitted, traditional vestments forbidden and the altar replaced with a wooden table.

The influence of Swiss reformers, particularly of Heinrich Bullinger, is to the fore here; indeed, there is what future ages would term a Calvinist slant to these revisions. As finally hammered out in his vastly influential *Institutes*, Calvin's theology accepted several elements found in Lutheranism – the supremacy of scripture as a regulator of faith, and justification by faith alone in particular. However, he also asserted that those 'elected' by Christ for salvation could not lose grace: the so-called doctrine of predestination. Calvin rejected both Luther's forthright insistence that Christ's body and blood were present at the eucharist and the 'sacramentarian' beliefs of Zwingli. For Calvin, the eucharist embraced a 'sacramental presence', where Christ's body and blood fed the souls of the faithful elect, while the bread and wine fed their bodies. Wary of breaking the Commandment prohibiting worship of graven images, Calvin rejected much of the ceremony and ritual retained by Lutherans. The English church seemed to be moving, if hesitantly, in the same direction.

While conservatives deplored the direction, radicals thought even the hesitation regrettable. John Knox, taken up by the duke, to Cranmer's irritation, and considered briefly by Northumberland for the see of Rochester, protested in characteristically forthright fashion against the retention of kneeling communicants, echoing pressure from Hooper and other like-minded clergy. The council was generally sympathetic but still shared Cranmer's doubts about 'glorious and unquiet spirits, who can like nothing not after their own fancy'. Nevertheless, just as the new prayer book was going to press, counsellors added on their own authority the so-called 'black' rubric, originally tipped in as an addition to the book rather than being reset in red ink as with other explanatory passages, explaining that kneeling implied nothing more than due respect and order. Maybe this was intended as a snub for Cranmer, or perhaps it should be seen as a response to the young Edward VI's increasingly strident expressions of religious evangelism.

If snub it was, this was no isolated gesture. Financial tensions were souring Cranmer's relationships with fellow counsellors. The administration was hungry for cash and the church was, as ever, a tempting target. In March 1551 the council recognized the king's immediate need for 'a mass of money' and accepted that commissioners should be empowered to seize church plate. But moves portrayed as the necessary alleviation of national poverty could also appear – often all too convincingly – as the gratuitous self-enrichment of privy counsellors and favoured adherents. A disillusioned archbishop hardly needed persuading that mammon ruled at court. Attempts to reduce the landed wealth of numerous bishoprics during 1552 and 1553 came uncomfortably close to home. Gardiner's replacement as bishop of Winchester, John Ponet, lost £3000 worth of episcopal lands in return for a salary of £1333 in 1551, and after Tunstall's deprivation, plans to divide the bishopric of Durham in two and hand its lands to the crown were frustrated only by Edward's death.

Cranmer, as he well realized, was defending a weak position: if bishops were indeed royal officers, their powers of jurisdiction founded upon the royal supremacy, was it not proper that they should be rewarded as royal functionaries and spared the burden of widespread estates? A compliant episcopate was useful to the council as an administrative tool, but bishops were not now allowed to forget the source of their power, particularly when some reformers were questioning scriptural authority for the office itself.

These tensions are illustrated by the fate of Cranmer's efforts to introduce a reformed code of canon law in the parliamentary session of 1553. His every attempt was frustrated by a council and consensus of common lawyers determined to prevent any extension of ecclesiastical jurisdiction. They are seen also in the complicated evolution of the archbishop's Forty-two Articles, a long-awaited doctrinal statement of the new English faith. Cranmer, as ever, took advice widely and progress was slow. The council's own amendments to his list, and its studied insult in referring a resubmitted draft to the six evangelically minded royal chaplains, may have led to few alterations but underlined a breakdown in trust. The Articles were finally issued by council in June 1553, when the king had less than a month to live; even at that late date they were busily circulated for subscription by Cranmer and his bishops.[11]

If Northumberland and Cranmer could agree on little else by 1553, they cooperated to demolish the remaining structures of religious conservatism. The Articles, while coming too late to make any impact on the Edwardian church, gave a final twist to the dagger in the back of conservative theology, specifically condemning Catholic teaching not just on purgatory and good works, which was only to be expected, but also on transubstantiation. Predictably, they walked more carefully through the minefield of conflicting protestant teaching: here, as Christopher Haigh writes, there was only 'theological compromise and determined ambiguity'.[12] Although they are employed in a somewhat different theological context, several articles are borrowed almost word for word from the German Augsburg Confession. Those powerless bugaboos, the anabaptists, could alone be denounced unambiguously, and denounced they were. Eighteen of the Forty-two Articles attack specifically anabaptist views. Cranmer's concentration on an easy target suggests a middle-aged man exaggerating the dangers of his younger days, for while anabaptists, in the broad, pejorative sense of the word, were far from unknown in England, they never posed a significant threat to the established church.

The late appearance of these new articles of faith is symptomatic of the problems that confronted, and ultimately frustrated, King Edward's reformation. Like the Catholic reaction that followed under Mary, the changes introduced by politicians and clergy never enjoyed time in which to put down roots. All along there were tensions between the reformed churchmen themselves: while some assisted enthusiastically in the erection of a reformed state church, for others the true church of Christ was a small brotherhood of the godly, men and women receptive to the written and spoken word of God, tested by enforced Henrician conservatism or by the worldly vacillations and half-measures of successive minority administrations.

This vision of two churches – an 'invisible', pure, small body and a 'visible' national body that was either corrupt or potentially so – infuses the writings of Edwardian protestants and Marian exiles and foreshadows the views of many stricter protestants or 'puritans' in the reign of Elizabeth. From one viewpoint, this distinction amounted to a realistic assessment of popular support for reform, taken by a new church dependent on the goodwill of a young king and his worldly ministers. Catholic resistance in England, the religious element in the 1549 rebellions, the slow initial progress of reformed religion among the masses, were to the 'zealots' all confirmation that Antichrist was at work in the world, stiffening and subverting the ignorant majority. Here were no grounds for self-doubt; the godly must needs suffer through ignorance and malice. Clerical discipline over the church as a whole was, at least initially, considered a tool of popery, inappropriate for the propagation of true religion: the secular magistrate was to wield the sword of discipline, the preacher to rely on the power of his word. By 1553 though – so slow was progress towards the new Jerusalem – Ponet, Latimer and others in positions of authority were calling for a restoration of excommunication, regarded by many protestants as a popish abuse of authority. Such censures were seen as a necessary protection for the wider community of Christians against the determinedly ungodly and the downright wicked.

Today, perhaps, it is insufficient to set all the blame on Satan and his legions. More down-to-earth explanations for the slow conversion of English hearts and minds may help persuade a modern audience. The familiar is frequently popular; change must enjoy time in which to earn the security of old custom. England's clerical patronage system, moreover, survived the vicissitudes of the reformation little altered. If the dissolution had taken many advowsons away from monastic houses, most had been presented instead to new lay landlords, for whom considerations of property generally outweighed any commitment to a particular form of religion. Livings could only be filled when an incumbent died or resigned. The achievement of conformity through the wholesale introduction of a like-minded clergy would have involved riding roughshod over the interests of the county families of Tudor England, an uncongenial task far beyond any sixteenth-century government.[13] Failure even to attempt the impossible, however, was scorned by the more zealous protestants who viewed such pusillanimity as a breaking faith with God. Parishioners were being abandoned to ignorance and sin. Hooper and Latimer pleaded with Edward and with his ministers to repent, reform and not to try the patience of the Lord.[14]

The recent rehabilitation of Northumberland has weakened Wilbur Jordan's argument that the choice of his successor was one made by Edward VI and foisted upon an unwilling royal servant.[15] Nevertheless, we should not conclude that the intelligent, affable, imperious young king had been, and remained in 1553, a mere cipher. That would be to ignore the realities of politics in a personal monarchy. Northumberland, admittedly embarked on policies that at no point ran against the king's known preferences, was of course aware of Edward's approaching majority, and ordered Cecil and Sir William Petre, the king's secretaries, to keep the boy fully informed on affairs of state. While Edward may not yet have been taking an active role in the making of policy, the fact that he would do so on a day not now far distant made it vital to win his unforced consent for important decisions. To this end the duke had bent not only his considerable personal charm, but also every patronage opportunity inherent in his position. Sir John Gates, vice-chamberlain and captain of the guard, remained his loyal follower, reporting all comings and goings at court. The king's tutors, William Thomas and Sir John Cheke, were also in full accord with the duke. So too was one closer than any other to the young Edward, Sir Henry Sidney, Northumberland's son-in-law, who, according to one ambassador, 'had acquired so great an influence next to the king that he was able to make all of his notions conform to those of the duke'. The deep mutual affection between king and subject is beyond doubt. Finally succumbing to what John Hayward calls 'the invincible malignity' of pulmonary tuberculosis, Edward died late in the afternoon of 6 July 1553, cradled in Sidney's arms.

It had been obvious for some time that Edward's days were numbered: contracted the previous winter, his disease had made inexorable and all too visible progress. The course of events by which the royal succession was altered in favour of the duke of Suffolk's daughter, fifteen-year-old Jane Grey – granddaughter of Henry VIII's younger sister Mary and married since May 1553 to Northumberland's son – forms yet another obscure chapter in the history of Tudor court politics. We have a draft in Edward's hand of the 'devise' for the succession, but the survival of this rambling and impractical document may mislead. The king was set against his eldest sister's succession, and he also ignored Elizabeth's claim, presumably on the grounds of illegitimacy, but it is improbable that in so great a matter a dying boy could have persuaded his adult counsellors to any course not in accord with their own inclinations. We may suspect in the decision to crown Queen Jane a general conspiracy undertaken by those who stood to lose by Mary's accession. There is now some reluctance to hold Northumberland solely responsible, though such hesitation is perhaps misplaced. All too aware of the princess's personal animosity the duke dreaded the prospect of a Queen

Mary, and the suspicion remains that he was determined to retain his position, come what may. It has been argued from the evidence of his correspondence with Cecil that Northumberland had wearied of power, longing only for a quiet retirement on his estates. Though perhaps tinged with hypochondria, ill-health certainly dogged the duke. As evidence, however, letters addressed to a single correspondent can too often fall into a conventional stylistic pattern for repeated expressions of weary resignation to carry weight.

Lay the responsibility where we will, the gamble was compromised, at Edward's death, by failure to secure Jane's rival. So incredible an oversight can only partly be explained by the unexpected speed of events, and by the apparent success of Mary's household in persuading Northumberland that the princess trusted his many protestations of loyalty and intended to accept the council's will. This still leaves questions unanswered. Edward's demise, though at the end mercifully swift, cannot possibly have come as a surprise to those in daily attendance upon him. The council was best placed to chart the progress of his decline, and events in late June 1553 show it taking precautions expected upon the imminent death of the monarch, summoning peers to London, increasing the night watches, securing Tower prisoners and calming the fears of foreign ambassadors. After the event, following the precedents of 1509 and 1547, Edward's death was kept secret for three days while attempts were made to forestall trouble and, belatedly, to detain Mary. Jane was then proclaimed in London, and, the news spreading, as far afield as Beaumaris in Wales and, on 27 July, Kilkenny in Ireland. Perhaps the duke judged that, faced with a declaration of the succession backed by the old council and by the force of Edward's will, Mary would be powerless to oppose him. Although many of Mary's supporters, including members of a recently arrived embassy from Charles V, also saw no prospect of her succession, this proved a fatal delusion.

Mary, lodged at Hunsdon in Hertfordshire, had sympathizers close to the king and was well informed. She set out on the night of 4 July for her estates in Norfolk, travelling via the houses of sympathizers. The gauntlet was cast at Northumberland's feet when she proclaimed herself queen at her own manor of Kenninghall on 9 July. Northumberland's policies of financial retrenchment now helped ensure the collapse of all his dreams: with his gendarmes disbanded, and no mercenary force closer than the Scottish border, the succession was left dependent on a stark choice of loyalties, exercised by those not sufficiently far from the scene to be able to wait upon events: the counsellors and courtiers in London, and the nobility, landowners and citizens of East Anglia. That choice, it soon grew clear, favoured Henry VIII's daughter and made possible the sole successful Tudor rebellion.

The decision was perhaps more finely judged than is at times allowed, for some East Anglian towns – notably King's Lynn, Great Yarmouth and Boston – showed at least an inclination towards Queen Jane, basing their decisions upon the capricious calculations of local politics rather than upon any loftier consideration.[16] Nevertheless, success took on its own momentum, the waverers going along with the majority. Perhaps it was the force of Henry VIII's will, backed by statute, which ensured overwhelming support for the

Marian cause, rather than simple respect for the legitimacy of her birth. Perhaps it was, but that simple respect should at no time be disregarded. Tudor society had a very close and very proper regard for the principles of inheritance.

For all her initiative and strength of character, Mary's success owed a great deal to the shortcomings of her opponents. Edward's counsellors might proclaim their choice, but the council's formal authority had died with the sovereign, and in any case its membership united only tentatively behind Northumberland. Jane's claim was itself weak, passing over as it did not only Mary and Elizabeth, but also Mary Stuart and Jane's own mother, the duchess of Suffolk. Rather surprisingly, Northumberland failed abjectly as a military commander. Having assembled a strong force with which to confront Mary, an appreciation of his rival's resources, the uncertain quality of troops hastily pressed to his command and, finally, the duke's loss of nerve ensured that the issue was settled without battle.[17] Mary was joined by increasing numbers of the local gentry, by King Edward's counsellors and by loyal peers. A majority of the council in London, led by the earl of Arundel, abandoned Jane. Northumberland marched to Cambridge, but with his army wracked by desertions he there performed a volte-face, proclaiming Mary as queen and submitting patiently to arrest. Although ready to publish the final, despairing profession of Catholicism from a man clearly distracted by the turn of events, Mary's new regime showed Northumberland no mercy. The duke was executed along with his intransigent associates, Sir John Gates and Sir Thomas Palmer, in August 1553.[18]

9 Queen Mary's Regime: England 1553–8

1557–8	Influenza epidemic
January 1558	Loss of Calais
November 1558	Deaths of Queen Mary and Cardinal Pole; accession of Elizabeth I

If recent revisionism has transformed the 'Good Duke' into a pragmatic muddler, and 'Black John' Dudley into a capable and well-intentioned states-man, what has it made of 'Bloody Mary'? Current interpretations shift our focus from the bigoted creature of English protestant tradition, some going so far as to present us instead with an astute and determined monarch whose twin policies of dynastic security through a Habsburg marriage and religious reconciliation with Rome met with initial success, only to be undone by gynaecological misfortune. Marriage with Philip of Spain was, undoubtedly, a gamble, and the pathetic picture of Mary in 1558, haunted by ever less credible delusions of pregnancy, displays in failure the extent of the risk taken. The situation two years into the reign, however, with the queen to all appearances pregnant and a nation manifestly enthusiastic over the prospect of an heir, presents the observer with a fleeting vision of what might have been.

The new monarch's position in August 1553 appeared far from secure. Mary was the first queen regnant in England's history, the turbulent and never fully recognized reign of Henry I's daughter Matilda in the twelfth century apart. Henry VIII's nightmares had materialized. At the same time, she could draw comfort from more auspicious omens. No viable male claimant was on hand to challenge for Mary's throne, while the many recent pledges of loyalty ex-pressed during the ferment of rebellion bolstered her immediate authority. The country enjoyed peace, and Northumberland's swift downfall had helped ensure that there was a strong field from which her officials and servants might be drawn.

At the heart of the court there was inevitable upheaval. Principal privy chamber offices fell into the hands of apolitical gentlewomen, though Mary's reliance on the tried and trusted senior officials of her former household at Hunsdon, men like Sir Robert Rochester, controller, and Sir Henry Jerningham, vice-chamberlain and captain of the guard, ensured that the privy chamber continued to exercise a vital role, both in providing the queen with information and in governing access to the royal person. Elsewhere, changes were more subtle. Mary's privy council, which numbered forty-three by October 1553, and which remained close to that size throughout her reign, was considerably larger than those of both her father in the 1540s and her sister in the 1560s.

The efficiency of any large privy council has been questioned, and that presided over by Mary was for long thought to be riven by faction, illustrat-ing both the queen's lack of discrimination in appointment and her inability to instil in servants the respect due a monarch. Such an interpretation, however, ignores the circumstances of Mary's succession; in the formation of her council the ambitions of three groups had to be accommodated. First came those who had rallied to her cause in July 1553; in appointing the likes of Edward Waldegrave and the earls of Bath and Sussex, all negligible as politicians in the days ahead, Mary recognized that the first obligation of a counsellor was unswerving loyalty. Attention had also to be paid to opponents of Northumberland's regime, men like the old duke of Norfolk and Stephen Gardiner, and also to many nominal backers of the last administration who were able to trade on the monarch's inclination to mercy and her obvious need for experienced counsel. Such men varied in the degree of support they had given Northumberland. While the most able statesman among them – Lord Paget – had given only the most reluctant backing to Jane Grey, the earls of Arundel and Pembroke, whose support had been, if grudging, more manifest, were also able to maintain that loyalty to the queen and distrust of Northumberland had at last prevailed in their deliberations. The capable Sir William Petre, Sir John Gage and Sir Thomas Cheyney were easily assimilated into the new regime. Selections, though, were made with caution. Of the thirty-three members of Edward's last council, only thirteen retained or had regained their places by November 1558.

A distinction must be drawn between the notional strength of the council and the numbers involved in day-to-day deliberations at the council table. Excluding those appointed through early necessity or as a sole result of loyalty to the queen, what we might term the working council was much smaller; according to David Loades's figures, thirty out of the fifty-one counsellors appointed by Mary during the course of her reign attended fewer than 20 per cent of the council meetings for which they were eligible.[1] The assumption of power and influence by the Edwardian politiques has been at times portrayed as a coup within government, an argument that would be more convincing were there evidence of resentment on the part of those relegated to subsidiary roles.[2]

The significance of council divisions may be exaggerated. Such dissent as there was is inconsistent, focusing as it does upon the conflicting ambitions of Paget and Stephen Gardiner, restored as bishop of Winchester and appointed lord chancellor in August 1553. Given mutual ambition, and Gardiner's fiery temperament, it is perhaps surprising that more serious discord was avoided. Disagreement in council turned on specific matters. Before Mary announced her intention to marry Philip of Spain, late in October, the majority of her council either backed Gardiner's opposition to the union or waited upon events. Paget encountered little support in advocating the course his queen eventually adopted. When Mary and Gardiner both wished to punish Princess Elizabeth in the aftermath of Wyatt's rebellion, however, the majority fell in behind Paget, and leniency. After Gardiner's death in 1555, signs of tension within the council appear to dissolve.

If we have at times been guilty of misinterpreting Marian politics there is a convenient scapegoat to hand: the foreign ambassador. Colourful and quotable, the dispatches of Charles V's envoy, Simon Renard – backed by the less well-informed reports of his French and Venetian counterparts Noailles and Michieli – recall many of the problems raised by Chapuys's communications twenty years earlier. Renard's letters eloquently convey the ambassador's own fears and display the natural tendency of one in a strange land to discern everywhere the work of 'factions' hostile to his master. Renard's dispatches, particularly after the arrival of Philip, who disliked and ignored him, also display an irritating self-absorption, which distorts the tale he tells. Noailles, busily attempting to disrupt the Anglo-Spanish amity, is hardly less partial. Nevertheless, as with Michieli's description of turmoil in the Commons during the 1555 session, the ambassador can on occasion light a torch in the darkness – it is, as ever, simply a case of judging how far to trust the shadows cast.

Ambassadorial evidence has for too long been allowed to decide a question of still more fundamental importance, that of the extent to which Mary, a woman carrying out what many regarded as man's work, determined her own policy. One dispatch from Renard has the queen, following unsatisfactory discussions on the problem posed by Princess Elizabeth, telling her council that they would never have defied her father's wishes so blatantly, and in spite of some vigorous recent attempts to present Mary as the mastermind behind state policies, the evidence is far from clear.[3] It is, nevertheless, notable how the principal goals of Mary's administration bear an intensely personal stamp. The longer struggle to restore the pre-reformation church was always vulnerable to the combined effects of shifting international politics, papal mistrust and shortage of time, but in the choice of her husband the queen demonstrated quite unambiguously that she alone was mistress of events.

There was never any question that the queen would marry, both to provide the country with an heir and to secure for herself the advice and guidance of a consort; Mary's age – she was thirty-seven in 1553 – demanded that the choice be made with dispatch. There were two viable candidates: Charles V's son and heir Philip, and Edward Courtenay, son of Henry VIII's victim, the marquess of Exeter, newly restored to his father's earldom of Devon, a handsome if intellectually and morally undistinguished young man in his midtwenties. Mary's choice, though, was clear: only some unforeseen diplomatic crisis would frustrate a Habsburg alliance. Events abroad in fact worked in her favour. Wishing to retire from public life, but facing a consequent obligation under the terms of Habsburg dynastic agreements to partition his lands between his own family and that of his younger brother Ferdinand, the Emperor Charles also saw the advantages of an English match for his son. The crown matrimonial of England would help guarantee for Philip – Philip II of Spain from 1556 – Habsburg possessions in the Low Countries, territories which showed a preference for rule by the Austrian branch of the family. Paget, who had for some years upheld the Imperial alliance, perceived the strength of Mary's determination and set himself at the head of those favouring the match with Philip. Gardiner, assured of his ability to persuade an inexperienced queen and apparently the only counsellor convinced of Courtenay's merits as opposed to the man's convenience, backed the English candidate so obstinately that his influence with the queen rapidly waned.[4] A treaty of marriage was approved by the end of 1553.

The speed with which the treaty was concluded illustrates mutual determination. Philip is granted the title of king but is tied to a string of provisions limiting his exercise of actual power. England is to remain at peace with France, unfettered by existing hostilities between the emperor and Henry II. Should the marriage prove childless and Mary predecease him, Philip is to have no further executive authority and no say in the succession. On the other hand, any child born to the couple will inherit England, the Low Countries and the Franche Comté; and should Philip's son by his first marriage die without issue Spain and all her possessions in the Mediterranean and the New World will also pass to Mary's offspring. Five years before, the Scots had agreed to marry their young queen into the royal house of France. Now the queen of England was, of her own free will, allying England to the other great continental power bloc, with what long-lasting dynastic implications no one could tell.

The treaty guaranteed England's independence, but many of Mary's subjects placed no trust in the terms of a treaty; the queen, they feared, would inevitably allow her new husband to dictate policies against the nation's best interests. The marriage was as unpopular with the Spanish estates, and with Philip himself. His true feelings are revealed in a declaration written into the Spanish records in January 1554, where he asserts that the forthcoming treaty should bind him to no course prejudicial to his own interests and those of his heirs. Fears on both sides, though, were irrelevant in the face of dynastic necessity. Englishmen disliked the notion of a Spanish match, but they were no more enamoured of continued uncertainty over the succession. With hindsight, and with the ghastly example of Darnley in Scotland ten years on, we may conclude too that Mary's marriage to Philip, for all the eventual disillusionment, was preferable to a union with the unsavoury Courtenay. In pursuing the line she did, the queen was only making the best of circumstances.

The sole manifestation of serious trouble emerged in January 1554. Four simultaneous uprisings were planned for the spring, but the incompetent dabblings of both Courtenay, disappointed in his suit for the queen but hoping instead for the hand of Princess Elizabeth, and the duke of Suffolk, pardoned for his leading role in his daughter's coup yet incapable of learning from good fortune, helped an alerted government nip three of them in the bud. Fresh memories of Northumberland's enterprise discouraged several would-be rebels. The surviving rebellion, however, was based in Kent, thus posing, like the peasants' revolt of 1381 and Jack Cade's insurrection in 1450, an immediate threat to the capital. By the last week of January, Sir Thomas Wyatt, son of Henry VIII's courtier-poet, a leading gentleman in the county and an experienced soldier, had some 3000 men in the field and high hopes of aid from France, whose ambassador had been embroiled in the plot from an early stage. Wyatt's power overawed the loyalist Kent gentry, leaving London, briefly, undefended. Mary, though, displayed great courage when addressing citizens in the Guildhall on 1 February, demanding their loyalty in the crisis and promising them that she would marry her foreign prince only with the assent of both council and kingdom. Hasty measures to assemble an adequate force in the middle of winter proved sufficient. Wyatt's insurgents circled London, gathering support, but when they at last approached from the west his army dwindled, Ludgate was barred against him, and following a sharp skirmish he surrendered at Temple Bar. After some thought of clemency Wyatt was executed, along with ninety of his followers. Despite their assertions that the rising was intended only to frustrate a Spanish marriage, suspicions that the rebels had been inspired by Edwardian protestantism, or worse still, had aimed at some more radical alteration in the state, were sufficient to send Suffolk, Jane Grey and her husband Guildford Dudley to the block, and, briefly, both Courtenay and Princess Elizabeth to the Tower.[5]

To the chagrin of Renard, Mary refused to permit further executions. The queen's distrust of Elizabeth was, however, aggravated by these events. She set this particular problem aside, discountenanced any attempt to conciliate or convert her sister, refused to recognize Elizabeth as her successor until the month before her death, and either took refuge in fantasies of pregnancy or left the issue resignedly to God. Fearing the succession of Mary Stuart, then Dauphine of France, Philip worked constantly to reconcile the sisters, hoping to marry Elizabeth to his own client Emmanuel Philibert, duke of Savoy, but Elizabeth balked at the prospect, while Mary preferred to keep a potential rival under surveillance at home.

Many of those who had acknowledged the strength of her title and supported Mary in the crisis of July 1553 did not share the queen's belief in a restored Roman Catholic church. Indeed, there was some initial confusion over Mary's own position. Her first declarations specify only such generalities as freedom of worship for Roman Catholics, and she allowed herself to be proclaimed supreme head of the English and Irish churches on 1 October. By late autumn, however, the queen was making her intentions clear: Roman authority was to be restored, employing the authority of crown in parliament to pull down that which had earlier been set up. Some counsellors remained uneasy at the prospect of reconciliation. Thomas Thirlby, bishop of Norwich, and the leading peers under Paget, Arundel and Pembroke, favoured a return to the religious status quo of January 1547. Though appreciating the wishes of their mistress, they feared for the future of church land now in lay hands. Mary weighed such doubts and proceeded cautiously, accepting the advice of Charles V and subordinating reconciliation to Rome to the completion of marriage negotiations. She and the more hesitant members of her council were, after all, united in their determination that the Edwardian religious statutes should be swept away.

There was little resistance in the face of such resolve, for the Edwardian church was in utter disarray. Convinced reformers, eventually some eight hundred of them, departed for the continent, where they set about making sense, in their writings and in private debate, of the swift, providential turn of events.[6] French and Dutch evangelicals welcomed to England under Edward VI and now obliged to depart, such as John à Lasco and Peter Martyr, spent

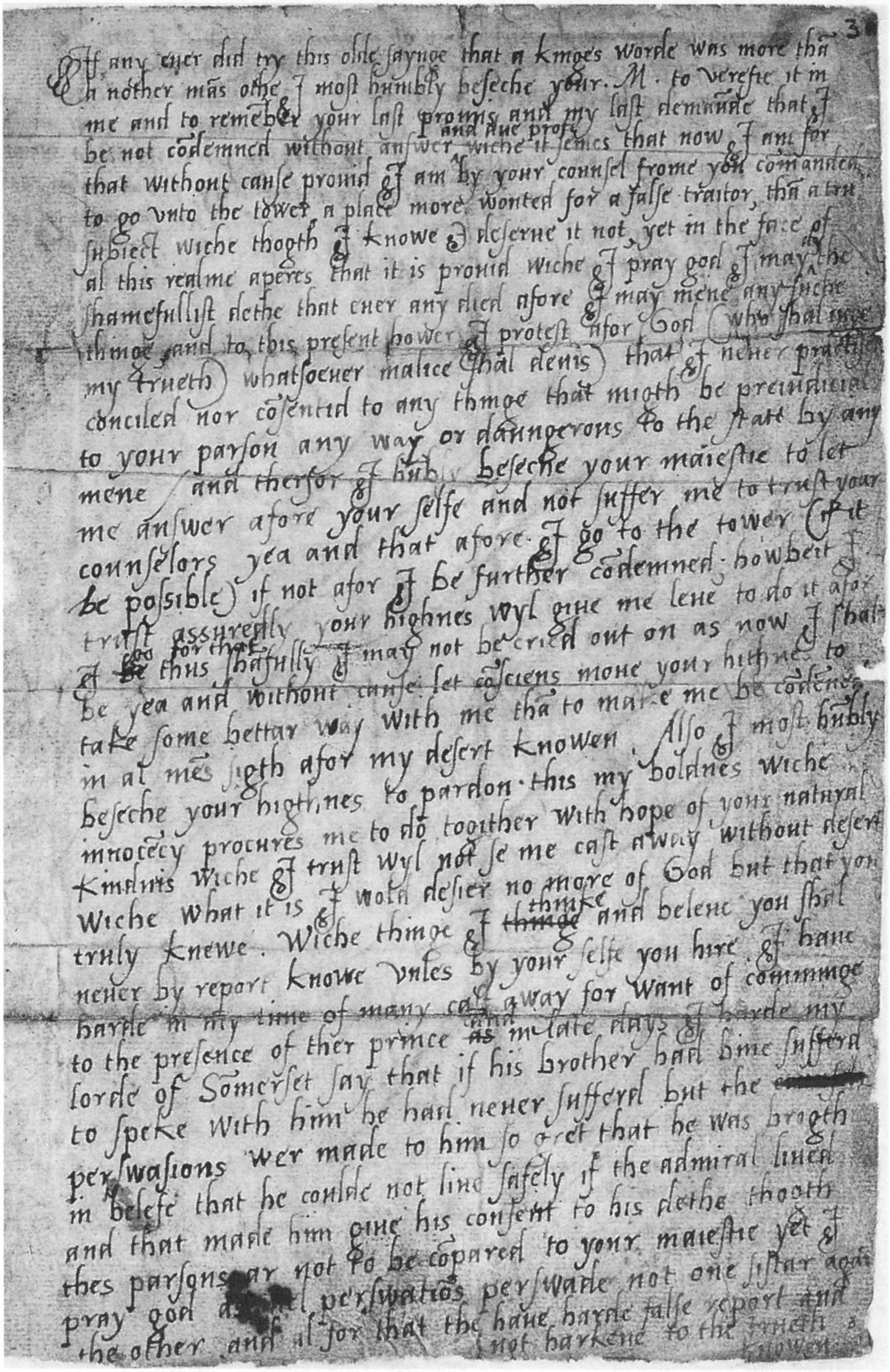

Plate 11 Letter from Princess Elizabeth to Mary I, 16 March 1554. Insisting upon her innocence of any complicity in Wyatt's rebellion, Elizabeth begs her sister not to believe malicious reports against her.

Source: Public Record Office

a troubled winter looking for alternative homes, and then added their weight to a propaganda campaign waged through the Swiss and German presses. This campaign, in its attempts to write up the Edwardian reforms for an educated readership on the continent, mirrored similar efforts sponsored to the opposite end by Mary's administration.[7]

At home, deprived Catholic bishops were restored without delay. Cranmer, offering to defend Edwardian innovation and openly protesting against the revival of the mass, was committed to the Tower in September, sentenced to death for treason in November (a sentence which under the common law stripped him of his see), and attainted in December. But Mary did not wish to see so gross a heretic die for treason, and for a while he was spared. From 1553, hundreds of protestant ministers – many unwilling to reject marriages contracted since 1549 – were deprived, at least 240 in Norwich diocese alone. Even Wyatt's nationalist rebellion failed to inspire any marked protestant resistance, most of those gentlemen who dared to take up arms coming, so far as we can tell, from the ranks of Henrician conservatives. Set against the largely non-political protestant propaganda of Mary's first years – to suffer for God was seen by many protestant exiles as preferable to resistance against a legitimate queen – Catholic authors like Miles Huggarde and John Christopherson gave aggressive support to the regime. Whether from novelty or commitment, London churches were full for the first services after the old fashion, while in April 1554 a staged disputation at Oxford between Catholic theologians, and Cranmer, Latimer and Ridley, produced the expected condemnation of evangelical beliefs.

Yet Edwardian forms survived, particularly in London and East Anglia. The very word protestant first became commonplace in England during Mary's reign, used by conservatives and evangelicals alike. Among the credulous and the wistful, rumours circulated that Edward VI was still alive: he followed in an ancient tradition of resurrected English kings. Reformist literature was acquired and circulated – an Index of prohibited books issued in 1555 and subsequent drastic penalties threatened against anyone possessing such subversive texts having little effect – and clandestine services catered for scattered rural congregations. More significant, in the long term, were the protestant communities noted in towns such as Colchester and Ipswich after 1553: small, harassed but resilient. Wherever there were organized congregations of protestants, capable of supplying mutual support, the task of reducing their faith proved all the harder.

Parliamentary opposition to religious legislation might suggest that the reformed religion also retained support in high places. When the Edwardian Acts of Uniformity were overturned in the first Act of Repeal, which came into force in December 1553, some eighty members of the Commons opposed the bill, while a companion bill to enforce church attendance was dropped and efforts to restore the bishopric of Durham foundered in the face of determined lobbying from the burgesses of Newcastle. Such opposition, however, was motivated as much by the fears of interested property holders as by any religious scruple. More serious problems beset Mary's second parliament during April and May 1554, although, again, closer examination suggests that these disputes did not turn on religion. After the catharsis of Wyatt's rising, legislation to facilitate the Spanish marriage passed both Houses without a stir, but the Commons only approved another attempt to restore the bishopric of Durham after a particularly hard-fought debate, while the prospect of full reconciliation to Rome provoked opposition from Paget and his associates in the Lords to measures reintroducing penal statutes against heretics. Mary's furious reaction showed that Paget had misjudged his mistress – he never fully regained her trust – but it was clear enough that the mood of the landowning class which had profited so markedly from Henrician alterations could not now be disregarded. Pending some specific declaration from Rome to guarantee men's titles to monastic lands, efforts at a constitutional reconciliation marked time.

Rome was willing enough to compromise. The opportunity offered by Mary's accession was quickly recognized by Pope Julius III, and by Julius's choice to lead a mission of reconciliation to England, Cardinal Reginald Pole. Then in his mid-fifties, Pole had been for a quarter of a century the most prominent English critic of England's reformation. Favoured with an attractive personality, loyal friends and clients, Plantagenet royal blood and impeccable connections, he had enjoyed a distinguished career in papal politics and had earned the goodwill of numerous European statesmen and clerics. There was a less promising side to his character: no skilful theologian, Pole had to live down increasingly suspect links with Gasparo Contarini's Oratory of Divine Love, extending in the 1540s to an association with the reformist Bernardino Ochino and with others subsequently condemned as heretics. Moreover, he had tactfully withdrawn from his co-presidency of the Council of Trent after deliberations on the theory of justification had closed the door on compromise with the Lutherans. Nevertheless, the queen was in friendly contact with the cardinal from the very start of her reign, and she welcomed Julius's choice of legate. Pole's charm again worked to his advantage. As Mary's ambassador in Brussels, Sir John Mason, suggested in a letter to the queen, 'it would be a right stony heart that in small time he could not soften'.

All, however, was not plain sailing. His open intransigence over the return of church lands – the idealistic Pole saw any policy that left secular landlords in possession as the squalid purchasing of assent for restoration of papal authority – threw doubt on his commitment to reconciliation. Even so, once Philip was in England, Julius was finally persuaded of the need for concessions over church property: he issued a directive to Pole in November 1554, ordering him to provide collective dispensations for all the so-called 'possessioners'. Specific papal instructions overriding his doubts, the way was at last clear for the cardinal's homecoming. Pole, his attainder hurriedly reversed, was received at court on 24 November and, thereafter, events moved with a swiftness unexpected after so dilatory a year. The realm was formally absolved by the legate six days later.

Although Pole still tried to insist that the dispensation promulgated on 24 December was an *ex gratia* concession by the present pope, pressure from all other interested parties ensured that the second Marian Act of Repeal, the statute that restored Roman primacy in England, amounted to a compromise in which secular control over former religious property was left unchallenged. Royal assent to this act in January 1555 permitted Pole to assume at long last the full authority of a papal legate.

Pole's attempts to re-establish the old church have traditionally attracted little sympathy.[8] Following, so the argument goes, the cardinal's personal convictions, efforts to win the hearts and minds of Englishmen and women were subordinated to a preoccupation with the restoration of Catholic ceremonial and with increasingly futile and savage efforts to enforce conformity. Wearied, even frightened by his own brushes with reformist theology, Pole took refuge in personal obedience to Rome and in an increasing adherence to formalism. 'But this I dare say,' he preached, in a rare sermon, 'whereunto Scripture doth also agree, that the observation of ceremonies for obedience sake will give more light than all the reading of Scripture can do.' Times were hard for those who were disobedient, and for those who questioned the prescribed ceremonial. The catalogue of imprisonings and executions – from February 1555 some 300 men and women were burnt, mostly in the southeast, many drawn from the artisan laity – provoked widespread disillusionment. Gardiner, at first supportive, soon came to regard executions as ineffective, while local authorities around London increasingly despaired of eradicating heretical beliefs in their counties. Persecution helped demonstrate that, although many Englishmen and women were content to return to the old ways, Edwardian protestantism had not altogether failed to put down roots. It has also left a lasting stain on Mary's reputation which the most charitable observer finds difficult to wipe away. Making full allowance for the times, and the circumstances that shaped her reign, it remains hard to excuse the actions of a monarch who, faced by no significant external or internal threat, and within the space of a few years, consigned hundreds of her subjects to the flames.

There is, though, another side to such considerations. King Edward's protestant church had also been imposed from above, and while clergy and commentators then and since stressed the need for a vigorous campaign of preaching and renewal, such a campaign would probably have commanded little immediate interest among the bulk of the population, thoroughly disenchanted with the constant turn and turn about in matters of religion. The emphasis placed in ecclesiastical visitations upon rooting out and depriving married priests, and upon assessing the material wealth of the English church, while it highlighted the huge task facing Marian reformers in the wake of Edwardian spoliation, was perhaps not misplaced, given the traditionalism of the English laity, its regularly expressed scorn of married clergy, and given also the significance of symbolism and tradition within the Catholic church.

One is left wondering who stood to be converted by persuasion. Cranmer possibly, and the former archbishop did indeed waver in his rejection of papal supremacy and Catholic ritual. He recanted several times during the final months of his life, after being forced to watch the burning of Latimer and Ridley at Oxford in October 1555. But Cranmer was hardly typical. Mary and Pole were in any case reluctant to spare one so tainted, one who had blatantly betrayed the pope's trust: his trial on heresy charges in September 1555, and his eventual execution in March 1556, hardly come as a surprise. Nor does his final, emphatic reaffirmation of protestant beliefs, made on the morning of his execution. At the end there was no ambiguity. 'As for the pope,' Cranmer cried, 'I refuse him, as Christ's enemy and antichrist, with all his false doctrine.'[9]

For all their backward glances at the vanished world of the 1530s, the queen and Pole accepted that times had moved on, that tastes had changed and that a simple return to the conditions of 1529 was no longer possible. No serious effort was made to restore the major shrines, for pilgrimages, like published *Lives* of saints, had gone out of fashion. The six new religious houses founded in Mary's reign were something of a token effort: they enjoyed a total endowment of only £2000, all of this coming from the crown.

Nor may one entirely dismiss the effects of principled repression. The heresy trials, however horrible their results, at least ensured that large numbers of potential protestant sympathizers, to borrow Latimer's regretful phrase, 'went with the world'. Apathy can sometimes appear indistinguishable from conformity. John Foxe's catalogue of martyrs has never failed to impress later generations, but his *Acts and Monuments* is itself a masterpiece dependent for its popularity upon the chance re-establishment of a regime hostile to much that Mary stood for. It is by no means improbable that persecution, in the context of a longer reign, might have helped cement the return to Rome.

Circumstances, though, conspired against the success of Mary's policies. The death of Julius III in March 1555 and Charles V's reluctance to support Pole's candidature in the conclaves that followed brought, after the brief pontificate of Marcellus II, the aged and acerbic Gian Pietro Carafa to the papal throne as Paul IV. Paul's vigorous support for Tridentine theology, and his deep hostility towards Spain, were soon causing disquiet in England. Carafa, moreover, had long doubted Pole's orthodoxy. Initially, relations remained cordial enough: Paul IV confirmed the English mission; in March 1556, following Cranmer's execution, he ratified Pole's appointment to the see of Canterbury and retained Pole's close friend, Giovanni Morone, as the vice-protector of the church in England. In September 1556, however, Philip's troops invaded the Papal States, and over the next year the situation dramatically worsened. Although England had still not entered the war, Paul revoked all legates in Philip's dominions in April 1557, Morone was arrested on suspicion of heresy in May, and Pole was recalled to Rome the following month, the pope appointing William Peto, a Henrician exile who had once preached against the divorce to Henry VIII's face, as cardinal and legate to England in his place. Peto, now old and ailing, and living in the Observant Friary at Greenwich, prudently declined the honour. Stung into retaliation, Mary refused to allow Paul's messenger into the country, and Pole, with great misgiving – for obedience to the papacy lay at the heart of his own beliefs – ignored the calls for his return.

If Paul's hostility towards Pole had flared up under the political dictates of war, it did not die back once peace was concluded between Philip and the papacy in September 1557. The Inquisition announced formal charges against

Morone, and while Paul restored the archbishopric of Canterbury's legatine status, he refused to restore Pole himself, turning a deaf ear to all appeals lodged by the English ambassador in Rome, Sir Edward Carne. Pole, despairing at such treatment, wrote, then burnt, an apologia defending his orthodoxy and appealed again and again to officials in the Vatican. All such efforts counted for nothing: during the last year of Mary's reign, English affairs in the curia stood still, the pope's hostility to Pole exacerbated by an increasing reluctance to transact formal business of any kind.

Pole's own worldweariness coincides with a loss of confidence throughout the English church. War, poor harvests and a devastating epidemic resembling influenza that swept the country in 1557–8, killing thousands, combined to impress upon contemporaries the magnitude of God's disfavour with the present state of affairs. Here was crisis on the grand scale. A disastrous harvest in 1556 pushed grain and related prices higher, when set against an average for the decade, than in any other year of the century. Lack of statistics – parish registers tended to fall victim to the disease along with incumbents – have led to an underestimation of both epidemic and famine. It now seems possible that the English population fell by 11 per cent in just two years, 1557–9. Perhaps 'influenza' killed Mary herself: reading the unsatisfactory descriptions of the queen's final illness this stands as an unprovable possibility.

An apparent decline in the surviving quantity of Catholic propaganda may also suggest malaise in the re-established church, although the paltry four known titles with a Catholic slant to appear in 1558 can just as easily represent a statistical aberration. The government had shown itself aware of the potential of print, and active in the dissemination of favourable printed propaganda, over the past four years.[10] Protestants abroad certainly seized on every apparent manifestation of God's wrath: the loss of Calais early in 1558 was grist to the mill. Towards the end of the reign, some exiles were insisting openly that tyrannous powers might be resisted, even to the point of violence. Such views, taken up by John Bale, the former bishop of Winchester John Ponet, Peter Martyr, John Knox and Christopher Goodman, had been and would be denounced by their co-religionists in the previous and succeeding reigns, when of course the boot sat on the other foot, yet the evident misfortunes endured by Mary's Catholic England allowed, even encouraged extreme voices to make their point.[11]

Polemical statements, though, do not provide impartial evidence for loss of morale. No one has ever found it easy to measure this elusive factor. That loss, we might suspect, was in any case transient, given permanent significance by Mary's death in November 1558. The hostility of Paul IV was unwelcome, but its significance was limited: as David Loades suggests, 'Rome had never occupied more than a peripheral place in the religious consciousness of Englishmen, and twenty years of constant anti-papal propaganda had also had its effect'.[12] If the church of Pole and Mary eschewed offers of help from the new Jesuit order, and sought to reform itself, the insular approach was broadly popular. The English political nation went cheerily to war in 1557, for their king and queen, and against France and the pope. Military setbacks and domestic calamities in 1557–8 might well have proved passing shadows in a longer reign.

Events in Mary's five parliaments have also received their share of attention in recent years. The old view of a radical House of Commons struggling against the dead hand of Marian reaction now stands discredited. Given the tendency in the 1540s and early 1550s for conservatism in the Lords to act as a brake on pro-protestant policies, there are, indeed, grounds for viewing Mary's parliaments as among the most cooperative in the entire century. Paget's orchestration of opposition in the Upper House during Mary's second parliament frustrated both the heresy bill and a move to bring Philip within the security offered by existing treason legislation, but Paget worked to the agenda set by his personal ambition, and was no protestant: the swift passage of very similar bills only months later shows that the disruptive forces at work in April 1554 had been essentially personal, and short term.

While dissent in the Lords might reflect the dissatisfaction of individual players amid the shifting fortunes of court and conciliar intrigue, that which surfaced occasionally in the Commons could be expected to illustrate wider hostility within the governing classes to some aspect of crown policy. In practice, though, it seldom did. A series of informal coalitions might emerge when legislation touched the raw nerves of family interest, or local privilege, but these could as easily dissolve or mutate with the next point under scrutiny. Difficulties in the Commons during the stormy parliament of 1555 revolved round Mary's restoration of first fruits and tenths to the church, while measures aimed at securing for the crown the property of protestant exiles not surprisingly alarmed many landowners.[13] Troubles encountered in squeezing a subsidy from the 1558 parliament do not necessarily suggest discord between parliament and privy council; a clear majority in both wished to reduce to a minimum the cost of a now unpopular and unsuccessful war.

Issues of property could indeed unite members of both Houses, but the strings of clientage do not appear to have been pulled in opposition to the crown. Individual peers might exercise their right to have a formal protest written into the *Lords Journal* – Viscount Hereford and Lord Cobham did so in 1555 over the restoration of first fruits and tenths – but nothing suggests that they took matters further and organized protest in the Lower House. Concerted protest was in any case more easily considered than achieved. Clients of the earl of Pembroke, the belligerent Sir John Perrot in particular, were quite willing to go against their patron's wishes in the debates on the exiles bill during 1555. Again, though, the motives for discontent might just as easily have been some personal resentment now beyond our grasp; Perrot was notoriously truculent. Henry Peckham opposed Marian religious policy and was eventually executed for his part in the abortive Dudley conspiracy of 1556, complaining of inadequate compensation for land in Sussex restored along with his dukedom to Norfolk. On the other hand, similar opposition from the former warden of New College, Oxford, Ralph Skinner, a man 'with little to lose, and much less to care for', may have been more principled. Without the means to delve into the souls and consciences of

Tudor MPs, surviving evidence seldom permits us to draw more definite conclusions.

With the personnel of revenue offices virtually unchanged under Mary, retrenchment continued to be the order of the day. Marian retrenchment, however, took at first a rather relaxed form. No financial crisis was imminent: Mary inherited a manageable debt of £185,000, one-third of which was owed to foreign bankers. Repayment of such sums highlighted the problems of liquidity confronting all early modern governments, and there was insufficient pressure to subordinate the political to the financial. Keen to restore the wealth of the church, and aware that little would be forthcoming from lay patronage or restitution, Mary regularly forgave and eventually suspended the debts on first fruits and tenths owed by new bishops, and her administration also waived, as a token of goodwill, the unpaid balance of the last Edwardian subsidy: perhaps some £30,000 to £40,000.

Such retrenchment as can be identified was small scale: garrisons in the Calais pale were reduced, and piecemeal sales of crown lands were licensed. After some effort at internal reorganization in February 1554, council commissions were established to examine defined areas of expenditure and, in still greater detail, revenue. But they appear to have achieved very little; household expenditure in the second year of the reign was 14 per cent up on 1552–3, at a time when regular crown revenue was static. By April 1554, the royal debt shows an increase of some 8 per cent on the July 1553 figure, annoying, but no incentive to further reform.

One Edwardian project was pursued. The multiplicity of autonomous revenue courts set up in the wake of the reformation – or rather the proliferation of salaried officials with parallel functions, and the increased level of competition between them – had for some time been a cause of concern. The court of general surveyors had been merged with augmentations at the beginning of Edward VI's reign, and further reform had been in the wind during March 1553, when parliament empowered the king to reorganize revenue courts by letters patent. In January 1554, after the passing of very similar enabling legislation, Mary sanctioned the absorption of the courts of augmentations and of first fruits and tenths by the Exchequer. Of the two, augmentations was the greatest prize; first fruits was possibly included in the merger at a late stage, the leniency shown new bishops suggesting that, in any case, its future was uncertain.

The enhanced Exchequer was not, however, the old writ large. Certainly, the lord treasurer now presided over all revenue administration in the country, the relatively small contributions of the court of wards and the duchy of Lancaster excepted. But, at the acknowledged cost of economic efficiency, both augmentations and first fruits continued to enjoy what amounted to an autonomous procedural existence. Long-term financial savings might be made, and the more modern methods of the newer courts did in time come to influence procedures in the Exchequer proper. More immediately, however, pensions to redundant officials swallowed most of the profit, while the practicalities of government dictated that over 50 per cent of crown revenues between 1555–8 passed through the hands of Nicholas Brigham, officially 'queen's teller', and unofficially a treasurer charged with the administration of funds marked out for Mary's personal use.[14]

The Antwerp money market remained essential, for banking services in England were still rudimentary in comparison with continental developments. Regular repayments on her loans made Mary a reliable risk, her experienced agent in the city, Thomas Gresham, ensuring that further advances were available, if only at a price. These were particularly important in providing the crown with an immediate supply of coin, some of this being used to settle debts in Antwerp itself. Such recirculation was necessary because the debased English specie was unattractive in an international market, and because Mary's agents found licences to export bullion from Flanders hard to secure; debts accumulated by the province's Habsburg rulers dwarfed those sums owed by the English crown.

In assuming that general purse-tightening in England could keep debt within bounds, however, the government overlooked the slow processes of Exchequer accounting and the cumulative burden of interest payments. More stringent measures soon became necessary, and by a complex process involving transfer, reallocation and parsimony, the Antwerp debt was greatly reduced between 1555 and 1557. Recourse was made to domestic taxation. The request for a subsidy from the 1555 parliament – in the first year of two ruinously poor harvests – met resistance, and was granted only through sacrifice of the accompanying fifteenths and tenths and through the acceptance of a new assessment based on a sliding scale for moveable property. Nevertheless, passed it was, while despite considerable foot-dragging and outright non-payment privy seal loans brought in an additional £140,000 in 1556–7 and, after the outbreak of war, in 1557–8.

Renewed conflict with France undid much of this good work. Despite the determination of Mary's counsellors to wage an economically prudent war – and in spite of further sales of crown lands and another subsidy granted by parliament in 1558 – military operations were inevitably very expensive. The administration returned to the Antwerp moneylenders. At her death, Mary bequeathed a debt of between £250,000 and £300,000 to her successor, somewhere near the 1551 level. In one respect only, wartime necessity prompted important economic reform. The revised book of rates, issued in April 1558, recalculated customs duties long rendered anachronistic by inflation, and, despite much initial dismay among the cloth merchants, provided a boost to ordinary finance in the years ahead. In general, however, war encouraged expediency and worked against a necessary restoration of the English currency.

Despite Philip's reservations – his own finances were in particularly dire shape at the time – the kings of France and Spain were again at war early in 1557. Aggravated by the machinations of Paul IV, Henry II's ambitions in Italy, coupled with long-standing frontier tensions round Metz, almost guaranteed trouble. Naturally, Philip hoped that England might be persuaded to join the conflict, particularly since one of the key theatres lay in Flanders.

The English council, weighing the financial consequences and mindful that Mary's marriage treaty had specifically catered for such an eventuality, proved reluctant. Their resistance, though, was gradually undermined. Ambiguities in the treaty – in particular the reaffirmation of a 1546 undertaking to aid the Netherlands in the event of invasion – and the queen's own inclination to support her husband led first to a financial commitment, then to the embarkation of a force of volunteers. Philip had left England after a stay of thirteen months in August 1555, and all Mary's entreaties had failed to lure him back again. Now, though, he swallowed his dislike of the country and its inhabitants in the interests of enlisting an ally for his war, returning for a short visit in March 1557.[15] Hostilities were all but guaranteed after the failure of a still mysterious French-sponsored invasion of England led by the pretender-in-exile Thomas Stafford, which landed at Scarborough in April 1557. Stafford's – indeed, Henry II's – motives remain obscure, but the escapade played into Philip's hands. Mary declared war in June.

The prospect of conflict at first proved popular among an English nobility and gentry hankering after the glamour of the battlefield; the earl of Westmorland, responding to a challenge from a Scots cousin to speak for his own nation rather than for Spain, declared that 'as long as God shall preserve my master and mistress together, I am and shall be a Spaniard to the uttermost of my power'. To begin with all went well. Paul IV was soon forced out of the struggle, and French forces in Italy suffered a series of setbacks. The Scots balked at any serious operation against England, while in Flanders a major French relief force was routed outside the besieged town of St Quentin in August. Arriving – perhaps culpably – late for this engagement, the English contingent under Pembroke joined in the storming of the town, and during the last weeks of the campaigning season Imperial forces consolidated their gains happy in the knowledge that the French had no adequate resources to deploy against them. The contending armies eventually settled into winter garrisons; during October, most of the English troops returned home.

With the recall of the duke of Guise from Italy, however, Henry II plotted an assault on Calais. After the dismal summer campaign France's honour was at stake, and nothing was left to chance. Guise, in command of a fresh army of 20,000 men, was informed by spies in the Pale of weaknesses in the defences, while the English, beset by inefficient intelligence, remained unaware of French intentions until it was too late. Following a brief siege Calais fell on 7 January 1558; the outlying garrisons of Hammes and Guisnes followed within the fortnight. The English forces, run down in the cause of economy, appear to have fought as well as anyone could have expected; the lord deputy of Calais, Lord Wentworth, was subsequently accused of treason, but was acquitted when tried in 1559. French success must be attributed to the tactical wisdom of Guise, to the town's obsolete defences, and to the bitter weather of January 1558, which froze and made passable the natural defences of the Calais marshes. Failure to launch an immediate counterstrike – as Guise's feverish rebuilding shows, the battered defences remained vulnerable – must be put down to a mutual lack of will on the part of the allies.

For the English council the loss of the Pale only confirmed their fears: England had been unable to afford this war. Opinion set firm against throwing good money after bad. They blamed Philip's reluctance to assist, and Anglo-Spanish relations grew every day more bitter. As the result of one short winter campaign, England's last remaining continental possession had fallen permanently under French control.[16]

Dismay following the loss of Calais encouraged significant alterations to the ways in which English armies were recruited. A standing army remained anathema to Englishmen, who held the common soldier in low esteem and refused to contemplate the necessary taxation. Troops, therefore, had to be assembled for particular expeditions. Hitherto, two levying processes had existed side by side. Under one, the crown had ordered individual peers and gentlemen to assemble contingents from among their tenants and servants. Under the other, leading gentry had acted as commissioners, drawing upon musters of able-bodied men in each county to supply quotas of troops. There was nothing inherently anachronistic about any system which could put armies of 30,000 men or more in the field. Henry VIII's two invasions of France, in 1513 and 1544, were both undertaken by formidable armies raised in this way.

Nevertheless, the crises of the 1540s and 1550s, coupled with a general perception that the quality of English soldiery was declining, prompted the council to consider reform. One solution lay in the recruitment of mercenaries, particularly German mercenaries. But the independent German princes, threatened by Charles V, were more interested in bringing about peace between England and France, and their views, and their diplomatic engagements with the contending powers, affected the market. In the costly, complicated business of outbidding rival powers for the most reliable and most experienced troops on offer the English agents were as novices when pitted against the networks established by France. As experience was gained in this game, so the pressing need for such troops slackened. After the 1540s England was not seriously threatened by a modern foreign army for forty years.[17]

An alternative lay in the recruitment of whole armies by contingents drawn from the county muster. With the decline of several great noble families, the dissolution of the monasteries, the rising costs of military equipment and the diminishing gentry households brought about by social change and the effects of inflation, administrations were having to request contingents from an ever greater number of landowners; administrative problems were mounting. In 1543, letters were sent across the south of England to gentlemen considered 'of power to make men' requiring them to supply statistics for able-bodied dependants and tenants, but while many recipients proved to be either dead or indigent, other viable contributors were overlooked. There were also signs in the 1540s that tenants were beginning to disregard the old unwritten customs that obliged them to serve with their lord in time of war. Repeated legislation suggests that the difficulties encountered were hard to overcome.

The system of recruitment from county musters also had drawbacks, associated with its own ancient roots. In theory, musters were organized by local

JPs, under the sheriff, but by the mid-sixteenth century this task had de-volved to specially appointed commissioners. Musters existed to check on compliance with personal military obligations, and although the burdens of maintaining a cavalry horse were amended in 1542, the duty of free men to bear arms was still defined by the 1285 statute of Winchester, confirmed as recently as 1511, under which a man with £10 in lands or 20 marks in goods was required to maintain a complete set of armour. Commissioners might view the able-bodied and specify what arms should be provided, but such obligations were difficult to enforce and were widely evaded: the 1557 musters show how 5889 able men in Sussex assembled between them only 1210 'harnesses', or sets of armour. There was another, still more unnerving problem associated with mustered troops. As the 1536, 1549 and 1554 risings showed, rebellion within the country, a more immediate menace to most Tudor governments than invasion, confronted the militia with divided loyalties; as an instrument of repression it was never wholly reliable.

Nevertheless, to administrations faced with a growing demand for man-power to supply armies in France and Scotland during the 1540s, the estab-lished and 'impersonal' formula of the muster was increasingly preferred to the bureaucratic nightmare arising from constant requests to a myriad local gentlemen. For all the snags of evasion by bribery and dependence on the not always effectual powers of the designated commissioners when set against vested county interest, the main difficulty facing the muster system was the way in which it sat uneasily alongside the older principle of personal contin-gents: large numbers of men might be held outside the county system to supply the commissioners' own retinues. Cromwell envisaged a reform of these anomalies in 1539, and in the 1540s Sir Thomas Wyatt, the future rebel, worked out a scheme which approached the system of 'trained bands' established under Queen Elizabeth, but it was only in 1558 that parliament-ary legislation introduced a system of assessment that spread the costs and obligation across all sections of society: the clause permitting a landlord to continue enforcing military obligations on tenants remained, for all but the great courtiers, a dead letter. Here was a realistic attempt to raise standards, both in the training and the equipping of men, and the attempt worked, even though no English administration could match the ever-increasing resources committed to Spanish and French armies.[18]

10 The Third Kingdom: Ireland, and Beyond, 1529–60

Chronology	
1534–5	Suppression of Kildare's rebellion
February 1536	Lord Leonard Grey appointed lord deputy
February 1537	Execution of Kildare and his five uncles at Tyburn
August 1539	O'Neill and O'Donnell defeated by Grey at Bellahoe
August 1540	Sir Anthony St Leger succeeds Grey as lord deputy
June 1541	Henry VIII declared king of Ireland; execution of Lord Leonard Grey
February 1542	Arrival of first Jesuit mission to Ireland
October 1542	Conn O'Neill created earl of Tyrone
June 1549	New English prayer book ordered to be used in Ireland
February 1550	French envoys establish links with Ulster lords
July 1550	Humphrey Powell licensed to establish printing press in Ireland
June 1555	Papal bull declares Ireland a kingdom
May 1556	Lord Fitzwalter, later earl of Sussex, appointed lord deputy
July 1557	Reformation legislation repealed in Ireland

Compared with the great continental powers – France, Spain and the Empire – both England and Scotland were politically united kingdoms. Both contained dominant language groups, legal forms and social elites. Almost every leading figure in the English and Scottish peripheries – in Wales, Cornwall, much of Ireland, the Western Isles, Caithness, Moray, Orkney and the shared borderlands – considered himself either English or Scots, or at least as a loyal servant of the English or Scottish crowns. This was particularly true of England, with its tradition of centralized government and its medieval ambitions on the continent. Throughout our period, its court and political society would be prepared, with reservations, to accept as English anyone from France, or Ireland, or Wales, or the northern borderland, who behaved in a credibly English fashion and who served the English king.

At the same time, efforts to bring outlying parts of the realm into greater conformity with traditions of government and law found in the south and east of England did not always run smoothly. However much Henry VIII and his ministers might legislate away the differences between lowland and border societies, those borders, whether against Scotland or Gaelic Ireland, remained frontiers, and each demanded particular personal abilities from the men set to govern them. The noble houses of the north – Percys, Dacres and Nevills – and of the Irish march – Butlers and Fitzgeralds – though never as wealthy as the leading court families, nevertheless maintained an ascendancy over their neighbours, an often fragile supremacy founded on crown favour.[1] Alterations that worked well enough in Wales, where the absence of a military frontier fostered a demilitarized society, where the crown was by far the biggest landholder, and where dominant families were closely associated with crown policies, fared less well in these areas. A continuing frontier dictated the priorities of local landowners. Operating within a culture of castles, raiding parties and, by southeastern standards, general lawlessness, great subjects could only serve their royal masters by developing armed retinues and, importantly, by maintaining a continuous personal presence in their countries. These proved costly burdens. At his death in 1489, the fourth Percy earl of Northumberland was spending 42 per cent of his income on retaining a broad cross-section of Northumbrian society. However, that which appeared essential to the local noble smacked of ambition to the distant crown: mutual suspicions of bad faith were never far away.

As the comparison with Wales suggests, parallels carry weight only so far. Each military borderland sustained its own characteristic individualism, fashioned by relations between the English crown and two very different competing societies. The Anglo-Scottish borders, though traditionally unruly and remote, reflected changing relationships between two sovereign powers, wary of disturbances along a land frontier. Anglo-Scottish amity might lead to concerted efforts at coercing the intransigent and the unruly, while antagonism fuelled border raids and larger-scale operations in which the borderers north and south played an enthusiastic and prominent part. With France's involvement in Scotland during the 1540s and 1550s, border unrest became one part of a wider European conflict, and gradually frontier society merged into the dominant shared cultures developing on both sides of the border.

Conditions were very different on the other frontier, with Gaelic Ireland. Here there was no separate state opposing English ambitions, no predatory continental power with serious designs of mischief or self-aggrandizement. Conflicts were internalized, between the anglicized and Gaelic parts of Ireland, and between a developing English mainland society and an increasingly alienated Anglo-Irish border culture, a border society which, as the years went by, tactically and purposefully accentuated its differences from England.

This book is concerned with the fortunes of the two nation states that shared, as they still share, the island of Britain. The seventy years under review, however, coincide with what once was seen as an inexorable and concerted drive by one of those states to impose its will and its systems of law and government over the second largest of the British Isles. That same process may more appropriately be summarized as a period in which successive English attempts at 'reform' in Ireland defeated a succession of statesmen, frustrated and perplexed more than one London administration, and resulted in calamity for the Irish themselves. Ireland is not and never has been England writ small, yet her story is so bound up with that of the English, later, the British crown, that we must consider here the ways in which events and decisions taken in England affected and were influenced by developments across the Irish Sea.

As viewed from London, Ireland presented not one but several distinct problems. The whole island, so Steven Ellis argues, was less a political entity than a debatable ground between English and Gaelic cultural and political systems.[2] As with all borderlands, the social and political balances vary as one travels through. The southern and eastern parts of the island, the so-called Pale round Dublin, the southern coast and its hinterland, had been heavily anglicized for nearly four hundred years following the Norman invasions of the twelfth century. In these regions, the key political relationship was that between the English authorities in Dublin and the predominant Anglo-Norman families – notably the Fitzgerald earls of Kildare and the Butler earls of Ormond.

In their own eyes, the Anglo-Norman aristocracy were Englishmen living in Ireland rather than a hybrid people bridging two cultures. The ninth earl of Kildare's military power was exercised, more often than not, in the service of the crown, and was regarded by most observers as a manifestation of royal authority. Nevertheless, the Anglo-Irish community, at every social level, possessed a sense of distinct identity. They were English, to be sure, but English born in Ireland. Ireland was their mother country, their Gaelic neighbours an unavoidable cultural influence. Seeing themselves as an autonomous 'middle nation' under the English crown, they had long resented the interference of 'foreigners', or 'new' men from England, and the persisting inadequacies and indifference of metropolitan government. Here were several paradoxes, of great significance in the years ahead.

Dublin offered the nearest approximation to a London-style government. There, spasmodically, sat an Irish parliament, complete with its separate houses for lords and commons, the latter rather smaller and geographically less representative than its English counterpart. Until their exclusion following opposition to the royal supremacy in 1536–7, there was also a third house for representatives or 'proctors' of the lower clergy. Parliament consisted of men drawn overwhelmingly from the south and east of the country. English kings generally employed it, if at all, to give statutory effect in Ireland to English legislation.[3] An Irish privy council, with limited executive powers, also met in Dublin from the early sixteenth century: there the governor, appointed by the crown, presided over select peers and administrators in a manner foreshadowing developments in England a generation later. In an effort to bind loyal magnates and gentlemen to royal policies, a larger council coexisted with the privy council, although, again as in England, this met only on great and urgent occasions. From its effective establishment in 1571 the court of Castle Chamber gave Ireland its own close approximation to the English Star Chamber.

Elsewhere, towns – particularly in Leinster, the easternmost of the four traditional provinces, and Munster in the south – provided the crown with bastions of loyalty. Again we have to extrapolate from the few available statistics with caution, but no Irish city approached the size of London, or even Edinburgh. Dublin had between 5000 and 8000 inhabitants by 1600, Galway on the west coast maybe 4000. Cork, Limerick and Waterford in the south were the only other urban centres with a population of more than 2000. All towns of any significance, Dublin included, were governed by their merchant trading oligarchies, as in England, although the degree of intermarriage and dynastic continuity among such oligarchies was frequently far more pronounced. This may reflect the defensive mind-set of these citizens, wary of or at odds with their Gaelic hinterlands. Faithful towns received their reward from a grateful crown in the form of favourable charters, exemptions from customs dues – though these were frequently ignored anyway – and, in the sixteenth century, grants of incorporation.[4]

While English law and systems of central and local administration modelled on English equivalents might have been far from moribund, their application was patchy at best, even in areas close to Dublin. The further into the north and west one travelled, the patchier that influence became. Local landowners serving as sheriffs and JPs administered English forms of local government in the Pale and the south as best they might. In more remote areas, the English structure of government was seldom more than a paper fiction, but the key players were again the resident Anglo-Irish families. They served both as political leaders in the deliberations of the English crown and as an interface between English government in Dublin and the Gaelic lords, for each head of an Anglo-Norman family also exercised his own overlordship in Gaelic society and fitted into those extensive networks of patronage that stretched across the island.

The study of Irish history in this period is bedevilled by the relative paucity of surviving records, and written sources to illuminate the essentially oral culture of Gaelic Ireland are particularly thin on the ground.[5] Such Gaelic literary texts as do survive – genealogies, poetry and chronicles or 'annals' – are difficult tools, particularly for historians used to the products of more bureaucratic systems.[6] Ireland is a small place, though, and the study of one

Plate 12 'Irish costumes', c.1567–76, from *Der Beschrijving der Britsche Eilanden*, by Lucas de Heere.
Source: British Library

kind of record can seldom safely be divorced from the other. When we discuss 'Gaelic society' we tend to have in mind the specific and not necessarily typical customs then prevailing in Ulster, or in parts of Connaught, the westernmost province, where English political influence had long been minimal. Even in those areas, however, an English cultural influence could be discerned, while a majority of those who spoke Irish as their native tongue – perhaps three-quarters of the total population – lived in parts of the country where English customs and mores had established themselves more decisively.

Authority in Gaelic Ireland rested in the lordships, great and small, the balance of power depending on the strength and cunning of individual lords. The lord's power in turn relied heavily on his armed following: on his ability to compel military service and exact tribute known as coyne and livery, in both money and kind, from subordinate territory. At the same time he had to pay for and billet, again on those subordinate lands, the Irish and Scots mercenary soldiers which stiffened these levies, and which might be crucial to victory in battle.

Succession to a lordship was governed by the custom known to the English as tanistry, under which the 'eldest and best' of a surname was nominated as tanist, or designated successor as chief of the family group. The chief was known simply by his patronymic: The O'Neill or The O'More, for example. Competition for a succession was almost invariably subject to complex nego-tiation and alliances. Again, the candidate's strong right arm frequently proved decisive.

Arbitrary this process certainly was, even allowing for the lord's accepted obligation to protect 'his own'. Tenants of a strong lord enjoyed a degree of security and were able to pursue more long-term forms of husbandry. If, on the other hand, the lord was absentee, or no match for his rivals, tenants might find themselves subject to demands from more than one source, life becoming correspondingly precarious. In practice there was no higher auth-ority – no king or court – to whom legal appeals might be made. The militar-ization of Irish society must be quantified to be fully appreciated. A survey in the 1540s numbered the combined strength of private armies at a conserva-tive 24,000. Even the least regarded of Irish lords could muster 500 followers, while greater men might command five or six times that figure. By contrast, only at times of great crisis did the sixteenth-century English garrison in Ireland exceed 2000.

Such uncertainty pleased nobody. While tenants daily faced insecurity, their lords looked askance at the effort and expenditure necessary to main-tain authority. Increasingly, as the century wore on, powerful men in all parts of Ireland were attracted to the 'compositions', ways of introducing a demilit-arized, settled society proposed by successive English administrations. Their interest was always leavened with caution: the promised blessings of these schemes presupposed that everyone in Ireland would lay down their arms and abandon their private armies at more or less the same time. As even the most optimistic observers were forced to concede, that scenario was never very likely.

In 1529, Tudor government in Ireland had settled into an equilibrium established over the previous four decades: English kings ruled through Anglo-Irish deputies, usually the earls of Kildare. Deputies enjoyed something of a free hand, although they could expect little military or financial support from London. Since the revival of the English crown under Edward IV in the 1470s, government through local magnates had served both monarch and magnate reasonably well. The local governor gained in authority from the outward trust shown him by the crown, while the crown welcomed a prac-tically self-sufficient system of government. If Irish revenues were tiny by

English standards, so too were costs. The salaries of a small Dublin bureau-cracy, and the demands of internal defence, were never supplemented by demands from London for contributions to English military projects on the continent, or other burdens imposed on English subjects.

There was a catch, of course; indeed, there were several catches. King had to trust deputy and deputy had to trust the king, but trust on both sides was always governed by suspicion. Earls of Kildare had backed the Yorkist cause in the Wars of the Roses and had supported pretenders to the throne seized by Henry VII. The ninth earl, deputy on and off since 1513, had dabbled in some dubious intrigues. Furthermore, royal reliance upon one family risked the transfer of that family's local and particular interests onto a national stage. On balance, though, no other policy offered commensurate advan-tages. Occasional efforts at more direct control, such as the lord lieutenancy of the earl of Surrey between 1520 and 1522, had demonstrated only the inadequacies of available Tudor resources. Viewed in military terms, and in a militarized borderland that perspective is instructive, the superiority of arms and armour enjoyed by the English lords was effective in keeping the Gaelic Irish at bay, but the difficult terrain of northern and western Ireland effec-tively cancelled out such advantages and discouraged any sustained attempt to extend the areas under Anglo-Irish control.[7]

In the early 1530s, however, this equilibrium was destroyed. The direct cause was a rebellion, ostensibly against proposed Henrician reforms, led by Lord Offaly, son and heir to the ninth earl of Kildare. King Henry's reforms were designed, with perhaps more puff than substance, to enhance and re-vitalize English law and crown authority in the Pale. The veil still rests upon many aspects of this climactic uprising: the timing is odd and the aims are obscure. It may be that the revolt was a gambit to persuade London against change, for no English government wanted to stir hornets' nests in Ireland. Perhaps it was even aimed, somehow, at bolstering Kildare's own prestige, at securing his position as deputy. But the gamble, if such it was, backfired wretchedly. Kildare and his son had intrigued with agents of both pope and emperor, and Henry VIII saw no merit in making concessions. Rumours of Spanish intervention and a rapid escalation of unrest combined to stiffen the king's determination. Decisively compromised by his son's actions, the old earl of Kildare died a prisoner in the Tower of London during September 1534. After the arrival of 2500 English troops at Dublin and Waterford that autumn, under the command of the Fitzgeralds' bitter enemy, Sir William Skeffington, the power of Ireland's paramount family was shattered in less than a year, along with the trust reposed in it by the English crown. Prom-ised his life, against Henry's wishes, the new earl of Kildare surrendered in August 1535.

The initiative thus lay with the English king and his ministers, though it was by no means a welcome burden. Military victory had cost upwards of £40,000 sterling. Conclusive against Kildare himself, it had left unreconciled many of his allies among the Fitzgerald affinity, the so-called 'Geraldines'. In the tense international climate of the 1530s, any territory held less than securely by the English crown remained a potential focus for foreign subversion. Disruption of the great family networks made life more difficult still. The Geraldines might be in eclipse, but Henry held their great rivals the Butler earls of Ormond at arm's length, suspicious of raising another overpowerful family.[8]

The ways in which Henry VIII, and his successors, responded to circumstances in Ireland were shaped by these fears, but influenced too by a succession of conflicting recommendations as to the best way of making Ireland more like England. 'Lawlessness' was widely considered, both in London and in Dublin, to be the curse of Ireland. Impose the blessings of English law, so the argument went, and the makings of a stable, friendly society would surely be at hand. Benevolent paternalism, encouraged by the steady if unspectacular spread of the English language through the century, particularly among the Gaelic elite, was long seen as the means to a desirable end. However, while successive English administrations appreciated the potential for trouble in Ireland, they were reluctant to devote the funds and time necessary to secure a region ranking low on any list of political priorities. Intermittent threats were met with intermittent intervention. Ulster, the northernmost and least anglicized province, geographically very close to Scotland, was also the least accessible to any would-be invader. Scotland, while she might from time to time hope to *embarrass* England through Ireland, would never choose to *invade* England through Ireland.

This is not to suggest that Ireland was ever altogether neglected. When the new supremacy legislation was set before an Irish parliament in 1536–7 – all the important measures, based closely on English legislation, passed with little dissent – Thomas Cromwell devoted many hours to Irish affairs. With characteristic energy he prepared crown business for the parliament and after the parliament, directing the operations of his agents and, from September 1537 to April 1538, the work of a group of investigatory commissioners in Dublin who were charged with examining the current state of Ireland. There was, however, no significant attempt to put new social and administrative legislation into effect. Significantly, whenever collection of crown debts fell far in arrears the principal response was to cut costs rather than improve returns. The royal garrison was halved to 340 men in September 1537 while ad hoc efforts continued to build a new, reliable dependency among Irish lords in place of the polity swept away in 1534.[9]

After Kildare's destruction a new deputy was required: Henry was faced with the choice of appointing another Anglo-Irish lord or selecting some English official for the task. He chose the latter, in the person of Leonard Grey, son of the earl of Dorset and Kildare's uncle, and in so doing set a precedent. For the rest of the century the powers of the crown were delegated to successive English 'viceroys', lords lieutenant or lords deputy, the lieutenancy usually being reserved for members of the royal house or prominent English noblemen. The decision placed reliable figures at the head of the Dublin administration, but had disadvantages too, extending beyond the predictable Anglo-Irish resentment of a newcomer. The crown's pursuit of reform in Ireland created opportunities for ambitious courtiers, willing to promise much for the prestige brought by high office. When the deputyship became the object of competition between court rivals, however, consistency and objectivity went out of the window. One weakness of the old system also preyed on the new. So long as the incumbent was vulnerable to sniping from rivals in London, his prestige in Ireland was dangerously undermined.

He was, indeed, all too vulnerable. The deputy's office was no sinecure. It came to demand military ruthlessness, personal standing and wealth, as well as the ability to execute an extensive brief supplemented by ill-informed and often obsolete directives from London. The deputy had to deal with intransigent Anglo-Irish lords, scheming Dublin officials and the unpalatable fact, bluntly analysed by the earl of Surrey in the 1520s, that a full military conquest of Ireland would prove prohibitively expensive and perhaps logistically impossible. Ideally, he had to remain mobile, ranging through Ireland in an attempt to establish personal links with local lords and to show his influence over the Dublin council, yet the cost of his progresses went against London's desire for low-key government. Above all, the governor lacked authority. While he might act in the name of the English king, Irishmen and compatriots, including colleagues on the council, were prepared to appeal over his head any decision with which they disagreed, and the crown not infrequently proved willing to entertain such appeals.

Analysing an awkward situation, Grey concluded that the only way to achieve his twin goals of pacification and economy lay in a show of military strength, and, exploiting his own kinship ties, through conciliation of Kildare's erstwhile supporters. However, in attempting this he alienated both the Butler connection, which did not receive expected advancement, and colleagues on the Dublin council, among them John Alen, chancellor from 1538, and Gerald Aylmer, chief justice of common pleas. Both Alen and Aylmer had influence in London, and coloured Grey's overtures with a sinister shade of personal ambition. For a time, the deputy enjoyed considerable success, countering every insinuation by his achievements. Eventually, however, the complexities of Irish politics, and a worrying though rather superfluous act of defiance from the Ulster lords O'Neill and O'Donnell in 1539 which attracted backing from James V, allowed his opponents their opening. In June 1540, the fall of Cromwell deprived Grey of the statesman who had protected his interests most assiduously. He was convicted of treason and executed in 1541. The precedent set by his deputyship was decidedly unpromising.

Just as unpromising was the fact that Grey's disgrace had at least in part been encouraged by his successor as deputy, Sir Anthony St Leger. A close ally of that old Irish hand the earl of Surrey, by now duke of Norfolk and one of Henry VIII's principal advisers, St Leger remains a controversial character. Brendan Bradshaw suggests that his crucial support for the act passed by the Irish parliament of 1541 recognizing Henry as king of Ireland should be seen as an enlightened attempt to mark all Irishmen alike as subjects of the same monarch, with the same duties and the same privileges. Hitherto, Ireland had been recognized in European courts as a lordship under the English crown, and in that medieval lordship the degree to which all Irishmen might be considered subjects of England's king simply by the fact of their birth in

Ireland had remained uncertain in theory, negligible in practice. The king as lord of Ireland had stood obliged to protect his subjects there, but as the Anglo-Irish had repeatedly reminded successive kings, the fact that they needed such protection recognized that the danger came from other Irishmen.

The anomalies inherent in creating a new Irish kingdom by statute are worth emphasizing. The very status of this Irish crown proved ambiguous: no Irish king visited his country for 148 years after 1541, none consequently enjoyed a coronation in Ireland or took a particular oath to defend his Irish subjects' rights and liberties. Constitutionally, this neglect in no way reduced the authority of Irish monarchs, but it contrasted sharply with the nature of their rule in England. Irish policy continued to be settled in the English council, while English parliaments, though without any Irish representation, retained the right to legislate for Ireland. English courts reserved powers to review Irish cases, with some business by-passing the Irish judicial system altogether. Still subordinate, still neglected, the new kingdom differed very little from the old lordship.

There was, in any case, a lot more to the 1541 Act than disinterested idealism. The lordship of Ireland enjoyed by former English monarchs had been a papal title, granted in the twelfth century, and some alteration was naturally desirable after the breach with Rome.[10] Creation of the kingdom of Ireland was a means to an end. Inexpensive pacification remained the keystone of English policy, St Leger concluding a series of so-called 'surrender and regrant' agreements with Irish lords. Surrender and regrant became both the symbol and the instrument of conciliatory anglicization. It recognized where power already lay; agreements were carefully tailored to suit a particular lord, each side to the bargain realizing that the pact enhanced its own authority. After negotiation with the chief concerned, who frequently showed an unexpected knowledge of English law, underlining the blurring of cultures, the deputy would receive the lord's homage to the king, and his acceptance of English institutions and customs. In return, the crown would grant back to the lord his possessions, now to be held of the king by knight service. Some of the more politically important lords, most notably Conn O'Neill in Ulster, who became earl of Tyrone during a ceremony in Greenwich in 1542, were granted English peerages or knighthoods in return for renunciation of their Gaelic titles. In concluding these agreements, lords theoretically accepted primogeniture and English styles of dress. Early surrender and regrant agreements, however, declined to specify too precisely the extent of the lord's obligations.

Here was no more than a beginning in what all sides realized would be a long process. Successive deputies concluded similar agreements, reaching ever further down the ranks of Gaelic society. In the short term, though, with Henry VIII suspicious of concessions and the Gaelic lords hesitant and procrastinating, the process of surrender and regrant was in effect suspended towards the end of 1543. For all his statesmanship, St Leger was hampered by restraints faced by Grey in 1536: the Butlers looked to him as their man, the Englishmen on the Irish council sought sometimes to work with him, sometimes to displace him, while the Geraldine connection remained a potential threat to stability. All that emerged from London were the same demands for economy and quiet.

St Leger formulated his own responses, some of which centred around the dubious practices of the vice-treasurer and later lord justice of Ireland, Sir William Brabazon. Brabazon seems to have used his good relations with Grey and St Leger to line his own pockets, and latterly the pockets of St Leger and other political cronies as well, through selective collection of taxes and rents, and through the sale or leasing of former monastic lands at low prices. To the opportunistic St Leger, disposal of monastic land offered great possibilities. In Ireland, dissolution had followed the English pattern. Smaller houses had vanished, followed by a general suppression. With only part of the island under effective English control, however, the process remained incomplete. Some 55 of the 140 or so monasteries, and a rather smaller proportion of the friaries and other mendicant houses, were dissolved in the late 1530s and early 1540s, though those which disappeared included all the wealthiest communities. Resulting largesse was spread deliberately widely to leading members of the community, Englishmen and Gaelic lords alike. By sharing in royal generosity these men were, in theory, allying themselves to the crown. For the moment, such conciliation worked. When accused of misgovernment St Leger pointed to his record, noted the peaceful state of Ireland, and asked an English government preoccupied elsewhere if it wished to reject the services of so successful a deputy.

King Henry, absorbed in war with France, was content to leave Ireland, and St Leger, well alone. While the deputy was eventually recalled in May 1548 by a new English administration under the duke of Somerset, all the essentials of what we might term St Leger's policy in Ireland are still in evidence during a confused period to 1556, in which Sir Anthony was repeatedly replaced and reinstated, allowing Sir Edward Bellingham (1548–9) and Sir James Croft (1551–2) each some twenty months in office. Such brief deputyships might hardly be expected to produce any radical departure from past practice, but there are signs of a far less tolerant approach emerging under the man who in 1556 replaced St Leger for the last time: Thomas Radcliff, Viscount Fitzwalter, who succeeded in 1557 to the earldom of Sussex.

Sussex, eventually appointed lord lieutenant in recognition of his rank, favoured direct action. He made repeated, expensive and futile attempts to crush a revolt by the powerful Ulster lord, Shane O'Neill, and his efforts to drive Scots mercenaries and settlers out of Ulster in 1557–8 – at a time when Scotland was allied to an enemy power – proved equally fruitless. Directness of method, on its own, did not amount to a new approach in Irish government. Sussex's two administrative treatises of 1560 and 1562 are models of caution and responsibility. These treatises have been much studied and very thoroughly analysed. Perhaps they have received too much attention. Whenever governors oblige us with self-justifications for their actions their words must be interpreted in the light of their experiences in Ireland, bearing in mind the image they wanted to convey at home. Here, direct methods march hand in hand with traditional ends. Sussex claimed to be working towards the deeply unoriginal goal of permitting each and every man in Ireland to 'live of his own'. This required domestic tranquillity. To secure tranquillity, conciliation was preferred towards all but the deeply intransigent; it cost less, both in manpower and money. Even after five years in Ireland, Sussex looked to a gradual process of anglicizing the Gaelic lords and de-Gaelicizing the Anglo-Irish, in part by weakening the dominance of the Fitzgerald and Butler factions through new peerage creations. For Sussex, factional alignments were the cause of Ireland's instability: they sustained private armies and encouraged defiance of English rule. Once royal bounty became apparent to lesser Irish lords, more and more would hasten to shed their subordinate positions within the great Geraldine or Desmond affinities.

Conciliation took some perhaps unexpected forms. In his 1562 treatise Sussex sought to leave scope for Gaelic law in deciding lesser cases, and he held out an olive branch to the experts in native Irish 'brehon' law, offering to recognize them as men qualified to plead before governor and council 'in all constitutions after the manner of them, and in all other matters after the order of brehon law or allowed customs'.[11] He further suggested that certain territories held by reliable collaborators should be excluded from the administrative reforms under consideration for Munster, Connaught and Ulster. The caution and pragmatism in all these proposals was unoriginal; Sussex only claimed to outperform the 'corrupt' St Leger in achieving common ends.

At times force was unavoidable, but the majority of Sussex's military operations sought to restore a status quo determined, sometimes in the teeth of feasibility, by former surrender and regrant agreements. The case of Shane O'Neill provides the most notorious example. Shane had been passed over by his father in favour of an adopted brother, Matthew, a move supported by the English despite Shane's claim by both primogeniture and military strength.

Sussex's reliance on military men to serve as 'seneschals' or 'captains', supervisors of the Gaelic septs, bears witness to his limited ambitions. Captains were put in place to preserve order, to take and enforce pledges of loyalty. Hints of any reform programme were absent from their instructions. In age-old Anglo-Irish tradition these captains often 'went native', carving out estates in their allotted areas, and turning a blind eye to coyne and livery and retaining. Some married into prominent local families. Others were themselves drawn from the ranks of Gaeldom.

Even in his support for plantations of English and Anglo-Irish settlers in the Irish midlands Sussex was doing little more than sustaining St Leger's original leases for settlement of lands forfeited by attainder. 'Plantation' in a 1550s context did not imply wholesale removal of population. Most early schemes envisaged small settlements, undertaken by men with military experience, around central defensive fortifications. In enterprises of this nature there was always a place for the farmers and labourers of Gaelic society: men who performed the menial tasks of a colony, freed from the oppression of erstwhile overlords. However hard it was to match these expectations on the ground, colonization was deliberately designed as an advertisement to Irish neighbours of the benefits of English society.

But at this point we might pause, and consider yet another Irish paradox. Though so many of Sussex's goals were unoriginal, and though so many of them were pursued in unoriginal ways, it is important to recognize that his rule nevertheless marked a distinct new phase in the history of Ireland. Sussex's impatient aggression, his intolerance of any form of dissent, and his enthusiasm for draconian enforcement of arbitrary penalties as a pre-emptive rather than a responsive measure, set a disturbing precedent. His captains went out into their Irish hinterlands armed with commissions of martial law, lacking salaries but lured by the promise of confiscated traitors' possessions. For traitor read tax offender, the vagabond poor, the peasant obliged to serve more than one master. The policy was cheap, savage, and for many Irishmen it appeared to represent the inescapable, dismal future.[12]

Religion as yet provided no focus for unrest within Ireland, in part because the religious situation in England remained fluid, and in part because, even in the areas under English control, Henrician and Edwardian reforms were half-heartedly enforced. Lack of enthusiasm for reform did not equate with enthusiasm for Rome: as in England, there was a good deal of conservative resistance to novelty, among native Irish and Old English alike. The introduction of new forms of service under Edward VI had provoked criticism in the parishes, but protests of this nature subsided when it became clear that the alterations were largely being ignored.

Little, in practice, changed under Queen Mary. She confirmed the return of St Leger as deputy in 1553, carrying instructions that religion should be that 'of old time used'. She deprived bishops for marriage and for studied opposition, and she obtained from Rome a declaration that Ireland was to be henceforth a kingdom, thus regularizing the changes made by her father. But only in 1557 was a parliament summoned in Dublin to reverse King Henry's legislation and restore Ireland to Rome.

At Elizabeth's accession, fresh attempts were made to establish a protestant church in Ireland. The Irish parliament of 1560 restored royal supremacy, sanctioned an ecclesiastical commission to oversee church reform, passed an Act of Uniformity more or less along English lines, and provided for the use of the Book of Common Prayer. The Act of Uniformity further required priests to conduct services in English or, if that was beyond them, in Latin. Significantly, perhaps, no concession was made to services in the vernacular. At the same time, the resulting Latin prayer book, given the form of its communion service, and its provision for reservation of holy communion and a requiem eucharist, was doctrinally more conservative than its English counterpart. The relatively easy passage of the bill through parliament, with little resistance from the bishops, suggests that both the retention of ceremonial and the implicit opposition to services in Gaelic represented the preferences of the Anglo-Irish hierarchy. This broad support from senior clergy in Ireland for the 1560 measures became a source of embarrassment for their Catholic heirs and successors, thirty years on.[13]

While no subsequent effort was made to follow English precedent and impose articles of religion on the Irish church, the reformation in Ireland came away from the parliamentary session of 1560 bearing a distinctly English stamp. In the long run, this proved a burden rather than an asset. That which enabled her church to establish itself in England during Elizabeth's long reign worked against it in Ireland, where there was no nationalistic card to play, where enforcement of religious legislation was less diligent, and where, in their resistance to coercion, the Catholic families of the Pale proved better organized and more persistent than the committed Catholic gentry across the water. Crucially, the 1560 settlement yoked Ireland's reformation to a government in Dublin that was weak in many parts of the land, and increasingly unpopular in others.

For Scotland, which never claimed any political authority in Ireland but which nevertheless was a political player there, England's new commitments offered an opportunity to embarrass, an unofficial but valued outlet for young men seeking glory on the battlefield, and scope for Gaelic western magnates to work upon and profit from the kinship and cultural links that bridged the North Channel between Argyll and Ulster. A glance at the map is instructive here. Ease of sea-borne communication contrasted with the rough landward approaches to Ulster that hampered every military operation directed from Dublin. Dabbling in Irish affairs was nevertheless considered a risky game by the Scots crown. The Anglo-Irishman's distrust of his Gaelic neighbours was echoed by that of the lowland Scot. Towards the end of the century, the English search for a 'solution' to Ireland began to provide a sorry model for the Edinburgh government's own efforts, inadequate, misconceived and underresourced, to extend the values, language and culture of the lowlands over Scotland's own Western Isles.[14]

The presence of Scots in Ulster, both as mercenary soldiers and as settlers in Antrim, contributed to the instability of local politics. Mercenaries, younger sons and adventurers known as redshanks or bonnaghts fought in the Ulster succession squabbles from the 1520s. Marriage alliances between Ulstermen and Scots from the Western Isles were not infrequently made with a view to securing the services of Scots mercenaries, and the result was a form of arms race among Ulster lords. Settlers came in waves, in the 1490s and in the 1540s, both times as a result of troubles besetting the lordship of the Western Isles. The English vacillated between seeing the Ulster–Scots connection as a foreign invasion of Ireland, or as a means of employing the potential of the lordship of the Isles to destabilize Scottish politics. Attempts to frustrate the former and to exploit the latter were, however, uniformly unsuccessful.

We have already touched upon Henry II's dynastic ambitions and the threats they posed to the sovereignty of both England and Scotland. The French king also dabbled, very half-heartedly, in the confused politics of Ireland. Here was a chance to divert English resources. The busy earl of Argyll suggested to a French agent visiting Scotland during that year of English crises, 1549, that France should aid Irish insurgents, or alternatively Argyll himself, for the earl professed himself willing to lead a descent on Ulster. This, and subsequent schemes fostered over the next few years by Irishmen in Scottish exile, was scrutinized by the French court and its agents. Envoys were sent to secure treaties between the French crown and leading Irish lords hostile to the English, the Irish contemplating French sovereignty in return for assistance in overthrowing English power.

Such schemes came to little. Attempts to play upon Henry II's religious orthodoxy by appealing for help against a heretic power foundered on the French king's pragmatism. For France, the whole business turned on maximizing annoyance to England, while minimizing her own commitment: Scotland was proving costly enough and Ireland was wholly unimportant by comparison. When confronted with the paramount threat of Habsburg power, France, for all her belligerence, preferred English neutrality to enmity. Nevertheless, the potential for trouble remained, while French intrigues in 1550s Ireland provided some small foretaste of Spanish strategy three decades on.[15]

Other Scots, paradoxically, perceived an English opportunity. The protestant lords of the congregation after 1560 expressed the view that Elizabeth would be well advised to subjugate Ireland. Then, they declared, 'the Queen would be the strongest Princess in Christendom upon the seas, and establish a certain monarchy by itself in the ocean, divided from the rest of the world'. These sentiments echo the ambitions of Elizabeth's great minister, William Cecil. When Cecil's initial 'British strategy' broke down in 1565, the most serious implications lay not in the transient change of fortune in Scotland but in Ulster politics, where Argyll was alienated and turned from friend to implacable foe. The 'postern gate', the weak point in England's defences, had transferred from Scotland to Ireland by the 1580s.

Consideration of the English experience in Ireland may warn us against expecting programmatic foreign policies in respect of other European states. Foreign policy is an unfortunate term which presupposes that monarchs and statesmen of the age, beset by the vicissitudes of what were essentially dynastic politics, thought in terms of, or had the resources and fortune to put into practice, fine theories of international statecraft.[16] The triumphs of English diplomacy in the early sixteenth century – Wolsey's Treaty of London in 1518, for example – kept England's options open, allowing her latitude to support one or other of the great European powers as seemed expedient. If this legerdemain amounted to policy then policy there was, but as such this was little more than glossed pragmatism: one's enemy's enemy was inevitably cast as one's friend, while one's principal trading partner might not casually be offended. For all their apparently consistent hostility, Henry VIII's relations with Scotland, and James V's relations with England, were opportunistic, often reflexive responses to genealogical accident and to shifting relationships with other nations, most notably France. So it was on a broader front. For the duration of the Tudor dynasty, successive English administrations pursued advantageous cooperation with the established ruler of the Low Countries, when there was one, while Scottish monarchs adhered to the security of alliances, first with France, then with England. But both could and did look elsewhere for friends as the need arose. Considerations of prestige also coloured the picture. English kings maintained a pretence to be kings of France, even though the medieval empire had shrunk to the Calais Pale; even though the 1536 incorporation of representatives from Calais in the English parliament amounted to a tacit rejection of any separate French kingdom; and even though opportunities to refashion that empire by exploiting French weaknesses were no longer available.

Successive administrations deplored the declining skills of English archers, skills that had fashioned such victories as Crécy, Poitiers and Agincourt, but archery alone had in fact won none of these battles, and there were deeper factors at work than skill shortages or questionably obsolete technology. England, with her smaller population, could not match the resources of France or those of Charles V's dynastic empire: she was a middle-ranking European power, and only her apparently impregnable position on the rim of Europe gave her any latitude for choice and security in foreign affairs. For Scotland, still less threatened, but still more peripheral, security was the greater, choice the smaller. Fortifications and new weapons cost money, but the greatest charge was that of raising and supplying soldiers, the ever larger bodies of men who could advance a king's honour in the field and pursue his territorial ambitions. Neither country could really afford to deploy a standing army or to purchase the Swiss and German mercenaries so important to wealthier France.

Political tensions may from time to time have strained Anglo-Habsburg harmony near to breaking point, but two imperatives dictated an alliance with the emperor throughout the first half of the century. First, England feared an overmighty France extending her power along the Channel coast, into Flanders. The security of Calais was only part and parcel of that broader consideration. Against this, the authoritative if indirect rule of Charles V, preoccupied with religious unrest in the empire and by the military advance of the Turks, appeared to hold French ambitions in check while at the same time offering welcome stability within the Low Countries themselves.

There was, secondly, a mighty economic impetus to the Habsburg alliance. England's – London's – overseas market was concentrated on Flanders, particularly on Antwerp. A majority of cloth exports went there, and by far the greater part of the continental return trade, in manufactures and exotic luxuries, was shipped from the city for consumption in London or for redistribution to provincial ports. Controlled by the London Company of Merchant Adventurers, English cloth accounted for perhaps 75 per cent of the nation's exports by value in the 1530s, and the proportion did not alter substantially throughout the century. A particularly exaggerated boom in the Antwerp market for English cloth came at the very end of Henry's reign, when debasement enhanced the competitiveness of English exports. This boom, however, brought with it higher prices, a leavening of inferior produce and a sudden collapse in the market during 1551. Thereafter, retrenchment and currency reform in England drew exports back to a stable yet still substantial level, around 100,000 shortcloths a year, which was maintained for the rest of the century.

Other markets were either moribund, inaccessible or insubstantial. The English wool staple in Calais survived until 1558, but compared to fourteenth-century statistics raw wool was now a minor export, some stages in the processing and 'finishing' of cloth having been brought home. Merchants of the Hanseatic League conducted such trade as there was with the Baltic ports, successfully blocking attempts by English merchants to break their monopoly. Trade in French woad, salt and wines and English cloth proved profitable, war permitting. Scottish fishermen exchanged their catches for grain at Newcastle, Hull and King's Lynn, as well as London. Spanish iron was available in exchange for cloth, a fact recognized by Henry VIII's foundation of an Andalusia Company to conduct trade with the port of Seville. But all of this was small scale by comparison. Since war was no friend to trade, English interests clearly lay in a stable Low Countries.

11 The Elizabethan Settlement: England 1558–63

Chronology

January 1559	Coronation of Elizabeth I; parliament assembles
April 1559	Treaty of Câteau-Cambrésis
May 1559	Acts of Uniformity and Supremacy receive royal assent; revised 1552 Book of Common Prayer introduced
December 1559	Matthew Parker installed as archbishop of Canterbury
1559	Publication of the Latin prototype edition of Foxe's *Acts and Monuments*
August 1562	Full recoinage brings eighteen years of debasement to an end
February 1563	Thirty-nine Articles agreed by convocation

When the dying Mary grudgingly named her half-sister as her successor, before a parliamentary delegation on 7 November 1558, she was acknowledging both the force of dynastic legitimacy that had ensured her own succession and the absence of any viable alternative candidate. The queen's husband, occupied elsewhere and deeply disenchanted with the English, remained absent and silent, but Philip had long accepted Elizabeth as heir presumptive to the English throne. In Mary's failure to produce a child lay the defeat of all her dreams. Her death, on 17 November, and the succession of her sister, passed off without trouble.

Like Mary before her, and like James I nearly half a century later, Elizabeth came to the throne widely welcomed, but an unknown quantity. A well-educated woman of twenty-five, she had never enjoyed any say in affairs of state. This enigma was in part self-fashioned: the vicissitudes of her early life had taught Elizabeth the virtues of caution and procrastination. Philip II's ambassador, the count of Feria, interviewed her days before Mary's death and, in an upbeat report, described her as confident in the strength of her position, and unlikely to encounter a challenge from Mary Stuart. The daughter of Anne Boleyn and the patron of protestant sympathizers in her sister's reign, Elizabeth might veer away from Mary's religious policy, but she might equally favour some practical alliance with a papacy willing to remove from her the stigma of bastardy. At the same time the ambassador noticed some ominous straws, caught in a gathering wind. Feria thought the queen 'inclined to govern through men who are believed to be heretics', and 'highly indignant about what has been done to her during the queen's life-time'. He appreciated too how Spanish influence had dwindled: 'They have', he wrote, 'received me well, but somewhat as they would a man who came with bulls from a dead pope.'[1]

Here the ambassador caught the mood of the times. To all intents and purposes, Mary's reign ended days before her death. While the queen's last illness dragged on, Elizabeth's privy council was already taking shape amid discussions at Hatfield House. Feria noted that Edward VI's secretary, Sir William Cecil, according to reports an 'able and virtuous man', though a heretic, was to resume his post, and though some enterprising trimmers such as Mason, Paget and Petre had all secured the heir's favour, there would clearly be many changes. In fact, the queen did not enjoy a completely free hand: her choice of counsellors in 1558 was as much a statement of political unity as her sister's had been in 1553. Ten of the first twenty Elizabethan counsellors had served under Mary. Nicholas Heath, archbishop of York, lost his position as lord chancellor but, in what appears to have been a conciliatory move towards the high clergy, was retained on the council until his opposition to the Elizabethan church settlement led to his removal, and deprivation, in 1559. The earls of Arundel, Pembroke, Derby and Shrewsbury, leading representatives of the nobility from Mary's council but important to Tudor regimes of every religious shade for the local authority they exercised, retained their seats, while the experienced marquess of Winchester was also kept on as lord treasurer. The conservative Winchester, however, sat at the council table irregularly, a circumstance not perhaps wholly explained by his advanced years.

New counsellors from the ranks of the peerage – the mediocre marquess of Northampton and the altogether more capable young earl of Bedford – reflect Elizabeth's affection for the house of Parr and a recovery in the Russell family's political fortunes. The clergy are almost entirely absent, and do not reappear. By the standards of earlier times it is remarkable that Matthew Parker, Pole's successor as archbishop of Canterbury, was never appointed to the council; among those in holy orders, only Dr Nicholas Wotton and Archbishop Whitgift served as counsellors during the next forty-five years.

Below the ranks of the peers, though, the balance between Marians and new blood swung the other way. While Mason, Petre and Sir Richard Sackville were retained, Sir Nicholas Bacon as lord keeper, Sir Ambrose Cave as chancellor of the duchy of Lancaster, Sir Thomas Parry controller of the house-hold, the queen's cousin, Sir Francis Knollys, and Cecil all, to some extent, represent Elizabeth's own preferences. Despite his long experience and cordial relations with the new queen, Paget was not appointed to the council. His reluctance to accept further religious change, together with the veiled hostility of other counsellors, ensured that the greatest statesman of Mary's regime was consigned to an honourable retirement ended only by his death in 1563.

In one respect Feria had read the signs well: William Cecil took an increas-ingly prominent role in the new administration. The son of a Northampton-shire gentleman, Cecil was then in his late thirties. Educated at Cambridge and Gray's Inn he had served Elizabeth's father and brother in important administrative positions and had undertaken diplomatic assignments for Mary. Elizabeth, inexperienced in matters of state, trusted him personally as much as she valued his proven political abilities. Across nearly forty years, that trust was never lost.

The conclusion of a war both burdensome and profitless had already been mapped out in negotiations before Mary's death. By November 1558, the only sticking point was England's unwillingness to accept the loss of Calais. The English feared that Philip II would renege on a promise to make no peace while the issue of Calais remained unresolved; the Spaniards suspected that their allies might welcome such unilateral action, identifying in this fashion a convenient foreign scapegoat for their own failings. France, for her part, would not return the town, representing as it did the sole tangible gain in a disastrous war. That the issues at stake were essentially those of honour was, by the end of the year, tacitly accepted on all sides, and Elizabeth told her ambassadors that she would agree to a continuing French occupation, for some token period, provided that an adequate subsidy was paid by way of compensation. This face-saving formula was duly adopted. In April 1559, peace was signed at Câteau-Cambrésis, France agreed to pay an indemnity and to return Calais after eight years, provided that no English action had abrogated the agreement. The façade of continuing English sovereignty, how-ever, fooled no one.

King Philip could work up no enthusiasm for an English regime at best schismatic, at worst heretical, but political necessity obliged him to tem-porize. The prospect which confronted him in 1559, and which continued to haunt him long after, was that of a union or alliance between England and France, threatening the security of his Netherlands possessions. The mar-riage of Mary Stuart to the Dauphin Francis, and Mary's claim to the Eng-lish throne, made that threat all too real. Spain preferred England as an ally, or at least as a benevolent neutral, while at the start of her reign Elizabeth saw France as the greatest external threat to her country's security. For the moment these conceits dictated diplomacy. Philip, after a suitable interval, sought Elizabeth's hand in marriage and negotiations for the match offered a convenient cloak for preserving an alliance against the French. Aided by a succession of amenable popes after the death of Paul IV in 1559, Philip was able to postpone excommunication of the English queen for as long as Eng-lish friendship remained desirable.

Yet it was a postponement of the inevitable, for Elizabeth's religious settlement, though not as radical as some about her might have wished, amounted to a total repudiation of Roman supremacy. In November 1558, England was a Catholic country with an orthodox episcopate, a resident cardinal archbishop at Canterbury and a revived monastic tradition. By November 1559 both the cardinal and his royal mistress were dead. Rome's authority had once again been extinguished in England. Virtually every one of Mary's surviving bishops had been removed, an act had been passed abolishing the new religious houses, another had restored first fruits and tenths to the crown. Mary's church had been swept away and in its place stood the curious doctrinal compromise that was Elizabethan protestantism. The processes by which this change was effected bewildered many contemporaries and have intrigued historians ever since. The favoured nineteenth-century picture, of a protestant queen brushing aside Catholic opposition in the 1559 parliament to impose upon England her desired church settlement, was challenged by Sir John Neale some fifty years ago. Neale suggested that Elizabeth's own preference was for a revived Henrician church similar to that bequeathed by King Henry to his son in 1547, and that only through pressure from returning protestant exiles in the Commons was she induced to move towards a conclusion modelled upon the 1552 reforms. Neale's belief – he was careful never to be too dogmatic when asserting these ideas – in the existence of a strident and influential 'puritan choir', which took the queen's initial supremacy bill and augmented it with measures aiming at protestant uniformity, was challenged in turn. His views came under fire from those who, examining the religious professions of specific exiles and known malcontents in 1559, appreciated that the first were, in parliamentary terms at least, a small group, which by no means spoke with the same voice,[2] and that the second were all too often men of conservative or indeterminate religious beliefs, whose motives must be sought elsewhere. The sixty-eight members from Mary's most fractious parliament, that of 1555, who were returned in 1559 were crucial to Neale's theories: he suspected that they worked in concert to shape the state religion. But as we have seen, the troubles of 1555 arose from a complicated brew of personal political grievances. Upon closer inspection, the religious leanings of these men frequently prove rather difficult to pin down.

And so it has become necessary to seek other 'explanations'. Perhaps Elizabeth's government did indeed pursue a '1547' – or a '1549' – solution; maybe it was Catholic opposition in the House of Lords that wrecked her initial ambitions and left her compelled to forge an alliance with more radically minded counsellors and churchmen. Cecil later accepted 'guilt' for the 1559 settlement, while Nicholas Bacon proved a less than impartial adjudicator in the staged Westminster Hall debate on religion during Easter Week 1559, arranging the arrest of the principal Catholic disputants, the bishops of Lincoln and Winchester, on grounds that they had, in retiring from a public religious disputation, been guilty of disobedience to the civil authority. Shades here of Oxford in 1554! Nevertheless, we must be careful not to misinterpret the religious conceits of these statesmen. Neither Cecil nor Bacon was a particularly zealous reformer. As Patrick Collinson has reminded us, Cecil was seventy-five years old before a university dispute obliged him, opening his eyes mightily in the process, to dwell on some of the darker implications of Calvinism. Bacon, consciously projecting a stoical, foursquare image, gives no clue that he knew or cared about the theological refinements of the protestant sects, and if both these pillars of the establishment may be termed 'mere Christian', do they not cast a grey shadow across swathes of territory formerly defined in sharp black and white?[3]

A particularly persuasive interpretation of events in 1559 has quite recently been advanced by Norman Jones.[4] Jones swings about to a surprisingly traditional view. He reminds us of the uncertain, even dangerous, position in which Elizabeth found herself: the loyalties of her nobility, judiciary or clergy remained untested in the very early days of the reign. He reminds us too that there is much we simply do not know about the events of this ill-documented parliament. Nevertheless, after scrutinizing the available evidence, Jones argues that a return to the 1552 prayer book was all along the queen's intention. Clear hints are given in Bacon's opening address to parliament in January 1559, where he calls specifically for a uniform order of religion and for the measured abolition of superstition and idolatry. Although parliament was not concerned solely with the settlement of religion – the definition by statute of Elizabeth's title to the throne and the practicalities of voting a subsidy weighed as heavily – that same settlement was tackled with vigour and trepidation. Jones counts three bills introduced in February as part of the administration's initiative to restore the 1552 prayer book, although he concedes that, since in both senses of the word the bills were lost, we cannot be sure of their origin or their content. Opposition to the bills, reintroduced in one composite on 21 February, was fiercest, not in the largely acquiescent Commons but in the Lords. There, eleven of the Marian bishops, the abbot of Westminster and influential peers led by Arundel and Winchester together comprised a formidable conservative force. In a small House the power of this combination was soon evident: the bill was sent to committee and subsequently emasculated; even Elizabeth's title of supreme head was conceded only grudgingly, to be suffered under duress at the monarch's insistence. Cowed by this example from the Upper House, the Commons passed the bill as amended and, without revoking the heresy laws, approved legislation ensuring the toleration of protestant worship.

The administration, in Jones's scenario, was caught completely off balance by the Lords' resolute hostility. A proclamation was prepared which, while requiring communion in both kinds at Easter services, conceded that the existing authorized forms of divine worship were to remain unchanged. Had Elizabeth really been prepared to settle for a Henrician solution, there the issue might have stood. However, no dissolution followed, and over the Easter recess the Westminster conference exposed encouraging divisions among the Catholic bishops and – thanks to the arrest of the two bishops – cost the conservatives two vital votes in the Lords. New bills were prepared, this time separating the issues of supremacy and uniformity; an admission of weakness, for ministers feared that the latter legislation might fail. 'Supreme governor' was substituted for 'supreme head' in the wording of the supremacy bill, possibly in an attempt to attract support from both religious extremes which, while differing in almost every other detail, shared a belief that no man, let alone any woman, should so presume on authority given to Christ alone. Or perhaps the move reflected Elizabeth's own determination that she would have things settled this way: the governorship of a subordinate church was more useful to her than any frankly insupportable claim to theocratic supremacy. Embracing also the abolition of heresy laws, and providing for communion in both kinds, the revised supremacy bill again encountered serious resistance in the Lords, which limited the scope of the new Commission for Ecclesiastical Causes in judging heresy. Nevertheless, the bishops, though united in opposition, this time failed to attract equivalent support from the conservative lay peers and the measure went through.

However, those same peers, hankering after the Six Articles and the return of a Henrician Catholicism, were less sanguine over the reimposition of the 1552 prayer book envisaged by the uniformity bill. The council may have modified the original draft in an attempt to allay their doubts, offering a slight return to 1549 in the form of consecration, and adopting more Catholic regulations on clerical dress and church ornaments. Such changes, though, failed to win over all the peers, the dissenters including both Winchester and Shrewsbury from the ranks of the council, and a considerable debate in committee ensued, the Lords eventually passing a bill shorn of many of its penal clauses by an unusually close margin: 21 votes to 18.

The oath included in the Act of Supremacy acknowledged the queen as supreme governor and denied the authority of any foreign prelate in England. It tested the commitment of Marian bishops, who showed resolution in adversity. With one exception, Anthony Kitchin in the relatively minor see of Llandaff, the bishops refused to acknowledge Elizabeth's governorship, and they were all deprived of their dioceses by the autumn.[5] While the high clergy took a stand, however, their lesser brethren were more accommodating. The vast majority of parish clergy accepted the new dispensation, and one may only speculate over the range of mental reservations, the ignorance, or indifference, then engaged. Faith among the laity was hardly scrutinized at all. The fine for non-attendance at the established church on Sundays and Holy days was set at one shilling a week; in practice, that penalty was seldom if ever enforced.

Thus the Elizabethan settlement, but was it in fact Elizabeth's settlement? To what extent did parliamentary legislation in 1559 reflect the queen's own beliefs? These questions are almost impossible to answer, for the clues are few and to a degree ambiguous. In considering what was best for her country, Elizabeth does appear to have looked beyond a return to her father's brand of 'Catholicism without Rome'. The reform of her chapel in 1558, the famous occasion when she walked out of the Christmas Day celebration of mass at the elevation of the host by the bishop of Carlisle, the constant preference given to reformed preachers and her authorization of the Westminster debate all point in the same direction. So too does her toleration of clerical marriage. Injunction 29 of the subsequent royal visitation of 1559

– the visitation which administered the oath and enforced use of the prayer book – explicitly declared it lawful. The spinster queen never mustered any enthusiasm for a married clergy. Early in her reign she deplored such unions in conversation with Matthew Parker, speaking so intemperately that Parker, himself a married man, recoiled in 'horror to hear such words to come from her mild nature and christianly learned conscience'. Nevertheless, she continued all her life to approve appointments and promotions of married clergy, including – as in the case of Bishop John Thornborough of Limerick – those with distinctly unsavoury marital histories. At least fifty-eight of the seventy-six bishops appointed under Elizabeth had married, some more than once. Weighing the scandals bred of a married clergy against the sins of sexual incontinence the queen opted, in the interest of general decorum within her church, to allow priests their wives.[6] There is a good deal of scorn here. Beneath Elizabeth's proper concern for the welfare of her church lies a wealth of evidence to illustrate her contempt for the moral failings of those who ministered to her kingdom's spiritual needs.

A still greater mystery surrounds the queen's personal beliefs. Insofar as we can discern her private convictions, Elizabeth inclined to a pragmatic evangelism: she made a point of embracing an English Bible upon her entry to London in 1559. This was no doubt a personal statement, but it also seems to have been a reaffirmation that the vernacular Bible was a symbol of the authority wielded by a monarch who walked in step with God. The queen's father would have approved. While crosses and other popish images were removed from parish churches up and down the land, Elizabeth herself kept a cross in her own chapel from 1559, and went on record to say that the public display of this traditional image of Christ's passion worked 'for the advantage of the church'. The Elizabethan compromise of 1559, implicitly lauded by Bacon in his closing speech to parliament in May, when he warned against extremism in both Catholic and protestant – 'both these alike break the rule of obedience' – echoes King Henry's agenda of a 'middle way' and provided a definitive statement of an Englishman's faith, defended by the queen to the day of her death. It is difficult not to suspect that for Elizabeth the settlement of religion in one particular fashion mattered, first because the business was settled, and second, because the queen had been seen to settle it in this particular way. While her reluctance to contemplate further reform may have hindered useful administrative as well as purely doctrinal alterations to the established church, the chaos of the past twelve years demanded stability. As in so many other ways, Elizabeth's longevity proved her most potent political weapon.[7]

Recent reversals of religious policy now also gave rise to innumerable disputes over land and property. Lands surrendered to the crown by certain new Edwardian bishops had been leased subsequently to third parties, but when Mary restored bishops deprived under Edward VI the surrenders made by protestant interlopers were deemed invalid. By 1559, there were many instances where two or more parties could claim title to the same piece of ground. In the Commons, during the two months before the Easter recess, the processing of private land bills occupied fully three weeks of business.

What Jones has called the 'land rush' of 1559 can appear an unedifying combination of greed and ostentatious religious zeal. The scrupulous legality underpinning each and every step of these bills, however, suggests that fear was the driving force. The landowning classes represented in parliament sought secure titles to the lands on which their prosperity was based and were concerned, wherever possible, to arrive at mutually agreeable, lasting settlements. Questions of religion deferred to good title, Marian bishops conducting occasionally successful defences of their leases and exchanges. The passage of bills concerning properties formerly belonging to the bishops of Winchester and London, in particular, illustrate the distinction drawn by conservative peers between the question of supremacy – which touched the material wealth of the crown, the church and themselves – and of uniformity, which concerned a man's spiritual journey through life. With the renewed impetus for reform after Easter, the Commons passed a bill to restore those who had received leases from Nicholas Ridley while bishop of London, but who had subsequently been deprived by Bonner. This bill the Lords, in an apparently unanimous decision, rejected.

That, though, is to simplify: the issues at stake in 1559 also raised questions of personal alliance, family honour and the hesitation born of changeable times. Bonner's determined search for justice, and the tangled problems in Winchester diocese, provoked the only significant divisions in an otherwise united bench of bishops. His stridency may have both alienated lay support in the Lords and stirred up anticlericalism in the Commons, prejudicing opportunities for compromise in the battles over supremacy and uniformity.[8]

The second parliament of the reign, in 1563, closed one loophole in the 1559 legislation. A treason act targeted any man or woman who offered explicit support for papal jurisdiction, declaring it high treason to uphold on two successive occasions the pope's power in England, or twice to refuse the oath of supremacy. It also demanded that all MPs and most lay officials should take the oath on entering office – a notable tightening up of 1559 provisions. But the act appears to have been the work of private initiative in the House of Commons, with only the most half-hearted backing from members of the privy council, and less support from the queen herself. To all intents and purposes it was left unenforced.[9]

The real significance of this session lies elsewhere. Links between debasement, inflation and economic malaise had been recognized by Cecil and his colleagues when, after consultation with the economist Sir Thomas Smith, they had recalled all debased currency in 1560–1. No one expected a complete remission from inflationary pressures, but there were hopes of greater stability in wages and prices. The 1563 Statute of Artificers, a wide-ranging attempt to regulate working practices and conditions, threw the burden of wage control on JPs, who were directed to set maximum wage rates annually for various occupations, after weighing local considerations. In the best early modern tradition, enforcement varied widely across the country: some justices were more strict, or more conscientious, than others. Whereas those of Chester realistically raised such maxima during the reign, the Rutland JPs permitted hardly any change in their own rates well into the next century.

While parliament debated the safety of the queen and the welfare of her subjects, it was left to the clergy in convocation to approve the newly established church's statement of belief, the Thirty-nine Articles. Similarities to the Forty-two Articles of 1553 are marked, though there is a more conservative slant to some questions of ceremonial, while paranoia against the receding anabaptist threat is less pronounced. It was a rather fractious session. Debates over the Articles were vigorous, and attempts to reform canon law were once again rejected. A bid to make further alterations to the prayer book failed too, as did efforts to abolish holy days, the compulsory wearing of the surplice, the use of organs in churches, and two significant rituals: the sign of the cross and kneeling to receive the sacrament. Several bishops had themselves advocated many of these alterations, but somewhat reluctantly they compromised their ideals in the interests of uniformity.[10] Failure to secure further church reform alarmed numerous English protestants. Insistence on the use of the surplice provoked refusals, followed by several deprivations. At the same time, the queen was none too keen even on the declaration of the faith arrived at by her convocation. Despite pressure from parliament in 1566, she refused to approve a bill giving statutory effect to the Thirty-nine Articles until 1571.

12 UnElizabethan England: England 1560–72

For those reared on the Hollywood version of Elizabethan history – or, indeed, on the interpretations provided by a host of romantic novelists – the first decade of the queen's reign presents an unfamiliar spectacle. Elizabeth is, technically at least, in communion with Rome, and Catholics retain important positions in her administration; Spain is a friendly, or at least a sympathetic, power. Rather than a sorry, scheming prisoner, Mary of Scotland is an active and constant threat to the Tudor crown, while the traditionally indecisive English queen gives her approval to some perilous initiatives in foreign policy. Stranger still, the hand of the 'Virgin Queen' is a sought-after and apparently attainable prize in the game of state diplomacy.

There was a general assumption, shared, perhaps, by the queen herself, that Elizabeth would marry and produce an heir. The alternative was uncertainty. Should Elizabeth die – and die she very nearly did, from smallpox in 1562 – the throne would pass either to the descendants of Henry VIII's elder sister Margaret, or to those of his younger sister Mary. Translating from dynasties to individuals, the heir presumptive was, in both cases, a woman: Mary Queen of Scots, and Catherine, younger sister of Jane Grey. The Stuart claim was considered the stronger, its deficiencies arising from xenophobia rather than from religion. Mary Stuart was indeed a Catholic, but it was assumed confidently, and perhaps correctly, that if she succeeded she would either swim with the political tide or be guided, as in France, by her husband.

Catherine Grey's claim rested on anti-Scottish sentiment and on a willingness to set aside the title of an elder child in favour of a younger. Nevertheless, so long as a Stuart succession meant the succession of Mary, Catherine's chances of succeeding Elizabeth could not be discounted. In 1561 Catherine incurred the wrath of Elizabeth through her clandestine marriage to the young earl of Hertford, Protector Somerset's son. Hertford and Catherine kept their marriage secret until Catherine's first pregnancy could be concealed no longer, but such secrecy proved their undoing. So hugger-mugger had been the marriage ceremony that upon examination no witness could be found. Their two sons pronounced illegitimate, the lovers languished in the Tower or under house arrest until Catherine's death in 1568. Even so, several counsellors openly supported Catherine's claim when it was feared Elizabeth might not survive the smallpox.

If the Stuart claim was the stronger, its strength posed a particularly menacing threat in 1559. A combination of French diplomacy and force of arms had driven England from the continent and had foreshadowed, through the marriage of Mary to the Dauphin Francis, the absorption of Scotland under the French crown. Henry II's grand design for a dynastic union of all three kingdoms eventually collapsed through – from the Valois standpoint – calamitous chance, but for the first two years of her reign Elizabeth, and her subjects, had to live with the fact that the French dauphine and queen was heir presumptive to the English throne.

While the desirability of marriage was easily accepted, the choice of bridegroom proved far more difficult. No candidate could command general support from queen and council. Philip II – held responsible for his late wife's religious policy and for the disastrous war with France – proposed, was rejected after a mutually acceptable interval, and subsequently backed rather half-heartedly another Habsburg suitor, Archduke Charles of Styria, son of Emperor Ferdinand I. Though neither side saw it as the perfect solution, negotiations persisted for a decade, Ferdinand, his son and successor Maximilian II, and Elizabeth all displaying a willingness to make concessions over the practice of Charles's religion and the limits of his authority in England.

Inevitably, the archduke had a French rival. After the death of Francis II in 1560, the new king of France, Charles IX, was for several years discussed as a possible husband, for all that he was still a child, seventeen years Elizabeth's junior. Other offers came from less familiar quarters. Even before his election to the throne of Sweden in 1560, Erik XIV threw his hat into the ring – pressing his claims by means of a magnificent embassy, headed by his brother John, duke of Finland. Marriage to Erik offered England a protestant prince, one, moreover, unlikely to press for expensive adventures in France, even if the Swedes had ambitions of their own in the Baltic. Nevertheless, the prospects for such a union were remote: Erik declined with the years into a morose insanity and, his suit long forgotten, was deposed by his formerly loyal brother in 1569.

Domestic suitors, after Mary's recent unhappy experience, also harboured hopes of success. Representatives from the latest generations of the Seymour and Dudley families were initially both in the running, but the unprepossessing Edward Seymour, earl of Hertford, had been tacitly rejected well before his marriage to Catherine Grey. By contrast, Robert Dudley, another son of the late duke of Northumberland and now Master of the Horse, remained to his death the great love of Elizabeth's life. The historian William Camden, no friend to Dudley, could not deny the deep affection, for all that he found the cause elusive: perhaps it emerged from shared tribulation under Mary Tudor, or perhaps 'from their first procreation, by a secret conjunction of the planets at the hour of their birth combining their hearts in one'.

Such was the mutual attraction that even the supremely cautious queen may have risked marriage. In the event, practical obstacles proved insurmountable. Dudley was already married, and the discovery of his unfortunate wife, dead at the foot of a short flight of stairs at Cumnor Place, near Oxford, in September 1560 roused a tremendous scandal. A coroner's jury absolved Dudley of complicity – accidental death or suicide remain the most credible explanations – but few were disposed to credit so convenient a resolution. Perhaps an even greater impediment arose from fears, vague yet impossible to discount, that the elevation of Northumberland's son might initiate perilous faction: Elizabeth herself once declared rather plaintively that it was not in Dudley's nature 'to seek revenge of former matters past'. Dudley's attempts – backed by the queen – to win the support of Philip II for the match by holding out the possibility of English representation at the reconvened Council of Trent failed when Cecil 'discovered' a domestic Catholic plot to overturn the 1559 settlement. The papal nuncio bearing an invitation was refused entry to England, Philip backed away, and prospects of a Dudley marriage all but vanished.

Plate 13 *Robert Dudley, earl of Leicester,* Anglo-Netherlandish school, Elizabeth's favourite *c.*1564.
Source: Private collection

Elizabeth might, reluctantly, have rejected him as a suitor, but Dudley lost only the supreme prize. For all his ambition, he had always shown that he could adapt to shifting fortune.[1] Ostentatious and extravagant, yet personally moderate, Dudley established himself as the leading patron, after Elizabeth herself, of arts, sciences and reformed religion. His household overflowed with ability, full of young men destined for great things. Much of his generosity, and his magnificent living, was financed directly or indirectly by the queen, who bestowed on him largesse far in excess of that granted to any other courtier.

Dudley also drew support from, and was a mouthpiece for, those servants of his father who had rejected compromise with Queen Mary's regime and who had passed the previous five years in conspiracy or exile. The men who had gathered round Northumberland, who had supported Wyatt in rebellion and who had dabbled in other plots against Mary's throne now tied themselves to the fortunes of the late duke's son. It was not just Robert, whose success is *sui generis*, but the Dudley entourage as a whole who found favour at the succession of Elizabeth. In the event they had to wait for the more significant honours, perhaps because of the concerns such advancement raised elsewhere at court, but the time of waiting was not long. The elevation of Dudley's close ally and elder brother Ambrose to the earldom of Warwick in 1561 shows in itself that the family was in many ways greater than the individual.[2]

Having so intimate a spokesman with the queen brought particular benefits when war was in the offing. Several of the Dudley clientele, Sir James Croft and Sir Thomas Finch for example, were experienced soldiers, and campaigning, either actual or in prospect, served to cement their allegiance. Dudley was a man after their own heart. For the first but not the last time he stepped forward as the advocate of military intervention overseas, urging the queen to seize her opportunity when civil war broke out in France during 1562. The war arose out of tensions in the Guise-dominated French court and from a sudden outburst of religious persecution which compelled the numerically inferior French protestants, or Huguenots, to look for help from England. They were encouraged by the English ambassador in Paris, Sir Nicholas Throckmorton, strongly protestant and suicidally outspoken, and by Dudley's client Henry Killigrew in the Huguenot-controlled Seine port of Le Havre. Like the Dutch rebels a decade and more later, the Huguenots in their peril magnified Elizabeth into a protestant saviour. 'It lies in her hands', wrote Killigrew, 'to banish idolatry out of France.'

Elizabeth was hardly tempted to risk war for such an objective. Exploiting the French crown's weakness to secure a Channel port was, however, another matter. Although laid to the account of her sister, the loss of Calais was still a recent and very raw wound. So Dudley's recommendations were heeded. Indeed, there were few dissenting voices; Cecil, less enthusiastic, went with the majority. Dudley was admitted to the privy council, while Warwick led a field army to France. The deal struck at Hampton Court between Elizabeth and the prince of Condé in September 1562 promised 6000 troops and a loan of £42,000 to the Huguenots in return for Le Havre, known to the English as Newhaven, a bargaining counter for the return of Calais. But the success of the adventure depended first on English willingness to pay the price of garrisoning Newhaven in strength, and second, on prolonged civil war in France. In swift succession, however, the Huguenots were trounced at

Dreux, Condé was taken prisoner and Guise, the moving spirit on the Catholic side, was assassinated. This round of blood-letting took heat out of
the situation. A peace was patched together and a united French siege army
forced the surrender of Newhaven, agreeing the evacuation of Warwick's
plague-ravaged forces. The Treaty of Troyes in April 1564 confirmed the loss
of both Calais and the indemnity paid by France since Câtcau-Cambrésis.
Though mercifully brief, the war had proved a costly failure; it taught the
queen a lesson she never forgot. Once more, however, Dudley rode the storm.
Elevated to the earldom of Leicester during marriage negotiations with Scotland in 1564, he remained one of Elizabeth's closest advisers.[3]

For all his faults, Dudley had represented a realistic husband for the English queen. As his hopes of marriage to Elizabeth receded, so the general desire
to see a settlement of the succession increased. The Scottish ambassador,
Sir James Melville, claimed that he had told Elizabeth in 1564 how he, for
one, had never been surprised by the queen's reluctance to marry. Her 'stately
stomach', he declared, would never permit her to yield the smallest part of
her present authority: 'king and queen both'. Perhaps he was right; certainly
the queen could summon no enthusiasm for any remaining suitor. The council
fretted mightily over the uncertain succession. In 1563 and 1566 they used a
compliant parliament as one mouthpiece for public anxiety on the subject;
not without justification, since the 1559 Act that recognized Elizabeth as
queen had explicitly based her claim on the Succession Act of 1543. Robert
Monson felt able to argue in the Commons in 1571 that attempts to preclude
discussion on the succession when the queen's own accession had rested on
statute amounted to nothing less than 'horrible treason'.

Queen Elizabeth was having none of this, rejecting attempts by subjects to
debate matters fit only for princes. Personal disinclination would perhaps
have given way before national interest: a united council might have persuaded her into a particular match. But the council never did speak with one
voice on the subject. Cecil opposed a Dudley marriage, Dudley could not
tolerate a union with Archduke Charles. Elizabeth played upon their divisions, lashing out alike at appeals and advice. Parliamentary petitions were
dismissed as merely insolent, while the hapless marquess of Northampton
was reminded of his own disastrous first marriage. Cecil sought at one point
to tie the granting of a subsidy to a settlement of the succession. In a perilous
undercover strategy, he worked through clients of a council colleague, Sir
Ambrose Cave, in the Commons. However, Elizabeth was also capable of
sweet yet indefinite promises to marry which mollified in the short term.
Cecil was an inveterate scribbler: many of his memoranda survive to instruct
and tantalize the historian. His frustration is reflected by the increasingly
despairing tone of such private jottings. One note composed at the end of the
1566–7 parliament speaks volumes in its brevity: 'The succession not answered,
the marriage not followed.'

If the backcloth against which it worked appears unfamiliar, the 'traditional' form of Elizabethan government emerges very early in the reign. The
queen preferred to take advice from a small group of counsellors, an inclination which entrusted to the chosen few a great deal of political authority and

patronage. The privy council, twenty strong in 1558, had just eleven members in the 1590s. Considerations of policy had forced the queen's hand at the start of her reign. Forty years on, she was bound only by the chains she herself had fashioned; two of the last men promoted to her council were a regional magnate, Gilbert Talbot, earl of Shrewsbury, and a trusted cousin, Edward Somerset, earl of Worcester. Both were personal selections and both, it may be noted with interest if without particular significance, were closet Catholics. The whole 'system', if such it can be called, worked on long service, intimacy and trust. Cecil, that pattern of the regime, served the queen for forty years, first as secretary then, after his promotion to the peerage as Lord Burghley in 1571, as lord treasurer. During the queen's reign, three men – Lord Hunsdon, Lord Scrope and Sir John Forster – could together muster ninety years in one or other of the three wardenships of the east, west and middle marches against Scotland. Elizabethan society was indeed gerontocratic, and the respect accorded to age, experience and long memory coincided with royal caution and conservatism. When the count of Feria wrote to Philip II in December 1559 that 'the kingdom is entirely in the hands of young folks, heretics and traitors', he was giving expression to a common English sentiment on the inadequacy of youth.

At court there was little conscious innovation, 1559 arrangements remoulding the existing household structure to reflect life without a male monarch. Catherine Parr's household served as a practical model for Elizabeth's domestic arrangements. Even the development of the bedchamber, which created a definite hierarchy within the privy chamber based on intimacy of access, was in some sense an echo of Northumberland's reforms under Edward VI, which had neutralized the powerful office of groom of the stool by placing it in commission. Following an initial 'purge', necessary when intimacy and trust were all important, the personnel of Elizabeth's bedchamber and the wider privy chamber served until death, severe illness or, occasionally, dishonour intervened. Elizabeth liked to keep things within the family. The ladies who surrounded her in her privy chamber were largely drawn from her extensive cousinship. Henry VIII's complex marital history stood his daughter in good stead. Several great Elizabethan families – Seymour, Carey, Sackville, Howard, Radcliff, Grey, Knollys and Blount – could all claim a fairly close relationship with a sovereign who saw fit to acknowledge the connection. In the 1560s, many of the queen's ladies had served her as princess, and in later years their daughters and granddaughters succeeded them. While these ladies assumed dignified but now apolitical posts within the chamber, so their husbands, brothers, fathers and sons served the queen on embassy, on the battlefield, as court officials and at the council table.

One change, however, was to be of great importance to the structure of government over the following half century. Under Henry and Edward the grooms of the stool had, through the flexibility of their office and their intimacy with the sovereign, usurped many of the duties notionally performed by the secretary. Cecil, the new queen's secretary, now seized them back again. The late Tudor secretary was an intermediary between monarch and council; though the dogsbody of both, his unique rights of access afforded him powers to shape policies and set agendas. Cecil also took over the administration of the privy coffers, leaving the intimate privy purse expenses in the hands of minor grooms of the privy chamber.

The secretaryship was not the only office to benefit. With a (nearly) all-female personnel, the privy chamber also lost much of its hard-won status within the household, and the role of the lord chamberlain, at the head of the entire 'above-stairs' establishment, became ever more significant. When access was all important, the chamberlain's power to allocate lodgings at court became a particular source of authority.[4]

Though the path to promotion was easier for relatives and trusted servants it was never, in fact, easy. Leicester had to wait nearly five years for his earldom, while Cecil himself laboured over a decade to earn, and never rose beyond, the rank of baron. In context, this represented high reward. Elizabeth's other courtiers, however capable, had to work hard for even the dignity of knighthood. A few close cousins, Henry Carey, Lord Hunsdon,[5] for example, or Thomas Sackville, Lord Buckhurst, might be promoted to the peerage, but the five promotions to earldoms – Elizabeth raised subjects no higher, apart from her restoration of Parr as marquess of Northampton – all took place before 1572. Otherwise, when titles fell by attainder or natural causes, new creations were rejected. It may be argued in Elizabeth's defence that she was careful to promote no one unable to afford the higher dignity expected from a peer. Nevertheless, she set a very rigorous standard.

Small numbers did not remove tensions within the council, but major stresses and strains at this highest level appear only transiently: in 1565–6 when Leicester had what can appropriately be described as a personal falling-out with the young fourth duke of Norfolk and Sussex, exacerbated by differences over the proposed Habsburg marriage;[6] in the crisis of the late 1560s, when Cecil came under fire from colleagues worried by his anti-Spanish stance; in the mid-1580s, when peace and war hung in the balance, alienating Burghley from his successor as secretary, Francis Walsingham; and finally in the 1590s, when the earl of Essex forsook a decade of practical cooperation with the Cecils. One should not underestimate the intensity of such eruptions. Equally, one should be careful not to exaggerate occasional ill-feeling. Voices raised in argument across the council table more commonly advocated differing approaches to the same problem, even variants on the same solution. On great matters of state Elizabeth's counsellors stood in broad agreement. Perceiving the queen's wishes, individuals took pains to preserve harmony. Cecil, Leicester and, later on, Walsingham and Christopher Hatton, all dined together regularly, shared information and made little effort to secure personal advantage from colleagues' mistakes. To a degree this is posturing, but we may not entirely discount claims made by both council heavyweights, Leicester and Cecil, that they strove only to compose disputes. Leicester specifically declared that he had 'never been willing to make quarrels in this court nor to breed any', while Cecil responded with his usual emollience. If this was a front, it was remarkably well maintained.[7]

Hidden in these generalities lies a key to the nature of faction in Elizabeth's court. If factions there be, they are discerned best of all if we take an

Plate 14 *Sir Francis Walsingham*, by John de Critz the Elder (attrib.), Queen Elizabeth's secretary of state, *c.*1587.
Source: National Portrait Gallery, London

unconventional step and consider the queen a faction in herself. Queen Elizabeth commanded deference, she alone took the great decisions of state. What the queen desired, the council, court and parliament were in general content to forward. The queen, however, often rested undecided, dragged her feet or changed her mind. Accordingly, her ministers and noblemen faced a stark choice: they might either combine to persuade Elizabeth against her instincts, or they might line up behind her. Such procrastination, rather than acting as a divisive force, tended to bring frustrated counsellors together in search of catalysts.

If there is at any time an exception to this characteristic, Elizabethan harmony, it is again to be found in the first decade of the reign. According to the Scottish envoy Melville, Leicester described Cecil in a moment of candour as 'his secret enemy'. But Leicester's involvement in the Norfolk plot of 1569, the clearest evidence of discord between the two men, remains decidedly ambivalent. Equally, the traditional contrast drawn between Leicester as the advocate of continental intervention and Cecil as the proponent of cautious disengagement comes into focus only with the steady decline towards open war noticeable from the late 1570s. In the 1560s there is really no such distinction. Cecil engineers a remarkably aggressive and forward foreign policy, which takes risks, suffers setbacks and costs a good deal of money. We must balance Cecil's pragmatism against a genuine protestant faith and his belief in the theory, popular among many of his compatriots, of a general Catholic conspiracy. Whether speaking from the heart or no, he certainly employed the popular, redolent apocalyptic language so characteristic of the age, denouncing 'the Anti-christ of Rome'.[8] In the invasion of Scotland, less enthusiastically in the Newhaven episode, in the release of Darnley and in the seizure of Spanish bullion ships in English harbours which caused a great diplomatic scandal in December 1568, Cecil is seen advocating or endorsing the 'forward policy', in concert with council colleagues, but also in the face of conservative opposition. Nicholas Bacon, the influential lord keeper, for instance, opposed any Scottish expedition so early in the reign. The queen's caution may already be manifest, but that of her secretary, which in time grows to match that of his mistress, is emerging only in his precise but increasingly non-committal *aides-mémoire*.

Twenty-five years ago, Geoffrey Elton proposed that we set parliament, alongside court and privy council, as a point of contact between rulers and their most influential subjects.[9] Despite its occasional nature, and the undeniable cost of legislation, the assembly of a parliament was a great event in the lives of lords and gentlemen across the Elizabethan shires. Potent considerations of prestige, self-advancement and public duty combined to ensure that this was so. As the century wore on, more and more towns were represented in the Commons. Here we see the crown responding generously to rising demand, as urban authorities sought to match the status achieved by rival boroughs and to reward accommodating local patrons by placing seats at their disposal. Even if their day-to-day concerns lay elsewhere, notably in the lesser law courts, 'parliament time' remained for the enfranchised towns an occasion on which to hear news, sense the drift of policy and make representations among the great.[10] Very occasionally they might try, with varying success, to promote a private act encouraging some specific individual or local interest.

Parliament's political significance in the reign of Queen Elizabeth was considerable, if largely unoriginal. As the succession debates show, it could be used by those in power to apply further pressure, through allies in the Lords or clients in the Commons, in the game of shifting an immobile queen into action. Taken beyond these transcendent questions, the motivations of such clients tend to be obscure. Their discernible religious persuasions, for instance, vary enormously, but a strong protestant or Catholic faith was in itself no barrier to personal advancement, particularly when a man was blessed with well-disposed friends on the council. Thomas Norton, long seen as a 'puritan' advocate of parliamentary liberties, was equally a reliable if occasional agent of the council, chosen for his experience in the Commons. Busy and intelligent, Norton co-wrote *Gorboduc*, an early Elizabethan English play, the political context of which has been much discussed. He and others like him enjoyed the 'game of parliament' for its own sake. There appeared to be no contradiction in working with or informing Cecil of developments in the Commons for the public good, advocating some advanced religious views, and speaking up for the interests and better organization of an institution for which long service had bred an undeniable affection.

Even if its intermittent nature placed a brake on its ability to play a sustained political role, as the passer of laws, as a channel of advice and consent, and as, in Norman Jones's words, 'a conduit for moral suasion', parliament had no equal. There are still, however, many gaps in our knowledge. We remain imperfectly informed on the nature of parliamentary elections, the ways in which MPs were selected and the fashion in which they exercised their obligation to represent constituencies. We still have too few studies of the Elizabethan House of Lords, that small but pre-eminent chamber which lent grandeur and relevance to parliament in equal measure.[11] While we can trace, if imperfectly, the life of a bill once introduced into either House, the genesis of legislation, the ways in which bills were touted and formulated, and the processes by which they were imposed, accepted or tacitly rejected in the country, remain among the great elusives of Tudor history.[12]

Again though, the 1560s stand apart. By 1570, the prospect of a royal marriage was already receding, and if few openly acknowledged the fact, the great impetus for debate that coursed through earlier sessions had ebbed away. Another facet of parliamentary life in the 1560s is also absent in later years. We still encounter in that first decade confident efforts on the part of the established clergy to introduce further reform of the English church through convocation and the House of Lords. Such efforts were inspired by three crusading ambitions: the desire to reform enduring medieval structures of patronage, ecclesiastical administration and canon law, to root out consequent corruption and ill-discipline in the clergy, and to introduce reforms that would reduce the 'Catholic' elements in both doctrine and the structure of the church. A few measures succeeded, notably the 1566 bill, shelved due to the delicate international situation but reintroduced in 1571, which turned the Thirty-nine Articles into a statutory statement of an Englishman's faith. Most, though, were blocked by a queen suspicious of innovation in religion and satisfied with the deliberate ambiguity of 1559.

Elizabeth's stand would have puzzled many of the Marian martyrs, not least Cranmer himself, who would almost certainly have preferred further reform in prayer book, articles of religion and canon law, and whose idea of a 'middle way' in religion was subtly different, but it was not without support. Despite exasperating the zealots and irritating some members of the council who supported alterations to the established church, the queen appears to have carried the majority of both council and parliament with her. Together they might look charitably on worthy proposals to educate the lower ranks of the clergy, such as those presented by Commons petition in 1576. But the House, like the queen, drew the line at efforts made repeatedly through the reign by a small group of radicals, including Job Throckmorton, William Strickland, and Peter and Paul Wentworth, to move towards a presbyterian church after the Genevan model. Elizabeth drew her own line still more precisely. So far as the queen was concerned, any parliamentary discussion of the English religion by law established transgressed prerogative, and she consistently vetoed even relatively moderate measures enjoying the support of both Houses, for example the bills of 1571, 1576 and 1581, which tried to introduce compulsory quarterly attendance at church.

Royal intransigence, and Elizabeth's broad interpretation of her prerogative, prompted some misgivings among a broad cross-section in parliament, but these misgivings could not in general shake their loyalty. When Strickland introduced a bill to reform the prayer book in the parliament of 1571, he was called before the council and banned from attending further sittings of the House on the grounds that he had trespassed upon matters only the queen might initiate or consider.[13] The Commons were dismayed but proceeded very tentatively to suggest that Elizabeth might deign to reconsider the matter. On this occasion, she took the hint, permitted his return and so defused the situation. It did not, however, alter her stance. In 1572 she directed the Lower House to avoid introducing any religious bills on private initiative. In 1576, Peter Wentworth launched into a passionate oration attacking the queen's decision on the grounds that it infringed the Commons' right to free speech, 'without the which the prince and state cannot be preserved or maintained'. Wentworth's speech was as much an attack on the lassitude of his colleagues, who were informed that 'the accepting of such messages [from the council] and taking of them in good part doth highly offend God'. Accordingly, it was the House that slapped him down: he spent a month in the Tower for his presumption.

Elizabeth, however, held her line at the price of lasting disillusion among more radical English protestants, already alarmed by the archbishop of Canterbury's drive to enforce the prescribed regulations on clerical dress, particularly the wearing of the surplice. This so-called vestiarian controversy resulted in some suspensions in 1565–6. England's universities struggled with the many issues raised. Cambridge in the late 1560s was convulsed by a debate initiated by the new Lady Margaret Professor of Divinity, Thomas Cartwright, in which he criticized the structure of the English church when compared against the model offered by the early Christians, and set out a justification for English presbyterianism. While Cartwright was ejected from his professorial chair and departed for Geneva in 1570, his arguments thereafter provided impetus both at a local and national level for the establishment of a presbyterian form of church administration.[14]

The stalling of further reform also provoked a protracted crisis of morale among the senior English clergy. Elizabeth's intolerance towards her bench of bishops is as striking as her practical tolerance of religious dissent itself. Bishops, in their own eyes, remained princes of the church, after the model of their pre-reformation forebears. That vision, indeed, became more pronounced as the Edwardian generation, which could recall exile and suffering, passed away. Elizabeth, however, while insistent that they maintain the dignity proper to senior crown servants, frequently wondered whether individual bishops were worth the endowment such a position demanded. For Elizabeth, bishops were workhorses of the state, to be driven and chastised where necessary. The conservatism of her regime did, admittedly, help give bishops a form of job security: no member of the episcopate was deprived during her reign, and the commissions issued for their appointment did not follow the Edwardian precedent of declaring that the office was to be held during royal pleasure. However, while conceding their right to decide purely religious controversies, so long as her royal wishes were recognized, and to 'decree rites and ceremonies', Elizabeth was quick to reprove any impertinent exercise of episcopal authority in other spheres. While the queen was characteristically inconsistent in levying these exactions, whenever the government needed money bishops might find themselves subjected to unfavourable exchanges of lands; and other property was extracted from them on disadvantageous terms to the benefit of favoured courtiers such as Hatton or Sir Walter Ralegh. Bishop Richard Cox of Ely in 1575 described Elizabeth, intemperately if with some cause, as a 'harpy', and one prominent peer as a ravening wolf.[15] When bishops died their dioceses were frequently left vacant for years at a time, while the queen, as was her right, reaped an income from episcopal lands. After Cox's death, for example, Ely was without a bishop between 1581 and 1599.

Bishops, it is true, never sank to the level of landless, salaried state servants; they all retained estates, and something of their medieval dignity. Measures such as the 1559 Act of Exchange replaced revenue from land with tenths, tithes and allied payments as the key to wealth in many sees, but these measures were less sweeping, and rather more temporary, than is sometimes suggested. Nevertheless, they had their effect: in inflationary times, it was all that the majority of early and mid-Elizabethan bishops could do to maintain their incomes at, in real terms, 1540s levels, particularly if they were ill-served by their officials. Compared with their predecessors, most bishops could draw on only limited personal resources to cushion the worst effects of these encroachments. We are hard put to define their social level, but may note that their children did not marry into the ranks of the lords temporal.

Across the religious divide, England's Catholics were trapped in an awkward and confusing limbo. The Council of Trent, which helped define what were and what were not Catholic beliefs, finished its deliberations only in 1563, and English Catholicism was not given fresh sustenance or direction until the arrival of missionary priests from the continent during the 1570s. That, however, is not to deny the strong continuity of Catholicism in several fundamentals: loyalty to the mass and to traditional ceremonial, and a proper reverence for the papacy. In the 1560s, the work of preserving Catholicism in England fell to those members of the pre-1559 priesthood unwilling to uphold the faith as laid down in parliament, and more effectively, perhaps, to groups of lay Catholics who found it impossible to swallow the new doctrines. Laymen, such as Dr Thomas Vavasour in York, do provide a real link between the gentry Catholicism of Mary's day and the recusancy of the 1580s, while the Marian priests, confronted with the 1559 settlement, were by no means the supine group of collaborators later commentators have suggested. But this, in essence, was the Catholics' difficulty. Laymen might conform, muttering fruitlessly, and one or two might find the strength or the stubbornness to protest. Priests might resist, resign livings, go into exile, conform or practise 'survivalism', but the response to state protestantism was individualistic in the extreme, lacking any organized leadership.[16]

There was, nevertheless, a sizeable majority at virtually every level of society and in almost every county in England, if not Catholic then (that vague but still very useful classification) religiously conservative. Here is a battlefield strewn with false signs and obscured by the fog of imprecise terminology, but this generalization is ever more difficult to refute.[17] Equally, there is no question that most Englishmen and women were prepared to conform to the church settlement imposed from above. Queen Elizabeth was herself no Catholic, yet her refusal to persecute, and her abrupt rejection of further protestant reform, nourished suspicions that she might be brought, either through marriage to the right man or through diplomatic advantage, to conformity. Such was the bait cast by the privy council, when they decided in 1567 that, to ease marriage negotiations with Archduke Charles, the Habsburg prince should be told that in England 'no quiet Catholic may need to forbear to resort to our churches and common prayers'. It was only after the queen's excommunication in 1570 that this studied neglect of covert Catholicism began to change, provoking corresponding disillusionment among the Catholics themselves.

The tenth year of Elizabeth's reign saw relations with Spain begin to deteriorate. In 1567, the duke of Alba marched north across Europe to the Spanish Netherlands, ostensibly to counter the increased signs of dissatisfaction among King Philip's Low Countries subjects. The arrival of this powerful force, permanently quartered in England's premier trading outlet, was watched in London with great dismay. When considered alongside the recent expulsion of an English ambassador from Madrid – most undiplomatically, he had called the pope 'a canting little monk' – and the increasing frequency of clashes between Spanish merchantmen and English privateers on the high seas, Alba's march assumed a most sinister complexion. Coincidental, but quite as important, was the final collapse of negotiations for a Habsburg marriage: for too many counsellors the religious compromises demanded proved indigestible. To Philip and his cousin, the Emperor Maximilian, this breakdown amounted to a deliberate affront and they attributed both failure and insult to the heresies prevailing in England. If the marriage bargaining had been conducted in an atmosphere remarkably free of religious dogmatism, its failure helped clarify and define some intractable future problems.

England's response to the worsening situation was abrupt and intemperate. In December 1568, Spanish ships sailing with bullion for troops in the Low Countries sought shelter from pirates and winter gales in south coast ports. After considerable and still obscure deliberation the queen and a majority on the council, with Cecil at their head, resolved to seize the rich cargoes, £85,000 being unloaded and carried to London. Elizabeth justified her actions on the grounds that the money still technically belonged to the Genoese lenders, and that she was entitled to take up the loan herself, but Alba did not see things in this light, and several conservative counsellors were appalled at the affront to Spain. The measures and countermeasures taken in response to this provocation led to a disruption of trade, which itself had lasting consequences. The cloth mart was threatened when its traditional home in Antwerp was, for the second time in five years, closed to English merchants. While many viewed this sanction with alarm, there were several among the London merchant community, ideologically driven, who rejoiced at the breaking of such dependence upon the ports of a Catholic power.[18] This immediate dispute was smoothed over, but despite the best endeavours of diplomats on both sides, which culminated in the 1574 Treaty of Bristol, Spain and England had both set out on a road that led, eventually, to open war.

The nation reaped one immediate benefit from unrest in the Low Countries. Flemish and Dutch families skilled in clothworking and other trades sought refuge in the more tranquil surroundings of English towns. There, though not always made welcome by xenophobic Englishmen and women, they settled at the direction and with the support of the privy council. Perhaps 50,000 refugees arrived in London between 1550 and 1585, many of whom moved on to other parts of the kingdom. Around one-third of Norwich's population were 'strangers', that is foreigners, in 1579.

The importance of the merchant community, domestic and immigrant, goes beyond the vital commerce they conducted. As informants and as substitute diplomats these families filled a crucial role in the early modern state. England long maintained a permanent ambassador only in France, and reliable information was often hard to come by, even at court: it is significant that the first news reaching the government detailing retaliatory seizures of English shipping in 1569 came from the lord mayor of London. The treasure ships imbroglio had still further consequences. New prominence of necessity accorded to trading connections with German cities led to a reappearance of that perennial Tudor mirage, the alliance with Lutheran Germany. As in the 1530s and 1540s, the overtures of 1568–9 were abortive, neither side then seeing any gain in an anti-Spanish pact. But the fact of these negotiations is itself significant.

In the short term, however, Cecil's handling of the bullion fleet led to a serious division of opinion in the privy council. The duke of Norfolk, the earls of Arundel and Pembroke, and Lord Lumley, all religious conservatives and supporters of what they saw as a natural alliance between Spain and England, looked on in horror at so blatant an insult. Subsequent events took their cue from the recent arrival, during May 1568, of Mary Stuart, seeking Elizabeth's support in her bid to recover her throne. Secret plans were developed to marry Norfolk – nominally protestant but with Catholic sympathies – to Mary, thus presenting the unwitting English queen with a *fait accompli* that would secure the succession and eclipse Cecil's influence. The scheme received unexpected support from Throckmorton and, more ambivalently, from Leicester. Both grasped the advantages in restoring Mary to the throne of Scotland by force of English arms, and the possibilities in a marriage with Norfolk that would immerse the duke in Scottish politics.

The projected marriage also attracted backing from two discontented northern peers. Contrary to some modern assumptions the north of England was no feudal backwater. Rather, as the first line of defence against an unpredictable neighbour, it was endowed with the best management an English administration could provide. Here we see in practice the Elizabethan policy of tight conciliar rule, based on a close circle of kinship, while shorn of the refinements necessary to keep the peace at court. Berwick was placed in the control first of the earl of Bedford, then of Lord Hunsdon. Lord Scrope, a reliable soldier, was appointed warden of the west march after the death of Lord Dacre in 1563. The implementation of these changes inevitably created losers as well as winners, principal among them the earls of Northumberland and Westmorland.

Representatives respectively of the great medieval houses of Percy and Nevill, their alienation is sometimes regarded as a consequence of Tudor curbs upon northern magnates. That interpretation, however, appears to stretch available evidence. Northumberland owed the restoration of his title to Mary and had never been on good terms with Elizabeth. His reconversion to Rome in 1567 had been a maverick personal action, and no government of whatever stamp could have been expected to place much trust in such a man. Westmorland was a close friend and ally of his brother-in-law, Norfolk. The extent to which he had been 'ignored' in the 1560s is difficult to assess; the Nevills had no more claim on wardenships or offices in the north than a number of other families then lacking employment, Dacre, for example, or Clifford. Nor does the earl ever appear to have acted through personal grievance. He disliked Cecil, was over-loyal to Norfolk and, when forced to take difficult decisions, he miscalculated.

His miscalculation had tragic consequences. Late in 1569 Elizabeth learnt of the proposed marriage and, in an ominous rage, vetoed the whole scheme. Terrified that negotiations which had verged on *lèse-majesté* would now destroy them, the plotters at court backed down, Norfolk writing urgently to his friends counselling submission to the queen's wishes. Leicester made great show of disclosing all he knew, and Elizabeth was disposed to be charitable. This did not suit Northumberland or Westmorland, since, absent from the court, their actions had extended to open treason: they had sought military aid from Spain and from the pope. Gloomily assessing the situation, neither man harboured any hopes of forgiveness. They embarked upon rebellion, believing that their erstwhile colleagues had left them with little choice. Westmorland, his anger declaring the extent of his former trust, denounced Norfolk, saying 'he was the undoing of them for by that message . . . their friends fell from them and gave them over'. After hurried counsel, the two earls called out their followers and marched upon Durham in November 1569. There, in an act full of symbolism, they celebrated mass in the cathedral after the old, Catholic rite.[19] At Darlington, they appealed for support against 'divers new set up nobles about the Queen's Majesty', who 'not only go about to overthrow and put down the ancient nobility of this realm, but also have misused the Queen's Majesty's own person'. It was the old complaint against 'new men', the appeal to a religiously conservative 'old nobility' heard in 1536, a tactic regularly employed by Catholic authors in the years to come.[20] At the same time the northern rebellion carried, unlike the events of 1536 and 1549, a clear if undefined threat to the monarch. As such, it foreshadowed treasons later in the reign.

Again like later treasons, it failed abjectly. Rebellion attracted, despite the further symbolic flaunting of the old five wounds banner of the Pilgrimage of Grace, only limited support. Mary Stuart, held at Tutbury when the revolt began, was hurried out of the rebels' clutches by another powerful northern peer, the earl of Shrewsbury. Possession of the Scottish queen had been vital to the rebels' plans and the enterprise now fell prey to a fatal loss of morale. Both earls fled to Scotland. While Westmorland escaped into continental exile, Northumberland was eventually handed back by the Scots and was executed in 1572. Elizabeth and her council resolved upon exemplary revenge, perhaps because the fright had, briefly, been considerable, more likely because the worsening international situation demanded an unambiguous response. Over 700 insurgents – more than one in ten of the active participants – were condemned to hang. Lands seized from traitors offered further scope for patronage in the region, while in 1572, as another turn of the screw on security, the council of the north was reorganized under the zealous earl of Huntingdon, a firm protestant, a southerner and, again, the queen's distant cousin. Huntingdon's appointment marked, in turn, a fresh phase in the enforcement of religious conformity through the north.

The northern rebellion marked, in retrospect, a shedding of gloves. All sides were beginning to realize that the Elizabethan settlement, like it, detest it or live with it, was here to stay, and that the one possible way to undo its effects was to remove the queen, its source and symbol. Events thereafter took on a continental dimension and a momentum all of their own. As with the Pilgrimage of Grace thirty-three years before, the rebels, and possibly also the court plotters, had been in negotiation with Rome, and once again Rome's response was inappropriate and delayed. In February 1570, Pius V, in a development regarded as inopportune by both France and Spain but warmly welcomed by English Catholic exiles, excommunicated the queen in his bull *Regnans in excelsis*, declaring her a tyrant and absolving Catholics in England from their duty of allegiance. The move misfired, for without military support from a foreign power it placed those Catholics in an impossible position. While Pius's successor Gregory XIII decreed in 1580 that the bull need only be observed once its enforcement became possible, the loyalty of English Catholics to their queen understandably fell under lasting suspicion. Elizabeth's privy council, acting through the parliament of 1571, retaliated by introducing a new treason bill, which made clear, after some mid-Tudor obfuscation, that to promote in deed, writing or speech the death or removal of the queen was an act of high treason. Another bill deemed as treason the possession, reception or dissemination of papal documents. At a more practical level, parliament passed a bill confiscating the goods, chattels and landed incomes of Catholic exiles, although with events in the 1555 session in mind no attempt was made to deprive refugees of the lands themselves.

This was widely considered insufficient. Thomas Norton's actions spoke for many. It was almost certainly with some council support that he tried to embellish the treason bill with a clause that retrospectively excluded from the succession anyone who had questioned the queen's title. The target, clearly, was Mary Stuart. Such was the feeling against Mary in the House that the amendment passed, albeit narrowly. The very notion of retrospective legislation, however, alienated several MPs, and after the Lords had greatly weakened the force of the proposed bill a compromise was adopted, covering future rather than past denials.

Mary's predicament during the first few years of her captivity was similar to that which Elizabeth had endured during her sister's reign. They shared the distinction of being the only viable successor to the reigning queen, so long as that queen remained childless. It was thus not surprising that the notion of a marriage between Mary and the duke of Norfolk initially provoked anger and alarm rather than calls for their immediate execution. Stripped of respectability by the collapse of the Norfolk–Leicester court alliance, however, the scheme metamorphosed into a thoroughly dangerous treason. Alba's army, in the fantasies of the Spanish ambassador in London, Guerau de Spes, and of a Florentine banker Roberto di Ridolfi, would invade England, deposing the queen and setting Mary, duly married to Norfolk, on her throne. Although much about the plot remains obscure, and Ridolfi's motives in particular lie open to question, there can be no doubt that both Mary and Norfolk either supported a genuine conspiracy or swallowed a carefully laid bait.

The discovery of the Ridolfi plot led to the conviction of Norfolk as a traitor. Only after much pressure in the parliament of 1572 – called on privy council initiative to debate the security of the realm – did the queen agree to his execution, yet on this occasion her procrastination has about it a degree of the premeditated. Elizabeth sacrificed the duke as a sop to those who would, for preference, have set Mary's neck on the block as well. A majority in the Commons, perhaps another in the Lords, and certainly yet another among the bishops were bent on Mary's death: a just, Biblical fate, akin to that which befell the wicked Jezebel. Let 'her head [be] cut off and no more harm done to her', one MP is supposed to have cried. 'The examples of the Old Testament,' observed Norton, 'be not few for the putting of wicked kings to death.' At the very least, parliament hoped to legislate away Mary's claim to the succession: 'an axe or an act?', pondered another member.[21]

The answer was neither. This, so far as Elizabeth was concerned, was not the way one treated anointed monarchs, still less the unadmitted heir to her throne. Her refusal dismayed most members of the council, and their clients, friends and representatives in the Commons. Cecil told Walsingham, then still establishing his career as ambassador in Paris: 'All that we have laboured for and had with full consent brought to fashion – I mean a law to make the Scottish Queen unable and unworthy of succession to the crown – was by her majesty neither assented to nor rejected, but deferred.' For deferred, read vetoed. But with war clouds gathering over Europe Mary could never again hope to shake away the fatal suspicions of protestant England. From that time on, every act of Catholic perfidy – notably the massacres of St Bartholomew's Day in August 1572, in which thousands of Huguenots died across France – was turned against her. When the bishop of London, Edwin Sandys, heard of the slaughter in Paris, he articulated the sentiments of many influential Englishmen in advising the council 'forthwith to cut off the Scottish Queen's head'.

13 The Elizabethan State: England in the 1570s and After

The word faction holds unattractive connotations for the modern reader, suggesting conflict, overriding personal ambition and divisive hostility. In Tudor England, too, it was pejorative: faction was a failing to which others succumbed. However, the picture advanced by many, from Sir Robert Naunton in the seventeenth century to Sir John Neale in the twentieth, of a court riven by faction, held together solely by Queen Elizabeth's cunning and character, has been successfully challenged precisely because the evidence for structured antagonism is too thin. Faction, broadly defined, certainly existed: contemporaries either sensed it or dreaded it, and without such a concept we would be hard put to describe some of the shifts within the late Tudor court. There were factions about the earl of Leicester, the Cecils and, later, the earl of Essex. Yet with the possible exception of Essex, all were built on

207

narrow issues or self-interested pragmatism, or at times on fear, and each and every one overlapped on broad fronts with the 'factions' of contemporaries. Elizabethan factions were responsive, they existed to oppose other factions, indeed, the definition of one's opponents might suffice to define a faction of one's own.

What elements underpin court faction? The competition for personal advancement, suggest some, policy differences, say others, patronage and the need to advance clients, argue others still. Surviving evidence for all three is ambivalent. If we suggest that court faction and county faction are two separate entities, the latter seldom if ever taking its direction from the former, we are nearer the truth, for certainly there are discernible and persistent gentry alliances in a number of shires. The game at court, however, was different. Elizabeth's favour was never exclusive: all her leading courtiers had access to her person, and if access was denied to lesser men that only left the select few in a still more fortunate position. As all prominent courtiers realized, the prestige won in being a good lord to those who sought preferment far outweighed any risky profit gained through intrigue against powerful colleagues near the queen. With give and take, all could be satisfied.[1]

This is not to deny the importance of good connections at court; rather, it emphasizes their importance. Court favours were vital, they required working at. Few clients were so devoid of connections that they had to tie their colours to one mast alone. Men dependent on a single patron, either by choice or by obligation, seldom found the path to promotion easy, even when the patron was as powerful as Burghley: Sir Edward Stafford, ambassador in France and a traitor who got away with selling secrets to Spain, and the altogether more deserving William Davison, scapegoat for the execution of Mary Stuart in 1587, are cases in point.[2] All too often, a 'faction', like a 'clientage', depended for its energy on the people seeking support and favour. The examples of the Bacon brothers, the disputing parties in Wiltshire who all sought support for litigation in the 1590s from various court figures, and the younger sons of the eighth earl of Northumberland who begged favours from their brother-in-law Essex, Cecil and their elder brother, the ninth earl, quite indiscriminately, testify to this conclusion.

'Faction' and 'patronage' are words which offer to define what is, essentially, indefinable: personal relationships, surveyed over a period of time, and described frequently at second or third hand. Each such relationship depended upon a mass of frequently competing influences: family loyalty, education, upbringing, religion, ambition (or lack of it), fear and royal favour. Each, ultimately, was governed by the human heart and will. Patronage, and the construction of factions, depended upon the mutual recognition of obligation and responsibility between individuals, and as with any other relationship between individuals the link may be fragile or sound, tested or experimental. Here lies the essential charm, and the danger, in any factional interpretation of historical events. Essex, in the 1590s, tried his best to help the historian, spelling out repeatedly that those who were not for him were, to his mind, against him. But Essex was isolated in his judgement; his rival Robert Cecil's 'faction' has rightly been described as 'the court itself'.[3]

Such divisions as are perceptible in the council of the 1570s lie between the risk-takers, led by Walsingham and Leicester, and the risk-avoiders, headed by the increasingly cautious Burghley, Sussex and Sir Christopher Hatton. Hatton, the son of an old Northamptonshire family, had risen to favour in the late 1560s: accomplished, a gifted orator, exceptionally tactful, he owed his fortune, and perhaps his opaque stance in religion, entirely to Elizabeth. It would not do to pretend that the differing strategies were easily reconciled. While Leicester advocated further military intervention on the continent, particularly in the troubled Spanish Netherlands, Burghley recalled (as Elizabeth certainly did) the debacle at Newhaven and doubted the value of inescapably expensive operations.[4] But a common opposition to the growing Spanish threat prevailed, and these divisions, deeply felt though they were, were never pursued to the knife. The queen held to a course – it can hardly be termed a policy – of wary neutrality. Her own preferred solution was undoubtedly shared by her counsellors: all hankered after an autonomous Spanish Netherlands, its independence guaranteed under the Spanish crown, but freed from any Spanish army of occupation and enjoying a measure of religious freedom. However, whereas Elizabeth, Burghley and the risk-avoiders continued to believe that such a settlement might eventually prove feasible, the risk-takers suspected that Spain must now find it intolerable. They were, in the end, proved right, but intransigence was by no means confined to the courts at Brussels and the Escorial.

The situation was a long while deteriorating. Alba's army had crushed revolt in the Low Countries during the late 1560s, but in April 1572 a group of Dutch protestant refugees – the so-called 'sea-beggars' – seized the port of Brill, and from then on a greater or lesser portion of the Netherlands provinces rejected Spanish rule. At first this *de facto* independence was precarious. English volunteers served against the Spanish in Holland, and English money helped finance the rebels' constant search for mercenary support, but Elizabeth declined to give them any official backing. Over more than a decade, only in the wake of the Spanish mutinies of 1576, when the entire Low Countries temporarily united against Philip II, was military intervention seriously considered – and Spanish success in wooing back the Catholic southern provinces again changed the queen's mind.

Hostility towards Spain had other consequences. Pragmatic alliance with France, internally divided but still sufficiently powerful to challenge Spanish ambition, brought with it the last serious prospect of a royal marriage. As Elizabeth entered her forties and the likelihood of a Tudor heir rapidly diminished, the clamour for any match also dimmed, although Leicester when laying on a fortnight of lavish entertainment for the queen at Kenilworth in 1575 made one last try, through drama, masque and verse, to force the issue. From 1579, however, a Spanish military recovery in Flanders under the methodical generalship of Alexander Farnese, prince of Parma, alarmed both London and Paris, while in the following year Philip seized the crown of Portugal, uniting the Iberian peninsula and two great empires. For a while it looked as if Elizabeth might accept the hand of King Henry III of France's younger brother and heir Francis, duke of Anjou. Anjou had been nominated

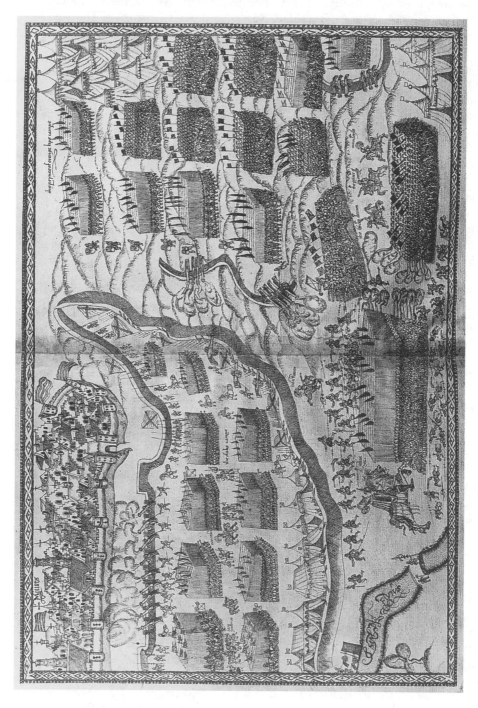

Plate 15 Fight in front of Mons, 1572, from Walter Morgan's illustrated Low Countries Chronicle. Sixteenth-century land warfare; note the combination of pikemen and musketeers in an infantry regiment, the latter forming a skirmishing fringe about the solid ranks of pikes.

Source: The Warden and Fellows of All Souls College, Oxford MS.129, fols 9v–10r

first as 'Defender of the Liberties of the Low Countries', then as 'Prince and Lord of the Netherlands', his titles reflecting a desperate search for international legitimacy by the Dutch.

For Elizabeth, the prospect of marriage and collaboration with the French royal family served to warn Philip II against taking too high a line with the Dutch. Just as important, the negotiations acted as insurance against French territorial ambitions in Flanders. For the French, the search for allies in the face of resurgent Spanish power coincided with the need to find a role for Anjou, whose proximity to the throne had already served as a focus for dissatisfaction. The duke visited England twice, in 1579 and 1581–2, to the fury of some protestants, to the frank incredulity of many, and to the alarm of Leicester and his clients, who, suspicious of French intentions in the Low Countries, worried at the friendly links established between the French prince and Burghley, Sussex and the crypto-Catholic circle round the earl of Oxford. Council advice was divided, Elizabeth tempted, but cautious. John Stubbs, a lawyer, lost his right hand in 1579 for writing a tract against the union, while Thomas Norton was consigned to the Tower in 1581 on account of his 'overmuch and undutiful speaking touching this cause'. On a more elevated literary plane the fears of Leicester's followers were expressed eloquently in Philip Sidney's unprinted *Letter to Queen Elizabeth* and in Edmund Spenser's *Shepheards Calender*.

These fears were far from unfounded. On one occasion Elizabeth announced publicly that she would marry her French suitor, only to withdraw the promise after a fraught night spent listening to doubts expressed very forcibly by the ladies of her bedchamber. The fact of wedlock accomplished, however, was less attractive to Elizabeth than the diplomatic possibilities in marriage negotiations. Whatever her own feelings, she could not ignore misgivings within her own council: Mary Tudor's marriage to Philip, against the wishes of several counsellors, had brought rebellion to the gates of London; Mary Stuart's equally unpopular marriage to Bothwell had cost her a throne. Anjou took his leave of England, laden with gifts, promises and compliments, but still a single man. These negotiations mark a watershed in the long story of the Elizabethan succession. Through the 1580s and 1590s, past childbearing age and confronting an international situation in which no foreign marriage alliance appeared attractive, the queen, her ministers and court magnified the advantages of Elizabeth's single state, emphasizing in the complex iconography of poetry, drama and art the notion that a virgin queen could yet be a mother to all her countrymen. Here was a message by no means universally popular; those involved, even, perhaps, Elizabeth herself, were making the best of an essentially undesirable situation.[5] Or perhaps disconcerting might be the better word: as Francis Bacon observed, once the line had safely died out, the last three Tudors had offered 'the strangest variety that in a like number of successions of any hereditary monarchy hath ever been known', and Elizabeth's predicament was of the three perhaps the strangest.

Prospects for the queen's marriage were debated hotly in literature, at court and in the English countryside, but they no longer figured prominently in parliamentary debate. In resigned deference to Elizabeth's wishes the issue

Plate 16 *Elizabeth I 'The Ditchley Portrait'*, by Marcus Gheeraerts the Younger, *c*.1592. This supremely impressive full-length portrait conveys a stylized image of the virgin queen. Note the uncovered bosom, then fashionable for unmarried Englishwomen, the map of England at her feet, and the way in which both sunshine and storm are used to emphasize her majesty.

Source: National Portrait Gallery, London

was set on one side. There was, after all, plenty of other business to occupy the intermittent sessions. Parliament still served its long-established purposes: it granted subsidies – though these, in real terms, became ever less substantial – and it passed laws, including private laws. While the origins of certain measures defy classification, figures for the Elizabethan parliaments down to 1581 suggest that nearly one in ten private bills introduced into either House eventually emerged as a public act, while one in three was accepted as a private statute. The success rate is higher than public legislation, and although the latter is better documented and the figures may thus be distorted, there is no doubting the importance of parliament, to its members and the men they represent, as a channel for the implementation of private legislation.

These traditional ends were pursued with a willingness that betokened common purpose throughout the elite of Elizabethan society. Members came from the same ruling class; most owed their seats to their wealth and connections, and saw attendance as a duty to God, queen, patron and country, indissolubly bound together. The queen was not alone in viewing parliament as a source of assent to her executive initiatives; members tended to regard business in the same light. They enjoyed freedom of speech in the Commons, but qualified this themselves as the freedom to speak 'sensibly', in accordance with perceived royal wishes. As the chancellor of the Exchequer, Sir Walter Mildmay, reminded Peter Wentworth in 1576, parliamentary freedom of speech 'never, nor ought to be extended so far as though a man in this House may speak what, and of whom he list'. Within parliament, Norman Jones observes, members set out to 'act as judges, sharing with the queen the responsibility of making law, for which they were answerable to God'.[6]

Parliamentary practice changed little through Elizabeth's long reign. If there is a case to be made for continuing institutional evolution, if parliament by the 1590s was, to quote Wallace MacCaffrey, 'something a good deal more than a merely petitionary or tax-granting body, something more than an advisory Council waiting to be asked its opinion', that case is far from clear cut.[7] Gradual such evolution certainly was, for long service, the foster-mother of institutional self-consciousness, was uncommon. Sixty-two per cent of all Elizabethan Commons MPs sat in just one parliament; only in 1586 did more than half the House enjoy previous parliamentary experience. Repeated considerations of public issues, and a more intimate linkage between council and membership in both Houses, perhaps fostered some sense of parliamentary identity, but evidence for this is also thin.

Though the council might wield great executive power, and while parliament might provide a legislative framework for this regulation, the administrative system of Elizabethan England, in common with most contemporary states, depended upon the goodwill of local landowners. In the absence of any central bureaucracy capable of supervising and correcting these local authorities, every aspect of Elizabethan government, from religious settlement to economic regulation, takes on a different hue depending upon the shire studied. English counties differed in their response to such direction, and they differed in their political make-up, and those differences differed over time. As Alison Wall notes, in a necessarily cautious assessment, while

SYMONDS of
C° Norfolk.

Plate 17 *Mr Symonds of Norfolk*, British school, *c*.1595. An English gentleman coursing and hawking across his estate, painting by an unknown local artist. Norwich is seen in the distance.
Source: Norfolk Museums Service, The Ancient House Museum, Thetford

we may discern some 'patterns of politics in English counties . . . they were complex'.

The complexity overshadows the patterns. In some counties, Suffolk for instance, local government had fallen exclusively into the hands of reliable protestant gentlemen by the late 1570s, with greater or lesser connivance from the privy council; in other counties, notably Nottinghamshire and Norfolk, this never really happened. In some shires – as with the Stanley earls of Derby in Lancashire, the Hastings earls of Huntingdon in Leicestershire, the Cecils in Hertfordshire or the Wynns in Caernarfonshire – a dominant local family directed the administration of justice and settled parliamentary returns harmoniously with other leading men of the county. In other counties still – Essex and Monmouthshire, for example – no single family dominated. Local gentry generally took their cue from social superiors, but in some counties might set their course against the authority of a leading nobleman, and through their own influence and connections at court defy his influence: this the marquess of Winchester in 1560s Hampshire learned to his cost.[8]

This variety of experience was reflected in the crown's relations with its local agents, and the interrelationships of those local men. More and more trust was placed in the religiously 'well affected' in each shire. Principal local officers had always been drawn from a relatively small pool of prominent and 'reliable' gentry, and following Elizabeth's religious settlement that pool shrank. From 1579, assize judges were ordered to administer the oath of supremacy to all JPs, and since the judges, at least after the deaths of Marian appointees allowed in men of a more conformist hue, were generally dependable in such matters, this was one direction from the centre efficiently carried through. However, those well affected in religion were by no means always as well disposed towards the laws they were supposed to enforce. The festering dispute between Sir Thomas Coningsby and Sir James Croft in Hereford-shire, which descended to armed violence as well as the law courts, is one particularly glaring instance from the 1580s.[9] Not everyone behaved so abrasively. Nevertheless, egocentricity often complemented a strong commitment to local affairs, and the means of excluding troublesome gentlemen from the influence conferred upon them by their birth was not always to hand.[10]

Limited resources dictated the twin approaches of central government to the handling of localities. On the one hand there was the informal, personal communication of counsellor to his friends, clients or agents in the shire, and on the other there was that ubiquitous and more formal instrument, the council letter. The sheriff and, above all, the JP were the recipients of most such council directions. Experts in finance or in law might be joined with these officials in ad hoc commissions, as the need arose, and in its myriad forms the commission becomes another symbol of Tudor administration. There were commissions to collect taxes and review financial institutions, others to supervise oath-taking, others to review the conduct and perform-ance of universities, or to advise on procedures for rebuilding forts and naturalizing foreigners. Some were investigatory, others, as with royal com-missions of our own age, investigative and advisory. They could on occasion exercise the broadest of functions: the Elizabethan High Commission, form-alized as a court around 1580, was empowered to supervise and enforce the religious settlement of 1559 across the land. If the subject for consideration offered prospects of financial return, the crown might license individuals to carry out the work, in return for a share of the profits. The most notorious example is the regular use, through Elizabeth's reign, of favoured 'searchers' to look for so-called concealed lands: lands, that is, belonging to the crown where the title had been obscured by ignorance and time, and which in consequence yielded no return to the royal coffers.[11]

The privy council's channel of communication with the localities through the sheriff and commission of the peace was augmented by the use of indi-vidual noblemen to serve as unofficial vice-regents or lieutenants in areas where they possessed extensive estates. The earls of Shrewsbury filled this role in Derbyshire, the earls of Derby in Lancashire. Eventually, these ad hoc yet effective arrangements were formalized. County lieutenancies, created in 1550 to muster levies as a preventative measure against any repeat of the

*How England
was managed*

1549 troubles, appear spasmodically, at times of political uncertainty, through the early years of Elizabeth's reign, and, by the end of the century, are emerging as permanent institutions. They offered a more direct channel for the council when issuing important orders: as Sir Thomas Smith warned William Cecil as early as 1549, by sending out council directives to sheriff and individual JP, central government was granting the county agents rather too much scope to stand back in the expectation that one of their colleagues would carry out the commission. Investing one man with both office and responsibility seemed the answer, to the council, to the man chosen for the prestige thus conferred, and to the locality, since the lieutenant was often a prominent counsellor offering county friends and clients an ear and even a voice at the heart of Elizabeth's court. The lieutenant was aware of the consensual element in local authority, while supervising and exhorting his JPs he was also well placed to conciliate and sympathize. Though the prominence of lieutenants might be advantageous in many ways, it also meant that this supreme county agent was often absent from his shire. Accordingly, favoured local gentlemen received appointments as deputy lieutenants in the 1590s, exercising in conjunction with assistants many of the lieutenant's functions.

Towns present another manifestation of delegated government. With London, and with other cities where it suited, the crown recognized the lord mayor and his brethren as the local officials of a separate county. By 1537, with the elevation of Exeter, thirteen urban centres in England enjoyed the legal status of a county borough, complete with their own 'sheriffs' and commissions of the peace. The men who received such authority, generally speaking a closed, self-perpetuating community of successful first- or second-generation merchants, were flattered by the attention of central government. They understood, however, that increased honour implied increased responsibility; and they showed, albeit through instincts not far removed from self-preservation, some concern for their poorer fellow citizens. Ruling town councils organized services and maintenance projects, while collecting taxes and watching for signs of unrest. Other, even less tangible factors worked against manifestations of urban discontent. Steve Rappaport's description of London as a multitude of little communities and 'worlds' within a great city, each requiring an individual's participation in its government, however mean that individual, helps explain why the sixteenth-century capital never succumbed to the temptations of revolt.

The economic problems encountered earlier in the century were less widespread by the 1570s, although towns reliant on certain industries bucked this hopeful trend. Unable to retain their hinterland against new competition from rural weavers, Coventry and Winchester faced severe problems. Other instances of decline might be attributed only to politics – as with Rye and the loss of Calais – or to nature, as with coastal erosion at Dunwich. But no one seems agreed on the criteria by which to measure stagnation and it has become apparent that the same evidence, slow population growth, for example, can point in different directions. London's growth and increasing monopolization of overseas trade certainly hurt several outports, but even

Into--trade

where the London economy did impinge on that of another English port, its rapid growth also created a market, for coal and foodstuffs, which could be exploited by enterprising provincial merchants in towns like Newcastle and King's Lynn.

These are some manifestations of those infinitely variable chains of authority which bound the queen and her court to the meanest labourer, in the farthest parish of the realm. For all their improvised and pragmatic nature, the links in these chains were often of surprisingly true metal. The weakest may well have been not those between court and the increasingly sophisticated layers of Elizabethan county agents, but those between these men and the voice of the county itself, the neighbours who kept their eyes open, or closed, depending on their inclination, who might inform, or withhold information, who would administer as churchwardens the poor law measures on a parochial basis, and who might, or might not, bring in when serving as jurymen in court a verdict appropriate to the known facts. Offering these local men a voice in county government was the surest way of winning them to a communality of outlook, but as Penry Williams observes, 'that cooperation, often grudging and partial, had to be won, for it could not be assumed'.[12]

Professional informers profited from these weaknesses. They were particularly active in the enforcement of social and economic legislation, where offenders might pay a forfeiture to the crown on conviction. Such legislation ranged in practice from measures against usury to those which attacked recusants. The activities of private informers were intensely resented at all levels of society, but wherever humble churchwardens, even JPs, could be coerced or bribed into winking at the faults of their social superiors they had a role to play. At parliament after parliament, government officials lamented the obvious discrepancy between well-intentioned legislation and the often non-existent processes of enforcement. Christopher Wray, in 1571, declared before the queen upon his election to the speaker's chair that legislation could only be considered 'a good law well made when it is well executed'. Overworked JPs, busy with enforcing all the other social and political demands of central government, were in no position to ferret out furtive commercial agreements, gather the necessary proofs and attend a central court of record over an often prolonged period. To whom else might central government turn?

The task confronting informers was seldom straightforward. Exchequer process could be desperately slow; few cases resulted in trial, let alone conviction. Whatever the rights and wrongs of a particular issue, the costs of interminable litigation frequently encouraged all parties to seek a compromise, and unrecorded sums of money changed hands out of court. Legislation of 1576 tightened up the rules under which informers and court officials worked in an effort to avoid blackmail and vexatious litigation. Little more, though, was done. Inaction reflected the council's ambivalence. While inclined to root out abuses, many counsellors were reluctant to surrender their control of licences to inform, or to discover offenders: these licences were remarkably lucrative. Even the most principled feared that legislation might deter honest men from commencing litigation. The council was equally unable, and unwilling, to tackle the problem that underlay so much of this ill-feeling towards informers: the impracticality of many penal laws, particularly those against usury and 'middlemen'.[13]

From 1574, a new phase in the history of post-reformation Catholicism opens with the arrival in England of Roman Catholic priests, trained in the seminary at Douai founded by the priest, theologian and author William Allen. Another seminary, at Rome, was established under Jesuit auspices in 1579. These training institutions aimed at the reconversion of England and Wales through the deployment there of an educated English Catholic priesthood. Here was a noble aim, underpinned by a grandiose vision, but over the next thirty years the missionary priests enjoyed only limited success. For all the conviction and discipline shown by these brave young men, and for all their thorough grounding in the Bible and English church history, they arrived in England ill-prepared for a life on the run. All too often their days of service were brief. Nor did they arrive in sufficiently large numbers: sixty-one priests trained at Douai had entered England by the end of 1578, around 500 came in all between 1574 and 1603. Fresh impetus was given to the English mission with the arrival of the first Jesuit priests – Edmund Campion and Robert Persons – in 1580, but the Jesuit fathers, like their predecessors, took a strategic decision which helped determine the nature of English Catholicism for centuries to come. They concentrated their attentions on the proven recusants – people who refused to attend the new church services – especially those among the gentry. The missionary priests did not seek wholesale conversions; theirs was to be a holding operation. As often as not they were themselves the sons of gentry families, and now they ministered as household chaplains to their own kind, particularly in regions most accessible to the continent, places – such as Essex and the Thames valley – not noted for their high concentrations of committed Catholics. Within its limits the strategy was successful, for Catholicism survived in England, but this was also a strategy which accepted, however tacitly, the enduring success of a new English religion.

Native Catholics in exile allowed themselves to be misled by recollections of an England fast disappearing. Allen, born and raised on the conservative Lancashire coast and forever impressed by the easy reversal of Edwardian protestantism during his years as an Oxford don in the 1550s, was particularly guilty of exaggerating commitment to the Catholic faith. The exiles turned hopefully to Spain. Philip II's armies, they reasoned, were capable of enforcing reconversion. But in so doing they wilfully ignored the obvious English hostility to foreign intervention. Only at the very end of his life, after the failure of the Armada, did Allen begin to face reality, bargaining for limited toleration of English Catholics, yet by then, given the prevailing intransigence governed by war, negotiations of this kind were all but impossible to initiate.[14]

By around 1580 we must begin to write of England as a protestant country: Elizabeth's longevity was giving her church time to put down lasting roots in the country which, as a whole, was prepared quietly to discard old ways and take to new, encouraged by the repeated insistence of secular authority and the enthusiasm of influential minorities in town and country-side. This twin process of rejection and acceptance remains one of the abiding mysteries of the long, slow English reformation.[15] The late medieval Catholic ceremonials, the Yuletide processions and mystery plays, which in the 1560s and into the 1570s had still coloured the seasonal 'months of ease' from December to June, began to disappear as first official and then public attitudes started to take a more austerely protestant line. The church seemed less willing to use popular culture, book and pamphlet illustration, drama or catchy ballad, as a didactic tool. At parish level Catholicism withered irredeemably. When the bishops at the turn of the century contrasted the 2,250,000 communicants of the established church with the 8600 officially recorded recusants they deliberately underestimated the latter figure, blurring over extensive token conformity. All the same, the contrast presented between a national religion confronting the timeless problems of lay ignorance and clerical poverty, and a small, if disciplined, minority denomination surviving on the idiosyncrasies of individual country gentlemen, is one that hardly requires emphasis.

The missionary priests insisted that they went about God's work; the English administration insisted that they peddled treason. In a tense international climate, the religious and political threads in the message they carried were hard to disentangle. Persons may, or may not, have advocated the murder of Elizabeth in an enigmatic letter written during 1583.[16] While forbidding discussion at Douai of any conspiracy against Elizabeth, Allen himself dabbled in plots, drawing on support among fellow exiles at the court of Spain. For such zealots, and the small minority of like-minded individuals among the English Catholics, Pius V's excommunication of the queen stirred dreams that removal of England's head of state might promote the nation's return to Rome. They pinned their hopes on the queen of Scots, and a trail of conspiracies through the 1580s sought to make Mary queen of England. After her execution in 1587 the plots continued, but removal of Elizabeth became an end in itself, little coherent thought going into the selection of an alternative Catholic claimant.

That is, however, to anticipate events. Mary Stuart remained a focus for trouble so long as she lived, but her continued imprisonment also gave Elizabeth welcome control over English relations with Scotland and the succession to her own throne. The captive queen had her uses. Sir Ralph Sadler, then chancellor of the duchy of Lancaster and an expert on Anglo-Scottish affairs, summed up an advantageous situation, early in 1570: 'As for the Queen of Scots,' he told Elizabeth, 'Your Majesty may so use her as she shall not be able to hurt you; and to that end surely God hath delivered her into your hands.' These pious considerations dictated the balancing of mercy and justice after the Ridolfi plot. In the decade following that conspiracy, Mary, conscious that hostile eyes were watching her every move, avoided any serious taint of intrigue, concentrating on her claims in Scotland, her French lands and access to the spas of Buxton.[17]

The papal excommunication of Elizabeth and the arrival of the missionary priests increased the administration's suspicion of domestic Catholics.

Although there had been exceptions in dioceses ruled by more radical or diligent bishops, efforts to impose conformity in the 1560s had usually stopped at attempts to control the influx of Catholic literature, as the religiously conservative historian John Stow found to his cost when his study was raided by the bishop of London's men in 1569. Tolerance now began to evaporate. The authorities' first steps were nevertheless rather tentative. Efforts to convert the more prominent Catholics of specific counties, notably the sons of such families attending university, occupied a great deal of council time, with limited success. Reason was backed by threats, and on occasion by imprisonment. The discovery of Campion's and Persons's mission, however, stirred a major panic and led in the parliament of 1581 to a statute which defined as treason any attempt to persuade Englishmen to accept Rome's 'pretended authority'.

Yet again, it was one thing to legislate, another to enforce these laws. Considerable scope remained for those who were Catholic in their hearts, who considered themselves Catholics, and who even took part in some form of organized worship, to evade punishment through token attendance at established services. The fulminations of stricter protestants, and a growing use from the 1580s of that opprobrious term 'church papist', point to frustration as well as radicalism. In 1581, the same act introduced a fine of £20 a month for recusancy in place of the former shilling a week, but the very size of this figure identified the statute's intended targets. Just as the Catholic missionary priests had opted to fight their battle in the country houses, so too did a hostile administration choose to harass the wealthy landowners, the men who might back any attempted military operation to place a Catholic on the throne, just as the gentry of East Anglia had done in 1553.

There was another disincentive to proceed against poorer Catholics. Since prosecutions might now be brought by private informers, the profit motive weighed heavily. Informers were rewarded, where the prosecution was successful, out of the penalties imposed on their wealthy targets: little would be gained from the pursuit of poorer victims. Further legislation, such as an act of 1587, pursued the same men, stopping up legal loopholes by which wealthier recusants had shifted their lands to trusts, or into the nominal control of conformist relatives and friends. In 1593 an attempt was made to frustrate physical evasion, when recusants were ordered by statute to remain within five miles of their chief residences. Recognizing that any Spanish invasion would require cavalry support from within the nation, the government seized the stables of leading Catholic gentlemen and made them pay collectively for a light cavalry force in Ireland.

Attempts to quantify the extent of Catholic persecution generate some revealing statistics. Ostensibly political processes against seminary priests and their lay supporters resulted in some 200 executions for treason in Elizabeth's reign, most in the years 1581–93,[18] but apart from these obvious targets the protestant administration concentrated on a highly selective list of wealthy and influential country gentry, the type who could shape attitudes in a locality. Between 1581 and 1586, fines for recusancy were collected from a mere sixty-nine Catholics, and the overwhelming majority of these were men resident in southern counties rather than in the more religiously conservative

north.[19] In 1592, during a major privy council assault on recusancy, just over 140 paid fines, most having secured reduced rates. The degree of persecution seems to have varied in response to the threat from Spain, and there are signs that, by the 1590s, Elizabeth's council believed that it had the measure of English gentry Catholicism. Practical manifestations of persecution – notably the collection of recusancy fines – were appreciably relaxed.

The activities of Catholic priests in England prompted the Elizabethan church to look more closely at its own shortcomings. Some of these were old problems. Visiting bishops, as their predecessors had done for centuries, took perverse pleasure in listing the deficiencies of their parish priests. Campaigns backed by council and by greater provision for training in the universities gradually improved the proportions of ministers possessing degrees or licensed as preachers. There were one in five graduate priests in Worcester diocese in 1560, one in two by 1620, and similar increases were recorded in other parts of the country. By the end of the century 75 per cent of incumbents in an 'advanced', wealthy place like the city of London possessed a degree: even more impressive, 50 per cent of London parish curates were by then also graduates. Education alone did not guarantee competence, of course, but given the complex structure of clerical patronage in England and the element of individual choice exercised by a multitude of patrons this was good progress, rather better, indeed, than many expected.

By the end of Elizabeth's reign her church was fast acquiring sufficient numbers of qualified preachers capable of disseminating the essentials of what remained, even then, a new faith. Most dioceses by 1603 could boast a ratio of at least one preacher to two parishes, the preachers preaching to a better-educated, generally more receptive audience, and encouraged by a huge increase in the publication of religious editions and catechisms aimed at a popular market. Editions of the English Bible poured off the presses and found their way into the homes of 'ordinary' men and women. Only in Wales and parts of the north-west, where poverty of livings, large parishes and enduring attachment to Catholicism blunted many reformist endeavours, was the position markedly less rosy, and there too the same trends were at least observed.

Church reformers had for centuries also criticized the discrepancies in wealth within the ecclesiastical hierarchy: in particular, their censures were levelled at the meagre incomes enjoyed by lesser clergy. Once the problem had centred on poverty among the unbeneficed clergy; now it turned on the numbers of under-endowed benefices, which struggled to maintain a clergyman and, very often, a clergyman's family in an age of inflation. Fewer men came forward for ordination in the 1540s, 1550s and 1560s, principally, perhaps, because the great source of work for the unbeneficed, in chantries, had disappeared along with the custom and fashion for obituary masses. Clerical deprivations under Mary and Elizabeth had reduced the numbers further and had helped tailor a situation in which most ordained priests held or expected to enjoy benefices. Poverty, of course, was relative: simple comparisons of clerical incomes take no account of such factors as the difficulties involved in collecting tithes from recalcitrant parishioners, the produce from glebe land which could cushion a benefice holder against price inflation, the subsidiary incomes to be earned from performing marriages, funerals, baptisms and churchings, and, of course, the great imponderable of inherited wealth and property. Nevertheless, many parishes commanded incomes below £5 a year, which, taken in isolation, left the incumbent scarcely better off than the agricultural labourers or smallholders in his congregation. Archbishop Whitgift suggested in 1584 that just 600 of England's 9000 parishes offered an adequate means of support to an educated man. Although there was a gradual improvement as both country gentry and town hierarchies began to invest in clerical incomes, and as clergymen with substantial glebe land turned entrepreneur, rising prices dented the prosperity of any clergyman dependent upon fixed cash tithe payments, and the position only really began to improve in the next century.

Not every problem was of long standing. Educated or not, wealthy or poor, the commitment of many parish priests to the Elizabethan settlement also gave their superiors cause for concern. That very accommodation shown by a majority of incumbents, prototype vicars of Bray up and down the land, to the various religious upheavals mid-century guaranteed that the Elizabethan church had inherited more than one generation of trimmers. Again the problem gradually eased, as men raised and trained in the post-1559 church took the places of elderly, conservative priests, but it had not vanished in the 1570s. Nor were replacements always as attached to the new faith as the administration might wish. Many owed their places to preferment from country gentlemen who held livings in their gift, and who may have themselves been ambiguous in matters of religion. Possession of Catholic sympathies had at no time deterred men of means from buying monastic lands and properties – and the livings that formed part of such property. Only a minority of lay patrons ever enquired closely into the qualifications, ability or doctrinal persuasions of the clergymen they preferred to livings: patronage, obligation to others, financial considerations and family ties were the factors that counted.

Ever since the breach with Rome there had been inherent tensions in the marriage between a protestant church and a national, established religion. Godly minorities seldom sat at ease with ignorant, irreligious, even popish multitudes. Foxe, in his *Acts and Monuments*, offered an official *modus vivendi*. Here, the native church in the form of Elizabethan protestantism was shown emerging from centuries of persecution and oppression by priestly obscurantists; Biblical truth was being given back to the people, dragged from the clutches of an un-English Roman church, obsessed with show rather than substance. What, though, of the role of the bishops and lesser clergy, at once denounced for corruption in days past, and now expected to lead their flocks along the paths of righteousness under the new dispensation? Foxe's vague insistence that priests lapsing into unsound doctrine and improper behaviour would be set aside by God, perhaps even in favour of laymen, rather suggested that chastisement was indeed beyond the powers of men, while his simultaneous defence and castigation of ecclesiastical hierarchies seemed then, and seems now, equally strained.[20]

Tensions between religious radicalism and an unreceptive administration provoked uncertainty. The presbyterian campaign for further church reforms in parliament during 1572 had failed to attract anything more than minority support, even in the Lower House. That minority was, nevertheless, not insignificant: the growing aggression of counter-reformation Catholicism was helping to promote the views of those elements within the English church which regarded further refinement of the Elizabethan settlement as a necessary weapon against threats from both without and within. This, they argued, the existing popish 'mingle-mangle' could never provide. In practical terms, the presbyterians demanded in place of the present church hierarchy the establishment and recognition of autonomous congregations under elected ministers and elders; representative councils or synods should supply the only guidance or direction from a higher earthly authority.

Their unspoken agenda was clear. A godly 'elect', the 'true church', might seek the prince's help in enforcing religious purity, but, ultimately, it could exist without him – or her. At this point these views parted company with those of otherwise sympathetic figures at the very heart of the Tudor polity. Leading statesmen might agree the desirability of alterations in church government, and might dislike the 'Romish' elements in the queen's religion. But that was the point: the queen's counsellors could never forget that it *was* the queen's religion, and that Elizabeth would tolerate no alteration.

Though the word has been misused down the years, there is no real harm in labelling the more vehement presbyterians puritans: the purification of the English church from Catholic 'error' as the means of confirming God's bond with His elect summarizes their agenda well enough. Like church papistry, puritanism is an umbrella term, reeking of the pejorative. There never was any cleanly defined puritan philosophy or theology: a shared adoption of Zwinglian or Calvinist theology, a conviction of the merits of good preaching and moral rectitude, a sense that England should take its rightful place at the heart of European reformed churches, all move us towards the inspiration behind rather than to any definition of puritanism. Patrick Collinson observes that, as a term of perception or stigmatization, puritanism sheds light on those who used it as much as those on whom it was conferred, informing us 'about both halves of a stressful relationship'.

Despite Elizabeth's hostility, political presbyterianism enjoyed considerable strength among the ruling classes in the 1570s. For a brief moment, in the middle of that decade, it even enjoyed the support of the archbishop of Canterbury. Nominated to the archbishopric on the death of Matthew Parker in 1575, Edmund Grindal was, however, suspended less than two years later. Grindal had seemed a sound enough choice. A favoured preacher at Edward VI's court he had, with the constant backing of Burghley, put in good service first as bishop of London, then as archbishop of York. But there was a sense in which the appointment had been a finely judged gamble, for Grindal's advanced beliefs were sufficiently well known. His successful confrontation of Catholicism at York had been backed up by a considered advocacy of reformed religion which had enjoyed strong support from like-minded members of the court, Leicester, Sir Francis Knollys and Walsingham.

Grindal's disgrace resulted from his refusal to obey a direct royal instruction in 1576. Elizabeth had ordered him to suppress the emerging custom by which clergy in a locality met, often in a convenient market town, to hear and discuss a small set of sermons on a particular scriptural text. These learned gatherings had, somewhat unfortunately, acquired the colourful designation 'prophesyings'. Here was a word with unpleasant connotations; it conjured visions of uncontrolled gatherings of reformist clergy, visions most displeasing to a queen who in any case questioned the need for vast armies of preachers. The fact that such assemblies gathered openly, in churches, before large congregations, was just as alarming. Having once rejected suppression, Grindal refused to back down or to compromise, making his suspension in 1577 inevitable. Only the efforts of sympathetic privy counsellors dissuaded Elizabeth from depriving him of his see. The queen recognized Grindal's right to take a stand on matters of genuine conscience, but considered the whole question of prophesying 'indifferent', among the *adiaphora*, and thus interpreted his actions as gross impertinence.

So Grindal remained archbishop, in name only, until his death in July 1583. An ecclesiastical commission was given powers to put an end to prophesying and to encourage tighter episcopal surveillance over dioceses. In practice suppression was never wholly successful, for clergy continued to assemble in 'combinations', for 'exercises', taking turns at public preaching, while many bishops, who had always seen meetings of this kind as a means to educate their parish clergy, sponsored endorsement and regulation of appropriate initiatives in convocation. Few market towns regretted the extra custom attracted by good preaching. Here was a manifestation, both of old-fashioned good fellowship – a hearty dinner was commonly provided – and of that growing sense of collegiality among clergymen which during the seventeenth century helped bring together ministers of the Church of England in a consciously distinct and mutually supportive society.

Intransigence on a point of principle might appear admirable, but it weakened the cause Grindal sought to advance. It also contributed to the generally low esteem in which the clerical hierarchy was held. Slowly, self-preservation was bringing the bishops to a doctrinaire conformity. With the nomination in August 1583 of John Whitgift, bishop of Worcester, as Grindal's successor, the government ensured that the archbishopric of Canterbury would rest in the hands of a disciplinarian, resolute in imposing episcopal surveillance of the clergy through High Commission and through his own relentless scrutiny. Whitgift was both leader of and exemplar to the late Elizabethan episcopate: he forged his career in attacks upon unorthodoxy. Harbouring no thought of concession to radical alteration he proved a redoubtable enemy to would-be presbyterian reformers, testing suspect preachers under oath on the substance of their beliefs. In debate with Thomas Cartwright and others, he had long ago come to the perhaps not-unfounded conclusion that, whatever the convenient status quo of recent years, presbyterianism was incompatible with the stability of England's monarchy.

To some of the older generation, including Burghley, these tactics smacked of the Spanish Inquisition, but for Whitgift radical presbyterians and puritans were the queen's enemies and had to be treated as such. As he pointed out in the 1584–5 parliament, preachers were a dangerous luxury when the country lacked sober, well-educated ministers to administer sacraments, and read prayers and homilies. Burghley might have his doubts, but the queen herself, and Whitgift's friends and fellow counsellors Hatton and Lord Buckhurst too, upheld this rigid approach. The queen appointed him to her privy council, a rare distinction for an Elizabethan cleric, and she chided her archbishop only when his intransigence stirred up discontent in parliament. Bishop Richard Cox of Ely described Whitgift as 'athleta Dei fortissimus', and Elizabeth would not have quarrelled with that. Whitgift was not necessarily against innovation in religion: he accepted that there might be more than one valid form of church government. Reform was something he was prepared to countenance, and enforce, provided that such reform was confined essentially to improving educational standards of parish clergy and was in accord with Elizabeth's wishes.

Elizabeth's wishes were vital, not only because she was head of the church but also because, as Whitgift and his colleagues were inclining to argue, her authority as head of state and head of the church was derived directly from God alone, her prerogative powers, in consequence, absolute. The common law judges were, in various test cases, increasingly disposed to take a similar view. As the century drew to its close, the various impulses towards religious reform which we might conveniently generalize as presbyterian gradually lost the support of everyone who counted, both in church and in council. The deaths of Walsingham and Leicester, and the pressing need for conformity in time of war, played into the hands of those opposed to further innovation.[21]

Thus presbyterian initiatives eventually had an effect, but that effect was one of reaction rather than agreement. The church was placed on its guard. Those favouring reform concentrated instead on the eradication of wilder heresies. Even the innocuous followers of a German mystic Hendrik Niclas – the so-called Family of Love – attracted a good deal of anxious government attention in the late 1570s, above all because their rather simplistic, Bible-centred beliefs included the convenient sanction of complete outward conformity to the oaths, services and other tests enjoined by authority. Yet in the countryside 'familists' lived quietly, and were left alone. Like the church papist, 'church protestants' were denounced violently as hypocrites and dissemblers, but much of the violence stemmed from the fact that, having chosen its battlefield, there was little that the government might do to challenge such men and women.[22]

By the 1580s and 1590s this reaction was gathering momentum, spearheaded by a new generation of bishops. Richard Bancroft and Thomas Bilson were using scripture to defend both the central role of a godly prince and, at least within England, the anciently ordained necessity of an episcopal hierarchy. The bishops were recovering confidence, fashioning themselves as the quashers of 'puritanism', essential agents of the royal supremacy. Always allowing for the variety of individual circumstance – Welsh and new, poorly endowed English sees like Peterborough and Oxford contrasted sharply with old-established Canterbury, Durham or Winchester, while personal wealth or the lack of it could make or mar a career – it is clear that the bishop's social standing and, more debatably, his prestige within his bishopric had declined by 1603. Signs of revival were, however, by then already present. If there was dissent in religion, if there was pressure to amend the 1559 settlement, Elizabeth knew where to place the blame; were not the governors of her church responsible for the tranquillity of their flocks? This recognition of responsibility itself enhanced the bishops' reputation and their own self-esteem. Self-confidence also drew on roots that were strong and deep. Bishops of the 1560s had rolled up their sleeves as, in John Jewel's words, 'pastors, labourers and watchmen', the very ideal of the primitive Christian prelate. Yet they, like their more ambitious successors, had recognized in this stance the antiquity of their office and the strengths to be derived from ancient precedents in a society impressed by lineage and descent.

With confidence came further claims. Bishops, such writers insisted, were not only necessary to good government, they were ordained by Christ. Why, they argued, should consensual, divinely sanctioned government give way to the election of ministers and elders, and the rule of an assembly? Just as a contested parliamentary election was viewed as bringing shame to a community, highlighting its divisions, so too did opponents of presbyterian reform contend that religious truth was as likely to be perceived by a learned minority as by an ignorant majority. Improved morale was reflected – though we are talking of individuals and individual variety – in the vigour many bishops brought to their labours. The energetic and ambitious Tobie Matthew, bishop of Durham, and archbishop of York under James I, who preached, according to his diary, 1992 sermons in forty-odd years from 1583, is just one example. New episcopal pretensions greatly alarmed the stricter protestant. Acceptance of the ancient authority of bishops verged on the recognition of the Roman church as a 'true' church, albeit grossed about with human errors. This view, espoused by James I, was at odds with those adopted by most in the early Elizabethan church.[23]

That alarm was, perhaps, exaggerated. The theological argument had in fact been won by the Calvinists in the church. Whitgift and Bancroft, his successor at Canterbury in 1604, married the hierarchy imposed by the Elizabethan settlement to strict interpretations of predestination – double predestination indeed – which aspiring, career-minded clergy questioned at their peril. In 1595, an academic dispute in Cambridge over predestination resulted in Whitgift's compilation of the so-called Lambeth Articles, a vehement restatement of Calvinist opinions. While Elizabeth tried to silence further debate she was not altogether successful; predestinarian beliefs held the day among the highest church authorities.[24]

In the heyday of its political importance under the Tudors, English presbyterianism played with some startlingly radical notions. Yet the presbyterians' assault on England's established church acknowledged the realities of society and aimed for any compromise that would shift the queen towards their own position, and enable them to impose presbyterian views on the country through act of parliament – from the top down. Like many fervent believers, they held the spiritual worth of the common Englishman and woman in low esteem. And for all their bibliocentric beliefs they appreciated – as Elizabeth did – that the histories of ancient Israel in the Old Testament, though one part of the Word of God, offered far too many disquieting precedents for social mayhem and every kind of political mischief. That they failed with tact as with bombast says much for their misunderstanding of Elizabeth's utter intransigence on the subject. It bears restatement that for her, the 1559 settlement was no mere staging post but the appropriate end of her nation's spiritual journey.[25]

How popular her stance was with the nation as a whole remains open to question. As in so many other areas – marriage, succession, foreign policy and national security – there is scope to see Elizabeth isolated against the great mass of the politically significant, gathered in the council, at court or in parliament. It is, though, equally valid to insist that the voices of the religiously committed, however loud, must not be allowed to speak for the majority of Englishmen and women, or even the majority of the Lords and Commons assembled. The shared conviction of committed protestants and Catholics – frequently expressed in their so-called 'complaint literature' – that 'rank Atheists and mock-gods', to quote from the puritan Arthur Dent's enormously popular *The plaine man's path-way to heaven*, formed a majority in the land, has about it more than a grain of truth. Alongside men more or less persuaded to particular points of view, and the incalculable number of people who conformed without thinking or out of respect for the law, stood a considerable though largely undocumented and uncounted group at the lower end of the social spectrum who went through life without troubling themselves over religion or church attendance, and who were insufficiently important or settled to merit more than a passing censure from authorities – in effect churchwardens – preoccupied elsewhere. The church gave up on these people: not one of the 154 churchwardens' presentments in Sudbury (Suffolk) deanery in 1593 was for absenteeism, and the picture is similar in other counties. Others stayed away from church because they, or the heads of their families, had ignored a summons to answer a charge in a church court, and had been excommunicated. Several thousands, apparently, fell into this category in late Elizabethan England, and few troubled to do penance and reverse the sentence, particularly if young or poor. Indeed, it is difficult to establish just how welcome were the very poorest in society at church services: no doubt the reception they received varied greatly, but we really do not know.

Alongside irreligion there persisted superstition and the love of tradition for its own sake: a continuation, frequently transmuted into some secular folk custom or domestic form, of such once-popular ceremonies as bells, fires and prayers for the dead on All Saints' Day (1 November), the hallowing of candles at Candlemas (2 February) and of wooden crosses cut from Palm Sunday foliage, as well as belief in magical and folk ceremonies and customs.[26] These were merely the most innocent of a great range of superstitions, believed and practised up and down the land. Many took notice of astrology or alchemy, pursuits then dignified as scientific which had long coexisted with state Christianity and which continued so to do, if with increasing tension, throughout the century.

*look out
for yourself
idea*

*local
problem —
but is
always
problem*

The poor had problems of their own. Niceties of a national creed faded into the background, as men, women and children struggled to find food and provide shelter for themselves and their loved ones. Such enduring hardships were repeatedly addressed by English parliaments. Led on, as so often in social legislation, by the example of London and other major towns, parliament took another step in 1572 towards a national codification for the control of the poor. Resulting legislation comprised the first major revision of the poor laws since 1531, although parliament had been tinkering with the problem across the intervening decades. Absolute poverty had always been first and foremost an urban phenomenon, and, whereas London imitated continental practices to contain the problem, other English towns and cities imitated London.

This process was empirical. After experimenting with voluntary collections in churches and at public preachings, town authorities up and down the country had introduced compulsory levies on their inhabitants to cope with the growing nuisance posed by beggars. London in 1547, Norwich in 1549, and York shortly afterwards, pioneered the way. The spate of London hospitals founded mid-century in former religious property – St Bartholomew's and St Thomas's for the sick and impotent, Bethlehem for the insane, Christ's Hospital to support orphans, Bridewell for the 'idle' vagrants – was also part of a coherent strategy to tackle the twin urban ills of idleness and poverty. Success varied. The most efficient schemes, in London, were swamped by sheer numbers as the city grew, while in other towns more modest resources were utilized, not always to good effect.

Poverty and unemployment – or underemployment – were not, of course, absent from the countryside beyond town walls. The scale of this particular problem remains elusive, although at a best guess some 10–20 per cent of the population may have lived below a level at which their income or other production met basic requirements. Statistics available for London and the south-east in the 1590s and 1600s suggest that this percentage of inhabitants took poor relief on an intermittent or a regular basis.

As in legislation of 1536, 1547, 1552, 1555 and 1563, the 1572 statute sought a compromise between savage punishments for able-bodied adult vagrants and a measure of compassion towards those rendered destitute through old age, widowhood, the death of parents or some other unavoidable misfortune. Again, the parish was considered the most effective unit for administration. Developing on the legislation of 1552 and 1563, the element of compulsion in alms-giving was increased. Hitherto, the only coercion, a threat of imprisonment by JPs in 1563, was exerted on those refusing to give anything. Now, attention was given to equalizing and rationalizing the amounts contributed. Those who gave derisory sums to the churchwardens under the old regulations might still shift and evade payment of their assessment, but evasion was slowly becoming far more difficult.

In 1572, JPs were given a more direct role in setting the rate at which relief was to be paid, establishing who did and who did not qualify. They also appointed the overseers, who put the scheme into practice: unpaid, obliged to serve and, in theory, selected annually from wealthier residents. Competing impulses lay behind such lawmaking, and the accompanying non-parliamentary regulations put out in the forms of royal proclamations and books of orders. The brew was complex, embracing fears of what the idle unemployed might do, concerns that society should be taking more account of poverty, and the inclination of many privy counsellors to build on local initiative and to extend central control. Legislation, both at a local and a national level, often appeared in the aftermath of difficult years, when minds were focused uncomfortably on the possibilities of social unrest.

An act passed in the next parliament, that of 1576, began to make more provision for that third, important class of the poor: those neither impotent nor idle but genuinely unable to find work. It required parishes to amass stocks of raw material – 'wool, hemp, flax, iron or other stuff' – on which the unemployed and underemployed might work. At the same time it recognized the need for compulsion in the form of 'houses of correction', along the lines of the established 'Bridewell' in London. There is, though, again difficulty in establishing the degree to which parishes complied. Though called for in the vagrancy legislation of 1547 and 1576, 'Bridewells' – as houses of correction were popularly known – only emerged in significant numbers after an act of 1610. So many factors varied across England: the size and cohesiveness of the parish itself, the enthusiasm and energy of JPs and churchwardens, and the wealth and generosity of local inhabitants. Legislation framed in the easy economic climate of the 1570s was on more than one occasion found insufficiently flexible twenty years later.

For the indigent poor life could seldom have been comfortable: comfort was never the goal of such legislation. Unsurprisingly, the law was especially unremitting against males. Women formed the majority of those assessed as poor; while men were expected to be capable of earning a livelihood, the widow with children was always recognized as more worthy of pity. Throughout the century unlicensed beggars, mostly males, might be whipped or mutilated. Although the full rigour of the law was seldom if ever enforced, vagrants convicted for the third time remained subject to the death penalty until 1593. Under legislation of 1598 these men were potentially liable to banishment or military service. Despite this severity, the 1570s social legislation, by throwing specific obligations on local justices and the parishes, played its part in a process which left Englishmen and women in 1603 of all social classes infinitely clearer as to their obligations, and their rights, in evil times.

14 England's Empire: Ireland, and Wider Horizons, 1560–1603

Chronology

January–February 1560	Legislation restores royal supremacy in Ireland and enforces Act of Uniformity
May 1560	Sussex appointed lord lieutenant
June 1561	Shane O'Neill proclaimed a traitor
April 1563	Parliament orders Welsh translation of prayer book
February 1565	Battle of Affane: earls of Desmond and Ormond summoned to England
May 1565	Shane O'Neill defeats Ulster Scots at Glenshesk
October 1565	Henry Sidney replaces the earl of Sussex as lord deputy
August 1566	Shane O'Neill proclaimed traitor for the second time; O'Neill burns Armagh cathedral
1567	New Testament published in Welsh
June 1567	Murder of Shane O'Neill
1569–70	Risings of James Fitzmaurice, Sir Edmund Butler and the earl of Thomond
March 1571	Sidney leaves Ireland
August 1573	Earl of Essex launches his Ulster plantation scheme
July 1575	Essex massacres inhabitants of Rathlin Island

September 1575	Sir Henry Sidney again installed as lord deputy
September 1576	Essex dies in Dublin
January 1577	Palesmen send delegation to London complaining of burdensome cess
1579–81	Nicholas Sanders, papal legate, active in Ireland
1579–83	Desmond rebellion
July 1580	Rising in the Pale under Viscount Baltinglass
November 1580	Massacre of Irish, Italian and Spanish troops at Smerwick
November 1581	Baltinglass goes into exile
November 1583	Earl of Desmond killed
January 1584	John Perrot appointed lord deputy
May 1587	Hugh O'Neill granted earldom of Tyrone
February 1588	Sir William Fitzwilliam replaces Perrot as lord deputy
March 1592	Foundation of Trinity College, Dublin

While trumpeting the virtues of Elizabethan peace, queen and council were all too aware that the tranquillity of the 1560s and 1570s owed a great deal to the distractions of other powers. As time wore on, and relations with Spain plumbed new depths, it became clear to everyone that this happy state of affairs would not last forever. England's protracted slide towards war had obvious consequences for relations with Scotland, since a hostile Scotland might once again offer support to England's continental enemies.

Scotland, however, showed little inclination to dabble in measures directed against England. Her chaotic internal politics were partly responsible, for successive minority regimes found it difficult to pursue any credible foreign policy at a time when the courts of Europe were wholly indifferent to Scottish affairs. It is also true, however, that the chains of shared religion forged after the Scottish reformation had an enduring effect on the relationship between the two British kingdoms. Such chains were very new, of course, and we are obliged to assess the nature of the steel, while testing the resilience of the links themselves. For conviction politicians north and south the bonds were sure enough. William Maitland could eulogize upon the impregnable unity offered by harmony within 'this microcosm of Britannye, separate from the continent world, naturally joined by situation and language, and most happily by religion'. But he and his correspondent Burghley, who shared these sentiments, realized privately that deep-rooted prejudices and distrust could not lightly be set aside. Maitland saw amity between equals, and out of politeness Burghley was careful to recognize that he was dealing with the representatives of a sovereign, independent power. Among Burghley's countrymen, however, assumptions of cultural and political superiority were deeply ingrained. Many in the southern kingdom, including luminaries like John Foxe and Lord Chancellor Ellesmere, committed the sin of conflating Englishman and Briton, some – though by no means all – going further and equating English history with British history. Still more blatantly, William Harrison in his 'Description of Britain', widely disseminated as a preface to 1577 and 1587 editions of Raphael Holinshed's *Chronicle*, insisted that English kings enjoyed a historic claim to Scotland, and described the Scots and their ancestors in unflattering terms. Scots from Hector Boece to George Buchanan and Sir Thomas Craig rose to challenges of this kind by asserting the antiquity of Scottish independence in massive, equally polemical histories.

Amity born of shared protestantism was in any case rather more complicated than at first appears, for the English and Scottish churches remained far apart, theologically and administratively. It consisted both of an alliance between presbyterians north and south of the border, and also a growing dialogue, hostile to much that the presbyterians stood for, between bishops in both countries. While the English presbyterian Christopher Goodman maintained his close contacts with the Scottish radicals, and George Buchanan profited from connections in the puritan circle round Sir Philip Sidney during the 1580s, Patrick Adamson, archbishop of St Andrews, went out of his way to court the English episcopate, and Bishop Bancroft of Worcester, sensing that Scottish presbyterians nourished English protestant dissent, laid into their beliefs in both sermon and print. The young James VI, for his part, always kept himself informed on the work of absolutist theologians and political thinkers in England.[1]

If the bricks of Anglo-Scottish friendship were supplied by shared religion and a meeting of political minds, broader forces provided the cement. Throughout the long reigns of Elizabeth and James VI, a common culture was developing, grounded on mutual defiance of a hostile Catholic Europe. In this apocalyptic, protestant world view, manifestations of God's will in current political events helped men and women north and south of the border sense divine purpose: for many a Scot, England's defeat of the Armada of 1588 was God's work, and so their triumph too. That common culture was grounded still more firmly on a mutual language, its compatibility emphasized to the literate members of both societies by the spread of printing, which in turn helped standardize – anglicize – both English and Scots. The same books were read, similar thoughts inspired. The Geneva Bible was officially adopted in Scotland, and, despite official disapproval, remained popular in England, available as it was in inexpensive editions complete with accompanying Calvinist commentary. Foxe included Scottish martyrs in his *Acts and Monuments*, and thought it quite natural to do so. Spoken Scots remained distinct from English, but, with religious texts leading the way, written Scots withered over a long period stretching beyond 1603 when confronted with the output of busy, commercially dominant London and English provincial printing presses.

A shared culture encouraged shared prejudices, and shared responses to other societies. As England pondered the question of Ireland, so Scotland faced parallel questions over the Highlands and Western Isles. The Scottish court's attitude to the west mirrors English policy in Ireland: optimism that a low-cost policy of 'civilizing through indirect rule' might suffice is replaced by a reluctant realization that it will not. Attempts to colonize the Hebridean island of Lewis as a stepping stone to other similar ventures, in the 1590s, proceeded alongside legislation similar to Irish surrender and regrant. The two administrations saw themselves confronted with one and the same problem, that of civilizing the uncivilized. The 1609 statutes of Iona launched an attack on 'Irish' culture in the west as forthright as any policy pursued by Elizabethan England. Clan chiefs were ordered to have their heirs educated in lowland Scotland, where they would receive tuition in English.

Self-interest was even more significant in securing a lasting amity. Anglo-Scottish friendship developed in response to the growing probability that James VI would succeed to the English throne. Significantly, that friendship was no longer bought and sold. Particularly towards the close of Elizabeth's reign, the distribution of English money to the well affected in Scotland is almost impossible to detect, the pension paid to James VI apart. There was a weary acceptance on both sides of the border that little purpose was served by financial commitments of this nature: for the English, long experience had taught them that the Scottish nobleman was apt to turn coat at a moment's notice, while for the Scottish noble himself, the sums on offer from a parsimonious queen simply proved an insufficient incentive. From 1586, England concentrated on paying James his annuity, hoping that he might acquiesce as would a client king to English policies and decisions. And the king's pension was trifling – £58,000 over sixteen years.[2] The ruling classes on both sides of the border sought greater if less immediately tangible benefits. For the nobility and gentry of England, a Scottish succession, hardly an attractive prospect in itself, at least offered stability and a new protestant dynasty. Their Scottish counterparts glimpsed the potential for enhanced prestige at the court of a king of all Britain, and the possibility of commensurate financial rewards. The cautious statesman, however, holds the golden, insubstantial daydream at arm's length. Friendship arising from these forces was built only slowly, and progressed despite as much as because of the conscious wishes of either political nation.

Here we can appreciate the lowest common denominator nature of such a shared identity. It was always easier to share self-interest, ideology and enemies, even to share enjoyment of the same literature and art, than it was to agree on common political forms or to adopt identical religious hierarchies. Self-interest, indeed, worked both ways; neither country could summon up any enthusiasm for the closer union envisaged, somewhat mistily, by their mutual sovereign after 1603. Even James, perhaps, considered union an extreme bargaining counter: it was not achieved in his reign, but, congenially for the king, Scotland got on with ruling itself while the court at London, the king's court, took on a more cosmopolitan, Anglo-Scottish hue, with Scots dominating the king's bedchamber.[3]

Self-interest led to cooperation over such matters as the suppression of intransigent borderers and a general improvement in relations. But while amity focused the eyes of Scottish noblemen on England, the English tended rather to indifference. English involvement in Scotland after the treaty of 1586 was minimal, returning to the pattern of the 1570s when the English government, preoccupied with events on the continent, more or less ignored the northern kingdom, relying on the goodwill of a compliant regency. When viewed over a long period, one perspective to Anglo-Scottish relations suggests that from 1560 onwards the English, hubris apart, were uninterested in the assimilation of Scotland, either by conquest or by political-dynastic union. That confident, rather cavalier neglect stands in contrast to the intermittent but persistent efforts of some Scottish peers and landowners to bind the two nations into a single state or confederacy. In the context of the 1580s and 1590s calculated English disinterest is qualified only by Queen Elizabeth's recreation. In a string of letters, Elizabeth lectured an infuriated James on the duties, dangers and obligations of kingship. It was good sport: she knew that the Scottish king had to swallow her advice, hoping that compliance would in time bring him her English crown.

On the English 'frontier' in Ireland the picture was very different. Far from disappearing, cultural divisions widened, while the cost to the English crown escalated rather than dwindled. English efforts at gradual, peaceful assimilation foundered on the rocks of mistrust and heavy financial demands. No English government liked spending money on Ireland, and the commitment to government on the cheap never disappears. The inescapable baseline for that costing, however, rose as the garrison in Ireland was augmented to counter fresh problems of internal security and developing continental threats. The royal garrison under Henry VIII was numbered in hundreds, the years of Kildare's rebellion apart, yet Protector Somerset's garrisoning mentality bred a new approach. In the reign of the highly cost-conscious Elizabeth the strength of the Irish garrison seldom fell below 1500. Parsimony in Ireland had always been the child of fear as well as neglect: the fear that Ireland could *potentially* cost England a great deal. Now the costs were real, and verging on the intolerable. R. W. Hoyle has calculated that in Elizabeth's reign, 8 per cent of English Exchequer receipts were paid over to the Irish treasurer for war: Ireland cost the queen around 75 per cent of the money she raised through taxation.[4]

A worsening international situation led to the improvement of strongholds around the coast and in the troubled midlands. Less perceptibly, it began to recast the role of the lord deputy, who grew with time into a military administrator, respected only for the army at his disposal. He appeared, moreover, to be a military administrator constantly torn between conciliation and repression. The earl of Sussex had advocated an initial increase in military expenditure, contending that through the swift suppression of trouble and the establishment of plantations this investment would surely pay dividends later. Military expenditure, however, was the worst enemy of economic government. With 2000 soldiers in regular pay each year between 1560 and 1563, expenditure in wages to soldiers alone ran at around Irish £20,000–25,000, at a time when revenue yields, despite Sussex's optimistic forecasts, averaged only Irish £4500 a year.

The Dublin administration found itself increasingly in debt, and increasingly dependent on payments out of the English Exchequer. Subventions were only the tip of an iceberg of indebtedness. English governments resorted to debasement, and persisted with that policy in Ireland long after it became inexpedient so to do at home. Vast quantities of debased coinage were imported, until even Lord Deputy Sussex realized the harm this was doing in 1558 and called for a halt. Immediate debts were paid, but the result was inflation, a decrease in real wages and a dislocation of the Pale economy throughout the 1550s.

In these new circumstances there was simply no scope to play the 'good lord'. Rather, there was all the scope in the world to aggravate the Anglo-Irish through increasingly burdensome demands for 'cess'. English commentators usually equated cess with the prerogative right of purveyance, the buying up of provisions at artificially low prices in order to supply the court. In fact, the vagueness and arbitrariness of cess made possible abuses out of the question in England. The principle as applied in Ireland seemed to cover the compulsory supply of transport and all manner of provisions at favourable rates, not only to the deputy, his household and retinue but to the English garrison as well. Repeated demands of this nature bred a defensive attitude among the wealthy men of the Pale, and bred, too, a new self-awareness in this community, long used to thinking of itself as English.

By the late 1560s this self-awareness had produced attempts at self-definition, or self-fashioning. The emerging term 'Old English' captures both the community's sense of loyalty to the crown and its distrust of new impositions. The Old English were convinced that 'new men', obtaining through court patronage posts hitherto monopolized by those born in Ireland, were eroding their own pre-eminence in Dublin and Pale society. They understood that these problems originated at a London court which regarded Irish service as a means to make a name, but comprehension made the fact no more palatable. Of course, Palesmen had for long been demanding some effective action by the English crown to bring the Gaelic Irish to heel, but again and again they cavilled at the cost, the means and the efficiency of any such attempt.

Successive viceroys underestimated, often deliberately, the difficulties of engineering reform with the meagre resources available. Sussex's belief that the solution of a few specific problems would lead to the steady improvement of the crown's position in Ireland offered the prospect of glory for himself and his followers, but left the growing financial burdens unconfronted and increased disillusionment among the Irish lords. These, he reasoned, were minor considerations which might sort themselves out once he had suppressed the Shane O'Neill rising, expelled the destabilizing Scottish settlements in Antrim, organized the midlands plantation and departed. Instead, the disillusion festered while Sussex made little progress in his key objectives. Three summers spent pursuing the elusive O'Neill lost him credibility and support on an increasingly critical English council. Plans to expel Scots settlers and halt the annual flow of 'redshank' mercenaries from Argyll were frustrated by inadequate resources, impatience and an ignorance of local conditions.

Sussex, a politique survivor from Mary's regime, was also vulnerable to enemies in England. He had some influential foes, particularly – and in this there was a good deal of the personal – the earl of Leicester. Leicester intrigued with Gerald Fitzgerald, earl of Kildare, half-brother to the executed rebel earl, and it was Kildare who helped him win the (temporary) submission of O'Neill. This was a massive loss of face for Sussex. Leicester also worked with an anti-Sussex coalition of English crown servants in Dublin which repeatedly laid charges of waste, oppression and incompetence at the lord lieutenant's door. In the best Dublin tradition, mud was flung in quantities sufficient to ensure that some stuck fast to the target. Sussex was eventually recalled in April 1564, but efforts to tie his name to the worst financial abuses were unsuccessful, and as a member of the London council and a confidant of the queen he in turn mocked and criticized his successors in Ireland.

Through his sustained campaign to replace Sussex with his own nominees Leicester also advocated the refinement of Sussex's simplistic approach, of his notion that Ireland could be secured and anglicized through conciliation linked to a handful of sharp military operations designed to remove the entrenched opponents of change. He was tempted by the same hopes of glory. Even though Sussex's experiences might have warned against such optimism, Ireland could offer an outlet, indeed, the only outlet, for Leicester's military following, while success there promised to enhance his authority in the queen's council.

Initially, though, very little was achieved. Sussex's departure left an effective power vacuum which alarmed the army captains, while trouble brewed in Munster. The earl of Ormond, worried by the political recovery of his great factional rival, clashed with Kildare's ally the earl of Desmond, who had returned from detention in England in 1564. Desmond was captured by Ormond after a bloody battle near Affane, near Lismore, in February 1565. In a miasma of royal displeasure, both earls were summoned to London to explain themselves. There they encountered contrasting fortunes. After months of examination, Desmond was censured and eventually ended up in the Tower, while 'Black Tom' Ormond became – much to Leicester's displeasure – a particular favourite of the queen.

Elsewhere Shane O'Neill, having won virtually all he sought including the title and rights of O'Neill, insisted that the English had reneged on recent promises. They had not, he said, created him earl of Tyrone, and he had yet to set eyes on the English noblewoman promised him as a bride. Once again he fell to arms, defeating the Antrim Scots at Glenshesk in 1565, seizing their principal strongholds and ravaging the countryside. Appeals for assistance from Ulster again persuaded the London council that O'Neill was not to be trusted, that the new administration was proving spineless, and that Sussex had been right all along in viewing Shane as a paramount threat to order.

These conclusions were not misplaced: weak leadership in Dublin had coincided with a flexing of muscles by those who saw their long resistance to Sussex at last paying dividends. Increasingly alarmed by the turn of events, Leicester secured the appointment as deputy of his friend and brother-in-law, Sir Henry Sidney. It is both ironic and a reflection on the close family ties that bound so many Elizabethan noble families that Sidney was also brother-in-law to Sussex. It was under Sussex that he had first gained experience of Ireland. With Kildare, numerous Gaelic chiefs, citizens of the Pale and leading men of the towns, whose prosperity and trade he assiduously and largely ineffectively sought to develop, Sidney was a popular choice, and that popularity was never entirely forfeited, testimony in itself to his political flexibility. Nevertheless, his position was fundamentally flawed. Sussex's political survival, the usual insistence on economy, dubious allies and the need to make progress on key matters as specified in a particularly thorough set of instructions all rendered the new deputy's task thankless.

Whether by personal inclination or by careful assessment of the situation as he found it, Sidney adopted what was essentially Sussex's 1562 plan, brought up to date. He supported the establishment of government by council in the three western and northern provinces, backed Sussex's scheme to settle the north-east coast in the hope of frustrating continued Scottish encroachment, and denounced the way in which the 'showpiece' midlands settlement in Laois-Offaly had been left to disintegrate in the face of Gaelic incursions. O'Neill, in particular, had to be taught a sharp lesson. All this he undertook to achieve with limited military support. Determined to secure the post, Sidney had bargained away the necessary resources: no more than Irish £15,500 per annum would be spent on the Irish garrisons, well below the existing figure.

The queen and council paid for garrisons in Ulster and for a renewed offensive, yet those were the only areas in which collective council anxieties completely discounted the hostility of Norfolk and Sussex. In every other direction – when recommending appointments to church and army and in the selection of advisers among the Dublin elite – Sidney encountered criticism and prevarication, not least from the queen herself. Much depended on support from Leicester, but even the earl's great influence had its limits. In frustrating any extension of Leicester's clientage in Ireland, Elizabeth managed to obstruct Sidney's attempts to woo Geraldine elements in the ranks of the Anglo-Irish at the expense of the pro-Sussex Butlers. All for balance, sympathetic towards the gallant Ormond and with a wary eye on her powerful earl, the queen ordered Sidney not to show undue preference for the Geraldines, and she rebuked him when he did.

Those rebukes became all the more angry when Sidney, like Sussex before him, failed to subdue Shane O'Neill. His task had admittedly been made more difficult by the earl of Argyll's new-found hostility towards the English, shared briefly by what in this context was a rather less important Edinburgh administration. It was rendered still more urgent by Shane's increasingly independent stance: he intrigued with both Scotland and France, and – a

another world

novelty – began subjecting his tenantry to military service. That perennial Geraldine troublemaker Desmond, whose actions Sidney had endeavoured to excuse, renewed his feuding with the Butlers in Munster, and in 1567 the deputy seemed to be losing control of the situation. 'For God's sake,' he wrote to Cecil that January, 'take me out of this world.' Having none of this self-pity, Elizabeth wrote to censure his 'darkness of judgement'.

Then, in June 1567, Sidney's luck changed. The O'Donnells and Mac-Donald Scots succeeded where successive English governors had failed: they killed Shane O'Neill. His severed head was pickled and sent post-haste to Dublin.[5] Rejoicing at his elimination, the London privy council at once set to work considering the merits of various reform measures, including schemes to colonize parts of Ulster, while Sidney personally affirmed the good intentions of Shane's successor as O'Neill, Turlough Luineach O'Neill. The deputy followed this up by reassuring Desmond's affinity in Munster that, although the earl himself had recently been arrested and dispatched to England, their interests would not be forgotten when the new model presidency under Sidney's associate, Sir Warham St Leger, was finally approved by the queen.

Elizabeth, however, remained suspicious of Sidney and required persuasion. While in London fighting for the adoption of his plans the deputy fell ill, and the council was unable to agree a way forward. The result was a paralysis in Irish affairs, and in 1568 Sidney's prolonged absence contributed to a general breakdown in law and order. Turlough and the O'Donnells, alike disappointed with the English crown, made common cause against the Dublin government, while James Fitzmaurice Fitzgerald, cousin to the absent Desmond, assumed command of a general revolt in Munster, leading family and other Geraldine connections against both the Ormond Butlers and the English.

As the man most familiar with the situation, the convalescent Sidney was sent once again to Ireland in 1568, bound by the usual orders to effect pacification without spending any money. He summoned a parliament in Dublin, pressing through a bill of attainder on the dead Shane O'Neill which simultaneously attempted to lay the foundations for an Ulster settlement. Sidney's proposals linked generous pardons to the confiscation of lands sufficient to pay a substantial rental income to the crown. The parliament showed disturbing signs of considerable Old English dissent, centring round Sir Edmund Butler, Ormond's brother and heir. But that opposition was limited, and was eventually to betray itself in open rebellion. In spite of delay and obstruction, Sidney secured the passage of a bill outlawing the extortion of coyne and livery by local lords, long a stumbling block to reform. Another measure proposed the division into counties of those parts of the country not as yet shired, while still another gave deputy and Dublin council full discretion in further surrender and regrant settlements.

All this, Sidney argued to London, was the only way to marry efficiency to economy: the O'Neill lands offered a source of wealth which he was keen to exploit. He encouraged private plans for colonizing Ulster and the south-west, on the grounds that these too would save money while spreading the merits of English civility. If he looked to a quiet settlement in Ulster, based on rents secured to the crown from O'Neill lands, Sidney was not prepared to forego the support of individual promoters. They had only to make their schemes work, and he would rest content.

In addition, he pressed once again for the proper establishment of provincial councils, at least in Munster and Connaught. Experience gained in one part of the British Isles was, not for the first or last time, being applied to another: Sidney had himself headed the Welsh council in the marches and was persuaded that what had worked in Wales, necessarily modified, stood every chance of working in Ireland. Without such regional government, he argued, any plans for a fully shired Ireland on the English model enjoyed little prospect of success.

Sidney's opportunistic pragmatism was dogged by unforeseen difficulties. The discovery of plots surrounding Mary Stewart and the rising of the northern earls distracted the London council. Even with the deputy back in Dublin no particular scheme for a plantation in Ulster commended itself, while the office of president in Munster remained unfilled. Turlough, now diplomatically cautious towards English authority, was unimpressed by Sidney's plan to establish a rental income for the crown from O'Neill lands, particularly since the idea lacked support from the privy council. He continued to bring in Scottish mercenaries and to impose his authority by force on lesser Ulster families.

A more insidious problem was the breakdown of amicable relations between deputy and Dublin council over the provisioning of troops, while in a still unexplained move, perhaps emerging from his strenuous parliamentary opposition, Sir Edmund Butler with the support of his younger brothers and a broad family following had made common cause with unreconciled Geraldines by the summer of 1569. Ormond, who may or may not have had some inkling of his brothers' intentions, and who may even have been one of their intended victims, criticized Sidney's actions in London. But his quarrel with Sidney was personal and he remained loyal to the crown, as did many local landowners, Turlough O'Neill in Ulster, and the important south-western towns, alike unimpressed by the rebel leader James Fitzmaurice's repeated efforts to cloak his actions in Gaelic tradition and his calls for a war of religion. Philip II was also unmoved by requests for Spanish aid. The few extra troops provided by the council proved sufficient. After some bloodshed the rebels were outmanoeuvred by government forces, and the Butler brothers made a less than enthusiastic submission to Ormond, freshly returned from England, in September.[6] The ensuing pacification was uncompromising. Fitzmaurice took ship for France, awaiting his day.

Suppression, however, proved costly. By March 1571, the crown had laid out £148,000 to finance Sidney's second term as deputy, and another £73,000 was owing. This outlay fatally compromised Sidney's position at court: amid general retrenchment, Elizabeth and her council were very reluctant to spend so much on Ireland. An auditor's report on Irish government between 1559 and 1569 showed that the total cost of administration had come to £348,000, and, more tellingly, that London had had to foot 90 per cent of this bill. In 1571 Sidney was recalled, to a distinctly chilly reception from the queen.

used
by enemies

Sidney himself was only one of the casualties. As the international situation deteriorated the failure of his reforms encouraged fears that an Ireland left in a state of 'traditional' disorder offered enemies of the kingdom great scope for mischief. Still, though, the argument lacked compulsion. Irish discontent had seldom fed on nationalism, or religion, but rather on local grievances, and so long as this remained the case no English government would consider spending money there, either to conciliate or to coerce. However, such money as was dispatched by London to Dublin was increasingly earmarked for military ends. It went to fill the pockets of a burgeoning military establishment, consisting, at the higher levels, largely of adventurers freshly arrived from England. In 1571 the Irish garrison numbered just over 2000.

Civil projects such as the establishment of presidencies after the English model were abandoned or replaced by what amounted to military government. The Irish experimental civil presidencies – in Connaught in 1569 and Munster in 1570 – had been set up at an unfortunate time, and in the wake of rebellion they were judged expensive and ineffective. That attempted amid high expectations in Connaught, long the least troublesome province, collapsed when the notably uncivil president, Sir Edward Fitton, lost the confidence of the earl of Clanricarde and found himself powerless to counter the passive resistance of Conor O'Brien, earl of Thomond. Both these powerful local families were heavily involved in the risings of 1569 and in further troubles during 1570. Fitton, and Sidney, drew obvious conclusions from this failure in civil government. Power, it was clear, would have to bridle insolence.

Of course, power would also have to be sustained, and in view of the English government's reluctance to provide funds money had to be found in Ireland itself. Here lay the crucial dilemma, central to the deterioration in relations between Irish government and the Pale society on which it depended. How was this funding to be obtained? In pacifying Munster, Humphrey Gilbert offered one answer. He solved the problem by all but returning to Irish methods of coyne and livery, interpreting provision of his troops as an act of loyalty, and rewarding supply with courtesy and protection, and failure to supply with exemplary correction. Sidney was clearly thinking along the same lines. Similar ideas, applied to the whole of Ireland and with due scope for composition, were advanced by Edmund Tremayne, clerk of the privy council, a self-declared expert on Irish problems who had served Sidney as private secretary in 1570–1 and who spoke on this occasion for his master. Tremayne saw intimidation as the key. Since Ireland was a country dominated by the private retinues of its great lords, stability was only possible if the queen imitated their actions and established an army of her own, composed of loyal subjects, which might overawe opposition and compel the payment of cess. Such a force, he argued, could be funded through a general taxation or 'composition' of feudal and military rights in particular lordships. Pressing his scheme ever more urgently, Sidney angled for his recall, employing all the usual courtier's tactics and spreading tales about the inadequacies of his replacement as deputy, Sir William Fitzwilliam.

Elizabeth was unhappy with any project for Ireland that required English money to 'prime the pump', distrusting suggestions that these policies might soon prove self-financing. Here was just such a scheme: armies fit to overawe Irish lords could never be purchased cheaply. With the ambitious and capable earl of Essex currently soliciting support for his plan to colonize Ulster at the expense of the Scots, Sidney had to bargain hard for permission to return. Not for the first time, he threw away in the bargaining the viability of his own plan. He accepted a pared-down force of 1100 men, to be divided among the presidencies, and undertook to leave Ireland self-sufficient within three years through the expenditure of no more than £60,000.

At least the bargaining went his way. In September 1575 Sidney returned to Ireland, where his plans at once ran into severe trouble. His attempt to persuade Palesmen to agree a tax substitute for a heavy cess demand implicitly acknowledged that cess had become, in effect, an alternative, annual, extra-parliamentary subsidy; expedient had grown into prerogative. In the aftermath of two poor harvests, landowners in the Pale refused to pay cess and ignored the proposed alternative. Their opposition was all but total, and well organized. In need of winter provision, Sidney was obliged to reduce his request for cess, but this only served to convince many Palesmen that the initial demand had been pitched far too high. Leading families refuted Sidney's argument that cess in all its guises depended only on royal prerogative, insisting that these exactions remained invalid without parliamentary sanction. Enjoying some support from Old English members of the Dublin council, they rejected even the reduced cess, and in an unauthorized move representatives travelled direct to London to argue their case.

Elsewhere, Sidney was only marginally more successful. After initial progress his attempts to win support from the provinces, from late 1576 all under new presidents of his own choosing, unravelled in mutual suspicion and in a rebellion by the earl of Clanricarde's sons in Connaught. The Clanricardes justified their revolt as a reaction to exploitation rather than in any more lofty terms. Whereas the Tremayne–Sidney blueprint had advised a cautious, even-handed approach, Sidney now found himself obliged to demand immediate tokens of submission. Elizabeth, totally disenchanted with the whole spectacle, began refusing the regular instalments of money which kept Irish government out of debt. While representations by Leicester and his circle eventually persuaded her to back Sidney and insist on the submission of the Pale, the resulting, grudging assent in Ireland to a year's composition at the original rate delayed rather than dispelled the sense of impending crisis.

Over budget and deep in debt, the deputy endured a final blow from the hand of William Gerrard, chancellor in Dublin and an erstwhile supporter, whom Sidney had sent to London to advocate his administration's policies. Gerrard had always tended to an independent view, and now, knowing full well what the result would be, he outlined a gradualist, non-military, low-cost approach, by which the Pale would be settled and slowly extended, its extension accompanied by the ever-wider application of English laws. Gradualism and minimal costs appealed to the council in London, and Sidney was again recalled, this time for good, in the spring of 1578. No deputy was appointed in his place. Quite deliberately, queen and council set the government of Ireland in the hands of lesser men, burdened with no grand vision.

Power now lay with the lord justice, lord chancellor and an autonomous military governor in Connaught, Sir Nicholas Malby. Malby embarked enthusiastically on a 'composition' of his province, itself the brain-child of Sidney, by which rent charges were substituted for both government cess and demands from Irish lords.[7]

The hope was that stability might return to an Ireland left to its own affairs. After twenty years of overambitious and underfunded Elizabethan government, however, with the Anglo-Irish families thoroughly rattled, the Palesmen grumbling under increased exactions and the Gaelic Irish dismayed at the increasing numbers of unregulated settlers, the Dublin government was seen universally as a partial force, and the hope was vain.

Judged as injections of English civility and culture into the body of Irish 'backwardness', sixteenth-century plantation ventures in Ireland were almost entirely unsuccessful. Not one prospered; most struggled for survival. The showpiece plantations in the Irish midlands were ravaged by continuous unrest and saw the aggressive accumulation of land into the hands of a few powerful landowners. Banditry simultaneously eroded any economic prosperity that the region had formerly possessed. Ulster plantations were even less successful. At odds with the Dublin government and abandoned by many of their fair-weather colleagues, Essex's settlers survived by edging their way into local society, and by tacitly reneging on more grandiose aspects of the initial plan. Like Sir Nicholas Bagenal's garrison at Newry, the Essex enterprise attuned itself to local politics; aware that the English authorities would, at a pinch, sacrifice all their interests in the name of economy, they had really little choice.[8] As ambition foundered, the frustrations of those who had hoped to make their fortunes in Ireland took increasingly ugly forms. Essex's irritation manifested itself in a number of violent incidents, most notoriously the slaughter of 500 Scots on Rathlin Island during the summer of 1575.

None of this made the settlers any less loyal to the crown, but it reduced their effectiveness as a *mission civilatrice*. Settlers who had to get on with the task of making a living in their new country naturally preferred to assimilate with rather than confront established neighbours, and governments in Dublin and London, despite repeated rebukes, were powerless to prevent the process. The strategists grew disillusioned, and disillusion gradually altered their fundamental thinking on plantations. By the 1580s, the goal was less the reform of native Irish, more the segregation of societies: the forced establishment of English families on the land of displaced Irishmen and women.

The Anglo-Irish were just as disenchanted. The Butlers were left alienated by Sidney's ill-concealed hostility, while the Geraldines, although ostensibly benefiting most from Sidney's periods in office, took little satisfaction from Sir Henry's lack of credit at court. Kildare resorted more and more to violence and intimidation to augment his authority in Leinster, distrusting support from London; distrust of Kildare among the English intensified accordingly. After Sidney's first departure the earl was arrested and dispatched to England, accused of various acts of violence which, by the unfriendly Fitzwilliam, were interpreted as attacks on crown authority. Although the charges were dropped and Kildare received again at court, he did not return to Ireland until 1578, his credit seriously weakened. He could, so his erstwhile supporters reasoned, neither look to the crown for backing nor enforce his authority in more time-honoured fashion, without crown interference.

Kildare's Desmond Geraldine relations shared his deepening distrust of English intentions. When permitted to return to Ireland in 1573, Desmond himself found his authority greatly compromised. The earl's power in Munster had always depended heavily upon the exercise of force: nominally subordinate families were notoriously turbulent, internal family quarrels, one of them between Desmond and his brother Sir John of Desmond, equally unsettling. The situation called for strength and cunning in prodigious quantities, but these qualities the unfortunate Desmond conspicuously lacked.

For a time he survived, thanks not least to his carefully cultivated friendship with the Munster president, Sir William Drury. But a composition of all rents and services for a substantial fixed cash rental, agreed in 1578, angered those who, having renounced allegiance to Desmond, now had to pay him a reduced rent. When James Fitzmaurice returned from the continent in July 1579 the extent of Desmond's impotence became clear. Summoned by the returning exile to a 'crusade' against the heretic English, many of the earl's followers deserted him. Sir John of Desmond also supported the insurrection. When Drury succumbed to a long illness and was replaced by Sir Nicholas Malby, Desmond lost a friend and gained an enemy. His chronic indecision took on a sinister aspect in English eyes, and he was eventually proclaimed a rebel. While Elizabeth did not wholly swallow the allegations laid against him, Desmond considered himself abandoned and joined in the revolt.[9]

It took four bloody years to crush the Desmond rebellion, which was given a fresh lease of life in 1580 when one of the leading noblemen of the Pale, James Eustace, third Viscount Baltinglass, unfurled the papal banner and rejected English authority. Spanish and Italian reinforcements in the service of the pope landed at Smerwick, but along with a number of insurgents they were obliged to surrender to the English in September 1580. All were then systematically butchered. One of the executioners, a young captain called Walter Ralegh, turned out the pockets of the corpses, found letters concerning 'some matters of secrecy', was ordered to convey them to court, and embarked on a dazzling career.

Baltinglass's rebellion spawned a more prosaic offshoot in which little religious motivation is now apparent. This was led by William Nugent, a poet in both English and Irish, the younger brother and agent of Lord Delvin.[10] These and other risings were suppressed, amid a general distaste in the Pale for the extreme – or at least capricious – methods employed. Fitzmaurice was killed early on, Sir John of Desmond was slain in January 1582, Baltinglass and Nugent escaped into exile. The latter's uncle, Nicholas Nugent, lately chief justice of the court of common pleas in Ireland, was executed on trumped-up charges, while Desmond was hunted down and killed in November 1583. To the further dismay of many Old English, forfeited lands were distributed among military followers of the ruthless new deputy, Lord Grey de Wilton.

Plate 18 *Sir Walter Ralegh*, 'The Cadiz Portrait', late 1590s. Elizabeth's favourite of the 1580s in middle age.
Source: National Gallery of Ireland

The rebels were not the only losers. Kildare's attempts to fill the role of *agent provocateur* in Baltinglass's rising again lost him his liberty. He was sent to the Tower, awaiting a trial the queen never saw fit to stage. The earl was eventually released, but died in 1585. Kildare, like his father before him, like 'Black Tom' Ormond, went quietly. Nothing better illustrates the anomalous position of these Anglo-Irish lords than the patient way in which they sub-mitted to detention, even on grave charges. As with the groundswell of anti-establishment politics in the Pale, their position was increasingly ironic: men who saw themselves as English were moved to what amounted to nationalist opposition by the actions of fellow Englishmen. They felt as though they were being treated like their Gaelic neighbours and subjected to government by well-connected parvenus out of England. Worst of all, they were being asked to pay for the bestowal of these 'blessings'. By the mid-1580s, an almost wilful incomprehension governed relations between the key Anglo-Irish families and the English authorities: the one side saw double-dealing and neglect, while the other saw disloyalty and ingrained resistance to reform.

Religion, and hostility to the notion that a woman might assume the supreme governorship of the church, motivated Baltinglass and some of his fellow conspirators, but even in the early 1580s such wholehearted commitment to Roman Catholicism was scarcely typical of the Pale. Twenty years on from the Elizabethan settlement, and a decade after Elizabeth's excommunication, the protestant religion was still only lightly enforced, if enforced at all, and religious views did not reflect political loyalties on either side. Deputies' priorities lay elsewhere; they waged war on or conciliated the enemies of the crown. The causes of pacification and economy were not served by imposing a new religion on the Pale, especially since English commissioners in 1563 had encountered a population which, while ignorant in religion, was yet 'conformable to laws'. Successive ecclesiastical commissions, and from 1564 an Irish court of High Commission, were either inactive or left no record on which to base a judgement; oaths of supremacy were seldom demanded from office holders. It all made for a very muddled picture. Ever since the 1530s, the papacy had appointed its own archbishops and bishops to Irish sees, and in areas outside English control these men wielded far greater authority than their protestant counterparts. Monasticism persisted and friars continued their work in the hinterland. Incumbents ran the spiritual life of their parishes more or less as they wished. Religious allegiances were as a result highly ambiguous. Early in the 1580s, Ireland remained to be won and lost by the contending parties.[11]

By the 1590s, however, the nature of Catholic opposition was altering. Greater lay commitment among powerful town oligarchies saw relations deteriorate between the protestant Dublin administration and those traditionally loyal linchpins of urban society. As the size of the army grew in the 1590s, compulsory billeting added to the towns' sense of alienation. Not one of them actively went over to rebellion, the special case of occupied Kinsale in 1601 apart. Old English townsmen, with long experience of their troublesome neighbours, had little reason to trust Hugh O'Neill and his Gaelic supporters. There were, however, innumerable instances where English governors suspected the loyalty of urban ruling groups, and several where such suspicions were well founded.

The contrasting fortunes of state protestantism in England and Ireland betray the importance of support from the local landowners and principal citizens for the success of any policy initiative in the early modern state. In Ireland, private influence exercised in support of the old faith by a disgruntled gentry worked against the widespread acceptance of protestantism. The curious result was that the Catholic church prospered most, not in Gaelic Ireland but in the English heartland, around Dublin, and in the south. Here, recusancy became a totem of the Anglo-Irishmen's sense of separate identity;

it set them apart from new settlers and from representatives of English government.[12] Gentry money maintained Roman rather than protestant clergy, and gentlemen sent their sons abroad to receive a Catholic education. The increasing numbers of continentally trained priests included many sons of prominent Anglo-Irish families, and it was natural enough that these men should afterwards focus their ministries on the parts of Ireland with which they were most familiar. Catholicism could not claim the parish church itself, but in practice this hardly mattered. While dismayed protestants early next century contemplated empty naves, the Catholic priesthood preached to large congregations in private houses. William Lyon, establishment bishop of Cork, Cloyne and Ross, declared in 1604 that his dioceses were 'overwhelmed with the palpable darkness of idolatry' and that no protestant marriages, christenings or burials had been recorded in over a decade. The days of compromise, token conformity, were over. When religion joined the cess as a point of conflict, the unanimity of the Palesmen opposed to English government was to prove every bit as strong.

Facing an open challenge, the protestant church failed to respond. One reason for this was the fact that in Ireland, backing for protestantism from the English crown was limited by that crown's deliberate policy of parsimony and neglect. Inadequate endowment, low expectations and poor educational standards among the clergy alike undermined optimistic central directives. Laymen owning benefices – some 60 per cent of livings were impropriated in Ireland, compared with 40 per cent in England – were seldom concerned to see their cures filled with suitably qualified men. The scale of stipends, always lower than England, became even more glaringly inadequate as the century progressed. Healthy incomes do not always imply a healthy church, but Ireland was clearly no place for the ambitious or talented. At the top, it was difficult to recruit high-calibre candidates to fill impoverished bishoprics. Wealthier bishops had little but contempt for many poorer colleagues, particularly those with an Irish background. Adam Loftus – an Englishman – successively archbishop of Armagh and Dublin, and chancellor in Ireland from 1581 to 1605, dismissed one of his successors at Armagh, the Irish-speaking John Garvey, as an inadequate preacher and possible Catholic. Lower down the hierarchy, as in Scotland, Wales and more remote parts of England, the majority of clergymen were reading ministers, religious traditionalists, scorned by the few English protestant clergymen who came to Ireland.

The consequences require little elaboration. What provision for education there was in Ireland rested largely in Catholic hands, and abler pupils increasingly sought tuition in foreign schools and colleges rather than at Oxford or Cambridge, popular with Irishmen before the reformation but now effectively closed to Catholics. Trinity College in Dublin, Ireland's first university and in the next century the centre of protestant training for the ministry, was founded as late as 1592.

Morale suffered throughout the church. Even an energetic and capable prelate like Hugh Brady, the Irish-speaking bishop of Meath during the 1560s and 1570s, began to despair at the lack of financial resources, the absence of an educated, Irish-speaking clergy and the want of appropriate texts. Brady, like his colleagues, found himself continually on the defensive, ministering to existing elite congregations rather than seeking the conversion of the uncommitted. This lethargy, bred in the absence of any significant challenge from Roman Catholicism, was eventually shaken off, but long before that happened a resurgent counter-reformation Catholic church had secured a decisive lead in the race for hearts and minds.[13]

Loss of morale can be measured against another yardstick. Wales faced similar problems – impoverished livings, administrative laxity, lay impropriation and non-residence – and was noted to the end of the century for strong if localized residual Catholicism. Wales produced similar dismal tales from bishops, dismayed at the 'extreme darkness' of residual popery and ignorance that had settled over far too many corners. Catholic seminary priests were busy there from the 1580s, and, as in Ireland, they were prepared to use the language of the countryside for their purpose: the first book printed in Wales was, indeed, a 1585 Catholic tract, *Y Drych Cristionogawl* (*The Christian Mirror*). Furthermore, several gentry families in the Vale of Glamorgan, Monmouthshire, Flintshire and Denbighshire all adhered loyally to Catholicism.

Nevertheless, the numbers of Welsh Catholics were small when set against the total churchgoing population. Even in Monmouthshire Catholics mustered only about 20 per cent of the total population, and the missionary priests, concentrating their efforts elsewhere on the assumption that Wales was 'safe', made little further headway. The English church gradually put down strong roots throughout Wales, securing vital gentry support, and morale within the church proved more resilient than in Ireland. Commitment and realism had been evident from an early stage. English protestants soon appreciated that, if the new faith was to make headway in Wales, it would have to do so through the medium of the Welsh language. State and church together might dream of a day when English supplanted the native tongue, but that day was, they realized, far distant. The first book printed in Welsh, the 1547 *Yn Y Llyvyr Hwn . . .*, contained basic religious texts: Ten Commandments, Lord's Prayer and Creed. Significantly, it was published on the initiative of a Welsh gentleman, Sir John Price of Brecon. The epistles and gospels used in protestant services were published in Welsh in 1551 by the antiquary William Salesbury, and although his idiosyncratic translations did not find favour with the bishops they were nevertheless used and disseminated. Three years after the Irish parliament of 1560 insisted on the use of English, or Latin, the Westminster parliament, probably at the instigation of Richard Davies, bishop of St David's, ordered publication of the Bible in Welsh. A full translation was not available until the late 1580s – in the form of a clear and scholarly text promoted by the untiring efforts of the scholar-cleric William Morgan – but a New Testament and prayer book had been published by 1567. In the same year, by coincidence, the Catholic exile Gruffudd Robert published a first Welsh grammar, with the express aim of raising literary standards to continental levels.

While the 1563 Act, thanks to a final proviso added in the House of Lords, also decreed that an English Bible should be made available in churches so that comparison of Welsh and English versions might advance literacy in English, there is no need to play down the pragmatism of developments so responsive to the fact that nine Welsh people in ten still spoke Welsh as their native tongue. Despite high if unquantifiable levels of illiteracy, and within the parameters of a small market which deterred commercial publishers, demand for Welsh-language publications seems to have been reasonably healthy, at least following Morgan's well-received Bible. Alongside humble catechisms and manuals, four new versions of the prayer book appeared in Welsh between 1586 and 1630, two Welsh translations of the Psalms were published by Thomas Salisbury in London in 1603, while Morris Kyffin's *Deffynniad Ffydd Eglwys Loegr*, a translation of John Jewel's 1562 *Apologia Ecclesiae Anglicanae*, appeared in 1595 and proved enduringly popular. This activity might be compared with the printed output of Irish Gaelic. Apart from a 1571 catechism, little else was forthcoming before the 1620s. The Highlands of Scotland were still worse served. Even in the context of a predominantly oral culture, it is still surprising to observe the apparent lack of printed evangelical endeavour: only one book is known to have been printed in Scots Gaelic before 1603.

The church in Wales was also ably led, its bishops never succumbing to that collective despair which gripped their counterparts in Ireland. William Morgan, indefatigable promoter of Bibles and liturgical works in Welsh, was appointed bishop of Llandaff in 1595 and translated to the richer see of St Asaph in 1601. Neither in his energy nor in his Welsh birth was Morgan an isolated figure: of sixteen bishops appointed to Welsh dioceses under Elizabeth, thirteen boasted Welsh ancestry. Not everyone was free from fault, but the majority were capable men and sound scholars. What we are seeing in Wales is the fashioning of a seventeenth-century church which was to be both a bastion of Welsh culture and a source of strong political and religious support for the London administration. The contrast with Ireland is, once again, all too evident.[14]

Just the same, we should be careful not to anticipate events. Shared Catholicism was more a subsequent symbol of distinctness and unity to the gentry of the Pale than a cause of their disaffection. As the rebel earl of Tyrone found to his cost in the 1590s, it formed one element in a shared sense of separateness and community combined with loyalty to the crown, which preserved the traditional Anglo-Irish reserve, even hostility, towards Gaelic co-religionists. The seventeenth-century Irish peer, as comfortable in London as in the midst of his Munster or Connaught estates, adapted his Catholicism to suit prevailing circumstances every time he crossed the Irish Sea.

There was still room during the deputyship of Sir John Perrot (1584–8) for one last attempt to effect a programme of reform for Ireland. Favoured by Walsingham and, rather less consistently, by Leicester, Perrot was an odd character. According to some, now discredited, rumours he was the bastard son of Henry VIII; certainly his physique and temper reminded observers of the late king. Savage and irrational in anger, he was nevertheless an accomplished courtier and an able self-publicist. Perrot's plans recall earlier programmes. There was the same detailed, if fanciful, financial costing, and the same promise to deliver benefits within a brief space of time. Like Sidney in 1575, Perrot resolved to establish a composition for cess throughout Ireland and to concentrate his military resources on curbing the effective independence of Ulster. The Scots were to be expelled and the Irish brought to heel. Elsewhere his approach was equally uncompromising; the rebellious inhabitants of Munster were to lose their lands to new settlers.

Perrot's abrasive tongue had, however, won him many enemies. He was more than usually reliant on the Old English Dubliners. This fact, and the growing likelihood of English intervention in the Low Countries, led him to adopt a surprisingly conciliatory approach to composition agreements, and that approach proved effective for some years in Connaught thanks to the generous terms offered to local lords, Clanricarde and Thomond. Yet Perrot was ultimately no more successful than any of his predecessors. When the plantation there went ahead, he alienated new settlers in Munster by refusing to exempt or favour them from the composition, and he made an enemy of Ormond by rejecting many of the earl's personal petitions. This was not entirely Perrot's fault; the London council had assumed general control over the settlement project and had favoured English emigrants above loyal Old English landowners. Nevertheless, when the first settlers arrived later in the 1580s, they found themselves caught up in a confused situation where no one was clear as to who, in the aftermath of rebellion, famine and demographic upheaval, enjoyed title to what.

When matters were eventually sorted out, the new settlers too found cause for grievance. Faced with loss of promised lands, difficulties in recruiting suitable tenant farmers ready to risk all in Ireland, and legal costs, they clawed what they might from existing tenants and kept what they could from the crown. Stirring the brew of discontent were Burghley's unwise efforts to encourage the identification or 'discovery' of crown lands by private informers.

A parliament called in Dublin with conciliatory intent – Perrot had hoped to put royal taxes of several kinds on a sound parliamentary footing and so to give parliament a regular say in national government – provided an opportunity for the Palesmen to vent their anger at recent developments. Some maintain that this parliament served as a catalyst in the fusion of a distinct, self-conscious Old English community. While the evidence for this is hardly straightforward, the sense of overwhelming grievance cannot be doubted. Rudderless as a result of divisions within the ranks of government supporters, the parliament proved wholly uncooperative, rejecting an attempt to introduce English measures against Catholicism. After much ado, a rather half-hearted compromise on taxation was achieved, but the whole sour experience helped ensure that no more than two further Irish parliaments were summoned in the following fifty years.[15] So far as the crown was concerned there was, indeed, no longer any financial justification for the assembly. Thanks to wholly inadequate methods of assessment and collection the Irish subsidy had effectively been abandoned as worthless in the 1570s.

Perrot's policy of coercion in Ulster fared no better. The Scots could not be ejected by the troops at his disposal. Meanwhile, Gaelic landowners in the province resisted attempts at land reform. Perrot's agents either failed entirely or, as so often in the past, survived through assimilation. Attempts to mediate between Bagenal, the ageing Turlough O'Neill and Hugh O'Neill, earl of Tyrone from 1585, served only to aggravate a whole range of mutual suspicions.

The result was predictable. Perrot's failings were seized upon by a formidable array of critics in London, to whom a disillusioned queen and council gave a not altogether grudging ear. The failure of yet another reformist package served to persuade students of the situation in Ireland, including the poet Edmund Spenser, that military force, however costly its deployment, was the only way to secure English control over a people naturally rebellious. As Machiavelli had taught in his *Discourses on Livy*, a decayed political system called for remedial coercion, even, if but for an interim period, tyranny. Sir Edward Waterhouse, surveying the sorry state of Ireland in 1574, had argued that justice could never prosper there until 'the sword hath made a way for the law'; the passing years seemed only to bear out his fears.

That military ruthlessness advocated by Spenser in his *A View of the Present State of Ireland* did not, however, command universal support, even among new settlers. Some resisted the suggestion that reform of Ireland on anything other than a piecemeal basis was appropriate. Others, like the Munster resident Sir William Herbert, who also recalled happier experiences in Wales, still backed reform by example, arguing that a morally and practically superior form of law and government would inevitably be taken up in due course by a more backward people. Exemplary colonies, strategically planted, were what was needed. Neither side won the debate, such as it was. Spenser's attitudes reflected a belief shared among some 'second-rank' courtiers hoping for careers and profits in Ireland that violence would be necessary, sooner rather than later, a belief soon superficially justified by O'Neill's rising.[16]

When Perrot was recalled in 1588, initially to the reward of a council seat but later to face trial and conviction for treason on fabricated charges,[17] his successor was that veteran of many Irish administrations, Cecil's client Sir William Fitzwilliam. Fitzwilliam's appointment, like his policies, smacked of wartime necessity. His role was to resolve individual problems swiftly, as they arose, and to keep costs down: gone was any hint of a proactive, programmatic policy. But Fitzwilliam too miscalculated. He pursued another of those futile vendettas against his predecessor, encouraging the already widespread belief that no consistency might be expected from an English governor. Particularly unwise were his arbitrary, ineffectual interventions in Ulster, which rewarded the lord deputy's military inferiors but profoundly disturbed the leading families. These actions contributed directly to the breakdown in relations which, in turn, fuelled Tyrone's estrangement and the disastrous nine years of war that followed.

Unwillingness to devote precious resources to the problems faced by English administrations in Ireland did not imply *neglect* of Ireland. William Cecil, for one, kept himself thoroughly well informed on the situation. The map of Ireland would have been familiar enough to Elizabeth's counsellors. Cecil loved maps for their own sake, and he used them to advantage: they were among the tools of his secretarial trade. He wrote memoranda with an eye on his maps, scribbled on them, and commissioned better ones. Appreciating this, we can appreciate Cecil's strategic priorities. Anyone who lets his mind dwell on maps must needs let his eye run along frontiers, conjure weaknesses, imagine points at which an enemy might strike. Cecil looked on, and saw the defence of England as a British problem. His entire political experience was underpinned by a belief in the desirability of presenting to the world a common defence based on the British islands.[18]

Cecil was not alone in making greater use of maps, as techniques improved: coastal defences were mapped during the invasion scare of 1539–40, and in Christopher Saxton's series of county maps dating from the 1570s – a project enthusiastically supported by Cecil and the queen – England's governors enjoyed a fine series of cartographic aids which were 'put to immediate use in every level of government'.[19] Maps also presented Cecil's countrymen with a wider vision of the world in which they lived and did business; they encouraged pursuit of the broadening horizon. In one manifestation of this trend, the later years of the century witness a literal sea change in established trading patterns. Merchant investment, largely unobtainable for the exploitation of new markets in early Tudor times, was now available, for the Low Countries wool mart appeared increasingly under threat. New markets were sought, if only as an insurance measure. After a pioneering voyage in 1553–4 by Sir Hugh Willoughby (who died *en route*) and Richard Chancellor, which aimed to find a short-cut to China and reached the court of Ivan IV via the north of Norway and the White Sea, an unspectacular though regular trade was initiated with Russia. A Muscovy Company was established in 1555 by a range of courtiers and London merchants, pooling resources and taking proportionate shares in any profits – an early example of the joint-stock company. A royal charter gave the company legal status and administrative continuity.

Following the decline of the Hanseatic League after the northern war of 1563–70, more and more English and Scottish ships ventured into the Baltic to trade with the ports of Poland and northern Germany. Poland, and the Baltic as a whole, offered naval supplies – tar, pitch, cordage, hemp – in exchange for the ubiquitous cloth. With Venice, the leading carrier, distracted by the Ottoman Turks, the Mediterranean was once again opened to English vessels. By the 1580s, the Ottomans were taking English and French produce on a regular basis and extending privileges to the ships of both countries. English cloth for Turkish silk was considered an appropriate exchange. Nor was Spain ever really closed to English trade, even in the war years after 1585. New trading companies abounded, reflecting the London merchant's hunger for profit and his cautious desire to spread risks. The Spanish Company was founded in 1577, the Eastland Company for the Baltic in 1579, the Barbary Company in 1585 (but reflecting years of trade with northwestern Africa), the Africa Company in 1588, the Turkey Company in 1581 and Venice Company in 1583, the latter two merging in 1592 to form a Levant Company. The famous East India Company was established in 1600, in response to profitable Dutch trading with the East Indies.

These trading companies were, at least in intention, monopolies along the lines of the Merchant Adventurers, but by comparison with that great association and the trade it represented the newcomers were still small fry. Richard Hakluyt wrote his famous *Principall Navigations* not merely to satisfy his countrymen's fascination for the exotic and unexplored, but also 'to find out ample vent of our woollen cloth'. That cloth was, and remained, all important to the nation's wealth. The reluctance to break a dependence on Antwerp, notwithstanding the ominous political developments of the 1560s and 1570s, indicates the fear of instability in a trade too precious to adjust. Even the disruption in 1576, when the city was sacked by unpaid Spanish soldiers, merely dented the trade. It was only when the Dutch rebels sealed off the mouth of the Scheldt in 1585 that the alternatives came into their own. Emden, Hamburg, Stade and Middelburg all at some time offered facilities to the Merchant Adventurers, and a more general diversification of trade, tacitly ignoring the staple, was born of prudence.

Increasingly, this diversified trade was conducted in English ships. By 1602, almost 50 per cent of tonnage entering the port of London was English: cloth transported to the Baltic was carried almost entirely by English vessels. These developments reflect protectionist parliamentary legislation and the growth of an internal market, which helped provide both the demand for luxuries and exotic essentials and some of the capital that shipbuilding required. External trade is but the more visible manifestation of a much wider commercial environment, in which the poorly documented home economy plays a vital part.

Much about English or Scottish trade in the sixteenth century is, though, still pragmatic and primitive according to standards set in the course of the following hundred years. Supply of adequate coin, in particular, remained deplorably short throughout the period. Elizabethan London's rudimentary exchanges offered none of the sophistication to be found in Antwerp and several Italian cities, though the Royal Exchange, established in 1571, was a belated if enterprising attempt to redress this balance.

If English trade did reasonably well in spite of the war with Spain, Scottish trade in the 1580s and 1590s was flourishing thanks to an absence of these pressures. The boom was export-driven, with wool products still dominant. Edinburgh again led the way and prospered most. Like London, the city all but monopolized a nation's wool trade, taking by the end of the century a dominant share of the hide and coal exports as well. In 1598 the city was exporting just under 200,000 sheepskins, 204,000 other skins and 36,700 hides. On both sides of the Anglo-Scottish border regional ports – Newcastle, Bristol, Norwich, York and Exeter in England, Perth, Aberdeen and Dundee in Scotland – prospered by making a virtue out of a rapidly expanding capital city, operating as natural marketplaces for their particular hinterlands and passing on the goods and produce relayed by coastal shipping.

These patterns of international trade were advanced and frustrated within complex patterns of European diplomacy, the full subtleties of which are still only gradually coming into focus. Scottish and English – particularly English – international relations used to be discussed in terms of France, Spain and the Low Countries, but important recent research has emphasized the part played by the states of Germany and by the Baltic nations in the overall picture.[20] Like her father before her, Elizabeth, when she thought the balance of power in Europe might shift against England, was prepared to sponsor elaborate diplomatic campaigns in Germany and in Scandinavia with a view to enlisting new allies.

The existence of the 'two protectorates', that of Spain over the forces of counter-reformation Catholicism and of England over the protestant north, was recognized by contemporaries, even if it has been belittled subsequently. Elizabeth paid lip service to such constructions. While her ambition was security, while her eyes remained fixed upon the Channel ports of France and Flanders, successive English administrations recognized that careful diplomacy among the often mutually discordant German principalities might produce useful propaganda, mercenaries to fight in France and the Low Countries, trade outlets and the possibility – never fulfilled – of concerted military action. That no united armies ever took the field is, perhaps, just as well. As the queen realized, her status as protectress of continental protestants was, in all but a loose, moral sense, unenforceable. Philip II's experiences, particularly his three bankruptcies, show the limitations of even the most powerful early modern state obliged to conduct forbiddingly expensive early modern wars. In the mid-1570s in particular, bankruptcy lost Philip an initiative in the Netherlands which he was never to regain.[21]

Correcting the perspective remains a problematic exercise: the motives shaping foreign policy are difficult to pin down. Elizabeth was, undoubtedly, cautious in all her dealings with foreign powers, but is caution deliberate inactivity or uncertain vacillation? Too often, it is impossible to say. Emmanuel Kouri captures our dilemma nicely: 'If', he writes, 'she [Elizabeth] had no policy, but just drifted with events, this lack of policy was what was required to achieve the ends she might have had.'[22]

15 The Loss of Peace: England 1580–9

| July 1589 | Assassination of Henry III of France; succession of protestant Henry IV |
| June–July 1589 | Counter-Armada |

The 1570s and 1580s witnessed sustained population growth, not only in England but across western Europe. After the disastrous influenza outbreaks of 1557–8, we observe a trend towards younger marriages and larger families, together with an absence of major mortalities. 'Plague' had by no means disappeared: two epidemics spreading to London from the continent, in 1563 and 1603, each killed nearly a quarter of the city's population. Epidemic disease of this kind was, however, increasingly an urban phenomenon, and intermittent summer outbreaks in all major English cities do not appear to have set a brake on population growth during Elizabeth's reign. Indeed, reliable figures suggest that, between 1566 and 1586, mortality rates in England were lower than at any time before the early nineteenth century.

Younger marriage is a relative concept. In relation to life expectancy, even in absolute terms, Elizabethans married late. Such averages as we have suggest that men embarked on matrimony for the first time in their mid- to late twenties, women three to five years earlier. Younger marriages were more common among the gentry, and so, too, were large families. Early marriage is also encountered in towns and in some rural communities like the Weald of Kent, but it was not a national norm: the young couple who contracted an 'over-hasty' union were generally unpopular. In a rural society, a new marriage established a new household and a new economic unit of production. An eldest son, in these circumstances, was unlikely to tie the knot until his father had died, or retired, and left him a means of subsistence in the shape of the family landholding. Few men engaged in apprenticeships, either in town or country, could have envisaged breaking the terms of their indentures to marry until their years were expired and they had accumulated the means to set up an independent home.

As a result, wide age differences in marriage were not uncommon. Men obliged to wait by economic circumstances frequently took much younger brides – to the extent that this was remarked upon by amused foreigners – and when the elderly husband died wealthy widows might attract younger men keen to wed money. On the other hand, many never even contemplated matrimony. Twenty-five per cent of women over forty in a survey conducted in Ealing during 1599 were still single, and evidence elsewhere suggests that this proportion was not abnormal.

Demographic changes perplexed and fascinated the Elizabethans themselves. Richard Hakluyt, writing in the 1580s, saw the link between population growth and fewer outbreaks of epidemic disease, while William Harrison that same decade took as read 'the great increase of people in these days'. This growth can, tentatively, be quantified. A population – for England alone – of around 2.8 million in 1550 had risen to a little over 4 million by the end of the century. Wales might add some 220,000 and 320,000 respectively. English and Welsh population grew by between 4.3 and 5.8 per cent in each decade from 1561 to 1586. These increases conformed to European trends, for by 1600 the total population of France may have risen to between 16 and 18 million, while the figure for Spain and Portugal together was something in the region of 11 million. All these statistics remain best guesses: we have no national census, only extrapolations from the local records in which England is particularly well served.

For much of the reign, growth was achieved without undue pressure on the food supply. While those of 1562 and 1574 were decidedly poor, there was no disastrous harvest before the mid-1580s, and the fall in cloth prices had lessened the incentive to set land aside for pastoral farming. Living standards, in an inflationary age where the fastest price increases were those of foodstuffs, appear to have risen for most of those who could produce a surplus for the market. Landlords in particular were beginning to accommodate rather than to ignore the effects of inflation, learning more about their estates, surveying them and managing them more skilfully. Contemporaries saw the prosperity in its outward manifestations, from peers with their new, extravagant 'prodigy houses', art collections, coaches, entertainments and elaborate funeral monuments, to the well-to-do yeomen, with their larger, chimneyed houses of brick and stone, feather beds, greater diversity of household furniture and pewter on the sideboard. The other face to so bright a picture highlights the effects of inflation on the small tenant farmers producing only a modest surplus, and still more on those who had to work for money. In a well-supplied labour market wages stagnated while prices edged upwards. Few were wholly dependent on cash remuneration, but for many, particularly in towns, wages were essential to their families' livelihood. For the unemployed, underemployed or incapacitated, the opportunities newly opened to landowners lay far out of reach.

Setting aside abnormal peaks in the difficult years of the mid-1590s, prices rose, very approximately, fourfold in the course of the sixteenth century. Without deflationary pressures – a surplus labour supply, lower wage levels, corresponding reductions in demand for non-essential goods, the outflow of bullion and a rising demand for scarce money relative to goods – the increase might have been still more spectacular, but it was novel enough in the opinion of contemporaries.[1] Observers gradually grew more sophisticated in their analyses of the phenomenon, recognizing that inflation was a European problem which could be stimulated in many different ways. This complexity was brought home to them when debasement was taken out of the equation, Elizabeth in 1562 having finally called in the base money still in circulation. Thereafter, money supply grew very slowly, but amounted to no more than £1 per head in circulation by 1600. Though moving steadily in that direction, England was still far from what today we might consider a money economy.

Risk-spreading and risk-taking also accompany inflationary pressures. There is a diversity to Elizabethan industry, hitherto quite absent, and largely the result of encouragement given to foreign émigrés. Refugees from Flanders help to establish new crops, like hops and oilseed rape, and they reinvigorate moribund urban cloth industries through the production of lighter, inexpensive new draperies. Here are the boom textile products of the later 1500s; at Norwich, Colchester, Reading and other centres, textile workers find they can utilize the coarser long-staple wool rejected by traditional broadcloth and worsted manufacture. Immigrants from Germany introduce gunpowder manufacture from 1561, and copper and calamine mining in 1564–5. By the 1580s the quality end of the English printing market, formerly dominated by continental presses, has fallen almost entirely into native hands. The number of printing houses in London doubles between 1550 and 1590. Artisans from northern France, Flanders and Italy prompt a great revival in English glassmaking during Elizabeth's reign, while paper manufacture is found at Dartford from 1588, again under German auspices. These prominent industries overshadow flourishing basic product manufacture across the range of domestic demand: pins, needles, soap, buttons, and so on. The market is, after all, expanding, swelling the demand for such low-technology essentials.

If population and prosperity had grown in the three decades of Elizabethan peace, both stagnated during the years of sustained military commitment that followed. Peace appeared ever more fragile as the 1580s progressed. Her strength and will sapped by internal strife, France proved unable to provide the strong backing now desperately needed by the protestant rebels of the Low Countries, and the prospect of English intervention against Philip II's advancing armies grew accordingly, year by year. There were calculated affronts on both sides. Elizabeth knighted the first Englishman to circumnavigate the globe, Francis Drake, on the deck of his ship the *Golden Hind* in April 1581, but the Spaniards regarded Drake, not unreasonably, as a pirate and a thief. The expulsion of the Spanish ambassador Bernardino de Mendoza in January 1584, following his complicity in a plot against Elizabeth's life, was countered by sanctions against English nationals in Spain. With tensions rising across northern Europe, parliament met late in 1584 to vote Elizabeth money and, specifically, to consider measures for the queen's safety.

Parliament had a specific measure in mind. Drafted by the privy council in October 1584, the so-called Bond of Association had met the fears of protestant Englishmen by focusing their anxieties into pledges of vengeance were the life of the queen to be assailed, or taken. Personal obligation had been invoked, to the queen, certainly, but also to the state she symbolized and, by implication, to an unnamed successor. Subscribers had undertaken to 'withstand, offend and pursue, as well by force of arms as by all other means of revenge', all who in any way should promote actions tending 'to the harm of her majesty's royal person', means of revenge being left unspecified. Technically a private, voluntary association of leading gentlemen, the Bond had been promoted by the council in terms which had made refusal almost impossible. Nevertheless, the measure had caught a mood in the times: gentlemen in the counties, protestants and, where they could work it, Catholics, had queued up to sign. Here was the protestant nation at work, united in what Burghley himself called a 'fellowship and society': united, indeed, to such a degree that it could envisage life without this queen, or any other monarch hostile to the national faith. No wonder that Elizabeth's response was distinctly ambivalent.

So blatant an appeal to mob violence also underlines the fragility of Elizabeth's regime; it must be seen against disturbing developments at home and abroad. The discovery at the end of the previous year of a tangled and widespread plot to murder the queen and set up Mary Stuart in her place, hatched by a Catholic gentleman Francis Throckmorton, had sharpened the fears of English protestants, while the assassination of the Dutch prince, William 'the Silent', at Delft in June 1584, had again highlighted the dangers run by rulers.

When parliament met in November 1584, however, doubts were expressed regarding the legality of the Bond. The Act 'for the surety of the queen's most royal person', which eventually emerged in 1585, departed from the terms of the oath of association in acquitting the heir of a 'pretended successor', such heirs having been specifically targeted in the Bond. The point of this was clear. Provided that he did not himself dabble in enterprises against Elizabeth, James VI might not be deprived of his claim to the throne, or harried by vengeful Englishmen, for crimes committed in the name of his mother. Clarification was desirable. There lay, in the original Bond, ample scope, literally for overkill. Like the confirmatory legislation that gave parliamentary sanction to a 1582 proclamation declaring Jesuits and seminary priests to be traitors, regardless of what they actually said or did, it had illustrated the fears and the prevailing knee-jerk reactions of the times.[2]

Act overshadows Bond in practical as well as legal import, for when Mary was ensnared during 1585–6 in the imaginative plotting of a young Catholic courtier, Anthony Babington, she was tried and sentenced to death under the provisions of that statute. One may justifiably suspect pre-planning in all that followed. Burghley, never personally hostile to Mary and hitherto at least ambivalent over her right of succession, now agreed with Leicester and Walsingham that the international situation and the survival of Mary's son alike dictated her destruction. The year 1586 saw a virtual replay of 1572, with parliament and bishops seeking Mary's death, and Elizabeth prevaricating. The prevarication, though, was less convincing. While the queen openly hesitated to confirm the sentence passed on her fellow monarch, she too wished Mary dead; only the means to an end were at issue. In the face of a concerted campaign directed skilfully and discreetly by Burghley, Elizabeth at last signed the death warrant. Mary was beheaded at Fotheringhay Castle in February 1587.[3]

The 1586–7 session of parliament was summoned with the express intention of sanctioning due process of law against Mary. It remained a single-issue session, despite one final bid by the advocates of presbyterian reform to gain acceptance for their programme. The day of Cartwright and his colleagues was done. Some puritans turned henceforth to separatism: men like Henry Barrow came to be seen as dangerous enemies of state. Intemperately zealous, Barrow was quite willing to tackle Elizabeth's godless government head on, disparaging all advice to bide a more enlightened day. 'If princes

Plate 19 Sketch of the execution of Mary Queen of Scots in the Great Hall of Fotheringhay Castle, Northamptonshire, 8 February 1587. Note the rather claustrophobic setting, and the fire in the hearth to warm a winter's morning.
Source: The Fotomas Index

resist or neglect,' he asked, rhetorically, 'where [do] they find the faithful ought to rest in their defaults and disorders until God change the prince's heart?' Another separatist, John Field, expressed these sentiments in a manner still more stark. 'Seeing we cannot compass these things by suit nor dispute,' he insisted, 'it is the multitude and people that must bring them to pass.' For the large majority of puritans, though, these opinions represented only a disturbing impossibility. They stayed within the church, even upholding the rule of bishops. It was still possible so to do, when most bishops, pricked of their pride, expounded broadly Calvinist beliefs, and when a majority of Elizabeth's privy counsellors shared these views.

But while puritans stayed within Elizabeth's church, they seemed to retain their place there only on sufferance. In the reaction against a series of anti-establishment satires published under the pseudonym Martin Marprelate, the so-called Marprelate tracts which appeared in 1588–9, puritanism was again defined and, perhaps for the first time in print, ridiculed in its failings. The satire backfired, for the tracts were refuted in the same scurrilous, facetious mode, a process that helped establish the foolish, lecherous, hypocritical stage puritan of early seventeenth-century drama and popular imagination. Skits on his character, indeed, for a time overshadowed debate over the puritan's precise beliefs.[4]

The threat to Elizabeth's life forced counsellors into some contingency planning. It was all very well agreeing to pursue assassins to the death and to disbar from succession any whose cause was advanced by such devilry, but supposing the queen *did* die – what then? Here lay uncharted waters. Elizabeth's death would strip her privy council, and any parliament then sitting, of all authority, and there was no useful historical precedent to follow. A draft bill for the succession dating from early 1585 shows Burghley, with the assistance of the fiercely anti-Catholic attorney-general John Popham, devising one way round the dilemma. Should the worst happen, members of the old privy council would, under this plan, combine with a reliable group of the non-conciliar nobility and the chief justices to establish a 'great council'. A council in this form would provide continuity of government until a parliament, consisting of those who had sat in the last session, could meet and decide where the right of succession lay. Officially, no particular guidelines were adopted – Elizabeth seems to have expressed her disapproval – although the composition and functions of a 'great council' which met after the queen's death in 1603 suggest that some elements of Burghley's plan had been taken to heart.

A succession of plots against Elizabeth's life added to the council's unease. No sooner was the Throckmorton conspiracy broken than a renegade MP and, embarrassingly, a Burghley client, William Parry, was convicted and executed for planning to pistol the queen from her horse. After Babington's efforts on behalf of the queen of Scots, plots like those envisaged by Dr Roderigo Lopez, a Portuguese Jew employed as a physician by Elizabeth convicted of scheming to supply the queen with a poisoned plaster, and by Edward Squire, who intended to poison the pommel of Elizabeth's saddle, add to a sense of futility inherent in all such enterprises. Their ineptness, though, emphasized the danger. However far-fetched in their detail, these plots kept attention focused uncomfortably on the point of weakness in personal monarchy. Remove the head – how that is done, provided that it is done, hardly matters – and the state, legally, politically and practically, is caught off guard. At such moments, as the most famous conspirators of all argued in 1605, while they ferried their barrels of gunpowder into the cellars of Westminster, all options are open.

When the Spaniards captured Dunkirk and Nieuport in 1583, an invasion of England mounted from Low Countries ports became militarily feasible. Such an enterprise was even then under consideration, as the two nations slipped closer and closer to open war. The assassination of William the Silent had persuaded many in England, and most on the council, that conflict was inevitable, although for the best part of another year Elizabeth continued to hope that Henry III might be persuaded to intervene in the Low Countries and that her own prestige, and her military and financial resources, might not have to be hazarded. Henry, however, declined, preoccupied by troubles at home, and his indifference threatened to open the way to a conclusive Spanish victory. In 1585, through the terms of the Treaty of Nonsuch, English forces were dispatched to the Low Countries and naval raids mounted on the coasts of Spain and Spanish America. Over the next two years troops under Leicester helped the Dutch stabilize a precarious position.

By 1588, though, Philip II could take stock of a promising military and diplomatic situation. Parma had again gone on the offensive, France was once more tortured by civil war. Leicester's costly and undistinguished campaigning had disillusioned his queen and the Dutch alike, while in January 1587 an English colonel, Sir William Stanley, perhaps fearing implication in the Babington plot, had surrendered Deventer to the Spaniards, going over with his men to the enemy. Poor returns on her investment led Elizabeth and her council to weigh the cost of continued military operations, even to the point of opening negotiations with the representatives of Spanish Flanders in Bourbourg. But her decision had unforeseen consequences. Signs of weakness in a power he had come to view as the nourisher of sedition and revolt in the Netherlands helped persuade Philip that England was vulnerable and that a well-conceived military operation might neutralize her for the foreseeable future.

Philip's strategic plan combined two schemes, one advanced by Parma, the other by the king's experienced naval commander, the marquis of Santa Cruz. Santa Cruz advocated a sea-borne assault. A preliminary strike against Ireland would be followed by invasion of the south coast of England, in overwhelming strength. Parma's strategy was, by contrast, that of a land commander. He proposed a swift operation mounted by 30,000 veterans, who would cross the Channel in barges, sweep through Kent and trap the queen in London. Philip, unwilling to cast either plan aside, blended them to the extent that Santa Cruz's Armada would provide an escort for Parma's invasion force in its crossing of the Channel, and would supply reinforcements and siege guns to batter English towns into submission. Surprise lay at the heart of both schemes, yet surprise was all but impossible to sustain. The assembly of stores and supplies in Spain, and well-publicized attempts to raise money for the venture in Rome, saw to that.[5]

The so-called Spanish Armada was in fact drawn from all parts of the Mediterranean and Iberian seaboard, from Portugal, Italy and the Levant. So disparate a force required, and was provided with, able leadership. The death of Santa Cruz in February 1588 was long considered a desperate blow to Spanish ambitions, but in his replacement, the duke of Medina Sidonia, Philip enjoyed the services of a determined and utterly conscientious admiral. Plans progressed steadily. A bold raid on the harbour of Cadiz by Drake in April 1587, and adverse winds in early summer 1588, delayed matters for upwards of a year, but on 21 July the fleet of some 130 ships set sail from Corunna.

Philip's Armada did preserve some element of surprise, for few in England imagined that an invasion would be launched so late in the summer. Before the Spanish were sighted off Plymouth on 29 July, the large English fleet assembled in that port had itself been planning an offensive. The English, too, had been frustrated by bad weather – always an unpredictable element in naval warfare before the days of steam – and by logistical delays so characteristic of the age.

During the last week of July and the first days of August, the Armada slowly made its way along the Channel. Sailing in the close crescent formation deployed successfully against the Turks at the battle of Lepanto in 1571 it presented a formidable aspect, so formidable, indeed, that in their initial encounters the English were awed into a long-range engagement, hoping to wear down the enemy by picking off stragglers. The Lord Admiral, Lord Howard of Effingham, was clearly impressed. 'We durst not', he wrote, describing the first day of fighting, 'adventure to put in amongst them, their fleet being so strong.'

Yet by 9 August this impregnable Armada was being driven by adverse winds far into the North Sea, the English engaged in a hot pursuit, not broken off until both fleets had cleared the Firth of Forth. Many explanations have been advanced for this reversal. Some of these have been discredited by modern archaeological findings, others by closer examination of the documentary evidence available in Spanish archives. The opposing fleets were not, in fact, so unequally matched. William Camden quite naturally magnified the power of an enemy soon to be humbled, but his enduringly popular description of 'lofty turrets like castles' is misleading. Apart from the troop transports, which were lightly armed and of little use in battle, the ships of the Armada were no larger than those under Lord Howard's command. The Armada's firepower, indeed, was inferior to that enjoyed by the opposing fleet. Its ordnance was lighter and varied significantly in calibre. All the same, investigation of Armada wrecks has shown that there was no general shortage of round-shot at the crucial battle off Gravelines. We are, indeed, now led to believe that it was English stocks of ammunition that fell to dangerously low levels, early in August. This in itself is an interesting corrective to older views, for the English guns and, less certainly, gun-carriages were technically superior and capable of maintaining a better rate of fire in the close-quarter fighting off the Isle of Wight and at Gravelines.

All these factors, however, important as they no doubt are in clarifying the tactics employed and the course of the fighting, cannot in themselves explain failure. The Armada arrived off Calais intact and able to proceed with the combined operation. Both sides, indeed, were disconcerted by the lack of damage their artillery duels had inflicted on the enemy. Nor had the Spanish at any time lost the initiative, for in the absence of reliable military intelligence their strategy remained a mystery to their opponents, who wondered to the end whether the invasion fleet was destined for England, Holland, or both at once. In Calais roads, however, Medina Sidonia encountered an obstacle of the Spaniards' own making. According to Philip's master plan, the Armada was to secure control of the Channel, thus allowing Parma's transports to put out from Dunkirk. The means by which control was to be secured was apparently not addressed. No one seems to have drawn the distinction between navigating a stretch of water under enemy fire, and neutralizing that enemy. Having fought his way up the Channel, Medina Sidonia appears from surviving dispatches to Parma to have assumed that the Army of Flanders, supported by Parma's own not-inconsiderable fleet, would be capable of a short navigation through the sandbanks and into open water.

His assumption was false. With a powerful Dutch squadron poised outside the harbour of Dunkirk such a manoeuvre would have involved running enormous risks, risks that Parma was reluctant to contemplate. The Flanders fleet of seventeen royal warships was seriously undermanned in the early days of August, since many crewmen were still engaged in bringing round the 170 troop transports from Antwerp to Nieuport. Now, inefficiencies in the channels of communication between admiral and general began to have grave consequences. Although bombarded with requests for information and material assistance from Medina Sidonia, the vagaries of sixteenth-century message-carrying ensured that Parma was unable to dispatch a reply until the fleet arrived at the rendezvous. These delays helped prolong the fatal interlude off Calais.

Seeing the Armada thus compromised, but still uncertain as to the timing of Parma's next move, the English floated eight fireships among the enemy on the night of 7 August. The Spaniards were expecting this – they had encountered fireships before – but they knew also that little could be done to frustrate these tactics. Although two of the ships were pulled aside using grappling hooks, the threat posed by the rest persuaded Medina Sidonia to take evasive action. He ordered all his vessels to disperse, and to regroup once the danger was past. For too many ships, struggling with wind and tide as well as with the enemy, this simply proved impossible, and in a confused battle fought in rough weather all the following day the immediate issue was decided. The story of this battle, like so much else about the actual fighting in August 1588, remains obscure; the fog of war even permits some determinedly revisionist historians to insist that the Spaniards won a victory of sorts when they effected a fighting withdrawal. Such arguments have about them the ring of propaganda following a twentieth-century engagement close by, on the sands of Dunkirk. It seems more likely that the English fleet's superior firepower in close-quarter fighting was at last brought to tell. Suffering high casualties, Spanish morale began to slip and, with the winds also against him, Medina Sidonia was unable to rally his fleet. The only route home lay 'north-about', round Scotland and down the coast of Ireland, where storms took their toll of the dispersed Armada. While most of the casualties were transports rather than warships, at least one-third of the ships that had sailed against England failed to return. Fifteen thousand men perished, the casualties among Philip's experienced naval officer cadre being particularly severe.

The Spanish court was baffled and demoralized by this reverse. For the count of Fuentes, 'the mere thought of it defies all understanding'. There was, in adversity, a resolute stiffening of resolve among Philip and his

Plate 20 *Allegorical painting of the defeat of the Spanish Armada,* by Robert Stevenson, *c.*1610.
Source: Private collection

council, but there was, too, an inevitable round of recriminations. Parma came in for particular blame. He was, briefly, accused of treason, of frustrating the design of the Armada to forward his own aspirations to sovereignty in the Netherlands. The duke, though, was a professional, honourable soldier who had worked hard at the task of assembling his invasion force; these charges never really rang true.[6] If blame must be apportioned for the failure of an obviously risky strategy it should fall on Philip and his staff officers, who for all their meticulous planning committed the crucial stage of the operation to providence, finding it convenient to believe that a fleet of 130 ships could secure a waterway thirty miles wide. Memories of Lepanto had guided Spanish thinking, but the English Channel proved to be no Gulf of Corinth writ large.

Few gambles, however, are taken without some prospect of success. While combined operations are seldom straightforward, the Armada plan shows, alongside its weaknesses, intelligence and logic. The 'what might have beens' of history may beguile us to little purpose, but it is worth noticing that Philip provided contingencies for the land campaign not evident in the crucial rendezvous off Flanders. As perceived from Madrid, the Armada was born of a transient improvement in the international situation. No one expected the absence of crises elsewhere to last, and the Armada, in consequence, was given specific, short-term objectives. Its goal was the rapid, hopefully inexpensive, elimination of England, not as a nation but as a player in the continental war. Parma was to advance swiftly on London and take the city by storm, but were he to be delayed, a sufficient show of force in Kent was deemed sufficient for his royal master's purpose.

The decayed state of town fortifications – even at Tilbury the defences were but half-finished in mid-August – may lead us to suspect that assumptions of an easy land campaign were not too far wide of the mark. On the other hand, the problems Parma would have encountered in landing[7] and reinforcing his army, and his relative weakness in heavy cavalry, argue that the outcome may not have been so clear-cut. The English forces were by no means so haphazardly organized or so poorly armed as some authorities suggest. Their preparation had occupied months of hard work by central and local officials in 1588, work which had spawned a prototype 'council of war', of great significance in later years, as the professionalism of what may be termed a staff system developed.

Leicester's troops apart, the defenders had little military experience. At the same time, despite their lack of numbers, veterans trained and stiffened the shire levies. In 1573, the government had taken a step of immense importance for the future, adapting Queen Mary's legislation of 1558 and establishing permanent militia units, the so-called trained bands. These bands, under local gentry command, consisted of men selected from the mustered militia and provided with military training for ten days every year. The costs of such training were met by the individual county through local taxes. Increasingly, these well-trained, well-equipped soldiers served under crown-appointed officers, and although drawn from the militia, where the obligation was for home defence only, they served overseas as well, particularly in the 1590s. Elizabeth's government throughout the reign made a point of reserving the best equipment for the trained bands, even at the expense of forces fighting on the continent. By the end of the century, the longbow had vanished from their armouries and their equipment was as modern as that provided to the levies of any other European state.

The crown maintained its control of the trained bands through the lords lieutenant. In 1585, recognizing the scale of the war to which it was committed, Elizabeth's administration had appointed lieutenants across much of her realm, giving them a subordinate staff, or the means by which one might be created. In practice, this meant that the lieutenant or his deputy was delegated to bargain with the gentlemen of the county over assessments for troop quotas and the cost of the bands. Central government money was seldom involved in this initial process of recruitment, training or transport within England. Despite obvious scope for corruption and complacency, this system devised by a penniless administration dependent upon local cooperation worked well enough when put to a very difficult and protracted test.

Here, by sixteenth-century standards, was a formidable line of home defence to confront any invader. The musters of 1587 revealed that the trained bands nationwide stood at a notional strength of 44,000, the full general muster of able-bodied at nearly three times this number. Though mobilization was, for reasons of cost, deliberately delayed by Elizabeth, Parma would have been faced on his landing by a well-armed and well-led force at least twice the size of his own.[8] Here we reach the true imponderable. The battle for Kent would have turned on the morale of the English forces, and that factor of morale, never tested, remains unquantifiable.

The Spanish Armada has passed so far into the Great Legend of English history that much of the story has been distorted and confused. The proud Spanish boast of an 'Invincible Armada' comes straight from the pages of a 1588 English propaganda pamphlet, *The Copie of a letter sent out of England to Bernardino Mendoza*, while the tale of an armour-clad queen rousing her men at Tilbury with an immortal speech appears to have been a broad embellishment of what actually happened.[9] But if over decades the Armada spawned legends, in the short term it generated anxieties verging at times upon paranoia. Before 1588, no Englishman quite knew what to expect of Spanish power. In the 1590s, the real or rumoured approach of a Spanish sail on the horizon awakened fears of a 'new Armada'. Hitherto the papacy had been, for protestant Englishmen, the nation's principal enemy, but after 1588, while popes came and went, the malevolent, ageing figure of Philip II took centre stage.[10]

For all its drama, and for all the potency of the myths thus spawned, the Armada was not itself a turning point in the long conflict. Nor did its failure mark any great change in strategy, for Spain never ruled out an invasion of England, other circumstances permitting. So far as the English were concerned, of greater consequence was the legacy of events in 1589. The failure of the Armada provided the Elizabethan administration, hitherto obliged by circumstance to pursue a defensive course, with an initiative. Important decisions would clearly have to be taken regarding the future conduct of the maritime war. The 'Counter-Armada' that emerged in 1589 was the product of much tortured debate during the previous winter. All sides were agreed on the need for a retaliatory strike against the surviving Armada vessels. Moderates on the council thought in terms of a limited operation on the lines of Drake's descent upon Cadiz in 1587, but while the precedent of Cadiz, with its rich return on investment, certainly attracted the 'hawks', they envisaged a more ambitious campaign, aimed at restoring to his throne the exiled Portuguese pretender Dom Antonio. The goal of such an adventure, they argued, should be nothing less than the seizure of Lisbon.

Fatal compromise was a perhaps inevitable result. In the long deliberations over policy, both the destruction of the Spanish fleet and the promotion of an uprising against Spanish rule in Portugal were adopted as goals of the operation, while joint-stock financing of the fleet obliged the planners to include a third aim: the seizure of an island base in the Azores and an assault on the Spanish silver fleet, returning from the Americas. This multiplicity of objectives bred confusion. Orders eventually issued were to some extent incompatible. No effort seems to have been made to alert Dom Antonio's phantom army of rebels, while Elizabeth's unwillingness to provide artillery cast doubt on the viability of operations against well-defended towns and harbours.

Whereas the queen insisted that the destruction of Armada galleons should take priority – the fact that an absent fleet would leave England undefended caused her much disquiet – her commanders, Sir Francis Drake and Sir John Norris, once at sea, paid only superficial attention to her directives and set their sights on the glory offered by success in Portugal. Not for the first time in this war of islands and water, the orders and assessments of a council hundreds of miles distant were given wilfully free interpretation.

The expedition was ill-starred. Adverse winds prevented its prompt departure, while a large proportion of the Dutch ships commandeered into service deserted once out of sight of land. The combined force of some 140 ships and 23,000 men embarked on a series of plundering sorties which resulted in the burning of Corunna and Vigo, and little else. Sixty Spanish warships in Santander were ignored. Lack of artillery and general apathy among the local population frustrated the invasion of Portugal. Standing bemused before the barricaded gates of Lisbon, Norris had little option but to retire and re-embark. Operations in the Azores were thwarted by southerly gales, while disease killed 30 per cent of the troops and sailors. Mutual recriminations in the aftermath of failure are once again unedifying; the queen's unwillingness to commit resources had contributed to failure, but the poor performance of ambitious captains and inexperienced troops had in turn helped remind Elizabeth of the waste in human and financial terms that accompanied offensive operations. Ghosts from the Newhaven expedition still troubled her dreams. Forgotten by posterity in the shadow of the Armada, the Portugal expedition was accepted by queen and council as a salutary lesson during the years of attritional warfare that followed.

16 A Nation at War: England in the 1590s

The 1590s present an altogether different picture of Elizabethan England. Recently, indeed, we have been invited to view this bleak period of war abroad, economic hardship and political tensions at home as a second, distinct,

Elizabethan reign. Unlike the summer chivalries of Henry VIII's French campaigns, the wars of the 1590s lasted for years and were fought on many fronts. To the battlefields of Normandy and Brittany, the pursuit of an increasingly threatening enemy in Ireland, and to unending siege and counter-siege in the Netherlands, was added a distant enterprise of oceans and unknown continents, as Englishmen, with or without the sanction of their government, sought public glory and private profit in a series of attacks upon Spanish possessions in the Atlantic and the new world.

Whether or not we are justified in writing of a new Elizabethan age, war and politics were certainly conducted by new men. The ageing queen was fast outliving her contemporaries: Leicester and Warwick, Walter Mildmay, Francis Walsingham and Christopher Hatton all died between 1588 and 1591. The loss of so many trusted and seasoned counsellors had a destabilizing effect, particularly on the queen herself. Elizabeth thereafter appears an increasingly marginalized figure, her grip on political events slowly loosening and her control over her privy council gradually weakening.[1] The picture can be overdrawn for it may not take due account of the failings and incompetence of so many others in time of war, but it is nonetheless substantially accurate. The queen found it particularly difficult to handle the generation gap opening up in her court. Favourites and counsellors of the 1590s she consistently treated as boys, suffering from all the failings of youth. Some traded on and enjoyed this royal indulgence, others grew irritated, the majority, more prudent, bided their time against the accession of a new monarch.

From the older generation of statesmen Burghley alone survived, and after 1591, though increasingly debilitated by illness, he dominated the council. Unique in the history of western European monarchies, Burghley's long pre-eminence grew still stronger in his last decade, for the queen's trust never faltered. The manner in which he secured the admission of his promising younger son as a counsellor in August 1591, when Robert Cecil was still only twenty-eight, testifies to that royal confidence, just as it illustrates a father's ambitions.

This Cecilian supremacy was implicitly recognized by almost every other political player. There was, however, one notable exception. Though working in harmony with the Cecils on many occasions, the queen's young favourite Robert Devereux, second earl of Essex, was never their wholehearted ally. Essex gained a seat in council during 1593 and laboured assiduously to acquire the skills of a statesman, and to build up a clientage of scholars and administrators through the distribution of patronage. Capable and engaging, when he chose to be, Essex's promotion to high office proved a serious miscalculation. The earl was a prickly character, quick to see an insult, and spurred on by a combination of high-minded aspirations and personal ambition. Burghley nevertheless noted his mistress's affection for the earl and worked hard to secure Essex's goodwill. While Essex and Robert Cecil were never very taken with one another, evidence of early animosity is elusive and in later years both made conscious, if at times rather ostentatious, efforts to work in harmony.

Leicester's stepson, Walsingham's son-in-law, Essex stepped willingly into dead men's shoes. Walsingham's death had opened an opportunity for anyone

EARL OF ESSEX.

Plate 21 *Robert Devereux, second earl of Essex,* by Marcus Gheeraerts the Younger, *c*.1596–9.
Source: The Master, Fellows and Scholars of Trinity College, Cambridge

prepared to manage and to fund the gathering of intelligence, and Essex, in the heyday of his personal favour with Elizabeth, and genuinely interested in European affairs, duly made the attempt. He sent his own protégés abroad, to advance his knowledge and reputation, and also to further their careers.[2] The charismatic favourite attracted many promising young men. Among his clients he counted the talented Bacon brothers, Anthony and Francis, Anthony Bacon having formerly been in Walsingham's service overseas. Sir Thomas Egerton, lord keeper from 1596, and that enigmatic, unpleasant character Henry Howard, younger son of the late duke of Norfolk, were among others who considered Essex their patron and ally.

Essex also took up the 'forward policy' pursued by Leicester and Walsingham. There were wars to fight against Catholicism on the continent, he urged, and there was glory to be won too, if only the queen was brave enough to hazard supplies, money and men. At the same time – and Walsingham would have looked askance at this – he saw scope to conciliate English Catholics. Essex's targets were the forces of hostile Catholic states rather than domestic Catholics, many of whom regarded the earl as their patron.[3] Making his own name as a soldier, he was successful in attracting to his circle young gentlemen of every religious persuasion, united by their ambitions of a military career. Among these 'swordsmen', however, were some wild spirits, men who brought loyalty and ill-advice to their patron in equal measure. Essex discovered that in a war-weary court and nation the opportunities to reward such adherents were few, the costs of maintaining a high lifestyle well beyond the capacity of his relatively modest estate. The counsel of outspoken warriors, moreover, sharpened already well-honed neuroses. Essex, particularly as his career foundered on military misfortune and royal displeasure, saw matters in sharply delineated terms: those not whole-heartedly for him were undoubtedly working to bring about his ruin. Fortunately for the Elizabethan state, Essex was alone in identifying patronage so directly as a display of personal, political power. Even more fortunately, he proved inept at the game.[4]

Straitened wartime financial circumstances had broader repercussions, aggravating the potential for corruption in Tudor methods of appointment to and the exercise of public office. 'It demands', as Roger Ashley has written, 'an effort of imagination to picture a bureaucracy made up of life tenancies, whose holders regarded their subordinates as personal servants and their papers of state as private property',[5] yet this was Tudor reality. The crown possessed some 1200 offices that were considered worth the attention of a gentleman, but while that number remained unchanged from the time of Henry VIII, the press of applicants had grown and the prices men were prepared to pay well-placed courtiers able to intercede with the queen, who signed most royal grants in person, escalated accordingly. Any casual glance at Burghley's papers for the 1580s and 1590s shows the strength of this competition.

At first sight, the attractions of public office are elusive. Such positions commanded small, fixed salaries, eroded by inflation. The master of the court of wards, for example, received £133, the captain of the gentleman pensioners £100, and these were senior posts. However, a system which institutionalized obsolete salary levels, and which in effect regarded office as a financial reward, invited the post-holder to exploit what he had secured. Exploitation does not of itself imply illegal practice: there is a distinction to be drawn between salaries and fees, on the one hand, and money 'incentives' or bribes on the other. All public offices, when undertaking work on behalf of an individual, imposed a scale of fees for such tasks as sealings of documents or the issuing of writs, and these fees can hardly be criticized in principle. Nevertheless, there was endless scope for 'creative accounting' and nothing was done to regulate those far more dubious further payments, intended to secure an official's 'goodwill' in expediting business.

Improved salaries might – arguably – have obviated this institutionalized venality, but the crown never seriously considered reform of this kind, just as it made little if any effort to increase rents from its landed estates in line with inflation. Elizabeth's government chose to live with the poverty born of this inflation: her ministers felt that at a time of poor harvests, high prices and wartime social tensions the risks inherent in raising ordinary income or taxation to pay for improvements were not worth taking. An administration which refused to revise Queen Mary's 1558 book of rates for fear of antagonizing merchants, and which made only a half-hearted effort to improve returns on rents of crown lands, was strapped for cash, and sales of offices brought in a useful income, lining ministers' own pockets at the same time.[6]

There evolved a rough and ready gauge of what was acceptable, depending on the magnitude of the office and the scales of its official fees. Successive lord treasurers, the marquess of Winchester and Lord Burghley, accumulated personal fortunes, yet this great office commanded great fees and neither Winchester nor Burghley was considered a peculiarly avaricious man by his contemporaries. On the other hand, when a minor office holder, like the teller of the Exchequer Richard Stonley, diverted thousands of pounds of state money to his own purposes, his actions were denounced and investigations were launched. With rudimentary auditing and prevailing standards of acceptable conduct few light-fingered officials were ever brought to book. William Painter busily manipulated the accounts during his thirty-four years as clerk of the ordnance, the great office of military supply, while George Goring, receiver-general of the court of wards between 1588 and 1594, died owing the crown £19,000. His official salary was £66, with £70 board-wages. Small wonder, perhaps, that at his death, four-figure sums were immediately offered for his post.

War imposed a huge strain upon a nation grown unaccustomed to conflict, and beset by the social consequences of successive outbreaks of plague and a run of rain-ruined harvests between 1594 and 1598. Lacking an adequate wartime bureaucracy, the council battled to keep abreast of the mass of paperwork involved, while the lord lieutenants and their county subordinates struggled to translate calls for manpower from London into county contingents on the ground. Overseas, on campaign, rudimentary communications placed a premium on the efficiency and commitment of the local commander. In the static warfare of the Low Countries the London council might retain a degree of administrative control over its contingents, but in mobile campaigning, or when the theatre of war was more remote, directions were commonly delayed or mislaid. Thus Lord Willoughby seldom heard from the council when his contingent accompanied Henry IV across Normandy in the autumn of 1589, Sir John Norris was plagued with contradictory and belated messages from Elizabeth when campaigning in Brittany, and the earl of Essex in Ireland exchanged increasingly irritated letters with the council in 1599, which crossed at intervals of anything up to a fortnight. Naval commanders found the direction of the campaign effectively in their hands once their fleets entered the open Atlantic.

The Elizabethan government faced from its field commanders, and has faced from historians ever since, criticism that the war was conducted with an unbecoming parsimony. The queen and Burghley were undeniably reluctant to commit troops, and cavilled at the cost of most military enterprises. Any objective assessment, however, must acknowledge the burdens even this caution imposed. The navy alone, maintained in peace as in war, its administration integrated into the developing Elizabethan bureaucracy, cost the crown £50,000 a year through the 1590s, even after internal economies and the widespread use of independently financed privateers in an auxiliary role. Campaigns deploying large numbers of English troops had been fought before, but the country was now faced with a protracted commitment on several fronts and the burden was oppressive. The calm years of the 1570s had permitted the accumulation of a modest £325,000 in the Exchequer treasuries, but the Treaty of Nonsuch imposed an annual commitment of £126,000 and the 1590s saw yearly expenditure run at something like five times the early 1580s figure. The total bill for the eighteen years of war which concluded Elizabeth's reign came to around £4,500,000, at the national level alone.

The human cost of war was heavier still. Some 90,000 men were conscripted for military service between 1585 and 1603, that is, about 11 or 12 per cent of the male population aged sixteen to thirty-nine. Prospects for an enlisted man's survival were poor, diseases such as typhoid cutting swathes through any new batch of recruits, while inadequate diet and sanitation killed men by the thousand on major naval expeditions without any assistance from the enemy. It is, therefore, hardly surprising that the muster commissioners – gentlemen all – selected their contingents from the landless labourers and the wandering vagrants in preference to the sons of gentry or yeoman farmers. The crown would have preferred to draw upon the higher discipline and commitment of the 'better sort', but in this as in so much else it was at the mercy of its agents in the countryside. When Elizabeth's council suggested in 1600 that the calibre of selected men in Wales was such that 'it would seem they were picked so as to disburden the counties of so many idle, vagrant and loose persons rather than for their ability and aptness to do service', it was both touching on the truth and demonstrating its own impotence to correct so lamentable a state of affairs.

Parsimony, therefore, may rather have been a manifestation of fiscal necessity, given the unavailability of the foreign loans which shored up, and helped bankrupt, the continental powers. More could have been done to milk the wealth of individual citizens through forced loans, through a campaign to improve yields from crown lands and, perhaps, by a rescaling of subsidy assessments, but the conservatism of the queen, her government's caution and an unwillingness to denude private resources ensured that, while England contained wealth, much of it remained in the pockets of the landed gentry. The government was half obliged, half content that this should be so.[7]

That official line had its merits; advantages were unlikely to accrue from a more extortionate approach, given the difficulties faced by the country and the self-serving objectives of England's allies. Elizabethan conservatism also cautioned against any return to debasement; the ageing queen and her long-serving lord treasurer remembered the 1550s all too clearly. Tried and tested methods were adopted to raise money for the wars. Crown lands and offices were sold; of the three great dispersals of crown lands during Elizabeth's reign, that of the early 1560s helped cement loyalties early in her reign, while the other two, in 1589–91 and 1599–1603 respectively, met the pressing needs of military operations. Loans were taken out, feudal exactions like purveyance and wardship exploited for all they were worth, and more and more subsidies were sought from parliament. The times were desperate, MPs were told again and again, the queen frugal, her subjects lightly taxed and duty bound to offer more and more. Subsidies, though, brought in less and less, as assessments were fossilized and exemptions increased. Sir Walter Mildmay reminded the 1585 parliament of facts conveniently ignored: 'If I should tell you', he said, 'how meanly the great possessions in the country, and the best aldermen and citizens of London, and the rich men of the realm are rated, you would marvel at it.'

Most of his audience would not, in fact, have been very surprised. They themselves were profiting from the decline in assessment, just as some among them benefited in various ways from the monies devoted to the military bureaucracy. Little was done to account for these sums; no effort was made to combat the great inefficiency and peculation plaguing every aspect of the war effort. In spite of the council's efforts to ensure probity, the system whereby specie was transferred in large, intermittent quantities for disbursal by a treasurer at war, and then on down the chain of command through a company captain, failed when the responsible official proved dishonest. Sir Thomas Sherley, treasurer at wars in the Low Countries, was caught in the act of profiteering, but Sir George Carey, a counterpart in Ireland, escaped detection in his lifetime, amassing a personal fortune running into thousands of pounds.

The position of company commander was pivotal to the efficiency of an army lacking any substantial general staff. The captain arranged for his men to be paid, fed, watered and equipped, and he made a tidy profit at the business. While many of the men appointed were simply not up to their military task, it was, as the council admitted to Lord Mountjoy in 1600, 'fit that Her Majesty be not driven to discontent' the many suitors who sought commissions. Professional soldiers like Sir Francis Vere might fulminate, but the well-connected gentleman amateur was in a position to take from the wars not only honour, but an immediate profit from the imprests on pays channelled through his hands. Many had, after all, paid heavily to secure appointment, and the coming of peace would end such opportunities. There were possibilities for corruption at every turn, particularly in Ireland where the absence of a monitoring bureaucracy was notorious: no military auditor or muster-master came to Ireland until the 1590s, the Irish ordnance office was grossly incompetent and corrupt, and there was no central office over-seeing the problems of supply. Everywhere, the Elizabethan army resembled less a coherent fighting force, more 'a loosely connected series of franchises', flexible, certainly, but demanding personal contact between a commander and his captains for any degree of efficiency.[8]

Many burdens of war were carried by the English county, for the Eliza-bethan war effort was substantially localized and the taxpayer faced local as well as national levies. The shires had themselves to raise and transport their contingents to the ports of embarkation at their own cost. This caused logistical headaches, particularly when demands were repeated over and over again. Kent alone spent nearly £11,000 in the seven years 1596–1602 raising men for the wars. The money was found through a county rate – a local subsidy – calculated on lands and goods. Again in Kent, rates set in 1594 were more than doubled in 1596, despite the dismal economic outlook. Occasional token reimbursements by the council did little to alleviate the problem.

These were hard days for all levels of society. Individual noblemen, as ever, suffered or flourished according to their particular circumstances. Some, like the third earl of Cumberland, left considerable debts to their successors, but others, like the ninth earl of Northumberland, turned a relatively poor estate into a prosperous source of landed income within a decade. The privileges of rank and access were useful assets in time of hardship: some noblemen were sustained by forms of royal patronage, notably the interest-free loan. Personal circumstances, though, operate against a backcloth of economic stagnation, and years of difficulty for tenants posed many headaches for their landlords.[9] War also brought economic hardship for merchants involved in foreign trade, and for exporters. Any demand for military materials and supply was offset by the closure of foreign markets, taxation of merchant communities and the new, physical risks thrown in the way of commerce. Most merchants, however, could ride their ill-fortune; the poorest members of society, beset by high prices and scarcity of foodstuffs, were in a far more difficult position.

In these years famine blighted the land. Areas that had experienced par-ticularly high population growth now endured correspondingly high rates of mortality,[10] largely through the diseases accompanying undernourishment, although in some remote areas of the upland north-west cases of starvation were recorded. While population totals still did not approach England's medi-eval peak, recent demographic growth had strained agricultural production, that strain pushing up grain prices, forcing competition for good farming land, and leaving even in years of good harvest a pool of indigent poor and a surplus of available labour. Statistics must remain tentative, but it has been estimated that in 1597 as many as 40 per cent of the population could not achieve a subsistence livelihood.

Poor harvests with attendant high grain prices, the return of epidemic disease in the 1580s, which took away numerous breadwinners, and the growing numbers of disabled veteran soldiers, maimed in the wars, all tested systems of poor relief. Procedures developed in the 1570s, when only the impotent required assistance, were now stretched to provide for others. Although legislators accepted this only grudgingly, early Tudor assumptions that the able-bodied poor could if necessary work for a living were fast becoming redundant. Many of the vagrants crowding English roads were now landless young men, in search of elusive employment.

Obliged to sustain the war effort, the English government learnt a good deal about England itself. Information on sources of wealth, sources of manpower and possible troublemakers was carefully assembled. But knowledge brought fresh concerns as well as further statistics, and Elizabeth's counsellors were the biggest worriers of all. Fear of social calamity was not necessarily an overreaction: major rebellions prompted by economic crises erupted across Europe during this troubled decade, notably in southern France, Hungary and Habsburg Austria, the latter a peculiarly bloody affair. In England there were minor riots in London and several counties, protests against high grain prices. Kent endured eleven such disturbances between 1585 and 1603, and there was also a small-scale rising in Oxfordshire during 1596. While not one of these local manifestations of discontent developed into a major threat, the council's overreaction to what happened in Oxfordshire is revealing.[11] Executions for felonies peaked in these years, the assize judges making examples of malefactors, and justices of the peace stood on their guard. As fears of a Spanish invasion subsided in September 1596 Edward Hext in Somerset warned Burghley about the threat posed by the 'wicked and desperate', their ranks stiffened by 'wandering soldiers and other stout rogues'.

Prudence accompanied severity. Legislation against enclosure in the 1597 parliament was in part a response to concerns voiced in Oxfordshire the year before. The disastrous harvest of 1586 had prompted the publication of a Book of Orders, which tried to regulate the sale of available foodstuffs and in which concern for the welfare of the indigent poor is readily apparent. The Book was reissued in 1596. Advice for local justices covered matters as diverse as the standardization of quarantine procedures and the organization of searches for grain. Corn was stockpiled in many towns for sale at under the market price in times of shortage, and these stockpiles supplied hundreds of the poor: over 700 a week in Coventry during 1598. Legislation in the parliaments of 1597 and 1601 tightened up the procedure for administering poor relief. It detailed the parish's responsibility to provide – through the beefed-up office of overseer, still appointed by JPs but now including churchwardens *ex officio* and meeting monthly in the parish church – the framework of a system of poor relief in England which remained unchanged in many essentials until the 1830s. Of limited immediate effect, these measures at least reflected both disquiet and pragmatic social concern.[12]

There were, however, some for whom the advent of war opened doors to new careers and new opportunities. Many gentlemen and younger sons of noblemen acquired knighthoods through Essex's generosity at the siege of Rouen in 1591 and in Ireland during 1599. Though furious at his largesse, the queen declined to cancel these distinctions. Profits accruing to the well-placed company captain were not limited to the creative management of imprests; he might also win prestige and a pension. Sir Richard Percy, younger brother of the ninth earl of Northumberland, brother-in-law to Essex and latterly colonel of the Kinsale garrison, served for seven and drew a pension for forty years. Able commanders, such as Vere in the Low Countries, Norris in Brittany and Mountjoy in Ireland, earned material rewards and, that intangible yet essential avenue to favour, the respect of queen and council. There were winners too, far from the battlefield, in the court itself. Robert Cecil, through his dispatch of the ever-increasing wartime workload, edged closer to the coveted position of pre-eminent counsellor.

Englishmen – often the same Englishmen – served over twenty years in the Low Countries, over five years in France and maintained a garrison in Ireland, which swelled and diminished according to circumstances throughout our period. Continuing war thus presented England with a *de facto* standing army. The privy council sought to maintain lists of reliable captains, while the captains themselves sought to keep in their companies the veteran, experienced soldier, boasting to the government of the military expertise under their command. The Dutch reforms of Prince Maurice provided a model for army drill, which most captains adopted with alacrity. Spain provided new recruits to her army with introductory training and experience in the relatively peaceful Italian garrisons. The English crown was never so well organized, but the forces in Ireland or Holland provided a core of experienced soldiers – particularly officers – and it was not unknown for combat-hardened troops from one theatre to supply immediate needs in another.

We have been dealing so far with generalities. Useful as they are, these generalities can only be tested by examining how the 'standing army' performed in practice. The scale of challenges facing the English government in the crisis of the 1590s will be appreciated more readily through an examination of each theatre in the 'global war'.

The late 1580s saw a gradual change in the nature of the Anglo-Dutch alliance. In 1585 the partnership had been unequal, the Dutch seeking the patronage of a greater power prepared to allow them the devolved autonomy which they had enjoyed fifty years earlier. Although Elizabeth had refused the crown of the rebel provinces when it was offered, her general the earl of Leicester – much to the queen's indignation – had accepted the title of governor in 1586. Dutch subservience had, however, already vanished by 1590. Leicester's partial statecraft, and his mediocre military performance, encouraged this transformation, while Elizabeth's independent negotiations with Parma, broken only by the approach of the Armada, helped convince the Dutch that in a war of survival subordination to an independent power was too risky a strategy. In these years, the Dutch discovered in an uneasy alliance between the States-General, under Jan van Oldenbarnevelt, Advocate of Holland, and the Netherlands nobility under Maurice of Nassau, a leadership of their own. The two English seats on the council of state, carefully negotiated under the Treaty of Nonsuch, soon counted for little, as that council was increasingly by-passed by the States assembly.

The growing independent viability of the United Provinces was by no means unwelcome to Elizabeth and her government. Alterations which reduced

England's commitment permitted the drafting of experienced troops from the Netherlands to other areas. The aristocratic generals of the 1580s – Leicester and Willoughby – were succeeded in the 1590s by professional bureaucrats and soldiers, Thomas Bodley, ambassador at The Hague from 1589, and Sir Francis Vere, who succeeded Willoughby with the lesser rank of serjeant-major-general in the same year. Both men knew their place in the new scheme of things. Vere in particular established a good working relationship with Prince Maurice, of great significance in the long years of campaigning ahead.

All of which is not to claim that the United Provinces' progress from, in Wallace MacCaffrey's phrase, 'dependency to alliance' proceeded in an atmosphere free from mutual suspicion. The English still tried to play Maurice against the States, and at times contemplated an independent peace. The nature of the war in the Low Countries indulged such wrangling, for the conflict had become attritional and slow-moving, the attentions of Parma, now a sick man, drawn increasingly to problems in France. In Flanders, the campaigning seasons of 1589 and 1590 were uneventful. The capture of Breda, the first major Dutch success in five years, was significant more in hindsight, as a change in the tide of war, than as an immediate catalyst for further military adventures. Maurice's successful operations in 1591, however – the key towns of Zutphen, Deventer and Nijmegen were taken that year – and his equally profitable campaigning in Friesland in 1592, set the pattern of future allied operations: Dutch-led and following a Dutch strategy, while drawing upon the useful, still at times crucial support of an English contingent under Vere, constantly drained of experience by drafts but nevertheless maintained conscientiously at around 5000 men. This figure included English garrison troops, particularly in Ostend, Flushing and Brill. Throughout the 1590s, Dutch and English cooperated to supply the temporary deficiencies in manpower that both sides encountered when concentrating forces for an offensive. The Dutch provided support for operations in Brittany and for the 1596 fleet, the English contributing 3000 men to the 1594 campaign against Groningen.

Continuing English financial and military aid duly assisted in the gradual establishment of a sovereign state in the Netherlands. From 1594, with the cautious Austrian Habsburg, Archduke Ernest, established as governor-general in Brussels, and with Dutch and English starting once again to consider the possibilities of peace, Elizabeth began pressing for some repayment of the debts owed her in the Low Countries, a tacit indication that she was dealing with an independent power. France's conclusion of a separate peace with Spain at Vervins in 1598 led to the confirmation of a formal alliance between England and the United Provinces. While both sides subsequently feared the other might follow France's example, the treaty of August 1598 formed the basis of an alliance that endured until the queen's death. It ended all English financial contributions apart from the maintenance of cautionary towns, reduced English representation on the council of state to a single seat, and arranged that the Dutch debt should be repaid in annual instalments of £30,000, English soldiers serving henceforth at the States' charge.

The assassination of Henry III, last of the Valois line, by a Catholic priest in July 1589 threatened a radical alteration in the European balance of power and made the English administration reassess its priorities. The tide of France's civil war, which seemed to have set decisively against Henry's opponents in the so-called Catholic League during that season's campaigning, now turned fiercely against the new king, Henry IV. Unlike his predecessor, Henry IV was a protestant, and while he immediately declared that he would not impose innovation upon the established church, he also refused to contemplate precipitate conversion. The new king very soon gained a reputation for his mastery of the royal arts of diplomacy, but at first he was something of an unknown quantity. Many of Henry III's Catholic supporters uneasily withheld their aid, and with his army melting away and no money to pay those who remained Henry raised his siege of Catholic Paris. This proved just the incentive that the League required, and by the close of August, after a month of feverish manoeuvring, the duke of Mayenne's armies had forced the royalists everywhere onto the defensive.

From the English point of view, positive aspects in the new situation – the accession of a protestant king and the prospect of a war to divert Spain from the Low Countries – were offset by the poverty of the new monarch and the uncertain strength of his armed forces. The question of assistance had to be weighed carefully, for while some effective continental counterbalance to Habsburg ambition was desirable, and while France remained the one power with the potential to play such a role, the long-term threat of a revived French crown, renewing expansionist policies in Flanders and Scotland, could never be discounted. More immediately, Elizabeth was determined to avoid any overcommitment of her resources in one theatre, while the devious new French king inspired little trust. Nevertheless, as in 1585, manifest necessity had its way.

English intervention in France spanned some five years, and the nature of this involvement changed over time. Lord Willoughby's initial expedition was designed to save Henry from destruction: only unilateral action by Willoughby took the assembled force of 3600 men to France after Henry's victory at Arques in September 1589 reduced the immediate threat to his throne. During the autumn, Willoughby's troops fought alongside the king's principal army in campaigning that secured Normandy for the royalist cause. Never again, however, did Elizabeth allow Henry so free a hand. While prepared to 'save' France from the Guise, the English were not inclined to throw money and men at enterprises solely designed to restore royal power in France. Casualties in Willoughby's army – one-sixth of the men embarked never returned – underlined their caution.

In 1590, there was no direct English intervention in the French civil war which, after the pattern of 1589, climaxed with an unsuccessful siege of Paris. This new investment, though, was raised by troops from Flanders under Parma, and the menace of Spanish intervention brought Henry and Elizabeth to negotiations once again. Considerations that led both sides to the table themselves illustrate the conflict of interests: while Henry sought assistance in dealing with the Spanish threat to Picardy and Normandy, the

English government took fright at Spanish landings in Brittany in October 1590, Philip II supporting the duke of Mercœur's struggle for independence. Henry saw this development as but one in a series of Spanish attempts to weaken his power in peripheral France. For the English, however, what amounted to a Spanish occupation of the Breton peninsula completely altered the balance of power in the Channel and provided the enemy with the ideal base for combined operations against England, the lack of which had so frustrated the Armada of 1588.

As a result of this ambivalence, two separate English expeditions were fitted out in 1591, one under the earl of Essex targeted Rouen, the vital seaport on the Seine, and another under the experienced Sir John Norris set sail for Brittany. Essex's adventure, designed to assist Henry's principal summer campaign, failed amid mutual recriminations. By the time Henry's belated but long-anticipated conversion to Catholicism divided his war-weary opponents, already dismayed by the death of Parma late in 1592, and brought him Paris as his great prize, English contingents serving with the main French army amounted to nothing more than a token force under Sir Roger Williams. In Brittany, by contrast, the continuing civil war, although in no way troubling the overall security of the French regime, kept a force of at least 2000 Englishmen engaged until the turn of 1594–5. Then, the comprehensive defeat of Spanish forces in the peninsula allowed these troops to be withdrawn, stimulating instead a bitter debate in council over future war aims. Essex advocated attacks on Spain itself, but Burghley and Elizabeth, disturbed by Henry IV's conversion and determined to give no undue advantage to France, maintained that military resources should henceforth be conserved against developing unrest in Ireland.

When Sir William Fitzwilliam succeeded Sir John Perrot as deputy his directions from the English council had emphasized the need for continuing calm. Ireland remained a low priority. Relative stability was, nevertheless, gradually eroded. Sir Richard Bingham's heavy-handed and less than impartial governorship of Connaught provoked rebellion in 1589 and alienated the council commission sent to assist him in quietening the province. While trouble smouldered in the west, both sides took their quarrels to court, Bingham soliciting the assistance of Walsingham, Fitzwilliam and a majority of the Dublin council seeking support from Burghley. Weaknesses in the deputy's authority were never more graphically displayed.

Ulster presented an even more serious threat to stability. English policy in the province rested upon a careful balancing of local families. Hugh O'Neill, earl of Tyrone, had long been supported as a counterweight to the authority of Turlough O'Neill, the clan chief. But Turlough's increasing infirmity and the deaths of Tyrone's two principal backers in London – Leicester and Hatton – encouraged the council to consider spreading their patronage elsewhere, notably to the sons of Shane O'Neill. Tyrone was acutely conscious that the loyalty shown by the earls of Ormond and Thomond had not always earned its reward in London. Relations were soured in 1590–1 by Fitzwilliam's execution of Hugh Roe MacMahon and subsequent dismemberment of the

MacMahon lordship in Monaghan into crown freehold properties, a murky affair which developed out of personal animosities between the deputy and MacMahon and which, to Tyrone, set a highly disturbing precedent. MacMahon had been Tyrone's client; his lands stood close to the earl's own powerbase.

Gradually, Tyrone's actions begin to betray his unease. In December 1591 he assisted Hugh Roe O'Donnell's escape from custody in Dublin, and he encouraged Hugh Roe's succession to the lordship of O'Donnell a few months later. The next year, Tyrone was called upon by the English to confront and defeat a subordinate. After much havering he obliged, but having been wounded he left the final suppression of Maguire to his brother-in-law and personal enemy, Sir Henry Bagenal, while O'Donnell offered the fugitive refuge.

Events in 1594 betray the depth of Tyrone's distrust. Having secured permission to raise a peace-keeping force, he began to levy troops. Scots mercenaries, heavily engaged in MacDonald–MacLean clan warfare at home, were difficult to recruit at that time. Tyrone looked elsewhere: he succeeded, spectacularly, in recruiting local men on much the same terms once extended to the Scots. Improvements in arable farming practice and relative political stability in Ulster made possible the supply of unprecedentedly large forces, while the increasing availability of firearms improved the effectiveness of his favoured guerrilla tactics, well suited to 'that country of straights'. Subsequently, Tyrone launched raids on Bagenal lands. Local efforts at conciliation failed, but the only immediate reaction from England was sympathetic to the earl. Fitzwilliam, in poor health and increasingly unable to control the Dublin council, was recalled and Bagenal was not permitted any retaliation.

Unfortunately, the new deputy only succeeded in aggravating an already tense situation. While his inheritance was unenviable, Sir William Russell, a soldier with little diplomatic experience, proved a singularly poor choice for this most exacting of political roles. Tyrone at once came to meet him in Dublin, but their encounter did nothing to ease the evident mutual disenchantment that had already developed.

Seeing no hope of an accord with the new deputy, Tyrone came out into open revolt, seizing the strategic forts of Enniskillen in the west and the Blackwater in the east, and worsting Bagenal's forces at Clontibret in June 1595. These actions proved the worth of some intensive training: the earl's army was well led by veterans from the continental wars, well organized in disciplined companies and well supplied with hand guns, many obtained from the Baltic via Scottish middlemen, or from Scots gunsmiths. Munitions were imported from Glasgow, there being little in the way of towns or urban industry in Ulster.

The conclusion of the Brittany campaign allowed the English scope to respond, but the return of Sir John Norris, president of Munster, and the dispatch of 1600 troops suggest their continuing hopes for an inexpensive solution to the crisis. Norris and Russell soon fell out. Still unwilling to commit further resources, and aware of Irish appeals for Spanish support going back at least three years, the queen agreed to negotiate with Tyrone, and hesitant, mutually suspicious, inconclusive diplomacy broken by episodic violence characterized the next two years. Seeking to expose the divisions among his opponents, Tyrone openly declared his trust in Norris, and Sir John, not unwittingly, played along, deprecating Russell at every opportunity. The recall of Russell, and the deaths of Norris and the new deputy Lord Burgh, left English policy in Ireland rudderless by the autumn of 1597.

Parallels with the situation in the Netherlands are discernible, but they must, at the same time, be argued with much caution. While there is something of William the Silent's artfulness in Tyrone's political acumen, Tyrone remained a marginal political figure, fighting a small war at the end of the civilized world. Whatever the rhetoric generated in the course of his revolt, Tyrone lacked the authority to rule an independent Ireland and recognized the power of his foes. Rome never lost sight of these realities: the diplomatic, anti-Spanish Clement VIII turned a deaf ear to his appeals for assistance. The pope's reluctance was echoed by important Catholics within Ireland, including most of the Old English families and the Jesuit provincial from 1599, Richard Field, none of whom trusted Tyrone's motives. His enemies, Irish and English, never failed to emphasize the fact that he had initially come out in revolt for personal rather than nationalistic or religious reasons. Like James Fitzmaurice before him, Tyrone played the cards of nationalism and religion for all they were worth, but in Ireland they were still as yet worth little. Again like Fitzmaurice, the earl was unable to persuade enough Old English landowners that his call for the overthrow of English government would not precipitate their own ruin at the hands of the 'wild Irish'. As the Jesuits and 'hispaniolized' Catholics found in England, the belief that shared religion would ensure widespread backing for insurrection and foreign intervention against a protestant sovereign proved wide of the mark.

Even more than the Dutch, Tyrone needed the prop of a foreign ruler. Only a Habsburg overlord, he argued, would sidestep the lack of general support for any Irish candidate. But in making his assessment he exaggerated the popularity of such an alliance at home, Spain's military capacity in the mid-1590s, and her commitment to war in Ireland. Spanish overtures were not at all to the taste of the Anglo-Irish, while the foreign rulers in question – Archduke Albert, Ernest's successor as governor of Flanders, was proposed as well as Philip – were even more reluctant than the queen of England to take on so open-ended a commitment. A Spanish envoy visited Ulster in 1596, and arms and supplies followed. The Spanish also mounted an expedition to Ireland in 1596, following the ravages caused by the English at Cadiz, but their fleet was dispersed by storms. Otherwise, Philip II proved as cautious as the pope.

Beset by these enduring weaknesses, Tyrone overplayed his hand. Perceiving a general wish in London to avoid the escalating costs of Irish war, the earl and his associates held out for ever higher terms, amounting by early 1596 to extensive pardons, a *de facto* freedom of religion and recognition of an autonomous Ulster. To much of this, particularly if hedged about with vague generalities, the queen was prepared to accede, but Tyrone, never trusting his enemies, was determined to secure the most prestigious terms possible. Hiram Morgan argues that he understood the risk that Elizabeth would call his bluff, but was constrained by considerations of personal prestige and authority in Ulster to raise the stakes throughout Ireland, supporting the intransigent and disgruntled to the dismay of many Irish lords, both Gaelic and Old English. Whether the decision was purely Tyrone's or whether it owed much to the promptings of subordinates, we are surely observing a miscalculation. The substantial foreign intervention feared by the London government and prayed for by Tyrone was never a realistic prospect.

As English commitments elsewhere diminished, the queen and her council gradually came to the conclusion that negotiations with Tyrone were futile. The point of no return was reached when Sir Henry Bagenal's army was defeated at Yellow Ford on the Blackwater near Armagh in August 1598, and when the Munster plantations were overwhelmed in a sudden rising that autumn. Although Bagenal's ineptitude contributed to the Blackwater disaster, Tyrone's adroitness as a military commander was displayed for the first time on a wider stage. Swift action was manifestly necessary to preserve English authority in Ireland.

For the past fifteen years the burden of Irish affairs had steadily increased to the point where it completely dominated council business, the bureaucracies of war and colonization merging into the heaviest workload of any active theatre. Never was this better illustrated than in the bustling preparations of 1598–9. Through the winter, plans were laid for the dispatch of an army consisting of 16,000 foot and 1300 horse, under Essex's command. Essex was considered the natural choice; indeed, as he ruefully acknowledged in a letter to Lord Willoughby in January 1599, he was shackled to his own carefully cultivated military reputation. In fact, a command on this scale was new to him; it would have been a new experience for any man in England. What happened next was not entirely due to Essex's ineptitude; he lacked a cadre of reliable staff officers versed in the ways of Irish campaigning. Nevertheless, the shambles of the 1599 campaign, in which Essex, abetted by a cautious Dublin council, wasted the summer marching across southern Ireland, indulged his personal followers with knighthoods and empty commands, held treasonable discussions with Tyrone, and then fled back to London to confront his detractors at court, matters less than the fact that the English government was now committed to a policy of repression in Ireland. A final overture from London gave Tyrone one last chance to misread the situation: he advanced proposals, very obviously aimed at the Anglo-Irish, into whose hands he declared he would commit the government of Ireland, for a settlement based upon the virtual independence of a Roman Catholic state. Cecil, on reading a copy of these demands, scribbled 'Utopia' in the margin. The Old English declined so obvious a lure, while the English prepared for war to the knife. At the close of 1599 there was little real prospect of recalling Essex's army; rather, it was supplied, and a new commander appointed, the capable Lord Mountjoy.[13]

Following the twin disasters of the Armada and Counter-Armada, a mutually unsuccessful war at sea dragged on throughout the 1590s. Despite the fears of both governments, and periodic panics in both London and Madrid, successful amphibious operations, conducted at long range, remained largely beyond the capacities of any sixteenth-century state. In the particular circumstances of the time, they were relegated to a subordinate role during the great political crisis of the early 1590s, re-emerging as an important factor once Henry IV had secured his throne, the Spanish had been driven out of Brittany, and the Dutch had evolved an enduring defence against Parma and his successors. With the prospect of further adventures in France now extinguished, Essex's espousal of an aggressive foreign policy that involved carrying the war once again to the coasts of Spain helped this process along.

The lessons of 1588–9 were learnt anew after 1595. For all the one-off success enjoyed by Lord Howard of Effingham, Essex and Sir Walter Ralegh at the sack of Cadiz in 1596 – a massive loss of face for the Spanish crown – the best planned seaborne operation remained at the mercy of a contrary wind, as the Spaniards found in 1596 and as both sides discovered in 1597. In these reverses there was ever an element of misfortune, yet given the realities of Biscay storm and Channel tide too much was still left, on both sides, to the inscrutable favour of God or to the whim of good fortune.

The blunted thrust and counter-thrust of the great armadas was merely one dimension of the seaborne war. Another focused on the small-scale, privately funded English expeditions which year after year pursued the annual fleet bringing silver to Spain from the mines of Peru, their captains dreaming too of the plunder to be won from stray carracks laden with eastern merchandise. Many of these voyages pass unrecorded,[14] but as regards those for which evidence survives, generally speaking the larger ventures backed financially by queen or courtiers, the tale is one of frustration and disappointed dreams. The capture of the great carrack *Madre de Dios* in 1592, while it whetted expectation in the hearts of many an adventurer, was never matched in any subsequent late Elizabethan naval operation. For all that they are glossed and set in national legend, reverses such as those suffered by Sir Richard Grenville in the *Revenge* off Terceira in 1591, by Thomas Cavendish in 1592, and by Sir Francis Drake and Sir John Hawkins, who both perished during an ill-fated expedition to the Caribbean in 1595–6, are far more typical of the English experience in water-borne warfare than the great descents on Spanish harbours in 1587 and 1596. No doubt the harassment of Spanish shipping had its effect, but in the absence of any quantifiable figures the temptation to exaggerate remains.

Two further points might be made. First, most larger joint-stock expeditions involved a high percentage of Dutch shipping, both because English resources alone were inadequate and because Elizabeth remained cautious when required to commit her resources to actions far from England. She had no wish to leave her coasts undefended. Second, England and Spain continued, albeit in a surreptitious fashion, the commerce by sea important to the economic well-being of both nations. Ideology was all very well, but the eternal verities of profit and livelihood ensured that both governments – and the Dutch too – turned a blind eye to all but the most blatant or troublesome examples of such trade.[15]

We might reflect, finally, on the once popular notion that ideological war against an external aggressor bent upon the destruction of religion and state may have been a forcing ground in the development of an English national consciousness. Here, certainly, is a theory which gains support from any cursory glance at the literary output of the 1590s, in particular the great history plays of William Shakespeare, with their clear and not so clear allusions to the present. The current French wars are compared with those of past, Lancastrian kings; as Essex goes to Ireland he is likened to the great national hero Henry V. Here as in other fields of study, the beauty of Shakespeare's language has drawn from sober commentators a great number of startling and far-reaching interpretations, although it may be as unsafe to generalize on public patriotism or incipient nationalism on the basis of the enigmatic playwright's output as it is to draw conclusions on the religious attitudes of England from the martyrology of John Foxe.

The Shakespearian canon was only the choicest bloom in a sudden flowering of late Elizabethan drama. A growth industry in the late sixteenth century, growing, indeed, almost from scratch, English commercial drama was, with few exceptions, conformist, advocating support for a regime more interested in control than repression. The patronage of counsellors – Nottingham and Hunsdon followed the example of Leicester and Pembroke – was an invaluable weapon against the opposition of puritan London. More extreme protestants, from Grindal during his time as bishop of London in the 1560s onwards, and alarmed city authorities looked askance at the falsity and moral and environmental dangers associated with playgoing. Theatres from James Burbage's at Finsbury in the 1570s to the Globe and the Rose south of London Bridge twenty years on were liable to closure on any presentable pretext – plague was the most popular – and needed all the patronage going. But the necessary price to be paid was one of regulation: players who were 'counsellors' men' knew where succour lay. The plays, particularly history plays, may voice the fears of Everyman at the prospect of disputed succession or tyrannical rule; they certainly voice the fears of privy counsellors.

The literary output of the age is astonishing, both in the now popular vernacular, at every cultural level from theological tract to popular ballad, and also in the fine, now greatly neglected Latin prose of John Rainolds, John Case and their contemporaries. Literary patronage from queen and aristocracy apparently declined in wartime: the innumerable dedications were not always answered with substantial financial encouragement. But the influence of this patronage was only felt, and marginally at that, towards the expensive end of a vast market. At least nine million books were printed in England during Elizabeth's reign, probably a considerable underestimate given the now incalculable numbers of inexpensive editions, where books rubbed shoulders with single-sheet broadsides, poems or songs. Literature of some kind was available to all. While massive works such as Foxe's *Acts and Monuments* or Hakluyt's *Principall Navigations* might cost pounds – astronomical sums in the sixteenth century – the cheapest theology and popular literature was on sale for a penny or so: within reach of most literate men and women. Libraries were growing: the polymath and necromancer John Dee owned over 4000 volumes, and while the size of his collection was perhaps unique many noblemen and scholars took pride in libraries running into the thousands. Francis Bacon ranked the discovery of printing alongside the practical compass and the utilization of gunpowder as the most influential inventions of his age, and that complex, erudite man was well qualified to judge.

All these books and pamphlets supplied a growing market. While the regional, cultural and gender differences in literacy levels remarked on earlier survive beyond 1600, the population of England and the percentage of that population able to read were rising steadily. An elementary education was widely available. Once a man or woman could read or write, there was, in theory, nothing to stop that person from teaching others in turn. Wherever that education was obtained – in noble households, at elementary or grammar schools, in the parson's study, in the church, at home or after hours in workshops – there is evidence, both impressionistic and statistical, to support this healthy conclusion. At the age of four, Thomas Hobbes, author of the philosophical treatise *Leviathan*, 'went to school in Westport Church'. There, in the space of four years during the 1590s, he learnt to 'read well, and number four figures'. Or so John Aubrey says.

Hobbes went on to greater things – private schools at Malmesbury and Westport, and thence to the University of Oxford – but his early education would have been familiar to thousands of other children across England. At least 80 per cent of south Cambridgeshire parishes possessed an elementary school of some kind in the years between 1574 and 1628, about 20 per cent of them throughout that period. The percentages *may* have been lower in the remoter west and north, but perhaps not drastically lower. Girls did miss out, thanks to prevailing attitudes which questioned the necessity of female education, but many women managed somehow to buck this particular trend, and a number of schools, particularly elementary schools, taught both sexes.

If the market grew, then so too did the quality and variety of works published. From the satire of Thomas Nashe to the Italianate sonnets so popular in the 1580s, from the prototype novels of John Grange and John Lyly to the allegorical works of Spenser, the last two decades of the century see an increase in output, fluency and, from time to time, the random spark of genius. Shakespeare, to be accurate, is as much a Jacobean as an Elizabethan author, yet his sonnets were already circulating in unpublished form by 1598, while the early histories and comedies had established his reputation by 1603.

Finally, let us look briefly at education beyond the stage of primers and elementary schools. Grammar schools educating promising boys in the classics were increasingly common in major towns by the end of the century. There were still only two English universities in 1603, but the sixteenth and early seventeenth centuries were years of expansion and prosperity in Oxford and Cambridge as the impetus for a graduate clergy coincided with an ever-increasing intake of young gentlemen and sons of noblemen, passing a year or so at university to further their general education. From Oxbridge the young man of means might proceed to an inn of court, where he would rub shoulders with those pursuing a career in law. In London, moreover, the court, dancing and fencing masters, and Gresham's College with its lectures on divinity and medicine, navigation and astronomy, all combined to provide what was in effect a broader-based 'third university' – long before Sir George Buck coined the term, early in the 1600s.

17 The Jacobean Minority: Scotland 1568–85

Chronology

August 1567	Earl of Moray named regent
May 1568	Battle of Langside; Mary flees to England
October 1568	Mary's fitness to rule Scotland considered by commissioners in England
January 1570	Moray assassinated
September 1571	Murder of the earl of Lennox
October 1572	Death of the earl of Mar; succeeded as regent by earl of Morton
November 1572	Death of John Knox
January–February 1573	Collapse of resistance to James VI outside Edinburgh
May 1573	Marian troops at Edinburgh Castle surrender
1574	Return of Andrew Melville from Geneva
1578	*Second Book of Discipline* approved by General Assembly
December 1580	Morton arrested
June 1581	Morton executed
August 1581	Esmé Stewart created duke of Lennox
1581	Beginning of regular taxation in Scotland
August 1582	James VI 'kidnapped' by the earls of Angus, Gowrie and Mar; collapse of Lennox regime

| July 1583 | Earl of Arran seizes control of government |
| November 1585 | Arran regime collapses |

The deposition of Mary and the coronation of James VI in July 1567 were the work of a minority among the Scottish nobles, and a minority itself divided by religion and by personal grudges, united only in a desire to replace the queen with her infant son. Many of those ranged against Mary at Carberry – from Catholics such as Lords Borthwick and Sempill to vacillating protestants like Alexander Gordon, bishop of Galloway, and the earl of Cassilis – were opposed to the Bothwell marriage rather than to the queen herself. Deposition provoked widespread unease, particularly after Bothwell's swift departure from the scene. He fled to Norway, only to be seized and imprisoned by the king of Denmark, dying in captivity, out of his mind and long forgotten, in 1578. Châtelherault was alienated, as was Alexander Gordon and, more surprisingly, Argyll, for so long Moray's loyal ally. These defectors transferred their loyalties to a strong 'queen's party', built around the Hamiltons, who detested Moray, with support from the prominent Catholic earls of Caithness, Crawford, Cassilis and Montrose.

James's coronation – attended, so Mary's supporters alleged, by a mere five earls and eight lords of parliament – set in train years of strife. Regaining her liberty in 1568, the queen displayed characteristic energy in making one final bid to recover her throne. Some 6000 loyalists rallied to her cause within a fortnight. She was, however, handicapped by the incompetence of her Hamilton advisers. Both sides seeking a decisive military action, the royal army was utterly defeated at Langside in May 1568. Mary fled south and threw herself on her cousin's mercy.

In retrospect this was a profound miscalculation. Although some peers, like Huntly and his Gordon kinsmen in the north-east and Argyll in the west, remained defiantly in arms, the queen's supporters were left leaderless, and Moray was skilful enough to play on their indecision. Though this did not become evident for some years, Mary's absence transformed what may have been a temporary reverse in 1567–8 into the permanent loss of her kingdom.

For the second time in a quarter of a century Scotland was condemned to a long minority. As in the 1540s, subsequent events highlight the symbolic importance of the infant monarch and many telling divisions among the Scots nobility. In the 1570s, however, Scotland was more or less left to resolve her own problems. France, immersed in her own bloody tragedies, was no longer particularly interested in Scottish affairs; Henry II's grand design had withered. Henceforth, French influence was largely confined to the cultural and the scholastic, fields where, admittedly, it remained both vital and enduring.[1] England, concerned at political developments on mainland Europe, set upon economies at home and relieved at the transience of French ambitions in the north, was content to see Scotland neutralized as an international player. The fugitive Mary proved, as years went by, more of an

Plate 22 *James VI as a boy*, by Arnold Bronckorst.
Source: © National Galleries of Scotland, Scottish National Portrait Gallery

embarrassment than an asset; by the 1580s the queen of Scots had become a factor in English rather than Scottish politics.

Queens are not lightly set aside. Successive regents found their position weakened by the very fact that they were subjects and not sovereigns, and also by the reflection that a ruler to whom they had formerly sworn allegiance, mother to the king in whose name they claimed to act, remained not only alive but also hostile to their every move. Nevertheless, the Scottish nobility learned to live with new circumstances very swiftly; attention turned from one generation to the next. While party lines broadly reflected religious divisions, distinctions between king's and queen's factions were also shaped by the struggle for recognition as heir presumptive to James, with the Hamilton and Douglas families, and their connections, set at one another's throats. At times this made for strange alliances. Protestants such as Argyll, the earl of Rothes and Lords Livingston and Boyd supported Mary, while Catholic Aberdeen cautiously backed the king. In the circumstances caution was understandable. Many nobles refrained from open commitment to either party, and a long list of towns followed suit, unless compelled to take sides by occupation or assault.

James Stewart, earl of Moray, served as regent from 1567 until his murder in January 1570. A skilful soldier, and openly protestant, his appointment symbolized the close alignment of reformed church and government glimpsed in 1567, though not seen again for more than half a century. Despite these strengths, Moray's authority was undermined by the still realistic prospect of a Marian restoration. In the early years of her English captivity, Mary showed a willingness to accommodate any conditions imposed by her cousin. She even hinted that, if religious conversion was the price she would have to pay for her throne, then she was prepared to turn protestant. Had Elizabeth seen fit to provide military support restoration would probably have followed, and in such circumstances open commitment, to either side, appeared to many Scots both risky and premature. At Moray's summer parliament in 1568, only four earls, nine lords, two bishops and nine commendators put in an appearance.

Even the failure of the 1569 rising in northern England led not to any improvement in the regent's position but rather to a weakening of his authority during the few weeks of life left to him. His plans in ruins, his forces routed, the rebel earl of Northumberland sought refuge among the border Scots, only to be betrayed into Moray's hands. England demanded the extradition of a traitor, while friend and foe alike among the Scots nobility urged the regent to stand firm against Elizabeth's bullying. Caught in an impossible position, Moray appeared weak, indecisive or obstructive. His backers began to have second thoughts about their man.[7]

Moray, nevertheless, was of royal blood and had been an obvious choice for the regency. His death ushered in a period of disruption in the central administration. The new regent, chosen by Elizabeth in July 1570 following brief English military intervention, was Darnley's father the earl of Lennox, an elderly, ailing anglophile. Lennox enjoyed little support among the Scottish aristocracy in general, and was particularly distrusted by the Hamiltons. The ensuing civil war nevertheless went his way: by the autumn of 1571 the queen's party had been severely weakened, particularly by the loss of Dumbarton Castle and the execution of the most able member of the Hamilton family, John, archbishop of St Andrews. Denied substantial English support, however, the regency was unable to press home its advantage. Increasingly desperate attempts by a bankrupt government to finance military operations resulted in the plundering of episcopal revenues destined for the church, aggravating mutual distrust between kirk and regency. In September 1571, Lennox was killed in the course of a muddled escapade, half kidnapping, half raid, led by the Marian Sir William Kirkaldy of Grange. Despite defections from the queen's camp, mainly by nobles alarmed at what they saw as intransigence among the Hamiltons, Edinburgh itself, Lord Herries in the southwest and Huntly in Aberdeenshire still defied the king's authority.

King James was still only five years old when his supporters chose a third regent. During his year in office John Erskine, earl of Mar, tried very hard to exploit divisions among Mary's party, conciliating and bribing waverers. Mar's successes were limited, for his own anglophilia served to maintain some semblance of unity in the queen's cause. Parliament, throughout this troubled period, was summoned less as a legislative assembly, more as a show of strength, or as a means of displaying support. Six rival parliaments were held in the space of a year, 1571–2. During 1571, indeed, the king's and queen's parties convened rival assemblies in Edinburgh, and if by then King James's supporters could secure a more weighty representation, sniper and artillery fire from Edinburgh Castle, still in enemy hands, obliged its members to take appropriate precautions. This session was subsequently immortalized as 'the creeping parliament'.

Mary Stewart's hopes of a return to Scotland were frustrated, not by any decisive move from the king's party but by events on the international stage. While France moved towards the self-absorption of civil war, the discovery of the Ridolfi plot brought home to Elizabeth that her best interests lay in some form of cooperation with the regency and persuaded her, had persuasion ever been needed, to keep Mary in England. Hitherto, a majority in Scotland had suspected that their queen would return, sooner or later, perhaps in some power-sharing arrangement. Henceforward, it became apparent that Scotland's future lay with James alone. News of the St Bartholomew's Day massacres shocked many nobles and gentlemen into reconsidering the wisdom of their support for a queen so closely tied to the French administration, while the threat of parliamentary forfeiture sowed doubts in the minds of others. Given her own failings, and the horrors perpetrated by her family, was the cause of an absentee queen worth the risk to life and estates? Following Mar's death in October 1572 yet another anglophile regent, James Douglas, earl of Morton, aided by English diplomacy and military force, broke the back of Marian resistance. At the so-called pacification of Perth in February 1573, Huntly and leading members of the Hamilton family acknowledged James as king of Scotland in return for the restoration of lands and property which they had lost in forfeitures during the civil war. Edinburgh Castle fell after an artillery bombardment by the English in May. Morton's summary executions of prominent prisoners were in keeping with the way in which the bitterness of civil war had intensified over the past three years.[3]

In his seven years of power – five of them as regent – Morton enjoyed a degree of good fortune denied his immediate predecessors. The deaths of two political heavyweights, Argyll and Châtelherault, removed any immediate threat of a challenge to his authority. Chancellor for much of the previous nine years, Morton was also an experienced administrator, but for all his wealth, energy and ruthlessness that experience was not always employed to good purpose. Even by the standards of his time he was an excessively venal man: the seventeenth-century historian John Spottiswoode, archbishop of St Andrews, exercised charitable understatement when observing that the regent had ever been 'inclined to covetousness'. Morton's efforts to line his own pockets through the sale of import licences for corn and wine is but one manifestation of this defect in his character. On occasion he lent money to the overburdened treasury, taking reimbursement from the profits of debasement.

Morton also relied heavily, and bestowed favours disproportionately, upon his own kin; his family were, after all, his sole reliable allies. Even setting aside such partiality, the regent's lack of tact alienated rather too many important colleagues. Among those left discontented were James Hume of Coldenknowes, William Ker of Cessford and John, Lord Maxwell, wardens, respectively, of the east, middle and west marches. All three combined against him in and after 1578. Regency Scotland cried out for a strong governor blessed with the instincts of a conciliator, but Morton lacked the necessary skills. His attempts to compose a feud between the earls of Argyll and Atholl during 1576 and 1577 succeeded only in antagonizing both men, while his efforts to unite the nobility in an anti-Hamilton purge during 1579 were singularly ill-judged.

The earl's financial negligence – concentrating on milking the resources of towns he resorted to general taxation only once, raising £4000 in 1575 for a border expedition – received little criticism at the time, but has since been considered symptomatic of economic ignorance and drift. Political calculation and administrative impotence explain some, but only some, of this apparent lassitude. Initial enthusiasm for debasement, and subsequent half-hearted attempts to remedy its pressing evils, courted general unpopularity and evaded the admittedly intractable problem of a shortfall in bullion. The Scots pound fell in value from around 4s English in 1560 to some 1s 8d by the end of the century. That shortfall only prompted further debasement, together with sustained efforts to secure money from the towns, and these efforts in turn alienated most of the influential Edinburgh burgesses.

Nevertheless, compared with the darkest days of civil war, crown authority was reviving. Justice ayres held throughout the realm reaped useful income, an estimated £16,000 in the years 1574–6. Aberdeen in particular, notionally loyal to the king but with strong Catholic sympathies at all levels of society, was in 1574–5 forced to pay heavily for its temporizing.[4] Royal borrowing did not again touch the levels required to finance the siege of Edinburgh Castle in 1573. On the other hand, those debts now required settlement, and repairs to the battered fortress themselves proved costly.

Morton's policies foreshadow in some respects those adopted successfully by the adult James VI. Regent and king were alike persuaded of the dangers posed by presbyterianism – even when that danger was frankly quite minimal, as it was for much of the 1570s – and of the need for caution in confronting those dangers. Morton listened to representatives of the new church, and welcomed the mediation of the Swiss theologian Theodore Beza on certain disputed points in a draft formula of kirk 'jurisdiction and polity' during 1575. He had, however, clear views on the limits of clerical power, and a series of new episcopal appointments by Morton and his predecessors – notoriously those of John and George Douglas, his kinsmen, to St Andrews and Moray respectively – was seen by the General Assembly as a challenge to its own authority. In one frank exchange of views, Morton is said to have told the presbyterian leader Andrew Melville, a graduate of St Andrews with first-hand experience of Genevan Calvinism and from 1580 principal of that great nursery of protestant ministers, St Mary's College at St Andrews, that 'there will never be quietness in this country till half a dozen of you be hanged or banished'. While planning no such purge, the regent was not necessarily jesting.

Morton, though, was really in no position to issue threats. Soon he stood in need of all the allies he could get. Possession of the king was fast becoming the key bargaining counter in an increasingly feverish atmosphere of court intrigue. A twelve-year-old monarch might take formal control of his government, but he remained the pawn of powerful subjects. In the course of 1578 a group of peers hostile to the regent, fronted by the disgruntled Atholl and Argyll, allied itself to James's guardian, Alexander Erskine, Master of Mar. Under their influence, the king was brought to accept Morton's resignation – offered in a tactical gambit which misfired – and to appoint a ruling council with wide powers. Temporarily outmanoeuvred, Morton won back control of the council through his support for the earl of Mar's successful claim against his cousin the Master for the custodianship of James's person, but his authority was henceforth irreparably compromised. Attempts to play on anti-Hamilton suspicions among other noble families failed to consolidate his precarious position.[5]

Though still sovereign in name only, the day was approaching when James would rule as well as reign: his nobles might contend for authority, but they did so with an eye to the future, courting royal affection and trust. Initially successful at this game, Morton was fatally outmanoeuvred through the immediate rapport that developed between James and Esmé Stewart, seigneur d'Aubigny, a charismatic cousin of Darnley who arrived from France in September 1579. James was smitten by this dazzling young man, the first in a series of royal favourites stretching across the years. By August 1581 Esmé Stewart, laden with favours, had been created duke of Lennox. To his side flocked all those hostile to Morton, and Morton, in poor health and unable to secure English support, was unequal to the challenge. In an interesting resurrection of past sins he was arrested on charges of complicity in Darnley's murder – which, laid against one of Rizzio's killers, may well have been justified – and was beheaded on the 'maiden', a precursor of the guillotine, in June 1581.

Religion features only intermittently in these factional manoeuvrings. The reformed church, much to its dismay, found itself shunted from a position of great though disorganized power into a siding where its influence was more effectively restrained. The General Assembly's welcome for Morton's re-organization of clerical finance in 1573 was less than wholehearted, for the clarification of that which had been shadowy spelt out the extent to which spiritual revenues had been annexed by the laity in recent years. Morton exacerbated the tensions, rewarding family and favourites through remissions of their obligations to pay clerical thirds, and through presents of religious properties.

In political terms, support from the General Assembly remained a useful adjunct to the regent's power, but the Assembly's growing extremism under the influence of Andrew Melville also offered a reservoir of discontent attractive to the enemies of weak regimes. That radicalism, which out-knoxed Knox with its anti-episcopal insistence on the equality of church ministers, its notion of the 'two kingdoms' – church and state with mutually exclusive jurisdictions – and with its approval of a *Second Book of Discipline* in 1578, was itself a symptom of marginalization. Plans for the privy council to sit in the General Assembly, mooted in the 1560s, were quietly forgotten. The new *Book of Discipline* remained a dead letter, its call for a reduction in the number of parishes never implemented, its demands for an increased financial contribution from the state and a wider role for the church in political life rejected by the 1578 parliament. The *Second Book* is best viewed as another step, and a stumbling step at that, in the fashioning of a distinctive Scottish protestantism. The growing authority of kirk-sessions over the everyday life of parishioners was a more telling advance. Other such steps include the early attempts to set up presbyteries in 1581, building upon existing 'exercises' in the central lowlands and along the east coast. Here were initiatives as significant as Morton's support for episcopal authority: they all shaped the Scottish church of the next century.

As the church pulled one way so the crown pulled another. Moves towards a 'Genevan' church coincided with a renewed emphasis on royal authority. What Morton began, King James, Patrick Adamson, archbishop of St Andrews, and the Arran administration of 1584–5 continued, unambiguously subjecting kirk to crown in parliamentary legislation of 1584 – the so-called 'Black Acts' – and demanding conformity by subscription from ministers. The General Assembly shied away from confrontation. Most ministers dutifully subscribed to the articles of subjugation, condemning at the same time the few stouter hearts who, like Melville, opted for formal protest and exile. Bishops also secured vital support from the lay administration, even though that backing was limited a little by conscience and principle. Morton, in particular, while ignoring increasingly shrill demands that his friend Adamson should prove his merits before the General Assembly in 1576, was prepared to see James Paton, bishop of Dunkeld, disciplined by the Assembly for non-residence, neglect of his benefice and pluralism.

Gordon Donaldson has argued that post-Morton Scottish politics begin, in the early 1580s, to divide again along religious lines, the protestant, anglophile lords mustering under the leadership of the earl of Gowrie and the earl of Angus, the conservative, continentally oriented 'Catholics' coming together behind Lennox, James Stewart, earl of Arran (another favourite of the king), and the earls of Atholl, Caithness, Erroll and Huntly. There remained, however, many who found the middle ground congenial, the majority of lords wearing their religion lightly and switching sides as opportunity dictated. For all the thunderings of protestant preachers and the endeavour of Jesuit missions – assisted early on by Robert Crichton, bishop of Dunkeld[6] – religion remained a token of unity between allies rather than a cohesive force in its own right. Lennox accepted the reformed faith without scruple, even though the presbyterian ministers, resentful of continuing government appointments to bishoprics and fully aware that Lennox and James had met Jesuit agents from the Spanish crown, never trusted his professions.

Lennox's fall was as abrupt as his rise. His pre-eminence depending solely upon the king's favour, he suffered most when in August 1582 – in the so-called Ruthven Raid – James was kidnapped by Gowrie and his confederates. All sorts of personal interests contributed to this escapade. The Master of Glamis had recently been fined the vast sum of £20,000 as a result of his feud with the conservative earl of Crawford, Angus and his Douglas cousins saw the operation as a means to recover forfeited lands, while the Edinburgh burgesses resented the banishment of a city minister, John Dury, who had raged unwisely against Lennox's administration.

The Raid and its aftermath serve as a reminder that possession of the king was an essential prerequisite of power. Forsaken even by his closest friends, Lennox returned to France, where he died in May 1583. Like Bothwell, Lennox was, at his death, already a forgotten figure; the one man who did not forget him was James. The Ruthven Raid marked the young king for life. James, who habitually forgave easily, harboured ever after an intense distrust not only of Gowrie but of the entire Ruthven family, as well as of the presbyterian 'conspiracy' he saw lurking behind them. The Raiders were, in fact, a disparate group of men, alienated, aggrieved or on the make, but the terrified king viewed them in a far more sinister light.

Fortunes soon changed once again. James contrived to escape his captors in June 1583 and rapidly received support from an alliance of northern, conservative earls, distrustful of the Raiders and their overtly anglophile activities. Without the king, Gowrie's authority matched that of Lennox in the speed with which it dissolved. By August, Arran, liberated from imprisonment under the Raiders, had assumed effective control of government. Spurning a ham-fisted embassy by Walsingham he was already stoking the fantasy of a Marian restoration in an effort to woo the Guise faction in France. Edinburgh's council was purged in favour of men more pragmatic and congenial to the crown than their radical predecessors. The city council was important as the local government body in Scotland's capital, and its composition fluctuated time and again as successive minority regimes came and went.[7]

Blessed with his shares of learning, wisdom and cunning – he is said to have been well educated in both Latin and Greek – Arran had also tasted the life of a mercenary soldier overseas. That blend of education and experience proved a significant, if transient, strength. An English-sponsored rebellion which captured Stirling in April 1584 was crushed, while Gowrie, a potential source of further discord, was arrested and executed that August. Despite his Catholic sympathies Arran was, at first, able to reach some degree of understanding with more pragmatic counsellors in the English court. In return for rejecting any entente with the Catholic powers, James was offered an annual pension of £4000 sterling in 1585.

Arran's diplomatic skills, however, failed to offset the weaknesses in his own position. Distrusted by the conservatives and detested by the presbyterians he was obliged to place trust in those who proved to be no friends, while at the same time adopting an authoritarian approach which thoroughly alarmed a greater part of the nobility. His go-between to the English, the Master of Gray, conspired with Walsingham and other hawkish English statesmen keen to be rid of the ambivalent earl. James, who had taken a fancy to Gray, was led to believe that Arran opposed the accord with England, while a run-of-the-mill border affray was interpreted by Edward Wotton, the English envoy, as a deliberate provocation. Gray persuaded Elizabeth to release Scottish lords detained in England since the abortive revolt of 1584, and their sudden return in arms precipitated the downfall of a regime no one was now prepared to back. Powerless, Arran fled the country.

The administration that emerged after these upheavals confirmed that the king, although technically a prisoner of the returning exiles, now wielded real power within his kingdom. The figure all sides expected to reimpose stability was at long last old enough to deliver such blessings. Angus, Mar and Glamis were joined in the council by conservative earls such as Huntly and Crawford, by Lords John and Claud Hamilton (also recalled from exile) to represent the Hamilton interest, and by members of Arran's regime, notably the duplicitous Gray. Another former member of Arran's circle, and a one-time supporter of the queen's party, the highly capable John Maitland of Thirlestane, was appointed James's chancellor and chief minister, remaining in office for nine crucial years.

18

The Personal Rule of James VI: Scotland 1585–1603

Writing at the turn of the seventeenth century, White Kennett, bishop of Peterborough and a historian of no mean quality, pondered the merits of past chroniclers. Queen Elizabeth, he reflected, had enjoyed the services of William Camden, while Charles I had the future earl of Clarendon on hand to set in memorable perspective the tragedy of his reign. 'Poor James I', by contrast, had encountered 'none but paltry scribblers'. Kennett, however, omitted to mention that James himself, an able if at times florid writer, had never neglected an opportunity to boast his own achievements. For the student of Scottish history during the king's long reign, the misfortune is that so much of this natural self-publicity comes in the form of remarks directed at an English audience after 1603. James was all too aware of the heartfelt xeno-phobia washing about him in London – Guy Fawkes's defiant insistence that he had intended to blow king and courtiers back to their Scottish mountains is merely the most explosive example of such talk – and while it suited him as a Scot to ignore the cruder manifestations of the sentiment, it also suited him, as an English king, to magnify his own capacities by playing on English perceptions of Scottish backwardness. Governing his northern kingdom, he conceded to Robert Cecil before 1603, was like riding a 'wild, unruly colt'. In a much-quoted speech to the English parliament in 1607, he reminded his audience that he now ruled Scotland with his pen, sitting at his desk three hundred miles and more from Edinburgh. The rule of his ancestors, in con-trast, had rested, never very convincingly, on the sword.

Not for the first or the last time, his new subjects failed to absorb the subtleties of their king's message. In James, the vainglory, though real enough, was usually employed to a purpose. Remarks about pens and swords were intended not simply as personal puff but as an indication to sceptical Eng-lishmen that, far from being a primitive backwater, Scotland was a kingdom worth joining in some form of political union. Kennett was almost right in his assessment, but not quite. James's real misfortune in historiographical terms is that this lack of understanding, mixed with the antipathy of the English for all things Scottish, produced its own telling legacy. Compared with Camden or Clarendon, perhaps, those who explored James's reign were literary lightweights, but the works of John Stow, Godfrey Goodman and Kennett himself provide together no mean reservoir of largely favourable interpretation. Nothing they wrote, however, proved so popular as the de-licious calumnies set down by Anthony Weldon, a sacked household official, who worked through in print his festering bitterness towards the king and the Scots.

It is Weldon, in his *Court and Character of King James*, who supplies many of the more salacious details on James's personality and private life, details that have since taken root as accepted historical fact. The overlarge tongue, the pompous pedantry, the insanitary habits on horseback – this is a long list. Take Weldon's evidence away and we are left with a more sober view of King James. Take away the entire experience of James's rule in England and we begin to perceive a very different monarch. James, wrote the Scottish historian Gordon Donaldson, was 'a man of very remarkable political ability and sagacity... He may not have been the ablest of the Stewarts, but he was assuredly the most successful of his line in governing Scotland and bending it to his will.'[1] Here, then, are two differing faces of one king, one man; the differences are hard indeed to reconcile.[2]

No amount of special pleading can hide the less attractive aspects of James's character. His rule both in Scotland and in England affords ample evidence of financial fecklessness and the occasional example of dogged vindictiveness against those he perceived as enemies. His occasional bouts of indolence are also well documented. The king lacked courage, indeed, made no attempt to hide the fact. In his *Basilikon Doron*, a book of counsel for his son, written in 1598, James advised Prince Henry to wear light armour if ever obliged to fight a battle, the better for running away in. Persisting commemoration of those two attempts on his life, the Gowrie conspiracy of August 1600 and the Gunpowder plot of 1605, owe much to the king's personal fears that such treasons might one day be repeated.

All these, however, are minor sins, set against those of numerous forebears on both sides of the border. The point central to every argument advanced by his detractors is that, in ruling England, James failed to make sufficient allowance for the differences in style and tradition between the monarchies of his two kingdoms; methods successful in Scotland did not always adapt well in England. This begs two questions: what were James's methods of ruling Scotland, and were they, indeed, successful?

In Scotland, as we have seen, much depended on the king's ability to persuade and coerce his nobles, the men with the real local power, to the pursuit of his own policies. That line between persuasion and coercion was frequently ill-defined. The art to Scottish kingship, as Mary understood in her first five successful years and forgot at the end of her reign, lay in the careful choice of the appropriate moment for action and in the isolation of the truly intransigent. James, even his detractors concede, had the touch for this game from his youth. When Henry Wotton visited Scotland shortly before Elizabeth's death he remarked upon James's respect for counsel, believing the king to be 'one of the most secret princes in the world'.

Secrecy is hardly a word that popular English tradition applies to James VI and I, but it is not inappropriate. James knew that, while his real powers were severely circumscribed, the monarchy enjoyed wide theoretical powers and was looked to, for all its faults, as a symbol of unity which permitted Scotland a place in the polity of European nations. This pride in an ancient crown is often forgotten, yet the contrast between the 1570s, when Elizabeth treated Scotland as, to quote Wallace MacCaffrey, 'a British governor-general of India might have dealt with a neighbouring native state', and her later, far more considered approach, is telling.[3] Elizabeth, it is true, never quite overcame a distinctly English contempt for Scotland, but in the 1580s and after she was obliged to pay much greater attention to her northern neighbour. Other states had also ignored the squabblings of the Scottish nobility during the 1570s – Morton's political biographer concedes that the regent's foreign policy amounts to little more than 'a survey of Anglo-Scottish relations'[4] – only to 'rediscover' a nation once again blessed with an adult king. His marriage to the sister of Christian IV of Denmark in 1589 displays James, and Scotland, as significant once more in the game of international politics.

James knew his own strengths and played to them. Fostering his image as monarch-in-waiting of all Britain, James and his ministers went further than any previous Scottish administration in their attempts to promote the transcendent, unifying force that was kingship. A flourishing court and patronage of artists and poets were, perhaps, no more than reflections of earlier Stewart practice, but the widespread use of print to promote acts of parliament, histories of Scotland and treatises on the nature of kingship was something of a novelty in the 1590s. Through his personal chairmanship of the council of the articles, the 'steering-committee' that selected business for consideration in any session, the king maintained control of the legislation set before Scottish parliaments. Even in this most bureaucratic aspect of Scottish government, James's key to success lay in personal management. The same king who sat on the council of the articles, speaking and voting on the issues to be settled by Scotland's parliament, in 1587 wined and dined his fractious nobles and then walked them, literally hand in hand, in alcoholic *bonhomie*, through the streets of Edinburgh. No doubt he relished the occasion. James, as Jenny Wormald has noted, enjoyed 'the blessed gift of laughter – sometimes sardonic laughter'.

And it takes two to hold hands. Noble families looked to the crown as a source of patronage, and none, not even the Hamiltons or Campbell earls of Argyll, was strong enough to threaten crown stability on its own. Mutual suspicion – the Hamiltons were almost universally distrusted, even by long-standing allies such as the Douglases – acted as a further check on ambition. The nobility was beset with its own weaknesses: a recent examination of their debts reminds us that in an inflationary age the Scots peerage came increasingly to depend upon a mix of crown patronage and mercantile credit to offset growing insolvency.[5] All the same, management of these proud, authoritative individuals was never straightforward. Not for nothing does the rascally, truculent nobleman remain a part of our mental picture of sixteenth-century Scotland.[6] James, recalling all too vividly the factional turbulence of his minority, characterized in *Basilikon Doron* the aristocrat's greatest failing as 'a feckless arrogant conceit of their greatness and power'. With no substantial bureaucracy or standing army, little could be done about some manifestations of the problem. Hereditary office holding, in particular, remained an unchallengeable fact of political life; only where the nobility stepped beyond the bounds of behaviour acceptable to the majority of their fellows could the king act.

On balance, though, the common cause fashioned by considerations of prestige and stability did what it had always done in Scotland, placing an adult king in a position of considerable strength. When the picaresque Francis Stewart, earl of Bothwell, dangerously powerful in the border shires, tried his hand at rebellion, he was, after a number of admittedly very alarming escapades, isolated, defeated and exiled. One of the most important highland clan chiefs, George Gordon, earl of Huntly, who had earlier overstepped the mark in murdering his rival in the north-east, the earl of Moray, was likewise defeated in open rebellion and banished from the realm. Bothwell, a dabbler in the black arts and, somewhat paradoxically, an occasional ally of more fractious elements in the kirk, ended his days as a conjuror casting horoscopes in Naples, but the king harboured in contrast a genuine affection for Huntly, who, following suitable expressions of regret, was allowed to return after a year in exile.[7]

In the early years of James's personal rule, the hand of his principal adviser, Sir John Maitland of Thirlestane, is everywhere discernible. Appointed chancellor in 1587, Maitland was trusted by the king; capable, if cautious, he in turn relied upon support from men of his own kind, the lairds. At the calculated cost of weakening long-term crown control of patronage, church property was used to establish many promising men and at the same time to reward those members of the nobility who conformed to royal wishes. Both lairds and towns laid the basis for future prosperity by taking advantage of the vogue for holding lands in feu.

On one important issue, the king and chancellor agreed to differ. Maitland, at the end of his life, was a staunch presbyterian; Andrew's nephew James Melville praised him as 'a great instrument in keeping the King off the Kirk and from favouring the Papists'. In contrast, from the earliest days of his personal rule, the influential group of Calvinist ministers about James looked askance at the king's own commitment to their beliefs. They sought a godly prince for Scotland, but did James have the necessary godliness in his heart?

Ever candid about his own beliefs, James throughout his life expressed a love of the 'middle way' in religion; to his moderate eye, wild Calvinist pastors were quite as threatening as subtle Roman priests. In his 1598 *The True Law of Free Monarchies* he developed the idea of divine-right kingship to establish his rule on 'principles other than those espoused by the presbyterian clergy in Scotland'. God alone, he suggested, might judge a monarch, or arbitrate between kings and their subjects.[8] James, though, had ground to make up: the Scottish reformed church had developed in an environment of either little or no royal control, and gloried in its independence. For all its plain speaking and frequent intransigence, for all its adoption of the texts on elective, accountable, popular sovereignty penned by James's feared former tutor and *bête noire*, the eminent scholar George Buchanan,[9] it was not that the Scottish General Assembly consisted of revolutionaries, intent on sweeping away royal power; it was rather that after so many years, this small, unrepresentative and divided body feared the changes an adult king might impose on the existing religious status quo.

Their fears were justified, although the tide turned only slowly: James was always cautious, and at first there were obvious limits to what might be achieved. He realized, reading Buchanan, that his mother's miserable career had burdened his own reign with particular problems, a particular obligation to reimpose royal authority, and his assertion of divine-right monarchy was the defensive statement of an ideal, a tactic rather than a dogma. Maitland persuaded James that concessions to the presbyterian ministers would bolster his position against the actions of less predictable nobles – memories of the alliance between church and peerage that had defeated Queen Mary remained fresh. There was also an element of financial calculation here, for in 1587 James had annexed the temporalities of Scottish benefices to the crown, a move that gave ammunition to advocates of presbyterian reform. Accepting Maitland's advice, James approved the 'Golden Acts' of 1592, which reaffirmed kirk privileges dented by the Arran regime's 'Black Acts' of 1584. He recognized the emerging system of presbyteries and the authority of the General Assembly, yet, significantly, he secured at the same time the king's right to specify both the time and the place of assembly, a retention of

Scottish bishoprics, and a definition of the church's role that left all matters of sedition, wherever found, within the sphere of secular authority.

These concessions were shrewd, buying time and forming the basis of James's efforts to 'tame' the church after Maitland's death in 1595. He exploited a strong position. The presbyterian church, its support among the nobility diminishing, its leadership tactically incompetent and its General Assembly seldom mustering more than a small minority of active ministers, hardly presented a united front; James recruited his most diligent bishops of the early 1600s from the ranks of gifted presbyterian ministers. By exercising his rights under the 'Golden Acts' and summoning the General Assembly to cities such as Perth and Montrose, where the local ministry was more conservative than in Edinburgh or St Andrews, and by taking it upon himself to set the agendas at these meetings, James worked on divisions and weaknesses, conciliating and persuading, promising a relentless pursuit of popery. At the same time he began enhancing the status and power of bishops, loyal ornaments and royal agents, as a real force in Scottish politics. These developments, however, so important to events over the following decades, were still embryonic in 1603. By that year, only six of the thirteen Scottish sees enjoyed an active incumbent. Although bishops might vote in parliament and sit on the privy council they as yet enjoyed no authority over ministers, remaining subordinate to the General Assembly and working with the courts and presbyteries in their dioceses.

The beleaguered General Assembly found it difficult to counter this steady extension of royal power within the church. Its hold on the Scottish population was still untested. Book prices were high enough and literacy levels still low enough to frustrate hopes of a committed lay protestantism: perhaps 25 per cent of adult males in the countryside could read in 1600. The kirk, moreover, was undergoing a prolonged crisis of manpower as the first-generation Catholic convert clergy – many of whom had been retained as low-paid readers – passed away. Qualified preachers were particularly thin on the ground. Only the crown could provide the resources to recruit and retain a universal, graduate clergy, and this, over the next three decades, it did, without help from the increasingly marginalized Melvillian extremists.[10]

Between king and radical presbyters, the strain of pragmatic cooperation followed by increasing dissociation found an outlet in mutual plain speaking. For James, the presbyterian ministers were dangerous republicans, 'very pests in the Church and Commonweal'. For the disgruntled Andrew Melville, James never amounted to anything more than 'God's silly vassal' and, in 1596, he told the king so to his face.

The lack of any concerted Catholic resistance to the reformation allowed both king and general assembly to indulge in such exchanges. The more eminent conservatives, both among the prelacy and the educated class, had long ago abandoned their more humble colleagues. James Beaton, archbishop of Glasgow, and the talented Ninian Winyet, along with a number of unreconciled colleagues, had departed into continental exile. Others had simply conformed, albeit superficially. As in England, the church papist was a common figure in the upper reaches of the nobility, with men as prominent as Thomas Hamilton, later earl of Haddington, John, Lord Maxwell, and Alexander Seton, later earl of Dunfermline and a long-serving lord chancellor, concealing Catholic beliefs behind a show of conformity.[11] None of this offended a pragmatic king, determined to curb outright dissent yet charitable when it came to preserving the dignity of his peerage. That dignity was, after all, an ornament to his own majesty.

Other changes followed the death of Maitland, but many of these fall into focus only in a study of seventeenth-century developments.[12] James had long recognized the importance of his privy council as an executive agency of royal power. The records are incomplete, but even in those that survive his assiduous attendance at council meetings is in marked contrast to his mother's record during her years of power. Formerly an amorphous body, shaped to meet the needs of a particular circumstance, the privy council was reconstituted from 1598 with thirty-two working counsellors, the king holding wide powers of appointment. Here was one strong incentive for the high nobility to make common cause with their king, and that incentive was advanced at an opportune moment. Maitland's passing removed some of the tension evident in the Scottish political scene of the early 1590s; the concentration of authority in one subject's hands had bred jealousy. As with Robert Cecil sixteen years later, James was in no hurry to replace a powerful minister, and the replacement when it came in both cases diminished the practical authority of the office in question.

The argument has been advanced that there were, in late sixteenth-century Scotland, two divergent streams of national consciousness, the one holding independence to be essential, the other, spurred by some particularly ingenious interpretations of the Book of Revelation and at times by the promise of personal enrichment, perceiving union with England as the natural, indeed, the desirable course. James, unsurprisingly, inclined to the latter school. His prospects of succession to the English throne held advantages and disadvantages for the king. Many a nobleman, with an eye on the largesse a wealthy, powerful monarch might bestow, stood true to his oath of obedience. The settlement of the long-standing Huntly–Argyll feud in 1603, personally brokered by the king, has about it more than an element of such calculation. Dissent is confined to the enigmatic events at Gowrie House on 5 August 1600, where the king persuaded himself that an attempt had been made on his freedom and his life. He may have been right, but the violent deaths of the young earl of Gowrie and his brother ensured that only one side of the story was ever told. At the same time James, lured by the prospect of English wealth, paid insufficient attention to the pressing financial, economic and social problems besetting Scotland in that most difficult of decades, the 1590s. Scotland's currency remained fragile and she was not spared the disastrous run of harvests that blighted so many European economies between 1594 and 1598. As the *Basilikon Doron* illustrates, James's grasp of economic niceties was never strong. His enthusiasm for peace led him to exaggerate the importance of political tranquillity to trade. Little effort was made to conceal his belief that merchants were mere parasites, feeding upon their fellow countrymen. Ingenuously (if we are kind), he also blamed merchants for debasement of the coinage, which in 1590s Scotland ran at levels unplumbed by any previous government on either side of the border.

It is no coincidence that the archives of central taxation in Scotland emerge as a useful source only in the 1590s. The scale of taxation granted and raised is entirely new; £100,000 was sought for James's marriage to Anne of Denmark, and whereas James's own baptism had cost the Scottish taxpayer £12,000, that of his son Henry, in 1594, cost £100,000. The charge of maintaining James's claim as Elizabeth's successor was itself high: visits to London by Scottish envoys in 1597 and 1601 called for grants totalling £200,000, while in 1601, after the failure of the Essex rebellion, James sought no less than £333,333, ostensibly frightened that he would have to fight for his inheritance.

While traditional forms and assessments of taxation, some still resting on thirteenth-century valuations, defied all attempts at reform, the increasing frequency of demand gradually produced mechanisms for collection and a general, if reluctant, acceptance of principle. The reality of collection was, in these circumstances, a muddle riven by inequality and ignorance of assessment. Under a system rightly characterized as 'feudal', only tenants-in-chief – freeholders, holders of clerical benefices, and burghs – were liable to taxation. They were, however, at liberty to milk the whole of their assessment from their own tenants.

The increase in feuing at first threatened to create a tax loophole, for feus were, in theory, outside the reach of existing taxation. While an act of 1581 empowered tenants-in-chief to require of their feuars a 'just' contribution towards the tax burden, no one, given the antiquated valuations, could decide what was just in this context. It was, at times, not even possible to say which of two noblemen held land of the other. Ministers on stipends and professional lawyers escaped the medieval net. Burgh taxation, more progressive, was hedged about by privilege.

Compromise, though common, was usually at the expense of the crown, and payment, when eventually made, was often incredibly slow. The 1596 taxation accounts were submitted only in 1607. Statistical ignorance of the nation's wealth itself contributed to the government's poverty. Landed property in teinds (equivalent to English tithes) was, as a form of rent, confirmed to be outside the scope of taxation on land. Only in 1594, when the government realized that at least 25 per cent of land by value was held in this fashion, was the holder of teinds included among those obliged to contribute to his superior's tax assessment. Even then, many successfully evaded the burden.[13]

During inflationary times the costs of monarchy were rising steeply; recognizing an obligation to try, James could muster no enthusiasm for domestic retrenchment. As yet another consequence of Maitland's death, the king gave an eight-strong panel – popularly known, for obvious reasons, as the 'Octavians' – wide powers to collect and spend royal revenues and to eliminate waste and mismanagement, not only in the court but across the whole range of government activities. Responding to this brave challenge, the Octavians duly promoted a general 5 per cent tax on imports, and backed a military expedition aiming to extract from the Highlands debts long owed to the crown. Within a year they had cut household expenditure by 20 per cent. After another twelve months, however, their practical authority had all but evaporated in the face of aroused vested interests, agricultural crises and – a fate common to economic panels of all ages – internal squabbling. Their pruning of pensions was particularly hard on a king who relied upon such grants to sustain the all-important royal largesse to his nobles: far too many royal lands had been feued by his ancestors for James to see alienation as a viable alternative.

Adding to their collective unpopularity, several Octavians inclined to Catholicism. This alarmed the church, helping provoke an unpleasant riot in Edinburgh during December 1596 which had as its principal target a leading member of the panel, Alexander Seton. Troubled by this open manifestation of unrest, in which numerous rich merchants had joined, James found more reasons to distrust the wilder kirk ministers and promptly imprisoned the ringleaders. At the same time, he was given convenient grounds for wondering whether the panel served any worthwhile purpose. Those many distasteful aspects of retrenchment, combined with the prospect of eventual succession to the riches of England, united to confirm such reflections.

Every Stewart monarch was confronted by perennial problems presented by two border areas, that along the frontier with England, and the great Celtic march comprising the Highlands and Western Isles. Given the growth of official cooperation with England, successive administrations in Edinburgh were able to take steps which, albeit gradually, brought the turbulent border families into line. No longer did Scottish kings see unrest in the area as a necessary price to pay for the defence of a vulnerable frontier against English encroachment. Indeed, the obligation to maintain good relations with his future kingdom now encouraged James to extirpate dissent throughout what he liked to call, after 1603, his 'Middle Shires'. The occasional raid to bestow a fleeting glimpse of royal justice, which had satisfied earlier Stewarts, was no longer considered sufficient.

Habits formed across centuries were not, of course, modified overnight, and the last years of the frontier witnessed their share of noisy feuds after the old fashion, among the Scots themselves as well as with the English. Blood was shed and high feelings aroused in the west march in clashes between the Maxwells and the Johnstones. Nevertheless, the systematic taking of bonds for good behaviour, and the appointment of reliable officials prepared to cooperate with English counterparts, saw a significant change of emphasis. While the unpredictable men on both sides – like Bothwell, Robert Ker of Cessford or Thomas Percy, constable of Alnwick – might still try to do things in the traditional way, they were increasingly called to account by the ever sharper hand of justice administered from both London and Edinburgh. The rescue by Scott of Buccleuch of Kinmont Willie Armstrong from Carlisle Castle in 1596 was, characteristically, followed by lengthy diplomacy and a token period of imprisonment for the offender in an English gaol. Percy, having killed a Scotsman in a border fray, was also consigned to prison. Honour was preserved; the retaliatory raid was, in all but the rarest cases, eschewed.

Relations between Edinburgh and the Celtic fringe were, as always, founded on a mixture of incomprehension and indifference. Mincing no words, James flayed the backwardness of the Highlands in his advice to Prince Henry, although he did go so far as to draw a distinction between those of the mainland, 'barbarous for the most part', and those of the Western Isles – 'utterly barbarous'. Years later, dismissing the protests of his closest ally in bringing civilization to the west, the bishop of the Isles, he took no action against Jesuit proselytizing in Argyll, reasoning that even Catholics were welcome to try to remedy highland backwardness. In the dismal economic conditions of the 1590s some efforts were made to tap the perceived wealth of the west, but as in the plan to settle the Island of Lewis with men from the lowlands after its forfeiture to the crown in 1598, these ran foul of local opposition, the hostility of alarmed highland chiefs and the inescapable fact that most lowlanders wanted no part in such ventures. They were, indeed, as reluctant to support, either with men or taxes, the traditional stamping of the royal will on these areas through raiding or progresses. For all James's early inclinations to tackle the problem more forcefully there was in practice little alternative to the centuries-old strategy of Scottish kings: the occasional display of military force and the playing of one clan chief against another, ensuring thereby that the perpetual unrest beyond the Highland Line did not lap over into the lowlands.

The story of Jacobean government in the 1590s is, we may conclude, one of growing crown authority and promise for the future. The skills acquired as king of Scotland, however, sat ill in an England accustomed to kings who flounced their regality and insisted upon the remoteness of majesty. James, vociferous in his assertion of the sacred in kingship, remained all his life a pragmatist in the translation of theory into practice. As illustrated by the bewilderingly complex and ultimately vain negotiations for an Anglo-Scottish union after 1603, the more dear to his heart a policy was, the more pragmatic his approach.[14]

Increasingly, the hand mocked while the heart fed. His English subjects disparaged James while they flattered him, were reluctant to credit his rule with any touch of dignity or enlightenment. The Jacobean court of the 1600s and 1610s was quite as sophisticated as, indeed, a great deal wealthier and more ostentatious than, its Elizabethan predecessor. The display of wealth is, perhaps, one of a court's foremost functions, yet history decrees that we picture James at the centre of the demeaning drunken debauchery so charmingly described, on the occasion of the king of Denmark's visit in 1606, by John Harington. Legend ever contains its ounce of truth, but the highly distasteful Overbury scandal of the mid-1610s cannot be allowed to characterize James's reign, any more than Catherine Howard's adultery besmirches that of Henry VIII, or the mysterious death of Amy Dudley taints the Elizabethan regime. At the end of her life, Elizabeth lamented the tendency of men in authority to seek out the 'rising sun' that was her successor. The elderly James, twenty-five years on, could well have reflected upon another eternal truth to political life: the glorification of a past age. The 'ideal' king of the Scots proved an unsatisfactory occupant of the English throne, while, arguably, in spending most of his remaining years south of the border he failed as a king of Scotland too. That is, however, another story.

19 The Elizabethan Dusk: England 1599–1603

The earl of Essex's abject loss of nerve in Ireland sealed his fall; within days of his precipitate return to London he was placed under house arrest. In desperation, Essex cast the blame elsewhere, accusing Cecil, indirectly, and Sir Walter Ralegh, directly, of having worked his ruin, but the evidence for a conspiracy is tenuous. Neither personal shortcomings nor the malice of colleagues can explain fully the disaster that overtook the earl between 1598 and 1601; the key lies rather in the attitude of Elizabeth.

Tensions had begun to emerge in court and council as the 1590s progressed, the natural consequence of open-ended war and the fundamentally different military strategies advocated. Nevertheless, no clearly perceptible 'factions' had appeared until at least 1596, or more realistically 1598–9, when the trial of strength had already been resolved. Incidents such as Essex's doomed attempts to secure the attorney-generalship for Francis Bacon in

1593–4, the debate on war policy which had followed Spain's defeat in Brittany in 1595, or Robert Cecil's appointment to the secretaryship in 1596 during Essex's absence on the Cadiz expedition, had provoked anger and private side-taking, but with the war, and the queen, demanding an outward show of unity and practical cooperation within the council all involved had striven for a *modus vivendi*. If, by 1598, the amity was more calculated and less convincing than in the past, it would probably have endured had Essex not, by his own actions, irreparably damaged his relationship with the queen.

That year, Essex's fortunes began to disintegrate catastrophically. He forfeited Elizabeth's affection and favour after a quarrel in council during June, which, as described by William Camden, has become the stuff of romance: in the course of discussions on Irish policy the earl, his advice scorned, turned his back on Elizabeth. Furious at the insult, Elizabeth boxed Essex's ears and the earl reached for his sword, before shocked fellow counsellors could intervene. The reconciliation that followed amounted to an empty gesture, while Burghley's death that August removed the only figure capable of repairing so deep a breach. Peace concluded between France and Spain reduced any prospect of further English campaigning on the continent, outside the attritional siege warfare of the Low Countries, while Tyrone's victories in Ireland confronted Essex, the leading advocate of military opportunism, with limited and unwelcome options.

The earl's hysterical letters from Ireland in 1599 show how keenly he felt the loss of royal favour; to his increasingly irrational mind, all news from England provided further evidence of the plots laid by his enemies, and the indifference of Elizabeth herself. The queen's side of their correspondence, by turns sharp and reassuring, did little to allay his suspicions. For Elizabeth, the earl's conduct in 1599 came very close to treason; the taste of treachery is not confined to Essex's correspondence, and there may have been more to hurried government preparations against a Spanish threat from Flanders that year than meets the eye. Evidence which emerged after Essex's death suggests that he did indeed contemplate a coup in England, making use of the army in Ireland, and although Elizabeth limited the earl's censure to a private dressing-down by the council at York House in June 1600, and suspension from the council, such a punishment was in itself a demonstration of contempt for her former favourite. If Essex had indeed been the son Elizabeth never had, he was a son disgraced and disinherited by the end of 1600.

More than a touch of fear lay behind Elizabeth's actions. Even at that late stage, the earl retained a stubborn popularity among those for whom the pursuit of peace advocated by Cecil and most council colleagues signalled an end to opportunities for glory in the field. Such embittered company fuelled Essex's increasing paranoia, his suspicions now given free reign through exclusion from the privy council and silence from the queen. Counsellors absorbed the queen's disgust and closed ranks behind her. The personal rivalry between Essex and Robert Cecil smouldered at court and in the country, but if this was faction in its most blatant guise, it was a hopelessly unequal contest; Essex held no court cards. Cecil alone retained Elizabeth's trust.[1]

As 1600 wore on, Essex appears less and less his own master. For one whose short-term debts alone exceeded £5000, the final blow came with Elizabeth's pointed refusal to renew the earl's monopoly of sweet wines, over the past decade the key to his solvency. 'An unruly horse', the queen is reported to have declared, 'must be abated of his provender, that he may be the easier and better managed.' Rather than submitting, the horse kicked out. On 8 February 1601 Essex, along with the earls of Southampton and Rutland, and some two hundred gentlemen, set off to capture the court at Whitehall, counting on support from the city of London. That support never materialized. There was sporadic fighting, the rebels retreated to Essex House, artillery was brought from the Tower to batter down the doors, and late on the same evening Essex and Southampton surrendered. So ended the 'rebellion of a single day', as Elizabeth contemptuously described it. Before February was out Essex had been tried, convicted of treason and executed; the queen, despite a multitude of pretty legends, showed little inclination to save him. Southampton, more fortunate, remained a prisoner in the Tower until King James's accession brought his release.

Essex's death heralds a period at once obscure and unedifying. All the romance and colour that attend the tragedy of Elizabeth's last great favourite fade away, giving place to a furtive scramble for the good favour of James VI. Elizabeth had all her life refused to name her successor, and she remained stubborn to the end. At the same time, any declaration had become almost superfluous. James, who had once cultivated Essex as the rising star in the English court, was now relieved of a contact long become a mere embarrassment and was eager to accept overtures from a far more promising quarter. Recognizing his opportunity, Cecil initiated approaches to emissaries from Scotland who arrived in London shortly after the collapse of Essex's rebellion.

Cecil was doing no more than acknowledging the obvious, for the logic and validity of the Stuart claim had become apparent to all. Spain's policy of steady disengagement from European conflict after 1598, coupled with the lady's reluctance to be considered, foiled the small group of Catholics who advocated the cause of the only viable overseas candidate, the Infanta Isabella, daughter of Philip II and at that time regent for the Spanish crown in Brussels. As for the other putative contenders, weariness with half a century of female rule ensured that the claim of James's cousin Arabella, or Arbella, Stuart was passed over – nothing in Arabella's character suggests that such neglect was unwise – while the child of the earl of Hertford and Catherine Grey, Edward Seymour, Lord Beauchamp, an Englishman and heir under the terms of Henry VIII's will, lacked either the personality or the desire to press his claim. 'Kingmakers', such as Thomas Wilson in his 'State of England' written in 1600, enjoyed the challenge of a genealogical game, carefully tracing lineages from the children of Henry III. Yet they succeeded only in persuading themselves that a Scottish succession was inevitable.

To many in England, high and low, this was an unappetizing prospect – as another of James VI's correspondents in these years, the earl of Northumberland, put it, 'the name of Scots is harsh in the ears of the vulgar' – but most were prepared, even determined, to make the best of the situation. A Stuart succession was not foisted upon Englishmen and women overnight; the probability had existed throughout Elizabeth's reign and, indeed, long before. The very old might recall across a span of seventy years talk of James V as heir presumptive to Henry VIII. For the English, James VI was a more palatable prospect than either his mother or grandfather. Partly to reassure James, partly to allay his own reservations, Northumberland resorted to inaccuracy: the king, he declared, was 'half English' and in any case had no good cause 'to be so far enamoured with the faith of [Scotsmen] that willingly they will repose a greater trust in them than in the English.' James, courteous if reserved, was pleased to concur.

Hindsight, though, is a dangerous ally to the historian of Elizabeth's final years. Convenient coincidence carries us along. Essex is executed in February 1601. Bereft of his erstwhile champion – he never forgot Essex's loyalty – James accepts the overtures of men formerly uncommitted, like Cecil, Northumberland and the earl of Nottingham, or more overtly hostile, like Ralegh. The rump of the Essex faction, notably Lord Mountjoy in Ireland and Henry Howard, move over to the Cecil camp and offer their services in both promoting goodwill between monarch and minister, and – just as congenial to Howard – sowing distrust between James and others, like Ralegh, Northumberland and Lord Cobham, who also sought royal favour. Such manoeuvring is carefully concealed from Elizabeth, all parties waiting impatiently for the aged queen to depart. Then Elizabeth, entering her seventieth year – what Camden, again with hindsight, described as her 'climacteric' – falls sick, dies, and the king inherits peacefully. All this takes a mere two years or so, and in most histories of the reign, little more is said.

The central documentary evidence for the last years of Elizabeth's reign – and indeed for the first Stuart decade – is surprisingly thin. State papers are scattered, while a Whitehall fire in 1619 denies us more than eleven years of the council registers, from January 1602. Too many significant figures, including the earls of Worcester and Nottingham, remain shadowy, and even Cecil remains an enigma awaiting his modern biographer. All the more reason, then, to pass over the period with dispatch. We have travelled an arduous road across forty-five years and may expect tranquillity at journey's end, livened only by the queen's last, 'golden' speech, an oration dwelling on the monarch's responsibility to and love for her people, delivered to an appreciative parliament in November 1601. Certain passages ring down the years. 'There will never queen sit in my seat with more zeal than I have to my country and care to my subjects, and that will sooner with willingness venture her life for your good and safety than my self. I thank God I never yet feared foreign or home enemy.' The splendid scene closes with Elizabeth's subjects crowded about her, beckoned close in confidentiality, kissing her hand and departing, one by one. A sense of valediction hangs heavy in the air.

It is, though, quite misleading. The danger lies, of course, in assuming that the queen's limited time was common knowledge. The 'golden speech', seen in another light, is an elegant self-justification on the vexing question of monopolies, developed into a discussion of what underpinned good monarchy. In yet a further interpretation it appears as just one more expression of what David Sacks has called the 'ritualized renewal of the bonds of society', the mutual obligation between crown and people exemplified by parliament.[2] The picture of a queen huddled in the council chamber with her peers and what in other countries would have been termed her 'lesser nobility' is an image both moving and enduring: the queen with her *amici principis*, her 'friends', her 'natural counsel', the men who advised her fearlessly and whose advice was taken in good part, according well with the Senecan ideal.[3] Elizabeth's health in 1602 remained good, she went on her usual progress in the summer and kept Christmas with accustomed ceremonial.

Admittedly, there were disquieting signs. The queen seemed increasingly prone to fits of melancholy; she brooded on historical precedent and, with Essex's treason fresh in her mind, the threat of deposition. Early in August 1601, William Lambarde the historian was granted an interview with his royal patron. They discussed the records under Lambarde's charge in the Tower, and the reign of an unfortunate forebear caught Elizabeth's attention. 'I am Richard II,' she said, 'know ye not that?' In August 1602, while on progress, she suffered some form of indisposition, Northumberland telling Cobham of her determination that the problem – whatever it was – should be kept secret: 'the next day she did walk abroad in the park lest any should take notice of it'. Aches and pains, however, are common enough, and we must doubt whether much significance was read into these symptoms at the time. As shall be seen, Elizabeth's decline when it came in late February and March 1603 was rapid. That it did not catch Cecil and the council unawares is testimony rather to the prudence of her ministers than to any clear presentiment of her fate.

Cecil's determination to secure his position with James is understandable, his parallel endeavours to disparage Sir Walter Ralegh much less excusable. Ralegh, cordially detested by many at court as the archetypal self-made man, appears to have posed little political threat: he lacked any significant clientage, held no major office and had never secured a seat on the privy council. All that Ralegh had achieved had been won through high favour with the queen during the 1580s, and the trust on which that favour was based had been shattered by his secret marriage to one of the queen's maids of honour in 1592. His marriage, indeed, exemplifies the man's shortcomings, to which Cecil can hardly have been blind: Ralegh, for all his charm, for all the adventurous genius he displays in other fields, lacked diplomatic skills and was an inept politician. His monumental blunders in 1603 – when he advocated continued war with Spain to a king heart-set on peace and wandered unwittingly into a particularly hopeless treason – are of a pattern with what passed before.[4] Of Elizabeth's four principal favourites, Ralegh was by some distance the weakest. Lacking the breeding of Leicester or Essex, he was fatally unable to match Hatton's intelligent urbanity.

How, then, are we to explain Cecil's hostility? Can we portray it as a miscalculation, the fortuitous absence of genuine rivals after the death of Essex, with senior figures like Buckhurst and Nottingham content to play his game and to profit from the association, leading him into the trap of seeing dangers where none existed? Should we, alternatively, consider the possibility that the one-time favourite possessed strengths which we have failed to identify? Or perhaps a clue lies in the company Sir Walter kept. There is an element of personal affront in Cecil's actions, and his accusations are directed as much against Lord Cobham as against Ralegh. When writing during 1602 to Mountjoy and to Sir George Carew in Ireland, Cecil alludes to Ralegh and Cobham's increasing hostility, which he regrets, but is trying to ignore. The centuries of attention lavished on Ralegh have failed to establish the significance of his friend; here, if anywhere, was the man Cecil feared. The picture we have of Cobham is the unedifying portrait of a hapless fop, led on to destruction under Ralegh's spell. This is, however, the picture drawn by his foes, and it is not entirely credible. As a courtier, Cobham was far from negligible: he possessed the very merits that Ralegh now lacked. His wealth was considerable, and as warden of the Cinque Ports he held a highly important security post. After Essex's disgrace, no court figure comes closer than Cobham to filling the role of queen's favourite, for he retained to the end Elizabeth's ear and sympathy. It is this intimacy, surely, which attracted Ralegh and which led Cecil to warn James, albeit obliquely, of the 'threat' that Cobham posed.

The full tide of revisionism has yet to touch the last parliament of the Tudor age, that of 1601, but the principal issues of debate are obvious enough, while many minutiae are vividly preserved in a detailed if still enigmatic record compiled by the MP Hayward Townshend. The crown sought, and obtained, four subsidies, the continuing struggles in Ireland and the Low Countries providing a justification readily accepted on all sides. In one particular area the council expected, and duly endured, a heated squabble in the Commons. The crown had taken to developing earlier arrangements whereby inventors and innovators were given sole rights to manufacture, trade in and benefit from a product or process. It was now using its discretionary powers to sanction the production and exportation of more commonplace items regulated or prohibited by statute, such as bottles, currants, iron and vinegar. Favoured courtiers creamed off profits, while informers busied themselves in scenting out those contravening the regulations. The catalogue of these 'monopolies' grew longer and longer. When the list of new grants was read out in the 1601 parliament one member of the Commons, William Hakewill, demanded with heavy irony, 'Is not bread there?'. Monopolies were deeply unpopular – they were seen as preventing men from earning a living at their vocations – but their exploitation offered a source of income to an administration hard pressed by the costs of war, and a means of rewarding courtiers and crown servants. The failure of the crown to keep its promise from the last parliament and scrutinize the abuses of existing privileges provoked bitterness, and even, perhaps, some kind of organized campaign for remedy. Nevertheless, the disgruntled members eventually accepted another gracious assurance from Elizabeth, and a token round of cancellations.

There was, too, an expected squall of protest concerning purveyance, even though by now most counties had accepted the proffered hand of royal compromise and had compounded for this particular burden, and no fewer than six, uniformly unsuccessful, bills to regulate taverns in the perennial Tudor struggle to contain insobriety. Otherwise one sees only the consensus inherent in the last Tudor poor law. Little, in short, distracted from what at times appears a conscious display of coherence in the aftermath of Essex's rebellion.

The nine years' war in Ireland ended with the submission of Tyrone at Mellifont, six days after Elizabeth died. English victory, however, had long since been assured. Tyrone had pinned his hopes on Spanish intervention, but after the death of Philip II in 1598, with his successor's ministers led by the duke of Lerma seeking a European peace, and with tentative negotiations commencing between England and Spain at Boulogne in 1600, the eventual dispatch of 3400 troops under Don Juan del Aguila represented a pragmatic compromise between factions in Madrid. Not wishing to abandon allies whose pressure might prove useful at the negotiating table, Philip III was nevertheless only able to commit this force after a conclusion of peace between France and the Spanish client Savoy in January 1601. He was unprepared, in both senses of the word, to supply the 6000 men demanded by Tyrone.

It has been argued that in landing at Kinsale, on the south coast, the Spaniards facilitated an English victory by obliging Tyrone to emerge from his Ulster power base and commit his forces to open battle. Certainly, the Irish had counselled their allies to invade Munster only if they came in great strength. After a recent, very thorough, pacification by its president, Sir George Carew, the province was little inclined to assist the Spanish. But such an interpretation gives insufficient credit to Mountjoy's swift blockade of Kinsale. Though precipitating heavy losses through disease during a winter siege, his rapid response did indeed throw down a challenge to Tyrone and eventually gave the English the pitched battle they sought, resulting in the utter defeat of the Irish and the forced withdrawal of the Spanish army. Campaigning in 1602 and 1603 amounted to a large-scale mopping-up operation, a round of crop-burnings and submissions, Tyrone negotiating all the while for an honourable surrender. The terms eventually granted, couched in vague phrases, left Tyrone and O'Donnell with the titles to their lands intact, and were more generous than either man had expected. At the same time, the reality of the military situation was not lost, either on the earls or their erstwhile followers.

Such terms were offered, as Elizabeth had insisted, only upon unconditional surrender, but they owe their detail to the personal convictions of Mountjoy and most other Englishmen in Ireland that conciliation should be attempted. Mountjoy had particular cause to sympathize with supplicant traitors. As a supporter of Essex he had been invited to participate in the plot by which the army in Ireland would be used to support the earl's pretensions. Mountjoy had survived, for the queen had been prepared to forgive her successful deputy a great deal, but he was obliged to forge closer ties with Cecil, whose own patronage of Carew in Munster had been seen as a check on the deputy's power. The privy council's transmission of fulsome royal congratulations to Mountjoy in June 1601, commending his military success in Ireland, has about it the stamp of an official indemnity against offences in the uncomfortably recent past.

For all the problems imposed by the absence of council registers, events surrounding the death of Queen Elizabeth provide us with a fine example of the way in which late Tudor government coped with political change. By any test the much-feared dynastic alteration ran a smooth course. What form of malady it was that killed the queen is still debated by medical historians, although at least some of the more lurid contemporary tales, which had her succumbing to curses placed upon pieces of Welsh gold, and upon a playing card (the Queen of Hearts, naturally) nailed to her chair, may be discounted. Contemporaries blamed melancholy prostration, and they may well have been right. For the last month of her life Elizabeth found it impossible to sleep. Grieving for her close friend of many years, Katharine Carey, countess of Nottingham, who died in February, she refused food, and both her health and her state of mind began to deteriorate. At length the queen collapsed, was obliged to take to her bed, and died within the fortnight.

The council strove to deny rumours of the queen's decline. Writing to Mountjoy in Ireland as late as 13 March they conceded that Elizabeth had been indisposed, but reassured the deputy that the royal physicians and the evidence of their own eyes had convinced them that there was 'no doubt of her safe and perfect recovery'. Such assurances, however, proved inadequate; the rumours intensified. Sir John Carey, commanding the garrison at Berwick, began to panic, while in the waking nightmares of Giovanni Scaramelli, the Venetian envoy, factions supporting James, Arabella Stuart and the earl of Hertford's son by Catherine Grey all tussled for the crown. The situation was, he summed up in one anxious dispatch, sufficient 'to make most men blench'.

Carey and Scaramelli were wrong, of course, but their alarm is illuminating, for fears of Scottish invasions and civil wars were widely shared. To accept the necessity of a Stuart succession was one thing; to assume that one's compatriots would concur quite another. In the weeks surrounding Elizabeth's death there were few parts of England in which the local authorities encountered no example of unwise gossip or disturbing rumour. Although he in fact did nothing to promote his son's claim, Hertford was commonly reported to be in open revolt, while the more obdurate Catholic gentry were said to be scurrying hither and thither, bent upon mischief. In response, the precautions taken by the council show a sense of proportion as well as prudence. A few notorious troublemakers among the recusant community were placed in custody. Vagabonds were rounded up, and extra guards set on prisons and other key buildings in London. Remembering 1553, perhaps, the council further ordered the close confinement of Arabella Stuart.

Meanwhile, policies for the changed world that would follow the queen's death were hammered out in some particularly obscure negotiations. The council here displayed that felicity of tact which characterized so many of its moves in 1603. Realizing that their authority would terminate the moment Elizabeth died, counsellors invited the principal non-conciliar noblemen then in London – Northumberland, Cobham and Lord Thomas Howard, the future earl of Suffolk – to join their deliberations, laying plans to co-opt further peers when the moment seemed right. A particular attempt was made to woo Northumberland, perhaps because the consent of a Percy to the Scottish succession would provide excellent propaganda, perhaps because when writing to James in 1602 he had made some attempt to speak for loyal Catholics. The earl was encouraged to renew his correspondence with James, and it looks as if some thought was given to appointing him 'protector' or regent of England for as long as the new king remained out of the country. Such sweetening served its turn. At that crucial moment no man in England displayed greater loyalty to the Stuart cause.

When Elizabeth died, early in the morning of 24 March, the transition of power went smoothly. A proclamation declaring James's succession was at once drawn up, signed by an imposing array of former counsellors and lords. The show of strength and unity was reinforced later that morning when the 'Great Council', as it was sometimes described, rode in a body into London, Cecil reading the proclamation at the court gates at Whitehall, and at Cheapside. The city authorities fell into line. While celebratory bonfires lit the sky, counsellors worked through the night, ensuring that messages were sent into the country, enclosing copies of the proclamation to be read in shire towns. Although Sir Robert Carey had, in an act of unlicensed opportunism, pre-empted them by more than twenty-four hours, official notification was despatched to James on the morning of 25 March, carried, significantly, by the brother of one prominent nobleman – Northumberland – and by the son of another, the earl of Worcester. Soon after, the clerk of the signet, Sir Thomas Lake, followed them, with orders to brief the king on the immediate needs of the English administration. It says a good deal for the efficiency of the council's measures that James, never the most sanguine of men, felt able to make a leisurely journey south. He did not arrive in London until early in May.

If the personnel of Elizabeth's administration survived almost intact, much else had indisputably altered. So ended seventy-five years of almost continuous dynastic uncertainty. England had its mature, male monarch, and, in the shape of James's two healthy sons, a secure succession. Soon it would also have peace: the Treaty of London ended hostilities with Philip III's dominions in August 1604. The great constitutional problems and possibilities of the next half century, and in some measure the great religious issues too, would henceforth turn on the very different constitutional realities ushered in by the Stuart succession.

In the history of the British Isles, the coincidence of Tyrone's submission and the end of the Tudor dynasty carries a great deal of symbolic significance, though precisely what it symbolizes is an issue still vigorously debated. Once upon a time the Stuart succession seemed to mark, from the English perspective, a successful if somewhat fortuitous conclusion to long-term Tudor strategies: local autonomy had been broken down, while royal authority had been extended across the king's dominions. Despite many vicissitudes, efforts aiming at political centralization, administrative uniformity and cultural imperialism had ultimately triumphed, and by 1603 there were no longer any

Plate 23 London from Southwark, *c.*1630. The earliest surviving oil painting specifically of London, showing the results of Tudor and early Stuart growth. Note the south bank theatres, the buildings and heads on poles on London Bridge, and old St Paul's Cathedral dominating the skyline.
Source: © Museum of London

military frontiers, those breeding grounds of alternative cultures and polities, within the islands. In recent years, the optimism and sense of progress lying behind this rather one-dimensional interpretation has been deliberately qualified, if not turned on its head, not least through the work of those historians who have focused their studies away from London and southeastern England. Steven Ellis, in examining the fortunes of English government in Ireland and the administration of England's Irish and Scottish frontiers, argues that the Tudors inherited a political system that had, in practice, worked, and replaced it with a united structure flawed by lasting bitterness and disillusion in Ireland, and by marginalization and underrepresentation in the north, and even in Wales. The impractical model of a subordinate yet theoretically sovereign Irish kingdom helped fuel instabilities and antagonisms which in turn contributed to that great crisis of the three kingdoms between 1638 and 1660, still inadequately familiar to us as the English Civil War.[5]

Yet this scenario is also a little disingenuous. Despite its many flaws, the united structure worked too. We stand in danger of building a new high road to civil war, focused on a mirage and unwarranted by the available evidence. Was Wales or the north really any more marginalized after 1603? Gentlemen in both areas hardly thought so, and the number of MPs representing both regions is not so dramatically out of step with their respective populations. Pre-1534 *laissez-faire* government-by-magnate was itself a threadbare, inefficient form of administration, a particular liability in time of internal crisis or external threat. Within the context of the 1580s and 1590s such a system was no answer at all. The shortcomings of late Tudor efforts at compromise, followed by military subjugation, are apparent only when set against higher standards and higher expectations, unrealistic in the light of the state's limited resources, of men, of an Irish bureaucracy, of reliable intelligence and of money during a difficult and costly European war.

By 1603, for all its weaknesses, the Tudor hold upon Ireland went far deeper than any straightforward military conquest. Despite Old English alienation from crown appointees and adventurers in Ireland, their loyalty to the crown itself remained strong, as did those personal ties which bound Palesmen to members of the English council. Alongside military conquest and the subjection of Gaelic Ireland here, surely, lay advantages for Elizabeth's successors. While the legacy was squandered, a seventeenth-century Anglo-Irishman's key grievance was that his king would not listen to him; at heart the Palesmen and women were frustrated loyalists, not nationalists, and so for centuries they remained. When, forty years on, England collapsed into civil war, the Stuarts found some of their staunchest supporters among the ranks of the Old English in Ireland.

Any attempt to display developing English policies towards Wales, Scotland and Ireland as three manifestations of a single administrative problem also verge on oversimplification. Each frontier posed different problems, which confronted a crown at different times, and in different ways which themselves changed with time. This the Henrician administration realized as far back as the 1530s; unlike Wales, no act of union was ever imposed, no attempt at direct rule seriously envisaged in Ireland. Ireland presented its own problems and was treated to its own, unhappy, attempts at solutions. We return, at last, to one of the truths which govern a sixteenth-century polity: English government was founded on a consensus between crown and essentially self-governing localities, agreed on the degree to which local control should be subsumed in the wider national considerations of defence, justice, religion and community. The Welsh ruling elite found that they could accept and adapt to this system; their Irish counterparts, very, very gradually, decided they could not. After 1603, Scots looked askance at the miseries endured by the kingdom of Ireland, rejecting this constitutional precedent as no fit model for Anglo-Scottish union. However, it may be doubted whether the Scots would have liked the Irish model, even if cultural assimilation had proceeded more happily: Scotland's history, heritage and aspirations, its sense of nationhood, differed fundamentally from those of the kingdom of Ireland. While some (perhaps not many) Englishmen might have welcomed a union with Scotland, or Ireland, based on the Welsh model of assimilation, most Scots and many Irish rejected such ideas out of hand as unworkable and, indeed, offensive. Neither the English conquest of Ireland nor any other recent continental model – Poland–Lithuania, Scotland–France or Portugal–Spain

– offered a particularly attractive framework for future political development, nor was there any useful theoretical justification of multiple monarchy to guide the royal hand, or the hands of his more sceptical ministers.

The Tudor north presented another, different problem. Far from being the drain on resources that was Ireland, the north of England was garrisoned at remarkably little cost throughout the reign of Elizabeth, while on both sides of the border self-interest, that most compelling of forces, dictated coopera-tion and military disengagement. The English frontiers against Scotland and Gaelic Ireland were different, local societies were dissimilar, and the relation-ships of those societies with the English, and Scottish, courts varied too. In making too much of parallels that individualism may become obscured.

Parallels, if sanctioned, might indeed be extended in some unexpected directions. The English lowlands, often dismissed as a prosperous and there-fore a tranquil 'core', were never entirely reliable. They could on occasion explode into violence far more threatening than that encountered in the peripheries. Three times within the space of five years, extensive, well-armed, effectively led and popular rebellions centred within one hundred miles of the capital came closer than any northern or western uprising to bringing down a Tudor administration. One, indeed, succeeded. Such disturbances were only the most extreme manifestations of deep-seated anxieties and discontents, all too close to London. Rather than any creeping expansion of lowland 'cores' into the respective hinterlands, a remarkable feature in English and Scottish constitutional history is the essential sameness of the picture: the king's writ runs under Henry VIII and James V where, more or less, it runs under Edward the Confessor and David I. The odd, frequently resented case apart, English kings over five centuries seldom ventured further north than York, or further west than the headwaters of the Thames. Scottish kings, responding to very different demands within a far less centralized polity, had always travelled more widely.

Distinctions between a militarized north and west and a peaceful south-east may hold good for the England of the Wars of the Roses, but as we have seen they appear increasingly unrealistic in any study of the developing Tudor state. Certainly Irish troops served in the north of England, in 1544–6, just as northerners were recruited for Ireland during the disturbances of the early 1530s, and Welsh archers served in both borderlands. Yet troops in their thousands from every other part of England fought in every Tudor war. Advocates of a particular policy in Ireland would naturally draw parallels, wherever possible, between their own ideas and achievements in Wales: who would not wish to be associated with a success story? What, though, is so significant about a commander or a governor calling upon his past experience, or an administration taking troops wherever they might most conveniently or most cheaply be found?

Coincidences and parallels should never lead us to lose sight of the ad hoc responses of successive administrations to successive crises and constitu-tional difficulties. Seen in this pragmatic light, the light which lit the paths of hard-pressed courtiers and counsellors at the time, the achievements of Stewart and Tudor monarchs in neutralizing, overcoming or making the best of innumerable problems, some of their own making, are inescapably impressive. Finally, however, we must introduce a note of caution. Whether these achievements worked to the good of all, even a majority of their subjects remains doubtful. The impact of state upon the individual was still limited, particularly in Scotland but also in England, even after the 1590s. Should it be assumed that what was right for the statesmen, the all-powerful cohorts of the gentry, and the loquacious clergymen, also benefited the anonymous mass of the silent and poor, the urban apprentice, the agricultural labourer, the widow with her children, the old man incapable of manual work and the maimed ex-soldier thrown upon charity? That is a question more easily asked than answered. Over and again we have to guess at the practical effects of well-intentioned legislation, just as we are obliged to conjecture the true feelings of the crown's humbler subjects. In many cases we remain in ignorance as to their sentiments; the evidence has not yet been sifted, or, at this remove, it is too often lost beyond recall.

We are left, then, with the qualified achievement of the governors, the more or less enthusiastic acquiescence of some of the governed, the thinly perceived ignorance or ambivalence of others. We are left with theoretically near-absolutist, in practice consensual societies, in which the means of compulsion are still limited, but in which central administration is becoming an ever more intrusive element, for good or ill, in the lives of citizens. Behold, here, the early modern state.

Notes

Introduction

1 The vapid term 'Atlantic archipelago' is from time to time deployed by those so wary of modern, nationalistic prejudices that they would deny these islands their ancient, familiar name. This phrase may serve to describe the Azores, or the Falkland Islands, but serves no useful purpose here.

2 Foremost among the pioneers: J. G. A. Pocock, 'British history: a plea for a new subject', *Journal of Modern History* 47 (1975), 601–28, and 'The limits and divisions of British history', *American Historical Review* 87 (1982), 311–36.

3 Hiram Morgan, 'British policies before the British state', in Brendan Bradshaw and John Morrill (eds), *The British Problem, c.1534–1707: State formation in the Atlantic archipelago* (London, 1996), pp. 66–88.

4 David Cannadine, 'British history as "a new subject": politics, perspectives and prospects', *Welsh History Review* 17 (1995), 313–31. At the same time, the author praises similar, much later, nationalistic enterprises in Scotland, Ireland and Wales for 'establishing new, non-Anglocentric interpretations'.

5 John Morrill, 'The fashioning of Britain', in S. G. Ellis and S. Barber (eds), *Conquest and Union: Fashioning a British state, 1485–1725* (London, 1995), pp. 8–39, quote at p. 13.

6 Hugh Kearney, *The British Isles: A history of four nations* (Cambridge, 1989).

1 Sixteenth-century England

1 See Michael L. Zell, 'The social parameters of probate records in the sixteenth century', *Bulletin of the Institute of Historical Research* 57 (1984), 107–13.

2 On the consequences of catastrophic fire see C. J. Kitching, 'Fire disasters and fire relief in sixteenth-century England: the Nantwich fire of 1583', *Bulletin of the Institute of Historical Research* 54 (1981), 171–87.

3 See Frederic A. Youngs Jr, 'Towards petty sessions: Tudor JPs and divisions of counties', in DeLoyd J. Guth and John W. McKenna (eds), *Tudor Rule and Revolution* (Cambridge, 1982), pp. 201–16.

4 John Guy, *Tudor England* (Oxford, 1988), p. 420.

5 On the dynamism of the sixteenth-century book trade see F. J. Levy, 'How information spread among the gentry, 1550–1640', *Journal of British Studies* 21/2 (1982), 11–34.

6   See A. L. Erickson, 'Common law versus common practice: the use of marriage settlements in early modern England', *Economic History Review*, 2nd series 43 (1990), 21–39.

7   Mortimer Levine, 'The place of women in Tudor government', in Guth and McKenna (eds), *Tudor Rule and Revolution*, pp. 109–23.

8   For Kent see G. W. Bernard, 'The fortunes of the Greys, earls of Kent, in the early sixteenth century', *Historical Journal* 25 (1982), 671–85; for Northumberland see R. W. Hoyle, 'Henry Percy, sixth earl of Northumberland, and the fall of the house of Percy, 1527–37', in G. W. Bernard (ed.), *The Tudor Nobility* (Manchester, 1992), pp. 180–211.

9   G. W. Bernard, 'The Tudor nobility in perspective', in Bernard (ed.), *The Tudor Nobility*, pp. 1–48.

10 Felicity Heal and Clive Holmes (eds), *The Gentry in England and Wales, 1500–1700* (Basingstoke, 1994), p. 19.

11 On the extreme complexities inherent in establishing just who might and who might not be considered a gentleman, see J. E. Hollinshead, 'The gentry of south-west Lancashire in the later sixteenth century', *Northern History* 26 (1990), 82–102.

12 On this intimacy see David Starkey, 'Court, council and nobility in Tudor England', in Ronald G. Asch and Adolf M. Birke (eds), *Princes, Patronage, and the Nobility: The court at the beginning of the modern age c.1450–1650* (Oxford, 1991), pp. 175–203.

13 Daniel Javitch, *Poetry and Courtliness in Renaissance England* (Princeton, 1978), p. 3.

14 See Steven Gunn, 'The structures of politics in early Tudor England', *Transactions of the Royal Historical Society*, 6th series 5 (1995), 59–90.

15 See Roger Schofield, 'Taxation and the political limits of the Tudor state', in Claire Cross, David Loades and J. J. Scarisbrick (eds), *Law and Government under the Tudors* (Cambridge, 1988), pp. 227–55.

16 On personal links between the two houses see Helen Miller, 'Lords and commons: relations between the two houses of parliament, 1509–1558', *Parliamentary History* 1 (1982), 13–24.

17 Jennifer Loach, 'Parliament: a "new air"?', in Christopher Coleman and David Starkey (eds), *Revolution Reassessed: Revisions in the history of Tudor government and administration* (Oxford, 1986), pp. 117–34.

18 For an exploration of enfranchisement see A. D. K. Hawkyard, 'The enfranchisement of constituencies 1509–1558', *Parliamentary History* 10 (1991), 1–26.

19 Compare Michael L. Zell, 'Economic problems of the parochial clergy in the sixteenth century', in Rosemary O'Day and Felicity Heal (eds), *Princes and Paupers in the English Church 1500–1800* (Leicester, 1981), pp. 19–43, with John Pound, 'Clerical poverty in early sixteenth-century England: some East Anglian evidence', *Journal of Ecclesiastical History* 37 (1986), 389–96.

20 See Andrew Hope, 'Lollardy: the stone the builders rejected?', in Peter Lake and Maria Dowling (eds), *Protestantism and the National Church in Sixteenth-century England* (London, 1987), pp. 1–35; J. F. Davis, 'Lollardy and the reformation in England', *Archive for Reformation History* 73 (1982), 217–36; R. G. Davies, 'Lollardy and locality', *Transactions of the Royal Historical Society*, 6th series 1 (1991), 191–212; Derek Plumb's contributions in Margaret Spufford (ed.), *The World of Rural Dissenters, 1520–1725* (Cambridge, 1995).

2 Divorce, Schism and Statute: England 1529–36

1 Maria Dowling, 'Anne Boleyn and reform', *Journal of Ecclesiastical History* 35 (1984), 30–46; Dowling (ed.), 'William Latymer's Cronickille of Anne Bulleyne', *Camden Miscellany 30* (London, 1990), pp. 23–66, esp. pp. 33–7; E. W. Ives, 'Anne Boleyn and the early reformation in England: the contemporary evidence', *Historical Journal* 37 (1994), 389–400; Thomas S. Freeman, 'Research, rumour and propaganda: Anne Boleyn in Foxe's "Book of Martyrs"', *Historical Journal* 38 (1995), 797–819. But for a recent suggestion that Anne was not the zealous reformer depicted by Dowling, Ives and (with qualifications) Warnicke, see G. W. Bernard, 'Anne Boleyn's religion', *Historical Journal* 36 (1993), 1–20.

2 E. W. Ives, 'The fall of Wolsey', in S. J. Gunn and P. G. Lindley (eds), *Cardinal Wolsey: Church, state and art* (Cambridge, 1991), pp. 286–315; and L. R. Gardiner, 'Further news of Cardinal Wolsey's end, November–December 1530', *Bulletin of the Institute of Historical Research* 57 (1984), 99–107.

3 Alistair Fox, 'Facts and fallacies: interpreting English humanism', 'English humanism and the body politic', both in Alistair Fox and John Guy (eds), *Reassessing the Henrician Age: Humanism, politics and reform 1500–1550* (Oxford, 1986), pp. 9–33, 34–51, quote at p. 34.

4 For a wide-ranging examination of the concept of royal supremacy see Henry Chadwick, 'Royal ecclesiastical supremacy', in Brendan Bradshaw and Eamon Duffy (eds), *Humanism, Reform and the Reformation. The career of Bishop John Fisher* (Cambridge, 1989), pp. 169–203.

5 See Thomas F. Mayer, 'On the road to 1534: the occupation of Tournai and Henry VIII's theory of sovereignty', in Dale Hoak (ed.), *Tudor Political Culture* (Cambridge, 1995), pp. 11–30; Hoak, 'The iconography of the crown imperial', in ibid., pp. 54–103.

6 Debate focuses on the true nature of the pardon of the clergy: see J. A. Guy, 'Henry VIII and the praemunire manoeuvres of 1530–1531', *English Historical Review* 97 (1982), 481–503; G. W. Bernard, 'The pardon of the clergy reconsidered', *Journal of Ecclesiastical History* 37 (1986), 258–82; Guy, *Journal of Ecclesiastical History* 37 (1986), 283–4; Bernard, *Journal of Ecclesiastical History* 37 (1986), 284–7.

7 For a résumé of this dispute see John Guy, 'Thomas More and Christopher St German: the battle of the books', in Fox and Guy (eds), *Reassessing the Henrician Age*, pp. 95–120.

8 See Susan Brigden, 'Thomas Cromwell and the "Brethren"', in Claire Cross, David Loades and J. J. Scarisbrick (eds), *Law and Government under the Tudors* (Cambridge, 1988), pp. 31–49, for an investigation of Cromwell's radical credentials.

9 On the concept of 'empire' see John Guy, 'Thomas Cromwell and the intellectual origins of the Henrician revolution', in Fox and Guy (eds), *Reassessing the Henrician Age*, pp. 151–78; S. E. Lehmberg, *The Reformation Parliament, 1529–1536* (Cambridge, 1970), p. 175.

10 R. Rex, 'The execution of the Holy Maid of Kent', *Historical Research* 64 (1991), 216–20.

11 On Fisher's resistance see J. J. Scarisbrick, 'Fisher, Henry VIII and the Reformation crisis', in Bradshaw and Duffy (eds), *Humanism, Reform and the Reformation*, pp. 155–68.

12 I am grateful to Dr Paul Ayris for allowing me to read his as yet unpublished work on Cranmer's visitation.

13 J. D. Alsop, 'The theory and practice of Tudor taxation', *English Historical Review* 97 (1982), 1–30; G. L. Harriss, 'Theory and practice in royal taxation: some observations', *English Historical Review* 97, 811–19; Alsop, 'Innovation in Tudor taxation', *English Historical Review* 99 (1984), 83–93. For a recent 'traditional' interpretation of the 1534 statute see R. W. Hoyle, 'Crown, parliament and taxation in sixteenth-century England', *English Historical Review* 109 (1994), 1174–96, and Hoyle's general remarks on Henrician finance in D. MacCulloch (ed.), *The Reign of Henry VIII: Politics, policy and piety* (London, 1995), pp. 75–99.

14 On the wider context of drama and literature in the reign see Seymour Baker House, 'Literature, drama and politics', in MacCulloch (ed.), *The Reign of Henry VIII*, pp. 181–201.

15 See J. D. Alsop, 'The structure of early Tudor finance c.1509–1558', in Christopher Coleman and David Starkey (eds), *Revolution Reassessed: Revisions in the history of Tudor government and administration* (Oxford, 1986), pp. 135–62.

16 For the Tudor settlement see J. Gwynfor Jones, *Early Modern Wales c.1525–1640* (Basingstoke, 1994), ch. 2; W. R. B. Robinson, 'The Tudor revolution in Wales', *English Historical Review* 103 (1988); Peter Roberts, 'The English crown, the principality of Wales and the Council in the Marches, 1534–1641', in Brendan Bradshaw and John Morrill (eds), *The British Problem, c.1534–1707: State formation in the Atlantic archipelago* (London, 1996), pp. 118–47.

17 For an introduction to the early years of Welsh representation see G. R. Elton, 'Wales in parliament, 1542–1581', in R. R. Davies et al. (eds), *Welsh Society and Nationhood* (Cardiff, 1984), pp. 108–21.

18 For a healthily broad approach to the question see John Guy, 'Thomas Wolsey, Thomas Cromwell and the reform of Henrician government', in MacCulloch (ed.), *The Reign of Henry VIII*, pp. 35–57; C. S. L. Davies, 'The Cromwellian decade: authority and consent', *Transactions of the Royal Historical Society*, 6th series 7 (1997), 177–96.

19 Christopher St German, for example. See J. A. Guy, 'The Tudor commonwealth: revising Thomas Cromwell', *Historical Journal* 23 (1980), 681–7; Guy, *Christopher St German on Chancery and Statute* (London, 1985).

20 See John Guy, 'The king's council and political participation', in Fox and Guy (eds), *Reassessing the Henrician Age*, pp. 121–47.

21 See David Dean, 'Image and ritual in the Tudor parliaments', in Hoak (ed.), *Tudor Political Culture*, pp. 243–71.

3 Pilgrimage, Dissolution and Reform: England 1536–40

1 On the fall of Anne Boleyn, as with other aspects of her career the subject of heated recent debate, see E. W. Ives, *Anne Boleyn* (Oxford, 1986); Retha M. Warnicke, *The Rise and Fall of Anne Boleyn: Family politics at the court of Henry VIII* (Cambridge, 1989) (reviewed by Ives in *Historical Journal* 34 [1991], 194–200); G. W. Bernard, 'The fall of Anne Boleyn', *English Historical Review* 106 (1991), 584–610, and the subsequent contributions by Ives, Bernard and Warnicke in *English Historical Review* 106 and 107; Warnicke, 'Family and kinship relations at the Henrician court: the Boleyns and the Howards', in Dale Hoak (ed.), *Tudor Political Culture* (Cambridge, 1995), pp. 31–53. Much has recently been made of reports that the foetus was deformed – a misfortune supposedly interpreted by

Henry as a divine censure upon his marriage. The evidence for this, however, first appears fifty years after the event. More significant, perhaps, are suggestions that this was Anne's first pregnancy since the birth of Elizabeth, reflecting on her capacity to bear further children (John Dewhurst, 'The alleged miscarriages of Catherine of Aragon and Anne Boleyn', *Medical History* 28 [1984], 49–56).

2   Specific charges of impropriety remain highly tenuous; see Warnicke, 'The eternal triangle and court politics: Henry VIII, Anne Boleyn, and Sir Thomas Wyatt', *Albion* 18 (1986), 565–79; 'Sexual heresy at the court of Henry VIII', *Historical Journal* 30 (1987), 247–68; 'The fall of Anne Boleyn revisited', *English Historical Review* 108 (1993), 653–65.

3   E. W. Ives, 'Anne Boleyn and the early reformation in England: the contemporary evidence', *Historical Journal* 37 (1994), 389–400.

4   For Cromwell's promotion to the vice-gerency see F. Donald Logan, 'Thomas Cromwell and the vicegerency in spirituals: a revisitation', *English Historical Review* 103 (1988), 658–67.

5   On the forces behind rebellion consider the different emphases in G. R. Elton, 'Politics and the Pilgrimage of Grace', in *Studies in Tudor and Stuart Politics and Government* (4 vols, Cambridge, 1974–92), III, pp. 183–215; Michael Bush, *The Pilgrimage of Grace: A study of the rebel armies of October 1536* (Manchester, 1996); and C. S. L. Davies, 'Popular religion and the Pilgrimage of Grace', in Anthony Fletcher and John Stevenson (eds), *Order and Disorder in Early Modern England* (Cambridge, 1985), pp. 58–91.

6   C. E. Moreton, 'The Walsingham conspiracy of 1537', *Historical Research* 63 (1990), 29–43.

7   J. M. W. Bean, *The Decline of English Feudalism 1215–1540* (Manchester, 1968), pp. 298–300; A. R. Buck, 'The politics of land law in Tudor England 1529–1540', *Journal of Legal History* 11 (1990), 200–17.

8   M. L. Bush, 'Captain Poverty and the Pilgrimage of Grace', *Historical Research* 65 (1992), 17–36.

9   R. W. Hoyle, 'The first earl of Cumberland: a reputation reassessed', *Northern History* 22 (1986), 63–94.

10 M. L. Bush, '"Enhancements and importunate charges": an analysis of the tax complaints of October 1536', *Albion* 22 (1990), 403–19. For the strong tradition of resistance to taxation in Yorkshire and Lancashire, see R. W. Hoyle, 'Resistance and manipulation in early Tudor taxation: some evidence from the north', *Archives* 20 (1993), 158–76.

11 On the increasingly apocalyptic nature and significance of political prophecy see Alistair Fox, 'Prophecies and politics in the reign of Henry VIII', in Alistair Fox and John Guy (eds), *Reassessing the Henrician Age: Humanism, politics and reform 1500–1550* (Oxford, 1986), pp. 77–94.

12 J. A. Guy, 'Privy council: revolution or evolution?', in Christopher Coleman and David Starkey (eds), *Revolution Reassessed: Revisions in the history of Tudor government and administration* (Oxford, 1986), pp. 59–85, esp. pp. 77–9; Starkey, 'Court, council and nobility in Tudor England', in Ronald G. Asch and Adolf M. Birke (eds), *Princes, Patronage, and the Nobility: The court at the beginning of the modern age c.1450–1650* (Oxford, 1991), pp. 175–203.

13 Amanda Bevan, 'The Henrician assizes and the enforcement of the Reformation', in R. Eales and D. Sullivan (eds), *The Political Context of Law* (London, 1987), pp. 61–76.

14 Tyndale had been betrayed into imperial hands and executed for heresy in Germany during 1536. See Thomas F. Mayer, 'If martyrs are to be exchanged with

martyrs: the kidnappings of William Tyndale and Reginald Pole', *Reformation History* 81 (1990), 286–307.

15 The picture is not uniform. Claire Cross, 'Monasticism and society in the diocese of York 1520–1540', *Transactions of the Royal Historical Society*, 5th series 38, 131–45, uses testamentary evidence to show Yorkshire houses still supplying 'succour to the living' and spiritual comfort to souls departed. Her study of wills suggests little or no tailing off in bequests during the 1530s.

16 Helen Miller, *Henry VIII and the English Nobility* (Oxford, 1986), p. 253.

17 See Susan Brigden, ' "The shadow that you know": Sir Thomas Wyatt and Sir Francis Bryan at court and in embassy', *Historical Journal* 39 (1996), 1–31.

18 On Cromwell's cooperative and generally successful administration of the western counties through local gentlemen see Mary L. Robertson, ' "The art of the possible": Thomas Cromwell's management of west country government', *Historical Journal* 32 (1989), 793–816.

19 See Maria Dowling, 'The gospel and the court: reformation under Henry VIII', in Peter Lake and Maria Dowling (eds), *Protestantism and the National Church in Sixteenth-century England* (London, 1987), pp. 36–77.

20 The king's backing for this legislation is examined in Glyn Redworth, 'A study in the formulation of policy: the genesis and evolution of the Act of Six Articles', *Journal of Ecclesiastical History* 37 (1986), 42–67.

21 On these events, Elton, 'Thomas Cromwell's decline and fall', *Cambridge Historical Journal* 10 (1951), 150–85, remains essential reading. On the spread of protestantism in London, and the authorities' abortive attempts at repression in 1540, see Susan Brigden, 'Popular disturbance and the fall of Thomas Cromwell and the reformers, 1539–40', *Historical Journal* 24 (1981), 257–78.

22 Anne gracefully accepted the king's 'liberality' in the form of a substantial annuity and precedence immediately below the new queen and royal issue. She died in 1557.

4 The Last Years of Henry VIII: England 1540–7

1 Syphilis and, more recently, scurvy, have been suggested as underlying causes of Henry's degeneration by those examining the far from adequate medical evidence available.

2 Richard Rex, *Henry VIII and the English Reformation* (Basingstoke, 1993). See also G. W. Bernard, 'The Church of England *c.*1529–*c.*1642', *History* 75 (1990), 183–206, esp. 184–6, and Diarmaid MacCulloch, 'Henry VIII and the reform of the church', in MacCulloch (ed.), *The Reign of Henry VIII: Politics, policy and piety* (London, 1995), pp. 159–80.

3 As is so often the case with sixteenth-century works, its official title, *A Necessary Doctrine and Erudition for any Christian Man*, cries out for abbreviation.

4 M. L. Zell, 'The Prebendaries' Plot of 1543: a reconsideration', *Journal of Ecclesiastical History* 27 (1976), 241–53; Diarmaid MacCulloch, *Thomas Cranmer: A life* (London, 1996), ch. 8.

5 Dale Hoak, 'The iconography of the crown imperial', in Hoak (ed.), *Tudor Political Culture* (Cambridge, 1995), pp. 54–103, esp. pp. 89–94; John N. King, 'The royal image, 1535–1603', in ibid., pp. 104–32.

6 Cromwell received the earldom of Essex after the death of Henry Bourchier, second earl. After Cromwell's attainder, and the king's sixth marriage, the title

was granted to Parr on the strength of his marriage to Bourchier's only daughter, Anne. Ironically, that marriage had by then broken down irretrievably.

7 See Maria Dowling, 'The gospel and the court: reformation under Henry VIII', in Peter Lake and Maria Dowling (eds), *Protestantism and the National Church in Sixteenth-century England* (London, 1987), pp. 36–77.

8 For an examination of this legislation, which arose from the individual concerns of towns and which enjoyed an ever-changing degree of government support, see Robert Tittler, 'For the "Re-edification of Townes": the rebuilding statutes of Henry VIII', *Albion* 22 (1990), 591–605.

9 Steven Gunn, 'The French wars of Henry VIII', in Jeremy Black (ed.), *The Origins of War in Early Modern Europe* (Edinburgh, 1987), pp. 28–51, examines Henry's continental expeditions.

5 Pre-Reformation Scotland, 1528–57

1 On the literary and cultural prejudice against the north in western tradition see Arthur H. Williamson, 'Scots, Indians and Empire: the Scottish politics of civilisation 1519–1609', *Past and Present* 150 (February 1996), 46–83.

2 See Sara Warnecke, 'A taste for newfangledness: the destructive potential of novelty in early modern England', *Sixteenth Century Journal* 26 (1995), 881–96.

3 See Alf Åberg, 'Scottish soldiers in the Swedish armies in the sixteenth and seventeenth centuries', in Grant G. Simpson (ed.), *Scotland and Scandinavia 800–1800* (Edinburgh, 1990), pp. 90–9.

4 Margaret H. B. Sanderson, *Scottish Rural Society in the Sixteenth Century* (Edinburgh, 1982), p. 169.

5 See Hector L. MacQueen, ' "Regiam Majestatem", Scots law, and national identity', *Scottish Historical Review* 74 (1995), 1–25.

6 Jenny Wormald, 'Bloodfeud, kindred and government in early modern Scotland', *Past and Present* 87 (May 1980), 54–97.

7 Technically, Scots, but the jury remains out on whether we have here a once-distinct tongue gradually merging with English, or simply a strong regional variant.

8 Nobility, high clergy and burgh commissioners. Freeholder lairds sat as shire commissioners as a fourth estate from 1587. See J. Goodare, 'The estates in the Scottish parliament, 1286–1707', in Clyve Jones (ed.), *The Scots and Parliament* (Edinburgh, 1996), pp. 11–32.

9 G. W. S. Barrow, *Kingship and Unity: Scotland 1000–1306* (London, 1981), p. 169.

10 Jenny Wormald, *Court, Kirk and Community: Scotland 1470–1625* (London, 1981), p. 12.

11 See Thomas Riis, 'Scottish–Danish relations in the sixteenth century', in T. C. Smout (ed.), *Scotland and Europe 1200–1850* (Edinburgh, 1986), pp. 82–96.

12 For an examination of the custumars' accounts see Isabel Guy, 'The Scottish export trade, 1460–1599', in Smout (ed.), *Scotland and Europe*, pp. 62–81.

13 George Hewitt, *Scotland under Morton 1572–80* (Edinburgh, 1982), p. 2, quoting David Hume of Godscroft.

14 For religious dissent before 1560 see James Kirk, 'The religion of early Scottish protestants', in Kirk (ed.), *Humanism and Reform: The church in Europe, England, and Scotland, 1400–1643. Essays in honour of James K. Cameron* (Oxford, 1991), pp. 361–411, quote at p. 388.

15 Mark Dilworth, 'The commendator system in Scotland', *Innes Review* 37 (1986), 51–72.

16 On the functions of bailies see Peter J. Murray, 'The lay administrators of church lands in the fifteenth and sixteenth centuries', *Scottish Historical Review* 74 (1995), 26–44.

17 T. M. Y. Manson, 'Shetland in the sixteenth century', in Ian B. Cowan and Duncan Shaw (eds), *The Renaissance and Reformation in Scotland: Essays in honour of Gordon Donaldson* (Edinburgh, 1983), pp. 200–13; Brian Smith, 'Shetland, Scandinavia, Scotland, 1300–1700: the changing nature of contact', in Simpson (ed.), *Scotland and Scandinavia*, pp. 25–37.

18 John Morrill, 'The fashioning of Britain', in S. G. Ellis and S. Barber (eds), *Conquest and Union: Fashioning a British state, 1485–1725* (London, 1995), pp. 8–39, quote at p. 19.

19 Some indication of Henry's military commitment to Scotland can be found in E. A. Bonner, 'Continuing the "auld alliance" in the sixteenth century: Scots in France and French in Scotland', in Grant G. Simpson (ed.), *The Scottish Soldier Abroad, 1247–1967* (Edinburgh, 1992), pp. 31–46.

20 On Pinkie in a Scottish context see D. Caldwell, 'The Battle of Pinkie', in Norman Macdougall (ed.), *Scotland and War, AD 79–1918* (Edinburgh, 1991), pp. 61–94.

21 Elizabeth Bonner, 'The recovery of St Andrews Castle in 1547: French naval policy and diplomacy in the British Isles', *English Historical Review* 111 (1996), 578–98.

22 Wormald, *Court, Kirk and Community*, p. 92.

23 Arran is henceforth referred to by his higher, French title.

6 The Reformation and the Reign of Queen Mary: Scotland 1557–67

1 The book had been published early in 1558, shortly before Mary Tudor's death! Regiment in this context means rule, or government.

2 See Jane Dawson, 'Two kingdoms or three?: Ireland in Anglo-Scottish relations in the middle of the sixteenth century', in Roger A. Mason (ed.), *Scotland and England 1286–1815* (Edinburgh, 1987), pp. 113–38.

3 See W. Ian P. Hazlett, 'The Scots Confession 1560: context, complexion and critique', *Reformation History* 78 (1987), 287–320.

4 Elaine Finnie, 'The House of Hamilton: patronage, politics and the church in the reformation period', *Innes Review* 36 (1985), 3–28.

5 See Jenny Wormald, ' "Princes" and the regions in the Scottish Reformation', in Norman Macdougall (ed.), *Church, Politics and Society: Scotland 1408–1929* (Edinburgh, 1983), pp. 65–84.

6 For St Andrews see Jane Dawson, ' "The face of ane perfyt reformed kyrk": St Andrews and the early Scottish reformation', in James Kirk (ed.), *Humanism and Reform: The church in Europe, England, and Scotland, 1400–1643. Essays in honour of James K. Cameron* (Oxford, 1991), pp. 413–35.

7 See Michael Yellowlees, 'The ecclesiastical establishment of the diocese of Dunkeld at the reformation', *Innes Review* 36 (1985), 74–85.

8 Julian Goodare, 'Scotland', in Bob Scribner, Roy Porter and Mikulas Teich (eds), *The Reformation in National Context* (Cambridge, 1994), pp. 95–110.

9 For a hostile analysis of Mary's statecraft see Jenny Wormald, *Mary Queen of Scots: A study in failure* (London, 1988). The queen is just as determinedly

defended by Michael Lynch in a review of this work, appearing in the *Journal of Ecclesiastical History* 41 (1990), 69–73, and in his introduction to *Mary Stewart, Queen in Three Kingdoms* (Oxford, 1988). Maurice Lee's review article, 'The daughter of debate: Mary Queen of Scots after 400 years', *Scottish Historical Review* 68 (1989), 70–9, surveys recent work on the subject.

10 The importance of the income from Mary's French lands is explored by M. Greengrass, 'Mary, dowager queen of France', in Lynch (ed.), *Mary Stewart, Queen in Three Kingdoms*, pp. 171–94.

11 On the Bannatyne MS see D. Fox and W. A. Ringler (eds), *The Bannatyne Manuscript* (London, 1980), and for more light on the political background to its compilation, Alasdair A. MacDonald, 'The Bannatyne Manuscript – a Marian anthology', *Innes Review* 37 (1986), 36–47.

12 A. A. MacDonald, 'Mary Stewart's entry to Edinburgh: an ambiguous triumph', *Innes Review* 42 (1991), 101–10, suggests that the ceremony was engineered by the strongly protestant town council, using the means at its disposal to exhort and threaten Mary into adopting the mantle of a protestant prince.

13 He died nearly fifty years later, in 1609.

14 On Huntly's authority in the north-east see Allan White OP, 'Queen Mary's northern province', in Lynch (ed.), *Mary Stewart, Queen in Three Kingdoms*, pp. 53–70.

15 Jane Dawson, 'The fifth earl of Argyle, Gaelic lordship and political power in sixteenth-century Scotland', *Scottish Historical Review* 67 (1988), 1–27.

16 For two, not necessarily mutually exclusive, interpretations of events leading up to the Darnley marriage see Jane Dawson, 'Mary Queen of Scots, Lord Darnley, and Anglo-Scottish relations in 1565', *International History Review* 8 (1986), 1–24, and Simon Adams, 'The release of Lord Darnley and the failure of the amity', in Lynch (ed.), *Mary Stewart, Queen in Three Kingdoms*, pp. 123–53.

17 We shall continue to use the familiar title, although Darnley was duke of Albany and king of Scotland from this month.

18 See Ian B. Cowan, 'The Roman connection: prospects for counter-reformation during the personal reign of Mary, Queen of Scots', and Julian Goodare, 'Queen Mary's Catholic interlude', both in Lynch (ed.), *Mary Stewart, Queen in Three Kingdoms*, pp. 105–22, 154–70.

19 Gordon Donaldson, *Scotland: James V to James VII* (Edinburgh, 1965), p. 120.

20 Michael Lynch suggests that there may even be hints at 'Charlemagne' in the names – he argues that the ceremonial employed at Stirling was a deliberate imitation of Valois pageantry in 1564–5, with the same goal of fostering reconciliation and unity ('Queen Mary's triumph: the baptismal celebrations at Stirling in December 1566', *Scottish Historical Review* 69 [1990], 1–21).

7 Protector Somerset: England 1547–9

1 E. W. Ives, 'Henry VIII's will – a forensic conundrum', *Historical Journal* 35 (1992), 779–804; see also R. A. Houlbrooke, 'Henry VIII's wills: a comment', *Historical Journal* 37 (1994), 891–9.

2 See Helen Miller, 'Henry VIII's unwritten will: grants of lands and honours in 1547', in E. W. Ives et al. (eds), *Wealth and Power in Tudor England: Essays presented to S. T. Bindoff* (London, 1978), pp. 87–105.

3 See A. J. Slavin, 'The fall of lord chancellor Wriothesley: a study in the politics of conspiracy', *Albion* 7 (1975), 265–86.

4 G. W. Bernard, 'The downfall of Sir Thomas Seymour', in G. W. Bernard (ed.), *The Tudor Nobility* (Manchester, 1992), pp. 212–40.

5 John Murphy, 'The illusion of decline: the privy chamber, 1547–1558', in David Starkey (ed.), *The English Court: From the wars of the Roses to the Civil War* (London, 1987), pp. 119–46.

6 On support from protestant Scots for a British union see Roger A. Mason, 'The Scottish Reformation and the origins of Anglo-British imperialism', in Roger A. Mason (ed.), *Scots and Britons: Scottish political thought and the Union of 1603* (Cambridge, 1994), pp. 161–86.

7 M. L. Bush, *The Government Policy of Protector Somerset* (London, 1975), pp. 37–8.

8 The book was in large measure Cranmer's own work, drawing as ever on a bewilderingly broad array of sources.

9 On Kett's rebellion see Diarmaid MacCulloch, 'Kett's rebellion in context', *Past and Present* 84 (August 1979), 36–59 (quote at p. 47); and his debate with Julian Cornwall in *Past and Present* 93 (November 1981), 160–73.

10 Joyce Youings, 'The south-western rebellion of 1549', *Southern History* 1 (1979), 99–122.

11 See James S. Berkman, 'Van der Delft's message: a reappraisal of the attack on protector Somerset', *Bulletin of the Institute of Historical Research* 53 (1980), 247–52.

12 A graphic, first-hand relation of these events can be found in A. J. A. Malkiewicz, 'An eye-witness's account of the coup d'état of October 1549', *English Historical Review* 70 (1955), 600–9.

8 The Dudley Supremacy and the Reign of Jane Grey: England 1549–53

1 See David Loades, 'Thomas Cranmer and John Dudley: an uneasy alliance, 1549–1553', in Paul Ayris and David Selwyn (eds), *Thomas Cranmer: Churchman and scholar* (Woodbridge, 1993), pp. 157–72.

2 H. James, 'The aftermath of the 1549 coup and the earl of Warwick's intentions', *Historical Research* 62 (1989), 91–7.

3 Dale Hoak, 'Rehabilitating the duke of Northumberland: politics and political control, 1549–1553', in Jennifer Loach and Robert Tittler (eds), *The Mid-Tudor Polity c.1540–1560* (London, 1980), pp. 29–51.

4 C. S. Knighton, 'The principal secretaries in the reign of Edward VI: reflections on their office and archive', in Claire Cross, David Loades and J. J. Scarisbrick (eds), *Law and Government under the Tudors* (Cambridge, 1988), pp. 163–75.

5 See Rex Pogson, 'God's law and Man's: Stephen Gardiner and the problem of loyalty', in ibid., pp. 67–89, and G. R. Redworth, *In Defence of the Church Catholic: A life of Stephen Gardiner* (Oxford, 1990).

6 Susan Brigden, 'The letters of Richard Scudamore to Sir Philip Hoby, September 1549–March 1555', *Camden Miscellany 30* (London, 1990), pp. 67–148.

7 For the complex diplomacy behind the Treaty of Boulogne, March 1550, see David Potter, 'The treaty of Boulogne and European diplomacy 1549–50', *Bulletin of the Institute of Historical Research* 55 (1982), 50–65.

8 Dale Hoak, 'The secret history of the Tudor court: the king's coffers and the king's purse, 1542–1553', *Journal of British Studies* 26 (1987), 208–31.

9 Barrett L. Beer, 'Episcopacy and reform in mid-Tudor England', *Albion* 23 (1991), 231–52.

10 Diarmaid MacCulloch, *Thomas Cranmer: A life* (London, 1996), p. 509.

11 On the late enforcement of the Forty-two Articles see Paul Ayris, 'Continuity and change in diocese and province: the role of a Tudor bishop', *Historical Journal* 39 (1996), 291–313, esp. 308–11.

12 Christopher Haigh, *English Reformations: Religion, politics and society under the Tudors* (Oxford, 1993), p. 181.

13 Barrett L. Beer, 'London parish clergy and the protestant reformation, 1547–1559', *Albion* 18 (1986), 375–91, illustrates how the careful study of a particular area can provide evidence supporting both the advocates of rapid and gradual reformation in England.

14 On the positions taken by Edwardian reformers see Catharine Davies, ' "Poor persecuted little flock" or "Commonwealth of Christians"; Edwardian protestant concepts of the church', in Peter Lake and Maria Dowling (eds), *Protestantism and the National Church in Sixteenth-century England* (London, 1987), pp. 78–102.

15 In *Edward VI: The threshold of power* (London, 1970); and in Jordan and M. R. Gleason, 'The saying of John late duke of Northumberland upon the scaffold, 1553', *Harvard Library Bulletin* 23 (1975), 139–79, 324–55.

16 See R. Tittler and S. L. Battley, 'The local community and the crown in 1553: the accession of Mary Tudor revisited', *Bulletin of the Institute of Historical Research* 57 (1984), 131–9.

17 The quality of Northumberland's armed forces in 1553 has recently been scrutinized: see R. C. Braddock, 'The character and composition of the duke of Northumberland's army', *Albion* 6 (1974), 342–56, and further discussion by W. J. Tighe and Braddock in ibid., 19 (1987), 1–11 and 13–17. See also J. D. Alsop, 'A regime at sea: the navy and the 1553 succession crisis', *Albion* 24 (1992), 577–90.

18 The task of disentangling responsibility for the scheme to set aside Mary's claim is complicated by mutual recriminations among the vanquished. Even on their walk to the scaffold, both the duke and Sir John Gates, while forgiving one another in the accustomed fashion, alleged that the other man bore some responsibility for their ruin. See N. P. Sil, 'The rise and fall of Sir John Gates', *Historical Journal* 24 (1981), 929–43.

9 *Queen Mary's Regime: England 1553–8*

1 David Loades, *The Reign of Mary Tudor: Politics, government and religion in England 1553–58* (2nd edn, London, 1991), pp. 404–11.

2 Dale Hoak, 'Two revolutions in Tudor government: the formation and organisation of Mary I's privy council', in Christopher Coleman and David Starkey (eds), *Revolution Reassessed: Revisions in the history of Tudor government and administration* (Oxford, 1986), pp. 87–115.

3 For one such attempt see Elizabeth Russell, 'Mary Tudor and Mr Jorkins', *Historical Research* 63 (1990), 263–76.

4 For a persuasive argument that Gardiner subsequently gave solid support to Philip see Peter Donaldson (ed.), *A Machiavellian Treatise by Stephen Gardiner* (Cambridge, 1975), and Donaldson, 'Bishop Gardiner, Machiavellian', *Historical Journal* 23 (1980), 1–16.

5 William B. Robison, 'The national and local significance of Wyatt's rebellion in Surrey', *Historical Journal* 30 (1987), 769–90. Courtenay was subsequently

exiled and, his name still linked with that of Elizabeth, became the target of Spanish assassination attempts. He died in somewhat suspicious circumstances and was buried, in Padua, in September 1556.

6   Joy Shakespeare, 'Plague and punishment', in Peter Lake and Maria Dowling (eds), *Protestantism and the National Church in Sixteenth-century England* (London, 1987), pp. 103–23.

7   Andrew Pettegree, 'The Latin polemic of the Marian exiles', in James Kirk (ed.), *Humanism and Reform: The church in Europe, England, and Scotland, 1400–1643. Essays in honour of James K. Cameron* (Oxford, 1991), pp. 305–29; Pettegree, 'The London exile community and the second sacramentarian controversy, 1553–1560', *Archive for Reformation History* 78 (1987), 223–51.

8   On Pole's role in Marian government see Rex Pogson, 'Reginald Pole and the priorities of government in Mary Tudor's church', *Historical Journal* 18 (1975), 3–20.

9   Diarmaid MacCulloch, *Thomas Cranmer: A life* (London, 1996), ch. 13; Rudolph W. Heinze, '"I pray God to grant that I may endure to the end": A new look at the martyrdom of Thomas Cranmer', in Paul Ayris and David Selwyn (eds), *Thomas Cranmer: Churchman and scholar* (Woodbridge, 1993), pp. 261–80.

10 See Jennifer Loach, 'The Marian establishment and the printing press', *English Historical Review* 101 (1986), 135–48.

11 For protestant resistance theory see Gerry Bowler, 'Marian protestants and the idea of violent resistance to tyranny', in Lake and Dowling (eds), *Protestantism and the National Church*, pp. 124–43.

12 David Loades, 'The piety of the Catholic restoration in England, 1553–1558', in Kirk (ed.), *Humanism and Reform*, pp. 289–304, quote at p. 293.

13 On first fruits see Patrick Carter, 'Mary Tudor, parliament and the renunciation of first fruits, 1555', *Historical Research* 69 (1996), 340–6. Exiles naturally condemned attempts to seize their lands. John Ponet's *Short Treatise of Politic Power* contained explicit references to the government's measures (see Barbara Peardon, 'The politics of polemic: John Ponet's *Short Treatise of Politic Power* and contemporary circumstance, 1553–1556', *Journal of British Studies* 22 [1982], 35–49).

14 See James Alsop, 'Nicholas Brigham (d 1558), scholar, antiquary, and crown servant', *Sixteenth Century Journal* 12 (1981), 49–67.

15 David Loades, 'Philip II and the government of England', in Claire Cross, David Loades and J. J. Scarisbrick (eds), *Law and Government under the Tudors* (Cambridge, 1988), pp. 177–94.

16 David Potter, 'The duc de Guise and the fall of Calais', *English Historical Review* 98 (1983), 481–512.

17 See David Potter, 'The international mercenary market in the sixteenth century: Anglo-French competition in Germany, 1543–50', *English Historical Review* 111 (1996), 24–58.

18 On the subject of 'military decline' and the remedies adopted see Jeremy Goring, 'Social change and military decline in mid-Tudor England', *History* 60 (1975), 185–97.

10   The Third Kingdom: Ireland, and Beyond, 1529–60

1   For comparisons of the different experiences of Wales and Ireland under the Tudors see Ciaran Brady, 'Comparable histories?: Tudor reform in Wales and Ireland', in S. G. Ellis and S. Barber (eds), *Conquest and Union: Fashioning*

a *British state, 1485–1725* (London, 1995), pp. 64–86; Brendan Bradshaw, 'The Tudor reformation and revolution in Wales and Ireland: the origins of the British problem', in Brendan Bradshaw and John Morrill (eds), *The British Problem, c.1534–1707: State formation in the Atlantic archipelago* (London, 1996), pp. 39–65.

2 For reflections on the ways in which historians have conceived and written of Irish history see Brendan Bradshaw, 'Nationalism and historical scholarship in modern Ireland', *Irish Historical Studies* 26 (1989), 329–51; Steven G. Ellis, 'Representations of the past in Ireland: whose past and whose present?', *Irish Historical Studies* 27 (1991), 289–308.

3 Under the terms of the so-called Poynings' Law, the Irish parliament, for example, might consider no measure that had not been first approved by king and council in England. It was summoned only six times between 1536 and 1603.

4 See Anthony Sheehan, 'Irish towns in a period of change, 1558–1625', in Ciaran Brady and Raymond Gillespie (eds), *Natives and Newcomers: The making of Irish colonial society, 1534–1641* (Dublin, 1986), pp. 93–119.

5 On Gaelic society see Kenneth W. Nicholls, *Gaelic and Gaelicised Society in Late Medieval Ireland* (Dublin, 1972). For a brief introduction see Mary O'Dowd, 'Gaelic economy and society', in Brady and Gillespie (eds), *Natives and Newcomers*, pp. 120–47.

6 For some of the problems and possibilities in the interpretation of bardic poetry see Bernadette Cunningham, 'Native culture and political change in Ireland, 1580–1640', in Brady and Gillespie (eds), *Natives and Newcomers*, pp. 148–70.

7 See Steven Ellis, 'The Tudors and the origins of the modern Irish states: a standing army', in Thomas Bartlett and Keith Jeffery (eds), *A Military History of Ireland* (Cambridge, 1996), pp. 116–35.

8 See Steven Ellis, 'Henry VIII, rebellion and the rule of law', *Historical Journal* 24 (1981), 513–31.

9 For a slightly more positive interpretation of Cromwell's contribution to the administration of Ireland see Steven Ellis, 'Thomas Cromwell and Ireland, 1532–1540', *Historical Journal* 23 (1980), 497–519.

10 For some introductory remarks on the constitutional relationship in the Middle Ages see James Lydon, 'Ireland and the English crown, 1171–1541', *Irish Historical Studies* 29 (1995), 281–94. Tudor historians unhappy with the papal grant as a justification of English authority over Ireland fell back on the myth of an Arthurian conquest detailed in the early twelfth century *Historia* of Geoffrey of Monmouth, or on other legends that suggested ancient subjection to the rulers of the larger island. Andrew Hadfield, 'British and Scythian: Tudor representations of Irish origins', *Irish Historical Studies* 28 (1993), 390–408.

11 See Nerys Patterson, 'Gaelic law and the Tudor conquest of Ireland: the social background of the sixteenth-century recensions of the pseudo-historical Prologue to the *Senchas már*', *Irish Historical Studies* 27 (1991), 193–215.

12 See David Edwards, 'Beyond reform, martial law and the Tudor reconquest of Ireland', *History Ireland* 5 (2) (Summer 1997), 16–21.

13 Henry A. Jefferies, 'The Irish parliament of 1560: the anglican reforms authorised', *Irish Historical Studies* 26 (1988), 128–41.

14 For a survey of the triangular relationship between the three kingdoms see Jane Dawson, 'Two kingdoms or three?: Ireland in Anglo-Scottish relations in the middle of the sixteenth century', in Roger A. Mason (ed.), *Scotland and England 1286–1815* (Edinburgh, 1987), pp. 113–38.

15 David Potter, 'French intrigue in Ireland during the reign of Henri II, 1547–1559', *International History Review* 5 (1983), 159–80.
16 For a survey of Henrician policy see David Potter, 'Foreign policy', in D. MacCulloch (ed.), *The Reign of Henry VIII: Politics, policy and piety* (London, 1995), pp. 101–33.

11 The Elizabethan Settlement: England 1558–63

1 M. J. Rodríguez-Salgado and Simon Adams (eds), 'The count of Feria's dispatch to Philip II of 14 November 1558', *Camden Miscellany 28* (London, 1984), pp. 302–44.
2 See N. M. Sutherland, 'The Marian exiles and the establishment of the Elizabethan régime', *Archive for Reformation History* 78 (1987), 253–84.
3 Patrick Collinson, 'Sir Nicholas Bacon and the Elizabethan *via media*', *Historical Journal* 23 (1980), 255–73.
4 See his article 'Elizabeth's first year: the conception and birth of the Elizabethan political world', in Christopher Haigh (ed.), *The Reign of Elizabeth I* (Basingstoke, 1984), pp. 27–53; and his book, *The Birth of the Elizabethan Age: England in the 1560s* (Oxford, 1993).
5 On the careers of the Marian bishops see Kenneth W. T. Carleton, 'English Catholic bishops in the early Elizabethan era', *Recusant History* 23 (1996), 1–15.
6 See Eric Josef Carlson, 'Clerical marriage and the English reformation', *Journal of British Studies* 31 (1992), 1–31.
7 For clues to Elizabeth's religious beliefs, see Patrick Collinson, 'Windows in a woman's soul: questions about the religion of Queen Elizabeth I', in his *Elizabethan Essays* (London, 1994), pp. 87–118.
8 See Norman L. Jones, 'Profiting from religious reform: the land rush of 1559', *Historical Journal* 22 (1979), 279–94; Gina Alexander, 'Bishop Bonner and the parliament of 1559', *Bulletin of the Institute of Historical Research* 56 (1983), 164–79.
9 There were several prosecutions under this act for first refusals of the oath, which were treated as praemunire offences, though harsh penalties were rare; see Leslie Ward, 'The treason act of 1563: a study of the enforcement of anti-Catholic legislation', *Parliamentary History* 8 (1989), 289–308.
10 See David Crankshaw, 'Preparations for the Canterbury provincial convocation of 1562–63: a question of attribution', in Susan Wabuda and Caroline Litzenberger (eds), *Belief and Practice in Sixteenth-century England* (St Andrews, 1998). I am grateful to Dr Crankshaw for allowing me to read a draft of his article.

12 UnElizabethan England: England 1560–72

1 See Richard C. McCoy, 'From the Tower to the tiltyard: Robert Dudley's return to glory', *Historical Journal* 27 (1984), 425–35.
2 See Simon Adams, 'The Dudley clientèle, 1553–1563', in G. W. Bernard (ed.), *The Tudor Nobility* (Manchester, 1992), pp. 241–65.
3 Wallace T. MacCaffrey, 'The Newhaven expedition, 1562–1563', *Historical Journal* 40 (1997), 1–21.

4   See Pam Wright, 'A change of direction: the ramifications of a female household, 1558–1603', in David Starkey (ed.), *The English Court: From the Wars of the Roses to the Civil War* (London, 1987), pp. 147–72.

5   Hunsdon, the son of Mary Boleyn, might possibly have been Elizabeth's half-brother; see Anthony Hoskins, 'Mary Boleyn's Carey children – offspring of King Henry VIII?', *Genealogists' Magazine* 25 (1997), 345–52.

6   On these negotiations: Susan Doran, 'Religion and politics at the court of Elizabeth I: the Habsburg marriage negotiations of 1559–1567', *English Historical Review* 104 (1989), 908–26.

7   See Simon Adams, 'Favourites and factions at the Elizabethan court', in Ronald G. Asch and Adolf M. Birke (eds), *Princes, Patronage, and the Nobility: The court at the beginning of the modern age c1450–1650* (Oxford, 1991), pp. 265–87.

8   Malcolm Thorp, 'Catholic conspiracy in early Elizabethan foreign policy', *Sixteenth Century Journal* 15 (1984), 431–48; Stephen Alford, 'Reassessing William Cecil in the 1560s', in John Guy (ed.), *The Tudor Monarchy* (London, 1997), pp. 233–53.

9   'Tudor government: the points of contact', in Elton, *Studies in Tudor and Stuart Politics and Government* (4 vols, Cambridge, 1974–92), III, pp. 3–57.

10 Robert Tittler, 'Elizabethan towns and the "points of contact": parliament', *Parliamentary History* 8 (1989), 275–88, questions the efficiency of parliament as a point of contact or 'political safety valve' for most English towns.

11 For some comparisons between the English parliament and the Castilian Cortes – without peers from 1539 and increasingly marginalized as a result – see Pauline Croft and I. A. A. Thompson, 'Aristocracy and representative government in unicameral and bicameral institutions. The role of peers in the Castilian Cortes and the English Parliament 1529–1664', in H. W. Blom et al. (eds), *Bicameralisme: Tweekamerstelsel vroeger en nu* ('s-Gravenhage, 1992), pp. 63–86.

12 Norman L. Jones, 'Parliament and the governance of Elizabethan England: a review', *Albion* 19 (1987), 327–46, quote at p. 346.

13 His intemperate outburst may have frustrated a more cautious scheme to further religious reform in parliament, fronted by Norton. See Thomas S. Freeman, '"The reformation of the church in this parliament": Thomas Norton, John Foxe and the parliament of 1571', *Parliamentary History* 16 (1997), 131–47.

14 See W. J. Sheils, 'Erecting the discipline in provincial England: the order of Northampton, 1571', in James Kirk (ed.), *Humanism and Reform: The church in Europe, England, and Scotland, 1400–1643. Essays in honour of James K. Cameron* (Oxford, 1991), pp. 331–45.

15 Eugene J. Bourgeois, 'The queen, a bishop, and a peer: a clash for power in mid Elizabethan Cambridgeshire', *Sixteenth Century Journal* 26 (1995), 3–15.

16 See Patrick McGrath and Joy Rowe, 'The Marian priests under Elizabeth I', *Recusant History* 17 (1984), 103–20.

17 For the conservatism in a county like Hampshire, outside both the protestant heartland of the south-east and the conservative north-west, see Ronald H. Fritze, 'The role of family and religion in the local politics of early Elizabethan England: the case of Hampshire in the 1560s', *Historical Journal* 25 (1982), 267–87.

18 Brian Dietz, 'Antwerp and London: the structure and balance of trade in the 1560s', in E. W. Ives et al. (eds), *Wealth and Power in Tudor England: Essays presented to S. T. Bindoff* (London, 1978), pp. 186–203.

19 R. Pollitt, 'An "old practizer" at bay: Thomas Bishop and the northern rebellion', *Northern History* 16 (1980), 59–84, sheds light on the tangled intrigues provoking rebellion in 1569.

20 Notably in the works popularly known as *The Papist's Commonwealth* (1572), *Leicester's Commonwealth* (1584) and *Burghley's Commonwealth* (1592). It is only the particular 'new men' who vary.

21 Gerald Bowler, '"An Axe or an Acte": the parliament of 1572 and resistance theory in early Elizabethan England', *Canadian Journal of History* 19 (1984), 349–59.

13 The Elizabethan State: England in the 1570s and After

1 See Alison Wall, '"Points of contact": court favourites and county faction in Elizabethan England', *Parergon* NS6 (1988), 215–26.

2 Mitchell Leimon and Geoffrey Parker, 'Treason and plot in Elizabethan diplomacy: the "Fame of Sir Edward Stafford" reconsidered', *English Historical Review* 111 (1996), 1134–58.

3 Important work has recently appeared on political structure and faction. For the early Tudor period see Steven Gunn, 'The structures of politics in early Tudor England', *Transactions of the Royal Historical Society*, 6th series 5 (1995), 59–90. For Elizabethan England see Simon Adams, 'Favourites and factions at the Elizabethan court', in Ronald G. Asch and Adolf M. Birke (eds), *Princes, Patronage, and the Nobility: The court at the beginning of the modern age c.1450–1650* (Oxford, 1991), pp. 265–87; Paul Hammer, 'Patronage at court, faction and the earl of Essex', in John Guy (ed.), *The Reign of Elizabeth I: Court and culture in the last decade* (Cambridge, 1995), pp. 65–86; and Natalie Mears, '*Regnum Cecilianum*? A Cecilian perspective of the court', in ibid., pp. 46–64, quote at p. 58.

4 On Sussex's opposition to intervention in the Low Countries in 1578, and his support for the Anjou marriage, see W. J. Tighe, 'The counsel of Thomas Radcliffe, earl of Sussex, to Queen Elizabeth I concerning the revolt of the Netherlands, September 1578', *Sixteenth Century Journal* 18 (1987), 323–31.

5 See Susan Doran, 'Juno versus Diana: the treatment of Elizabeth I's marriage in plays and entertainments, 1561–1581', *Historical Journal* 38 (1995), 257–74.

6 Norman Jones, 'Parliament and the political society of Elizabethan England', in Dale Hoak (ed.), *Tudor Political Culture* (Cambridge, 1995), pp. 226–42, quote at p. 242.

7 Wallace T. MacCaffrey, *Queen Elizabeth and the Making of Policy 1572–1588* (Princeton, 1981), p. 499.

8 Alison Wall, 'Patterns of politics in England, 1558–1625', *Historical Journal* 31 (1988), 947–63, quote at p. 947.

9 See W. J. Tighe, 'Courtiers and politics in Elizabethan Herefordshire: Sir James Croft, his friends and his foes', *Historical Journal* 32 (1989), 257–79.

10 A. J. Fletcher, 'Honour, reputation and local officeholding in Elizabethan and Stuart England', in A. J. Fletcher and John Stevenson (eds), *Order and Disorder in Early Modern England* (Cambridge, 1985), pp. 92–115, at p. 103.

11 C. J. Kitching, 'The quest for concealed lands in the reign of Elizabeth I', *Transactions of the Royal Historical Society*, 5th series 24 (1974), 63–78.

12 Penry Williams, *The Tudor Regime* (Oxford, 1979), p. 420.

13 See D. R. Lidington, 'Parliament and the enforcement of the penal statutes: the history of the act "In Restraint of Common Promoters" (18 Eliz. I c. 5)', *Parliamentary History* 8 (1989), 309–28.

14 On Allen see Eamon Duffy, 'William, Cardinal Allen, 1532–1594', *Recusant History* 22 (1995), 265–90.

15 For reflections on the pace and nature of the reformation see Patrick Collinson, 'England', in Bob Scribner, Roy Porter and Mikulas Teich (eds), *The Reformation in National Context* (Cambridge, 1994), pp. 80–94.

16 John Bossy, 'The heart of Robert Persons', in Thomas M. McCoog (ed.), *The Reckoned Expense. Edmund Campion and the early English Jesuits* (Woodbridge, 1996), pp. 141–58.

17 On Mary's captivity see P. J. Holmes, 'Mary Stewart in England', in Michael Lynch (ed.), *Mary Stewart, Queen in Three Kingdoms* (Oxford, 1988), pp. 195–218.

18 Compared with four heretics burnt in forty-five years.

19 See MacCaffrey, *Queen Elizabeth and the Making of Policy*, p. 142.

20 For an examination of his propaganda on behalf of the religious settlement see Jane Facey, 'John Foxe and the defence of the English church', in Peter Lake and Maria Dowling (eds), *Protestantism and the National Church in Sixteenth-century England* (London, 1987), pp. 162–92.

21 On Whitgift's reforms see Hirofumi Horie, 'The origin and the historical context of Archbishop Whitgift's "Orders" of 1586', *Archive for Reformation History* 83 (1992), 240–57. On the changing face of the Elizabethan church in the 1580s and 1590s see John Guy, 'The Elizabethan establishment and the ecclesiastical polity', in Guy (ed.), *The Reign of Elizabeth I*, pp. 126–49.

22 On the Family of Love see J. W. Martin, 'Elizabethan familists and English separatism', *Journal of British Studies* 20 (1980), 53–73.

23 Peter Lake details the concepts of authority advanced by the presbyterians and their opponents in 'Presbyterianism, the idea of a national church and the argument from divine right', in Lake and Dowling (eds), *Protestantism and the National Church*, pp. 193–224.

24 But consider too an alternative thesis, advanced most forcibly by Peter White in *Predestination, Policy and Polemic: Conflict and consensus in the English church from the Reformation to the Civil War* (Cambridge, 1992), that the majority of English bishops aimed rather for a true 'via media' between Rome and Geneva, and were hostile to strict Calvinism.

25 Michael McGiffert, 'Covenant, crown, and commons in Elizabethan puritanism', *Journal of British Studies* 20 (1980), 32–52.

26 See Ronald Hutton, 'The English Reformation and the evidence of folklore', *Past and Present* 148 (August 1995), 89–116.

14 England's Empire: Ireland, and Wider Horizons, 1560–1603

1 See Jane Dawson, 'Anglo-Scottish protestant culture and integration in sixteenth-century Britain', in S. G. Ellis and S. Barber (eds), *Conquest and Union: Fashioning a British state, 1485–1725* (London, 1995), pp. 98–9; Jenny Wormald, 'Ecclesiastical vitriol: the kirk, the puritans and the future king of England', in John Guy (ed.), *The Reign of Elizabeth I: Court and culture in the last decade* (Cambridge, 1995), pp. 171–91.

2 Keith M. Brown, 'The price of friendship: the "Well Affected" and English economic clientage in Scotland before 1603', in Roger A. Mason (ed.), *Scotland and England 1286–1815* (Edinburgh, 1987), pp. 139–62.

3   See Jenny Wormald, 'James VI, James I and the identity of Britain', in Brendan Bradshaw and John Morrill (eds), *The British Problem, c.1534–1707: State formation in the Atlantic archipelago* (London, 1996), pp. 148–71.

4   R. W. Hoyle, 'Place and public finance', *Transactions of the Royal Historical Society*, 6th series 7 (1997), 197–215, at p. 203.

5   The killers seem to have acted, at least in part, at English instigation. See C. Brady, 'The killing of Shane O'Neill: some new evidence', *Irish Sword* 15 (1982), 116–23.

6   David Edwards, 'The Butler revolt of 1569', *Irish Historical Studies* 28 (1993), 228–55.

7   Bernadette Cunningham, 'The composition of Connacht in the lordships of Clanricard and Thomond, 1577–1641', *Irish Historical Studies* 24 (1984), 1–14.

8   See too Hiram Morgan, 'The colonial venture of Sir Thomas Smith in Ulster, 1571–1575', *Historical Journal* 28 (1985), 261–78.

9   Ciaran Brady, 'Faction and the origins of the Desmond rebellion of 1579', *Irish Historical Studies* 22 (1981), 289–312.

10 Helen Coburn Walshe, 'The rebellion of William Nugent', in R. V. Comerford et al. (eds), *Religion, Conflict and Coexistence in Ireland: Essays presented to Monsignor Patrick J. Corish* (Dublin, 1990), pp. 26–52.

11 K. Bottigheimer, 'The failure of the reformation in Ireland: *une question bien posée*', *Journal of Ecclesiastical History* 36 (1985), 196–207.

12 See Steven G. Ellis, 'Economic problems of the church: why the reformation failed in Ireland', *Journal of Ecclesiastical History* 41 (1990), 239–65.

13 See Helen Coburn Walshe, 'Enforcing the Elizabethan settlement: the vicissitudes of Hugh Brady, bishop of Meath, 1563–1584', *Irish Historical Studies* 26 (1989), 352–76.

14 See Philip Jenkins, 'The Anglican church and the unity of Britain: the Welsh experience, 1560–1714', in Ellis and Barber (eds), *Conquest and Union*, pp. 115–38.

15 Victor Treadwell, 'Sir John Perrot and the Irish parliament of 1585–6', *Proceedings of the Royal Irish Academy* 85, C, no. 10 (1985), 259–308.

16 Brendan Bradshaw, 'Robe and sword in the conquest of Ireland', in Claire Cross, David Loades and J. J. Scarisbrick (eds), *Law and Government under the Tudors* (Cambridge, 1988), pp. 139–62. For an examination of Spenser's extreme policy see Ciaran Brady, 'Spenser's Irish crisis: humanism and experience in the 1590s', *Past and Present* 111 (May 1986), 17–49, and the subsequent debate between Brady and Nicholas Canny, *Past and Present* 120 (August 1988), 201–15.

17 One explanation for this curious episode is offered by Hiram Morgan, 'The fall of Sir John Perrot', in Guy (ed.), *The Reign of Elizabeth I*, pp. 109–25.

18 See Jane Dawson, 'William Cecil and the British dimension of early Elizabethan foreign policy', *History* 74 (1989), 196–216.

19 P. D. A. Harvey, *Maps in Tudor England* (London, 1993), p. 65.

20 See the review article by Andrew Pettegree in *Historical Journal* 31 (1988), 965–72.

21 A. W. Lovett, 'The Castilian bankruptcy of 1575', *Historical Journal* 23 (1980), 899–911.

22 E. I. Kouri, 'For true faith or national interest? Queen Elizabeth I and the protestant powers', in E. I. Kouri and Tom Scott, *Politics and Society in Reformation Europe* (London, 1987), pp. 411–36, quote at p. 428.

15 The Loss of Peace: England 1580–9

1   J. R. Wordie, 'Deflationary factors in the Tudor price rise', *Past and Present* 154 (February 1997), 32–70.

2   See David Cressy, 'Binding the nation: the bonds of association, 1584 and 1696', in DeLoyd J. Guth and John W. McKenna (eds), *Tudor Rule and Revolution* (Cambridge, 1982), pp. 217–34.

3   Burghley's role in events leading up to Mary's execution are detailed in Allison Heisch, 'Arguments for an execution: Queen Elizabeth's "white paper" and Lord Burghley's "blue pencil"', *Albion* 24 (1992), 591–604.

4   See Patrick Collinson, 'Ecclesiastical vitriol: religious satire in the 1590s and the invention of puritanism', in John Guy (ed.), *The Reign of Elizabeth I: Court and culture in the last decade* (Cambridge, 1995), pp. 150–70.

5   G. Parker, 'The worst-kept secret in Europe? The European intelligence community and the Spanish Armada of 1588', in K. Neilson and B. McKercher (eds), *Go Spy the Land: Military intelligence in history* (Westport, CT, 1992), pp. 49–72.

6   Hugo O'Donnell, 'The Army of Flanders and the invasion of England, 1586–8', in M. J. Rodríguez-Salgado and Simon Adams (eds), *England, Spain and the Gran Armada, 1585–1604: Essays from the Anglo-Spanish conferences, London and Madrid 1988* (Edinburgh, 1991), pp. 216–35.

7   It appears that the landing-place was to have been off Sandwich, a natural harbour for so large a fleet, but one which offered significant advantages to the defenders. See Simon Adams, 'The battle that never was: the Downs and the Armada campaign', in ibid., pp. 173–96.

8   See John S. Nolan, 'The muster of 1588', *Albion* 23 (1991), 387–407, and his important broader essay on 'The militarisation of the Elizabethan state', *Journal of Military History* 58 (1994), 391–420.

9   See Susan Frye, 'The myth of Elizabeth at Tilbury', *Sixteenth Century Journal* 23 (1992), 95–114. Happily, others are prepared to argue for the story's accuracy: Janet M. Green, '"I my self": Queen Elizabeth I's oration at Tilbury camp', *Sixteenth Century Journal* 28 (1997), 421–45.

10 Julian Lock, '"How many tercios has the Pope?" The Spanish war and the sublimation of Elizabethan anti-popery', *History* 81 (1996), 197–214.

16 A Nation at War: England in the 1590s

1   John Guy, 'The 1590s: the second reign of Elizabeth I?', in John Guy (ed.), *The Reign of Elizabeth I: Court and culture in the last decade* (Cambridge, 1995), pp. 1–19.

2   On Essex's attempts to establish an intelligence 'network' see Paul Hammer, 'The uses of scholarship: the secretariat of Robert Devereux, second earl of Essex, c.1585–1601', *English Historical Review* 109 (1994), 26–51; 'Essex and Europe: evidence from confidential instructions by the earl of Essex, 1595–6', *English Historical Review* 111 (1996), 357–81.

3   See Hammer, 'An Elizabethan spy who came in from the cold: the return of Anthony Standen to England in 1593', *Historical Research* 65 (1992), 277–95, at 290–1. There was a strong Catholic representation in Essex's disastrous 1601 rebellion.

4   For a broader view see Simon Adams, 'The patronage of the crown in Eliza-bethan politics: the 1590s in perspective', in Guy (ed.), *The Reign of Elizabeth I*, pp. 20–45.

5   'Getting and spending: corruption in the Elizabethan ordnance', *History Today* (November 1990), 48. On corruption see R. C. Braddock, 'The rewards of office-holding in Tudor England', *Journal of British Studies* 14 (1975), 29–47.

6   R. W. Hoyle, 'Place and public finance', *Transactions of the Royal Historical Society*, 6th series 7 (1997), 197–215.

7   Patrick Collinson, 'The monarchical republic of Queen Elizabeth I', *Bulletin of the John Rylands Library* 69 (1987), 394–424.

8   Ciaran Brady, 'The captains' games: army and society in Elizabethan Ireland', in Thomas Bartlett and Keith Jeffery (eds), *A Military History of Ireland* (Cambridge, 1996), pp. 136–59, quote on p. 151.

9   On the fortunes of Elizabethan noblemen see Susan Doran, 'The finances of an Elizabethan nobleman and royal servant: a case study of Thomas Radcliffe, 3rd earl of Sussex', *Historical Research* 61 (1988), 286–300, and works there cited at 286–8.

10 The Avon valley is one, admittedly extreme, example; see J. M. Martin, 'A Warwickshire market town in adversity: Stratford-upon-Avon in the sixteenth and seventeenth centuries', *Midland History* 7 (1982), 26–41.

11 See J. Walter, 'A "Rising of the people"? The Oxfordshire Rising of 1596', *Past and Present* 107 (May 1985), 90–143.

12 Re the preceding paragraphs see Jim Sharpe, 'Social strain and social dislocation, 1585–1603', in Guy (ed.), *The Reign of Elizabeth I*, pp. 192–211. The Hext quote is at p. 192.

13 For the war see Hiram Morgan, *Tyrone's Rebellion: The outbreak of the Nine Years' War in Tudor Ireland* (Woodbridge, 1993), and also Morgan's comparison with the Netherlands revolt, 'Hugh O'Neill and the nine years war in Tudor Ireland', *Historical Journal* 36 (1993), 21–37.

14 Kenneth R. Andrews, *English Privateering Voyages to the West Indies*, Hakluyt Society, 2nd series 111 (1959).

15 See Pauline Croft, 'English commerce with Spain and the Armada War, 1558–1603', in M. J. Rodríguez-Salgado and Simon Adams (eds), *England, Spain and the Gran Armada, 1585–1604: Essays from the Anglo-Spanish conferences, London and Madrid 1988* (Edinburgh, 1991), pp. 236–63; Croft, 'Trading with the enemy, 1585–1604', *Historical Journal* 32 (1989), 281–302.

17 *The Jacobean Minority: Scotland 1568–85*

1   See John Durkan, 'The French connection in the sixteenth and early seventeenth centuries', in T. C. Smout (ed.), *Scotland and Europe, 1200–1850* (Edinburgh, 1986), pp. 19–44.

2   See Ronald Pollitt, 'The defeat of the northern rebellion and the shaping of Anglo-Scottish relations', *Scottish Historical Review* 64 (1985), 1–21.

3   For an analysis of the civil war and its outcome, see Ian B. Cowan, 'The Marian civil war, 1567–1573', in Norman Macdougall (ed.), *Scotland and War, AD 79–1918* (Edinburgh, 1991), pp. 95–112.

4   Allan White OP, 'The Regent Morton's visitation: the reformation of Aberdeen, 1574', in A. A. MacDonald et al. (eds), *The Renaissance in Scotland: Studies in litera-ture, religion, history and culture offered to John Durkan* (Leiden, 1994), pp. 246–63.

5 Elaine Finnie, 'The House of Hamilton: patronage, politics and the church in the reformation period', *Innes Review* 36 (1985), 3–28, at p. 22.

6 John Durkan, 'William Murdoch and the early Jesuit mission in Scotland', *Innes Review* 35 (1984), 3–11.

7 Complicating the foundation of Edinburgh's Town College – later to become Scotland's fourth university – in 1583, see Michael Lynch, 'The origins of Edinburgh's "Toun College": a revision article', *Innes Review* 33 (1982), 3–14.

18 The Personal Rule of James VI: Scotland 1585–1603

1 Gordon Donaldson, *Scotland: James V to James VII* (Edinburgh, 1965), pp. 214–15.

2 For the central argument to this chapter, Jenny Wormald, 'James VI and I: two kings or one?', *History* 68 (1983), 187–209. On the xenophobia of 1603 see Wormald, 'Gunpowder, treason and Scots', *Journal of British Studies* 24 (1985), 141–68.

3 Wallace T. MacCaffrey, *Elizabeth I: War and politics, 1588–1603* (Princeton, NJ, 1992), pp. 304–5.

4 George R. Hewitt, *Scotland under Morton 1572–80* (Edinburgh, 1982), p. 168.

5 Keith M. Brown, 'Noble indebtedness in Scotland between the reformation and the revolution', *Historical Research* 62 (1989), 260–75. Brown's wider thesis, of a financially led 'crisis' in the Scottish aristocracy, has not passed unchallenged; see G. W. Bernard (ed.), *The Tudor Nobility* (Manchester, 1992), p. 8.

6 See Keith M. Brown, 'The nobility of Jacobean Scotland, 1567–1625', *History Today* 34 (December 1984), 15.

7 On Bothwell's bizarre career see Edward J. Cowan, 'The darker vision of the Scottish Renaissance: the devil and Francis Stewart', in Ian B. Cowan and Duncan Shaw (eds), *The Renaissance and Reformation in Scotland: Essays in honour of Gordon Donaldson* (Edinburgh, 1983), pp. 125–40.

8 Roger A. Mason, 'George Buchanan, James VI and the presbyterians', in Roger A. Mason (ed.), *Scots and Britons: Scottish political thought and the Union of 1603* (Cambridge, 1994), pp. 112–37.

9 Years later, in the 1620s, the king still had nightmares in which he was visited by the terrible old man.

10 See Michael Lynch, 'Preaching to the converted: perspectives on the Scottish Reformation', in A. A. MacDonald et al. (eds), *The Renaissance in Scotland: Studies in literature, religion, history and culture offered to John Durkan* (Leiden, 1994), pp. 301–43.

11 For Seton see Maurice Lee, Jr, 'King James's popish chancellor', in Cowan and Shaw (eds), *The Renaissance and Reformation in Scotland*, pp. 170–82. For Maxwell see Keith Brown, 'The making of a politique: the counter reformation and the regional politics of John, eighth lord Maxwell', *Scottish Historical Review* 66 (1987), 152–75.

12 See Michael Lynch, 'Response: old game and new', *Scottish Historical Review* 73 (1994), 47–63.

13 The complicated structure of direct taxation is explored by Julian Goodare, 'Parliamentary taxation in Scotland, 1560–1603', *Scottish Historical Review* 68 (1989), 23–52.

14 As Bruce Galloway showed in his *The Union between England and Scotland 1603–1608* (Edinburgh, 1986), while James bargained for a close union his underlying aim was simply that English and Scot might be united 'in hearts and minds'.

19 The Elizabethan Dusk: England 1599–1603

1 Natalie Mears, '*Regnum Cecilianum*? A Cecilian perspective of the court', in John Guy (ed.), *The Reign of Elizabeth I: Court and culture in the last decade* (Cambridge, 1995), pp. 46–64.

2 David Harris Sacks, 'The countervailing of benefits: monopoly, liberty, and benevolence in Elizabethan England', in Dale Hoak (ed.), *Tudor Political Culture* (Cambridge, 1995), pp. 272–91. Elizabeth's speech is from T. E. Hartley (ed.), *Proceedings in the Parliaments of Elizabeth I* (3 vols, Leicester, 1981–95), III, p. 496.

3 On the nature of counsel in Tudor England see John Guy, 'The rhetoric of counsel in early modern England', in Hoak (ed.), *Tudor Political Culture*, pp. 292–310.

4 Mark Nicholls, 'Sir Walter Ralegh's treason: a prosecution document', *English Historical Review* 110 (1995), 902–24.

5 Steven G. Ellis, 'Tudor state formation and the shaping of the British Isles', in S. G. Ellis and S. Barber (eds), *Conquest and Union: Fashioning a British state, 1485–1725* (London, 1995), pp. 40–63.

Further Reading

As a general rule this guide to further reading selects from works published since 1980, though some important earlier texts have also been listed. It includes no work published after December 1997. Articles in journals are detailed in footnotes against relevant paragraphs in the text, and have been omitted here. For reasons of space I have avoided the inclusion of overmany local studies; those noted below represent a proliferation of excellent works relating to the counties and regions of England and Scotland.

1 British Dimensions

The current trend towards viewing English, Scottish, Welsh and Irish history from a pan-British standpoint is exemplified by S. G. Ellis, *Tudor Frontiers and Noble Power: The making of the British state*, Oxford, 1995; S. G. Ellis and S. Barber (eds), *Conquest and Union: Fashioning a British state, 1485–1725*, London, 1995; A. Grant and K. Stringer (eds), *Uniting the Kingdom?: The enigma of British History*, London, 1995; Brendan Bradshaw and John Morrill (eds), *The British Problem, c.1534–1707: State formation in the Atlantic archipelago*, London, 1996.

2 England: General Works

For important general studies on the Tudor state see John Guy, *Tudor England*, Oxford, 1988; Alan G. R. Smith, *The Emergence of a Nation State: The commonwealth of England, 1529–1660*, London, 1984; Penry Williams, *The Tudor Regime*, Oxford, 1979. Rosemary O'Day, *The Longman Companion to the Tudor Age*, London, 1995, is a useful collection of facts and dates.

MONARCHY AND COURT

John Guy's introduction and linking commentary to his reader *The Tudor Monarchy*, London, 1997, offer many important insights. On the court see David Loades, *The Tudor Court*, London, 1986, a wide-ranging survey, and David Starkey (ed.), *The English Court: From the Wars of the Roses to the Civil War*, London, 1987.

NOBILITY AND GENTRY

G. W. Bernard (ed.), *The Tudor Nobility*, Manchester, 1992, contains some important essays. Bernard's introduction illustrates the diversity of experience among sixteenth-century noblemen, and notes the mutual dependence between nobles and crown. Kate Mertes, *The English Noble Household, 1250–1600*, Oxford, 1988, provides a general introduction to the nobleman's domestic environment, while Barry Coward, *The Stanleys, Lords Stanley and Earls of Derby, 1385–1672*, Manchester, 1983, offers a study of one important noble family across several generations. The burgeoning gentry class is discussed in Felicity Heal and Clive Holmes (eds), *The Gentry in England and Wales, 1500–1700*, Basingstoke, 1994.

GOVERNMENT AND LOCAL GOVERNMENT

On the mechanics of government see the chapter introductions in G. R. Elton, *The Tudor Constitution*, 2nd edn, Cambridge, 1982; R. W. Heinze (ed.), *The Proclamations of the Tudor Kings*, Cambridge, 1976.

Many of Elton's works are listed below, but any student of the period should also be aware of the convenient gatherings of his essays and articles, *Studies in Tudor and Stuart Politics and Government*, 4 vols, Cambridge, 1974–92. Elton was the recipient of several festschriften, among them Claire Cross, David Loades and J. J. Scarisbrick (eds), *Law and Government under the Tudors*, Cambridge, 1988; DeLoyd J. Guth and John W. McKenna (eds), *Tudor Rule and Revolution*, Cambridge, 1982. Important reconsiderations of Elton's theories can be found in Christopher Coleman and David Starkey (eds), *Revolution Reassessed: Revisions in the history of Tudor government and administration*, Oxford, 1986, with, among others, chapters by Starkey on the court's role in government, Guy on the evolution of the privy council, and Hoak on Mary Tudor's privy council. A summary of current research is provided by Steven J. Gunn, *Early Tudor Government, 1485–1558*, Basingstoke, 1995.

The workings of the Tudor state deserve much more detailed study. Penry Williams, *The Tudor Regime*, Oxford, 1979, is a fine survey. The introduction to one ostensibly local study, R. G. Lang (ed.), *Two Tudor Subsidy Assessment Rolls for the City of London: 1541 and 1582*, London Record Society, 1993, provides clues to the organization of a subsidy, and some reasons behind the declining effectiveness of the tax. On fiscal policy and administration, F. C. Dietz, *English Public Finance 1485–1641*, 2 vols, London, 1964, remains the only substantial compilation of relevant statistics, though its data and conclusions must be interpreted with great care. Tudor monetary policy is discussed in Christopher E. Challis, *The Tudor Coinage*, Manchester, 1978.

For an exemplary study of local administration see Diarmaid MacCulloch, *Suffolk and the Tudors: Politics and religion in an English county 1500–1600*, Oxford, 1986.

PARLIAMENT

Jennifer Loach, *Parliament under the Tudors*, Oxford, 1991, is a general introduction. Michael A. R. Graves, *The Tudor Parliaments: Crown, Lords and Commons, 1485–1603*, London, 1985, offers a useful summary of then current work. Graves's views on the pre-Elizabethan parliaments are echoed in his *Early Tudor Parliaments, 1485–1558*, London, 1990. Electoral process has been little studied, but an honourable exception is Mark Kishlansky, *Parliamentary Selection: Social and political choice in early modern England*, Cambridge, 1986, which details the methods of selecting MPs and emphasizes the rarity of contested elections. In the misleadingly named History of Parliament series are S. T. Bindoff, *The House of Commons 1509–1558*, 3 vols, London, 1982; P. W. Hasler (ed.), *The House of Commons 1558–1603*, 3 vols, London, 1981, useful and meticulous biographical registers of Tudor MPs, but *not* histories of the institution.

FOREIGN POLICY

Susan Doran, *England and Europe, 1485–1603*, 2nd edn, London, 1996, offers a convenient introduction to Tudor foreign policy. Increasingly, specific studies are challenging the traditional focus on France, Spain and the Netherlands. See the work of E. I. Kouri and H. Zins below.

RELIGION

The debate over whether England experienced a 'fast' reformation, advanced with general popular support, or a 'slow' reformation carried through by monarchs and statesmen against the wishes of a majority of the population, remains unresolved. The case for the former is advocated elegantly in A. G. Dickens, *The English Reformation*, 2nd edn, London, 1989. The other camp emphasizes the strengths of late medieval Catholicism in England. Consult Eamon Duffy, *The Stripping of the Altars: Traditional religion in England c.1400–c.1580*, New Haven, 1992; Christopher Haigh (ed.), *The English Reformation Revised*, Cambridge, 1987; Haigh, *English Reformations: Religion, politics and society under the Tudors*, Oxford, 1993; and, the case stated most blatantly, J. J. Scarisbrick, *The Reformation and the English People*, Oxford, 1984.

David Loades, *Revolution in Religion: The English Reformation, 1530–1570*, Cardiff, 1992; D. MacCulloch, *The Later Reformation in England, 1547–1603*, Basingstoke, 1990; Rosemary O'Day, *The Debate on the English Reformation*, London, 1986; William J. Sheils, *The English Reformation, 1530–1570*, London, 1989, are all succinct attempts to synthesize the two positions.

Native English dissent has received considerable attention in recent years. John F. Davis, *Heresy and Reformation in the South-east of England, 1520–1559*, London, 1983; Margaret Spufford (ed.), *The World of Rural Dissenters, 1520–1725*, Cambridge, 1995, include some of the most up-to-date work on Lollardy. Also important on the survival and influence of Lollardy is Margaret Aston, *Lollards and Reformers: Images and literacy in late medieval religion*, London, 1984.

A number of works explore the development of English protestantism: Diarmaid MacCulloch, *Building a Godly Realm: The establishment of English protestantism, 1558–1603*, London, 1992, provides an overview useful for the whole period. Peter Lake and Maria Dowling (eds), *Protestantism and the National Church in Sixteenth-century England*, London, 1987, considers several important topics. David Loades, *Politics, Censorship and the English Reformation*, London, 1991, focuses on the impact of printing. Joseph William Martin, *Religious Radicals in Tudor England*, London, 1989, looks at the enduring if limited impact of the 1550s exiles, while Carl R. Trueman, *Luther's Legacy: Salvation and English reformers 1525–1556*, Oxford, 1994, examines the impact of Lutheranism on English reform. The works by Patrick Collinson listed in section 5 below are essential reading. Peter White in *Predestination, Policy and Polemic: Conflict and consensus in the English Church from the Reformation to the Civil War*, Cambridge, 1992, looks at the various doctrinal questions preoccupying senior churchmen across a turbulent century. Ian Green, *The Christian's ABC: Catechism and catechizing in England, c.1530–1740*, Oxford, 1996, examines the ways in which future generations of Englishmen and women were inducted into their new faith.

Several works focus on religion at a local or parish level, trying with various degrees of effort and success to draw conclusions applicable to the country as a whole. Keith Thomas, *Religion and the Decline of Magic*, London, 1971, remains a seminal work on popular religion. Beat Kümin, *The Shaping of a Community: The rise and reformation of the English parish c.1400–1560*, Aldershot, 1996, examines popular religious attitudes in the parishes of early Tudor England, focusing on the role of the laity and the office of churchwarden. Andrew Pettegree (ed.), *The Reformation of the Parishes: The ministry and the reformation in town and country*, Manchester, 1993, studies both the congested urban parish and the remote countryside. Robert Whiting, *The Blind Devotion of the People: Popular religion and the English Reformation*, Cambridge, 1989, highlights the degree of passive conformity in a study of Exeter diocese which shows most people complying with religious change imposed from above.

Other regional studies of the impact of reformation include Margaret Bowker, *The Henrician Reformation: The diocese of Lincoln under John Longland 1521–1547*, Cambridge, 1981; Susan Brigden, *London and the Reformation*, Oxford, 1989; Claire Cross and Noreen Vickers (eds), *Monks, Friars and Nuns in Sixteenth century Yorkshire*, Leeds, 1995, a biographical register; Peter Marshall, *The Face of the Pastoral Ministry in the East Riding, 1525–1595*, York, 1995; Martha C. Skeeters, *Community and Clergy: Bristol and the Reformation c.1530–c.1570*, Oxford, 1993; and Susan J. Wright (ed.), *Parish, Church and People: Local studies in lay religion 1350–1750*, London, 1988, which includes fine essays by Palliser and Alldridge.

On the highest echelons in Tudor clerical society see Felicity Heal, *Of Prelates and Princes: A study of the economic and social position of the Tudor episcopate*, Cambridge, 1980; and also Rosemary O'Day and Felicity Heal (eds), *Princes and Paupers in the English Church 1500–1800*, Leicester, 1981. For their lesser brethren see Peter Marshall, *The Catholic Priesthood and the English reformation*, Oxford, 1994.

On English monasticism on the eve of the dissolution see David Knowles, *The Religious Orders in England*, vol. 3: *The Tudor Age*, Cambridge, 1959/repr. 1971. Essays in A. G. Dickens, *Late Monasticism and the Reformation*, London, 1994, are also valuable.

Finally, numerous essays in Anthony Fletcher and Peter Roberts (eds), *Religion, Culture and Society in Early Modern Britain: Essays in honour of Patrick Collinson*, Cambridge, 1994, deserve close attention.

GENERAL SOCIAL AND ECONOMIC

General works and collections of essays include J. P. Cooper, *Land, Men and Beliefs: Studies in early modern history*, London, 1983; Mervyn James, *Society, Politics and Culture: Studies in early modern England*, Cambridge, 1986 (including articles on the Lincolnshire rebellion and the 1569 northern rebellion); Peter Laslett, *The World We Have Lost: Further explored*, 3rd edn, London, 1983; J. A. Sharpe, *Early Modern England. A social history 1550–1760*, London, 1987; Keith Wrightson, *English Society, 1580–1680*, London, 1982; and, an excellent introduction to Tudor conditions, Joyce Youings, *Sixteenth-century England*, London, 1984.

The appearance of rural England is examined by Oliver Rackham, *The History of the Countryside*, London, 1986. The best introduction to early modern agriculture is Joan Thirsk (ed.), *The Agrarian History of England and Wales*, vol. 4, Cambridge, 1967; and the same author's *England's Agricultural Regions and Agrarian History, 1500–1750*, London, 1987. For population statistics see E. A. Wrigley and R. S. Schofield, *The Population History of England 1541–1871: A reconstruction*, 2nd edn, Cambridge, 1989. On the upward movement in prices during the century see R. B. Outhwaite, *Inflation in Tudor and Early Stuart England*, 2nd edn, London, 1982. C. E. Challis, *The Tudor Coinage*, Manchester, 1978, examines the inflationary effects of government fiscal policy. The hardships thus caused, and attempted remedies by Tudor administrations, are detailed in Paul Slack, *Poverty and Policy in Tudor and Stuart England*, London, 1988; and Slack's *The English Poor Law 1531–1782*, Basingstoke, 1990.

For an examination of the various issues raised by increasing literacy see David Cressy, *Literacy and the Social Order: Reading and writing in Tudor and Stuart England*, Cambridge, 1980; Eugene R. Kintgen, *Reading in Tudor England*, Pittsburgh, 1996; Rosemary O'Day, *Education and Society, 1500–1800*, London, 1982.

On the festivities and shared ceremonies that marked out the year see David Cressy, *Bonfires and Bells: National memory and the protestant calendar in Elizabethan and Stuart England*, London, 1989; Ronald Hutton, *The Rise and Fall of Merry England: The ritual year, 1400–1700*, Oxford, 1994. On the developing horror of witchcraft see A. Macfarlane, *Witchcraft in Tudor and Stuart England*, London, 1970.

For studies of provincial societies which shed light on a much wider stage the reader should consult, among others, Peter Clark, *English Provincial Society from the Reformation to the Revolution: Religion, politics and society in Kent, 1500–1640*, Hassocks, 1977; M. James, *Family, Lineage and Civil Society: A study of society, politics and mentality in the Durham region, 1500–1640*, Oxford, 1974; and Marjorie Keniston McIntosh, *A Community Transformed: The manor and liberty of Havering, 1500–1620*, Cambridge, 1991.

Works on specific social subjects include Peter Clark, *The English Alehouse: A social history 1200–1830*, London, 1983; Felicity Heal, *Hospitality in Early Modern England*, Oxford, 1990; P. D. A. Harvey, *Maps in Tudor England*, London, 1993, a survey of the significance of maps in Tudor society which can profitably be read together with David Buisseret, *Monarchs, Ministers and Maps: The emergence of cartography as a tool of government in early modern Europe*, Chicago, 1992.

THE FAMILY

R. A. Houlbrooke, *The English Family, 1450–1700*, London, 1984, offers an overview of relationships within the early modern family. On childhood and adolescence see Ilana Krausman Ben-Amos, *Adolescence and Youth in Early Modern England*, New Haven, 1994; Hugh Cunningham, *Children and Childhood in Western Society since 1500*, London, 1995; and Linda A. Pollock, *Forgotten Children: Parent–child relations from 1500 to 1900*, Cambridge, 1983. On marriage, see Eric Josef Carlson, *Marriage and the English Reformation*, Oxford, 1994; Alan Macfarlane, *Marriage and Love in England: Modes of reproduction, 1300–1840*, Oxford, 1986; and R. B. Outhwaite (ed.), *Marriage and Society: Studies in the social history of marriage*, London, 1981. The final ritual is considered in Clare Gittings, *Death, Burial and the Individual in Early Modern England*, London, 1984. See also the recent study by David Cressy, *Birth, Marriage and Death. Ritual, religion, and the life-cycle in Tudor and Stuart England*, Oxford, 1997.

TRADE AND INDUSTRY

D. C. Coleman, *Industry in Tudor and Stuart England*, London, 1975; *The Economy of England, 1450–1750*, Oxford, 1977; S. M. Jack, *Trade and Industry in Tudor and Stuart England*, London, 1977, remain important introductory texts. Eric Kerridge, *Trade and Banking in Early Modern England*, Manchester, 1988, examines the ways in which trade was funded. On specific industries John Hatcher, *The History of the British Coal*

Industry, vol. 1, Oxford, 1993; G. D. Ramsay, *The English Woollen Industry, 1500–1750*, London, 1982; and Michael Zell, *Industry in the Countryside: Wealden society in the sixteenth century*, Cambridge, 1994, are particularly recommended.

FAMINE AND DISEASE

A. B. Appleby, *Famine in Tudor and Stuart England*, Liverpool, 1978, explores a melancholy subject. On the effects of plague and other epidemic disease over the past two centuries the reader should consult John Hatcher, *Plague, Population and the English Economy, 1348–1530*, London, 1977. For its continuing influence, particularly in an urban environment, see Paul Slack, *The Impact of Plague in Tudor and Stuart England*, London, 1985.

TOWNS

General studies of the sixteenth-century town include Jonathan Barry (ed.), *The Tudor and Stuart Town: A reader in English urban history 1530–1688*, London, 1990; Peter Clark (ed.), *The Early Modern Town*, London, 1976; and A. D. Dyer, *Decline and Growth in English Towns, 1400–1640*, Basingstoke, 1991. On conditions and enterprise in specific cities see D. M. Palliser, *Tudor York*, Oxford, 1979; Steve Rappaport, *Worlds Within Worlds: Structures of life in sixteenth-century London*, Cambridge, 1989; and David Harris Sacks, *The Widening Gate: Bristol and the Atlantic economy, 1450–1700*, Berkeley and London, 1991.

WOMEN

M. Prior (ed.), *Women in English Society 1500–1800*, London, 1985, and Margaret R. Sommerville, *Sex and Subjection: Attitudes to women in early-modern society*, London, 1995, are among an ever-growing crop of works studying the place of women in sixteenth-century England. Amy Erickson, *Women and Property in Early-modern England*, London, 1993, reconsiders long-held beliefs regarding the legal status of women.

LAW AND CRIME

J. A. Sharpe, *Crime in Early Modern England 1550–1750*, London, 1984, offers an introduction to offences and courts. J. H. Baker, *The Legal Profession and the Common Law: Historical essays*, London, 1986, is essential reading. A. W. B. Simpson, *A History of the Land Law*, 2nd edn, Oxford, 1986, clarifies many complexities. On specific courts see M. Blatcher, *The Court of King's Bench, 1450–1550*, London, 1978; and John Guy, *The Court of Star Chamber and its Records to the Reign of Elizabeth I*, London, 1985.

John Bellamy, *Criminal Law and Society in Late Medieval and Tudor England*, Gloucester, 1984, is essential. Bellamy's *The Tudor Law of Treason: An introduction*, London, 1979, discusses what contemporaries considered the vilest crime of all rather more soberly than Lacey Baldwin Smith, *Treason in Tudor England: Politics and paranoia*, London, 1986, an investigation of the psychology behind treasonous behaviour. A less serious but far more widespread offence is discussed in Roger B. Manning, *Hunters and Poachers: A social and cultural history of unlawful hunting in England, 1485–1640*, Oxford, 1993. On lawyers and related professions see C. W. Brooks, *Pettyfoggers and Vipers of the Commonwealth: The 'lower branch' of the legal profession in early modern*

England, Cambridge, 1986; E. W. Ives, *The Common Lawyers of Pre-Reformation England: A case study*, Cambridge, 1983; and three works by or edited by Wilfrid Prest: *Lawyers in Early Modern Europe and America*, London, 1981; *The Rise of the Barristers: A social history of the English Bar, 1590–1640*, Oxford, 1986; *The Professions in Early Modern England*, London, 1987.

ART AND LITERATURE

Stephen Greenblatt, *Renaissance Self-fashioning: From More to Shakespeare*, Chicago, 1980, provides essential general reading. For examples of noble patronage of artists and scholars see French R. Fogle and Louis A. Knafla, *Patronage in Late Renaissance England*, Los Angeles, 1983.

On the cultural influence of printing see Elizabeth Eisenstein, *The Printing Press as an Agent of Change*, 2 vols, Cambridge, 1979, reissued in single volume, 1980. On Tudor literature see John N. King, *English Reformation Literature: The Tudor origins of the protestant tradition*, Princeton, 1982; and Lawrence Manley, *Literature and Culture in Early Modern London*, Cambridge, 1995, but consult also the works listed under specific periods below.

On art and political culture at court see Sydney Anglo, *Images of Tudor Kingship*, London, 1992; John N. King, *Tudor Royal Iconography: Literature and art in an age of religious crisis*, Princeton, 1989; and Dale Hoak (ed.), *Tudor Political Culture*, Cambridge, 1995.

On the architecture of the period see H. M. Colvin (ed.), *The History of the King's Works, IV: 1485–1660 (Part II)*, London, 1982; Colin Platt, *The Great Rebuildings of Tudor and Stuart England: Revolutions in architectural taste*, London, 1994; Simon Thurley, *The Royal Palaces of Tudor England: Architecture and court life, 1460–1547*, New Haven, 1993; and Robert Tittler, *Architecture and Power: The town hall and the English urban community, c.1500–1640*, Oxford, 1991. Nigel Llewellyn, *The Art of Death: Visual culture in the English death ritual, c.1500–c.1800*, London, 1991, sheds light on the sixteenth-century English person's management of mortality.

On theatre and music see Paul White, *Theatre and Reformation: Protestantism, patronage and playing in Tudor England*, Cambridge, 1993, which addresses the political uses of staged drama in London and across the kingdom; and David Wulstan, *Tudor Music*, London, 1985.

MILITARY/REBELLION

Richard Harding, *The Evolution of the Sailing Navy, 1509–1815*, Basingstoke, 1995; David Loades, *The Tudor Navy: An administrative, political and military history*, Aldershot, 1992; and N. A. M. Rodger, *The Safeguard of the Sea: A naval history of Britain*, vol. 1, 660–1649, London, 1997, introduce the sixteenth-century navy. The army is best examined through studies of specific periods as detailed below. Gilbert John Millar, *Tudor Mercenaries and Auxiliaries, 1485–1547*, Charlottesville, 1980, is an introduction to developments early in the century, but not all its conclusions have proved sound.

On major unrest within the Tudor state, Anthony Fletcher, *Tudor Rebellions*, 3rd edn, Harlow, 1983 (4th edn with Diarmaid MacCulloch, London, 1997), remains the standard introduction, with a useful bibliography. Paul Slack (ed.), *Rebellion, Popular Protest and the Social Order in Early Modern England*, Cambridge, 1984, offers a compilation of articles from the journal *Past and Present*, including useful essays on the Pilgrimage of Grace by C. S. L. Davies, Kett's rebellion by Diarmaid MacCulloch, and on food riots by John Walter and Keith Wrightson. Anthony Fletcher and John Stevenson (eds), *Order and Disorder in Early Modern England*, Cambridge, 1985, contains essays by C. S. L. Davies on the Pilgrimage of Grace, Margaret Spufford on puritanism and social control, and Fletcher on honour, reputation and local office holding.

POLITICAL THOUGHT

Useful works on the subject include Paul A. Fideler and T. F. Mayer (eds), *Political Thought and the Tudor Commonwealth: Deep structure, discourse, and disguise*, London, 1992; John G. A. Pocock (ed.), *The Varieties of British Political Thought, 1500–1800*, Cambridge, 1993; Quentin Skinner, *The Foundations of Modern Political Thought*, 2 vols, Cambridge, 1978; and Neal Wood, *Foundations of Political Economy: Some early Tudor views on state and society*, London, 1994.

3 England: The Reign of Henry VIII

Several studies and collaborative works attempt broadly conceived explorations of the reign. These include Uwe Baumann, *Henry VIII: In history, historiography and literature*, Frankfurt, 1992; G. R. Elton, *Reform and Reformation: England 1529–1558*, London, 1977; Alistair Fox and John Guy, *Reassessing the Henrician Age: Humanism, politics and reform 1500–1550*, Oxford, 1986; and D. MacCulloch (ed.), *The Reign of Henry VIII: Politics, policy and piety*, London, 1995.

BIOGRAPHIES

A wholly satisfactory biography of King Henry remains to be written. The unsympathetic study by J. J. Scarisbrick, *Henry VIII*, London, 1968, is still, perhaps, the best available. All too often the king is examined through the perspectives offered by his successive marriages. Such uxorial history has seldom proved satisfactory, although David Loades, *The Politics of Marriage: Henry VIII and his queens*, Stroud, 1994, provides some telling comments.

Cromwell apart, most of the king's spouses, courtiers and statesmen fare better. Amid much that is romantic to the exclusion of fact and common sense, Garrett Mattingly, *Catherine of Aragon*, London, 1942; E. W. Ives, *Anne Boleyn*, Oxford, 1986; and Retha M. Warnicke, *The Rise and Fall of Anne Boleyn: Family politics at the court of Henry VIII*, Cambridge, 1989, have much to offer, though Warnicke's work, as her subtitle implies, offers provocative theory rather than straightforward biography and her conclusions remain controversial. For Wolsey see Peter Gwyn, *The King's Cardinal: The rise and fall of Thomas Wolsey*, London, 1990, a long, very useful biography, and S. J. Gunn and P. G. Lindley (eds), *Cardinal Wolsey: Church, state and art*, Cambridge, 1991. Thomas More is particularly well served by John Guy, *The Public Career of Sir Thomas More*, Brighton, 1980; and Richard Marius, *Thomas More. A biography*, London, 1985. The career of More's companion in opposition to the Boleyn marriage, John Fisher, has also attracted work of high quality, notably Brendan Bradshaw and Eamon Duffy (eds), *Humanism, Reform and the Reformation. The career of Bishop John Fisher*, Cambridge, 1989; and Richard Rex, *The Theology of John Fisher*, Cambridge, 1991. The life of More's influential mentor, Erasmus, is examined in James D. Tracy, *Erasmus of the Low Countries*, Berkeley, 1996. A new biography of Bishop John Stokesley: Andrew A. Chibi, *Henry VIII's Conservative Scholar*, Berne,

1997, elucidates many 1530s developments. On the other side of the opening religious divide, Diarmaid MacCulloch's *Thomas Cranmer: A life*, London, 1996, casts the archbishop in a sympathetic and convincing light, while Paul Ayris and David Selwyn (eds), *Thomas Cranmer: Churchman and scholar*, Woodbridge, 1993, offer a substantial series of studies, covering all aspects of Cranmer's career. David Daniell, *William Tyndale: A biography*, New Haven and London, 1994, is at its best discussing Tyndale's literary output.

The Henrician nobility, both as individuals and as a group, have recently received a good deal of scholarly attention. Apart from Helen Miller, *Henry VIII and the English Nobility*, Oxford, 1986, a general study; G. W. Bernard, *The Power of the Early Tudor Nobility: A study of the fourth and fifth earls of Shrewsbury*, Brighton, 1985; and S. J. Gunn, *Charles Brandon, Duke of Suffolk, c.1484–1545*, Oxford, 1988, are recommended.

POLITICS AND COURT LIFE

The capacities and limitations of Tudor government are explored in G. R. Elton, *Policy and Police: The enforcement of the reformation in the age of Thomas Cromwell*, Cambridge, 1972. G. W. Bernard (ed.), *War, Taxation and Rebellion in Early Tudor England: Henry VIII, Wolsey, and the Amicable Grant of 1525*, Brighton, 1986, discusses an interplay of financial, military and political affairs relevant to any consideration of developments after 1529.

For the Henrician court, David Starkey, *The Reign of Henry VIII: Personalities and politics*, London, 1985, provides a brief, telling survey, stressing the importance of the privy chamber. See also Starkey (ed.), *Henry VIII: A European court in England*, London, 1991. Joseph Block, *Factional Politics and the English Reformation 1520–1540*, Woodbridge, 1993, attempts, not entirely successfully, to establish that court faction was 'driven by religious ideology'.

PARLIAMENT

S. E. Lehmberg, *The Reformation Parliament, 1529–1536*, Cambridge, 1970; and *The Later Parliaments of Henry VIII, 1536–1547*, Cambridge, 1977, remain essential reading, also introducing the work of convocation.

RELIGION AND THE BREAK WITH ROME

On the church in England before the break with Rome see J. Thomson, *The Early Tudor Church and Society, 1485–1529*, London, 1993. Alongside the more broadly conceived works on the reformation listed above, Richard Rex, *Henry VIII and the English Reformation*, Basingstoke, 1993, offers a persuasive analytical study of the king and his church. On a specific tactic in the break with Rome see Edward Surtz and Virginia Murphy (eds), *The Divorce Tracts of Henry VIII*, Angers, 1988.

PILGRIMAGE OF GRACE

For the Pilgrimage see Michael Bush, *The Pilgrimage of Grace: A study of the rebel armies of October 1536*, Manchester, 1996. M. H. and R. Dodds, *The Pilgrimage of Grace, 1536–1537, and the Exeter Conspiracy, 1538*, Cambridge, 1915, is still of use for its careful narrative of events. S. M. Harrison, *The Pilgrimage of Grace in the Lake*

Counties 1536–37, London, 1981, provides an interesting local study of an overlooked area.

SOCIETY

An introduction to 1530s concerns regarding social stability is provided by G. R. Elton, *Reform and Renewal: Thomas Cromwell and the Common Weal*, Cambridge, 1973. John C. Chandler (ed.), *John Leland's Itinerary: Travels in Tudor England*, Stroud, 1993, offers an accessible version of Leland's snapshot of English life under Henry VIII, but regrettably excludes Leland's chapters on Wales.

ART AND LITERATURE

The deleterious effects of the reformation on visual culture are examined in Margaret Aston, *England's Iconoclasts: Laws against images*, Oxford, 1988; and in the same author's *The King's Bedpost. Reformation and iconography in a Tudor group portrait*, Cambridge, 1993.

The literature of the 1530s and 1540s is examined in Alistair Fox, *Politics and Literature in the Reigns of Henry VII and Henry VIII*, Oxford, 1989; H. A. Mason, *Humanism and Poetry in the Early Tudor Period: An essay*, 2nd edn, London, 1980; Janel Mueller (ed.), *Katherine Parr* (in the Early Modern Englishwoman series), Aldershot, 1996.

Among other achievements, two works by Greg Walker bridge the awkward gap between 'court' and 'popular' culture: *Plays of Persuasion: Drama and politics at the court of Henry VIII*, Cambridge, 1991; *Persuasive Fictions: Faction, faith and political culture in the reign of Henry VIII*, Aldershot, 1996. Sydney Anglo, *Spectacle, Pageantry, and Early Tudor Policy*, 2nd edn, Oxford, 1997, studies the purposes behind overt displays of courtly refinement. One aspect of popular culture is examined in Sharon L. Jansen, *Political Protest and Prophecy under Henry VIII*, Woodbridge, 1991.

POLITICAL THOUGHT

The important works of Thomas Starkey are closely examined in T. F. Mayer, *Thomas Starkey and the Commonweal; humanist politics and religion in the reign of Henry VIII*, Cambridge, 1989; Mayer (ed.), *Thomas Starkey: Dialogue between Pole and Lupset*, London, 1989.

MILITARY

Charles Cruickshank, *Army Royal. Henry VIII's invasion of France, 1513*, Oxford, 1969, offers a snapshot of early Tudor military planning, and its limitations.

HUMANISM

Maria Dowling, *Humanism in the Age of Henry VIII*, London, 1986, is essential. T. F. Mayer, *Thomas Starkey and the Commonweal; humanist politics and religion in the reign of Henry VIII*, Cambridge, 1989, offers many important insights from the starting point of Starkey's work.

4 England: The Mid-Tudor Period

The reigns of the third and fourth Tudor monarchs used to be discussed in terms of crisis and instability. Such generalizations have rightly been replaced by more sober, pragmatic and positive analyses. See Jennifer Loach and Robert Tittler (eds), *The Mid-Tudor Polity c.1540–1560*, London, 1980; David Loades, *The Reign of Mary Tudor: Politics, government and religion in England 1553–58*, 2nd edn, London, 1991; Loades, *The Mid-Tudor Crisis, 1545–1565*, London, 1992; Loades, *The Reign of King Edward VI*, Bangor, 1994; and Robert Tittler, *The Reign of Mary I*, London, 1983.

BIOGRAPHIES

For the short life of Edward VI – and for contemplation of the what-might-have-been – see Wilbur K. Jordan, *Edward VI: The young king*, London, 1968, and *Edward VI: The threshold of power*, London, 1970. Jordan's interpretation of political events and the extent of the young king's authority has been challenged, but these two works still offer a detailed account of the reign. John Hayward, *The Life and Raigne of King Edward the Sixth*, ed. Barrett L. Beer, Kent, OH, 1993, provides a valuable if rather dry edition of an engaging, contemporary political narrative.

The duke of Somerset deserves a full modern biography. Jennifer Loach, *Protector Somerset: A reassessment*, Bangor, 1994, is slight, though reliable. M. L. Bush, *The Government Policy of Protector Somerset*, London, 1975, offers some insights into Somerset's character. In recent years more attention has focused on the duke of Northumberland. David Loades, *John Dudley, Duke of Northumberland, 1504–53*, Oxford, 1996, is now the book to read, although B. L. Beer, *Northumberland: The political career of John Dudley, earl of Warwick and duke of Northumberland*, Kent, OH, 1973, can also be read with profit. For Cranmer see Diarmaid MacCulloch, *Thomas Cranmer: A life*, New Haven, 1996. Among works relating to other prominent statesmen and bishops, Samuel Rhea Gammon, *Statesman and Schemer: William, first Lord Paget, Tudor Minister*, Newton Abbot, 1973; E. W. Hunt, *The Life and Times of John Hooper (c.1500–1555) Bishop of Gloucester*, Lewiston, 1992; Glyn R. Redworth, *In Defence of the Church Catholic; a life of Stephen Gardiner*, Oxford, 1990; Narasingha P. Sil, *William, Lord Herbert of Pembroke (c.1507–1570): Politique and patriot*, Lewiston, 1988; and D. Willen, *John Russell, First Earl of Bedford: One of the king's men*, London, 1981, are all worth reading.

Many of these works relate also to Mary's reign. The best biography is David Loades, *Mary Tudor; a life*, Oxford, 1989. W. Schenk, *Reginald Pole, Cardinal of England*, London, 1950, is all too brief.

POLITICAL

M. L. Bush, *The Government Policy of Protector Somerset*, London, 1975, remains the best overall examination of Somerset's regime, with Dale Hoak, *The King's Council in the Reign of Edward VI*, Cambridge, 1976, analysing the competition for and exercise of authority among Edward VI's counsellors. For Mary's reign see David Loades, *The Reign of Mary Tudor*, 2nd edn, London, 1991. As a fascinating supplement see Barrett L. Beer and Sybil M. Jack (eds), *The Letters of William, Lord Paget of Beaudesert, 1547–1563*, in *Camden Miscellany 25*, London, 1974.

REBELLION

This was a turbulent period. B. L. Beer, *Rebellion and Riot: Popular disorder in England during the reign of Edward VI*, Kent, OH, 1982, looks at manifestations of popular unrest. Besides Fletcher (above), Julian Cornwall, *Revolt of the Peasantry 1549*, London, 1977, examines both the western and Norfolk rebellions. On Mary Tudor's successful rebellion see D. MacCulloch (ed.), 'The Vita Mariae Angliae Reginae of Robert Wingfield of Brantham', in *Camden Miscellany 28*, London, 1984, an eyewitness account of events in July 1553 from the Marian side. David Loades, *Two Tudor Conspiracies*, Cambridge, 1965, is the only full-length study of Wyatt's dangerous rebellion and its more obscure postscript, the Dudley conspiracy of 1556.

PARLIAMENT

Michael A. R. Graves, *The House of Lords in the Parliaments of Edward VI and Mary I: An institutional study*, Cambridge, 1981, provides a pioneering study of the Tudor Upper House. A detailed study of each Marian parliament can be found in Jennifer Loach, *Parliament and the Crown in the Reign of Mary Tudor*, Oxford, 1986.

RELIGION

In Paul Ayris and David Selwyn (eds), *Thomas Cranmer: Churchman and scholar*, Woodbridge, 1993, many personal, political and religious issues of the mid-Tudor period are explored by a multidisciplinary team. The final years of the chantries are examined in Alan Kreider, *English Chantries: The road to dissolution*, Cambridge, MA, 1979. In *Foreign Protestant Communities in Sixteenth-century London*, Oxford, 1986, and *Marian Protestantism: Six studies*, Aldershot, 1996, Andrew Pettegree asserts the influence of continental protestantism and the resilience of the English protestant church under Mary. D. Andrew Penny, *Freewill or Predestination: The battle over saving grace in mid-Tudor England*, Woodbridge, 1990, examines a key point of protestant theology.

5 England: The Reign of Elizabeth I

Christopher Haigh (ed.), *The Reign of Elizabeth I*, Basingstoke, 1984, offers an important series of essays covering all aspects of the queen's reign, while Haigh, *Elizabeth I*, London, 1988, seeks to analyse the queen's exercise of political power. D. M. Palliser, *The Age of Elizabeth: England under the later Tudors*, London, 1983, surveys English economic and social history in the reigns of Henry VIII's children, and includes a fine bibliography.

The two 'uncharacteristic' decades in the reign have recently received impressive special treatment: Norman L. Jones, *The Birth of the Elizabethan Age: England in the 1560s*, Oxford, 1993, is the first in a projected series of period studies, while John Guy (ed.), *The Reign of Elizabeth I: Court and culture in the last decade*, Cambridge, 1995, provides an important collection of essays to illuminate many aspects of politics, religion and society in the 1590s.

BIOGRAPHIES

Much nonsense has been written about Elizabeth I, a good deal of it arising from the ambitious misreading of an essentially unfathomable character. The following works are among those which respect the abiding mystery, while making useful contributions to a credible portrait. Susan Bassnett, *Elizabeth I: A feminist perspective*, Oxford, 1988; Susan Frye, *Elizabeth I: The competition for representation*, Oxford, 1993; Wallace T. MacCaffrey, *Elizabeth I*, London, 1993; Susan Doran, *Monarchy and Matrimony: The courtships of Elizabeth I*, London, 1996 (Doran challenges the notion that Elizabeth was averse to the idea of marriage); and Carole Levin, *The Heart and Stomach of a King: Elizabeth I and the politics of sex and power*, Philadelphia, 1994, which despite some broad and rather questionable generalizations is good on the ramifications and insecurities engendered by female succession and dynastic uncertainty.

The quality of biographical studies for Elizabeth's courtiers and statesmen is predictably variable. Leicester is the subject of several rather slight studies, of which Derek Wilson, *Sweet Robin: A biography of Robert Dudley, earl of Leicester 1533–1588*, London, 1981; and Alan Haynes, *The White Bear*, London, 1987, are the most accessible. Simon Adams, *Household Accounts and Disbursement Books of Robert Dudley, Earl of Leicester, 1558–1561, 1584–1586*, Cambridge, 1995, goes beyond its superficially domestic remit to provide a series of insights into Leicester's character, and Elizabethan politics and society. On William Cecil: Conyers Read, *Mister Secretary Cecil and Queen Elizabeth*, London, 1955, remains influential, a ponderous but invaluable source of information on Elizabeth's foremost minister. Conyers Read is also the starting point for any study of Walsingham: *Mr Secretary Walsingham and the Policy of Queen Elizabeth*, 3 vols, London, 1925, reprinted 1978. Robert Cecil awaits a scholarly modern biography: Alan Haynes, *Robert Cecil, Earl of Salisbury, 1563–1612: Servant of two sovereigns*, London, 1989, provides a sound introduction, but the reader is also recommended to consult the numerous periodical articles by Pauline Croft. Alice Gilmore Vines, *Neither Fire Nor Steel: Sir Christopher Hatton*, Chicago, 1978, is the only recent study of Elizabeth's capable, amiable and enigmatic counsellor.

Among many biographies of lesser figures in or fiercely opposed to the regime, the following may be singled out: Claire Cross, *The Puritan Earl: The life of Henry Hastings, third earl of Huntingdon*, London, 1966; John Cummins, *Francis Drake: The lives of a hero*, London, 1995; Katherine Duncan-Jones, *Sir Philip Sidney: Courtier poet*, London, 1991; Francis Edwards SJ, *Robert Persons. The biography of an Elizabethan Jesuit 1546–1610*, St Louis, MO, 1995; Michael A. R. Graves, *Thomas Norton: The Parliament man*, Oxford, 1994; David McKeen, *A Memory of Honour: The life of William Brooke, Lord Cobham*, 2 vols, Salzburg, 1986; Alan G. R. Smith, *Servant of the Cecils: The life of Sir Michael Hickes, 1543–1612*, London, 1977; Virginia F. Stern, *Sir Stephen Powle of Court and Country: Memorabilia of a government agent for Queen Elizabeth I, chancery official, and English country gentleman*, Selinsgrove, PA, 1992; and Brian H. G. Wormald, *Francis Bacon: History, politics and science, 1561–1626*, Cambridge, 1993.

POLITICS/GOVERNMENT

The best coverage of political and diplomatic affairs is to be found in the three volumes by Wallace T. MacCaffrey, *The Shaping of the Elizabethan Regime*, Princeton, 1968; *Queen Elizabeth and the Making of Policy 1572–1588*, Princeton, 1981; *Elizabeth I: War and politics, 1588–1603*, Princeton, 1992. Studies of the all-important privy council as an administrative instrument are disappointingly few, though M. B. Pulman, *The Elizabethan Privy Council in the 1570s*, Berkeley, 1971, is well worth reading. On the burgeoning Elizabethan bureaucracy see Richard Winship Stewart, *The English Ordnance Office, 1585–1625: A case study in bureaucracy*, Woodbridge, 1996, which illustrates the heavy and multifarious costs of warfare, while Virginia F. Stern, *Sir Stephen Powle of Court and Country: Memorabilia of a government agent for Queen Elizabeth I, chancery official, and English country gentleman*, Selinsgrove, PA, 1992, highlights the differing priorities of crown servants. The land as a source of royal power is explored in R. W. Hoyle (ed.), *The Estates of the English Crown, 1558–1640*, Cambridge, 1992.

Among many good local studies which investigate relationships between local and national government see A. Hassell Smith, *County and Court: Government and politics in Norfolk 1558–1603*, Oxford, 1974; and S. J. and S. Watts, *From Border to Middle Shire: Northumberland 1586–1625*, Leicester, 1975.

FOREIGN POLICY

John Warren, *Elizabeth I: Religion and foreign affairs*, London, 1993, is an excellent introduction. MacCaffrey's trilogy, and R. B. Wernham, *After the Armada: Elizabethan England and the struggle for western Europe, 1588–1595*, Oxford, 1984; *The Return of the Armadas: The last years of the Elizabethan war against Spain, 1595–1603*, Oxford, 1994, are essential. E. I. Kouri, *England and the Attempts to Form a Protestant Alliance in the Late 1560s: A case study in European diplomacy*, Helsinki, 1981; Kouri, *Elizabethan England and Europe: Forty unprinted letters from Elizabeth I to protestant powers*, London, 1982; and H. Zins, *England and the Baltic in the Elizabethan Era*, Manchester, 1972, help broaden the traditional focus on France, Spain and the Netherlands.

PARLIAMENT

D. M. Dean and N. L. Jones (eds), *The Parliaments of Elizabethan England*, Oxford, 1990; T. E. Hartley, *Elizabeth's Parliaments*, Manchester, 1992, are fine introductions. For examinations of the individual parliaments see G. R. Elton, *The Parliament of England 1559–1581*, Cambridge, 1986; D. M. Dean, *Law-making and Society in Late Elizabethan England: The parliament of England, 1584–1601*, Cambridge, 1996; and T. E. Hartley (ed.), *Proceedings in the Parliaments of Elizabeth I*, 3 vols, Leicester, 1981–95. On the crucial first parliament of the reign see Norman L. Jones, *Faith by Statute: Parliament and the settlement of religion 1559*, London, 1982.

Though superseded in many of its conclusions by more recent research, J. E. Neale's *Elizabeth I and her Parliaments*, 2 vols, London, 1953–7, is full of important factual detail.

RELIGION

Susan Doran, *Elizabeth I and Religion, 1558–1603*, London, 1994; and Andrew Foster, *Church of England 1570–1640*, Longman, 1994, offer outline introductions to the 'Elizabethan Reformation'. The 1559 settlement is best explored in Norman L. Jones, *Faith by Statute: Parliament and the settlement of religion 1559*, London, 1982. Patrick Collinson's numerous works are essential reading for students of the late sixteenth-century established church: *The Elizabethan Puritan Movement*, London, 1967; *Archbishop Grindal, 1519–1583: The struggle for a reformed church*, London, 1979; *The*

Religion of Protestants: The church in English society, 1559–1625, Oxford, 1982; *Godly People: Essays on English protestantism and puritanism*, London, 1983; *From Iconoclasm to Iconophobia: The cultural impact of the second English reformation*, Reading, 1986; *The Birthpangs of Protestant England: Religious and cultural change in the sixteenth and seventeenth centuries*, London, 1988; *Elizabethan Essays*, London, 1994; *From Cranmer to Sancroft: English religion in the age of reformation*, Cambridge, 1994. On the role of the universities in nurturing the state church see C. M. Dent, *Protestant Reformers in Elizabethan Oxford*, Oxford, 1983; Winthrop S. Hudson, *The Cambridge Connection and the Elizabethan Settlement of 1559*, Durham, NC, 1980. On the recovering self-esteem of the priesthood see Rosemary O'Day, *The English Clergy: The emergence and consolidation of a profession 1558–1642*, Leicester, 1979.

For discussion of the theological debates within the Elizabethan church see Peter Lake, *Anglicans and Puritans? Presbyterianism and English Conformist Thought from Whitgift to Hooker*, London, 1988; Nicholas Tyacke, *Anti-Calvinists: The rise of English Arminianism c.1590–1640*, Oxford, 1987. The court sermon is explored in Peter E. McCullough, *Sermons at Court, 1559–1625: Religion and politics in Elizabethan and Jacobean preaching*, Cambridge, 1997.

On Elizabethan Catholicism see John Bossy, *The English Catholic Community, 1570–1850*, London, 1975; Alan Dures, *English Catholicism, 1558–1642*, Harlow, 1983, a general introduction; P. J. Holmes, *Elizabethan Casuistry*, Catholic Record Society 67, London, 1981; Holmes, *Resistance and Compromise: The political thought of the Elizabethan Catholics*, Cambridge, 1982; and Alexandra Walsham, *Church Papists: Catholicism, conformity and confessional polemic in early modern England*, London, 1993, a corrective to recent evaluations of post-reformation English Catholicism which concentrate on recusancy.

Both protestants and Catholics strove mightily to secure converts to their own faith. Michael C. Questier, *Conversion, Politics and Religion in England, 1580–1625*, Cambridge, 1996, gauges the successes and failures of such initiatives, and some of the complex impulses that prompted conversion. The efforts of Jesuit missionary priests, their tactics, successes and failures, are examined in several excellent essays in Thomas M. McCoog (ed.), *The Reckoned Expense. Edmund Campion and the early English Jesuits*, Woodbridge, 1996. Specific studies of radical protestant groups include Christopher W. Marsh, *The Family of Love in English Society, 1550–1630*, Cambridge, 1993. On that seminal text in the history of English protestantism, Foxe's *Book of Martyrs*, see David Loades (ed.), *John Foxe and the English Reformation*, Aldershot, 1997: essays on the composition and enduring influence of *Acts and Monuments*.

TREASON AND REBELLION

Alan Haynes, *Invisible Power: The Elizabethan secret services, 1570–1603*, Stroud, 1992, introduces a fascinating subject. On the sole major English rebellion of the reign see Sir Cuthbert Sharp, *The Rising in the North: The 1569 rebellion*, ed. R. Wood, Shotton, 1975.

MILITARY

The starting points for any study of the army are C. G. Cruickshank, *Elizabeth's Army*, 2nd edn, Oxford, 1966, and Lindsay Boynton, *The Elizabethan Militia, 1558–1638*, London, 1967/1971. On the problems of supply see Richard Winship Stewart, *The English Ordnance Office, 1585–1625: A case study in bureaucracy*, Woodbridge,

1996. For an excellent study of a single campaign see Howell A. Lloyd, *The Rouen Campaign, 1590–1592: Politics, warfare and the early-modern state*, Oxford, 1973. The military commitment of the 1590s is discussed more broadly in MacCaffrey, *Elizabeth I: War and politics, 1588–1603*, Princeton, 1992.

THE ARMADA

Colin Martin and Geoffrey Parker, *The Spanish Armada*, Harmondsworth, 1988, is the best of numerous books on the Armada that appeared during 1988. M. J. Rodríguez-Salgado and Simon Adams (eds), *England, Spain and the Gran Armada, 1585–1604: Essays from the Anglo-Spanish conferences, London and Madrid 1988*, Edinburgh, 1991, provides essential reading for students of the Anglo-Spanish naval war, with essays by British and Spanish historians. Peter Pierson, *Commander of the Armada: The seventh duke of Medina Sidonia*, New Haven, 1989, offers a welcome biography of Philip II's admiral, perhaps less convincing on the events of 1588 than when touching the rest of the duke's career. Garrett Mattingly, *The Defeat of the Spanish Armada*, 2nd edn, London, 1983, was for long the essential work on the subject, and still provides a memorable read. Also of interest are B. T. Whitehead, *Brags and Boasts: Propaganda in the year of the Armada*, Stroud, 1994, and Lisa Ferraro Parmelee, *Good Newes from Fraunce: French anti-League propaganda in late Elizabethan England*, Rochester, NY, 1996.

SOCIETY

On the Englishman's view of his own polity see Mary Dewar (ed.), *De Republica Anglorum by Sir Thomas Smith*, Cambridge, 1982. A lowly office upon which much responsibility was placed by social superiors is examined in J. R. Kent, *The English Village Constable, 1580–1642*, Oxford, 1986.

The problems brought about by increasing population, harvest failure and wartime social dislocation during the 1590s are examined in A. L. Beier, *Masterless Men: The vagrancy problem in England, 1560–1640*, London, 1985. The volatility but essential loyalty of the capital towards its rulers is explored by I. W. Archer, *The Pursuit of Stability: Social relations in Elizabethan London*, Cambridge, 1991.

Alan Haynes, *Sex in Elizabethan England*, London, 1997, offers an introduction to his subject based on the literature of the age. The same topic is considered from a legal standpoint in Martin Ingram, *Church Courts, Sex and Marriage in England, 1570–1640*, Cambridge, 1987.

LAW

Louis A. Knafla, *Kent at Law, 1602. Vol 1. The County Jurisdiction: Assizes and sessions of the peace*, London, 1994, attempts to comprehend the totality of the English legal system and its effects on Englishmen and women by focusing on all available records for a single county in a single year. A specific offence against Divine Law is considered in Norman L. Jones, *God and the Moneylenders: Usury and law in early modern England*, Oxford, 1989.

LITERATURE AND ART

On theatre see Marie Axton, *The Queen's Two Bodies: Drama and the Elizabethan succession*, London, 1977; Andrew Gurr, *Playgoing in Shakespeare's London*, Cambridge,

1987. Shakespeare, whose life is thinly documented, is nevertheless the subject of innumerable studies and biographies, among the best being Peter Levi, *The Life and Times of William Shakespeare*, London, 1988; and Stanley Wells, *Shakespeare, A Dramatic Life*, London, 1994.

On the visual arts, and in particular the representation of Elizabeth herself, see Susan Frye, *Elizabeth I: The competition for representation*, Oxford, 1993; Helen Hackett, *Virgin Mother, Maiden Queen. Elizabeth I and the cult of the Virgin Mary*, Basingstoke, 1995; Roy Strong, *Gloriana: The portraits of Queen Elizabeth I*, London, 1987.

A specific study of noble support for artists can be found in Michael Brennan, *Literary Patronage in the English Renaissance: The Pembroke family*, London, 1988. John N. King, *Spenser's Poetry and the Reformation Tradition*, Princeton, 1990; and Blair Worden, *The Sound of Virtue: Philip Sidney's* Arcadia *and Elizabethan politics*, New Haven, 1997, supply the background to Spenser's and Sidney's work. Other attempts to set major works in context are G. J. R. Parry, *A Protestant Vision. William Harrison and the reformation of Elizabethan England*, Cambridge, 1987; D. C. Peck (ed.), *Leicester's Commonwealth: The copy of a letter written by a Master of Art of Cambridge (1584) and related documents*, Athens, OH, 1985. Richard McCoy, *Rites of Knighthood: The literature and politics of Elizabethan chivalry*, Berkeley, 1989, examines the ways in which court culture adopted the rituals of both a historical and an invented past.

Accounts of visits to England in this period are to be found in Peter Razzell (ed.), *The Journals of Two Travellers in Elizabethan and Early Stuart England: Thomas Platter and Horatio Busino*, Caliban, 1995. Contemporary doubts on the utility of foreign travel are examined in Sara Warneke, *Images of the Educational Traveller in Early-modern England*, Leiden, 1995.

6 Scotland

Gordon Donaldson, *Scotland: James V to James VII*, Edinburgh, 1965, is a standard introduction to sixteenth-century history, still of great value for the insights it offers. An important, more recent work, covering a slightly shorter period in a different way, is J. Wormald, *Court, Kirk and Community: Scotland 1470–1625*, London, 1981. The sixteenth-century chapters in Michael Lynch, *Scotland: A new history*, revised edn, London, 1992, are among the very best in a fine book.

Collections of essays with material relevant to the period include Ian B. Cowan and Duncan Shaw (eds), *The Renaissance and Reformation in Scotland: Essays in honour of Gordon Donaldson*, Edinburgh, 1983; John Dwyer et al. (eds), *New Perspectives on the Politics and Culture of Early Modern Scotland*, Edinburgh, 1982; A. A. MacDonald, M. Lynch and I. B. Cowan (eds), *The Renaissance in Scotland: Studies in literature, religion, history and culture offered to John Durkan*, Leiden, 1994; and Norman Macdougall (ed.), *Church, Politics and Society: Scotland 1408–1929*, Edinburgh, 1983.

BIOGRAPHIES

Patricia Hill Buchanan, *Margaret Tudor: Queen of Scots*, Edinburgh, 1985, is a readable attempt to rescue Queen Margaret from obscurity. Caroline Bingham, *James V, King of Scots, 1512–42*, 1971, is the only readily available biography of a complex and enigmatic character. By contrast there is no shortage of texts, ancient or modern, concerning James's daughter. Mary Stewart rouses extreme emotions. The best recent studies are Michael Lynch (ed.), *Mary Stewart, Queen in Three Kingdoms*, Oxford,

1988 (Lynch in his introduction puts a fairly positive gloss on Mary's reign), and Jenny Wormald, *Mary Queen of Scots: A study in failure*, London, 1988 (a damning portrait of a queen both reluctant and incompetent). For James VI see Maurice Lee, *Great Britain's Solomon: James VI and I in his Three Kingdoms*, Urbana, 1990, and as an introduction S. J. Houston, *James I*, 2nd edn, Harlow, 1995.

Biographical studies of other sixteenth-century statesmen, ministers and peers include P. D. Anderson, *Robert Stewart, Earl of Orkney, Lord of Shetland, 1553–1593*, Edinburgh, 1982; Anderson, *Black Patie: The life and times of Patrick Stewart, Earl of Orkney, Lord of Shetland*, Edinburgh, 1992; William Blake, *William Maitland of Lethington 1528–1573: A study of the policy of moderation in the Scottish Reformation*, Lampeter, 1990; W. Stanford Reid, *Trumpeter of God: A biography of John Knox*, New York, 1974, a thoughtful, balanced profile of Knox, a good introduction; Margaret H. B. Sanderson, *Cardinal of Scotland: David Beaton, c.1494–1546*, Edinburgh, 1986; Sanderson, *Mary Stewart's People*, Edinburgh, 1987.

GOVERNMENT/POLITICS

Introductions to the various chapters in Scottish Record Office, *Guide to the National Archives of Scotland*, Edinburgh, 1996, provide a convenient survey of government and administrative bodies. Gordon Donaldson, *All the Queen's Men: Power and politics in Mary Stuart's Scotland*, London, 1983, sheds light on the government of a decentralized kingdom. For the 1570s see George Hewitt, *Scotland under Morton 1572–80*, Edinburgh, 1982. Most detailed studies of administration and political life focus on the better-documented personal rule of James VI. These include Maurice Lee, *Government by Pen: Scotland under James VI and I*, Urbana, 1980.

PARLIAMENT

R. S. Rait, *The Parliaments of Scotland*, Glasgow, 1924, remains a standard work on the Scottish assembly. However, Margaret D. Young (ed.), *The Parliaments of Scotland: Burgh and shire commissioners*, 2 vols, Edinburgh, 1992–3, is a rich source of biographical material for the Scottish 'Commons'.

REGIONAL STUDIES

Detailed accounts of politics and society beyond the Highland Line are scarce. William F. Skene, *Celtic Scotland*, 2nd edn, Edinburgh, 1886, remains a rich source of otherwise elusive information. The two northern island groups, relatively recent additions to the Scottish crown, are discussed in William P. L. Thomson, *History of Orkney*, Edinburgh, 1987; Donald J. Withrington (ed.), *Shetland and the Outside World, 1469–1969*, Oxford, 1983.

RELIGION AND REFORMATION

Ian B. Cowan, *The Scottish Reformation: Church and society in sixteenth century Scotland*, London, 1982, is an essential introduction, which highlights the need for more local investigation on the impact of religious reform in a decentralized kingdom. Gordon Donaldson, *Scottish Church History*, Edinburgh, 1985, provides a broader study. The two *Books of Discipline* are examined in J. K. Cameron, *The First Book of Discipline*, Edinburgh, 1972; and James Kirk (ed.), *The Second Book of Discipline*, Edinburgh,

1980. James Kirk (ed.), *The Books of Assumption of the Thirds of Benefices. Scottish ecclesiastical rentals at the reformation*, Oxford, 1995, supplies vital statistical information, with an introduction discussing the state of the mid-sixteenth-century church. Important for the church under James VI are W. R. Foster, *The Church before the Covenants: The church of Scotland, 1596–1638*, Edinburgh, 1975; and James Kirk, *Patterns of Reform: Continuity and change in the reformation kirk*, Edinburgh, 1989.

On specific aspects of reform see James Kirk (ed.), *Humanism and Reform: The church in Europe, England, and Scotland, 1400–1643. Essays in honour of James K. Cameron*, Oxford, 1991; Michael Lynch, *Edinburgh and the Reformation*, Edinburgh, 1981, which depicts a resilient Catholicism within Edinburgh; and D. G. Mullan, *Episcopacy in Scotland: The history of an idea, 1560–1638*, Edinburgh, 1986.

For John Knox, his career, writings and influence, see W. Stanford Reid, *Trumpeter of God: A biography of John Knox*, New York, 1974; Richard G. Kyle, *The Mind of John Knox*, Lawrence, KS, 1984, attempts the identification of Knox's mentors and his Old Testament-based theories of resistance. *History of the Reformation in Scotland*, ed. William Croft Dickinson, London, 1949, is a convenient edition of Knox's masterpiece.

SOCIAL/ECONOMIC

Margaret H. B. Sanderson, *Scottish Rural Society in the Sixteenth Century*, Edinburgh, 1982, offers a detailed, methodical introduction. R. A. Houston and I. D. Whyte (eds), *Scottish Society 1500–1800*, Cambridge, 1989, includes several interesting contributions, even if many are weighted towards later, better-documented centuries. Jenny Wormald, *Lords and Men in Scotland: Bonds of manrent 1442–1603*, Edinburgh, 1985, examines one of the instruments used to secure social cohesion. The fiscal base is examined in I. Stewart, *The Scottish Coinage, With Supplement*, London, 1967, the most accessible work on the subject, though for more detail see E. Burns, *The Coinage of Scotland*, Edinburgh, 1887.

On the developing witchcraft hysteria see Christina Larner, *Enemies of God: The witch-hunt in Scotland*, London, 1981.

MILITARY

Norman Macdougall (ed.), *Scotland and War, AD 79–1918*, Edinburgh, 1991, includes contributions by David Caldwell on the battle of Pinkie and Ian Cowan on the Marian civil war. On the continuing significance of the Scottish mercenary Grant G. Simpson (ed.), *The Scottish Soldier Abroad, 1247–1967*, Edinburgh, 1992, includes a chapter by Elizabeth Bonner on the Auld Alliance in the sixteenth century.

CULTURAL

On architecture see D. Howard et al., *The Architecture of the Scottish Renaissance*, Edinburgh, 1990; and Richard Fawcett, *Scottish Architecture: From the accession of the Stewarts to the reformation, 1371–1560*, Edinburgh, 1994, the first volume to appear in a new Architectural History of Scotland.

Literature is introduced by R. D. S. Jack (ed.), *The History of Scottish Literature, Volume 1: Origins to 1660*, Aberdeen, 1988; the visual arts by Duncan Macmillan, *Scottish Art, 1460–1990*, Edinburgh, 1990; and music in John Purser, *Scotland's Music*, Edinburgh, 1993.

LAW

H. L. MacQueen, *Common Law and Feudal Society in Medieval Scotland*, Edinburgh, 1993, is illuminating on the development of the Scottish legal system, with many insights on changes in the sixteenth century. On the survival of personal forms of justice see Keith M. Brown, *Bloodfeud in Scotland, 1573–1625: Violence, justice and politics in an early modern society*, Edinburgh, 1986.

POLITICAL THOUGHT

John MacQueen (ed.), *Humanism in Renaissance Scotland*, Edinburgh, 1990, introduces its subject in an engaging way. Marvin A. Breslow (ed.), *The Political Writings of John Knox: The First Blast of the Trumpet against the monstrous regiment of Women and other selected works*, Washington, 1985, provides a handy introduction to Knox's writings. Roger A. Mason (ed.), *On Rebellion, by John Knox*, Cambridge, 1994, also stresses the religious motivation and Scottish application of Knox's work. On several aspects of the issue of union see Roger A. Mason (ed.), *Scots and Britons: Scottish political thought and the Union of 1603*, Cambridge, 1994; and Arthur H. Williamson, *Scottish National Consciousness in the Age of James VI: The Apocalypse, the Union, and the shaping of Scotland's public culture*, Edinburgh, 1979. The opinions of the first king of Great Britain are considered in Johann P. Sommerville (ed.), *King James VI and I: Political writings*, Cambridge, 1994.

FOREIGN AFFAIRS

On the relationship with England see William Ferguson, *Scotland's Relations with England: A survey to 1707*, Edinburgh, 1977; Bruce Galloway, *The Union of England and Scotland, 1603–1608*, Edinburgh, 1986; Roger A. Mason (ed.), *Scotland and England 1286–1815*, Edinburgh, 1987; and Arthur H. Williamson, *Scottish National Consciousness in the Age of James VI: The Apocalypse, the Union, and the shaping of Scotland's public culture*, Edinburgh, 1979, a persuasive if at times highly theoretical analysis of divisions between the 'British' and 'Scottish' schools of thought on Scotland's national destiny.

For Spain see Albert J. Loomie, *Spain and the Early Stuarts, 1585–1655*, Aldershot, 1996, an enlightening collection of essays. The links between Scotland and the Scandinavian kingdoms, however, remained strong throughout the century. See Thomas Riis, *Should Auld Acquaintance Be Forgot: Scottish–Danish relations 1450–1707*, Odense, 1988; and Grant G. Simpson (ed.), *Scotland and Scandinavia 800–1800*, Edinburgh, 1990. T. C. Smout (ed.), *Scotland and Europe 1200–1850*, Edinburgh, 1986, includes essays on the sixteenth-century Scottish export trade, Scots–Danish relations, overseas visitors to Scotland and cultural ties with France.

7 Wales

Wales has been well served by modern general histories. Among the most useful are: T. Herbert and G. E. Jones, *Tudor Wales: Welsh history and its sources series*, Cardiff, 1988; Philip Jenkins, *A History of Modern Wales 1536–1990*, London, 1992; J. Gwynfor Jones, *Wales and the Tudor State*, Cardiff, 1989; Jones, *Early Modern Wales c.1525–1640*, Basingstoke, 1994; and Glanmor Williams, *Recovery, Reorientation and Reformation:*

Wales, c.1415–1642, Oxford, 1987. On the importance of the gentry in securing the Tudor settlement see Gareth Jones, *The Gentry and the Elizabethan State*, Llandybie, 1977. The essential work on the council in the marches remains Penry Williams, *The Council in the Marches of Wales under Elizabeth I*, Cardiff, 1958. On the church in Wales and the slow but effective reformation see, in addition to the above, Glanmor Williams, *The Welsh Church from Conquest to Reformation*, revised edn, Cardiff, 1976; Isaac Thomas, *William Morgan and his Bible*, Cardiff, 1988; and J. Gwynfor Jones, *The Translation of the Scriptures into Welsh*, Cardiff, 1988.

The impact of acts incorporating medieval Wales into the English state are explored in Glanmor Williams, *Wales and the Act of Union*, Bangor, 1992. For more specific studies see R. R. Davies et al. (eds), *Welsh Society and Nationhood*, Cardiff, 1984, relevant articles by Elton and Quinn; J. Gwynfor Jones (ed.), *Class, Community and Culture in Tudor Wales*, Cardiff, 1989; Jones, *Concepts of Order and Gentility in Wales, 1540–1640*, Llandysul, 1992; A. C. Reeves, *The Marcher Lords*, Llandybie, 1983; E. Rowan (ed.), *Art in Wales, 2000BC–1850AD*, Cardiff, 1978; I. Soulsby, *The Towns of Wales*, Chichester, 1983.

In a long-term view of the development of a political and cultural identity within the modern boundaries of Wales, Gwyn A. Williams, *When Was Wales? A History of the Welsh*, Harmondsworth, 1985, advances some provocative ideas.

8 Ireland

Methods to access the history of Ireland in the sixteenth century are discussed in R. D. Edwards and M. O'Dowd, *Sources for Early Modern Irish History, 1534–1641*, Cambridge, 1985. There have been a number of excellent general studies published in recent years, among them: Nicholas Canny, *From Reformation to Restoration: Ireland 1534–1660*, Dublin, 1987; Steven G. Ellis, *Tudor Ireland: Crown, community and the conflict of cultures 1470–1603*, London, 1985; Colm Lennon, *Sixteenth-century Ireland. The incomplete conquest*, Dublin, 1994; and T. W. Moody, F. X. Martin and F. J. Byrne (eds), *A New History of Ireland, Volume 3: Early Modern Ireland, 1534–1691*, Oxford, 1976. Significant essays are included in R. V. Comerford, Mary Cullen, Jacqueline R. Hill and Colm Lennon (eds), *Religion, Conflict and Coexistence in Ireland: Essays presented to Monsignor Patrick J. Corish*, Dublin, 1990.

The opinions of contemporary Englishmen are illustrated in James P. Myers, *Elizabethan Ireland: A selection of writings by Elizabethan writers on Ireland*, Hamden, CT, 1983.

CONSTITUTIONAL/POLITICAL

Brendan Bradshaw, *The Irish Constitutional Revolution of the Sixteenth Century*, Cambridge, 1979, is a starting point for any study. Steven G. Ellis, *Tudor Ireland: Crown, community and the conflict of cultures 1470–1603*, London, 1985, and *Reform and Revival: English government in Ireland, 1470–1534*, Woodbridge, 1986, takes a fresh look at Tudor administrations. Ciaran Brady, *The Chief Governors: The rise and fall of reform government in Tudor Ireland, 1536–88*, Cambridge, 1994; and Jon G. Crawford, *Anglicizing the Government of Ireland. The Irish privy council and the expansion of Tudor rule, 1556–1578*, Dublin, 1993, examine the impetus behind and the implementation of 'programmatic change'. S. G. Ellis, *The Pale and the Far North: Government and society in two early Tudor borderlands*, Galway, 1988, attempts comparisons between 'English Ireland' and the northern English counties.

Some recent biographical studies offer useful insights into the complex religious and political problems, for example Colm Lennon, *Richard Stanihurst, the Dubliner, 1547–1618*, Dublin, 1981.

RELIGION

On the varying fortunes of two churches see Patrick J. Corish, *The Irish Catholic Experience: A historical survey*, Dublin, 1985; Alan Ford, *The Protestant Reformation in Ireland, 1590–1641*, Frankfurt am Main, 1985. On the course and consequences of Henrician legislation against religious houses see Brendan Bradshaw, *The Dissolution of the Religious Orders in Ireland under Henry VIII*, Cambridge, 1974.

MILITARY

Thomas Bartlett and Keith Jeffery (eds), *A Military History of Ireland*, Cambridge, 1996, offers a collection of authoritative essays, including those for the sixteenth century by Ellis and Brady. Nicholas Canny, *The Elizabethan Conquest of Ireland: A pattern established 1565–1576*, Hassocks, 1976, remains essential reading. On the Irish military presence overseas see Grainne Henry, *The Irish Military Community in Spanish Flanders, 1586–1621*, Blackrock, 1992.

The two pivotal risings of the sixteenth century are studied in Laurence McCorristine, *The Revolt of Silken Thomas*, Dublin, 1987, a general survey of the Kildare rebellion; and Hiram Morgan, *Tyrone's Rebellion: The outbreak of the nine years' war in Tudor Ireland*, Woodbridge, 1993. The burden imposed by the nine years' war on English government and society is thoroughly explored in John McGurk, *The Elizabethan Conquest of Ireland*, Manchester, 1997.

SOCIAL AND ECONOMIC

There are several important essays in Ciaran Brady and Raymond Gillespie (eds), *Natives and Newcomers: The making of Irish colonial society, 1534–1641*, Dublin, 1986. Colm Lennon, *The Lords of Dublin in the Age of Reformation*, Blackrock, 1989, looks at the neglected Dublin city archives and sheds light on society in the capital. English settlement in the south is examined in Michael MacCarthy-Morrogh, *The Munster Plantation: English migration to southern Ireland, 1583–1641*, Oxford, 1986.

FOREIGN AFFAIRS AND CONTEXT

Nicholas Canny, *Kingdom and Colony: Ireland in the Atlantic world, 1560–1800*, Baltimore, 1988, offers some interesting broad perspectives. William Palmer, *The Problem of Ireland in Tudor Foreign Policy, 1485–1603*, Woodbridge, 1994, highlights how the perceived threat of invasion from Ireland influenced English foreign policy, while possibly exaggerating the importance of Ireland in policy determination.

9 Europe and the Wider World

Many important essays can be found in E. I. Kouri and Tom Scott (eds), *Politics and Society in Reformation Europe*, London, 1987.

NATIONAL HISTORIES

For histories in English of the various nation states and other political systems of sixteenth-century Europe see Jean Bérenger, *A History of the Habsburg Empire, 1273–1700*, translated by C. A. Simpson, London, 1994; Emmanuel Le Roy Ladurie, *The Royal French State, 1460–1610*, Oxford, 1994; Geoffrey Parker, *The Dutch Revolt*, revised edn, London, 1985; Parker, *Spain and the Netherlands, 1559–1659*, London, 1979; David Potter, *A History of France, 1460–1560: The emergence of a nation state*, Basingstoke, 1995; Michael Roberts, *The Early Vasas: A history of Sweden 1523–1611*, Cambridge, 1968; M. J. Rodríguez-Salgado, *The Changing Face of Empire: Charles V, Philip II and Habsburg authority, 1551–1559*, Cambridge, 1988.

Karl Brandi, *The Emperor Charles V*, London, 1939/repr. Brighton, 1980, remains the best study in English of the emperor's career, while for his long-time French protagonist see R. J. Knecht, *Renaissance Warrior and Patron: The reign of Francis I*, Cambridge, 1994. An important if generally benevolent picture of Philip II is provided by Henry Kamen, *Philip of Spain*, London, 1997.

On the French wars of religion see Mark Greengrass, *The French Reformation*, Oxford, 1987; N. M. Sutherland, *The Huguenot Struggle for Recognition*, New Haven, 1980; Sutherland, *Princes, Politics and Religion 1547–1589*, London, 1984; and R. M. Kingdon, *Myths about the St Bartholomew's Day Massacre 1572–1576*, London, 1988.

ROYAL COURTS

Ronald G. Asch and Adolf M. Birke (eds), *Princes, Patronage, and the Nobility: The court at the beginning of the modern age c.1450–1650*, Oxford, 1991, includes essays on English and European courts by, among others, Starkey, Adams, Rodríguez-Salgado, Press and Schalk.

TRADE AND EXPLORATION

On the primary trade with the Netherlands see Ralph Davis, *English Overseas Trade 1500–1700*, London, 1973, a useful introduction; Wolf-Rudiger Baumann, *The Merchant Adventurers and the Continental Cloth Trade*, Berlin, 1990; Douglas R. Bisson, *The Merchant Adventurers of England: The company and the crown, 1474–1564*, Newark, DE, 1993, a traditional, politically grounded study of this curious relationship; and G. D. Ramsay, *The Queen's Merchants and the Revolt of the Netherlands*, Manchester, 1986.

Widening our horizons, Kenneth R. Andrews, *Trade, Plunder and Settlement: Maritime enterprise and the genesis of the British Empire, 1480–1630*, Cambridge, 1984, provides a fine, well-referenced survey of Tudor mariners and adventurers. D. B. Quinn and A. N. Ryan, *England's Sea Empire 1550–1642*, London, 1983, is a most authoritative investigation, and contributions to Cecil H. Clough and Paul E. H. Hair (eds), *The European Outthrust and Encounter. The first phase, c.1400–c.1700: essays in tribute to David Beers Quinn on his 85th birthday*, Liverpool, 1994, contain much that is of interest.

EUROPEAN REFORMATION

G. R. Elton (ed.), *The Reformation 1520–1559*, New Cambridge Modern History, vol. 2, 2nd edn, Cambridge, 1990, is a thorough and well-updated introduction. Andrew Pettegree (ed.), *The Early Reformation in Europe*, Cambridge, 1992; and Pettegree,

Alastair Duke and Gillian Lewis (eds), *Calvinism in Europe 1540–1620*, Cambridge, 1994, both explore significant issues in sixteenth-century reformation and counter-reformation. Bob Scribner, Roy Porter and Mikulas Teich (eds), *The Reformation in National Context*, Cambridge, 1994, surveys the state of current research across Europe and includes chapters on England and Scotland by Patrick Collinson and Julian Goodare.

Specific studies include Amy Nelson Burnett, *The Yoke of Christ: Martin Bucer and Christian Discipline*, Kirksville, MO, 1994, a useful work on the career of the Strasbourg reformer, with a valuable bibliography; Ole Peter Grell, *Calvinist Exiles in Tudor and Stuart England*, Aldershot, 1996.

MILITARY

J. R. Hale, *War and Society in Renaissance Europe, 1450–1620*, London, 1985, provides a lucid examination of sixteenth-century European warfare and its social implications.

CULTURE

Interesting reading on some aspects of a vast subject is provided by J. V. Field and Frank A. J. L. James (eds), *Renaissance and Revolution: Humanists, scholars, craftsmen and natural philosophers in early modern Europe*, Cambridge, 1993; Jean-François Gilmont (ed.), *The Reformation and the Book*, Ashgate, 1997; Charles G. Nauert, Jr, *Humanism and the Culture of Renaissance Europe*, Cambridge, 1995; Roy Porter and Mikulas Teich (eds), *The Renaissance in National Context*, Cambridge, 1992.

Index

Illustrations indexed in italic